Lecture Notes in Computer Science 9192

Commenced Publication in 1973
Founding and Former Series Editors:
Gerhard Goos, Juris Hartmanis, and Jan van Leeuwen

More information about this series at http://www.springer.com/series/7409

Panayiotis Zaphiris · Andri Ioannou (Eds.)

Learning and Collaboration Technologies

Second International Conference, LCT 2015
Held as Part of HCI International 2015
Los Angeles, CA, USA, August 2–7, 2015
Proceedings

 Springer

Editors
Panayiotis Zaphiris
Department of Multimedia
  and Graphics Arts
Cyprus University of Technology
Lemesos
Cyprus

Andri Ioannou
Department of Multimedia
  and Graphics Arts
Cyprus University of Technology
Lemesos
Cyprus

ISSN 0302-9743   ISSN 1611-3349 (electronic)
Lecture Notes in Computer Science
ISBN 978-3-319-20608-0   ISBN 978-3-319-20609-7 (eBook)
DOI 10.1007/978-3-319-20609-7

Library of Congress Control Number: 2015941494

LNCS Sublibrary: SL3 – Information Systems and Applications, incl. Internet/Web, and HCI

Springer Cham Heidelberg New York Dordrecht London
© Springer International Publishing Switzerland 2015

Printed on acid-free paper

Springer International Publishing AG Switzerland is part of Springer Science+Business Media
(www.springer.com)

Foreword

The 17th International Conference on Human-Computer Interaction, HCI International 2015, was held in Los Angeles, CA, USA, during 2–7 August 2015. The event incorporated the 15 conferences/thematic areas listed on the following page.

A total of 4843 individuals from academia, research institutes, industry, and governmental agencies from 73 countries submitted contributions, and 1462 papers and 246 posters have been included in the proceedings. These papers address the latest research and development efforts and highlight the human aspects of design and use of computing systems. The papers thoroughly cover the entire field of Human-Computer Interaction, addressing major advances in knowledge and effective use of computers in a variety of application areas. The volumes constituting the full 28-volume set of the conference proceedings are listed on pages VII and VIII.

I would like to thank the Program Board Chairs and the members of the Program Boards of all thematic areas and affiliated conferences for their contribution to the highest scientific quality and the overall success of the HCI International 2015 conference.

This conference could not have been possible without the continuous and unwavering support and advice of the founder, Conference General Chair Emeritus and Conference Scientific Advisor, Prof. Gavriel Salvendy. For their outstanding efforts, I would like to express my appreciation to the Communications Chair and Editor of HCI International News, Dr. Abbas Moallem, and the Student Volunteer Chair, Prof. Kim-Phuong L. Vu. Finally, for their dedicated contribution towards the smooth organization of HCI International 2015, I would like to express my gratitude to Maria Pitsoulaki and George Paparoulis, General Chair Assistants.

May 2015

Constantine Stephanidis
General Chair, HCI International 2015

HCI International 2015 Thematic Areas
and Affiliated Conferences

Thematic areas:

- Human-Computer Interaction (HCI 2015)
- Human Interface and the Management of Information (HIMI 2015)

Affiliated conferences:

- 12th International Conference on Engineering Psychology and Cognitive Ergonomics (EPCE 2015)
- 9th International Conference on Universal Access in Human-Computer Interaction (UAHCI 2015)
- 7th International Conference on Virtual, Augmented and Mixed Reality (VAMR 2015)
- 7th International Conference on Cross-Cultural Design (CCD 2015)
- 7th International Conference on Social Computing and Social Media (SCSM 2015)
- 9th International Conference on Augmented Cognition (AC 2015)
- 6th International Conference on Digital Human Modeling and Applications in Health, Safety, Ergonomics and Risk Management (DHM 2015)
- 4th International Conference on Design, User Experience and Usability (DUXU 2015)
- 3rd International Conference on Distributed, Ambient and Pervasive Interactions (DAPI 2015)
- 3rd International Conference on Human Aspects of Information Security, Privacy and Trust (HAS 2015)
- 2nd International Conference on HCI in Business (HCIB 2015)
- 2nd International Conference on Learning and Collaboration Technologies (LCT 2015)
- 1st International Conference on Human Aspects of IT for the Aged Population (ITAP 2015)

Conference Proceedings Volumes Full List

Learning and Collaboration Technologies

Program Board Chairs: Panayiotis Zaphiris, Cyprus and Andri Ioannou, Cyprus

- Ruthi Aladjem, Israel
- Abdulaziz Aldaej, UK
- Martin Ebner, Austria
- Maka Eradze, Estonia
- Habib M. Fardoun, Saudi Arabia
- Mikhail Fominykh, Norway
- David Fonseca Escudero, Spain
- Mustafa Murat Inceoglu, Turkey
- Tomaž Klobučar, Slovenia
- Maarten de Laat, The Netherlands
- Edmund Laugasson, Estonia

- Birgy Lorenz, Estonia
- Ana Loureiro, Portugal
- Maria Mama-Timotheou, Cyprus
- Antigoni Parmaxi, Cyprus
- Christophe Reffay, France
- Nicos Souleles, Cyprus
- Sonia Sousa, Portugal
- Aimilia Tzanavari, Cyprus
- Stefan Trausan-Matu, Romania
- Johnny Yuen, Hong Kong
- Maria Zenios, Cyprus

The full list with the Program Board Chairs and the members of the Program Boards of all thematic areas and affiliated conferences is available online at:

http://www.hci.international/2015/

HCI International 2016

The 18th International Conference on Human-Computer Interaction, HCI International 2016, will be held jointly with the affiliated conferences in Toronto, Canada, at the Westin Harbour Castle Hotel, 17–22 July 2016. It will cover a broad spectrum of themes related to Human-Computer Interaction, including theoretical issues, methods, tools, processes, and case studies in HCI design, as well as novel interaction techniques, interfaces, and applications. The proceedings will be published by Springer. More information will be available on the conference website: http://2016.hci.international/.

General Chair
Prof. Constantine Stephanidis
University of Crete and ICS-FORTH
Heraklion, Crete, Greece
Email: general_chair@hcii2016.org

http://2016.hci.international/

Contents

Adaptive and Personalised Learning and Assessment

Virtual Worlds and Virtual Agents for Learning

Collaboration and Learning

Serious Games

ICT in Education

Technology-Enhanced Learning

An Eye-Tracking Analysis of Spatial Contiguity Effect in Educational Animations

Tugba Altan[⊠] and Kursat Cagiltay

Middle East Technical University, Ankara, Turkey
{taltan,kursat}@metu.edu.tr

Abstract. The purpose of this study is to examine spatial contiguity effect on multimedia learning with an instructional animation using eye-tracking. The research method was experimental method and the study was conducted with a user group consisting of 12 participants (6 female and 6 male). The data collection tools were a demographic survey, a prior knowledge test, a retention test and an eye-tracker. The collected data were analyzed using descriptive statistics and non-parametric statistics including Mann-Whitney U Test. According to the results there were no statistically significant difference in terms of learning outcomes, total fixation time on relevant texts and images, fixation count on relevant texts and images, and mean fixation duration on relevant images between spatial and non-spatial group according to the research results. However, mean fixation duration on relevant texts was significantly higher for spatial group than non-spatial group. According to mean ranks on all measures of eye tracking data, there may be tendency that participants in spatial group spent more time and attention on relevant text as non-spatial group spent more time and attention on narration and relevant images.

Keywords: Eye-tracking · Spatial contiguity effect · Educational animations · Multimedia

1 Introduction

A multimedia learning material includes both words (spoken or printed) and pictures (static graphics, illustrations, photos, animations or videos etc.). Multimedia learning theory indicates people learn more when words and pictures are used together than only words are used. This assertion has been developed based on dual channel, limited capacity and active processing assumptions [7]. These assumptions are results of cognitive science attempts for understanding how human brain works and how humans learn.

Cognitive load theory seeks ways for efficiency in learning via trying to determine how we can use limited human cognitive capacity and so, it provides some principles for designing learning environments efficiently. According to Clark, Nguyen and Sweller (2006) [3] cognitive load theory is useful for all instructional and learning situations because it's universal (can be applied to all instructional situations), provides some principles and guidelines for instructional design, evidence based, helps for efficient learning and leverages human cognitive learning process. Also the rationale

© Springer International Publishing Switzerland 2015
P. Zaphiris and A. Ioannou (Eds.): LCT 2015, LNCS 9192, pp. 3–13, 2015.
DOI: 10.1007/978-3-319-20609-7_1

for cognitive load is that "cognitive load depends on the interaction of... learning goals and its associated content, the learner's prior knowledge and the instructional environment." (p. 14) and so, it's important to reduce extraneous load when novice learners are dealing with complex content [3].

Cognitive load theory provides some principles for dealing with extraneous and intrinsic load and increasing germane load. For reducing extraneous load, we can use worked examples, completion, split attention, modality, expertise reversal, guidance fading and goal-free form of problems cognitive load effects. For increasing germane load, we can use variable examples and imagination effects of cognitive load [12]. These principles are also multimedia learning theory design principles [7].

Although, multimedia learning theory and cognitive load theory provide beneficial implications to design multimedia materials, there are some limitations of these theories. Firstly, cognitive load theory accept cognitive load as work load and take no notice of psychological effects of individuals' beliefs, expectations, and goals to cognitive load [9]. Second, theories depend on highly controlled experimental studies [3, 7]. Mayer (2010) [7] indicates learning materials should be designed in a way consistent with a research based theory that provides evidence for how people learn and how to help people learn. At this point, eye tracking research helps to test multimedia learning theory principles in a unique way. In fact, some researchers conducted studies to test some of the principles and provided theoretical implications.

Boucheix and Lowe (2010) [1] tested signaling effect and their findings indicated that visual signals guide learners' attention and there is a strong link between eye-fixations and learning outcomes. Another research result demonstrated a similar relationship between signaling effect and attention but inconsistent link between eye fixations and learning outcomes [4]. Also, Ozcelik, Arslan-Ari and Cagiltay (2010) [11] revealed that signaled group's performance is better than nonsignaled group's on transfer and matching test and similarly signaling guide attention. Differently, some researchers tested the effect of prior knowledge in multimedia learning. They found that experts spend more time looking at relevant areas of multimedia material than novices and so, prior knowledge guides the attention [2, 5].

Schmidth- Weigand, Kohert and Glowalla (2010) examined modality effect and the effect of pacing on learner's attention. Research results revealed that there is spending more time looking at relevant areas of an animation for animation-narration together material than animation and on screen text material. There is no strong link between eye-fixations and learning outcomes for slow or learner-paced presentation rate. Similarly, Meyer, Rasch and Schnotz (2010) [9] indicated that there are no strong effects of fast-to-slow or slow-to-fast pace on eye fixations, priming attention and overall comprehension. Ozcelik, Karakus, Kursun and Cagiltay (2009) [12] examined the effect of color coding on multimedia learning. Their results demonstrated that color coding help to guide attention to relevant information and increased retention and transfer performance.

The literature demonstrates that researchers studied attention on multimedia learning with eye-tracking mostly. According to multimedia learning theory, split attention occurs when the layout and the dependent information are presented in separate locations or pages. So, learner needs additional mental energy to integrate the separated information sources. It makes use of limited working memory capacity and increases extraneous cognitive load [3]. There are two kinds of split attention effect; temporal contiguity and spatial contiguity. While presenting words and pictures at the same time creates temporal contiguity, presenting corresponding word and picture next to each other creates spatial contiguity [7].

Johnson and Mayer (2012) [6] examined spatial contiguity effect on multimedia learning with eye-tracking. They found the groups that a multimedia material consistent with spatial contiguity effect was presented made significantly more eye-movements from text to diagram and diagram to text, and from text to the relevant part of the diagram than the groups that a multimedia material inconsistent with spatial contiguity effect was presented. Their results provided evidence that spatial contiguity effect helps to integrate corresponding words and pictures and encourages meaningful learning. However, they suggest to test this principle with instructional animations and materials including different learning topics in further studies. Hence the aim of this study was to examine spatial contiguity effect on multimedia learning with an instructional animation using eye-tracking.

1.1 Research Questions

1. Is there a significant difference between learning outcomes of spatial contiguity group and non-spatial contiguity group after learning with an instructional animation?
2. Is there a significant difference between eye movements of spatial contiguity group and non-spatial contiguity group after learning with an instructional animation?

2 Methodology

2.1 Research Method

In this study, as a research method post-test experimental method with experimental and control groups was used. Participants were assigned to two groups randomly; spatial contiguity group and non-spatial contiguity group.

2.2 Participants

This study was conducted with a user group consisting of 12 participants (6 female and 6 male). The participants were determined by convenience sampling method. Ten participants were graduate students at the department of Computer Education and Instructional Technology at METU, one of the participants was an undergraduate student at the department of Linguistics at Ankara University and the other participant had a B.S. degree from Chemical Engineering Department at Gazi University.

The multimedia material used for the study was in English so participants were selected in terms of this criterion. All the participants were Turkish native speakers but they are good at English. Eleven participants had at least 65 score in one of the English Qualifying Exams (KPDS, ÜDS or METU English Proficiency Exam) and the other participant had his undergraduate education in English at his department at university. Participants' ages were between 25–30 years.

2.3   Multimedia Learning Material

A multimedia learning material including animations was used for this study. Two versions of the material were used; consistent one and inconsistent one with spatial contiguity principle of multimedia learning theory. The multimedia material was an animation about schizophrenia treatment and side effects of the treatment (http://www. explania.com/en/channels/health/detail/schizophrenia-treatments-side-effects) and it was developed consistently with spatial contiguity effect. It was downloaded from the web site www.explania.com that includes free educational animations about a variety of topics. The web site allows visitors to embed animations into their own web sites or use them for their own purposes. So, the author downloaded the animation and also created an inconsistent version of animation in terms of spatial contiguity effect by using Adobe Flash CS6 software. The animation was in English Language.

Figure 1 represents the version of animation that is consisted with spatial contiguity principle of multimedia learning theory while Fig. 2 represents the inconsistent version of the animation.

The animation covers general treatment and medication of schizophrenia and possible side effects of medication. At the beginning of the animation, learners are informed about the purpose of the animation. After the introduction, who decides the treatment for schizophrenia and how he/she decides are explained to learners.

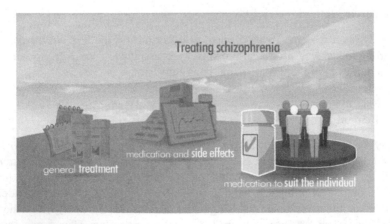

Fig. 1. Screen capture of animation with spatial contiguity effect

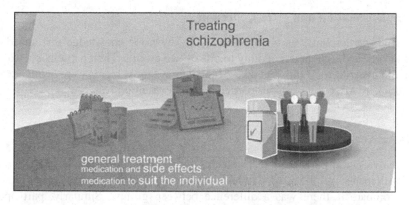

Fig. 2. Screen capture of animation without spatial contiguity effect

Also, animation provides information about what treatment covers, differences between old and new medication, positive effects and side effects of medication, what a patient should do if he/she has any of side effects and the important points that patients should pay attention during the treatment.

2.4   Apparatus

A computer, a headphone and an eye-tracker were used for collecting the participant's eye movement data during experiment. Eye tracker was Tobll 1750 Eye Tracker which was integrated within the monitor.

2.5   Instruments

A demographic survey, a prior knowledge test and a retention test were used as data collection tools. Demographic survey, prior knowledge test and retention test were developed by the author. The instruments (demographic survey, prior knowledge test and retention test) were reviewed by a physician, a clinical psychologist and a psychologist that works in METU Health Centre to provide content validity. Also, an English teacher reviewed the clarity of the language because of the instruments were in English. The English teacher is a PhD student at METU as well. After that instruments were pilot tested with a PhD student at department of Computer Education and Instructional Technology at METU.

Demographic survey included questions about participants' demographic information such as age, gender, education, English Language level. Prior knowledge test included 8 Likert-type questions about schizophrenia and side effects and participants marked the appropriate statement from selections (I don't know at all, I don't know, I somewhat know, I know, I know well). Retention test included 7 multiple choice questions and 3 true/false questions about schizophrenia and side effects.

2.6   Implementation and Data Collection

Firstly, each participant was tested individually by prior knowledge test and demographic survey and assigned randomly to one of two groups. Then participants watched multimedia material for 3 min and 43 s while their eye movements were being recorded by eye-tracker. After this session, participants had retention test.

2.7   Data Analysis

In data analysis, non-parametric test statistics was used because sample size was below thirty. Participants' prior knowledge test scores were analyzed with Mann-Whitney U Test to compare if there was a difference between groups. Similarly, participants' retention tests scores were analyzed with Mann-Whitney U Test to identify if there was a difference between test results of each group. Furthermore, participants' eye-fixation data were analyzed with Mann-Whitney U Test to determine if there was a difference between results of two groups. In all statistical analysis, significance level was taken as 0.05.

For eye tracking data analysis, each participant recording firstly was divided to 19 scenes in terms of narration and relevant images and texts. Then, two area of interests were determined on each scene in terms of relevant texts and relevant images. After that, total fixation time, fixation count and mean fixation duration calculated on Tobii studio for each scene and the results were calculated for each participant.

3   Results

3.1   Results of Test Scores

A Mann-Whitney U Test was administered in order to compare experimental and control groups' prior knowledge on the subject matter. The test result demonstrated that there was no statistically significant difference between two groups' prior knowledge on schizophrenia treatments and side effects ($U = 14$, $p > 0.05$). The results are presented below in Table 1.

Two groups' retention test scores were also compared by Mann-Whitney U Test in order to determine if there was a significant difference between test scores. Analysis results demonstrated there was no significant difference between two groups' retention test scores ($U = 11.500$, $p > 0.05$); however, spatial group's test score mean (7.58) was higher than non-spatial group's test score mean (5.42). Table 2 demonstrates the results.

Table 1. Mann-Whitney U test results of prior knowledge test

Groups	N	Mean Rank	U	Z	p
Non-spatial	6	7.17	14	−647	0.517
Spatial	6	5.83			

Table 2. Mann-Whitney U test results of retention test

Groups	N	Mean Rank	U	Z	p
Non-spatial	6	5.42	11.500	−1.090	0.276
Spatial	6	7.58			

3.2 Results of Eye Movement Measures

Eye movement measures were analyzed with Mann-Whitney U Test in order to understand if there was a significant difference between spatial and non-spatial groups' total fixation time, fixation count and fixation duration mean on both relevant images and relevant text in two versions of the animation. Results were presented in terms of total fixation time, fixation count and fixation duration mean.

3.2.1 Total Fixation Time

According to Mann-Whitney U test results, total fixation time on relevant texts was higher for the participants in spatial group (6.83) than the participants in non-spatial group (6.17). However, this difference was not statistically significant (U = 16, p > 0.05). Table 3 demonstrates the test results of total fixation time on relevant text for both of the groups.

Total fixation time on relevant images was higher for the participants in spatial group (6.67) than the participants in non-spatial group (6.33); however, this difference was not statistically significant (U = 17, p > 0.05). Table 4 demonstrates the test results of total fixation time on relevant images for both of the groups.

3.2.2 Fixation Count

According to Mann-Whitney U test results, fixation count on relevant texts was higher for the participants in spatial group (6.67) than for the participants in non-spatial group (6.33). However, this difference was not statistically significant (U = 16, p > 0.05). The results were the same as total fixation time for both of the groups. Table 5 demonstrates the test results of fixation count for both groups.

Similarly, there was no statistically significant difference between two groups in terms of fixation count on relevant images (U = 16, p > 0.05). However, fixation count on relevant images for the participants in non-spatial group (6.83) was higher than for

Table 3. Mann-Whitney U test results of total fixation time on relevant texts

Groups	N	Mean Rank	U	Z	p
Non-spatial	6	6.17	16.00	−0.320	0.749
Spatial	6	6.83			

Table 4. Mann-Whitney U test results of total fixation time on relevant images

Groups	N	Mean Rank	U	Z	p
Non-spatial	6	6.33	17	−0.160	0.873
Spatial	6	6.67			

the participants in spatial group (6.17). These results were different for fixation count on relevant images than fixation count for relevant texts. The results were presented in Table 6.

3.2.3   Mean Fixation Duration

Another Mann-Whitney U test was administered to analyze mean fixation duration on relevant text and pictures for spatial and non-spatial groups. According to results in Table 7, mean fixation duration on relevant text was significantly higher for the participants in spatial group than for the participants in non-spatial group ($U = 3$, $p < 0.05$, $r = 0.16$). This result indicated that the participants in spatial group (Mean Rank = 9) spent more time on relevant text than the participants in non-spatial group (Mean Rank = 4).

However, mean fixation duration on relevant images was not significantly different for the participants in spatial group than for the participants in non-spatial group ($U = 15$, $p > 0.05$) and mean fixation duration on relevant images for non-spatial group (Mean Rank = 7) was higher than the spatial group (Mean Rank = 6) according to results in Table 8.

To sum up, test results for mean fixation on relevant images were totally different than the test results for mean fixation on relevant texts. Participants in both of the groups spent similar time on relevant images.

Table 5. Mann-Whitney U test results of fixation count on relevant texts

Groups	N	Mean Rank	U	Z	p
Non-spatial	6	6.17	16	−0.320	0.749
Spatial	6	6.83			

Table 6. Mann-Whitney U test results of fixation count on relevant images

Groups	N	Mean Rank	U	Z	p
Non-spatial	6	6.83	16	−0.320	0.749
Spatial	6	6.17			

Table 7. Mann-Whitney U test results of mean fixation duration on relevant texts

Groups	N	Mean Rank	U	Z	p
Non-spatial	6	4	3	−2.544	0.011
Spatial	6	9			

Table 8. Mann-Whitney U test results of mean fixation duration on relevant images

Groups	N	Mean Rank	U	Z	p
Non-spatial	6	7	15.00	−0.561	0.575
Spatial	6	6			

4 Discussion and Conclusion

The aim of this study was to examine spatial contiguity effect on multimedia learning with an instructional animation using eye-tracking. For this purpose, both eye tracking data and retention test scores (learning outcomes) were analyzed. Results revealed that there was no significant difference in prior knowledge between participants in spatial and non-spatial groups. After watching the animation, the participants in spatial group had higher scores on retention test than participants in non-spatial group. However, this difference was not statistically significant. This result was similar to Ozcelik et al.'s (2010) [11] research results involving signaling effect and eye tracking, de Koning et al.'s (2010) [4] research results involving animation, visual cues and eye tracking and Johnson and Mayer's (2012) [6] research results involving spatial contiguity effect and eye tracking. However, a transfer test was not conducted in this study so it can't be said that spatial contiguity effect is not effective on learning.

Eye tracking data were analyzed in terms of total fixation time, fixation count and fixation duration mean measures. Results revealed that total fixation time on relevant texts and total fixation time on relevant images were higher for the participants in spatial group than the participants in non-spatial group; however, this difference was not statistically significant. These results differ from Ozcelik et al.'s (2010) [11] research results; they indicated that total fixation time on relevant information (relevant labels and relevant picture parts) was significantly higher for signaled group. However, their study focuses on a different multimedia principle so the difference may be related to this fact. Johnson and Mayer's (2012) [6] research results indicated that there were no significant differences between experimental and control group in terms of total fixation times on relevant text and relevant pictures. These results were similar to the results of the present study. Also, research results revealed that in both groups participants had higher fixations on text than diagrams [6]. The present research results have some similarities to this results. As mean ranks were examined, spatial group had higher total fixation time on relevant text than relevant images. However, non-spatial group had higher total fixation time on relevant images than relevant texts. Although these differences are not statistically significant, it may be non-spatial group paid attention to relevant images and narration in animation as spatial group paid more attention to relevant text next to relevant images in animation.

Another eye tracking data analysis result indicated that there was no statistically significant difference between two groups in terms of fixation count on relevant texts and relevant images. However, fixation count on relevant text for the participants in spatial group was higher than for the participants in non-spatial group as fixation count on relevant images for the participants in non-spatial group was higher than for the participants in spatial group. Similar to previous results of this study, the result is different from Ozcelik et al.'s (2010) [11] research results. They found that fixation count on relevant text and relevant pictures were significantly higher for signaled group. However, this result considered that spatial group may have paid attention to relevant texts as non-spatial group may have paid attention to narration and relevant images again.

According to results in this study, mean fixation duration on relevant text was significantly higher for the participants in spatial group than for the participants in non-spatial group. This result is similar to Ozcelik et al.'s (2009) [12] research results indicating average fixation duration was longer for participants using color-coded material than for participants in control group. However, present research results are different from Ozcelik et al.'s (2010) [11] research results; they found no significant difference on mean fixation duration for both of the groups. Another research result was that mean fixation duration on relevant images was not significantly different for the participants in spatial group than for the participants in non-spatial group in present study. This result is similar to Ozcelik et al.'s (2010) [11] research results.

In conclusion, there were no statistically significant difference in terms of learning outcomes, total fixation time on relevant texts and images, fixation count on relevant texts and images and mean fixation duration on relevant images between spatial and non-spatial group according to research results. However, mean fixation duration on relevant texts was significantly higher for spatial group than non-spatial group. According to mean ranks on all measures of eye tracking data, there may be tendency that participants in spatial group spent more time and attention on relevant text as non-spatial group spent more time and attention on narration and relevant images. So more research is needed to examine if such an assumption is true. Also, some researchers revealed that prior knowledge guides the attention [2, 5] and this result may be examined for spatial contiguity effect in further research.

In this study, there were some limitations in terms of number of participants, subject matter, data collection tools and eye tracking data analysis. Using a larger sample can allow to conduct more statistical analysis and obtain more generalizable results for the future research in the same topic. In this research, only retention test was used, but it is important to use transfer test and other performance tests to measure learning outcomes accurately. In eye tracking analysis, mean fixation duration, total fixation time and fixation count were used as eye tracking measures. Johnson and Mayer (2012) [6] indicated that they used integrative transitions from text to image and from image to text, text-to image transitions and corresponding transitions as measures to analyze the eye tracking data. It seems using these measures can be effective to analyze and interpret the eye tracking data in future research. This study was conducted using an animation about schizophrenia and side effects. Further research is needed to examine spatial contiguity effect on multimedia materials in different subject matters.

References

1. Boucheix, J.-M., Lowe, R.K.: An eye-tracking comparison of external pointing cues and internal continuous cues in learning with complex animations. Learn. Instr. 20(2), 123–135 (2010)
2. Canham, M., Hegarty, M.: Effects of knowledge and display design on comprehension of complex graphics. Learn. Instr. 20(2), 155–166 (2010)
3. Clark, C., Nguyen, F., Sweller, J.: Efficiency in learning: Evidence-based guidelines to manage cognitive load. Pfeiffer, San Francisco, CA (2006)

4. De Koning, B.B., Tabbers, H.K., Rikers, R.M.J.P., Paas, F.: Attention guidance in learning from complex animation: seeing is understanding? Learn. Instr. **20**(2), 111–122 (2010)
5. Jarodzka, H., Scheiter, K., Gerjets, P., Van Gog, T.: In the eyes of the beholder: how experts and novices interpret dynamic stimuli. Learn. Instr. **20**(2), 146–154 (2010)
6. Johnson, C.I., Mayer, R.E.: An eye movement analysis of the spatial contiguity effect in multimedia learning. J. Exp. Psychol. **18**(2), 178–191 (2012)
7. Mayer, R.E.: Unique contributions of eye-tracking research to the study of learning with graphics. Learn. Instr. **20**(2), 167–171 (2010)
8. Mayer, R.E.: Cognitive theory of multimedia learning. In: Mayer, R.E. (Ed.), Cambridge Handbook of Multimedia Learning, pp. 31–48. Cambridge University Press (2005)
9. Meyer, K., Rasch, T., Schnotz, W.: Effects of animation's speed of presentation on perceptual processing and learning. Learn. Instr. **20**(2), 136–145 (2010)
10. Moreno, R., Park, B.: Cognitive load theory: Historical development and relation to other theories. In: Plass, J.L., Moreno, R. Brünken, R. (Eds.), Cognitive Load Theory: Theory and application, pp. 9–28. Cambridge University Press, New York (2010)
11. Ozcelik, E., Arslan-Ari, I., Cagiltay, K.: Why does signaling enhance multimedia learning? Evidence from eye movements. Comput. Hum. Behav. **26**, 110–117 (2010)
12. Ozcelik, E., Karakus, T., Kursun, E., Cagiltay, K.: An eye-tracking study of how color coding affects multimedia learning. Comput. Educ. **53**(2), 445–453 (2009)
13. Sweller, J.: Cognitive load theory: Recent theoretical advances. In: Plass, J.L., Moreno, R., Brünken, R. (Eds.), Cognitive Load Theory: Theory and application, pp. 29–47. Cambridge University Press, New York (2010)

Audio Cues: Can Sound Be Worth a Hundred Words?

Jatin Bajaj[1]($^{\boxtimes}$), Akash Harlalka[1], Ankit Kumar[1],
Ravi Mokashi Punekar[1], Keyur Sorathia[1], Om Deshmukh[2],
and Kuldeep Yadav[2]

[1] Indian Institute of Technology Guwahati, Guwahati, Assam, India
{jatinbajaj1993,akash.harlalka,
kumar.ankiit7}@gmail.com,
{mokashi,keyur}@iitg.ernet.in
[2] Xerox Research Center India, Bengaluru, India
{omdeshmukh,r.kuldeep}@xerox.com

Abstract. Multimedia content is increasingly being used in the context of e-learning. In the absence of classroom-like active interventions by instructors, multimedia-based learning leads to disengagement and shorter attention spans. In this paper, we present a framework for using audio cues interspersed with the content to improve student engagement and learning outcomes. The proposed framework is based on insights from cognitive theory of multimedia learning, modeling of working memory and successful use of audio in the film industry. On a set of 20 freshmen engineering students, we demonstrate that the systematic use of audio cues led to 37.6 % relative improvement in learning outcome and 44 % relative improvement in long-term retention. Post-study interviews establish that the associated students improved recall and engagement to the presence of audio cues.

Keywords: Cognitive theory of multimedia learning · Working memory · Audio cues · E-learning performance · Student retention

1 Introduction

Increasing use of technology in the educational domain has given rise to new models of learning such as flipped classrooms [1], blended learning [2] and Massive Open Online Courses (MOOC) [12]. Using multimedia educational content is a central aspect in all of these models. This has in turn led to active research in the design of multimedia instructional content [9], efficient ways of content delivery [3] and the effect of such content on student engagement and performance [11]. The aspects of design research encompass issues such as video production style, duration of a typical module, and cognitive load of the content. Content delivery is being studied to understand how best to cater to the diverse set of devices and be robust to lossless and variable-speed delivery channels. Student engagement and performance is being studied by analyzing various behavior parameters such as the time spent on lectures, interactions with peers and instructor, performance on in-video quizzes and dropout rates.

© Springer International Publishing Switzerland 2015
P. Zaphiris and A. Ioannou (Eds.): LCT 2015, LNCS 9192, pp. 14–23, 2015.
DOI: 10.1007/978-3-319-20609-7_2

The use of multimedia in e-learning is however heavily skewed towards video content [10]. Speech and audio content is used only for conveying information whereas the potential use of audio for associative memory is largely ignored. Several studies have shown that the attention span for an instructional video is only about 6 min [11] further highlighting the non-engaging nature of current e-content. This is also reflected in the poor course completion rates of several leading MOOCs [12].

In this paper we are interested in evaluating the role audio cues can play in improving student engagement and learning outcomes in the context of multimedia e-learning. We propose a framework for synergistic combination of audio cues and the learning content. The theoretical underpinnings of the framework are based on cognitive theory of multimedia learning, models of working memory and successful use of audio in the film industry. While audio cues have been used in communicating emotions to computers [13], for conversation visualization [14] and to aid people with disabilities [15], ours is the first attempt to study the efficacy of audio cues in an educational setting.

The rest of the paper is organized as follows. In Sect. 2 we present the theoretical motivation for the proposed framework followed by detailed explanation of proposed audio-cue setup in Sect. 3. Experimental setup, results of user studies and discussions are explained in Sects. 4–6 respectively.

2 Theoretical Underpinnings for Audio Cues

Authors in [8] have done pioneering research work in formulating the Cognitive Theory of Multimedia Learning (CTML). CTML is based on three basic principles of learning: **C1** dual channels of processing for auditory and visual information, **C2** limited processing capacity of each channel, and **C3** active coordination of cognitive processes. The theory of working memory [7] also supports dual channel by the following postulation: **M1:** human brain system has two independent but interconnected subsystems phonological loop for capturing speech-based information and visuo-spatial sketch for capturing visuo-spatial imagery. The interconnection allows for visual information to be represented as speech-like information using sub vocalization.

CTML further specifies five cognitive processes where relevant information is selected from these two channels to form two independent models of the input message followed by integration with the long-term memory (i.e., prior knowledge).

While there is extensive research study on the role speech plays in providing verbal redundancy and facilitating dual coding in visual and auditory channels in the context of multimedia educational content [5] there is no study on using audio cues to facilitate coherent binding of information that is spread over time: an important aspect for active coordination of cognitive processes. Authors in [10] surveyed 12 award-winning instructional software products and came to the conclusion that sound is used largely for instructional purposes and not to drive any associative learning.

Authors in [6] propose a Structured Sound Function (SSF) model for use of sound in instructional content. Specifically, they mention that when sound is assigned to a visual event, it should serve one of the five purposes: **S1:** connect to a past/future event, **S2:** present a point of view, **S3:** establish a place, **S4:** set a mood, and **S5:** relate to a character.

One domain where sound is used very effectively is the film industry: be it to enhance the narrative, to immerse in an illusion, to accentuate a mood, or to add continuity across a number of temporal events. Authors in [4] make four recommendations from the film industry for using sound in e-learning: **F1:** consider sound's use from the start of the design process, **F2:** identify key storytelling elements to be amplified by sound, **F3:** capitalize on the way people listen to sounds, and **F4:** be systematic about how sounds are incorporated. For F3, the authors suggest that the four types of listening modes should be utilized: **L1:** reduced, where listener only pays attention to the main qualities of the sound and incurs minimal cognitive load, **L2:** causal, where the sound is associated with a descriptive category that could have likely cause the sound, **L3:** semantic, where the meaning behind the sound is decoded (e.g. Emotion in the spoken message), and **L4:** referential, where the sound evokes image(s) of familiar things. L4 is particularly useful in the context of dual-channels of information coding (C1).

Based on these findings, we build our framework as follows:

(The corresponding primary findings are mentioned in the parenthesis.)

(a) Identify important learning concepts to be retained based on applicability in exams and future course work [F2].
(b) Study the coursework to identify which concepts talk across a multitude of lectures and hence need a common binding [S1, F1].
(c) Identify concepts which, while not central, are good-to-know and can be reinforced through reduced listening [C1, C2, L1].
(d) Identify concepts which tend to occur together and/or can be most confusing and hence should use audio cues which evoke very different associations [C2, L3, L4].
(e) Identify events which can easily be connected with a visual image and identify corresponding sounds that can evoke these images [C2, L4, M1].

It is important to base the usage of audio cues in educational multimedia content on strong theoretical foundation as inappropriate usage may not only not enhance learning but may act as one of the detriments to learning [4].

3 Audio-Cue Framework Applied to a Narrative

We are in the process of formulating a systematic audio-cue framework for two data-intensive semester-long eleventh grade courses on Chemistry (which includes a list of chemical reagents along with their reactionary properties towards each other) and History (which includes major battles or events, the corresponding timelines, important parties involved and the outcome) working closely with a local high school administration. But to evaluate the efficacy of audio cues in learning outcomes and retention, we first built the framework in the context of an imaginary narrative that draws on basics of Mathematics, Physics and Chemistry. We also plan to use the insights generated from this study on the narrative to further influence the audio-cue framework formulation for the courses.

Here is a brief description of the narrative: After a long party, Marc, the main character, has difficulty falling asleep and is hallucinating. In each episode of hallucination, he goes on a new expedition with his friends: On one such expedition he experiences zero-gravity free fall; on another, he has to navigate through a castle; and in yet another, one of his friends is bit by a snake and the team has to create an antidote through a combination of chemicals (purely fabricated combination using the products commonly found in a kitchen whose combination can create effects akin to those created by chemical reactions. Hence creating situation similar to a chemical reaction (purely fabricated combination) while not creating any bias.

The narrative is divided into two different videos (part-1 and part-2) to simulate two lectures on the same topic. Each video is about 4 min 30 s long in accordance with the average attention span of video lectures [11]. Using the design principles mentioned in the previous section, we first identified the highlights of the narrative that we would like the students to remember and based on the kind of information or event, the sound cues were pre-cued/post-cued or played simultaneously.

- Pre-cued: To hint listener about a forthcoming event.
- Simultaneous: to add more emphasis and clarity to an ongoing event by establishing the place or the activity through the sound clip running in the background.
- Post-cued: To emphasize on the information that was just narrated and shown on the screen e.g. names of people, numbers, scientific term.

Accordingly we formulated appropriate post-video questions. Two important characters in the narrative were assigned two distinct audio cues (high pitch vs. low pitch), each important event location in the hallucinations was assigned an appropriate audio effect (e.g., a long hallway had 'echoes', the free-flow event had 'high speed wind noise'), important concepts were preceded by a consistent audio cue (e.g., every instance of acidity was associated with a consistent 'burp' cue). Appropriate chemical reactions were peppered with corresponding likely audio effect (e.g., to evoke images of strong repulsive smell, the audio of an uncomfortable cough was used, adding water to a chemical compound had the sound of 'water flowing through a tap'). The quiz corresponding to the part-1 video had 10 questions: 5 had highlighting specific audio cues associated with the likely answers whereas the other 5 had no cues. Similarly, the quiz corresponding to the part-2 video had 10 questions, 6 of which had specific associated audio cues. The questions were not in the chronological order of the narrative to avoid likely temporal bias.

In the experiments described here we used the audio narration of the above narrative with synchronized scrolling of the corresponding text on the video (similar to closed-captioning but on full screen). We used such a setup for our current experiments for two main reasons: (a) make optimal and synergistic use of the dual channels [C1 and C2], and (b) in practical e-learning situations, we have very little scope of adding relevant visual content to a video whereas audio cues can be inserted with relative ease. Two versions of the videos were created: the Narration Only (NO) version had no audio cues whereas the Audio-Cues (AC) version had audio cues interspersed with the audio-visual narration. The visual message was exactly the same in both the version.

4   Experimental Setup

We recruited 20 college freshmen students (18–20 years old) for this study and split them into two equal groups: the Narration-Only group (NO) and the Audio-Cues (AC) group. The NO group was shown the NO version of the videos whereas the AC group was shown the AC version of the videos. The students were informed about the end-of-the-video quiz. They were also told that they have to answer more than eight questions correctly, failing which they will have to watch the video and give the quiz again. The part-2 video was shown only after the students passed the part-1 quiz. Each student was presented the video on a 15-in. laptop computer along with a pair of earphones in a quiet room. The students were asked to complete each attempt of the part-1 quiz in five minutes and each attempt of the part-2 quiz in 10 min.

The questions were a mix of multiple choice, one word or one sentence, explanatory types. In the sentence long questions, marks were solely awarded on the mention of one or two keywords. For easy recall, the questions were asked in the chronological order (the order in which the events occurred in the narration).

The students were called in for a surprise quiz five days after they watched the part-2 and were given the same quizzes as earlier. This was done to evaluate their long-term retention (as per the forgetting curve, humans tend to forget nearly 80 % of the content within 4–5 days in the absence of any revision). At the end of this surprise quiz, we had an informal exit-interview with the students to gather their feedback on the entire process.

5   Results

Figure 1 shows the average student performance across multiple attempts for the NO and the AC group for part-1 and part-2 of the video narratives. As expected the performance improves after every attempt. Students in the AC group show much better performance than those in the NO group in the first attempt itself. The average performance of AC group students combined across the two parts of the videos in the first attempt is 11.7 whereas that of the NO group students is 8.5, which shows that audio cues lead to a 37.6 % relative improvement in learning outcome. Moreover, students in the AC group reach the passing criterion much quicker than those in the NO group: For example, only 1 student in the AC group needed three attempts while there were 3 such students in the NO group for part-1 video. In the case of part-2 video, 5 students in the NO group needed 3 attempts to reach pass the quiz whereas all the students in the AC group passed the quiz in the second attempt. The significant jump in performance of AC students in the part-2 video as compared to that of the NO students could be because of the multiplicative effect where the students 'learn' to optimally utilize the audio cues. Further experiments are needed to validate the existence of such an effect.

As mentioned in Sect. 3, answers to only about 50 % of the questions had corresponding specific audio cues. To test whether the improvement in the AC group performance was only due to these 'audio-cued questions', we analyzed the question-wise performance of the students in both the groups and across the two parts of the video. Figures 2 and 3 shows the average number of correct answers by the students of

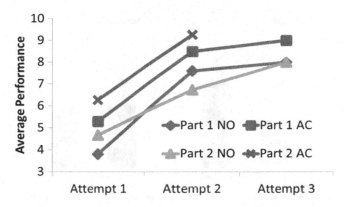

Fig. 1. Performance of students in the NO and the AC group on part-1 and part-2 video across multiple attempts.

NO and AC groups on audio-cued and non-cued questions for part-1 and part-2 videos. Notice that while the AC group performs better on the audio-cued questions, their performance on the non-cued questions is also better than that of the NO group. This leads us to believe that the audio-cuing phenomenon has a positive effect on the overall learning experience, which we term as the spread effect.

Figure 4 compares the average long term retention performance of students in NO and AC groups in terms of number of correct answers to the two quizzes. While the NO group answers about 12 questions correctly, the AC group answers about 17.3 questions correctly demonstrating a relative improvement of about 44 % in long term retention due to the use of audio-cues.

Figure 5 compares the performance of the NO and the AC group students for each of the 10 questions in the part-2 video quiz across multiple attempts. Each question has two horizontal bars. The bottom bar shows the performance for the NO group and the top bar show the performance for the AC group. The questions with

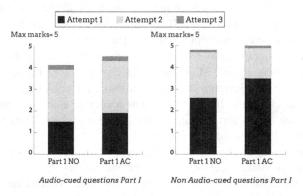

Fig. 2. Average number of correct answers by the students of NO and AC groups across multiple attempts to (i) audio-cued questions in part-1 video (5 questions), (ii) non-audio cued questions in part-1 video (5 questions).

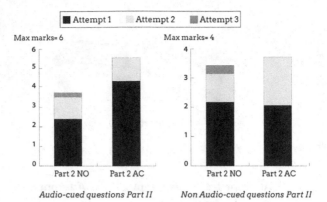

Fig. 3. (iii) audio-cued questions in part-2 video (6 questions), and (iv) non-audio-cued questions in part-2 video (4 questions).

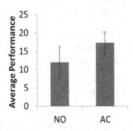

Fig. 4. Average long-term retention performance of students in NO and AC groups in terms of number of correct answers to the quiz questions.

specific audio cues are indicated separately on the y-axis. Performance on all the questions is improved by the use of audio-cues except for one question (question 3 from the top). This question asks the subjects to mention all the four ingredients used to create the antidote for snake bite. This can likely be attributed to the high cognitive load of recollecting multiple names. The other question with interesting behavior is the top most question which has poor performance by the NO group but substantial improvement by the AC group. This question asks the user to 'name the person who sobbed when Suzanne was bit by a snake'. The NO video only mentions the name 'Johanna' whereas the AC video has a special audio cue assigned to this character as well as plays 'girl sobbing' sound. These multiple cues helped the AC group to easily recollect the correct answer.

Similarly, there was one question in the quiz of part-1 video to test if students would latch on to secondary details that are provided only through audio-cues. The question was 'what is the castle door made of?'. The narration had no mention of the type of the door and the audio cue had a creaking sound of a rusty iron door. None of the NO group students could answer the question correctly, but 60 % of the AC group students caught on to the audio cue in the first attempt.

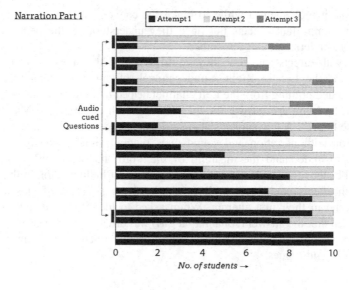

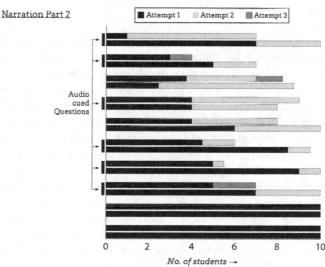

Fig. 5. Performance of the NO and the AC group students for each of the 10 questions in the part-1 and part-2 videos across multiple attempts. For each question, the bottom horizontal bar represents the performance of the NO group and the top bar represents the performance of the AC group.

This has significant ramifications for instructional multimedia content in that subtle associations (such as reminder of where a historic battle was fought) can be effectively reinforced through appropriate audio-cues rather than having to spell those out in the main lecture. Finally, as we conducted post-study interviews with the students, almost all the AC students attributed their high performance to the audio cues. Several of them mentioned that it took them a while to make the connection that the audio cues are reinforcing the important aspects but once they understood it, the part-2 video was much easier to understand and remember.

Subjects with effects said that they could visualize the story by identifying the sound cues and the Left or Right sound channel activation. For example sound of crickets and sound coming from the Left channel helped them in creating an imagery of the path took by Marc and answer the question- "Which direction did Marc turn in to switch on the light?". A few subjects also said that at times it was difficult for them to concentrate on both narration and sound cues running simultaneously. All subjects needed help to understand the meaning of the word 'hallucination'. Students with effects could better relate and understand the situation of hallucination in the narrative. Subjects with effects could very well comprehend the situation of closed well and concept of echo in their first attempt. When asked to identify the character sobbing, subjects replied that the answer (Johanna - a girl) was obvious; however, they could not tell why! The gender of the character was implicitly embedded in the listener's memory by the effect of audio cues.

6 Discussions

In this work, we presented our initial results on a framework for the use of audio-cues in educational multimedia content. The framework is based on insights from cognitive theory of multimedia learning, modeling of working memory and successful use of audio in the film industry. We demonstrated that a systematic use of audio cues can indeed improve student performance and engagement. We are currently formulating the use of audio cues for two semester-long courses: Chemistry and History. We are conducting in-field studies to collate sounds that naturally occur in classrooms and to identify their associations (e.g., sounds corresponding to tapping of the chalk on the board or slapping the duster on the table to capture students' attention, teacher's footsteps for close monitoring, student murmur for classroom discussion, etc.).

Further research on the retention capabilities of students shows that the capability to recall content is a complex phenomenon. Most students may not be able to recall the content visually presented to them but audio cues may serve as a brilliant medium to provide hints, we can call them audio anchors. Audio anchors may serve as a great help to students who are not able to answer the question presented to them in the right away but are able to recall the answer once given a small hint or a head start in words. The audio anchors will serve as an effortless memory anchor and will help in recalling the content.

Our initial findings on use of audio cues for improving learning outcomes and student retention have been encouraging. To conclude, our study shows that the answer to the question raised in the title of this paper is in the affirmative!

Acknowledgments. We gratefully acknowledge Safinah A. Ali for all her help and assistance in building our audio cue framework.

References

1. Tucker, B.: The flipped classroom. Educ. Next **12**(1), 82–83 (2012)
2. Horn, M.B., Staker, H.: The rise of K-12 blended learning. Innosight Institute (2011)
3. Zhao, X., Okamoto, T.: Adaptive multimedia content delivery for context-aware u-learning. Int. J. Mob. Learn. Organ. **5**(1), 46–63 (2011)
4. Bishop, M.J., Sonnenschein, D.: Designing with sound to enhance learning: four recommendations from the film industry. J. Appl. Instr. Des. **2**(1), 5–15 (2012)
5. Mayer, R.E., Moreno, R.: Aids to computer-based multimedia learning. Learn. Instr. **12**(1), 107–119 (2002)
6. Mann, B.L.: The evolution of multimedia sound. Comput. Educ. **50**(4), 1157–1173 (2008)
7. Baddeley, A.: Working memory. Science **255**(5044), 556–559 (1992)
8. Mayer, R.E.: Cognitive theory of multimedia learning. In: The Cambridge Handbook of Multimedia Learning, pp. 31–48 (2005)
9. Clark, R.C., Mayer, R.E.: E-learning and the Science of Instruction: Proven Guidelines for Consumers and Designers of Multimedia Learning. Wiley, San Francisco (2011)
10. Bishop, M.J., Amankwatia, T.B., Cates, W.M.: Sound's use in instructional software to enhance learning: a theory-to-practice content analysis. Educ. Tech. Res. Dev. **56**(4), 467–486 (2008)
11. Guo, P.J., Kim, J., Rubin, R.: How video production affects student engagement: an empirical study of mooc videos. In: Proceedings of the First ACM Conference on Learning@ scale Conference, pp. 41–50. ACM (2014)
12. http://www.insidehighered.com/news/2013/03/08/researchers-explore-who-taking-moocs-and-why-so-many-drop-out
13. Sebe, N., et al.: Emotion recognition based on joint visual and audio cues. In: 18th International Conference on Pattern Recognition, ICPR 2006, Vol. 1. IEEE (2006)
14. Bergstrom, T., Karahalios, K.: Seeing more: visualizing audio cues. In: Baranauskas, C., Abascal, J., Barbosa, S.D.J. (eds.) INTERACT 2007. LNCS, vol. 4663, pp. 29–42. Springer, Heidelberg (2007)
15. Velasco-Álvarez, F., Ron-Angevin, R., da Silva-Sauer, L., Sancha-Ros, S., Blanca-Mena, M.J.: Audio-cued SMR brain-computer interface to drive a virtual wheelchair. In: Cabestany, J., Rojas, I., Joya, G. (eds.) IWANN 2011, Part I. LNCS, vol. 6691, pp. 337–344. Springer, Heidelberg (2011)

Using Augmented Reality Technology in Assisting English Learning for Primary School Students

Salin Boonbrahm, Charlee Kaewrat, and Poonpong Boonbrahm[✉]

School of Informatics, Walailak University,
Nakorn Si Thammarat 80161, Thailand
{salil.boonbrahm,charlee.qq,poonpong}@gmail.com

Abstract. Motivation is the most important part in childhood education. Many schools have invested a lot in information technology with the hope that it will create some motivation in learning but there is no significant proof that it worked. Augmented Reality may be the answer, since it provides children to interact with virtual object while still in the real world environment. In this research, we have created 3 AR experiments to prove the concept that AR can motivate children in learning English. These AR experiments will concentrate on writing, reading and conversation. Different AR techniques were used for this purpose i.e. marker-marker interaction and user-defined target. The results agree with the prediction that children really enjoy and eager to learn more.

Keywords: Augmented reality · Language learning

1 Introduction

Teaching English to children whose mother's tongues are not English face many difficulties due to differences in background, knowledge, and culture, but the most important thing is the lack of motivation. Most children are not interested in learning a new language. The obvious reason is that they see no need to learn new language. But in reality, they cannot ignore the fact that English language is used as a mean of modern day universal communication. For example, ASEAN community which will start in 2015 shall use English as its official language and if the children cannot use the language properly, then they will be at a disadvantage. To solve this problem, many schools have invested in information technology for the purpose of using them as tools to support learning especially English language learning. With the software, in the form of Computer Aided Instruction (CAI), children can play and learn at the same time, this makes them eager to learn. Due to the fact that the output from CAI is not interactive and usually, they are in the form of routine 2D or 3D animation, after a while, the interest dies down and not so many people use them anymore. In this paper, we have proposed to use Augmented Reality to spice up English class in the hope of motivating children to learn English. Augmented Reality (AR) is a live view of a real-world environment whose elements are superimposed by computer-generated virtual objects such as texts or 3D computer models. AR technology can be divided into 2 categories

© Springer International Publishing Switzerland 2015
P. Zaphiris and A. Ioannou (Eds.): LCT 2015, LNCS 9192, pp. 24–32, 2015.
DOI: 10.1007/978-3-319-20609-7_3

i.e. marker-based AR and markerless AR. Marker is the 2D figure that carrying out information to be displayed on top of real space (Fig. 1).

For markerless AR, its applications can be grouped into 2 types: image-based AR and location-based AR. Image-based AR needs specific labels to register the position of 3D objects on the real world image (Fig. 2). In contrast, location-based AR uses position data such as data from GPS to identify the location (Fig. 3). In our work, we have decided to use marker-based AR because we want children to learn not only by using computer but also by interacting with real object as well. Besides that, by using marker-based AR, there are many more ways that the children can play around with them.

Fig. 1. Marker AR [1]

Fig. 2. Image-based AR [1]

Fig. 3. Location-based AR [2]

Due to the advancement of technology especially in the field of mobile technology, AR is now available for everyone who has a smart phones or tablets. Up to now, there are many applications of AR for education available in the market, but most of them just display 3D objects or animations when look through mobile phones with suitable software.

2 Related Work

Augmented Reality Technology has been applied to many areas in education such as medical sciences, engineering, arts, and languages. The example of applying AR in medical science is used as a tool for studying human anatomy [3]. This tool provides visualization of bones and important organs in the abdomen. While the use of AR in environmental studying can be done outside the classroom [4], the students can investigate the real environment together with the use of virtual media.

AR can be used for helping children developing their skills and understanding the lessons. Many researchers have investigated about the challenge and how to use augmented in Education. Fan et al. [5] pointed out the significance of AR based experiment in education and mentioned that AR technology will bring lots of new features for experimental education. The paper also summarized the AR based experiments in many subjects ranging from Medicine to Arts and Humanity. To apply AR in language learning, Meda et al. [6] has developed a mobile based augmented reality application that can detect English text and translate into Telugu language in real time. Students can use this application for translating English text available in text books and get appropriate Telugu meaning instantly. Barreira et al. [7] conducted the experiment in comparing the use of Augmented Reality games (MOW: Matching Objects and Words) and traditional teaching methods, for learning words in different languages. The results indicate that children who used the Augmented Reality games had a superior learning progress than those who used only traditional methods. For the motivation in learning, the result from Serio et al. [8] has shown that the use of augmented reality technology in learning environments had a positive effect on the motivation of middle-school students in visual arts course. In our experiment, we will design the AR games for English language learning to encourage Thai students to learn the language.

3 Experimental Setup

In language learning, there are three areas that children have to conquer; namely writing, reading and speaking. To motivate children in these three areas, designing suitable augmented reality experiments have to be examined. Since we have decided to use marker-based techniques, all these three experiments will be designed based on markers.

In this experiment, Unity 3D game engine is used on Qualcomm's Vuforia platform. Unity is a fully integrated development engine which is used for creating games and other interactive 3D content and Vuforia platform makes it possible to write a

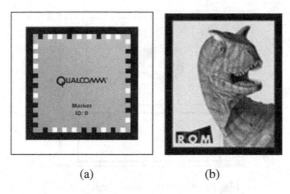

Fig. 4. (a) Frame marker [9] and (b) User defined target [10]

single native application that runs on almost all smartphones and tablets. In Vulforia, marker can be defined into two categories: "frame markers" and "user-defined target" (see Fig. 4). "Frame markers" are black and white squares with a code embedded around the edge and "user-defined target" is the images or objects for things that can be tracked by the software. In our experiment, markers in both categories will be used.

In the first experiment, motivate writing; we have designed the children to create their own user-defined target i.e. an alphabet. If they write the alphabet correctly, then that alphabet will become the "marker" that will display 3D object related to that alphabet. In the second and third experiment, we have used the marker marker inter-action technique to help children enjoy reading and conversation. In reading experiment, all the alphabets are markers, so when children put these alphabets together, if the combinations mean something, then 3D animation of the thing related to that meaning will appear above the markers. Same as in the third experiment except that in this experiment, only two markers interact with each other and conversation related to that interaction will appear.

4   Testing the Concept

We have made 3 experiments with different techniques to investigate how to motivate children in early age i.e. primary school, Grade 1-5, in English learning. The first one deals with how to improve children handwriting. The second experiment is about using the techniques of marker combination to improve skill in word. And the last one is about using AR in motivating English conversation. Details on each experiment are as follow.

4.1   Improve English Handwriting

In this experiment, children are encouraged to make their own marker by using their own handwriting. If they write them nicely as an example, then it will become the marker and 3D animation related to that alphabet will pop up on the screen of an iPad or any smart phones which have suitable software. For this purpose, we have designed

Fig. 5. Alphabets writing guideline

Fig. 6. User defined target with AR effect

a pattern with alphabets writing guideline (Fig. 5), so that children can practice writing an alphabet. For example, if a series of "W" or "w" is written nicely then a whale will pop up and swim around (Fig. 6).

4.2 Improve Ability to Assemble Word

For this second experiment, we try to motivate English learning for children by using the techniques of marker combination to form words. Children can mix any alphabet they want and if it matches the name of any animal, that animal will pop up and start doing some activity. For this experiment, we have made an alphabet card with the picture of the alphabet as a marker (Fig. 7).

Using the marker-marker interaction techniques as a combination of marker in proper order, we can get the new marker composed up to four alphabet markers (Fig. 8). This new makers can display virtual object such as animal on top of the markers. For example, if they put four markers representing b, e, a, r in this order, then a 3D bear will pop up and start growling (Fig. 9).

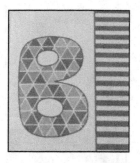
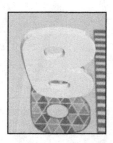

Fig. 7. Alphabet card as a marker

Fig. 8. A new marker composed of four individual markers

Fig. 9. AR effect caused by combination of markers

4.3 Motivating English Pronunciation and Conversation

The third experiment is for children in higher grade, a marker-marker interaction technique is used to form a conversation game. Markers can represent people or object of interests such as food, place or household equipment. If one marker represents a person, when we using a smart phone or a tablet to activate AR activity, then that person will talk about himself or herself. If we put another marker that represents another person, then they will start talking to each other. If we take the marker apart, they will say goodbye to each other (see Fig. 10). If one marker represents a person and

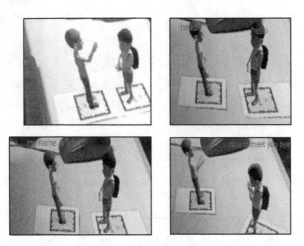

Fig. 10. Conversation between two students

the other marker represents an object such as a microwave oven, then that person will tell something that related to a microwave oven.

Children can learn English conversation or how to elaborate and even how to pronounce words.

The idea of these experiments is to let the children interact with activities so that motivation in learning will occurred. These activities can run on any smart phone or tablet or PC, making them suitable for learning in class or at home.

5   Results and Discussion

We have selected a primary school in Nakorn si Thammarat province which located in the southern part of Thailand for testing this concept. The participating children are students in Grade four and five (Figs. 11 and 12).

For each experiment, the children were divided into two groups of ten students. One group doing the experiment without knowing about Augmented Reality and the other group were explained about what will happen if they did the experiment

Fig. 11. Students with hand writing experiment

Fig. 12. Students with word assembly experiment

correctly. The students in Grade 4 are selected for the hand writing experiment, a group that knows what will happen seem to concentrate on completing the hand writing exercise nicely while students in the other group want to finish the exercise by using small amount of time. The average time spending on the first group is a little bit higher than the other group but the percentage of perfection is also higher. The same results also applied for the second experiment on word assembly. This indicates that the motivation in learning is increasing. The students enjoy taking more time to study and explore the result. For the third experiment about conversation, we only observe the participation of the students and found that they do not afraid of making a conversation in English. To conclude the results of three experiments, although it may not show significant difference between using AR and non-AR to do the exercises, this may be because hand writing exercise is easy for most of the students. We found that the students who have no experience in using AR can learn to use AR tool very fast and showing their enthusiasm to do the exercise carefully.

References

1. Augment Reality LAB. http://www.arlab.com/blog/markerless-augmented-reality/
2. Brand, R.: Nokia Maps to get augmented reality functionality. Windows Phone News. http://www.windowscentral.com/nokia-maps-get-augmented-reality-functionality
3. Blum, T., Kleeberger, V., Bichlmeier, C., Navab, N.: Mirracle: An augmented reality magic mirror system for anatomy education. In: IEEE Virtual Reality 2012, pp. 115–116. IEEE (2012)
4. Kamarainen, A.M., Metcalf, S., Grotzer, T., Browne, A., Mazzuca, D., Tutwiler, M.S., Dede, C.: EcoMOBILE: Integrating augmented reality and probeware with environmental education field trips. Computers & Education **68**, 545–556 (2013). Elsevier
5. Fan, P., Zhou, M., Wang, X.: The significance and effectiveness of augmented reality in experimental education. In: 2011 International Conference on E -Business and E -Government (ICEE), pp. 1–4. IEEE (2011)
6. Meda, P., Kumar, M., Parupalli, R.: Mobile augmented reality application for telugu language learning. In: 2014 IEEE International Conference on MOOC, Innovation and Technology in Education, pp. 183–186. IEEE (2014)
7. Barreira, J., Bessa, M., Pereira, L.C., Adão, T., Peres, E., Magalhães, L. In: 7th Iberian Conference on Information Systems and Technologies, MOW: Augmented Reality Game to

Learn Words in Different Languages: Case study: Learning English names of animals in elementary school, pp. 1–6. IEEE (2012)

8. Serio, A.D., Ibáñez, M.B., Kloos, C.D.: Impact of an augmented reality system on students' motivation for a visual art course. Computers & Education **68**, 586–596 (2013). Elsevier

9. Qualcomm Vuforia Developer Portal. https://developer.vuforia.com/resources/dev-guide/frame-markers

10. Royal Ontario Museum. http://www.rom.on.ca/en/exhibitions-galleries/exhibitions/past-exhibitions/ultimate-dinos/augmented-reality

G-NETS – Gesture-Based Nursing Educational Training Support System

Jen-Wei Chang[1], Chang-Fang Huang[2], Robert L. Good[3], and Chun-Chia Lee[4(✉)]

[1] Department of Electrical Engineering, National Taiwan University, Taipei, Taiwan (R.O.C.)
`jenweichang@ntu.edu.tw`
[2] Department of Nursing, Fooyin University, Kaohsiung, Taiwan (R.O.C.)
`ns096@fy.edu.tw`
[3] Department of English, National Kaohsiung First University of Science and Technology, Kaohsiung, Taiwan (R.O.C.)
`rgood@nkfust.edu.tw`
[4] Department of Information Management, Fooyin University, Kaohsiung, Taiwan (R.O.C.)
`chunchia.derek@gmail.com`

Abstract. This study aimed to apply gesture-based cognition learning technology to develop an educational training support system (G-NETS) for physical assessment practicum. The processes of G-NETS system development can be divided into two stages: user-centered design (UCD) development and system verification. Eventually, the quantitative and qualitative analysis is conducted to evaluate nursing students learning performance, attitude, cognitive load, and technology acceptance. Results reveal that G-NETS can help the clinical nursing instructors to access the learners' information easily, to monitor the student's learning behavior in clinical courses, and to give them timely support and feedbacks accordingly. That in turn can reduce the percentage of mistakes and increase the quality of clinical practicum learning process. In the future, this study can be applied to clinical education, the training of new clinical nursing staff, other subjects of clinical practicum training, which expand the beneficial results of practical training and clinical teaching.

Keywords: Gesture-based learning · Natural user interface (NUI) · Clinical nursing practicum · Cognitive task analysis · Clinical training support system

1 Introduction

Clinical nursing practicum is a critical clinical teaching unit for clinical nursing students, especially in physical assessment practicum, which includes complex application of combined knowledge with clinical skills [1]. In practicum courses, students would be divided into different groups to conduct standard operating process in physical assessment practicum. Then, the clinical teaching instructors assist to correct their motions and processes of physical assessment. However, clinical nursing instructors encounter more challenges because of insufficient and lack of experienced assistants [2]. In such

© Springer International Publishing Switzerland 2015
P. Zaphiris and A. Ioannou (Eds.): LCT 2015, LNCS 9192, pp. 33–42, 2015.
DOI: 10.1007/978-3-319-20609-7_4

circumstances, it is difficult for clinical nursing instructors to build effective and highly interactive support to nursing students in physical assessment practicum course [3, 4]. Therefore, how to improve these clinical difficulties has becoming crucial issues for clinical nursing instructors [4–6].

Recently, development of gesture-based technology creates emerging opportunities for instructors to provide students easier and more intuitive ways to interact with the course contents in interactive learning environments than ever before [7, 8]. For instance, Kinect [9], a motion-sensing input device developed by Microsoft for Xbox360, allows nursing students to use their body motions, such as swiping, jumping and moving, to interact with the content on the screen. Gestures play as an important roles of non-verbal communication within demonstration and presentation tasks, which can support the construction of a complete mental representation of the discourse content [10–12]. NMC Horizon Project report indicated that gesture-based learning (for instance, Microsoft Kinect, Nintendo Wii and Sony PlayStation Move) would be 4-5 years time-to-adoption educational technology in higher education [7].

Therefore, this study aimed to apply gesture-based cognition learning technology to develop an educational training support system (G-NETS) for physical assessment practicum. G-NETS can be anticipate to help the clinical nursing instructors to access the learners' information easily, to monitor the student's learning behavior in clinical courses, and to give them timely support and feedbacks accordingly. That in turn can reduce the percentage of mistakes and increase the learning quality of clinical practicum students.

2   Development of G-NETS

For increasing the effectiveness of G-NETS in learning, the design concepts of G-NETS system development take user-centered design (UCD) theory into consideration [13]. User-centered design (UCD) method is widely used in the practicum learning to facilitate instructor-student interaction, instructor need various information support including access student's profile, monitor student's learning behavior, on-line learning support and immediate feedback [14–16]. This method has become increasingly prominent as a model of instruction.

Following UCD development steps, we explored instructor's teaching requirement and contexts of physical assessment practicum through ethnographic study. Task analysis was then conducted to confirm instructor's teaching activities and analyze the information processing in physical assessment practicum. To identify nurse's decision-making skills and cognitive process in physical assessment, cognitive task analysis (CTA) [17, 18] is also employed to capture the knowledge that nursing students perform complex nursing tasks, including patient's medical record reading, physiological signals evaluation, pathological data collection, and situation summarization and diagnosis.

After all, this study developed the gesture-based training support system (G-NETS) based on the CTA analysis and the gesture interaction requirement. Visual Studio 2010 C# language, NET Framework 4.0, and Microsoft Kinect SDK is used for developing the system [9]. Eventually, nursing students were recruited to conduct a usability testing for evaluating the overall performance of G-NETS. This study also collected the feedback from in-depth interview of the nursing students.

3 G-NETS - Cardiovascular System Assessment as an Example

Clinical physical assessment course includes many clinical learning units (systems). This study took cardiovascular system as an example. G-NETS comprise two modules: module 1 for basic physical assessment practicum & module 2 for case simulation of physical assessment. The nursing student firstly logs onto the G-NETS and chooses module to practice. Then, G-NETS will show the purpose of unit and tasks need to complete. In the cardiovascular system unit, the students will fulfill the following purposes: (1) Identify cardiovascular anatomy; (2) Understand normal and abnormal heart sounds; the (3) Identify the inspection results between normal and abnormal.

3.1 Module 1: Basic Physical Assessment Practicum

After reading the statement of purposes and related tasks in module 1, G-NETS will randomly choose a set from the database of basic physical assessment practicum. Each basic practicum set includes a series of standards assessment problems. The nursing student will follow system guidance to practice the assessment problems step by step. Followings are example problems:

Example 1: Identify the Position of Cardiovascular Anatomy. G-NETS will randomly generate first type of problems, such as "Please point out the position of AO in the cardiovascular anatomy?" The nursing students need to identify where the position of AO in the cardiovascular anatomy is (see Fig. 1). They then move their hand to the position of number and push the number button when they decide an answer. If the answer is correct, G-NETS will go next item. If it is wrong, G-NETS will prompt the correct answer. Then, the students need to practice the same problem again until the answer are correct.

Example 2: Understand Cardiac Circle and Identify Normal and Abnormal Heart Sounds. After passing the cardiovascular anatomy, G-NETS will show the cardiac circle. When finishing the learning of cardiac circle, G-NETS generates second type of problems, such as "Please indicate the position when you hear the normal and abnormal heart sounds". Again, the nursing students need to identify where the position of heart sounds in the cardiovascular anatomy (see Fig. 2). They then will move their hand to the position of number and push the number button when they think of an answer. If the answer is correct, G-NETS will go next problem. If it is wrong, G-NETS will prompt the correct answer. Then, the students need to practice again until the answer is correct.

When all testing problems are correct, G-NETS will present "Passing module 1. Please go to module 2". Through the processes, the student is able to familiarize with complete steps and skills of physical assessment.

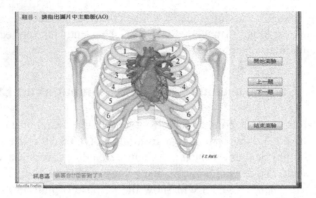

Fig. 1. Identify the position of cardiovascular anatomy

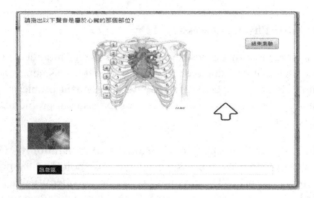

Fig. 2. Normal and abnormal heart sounds

3.2   Module 2: Case Simulation

Once the nursing students enter into module 2, the G-NETS chooses a case from the scenario case database for practicing physical assessment. The students are guided through the standard operating process (SOP) of physical assessment. The students has to judge his/her answers according to the case information offered by G-NETS. The processes includes five stages: (1) Read the patient history information; (2) Review the system of body: such as Respiratory system, Gastrointestinal system, Hematological system, Genitourinary system, Musculoskeletal system, Neurological system; (3) Collect pathology information using inspection, palpation, percussion, auscultation; (4) Diagnose the question from pathology information; (5) Determine the instance treatment according to the given information. Following is an example of physical assessment case.

Step 0: Select a Case. Firstly, the nursing student selects a case from scenario case database (see Fig. 3).

Fig. 3. Case selection

Step 1: Read Case Information. In the same time, the G-NETS will show the patient's information. In this case, patient's information is, "Mr. Lin, 57 years old man, a manager of a electrical company. He felt chest pain severely at meeting. He was sent to emergency department for further management. You are his in charge student nurse, how do you to collect the patient subjective and objective data to identify the patient's problem and give the nursing intervention immediately". (See Fig. 4).

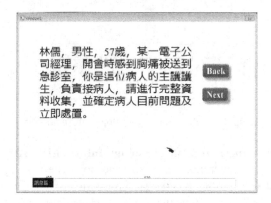

Fig. 4. Case background

Step 2: Review System of Body. The second stage will review the system of body. In G-NETS, we adopt question & answer method to simulate the system review environment. The G-NETS show the question like nursing expert, and then the nursing student push the answer button to listen and present the patient answer. When finishing all the question & answer items, students can practice and listen once again (Fig. 5).

Step 3: Collect Pathology Information. Like Step 2, to simulate collection of pathology information, the G-NETS still adopt question & answer method. The G-NETS system show the question like nursing expert, and then the nursing students push the answer button to listen and present the patient answer. When finishing all the questions, students

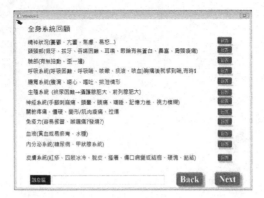

Fig. 5. System review

can practice and listen once again. (See Fig. 6) The pathology information includes present history, daily activities, past history, family history.

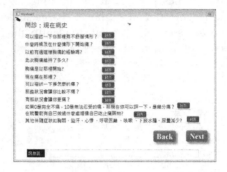

Fig. 6. Collection of pathology information

Step 4: Diagnose the Question from Pathology Information. After finishing Step 1 to Step 3, G-NETS will generate a diagnosis question. The nursing student needs to diagnose possible diseases from pathology information. They can move the answer button in left side to the answer frame in the right side (see Fig. 7). When all the answers are correct, the G-NET will present "Pass" and then go to next step.

Step 5: Determine the Instance Treatment According to the Given Information. In this step, the G-NETS system show the instance treatment procedures like nursing expert, and then the nursing students push the answer button to listen and review the suggestion answer accordingly. When finishing all the procedures, students can choose to practice and listen once again. (See Fig. 8)

After finishing all steps in module 2, the student then can learn other cases. When finishing all cases in module 2, G-NETS will present "Congratulation". Through this method, the nursing students will learn how to make a physical assessment, that increases the effectiveness of learning.

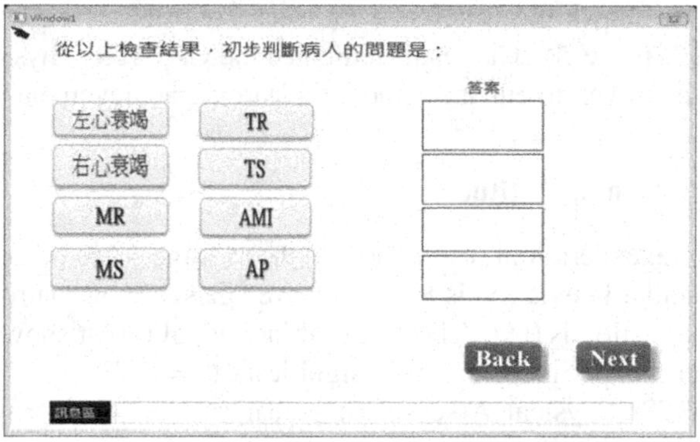

Fig. 7. Diagnose the pathology question

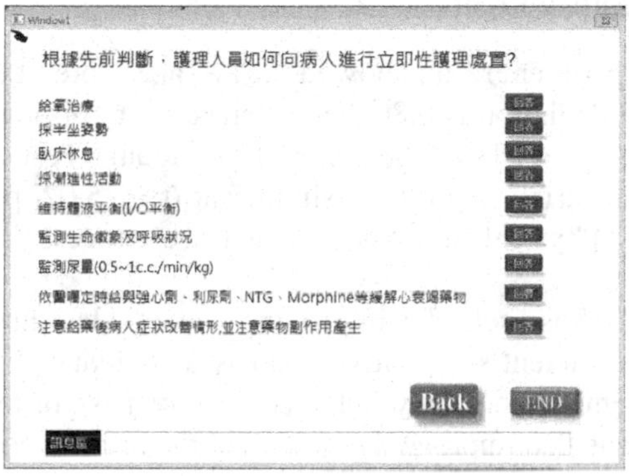

Fig. 8. Instance treatment

4 Result and Discussion

To understand the results of G-NETS on physical assessment courses, two fourth- grade classes of nursing department had been selected as subjects. The experimental group, including fifty-one students, was guided by G-NETS to conduct physical assessment courses, while the control group with forty-eight students was guided by the traditional learning approach. All of the students were taught by the same instructor whose teaching experiences for more than ten years. The evaluation tools in this study included learning achievement test of exams, questionnaires of learning attitude, cognitive load, and the acceptance of the G-NETS. Followings are experimental results.

4.1 Analysis of Learning Achievements

After the experiment, the data analysis comprises learning achievements, learning attitude, and cognitive load. For learning achievements, experiment result showed the average score of experiment group is 71.88, and the standard deviation is 8.17. The average score of control group is 64.30, and the standard deviation is 10.04. The result of individual t-Test shows the difference between control and experiment group is significant(t = 4.13, p < .05). The result indicated the G-NETS' Physical Assessment guidance process is proven to enhance student's learning achievements.

4.2   Analysis of Learning Attitude

For learning attitude, experiment result showed the average score of experiment group is 5.09, and the standard deviation is 8.17. The average score of control group is 4.50, and the standard deviation is 0.66. The result of individual t-Test shows the difference between control and experiment group is significant (t = 4.73, p < . 05). The result showed the G-NETS' Physical Assessment guidance process is proved to enhance student's self-learning attitude.

4.3   Analysis of Cognitive Load

For cognitive load, experiment result showed the average score of experiment group is 4.01, and the standard deviation is 0.80. The average score of control group is 64.30, and the standard deviation is 10.04. The result of individual t-Test shows the difference between control and experiment group is significant (t = -5.02, p < . 05). The result denoted the G-NETS Physical Assessment guidance process is proven to reduce student's cognitive load.

In summary, G-NETS is useful for improving student's learning achievements and learning attitude, and student's cognitive load is also reduced. The gesture-based teaching support system can not only enhance effectiveness in technology-mediated cognitive processing but also improve the quality of the nursing course.

4.4   Qualitative Analysis

Besides above quantitative analysis, this study also initially evaluates the influence of G-NETS on teaching and assessment performance using qualitative data analysis. We randomly selected and interviewed with several clinical instructors and their course students. The qualitative analysis includes the clinical instructor's subjective experience, opinions, and suggestions on G-NETS. Several instructors considered the gesture based physical assessment could effectively enhance students' learning motivation because of its novelty. Most physical assessment course instructors recognized G-NETS's positive influence on student's learning achievements, and would like to apply this system to other courses in the future. However, some instructors questioned the G-NETS' performance from the technical points of view. They considered the application of G-NETS' only focus on the course test and knowledge-based training, the teaching of main technical movement (such as inspection, auscultation, percussion, and palpation) is limited in current system. Therefore, they suggested G-NETS can be used as learning support tools in the current training of technical course.

Specifically, most instructors agree G-NETS can effectively reduce the workload of instructors. Instructors can't take care of multiple students' course practice when they are placing in the physical course. Students can learn by themselves and increase their mastering of physical assessment course through G-NETS' support. Additionally, G-NETS allows students to sense the effectiveness of physical practice intuitively. G-NETS increases student's self-learning opportunity and motivates student's self-challenging capability. Some students reported the G-NETS could instruct them step by step, especially for unfamiliar learning unit in the course. Although the G-NETS support has been recognized as being effective, some students reported G-NETS is time-consuming because the system allows them to proceed to next unit after they answer overall questions correctly. This design is used for improving student's mastering but also require them to take time. Students also reported the G-NETS is too monotonous for them and needs to increase some interesting design. Students also mentioned usability issue of the G-NETS. They found the gesture system sometimes out of tune because it fails to detect the gesture movement, which may reduce student's learning motivation.

5 Conclusion

This study aimed to apply gesture-based cognition learning technology to develop an educational training support system (G-NETS) for physical assessment practicum. Results reveal that G-NETS can help the clinical nursing instructors to access the learners' information easily, to monitor the student's learning behavior in clinical courses, and to give them timely support and feedbacks accordingly. That in turn can reduce the percentage of mistakes and increase the quality of clinical practicum learning process. This research finding of this study can be applied to clinical education, the training of new clinical nursing staff, other subjects of clinical practicum training, to expand the beneficial results of practical training and clinical teaching. Future work will attempt to account for, and evaluate the design of more context-aware gesture-based educational training support system. In doing so, will validate broad guidelines for the development of teaching support system for a range of nursing educational settings.

Acknowledgements. This study is supported in part by the Ministry of Science and Technology, Taiwan, under contract numbers MOST 102-2221-E-242-002- and NSC103-2221-E-242-004-.

References

1. Gillespie, M., McFetridge, B.: Nurse education–the role of the nurse teacher. J. Clin. Nurs. **15**(5), 639–644 (2006)
2. Kuen, M.: Perceptions of effective clinical teaching behaviors in a hospital-based nurse training program. J. Adv. Nurs. **26**(6), 1252–1261 (1997)
3. Watson, S.: The support that mentors receive in the clinical setting. Nurse Educ. Today **20**(7), 585–592 (2000)
4. Hautala, K.T., Saylor, C.R., O'Leary-Kelley, C.: Nurses' perceptions of stress and support in the preceptor role. J. Nurs. Staff Dev. **23**(2), 64–70 (2007)
5. Benner, P.: From Novice to Expert. Addison Wesley, Sydney (1984)

6. Hurst, K., Dean, A., Trickey, S.: The recognition and non-recognition of problem solving stages in nursing practice. J. Adv. Nurs. **16**, 1444–1455 (1991)
7. Johnson, L., Smith, R., Willis, H., Levine, A., Haywood, K.: The 2011 horizon report. The New Media Consortium, Austin, TX (2011)
8. Sheu, Feng-Ru, Chen, Nian-Shing: Taking a signal: A review of gesture-based computing research in education. Comput. Educ. **78**, 268–277 (2014)
9. Microsoft (2012). Kinect for Windows. http://www.microsoft.com/en-us/kinectforwindows/develop/
10. Chang, C.-Y., Chien, Y.-T., Chiang, C.-Y., Lin, M.-C., Lai, H.-C.: Embodying gesture-based multimedia to improve learning. Br. J. Educ. Technology **44**, E5–E9 (2013)
11. Chao, K.-J., Huang, H.-W., Fang, W.-C., Chen, N.-S.: Embodied play to learn: exploring kinect-facilitated memory performance. Br. J. Education. Tech. **44**, E151–E155 (2013)
12. Hung, I.-C., Lin, L.-I., Fang, W.-C., Chen, N.-S.: Learning with the body: an embodiment-based learning strategy enhances performance of comprehending fundamental optics. Interact. Comput. **26**, 360–371 (2014)
13. Nielsen, J.: Guerrilla HCI: using discount usability engineering to penetrate the intimidation barrier, Cost-justifying usability. Academic Press, Orlando, FL (1994)
14. Vredenberg, K., Isensee, S., Righi, C.: User-Centered Design: An Integrated Approach with CD-ROM. Prentice Hall PTR, Upper Saddle River, NJ (2001)
15. Constantine, L.: Beyond user-centered design and user experience: designing for user performance. Cutter IT J. **17**, 16–25 (2004)
16. Tullis, T., Albert, W.: Measuring the User Experience: Collecting, Analyzing, and Presenting Usability Metrics. Morgan Kaufmann Publishers, San Francisco, CA (2008)
17. Maarten, S.J., Chipman, S.F., Shalin, V.L.: Cognitive task analysis. Psychology Press, New York (2000)
18. Militello, L.G., Hutton, R.J.B.: Applied Cognitive Task Analysis (ACTA): a practitioner's toolkit for understanding cognitive task demands. Ergonomics **41**, 1618–1641 (1998)

Dual-Coding Strategy for the Chinese Characters Learners: Chinese PCS Editor

Chi Nung Chu[✉]

Department of Management of Information System, China University of Technology,
No. 56, Sec. 3, Shinglung Rd., Wenshan Chiu, Taipei 116,
Taiwan, People's Republic of China
nung@cute.edu.tw

Abstract. This paper discusses the efficacy of self-generated visualization on pitch recognition for the music sight-singing learning from the Internet. The self-generated visualization on music sight-singing learning system incorporates pitch recognition engine and visualized pitch distinguishing curve with descriptions for each corresponding stave notation on the web page to bridge the gap between singing of pitch and music notation.

This paper shows the conducted research results that this web-based sight-singing learning system could scaffold cognition about aural skills effectively for the learner through the Internet.

Keywords: Computer assisted language learning · Picture communication symbols · Chinese PCS editor · Dual coding theory

1   Introduction

Word identification is the essential skill to the process of reading [1]. The whole reading process involves two separate but highly interrelated areas - word identification and comprehension [2, 6, 8]. It requires readers familiar with letters of the alphabet and phonemic awareness. If a reader has difficulties in automatic word recognition significantly, that will affect the reader's ability to effectively comprehend what they are reading [7, 14]. Development of phonemic awareness is necessary to learn how to map speech to print. However written Chinese is a logographic orthography that differs greatly from alphabetic writing systems. The orthography–phonology relationship in alphabetic scripts is transparent. It is even harder for the text decoding difficulty readers to develop Chinese phonological ability.

The dual coding theory referred to the idea that visual and verbal information are processed differently and along distinct channels in the human mind, creating separate representations for information processed in each channel [11]. The mental codes corresponding to these representations are used to organize incoming information that can be acted upon, stored, and retrieved for subsequent use. Both visual and verbal codes can

© Springer International Publishing Switzerland 2015
P. Zaphiris and A. Ioannou (Eds.): LCT 2015, LNCS 9192, pp. 43–49, 2015.
DOI: 10.1007/978-3-319-20609-7_5

be used when recalling information [13]. Readers can facilitate two codes each due to the different sensory experiences from which they originated to read. Reading materials can also be presented in some other forms associated with texts to increase the efficiency of readers' recall and retention [3, 4, 10, 12]. Picture Communication Symbols (PCS) are a set of colour and black & white drawings which are easy to learn by children with little or no speech [5, 9].

With the development of digital technology, better texts in alternative picture and vocal environment can be created for children with the opportunities of multi-sensory interactions. In this paper, the Chinese PCS Editor was designed to provide children with Chinese picture-based sentence construction environment. The children's Chinese characters learning efficiency can be increased through the scaffolding process in the development of language abilities.

2   System Architecture

Based on Microsoft platform, the design of Chinese PCS Editor integrates PCS database developed by Unlimiter for use in augmentative and alternative communication (AAC) system [15], IBM ViaVoice Chinese Text-To-Speech Engine and Microsoft sound recorder (Fig. 1).

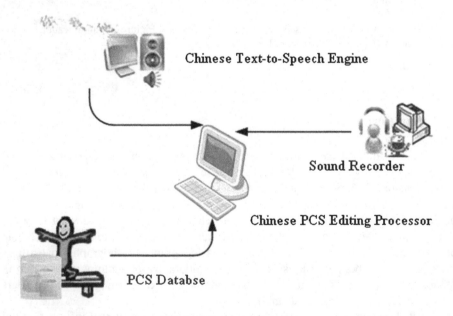

Fig. 1. System architecture

Usually children have developed their own picture and vocal vocabularies before they learn to identify word vocabularies. PCS database consisting of a core library of more than 3,000 symbols provides users for developing their own PCS starting from zero for certain needs to the Chinese characters with limited word identification capabilities. Chinese Text-to-Speech Engine converting Mandarin text into speech allows users to use their computer to identify the Chinese characters verbally. Sound recorder can be helpful to users as a memory aid and as an alternative to writing.

3   User Interface

The Chinese PCS Editing Processor consists of PCS Producer and PCS Editing Board (Fig. 2).

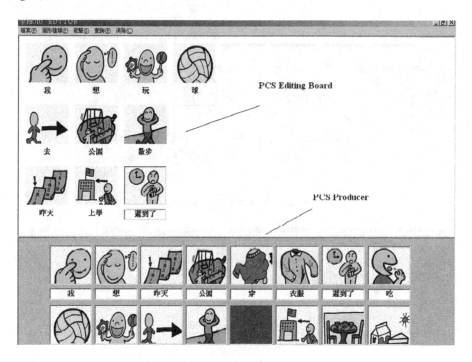

Fig. 2. Chinese PCS editor

The setting of PCS Producer includes the number of input PCS plates and the specified PCS setup. The choices of input PCS plates are divided into 2, 4, 6, 8 or 16. Users could manipulate the "Query" function provided on the function bar of Chinese PCS Editor to setup the specified PCS into one PCS plate (Fig. 3). For the unavailable PCS in the PCS database, users could either input the text directly or add picture/photograph by themselves for the PCS Editing Board further use.

PCS Editing Board is where the users write the sentences by dragging the target PCS from the PCS Producer. The Chinese PCS Editor could save and open the PCS sentences for users for later use and practice (Fig. 4).

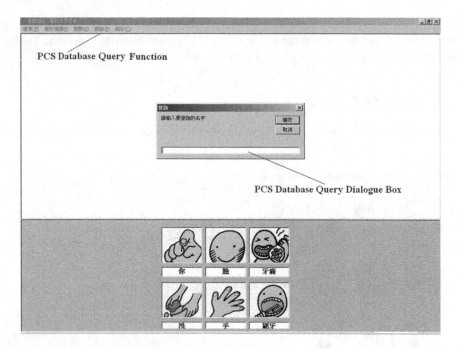

Fig. 3. PCS database query

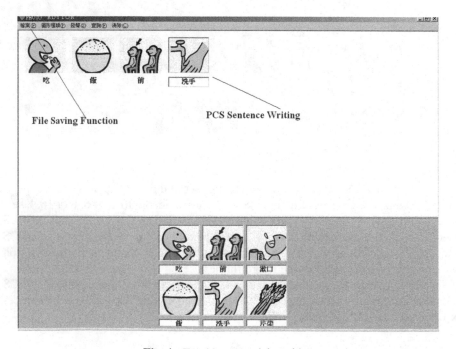

Fig. 4. Teaching materials making

As the output of speech is automatically produced by the Chinese Text-to-Speech Engine, users could repeatedly select a PCS word or PCS sentences to listen. At the same time, users could also express themselves through the PCS writings with the spoken out from the Chinese Text-to-Speech Engine. Any PCS dragged to the PCS Editing Board would be read out immediately to impress the users for learning purpose.

For any PCS in the PCS plate of PCS Producer, users could alter relative PCS words from the PCS database by clicking the right button of mouse, such as replacing "ball" with "basketball" (Fig. 5).

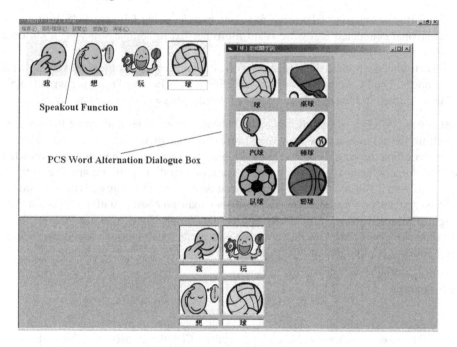

Fig. 5. PCS word alternations

In brief, Chinese PCS Editor works as a Word Processor with PCSs instead of words. And it is totally a software solution for the assisted Chinese character learning. Users could manipulate it easily in short time and make learning efficiently.

4   Benefits Evaluation

This Chinese PCS Editor was designed as a support for children in the learning process of Chinese characters at one elementary school in Taipei. The posttest scores (M = .56, SD = .19) were significantly greater than pretest scores (M = .39, SD = .20), $F(1, 93) = 87.73$, $p < .001$. Although there was no overall significant effect of tutoring conditions on posttest scores, learning with Chinese PCS Editor produced significant word identification and reading comprehension.

5   Conclusion

There are three anticipated effects from the completion of Chinese PCS Editor for children in the learning process of Chinese characters as the follows:

1. Encouraging the special education professionals and speech language pathologists developing digitalized PCS training materials. The operational interfaces of Chinese PCS Editing Processor are simplified to reduce the learning curve for the expertise users.
2. Providing easier use of learning environment. As using Chinese PCS Editor, the additional connected hardware is no more needed in comparison with traditional PCS drawing board.
3. Developing the potential of children with communication disorders for writing with symbols. The PCS editing function of Chinese PCS Editing Processor would facilitate children in the cognitive process of words, phrases, sentences and paragraph.

The Chinese PCS Editor for children with Chinese character identification difficulty tries to scaffold the unfamiliar texts from their pre-established picture and vocal vocabularies. While decoding the actual Chinese words, children could focus their attention on what the text actually means. With the eased burden of decoding, children are free to think about and gain. Children can thus derive more benefit from reading activities. Children will have greater opportunities for independence than ever before with such design. The design of Chinese PCS Editor could reduce the complexity of making PCS teaching materials and time for the special education educators, rehabilitation specialist/therapist and parents of communication disorders.

References

1. Baker, E.L., Atwood, N.K., Duffy, T.M.: Cognitive approaches to assessing the readability. In: Davidson, A., Green, G.M. (eds.) Linguistic Complexity and Text Comprehension: Readability Issues Reconsidered, pp. 55–83. Lawrence Erlbaum Associates Inc., Hillsdale (1988)
2. Catts, H.W., Fey, M.E., Tomblin, J.B., Zhang, X.: A longitudinal investigation of reading outcomes in children with language impairments. J. Speech Lang. Hear. Res. **45**, 1142–1157 (2002)
3. Ehri, L.C., Deffner, N.D., Wilce, L.S.: Pictorial mnemonics for phonics. J. Educ. Psychol. **76**, 880–893 (1984)
4. Fulk, B.M., Lohman, D., Belfiore, P.J.: Effects of integrated picture mnemonics on the letter recognition and letter-sound acquisition of transitional first-grade students with special needs. Learn. Disabil. Q. **20**, 33–42 (1997)
5. Fuller, D., Lloyd, L.: Toward a common usage of iconicity terminology. Augmentative Altern. Commun. **7**, 215–220 (1991)
6. Kieras, D., Just, M.: New Methods in Reading Comprehension Research. Erlbaum, Hillsdale (1984)
7. Lyon, G.R.: Towards a definition of Dyslexia. Ann. Dyslexia **45**, 3–27 (1995)
8. Mercer, C.D., Mercer, A.R.: Teaching Students with Learning Problems. Merrill Prentice Hall, Upper Saddle River (2001)

9. Mizuko, M.: Transparency and ease of learning of symbols represented by Blissymbolics, PCS, and Picsyms. Augmentative Altern. Commun. **3**, 129–136 (1987)

10. Moreno, R., Valdez, A.: Cognitive load and learning effects of having students organize pictures and words in multimedia environments: the role of student interactivity and feedback. Educ. Technol. Res. Dev. **53**(3), 35–45 (2005)

11. Paivio, A.: Mental Representations: A Dual Coding Approach. Oxford University Press, Oxford (1986)

12. Sadoski, M., Paivio, A., Goetz, E.T.: Commentary: a critique of schema theory in reading and a dual coding alternative. Read. Res. Q. **26**, 463–484 (1991)

13. Sternberg, R.J.: Cognitive Theory, 3rd edn. Thomson Wadsworth, Belmont (2003)

14. Torgesen, J.K., Rashotte, C.A., Alexander, A.W.: Principles of fluency instruction in reading: relationships with established empirical outcomes. In: Wolf, M. (ed.) Dyslexia, Fluency, and the Brain. York Press, Timonium (2001)

15. Yang, G.-P.: Multi-Media Wizard. Assistive Technology Engineering Lab, Taiwan (1995)

Exploring Student Interactions: Learning Analytics Tools for Student Tracking

Miguel Ángel Conde[1(✉)], Ángel Hérnandez-García[2], Francisco J. García-Peñalvo[3], and María Luisa Séin-Echaluce[4]

[1] Department of Mechanics, Computer Science and Aerospace Engineering, University of León, Campus de Vegazana S/N, 24071 León, Spain
miguel.conde@unileon.es
[2] Departamento de Ingeniería de Organización, Administración de Empresas y Estadística, Universidad Politécnica de Madrid, Av. Complutense 30, 28040 Madrid, Spain
angel.hernandez@upm.es
[3] Department of Computer Science, Faculty of Science, University of Salamanca, Plaza de los Caídos S/N, 37008 Salamanca, Spain
fgarcia@usal.es
[4] Department of Applied Mathematics, School of Engineering and Architecture, University of Zaragoza, María de Luna 3, 50018 Zaragoza, Spain
mlsein@unizar.es

Abstract. This paper presents four categories of learning analytics tools: dashboards, ad hoc tools, tools for analysis of specific issues, and learning analytics frameworks, and details the characteristics of a selection of tools within each category: (1) Moodle Dashboard and Moodle default reporting tool; (2) Interactions and Teamwork Assessment Tool; (3) SNAPP, GraphFES and Moodle Engagement Analytics; and (4) VeLA and GISMO. The study investigates how these tools can be applied to the analysis of courses by using real data from a course that made intensive use of forums, wikis, web resources, videos, quizzes and assignments. The discussion that follows points out how the different tools complement each other, and suggests the implementation of basic dashboards in learning platforms and the use of external frameworks for learning analytics.

Keywords: Learning analytics · User interactions · Moodle · Student tracking

1   Introduction

The application of Information and Communication Technologies (ICTs) to learning processes offers a new way to deliver instruction in face-to-face and distance learning. The best example of this is the use of learning platforms, such as Learning Management Systems (LMS). LMS give support to online and blended learning. In online and blended learning, due to the lack of face to face interaction, instructors and course coordinators need tools to track students. LMS register large amounts of information about student interactions, but this information is usually stored in the LMS databases as raw data, and thereby the extraction of meaningful information usually requires

© Springer International Publishing Switzerland 2015
P. Zaphiris and A. Ioannou (Eds.): LCT 2015, LNCS 9192, pp. 50–61, 2015.
DOI: 10.1007/978-3-319-20609-7_6

further processing [1]. The records in LMS logs store abundant information about student and teacher interactions –as well as access to resources and system functions. This information may give an idea of how and when students perform their assignments and tasks, course engagement, etc. However, extraction of meaningful data and transformation of this information into actionable knowledge is a difficult task. New educational disciplines, such as educational data mining, academic analytics or learning analytics offer different but convergent perspectives, methodologies, techniques and tools aiming to facilitate this transformation process.

Educational data mining includes a series of techniques oriented to extraction of educational data through statistical machine learning and data-mining algorithms, for analysis and solution of educational research issues [2]. Academic analytics takes a different approach, focusing on the analysis of institutional data about students; therefore, it has a stronger focus on institutional policy decision making [3, 4]. Finally, the main goal of learning analytics is "the measurement, collection, analysis and reporting of data about learners and their contexts, for purposes of understanding and optimizing learning and the environments in which it occurs" [5].

From the above, it is patent that, although there are some differences between the three disciplines, they have as a common objective the understanding of teaching and learning in order to make informed instructional decisions oriented toward the improvement of learning processes [6].

There is currently a wide choice of tools that facilitate educational data extraction and analysis for learning analytics purposes. A first broad categorization of these tools would include [7]:

- Cross-platform and platform-specific general purpose dashboards. Dashboards provide information about platform activity of the different learning agents –mainly, students and teachers–, generally in a visual and condensed form.
- Ad hoc tools. The design and implementation of ad hoc tools seeks to perform tracking and analysis of very specific types of information adapted to very specific contexts.
- Learning analytics tools for analysis of specific issues. These tools aim to provide information, and usually have very specific types of representation. It is also very common that they offer cross-platform capabilities.
- Learning analytics frameworks and tools. The design of learning analytics frameworks is directed toward standardization of learning ontologies and their implementation in different systems. They also pursue the exploration of student behaviors in different educational contexts and offer the user customizable visual representations of the information.

Taking into account the great variety of applications for learning analytics, this research study aims to describe some of them, and apply and compare their results using a common dataset from courses taught in a Moodle LMS. The results of this comparison will highlight the usefulness, advantages and disadvantages of the different approaches and perspectives, and how they can complement each other. This study has therefore two differentiated parts: first, it introduces the different learning analytics tools that will be analyzed, and then the empirical work will cover the results, including a comparison of the tools after analysis of datasets from existing courses. Finally, this study will wrap up the conclusions about the results from applying the different tools.

2 Analysis of Tools for Learning Analytics

This research covers both cross-platform and LMS-specific tools. Different versions of Moodle are required for testing of the different tools, as not all analytic tools are available for all the versions of Moodle. Most of these tools analyze user interaction from LMS log data. That means that most of the tools extract and transform data from the *mdl_log* database table. Until version 2.7 each developer could potentially add their logs to this table from an application, leading to log formats that could be "not standard". This problem is solved by the definition of a new log system in Moodle version 2.7. The new log system gathers more detailed information about user interaction that the previous system and, more important, it provides a standard API to write and read logs and increase system performance. Both log systems may coexist in Moodle installations with version numbers 2.7 and higher. Nevertheless, taking advantage of the new log system capabilities requires an adaptation of the different tools, and some of them have not updated to compatible versions yet. Therefore, the comparison presented in this study entails the use of different Moodle versions –note that the main objective of this research is to compare tools for learning analytics, not to address the problems related to how logs are stored in Moodle. The following subsections describe and analyze the different tools, according to the categorization showed in Sect. 1.

2.1 General Purpose Dashboards

Dashboards provide information about students or teachers activity in the platform, and present it in an aggregated and visually rich form –mainly tables and graphs with varying degrees of interactivity. Dashboards can be applied to different platforms [8, 9], or to a specific one [10]. These tools are primarily focused on the description of the activity carried out in LMS using very specific metrics, showing some relevant indicators at a glance, but they do not generally offer further information about how those metrics relate to each other. The main dashboard application for Moodle is Moodle Dashboard. There are other dashboards for Moodle, such as LearnGLASS or GoogleAnalytics, but these require adaptation and mapping of users' accounts to external systems and/or hardcoding Moodle source code.

Moodle Dashboard is provided as a block, and it allows users to graphically or literally display the result of any query made in Moodle. When used in standard course formats, the block gives access to an extra page that displays the data rendered for the specified query. There are different options to visualize the information returned from the queries: tables (linear tables, tabular tables and tree views), plots (line graphs, bar graphs, pie graphs, and "doughnut" graphs), geospatial and map graphs, and timelines. Moodle Dashboard may display the rendered data directly, but it may also combine with other blocks to form a complex, highly customizable dashboard. It has powerful data filtering capabilities, as well as a functionality to automatically generate data exports [11]. Moodle Dashboard is supported up to Moodle version 2.5.

Apart from Moodle Dashboard, the default Moodle reporting tool might also be considered a dashboard. Moodle reporting tool facilitates analysis of information about users' interactions in the platform, in different contexts. The different contexts available are site, course or activity, and the reports show information about user comments, course activity (most active, courses with most enrolled users, highest participation), LMS events logs (information of user's interaction in the LMS) and live logs (interactions occurring at a specific moment), and graphs and statistics about users' activity and view/post actions. Further filtering of this information is possible. On a course and activity level, it is also possible to gather information about course and activity completion, time spent to complete an activity, and grading information.

2.2   Ad Hoc Tools for Learning Analytics

Ad hoc tools are designed to track or analyze very specific bits of information, and to address a specific need in a very concrete context, with a set of defined constraints and conditions. The main problem of these solutions is that they are generally neither flexible nor scalable. This section describes two of these tools: (1) Interactions, a Moodle plug-in that groups types of interactions for later analysis, and (2) a web service that facilitates individual assessment of students in teamwork contexts.

Interactions is a plug-in that runs in Moodle versions 1.9 and 2.0 to 2.3. The plug-in is installed as a reporting block that adds functionality to the default reporting tool, with independent access permissions. Basically, Interactions adds a library that expands that functionality –including filtering capabilities– by creating a MS Excel spreadsheet with two different worksheets. The first one is an exact replica of the MS Excel file from the log reporting tool. The second worksheet processes each record and assigns it to a category within three different classifications (by agent, by frequency of use, and by participation mode) [6]. Experts on Moodle and eLearning participated in establishing the correspondence between actions and categories. The final output shows the total number of interactions of each category for each user in the platform. Because the results are already in Excel format, graphs can easily be derived from the output. Furthermore, the format allows easy integration with statistical analysis tools such as SPSS. It is noteworthy that the assignment of each record to any given category (a record can fall into one and only one category for each classification group, but it may appear in all the groups) is hardcoded in the processing library, and therefore any change to those assignments requires modification of the plug-in code.

The other tool is an ad hoc web service to assess student's performance in teamwork contexts. Building from Fidalgo-Blanco et al.'s [12] work, the web service proposes an approach to validate data about interactions as predictors of individual performance in teamwork contexts based on the Comprehensive Training Model of the Teamwork Competence (CTMTC) framework [13]. CTMTC indicates how to collect evidences from three sources: forums, cloud-based file storage services, and wikis. The system extracts students' interactions, enabling assessment of individual students and detection of conflicts. The tool uses the Moodle Web service layer [14] and extracts data from Moodle logs, focusing on forum posts and threads. It works in Moodle versions from 2.1 to 2.6 (its use in Moodle 2.7 or higher would require adaptation to the new log system). The tool allows choosing a forum within the course and then display the data for the student interactions with their peers, and has three different view modes: forum-based, team-based and thread-based. The tools gives information about the number of total messages in the forum/team/thread, as well as the number of people registered (the total number of team members), average participation of each student, the list of teams and the total list of students with their respective of the number of messages, creation dates of the first and last thread, list of threads (with the date of creation), and team members and degree of participation. In addition, rules of action can be defined based on thresholds set upon the number of messages [15].

2.3   Learning Analytics Tools for Analysis of Specific Issues

This set comprises tools of application focused on specific data and offering a very specific type of representation. These applications have very particular functionalities, and therefore they may or not fit institutional and personal needs. Some examples of cross-platform tools in this category are LEMO, SNAPP, StepUp!, while LMS-tied tools include Moodle Engagement Analytics, Moodle Learning Analytics Enriched Rubric or GraphFES.

Our analysis will focus on two tools for social network analysis –SNAPP (cross-platform) [16] and GraphFES (Moodle exclusive)–, which facilitates detection of disconnected students and gives information about the social interactions in the class, and Moodle Engagement Analytics [17], a Moodle block that provides information about at-risk students.

GraphFES (Graph Forum Extraction Service) is a web service that connects to both types of Moodle logs (legacy log and the new standard log) and extracts information from all the message boards in a given course. All the information that GraphFES collects is then processed to create three different graphs: (1) a graph including all the messages added by all users and how they relate to each other (i.e., a map of all the posts and how they are connected and organized in threads); (2) a graph connecting all the users in the course based on who has read contents posted by others, and how many times; (3) a similar graph to the previous one, but in which relations between course users are based on who replies to whom. GraphFES builds the social network graph and returns it as a .gefx file that can be opened in Gephi. The main idea behind GraphFES is that social network analysis is best done outside of the learning platform, using SNA specialized tools such as Gephi. Some advantages and applications of Gephi to the analysis of higher education courses from a social learning analytics approach can be found in [18, 19].

SNAPP (Social Networks Adapting Pedagogical Practice) [16] works as a book-marklet that extracts information from message boards in Sakai, Blackboard, Moodle and Desire2Learn, and then builds up the resulting social network in a Java applet. There are two versions of SNAPP (v.1.5 and v.2.1), and their functionalities are similar. SNAPP is structured in tabs, the first three of which are interactive. The first tab shows the graph of the social network from the interactions and allows the user to manipulate the graph by filtering, applying different layouts to the social graph and selecting individual nodes – nodes in SNAPP represent participants in the message board. SNAPP v.2.1 also displays a timeline of the messages posted in the forum. A second tab displays the values of the number of posts per user in v.1.5 and the main social network parameters (degree, in- and out- degree, betweenness and eigenvector centrality, and network density) in v.2.1. Finally, the third tab allows exporting the graph in GraphML and VNA formats in v.1.5, or writing annotations in v.2.1. (export capabilities are included in the first tab in v.2.1., adding the ability to export to.gefx format).

Engagement Analytics is a Moodle plug-in provided as a block that gathers and shows information, in the form of indicators, about student progress. As the name suggests, the block gives users insight on the level of engagement of a student, where engagement refers to activities which have an impact on student success in an online course. The block provides real-time ("live") information about students' interaction with resources, and incorporates a set of indicators and a risk alerting algorithm. This information may be useful for teachers to detect at-risk students and make decisions about when to intervene in order to avoid student failure. The indicators included in Engagement Analytics relate to student assessment, students' participation in forums and number student login frequency, and it is possible to assign each indicator different weights to describe and model students' risk of failure in a more customized way. Indicators comprise different items, and item weights can also be modified. This plugin is available from Moodle 2.2 up to Moodle 2.7, and the plug-in allows extension of the predefined indicators.

2.4 Learning Analytics Frameworks and Tools

The fourth category of tools includes applications and frameworks that can be applied to several platforms or contexts to explore different aspects of learning using different visual representations. Some examples of this kind of tools are SAM, VeLa or GISMO (this analysis covers the latter two).

VeLA (Visual eLearning Analytics) [20] is a framework that uses web services to extract information from LMS logs. VeLA provides different representations of the information and displays it in an interactive way. For example, users can filter, search, or change dynamically the representation of the information. VeLA offers four different functionalities: (1) a semantic spiral timeline that facilitates tracking users' platform activity during specific periods of time; (2) an interactive semantic tag cloud that allows users to analyze the most relevant terms and concepts used in a course; (3) a social graph that shows users' interactions; and (4) a tool to compare and establish relationships among the data stored in the LMS and users' activity. VeLA is supported by visual analytics techniques.

GISMO is a graphical interactive monitoring tool that provides visualization of students' activities in online courses. GISMO is a plug-in available for Moodle versions 1.9.X and 2.X. that enables teachers to examine diverse information about students, such as the course attendance, reading of materials, or assignment submission. GISMO provides comprehensive visualizations that give an overview of the whole class, not only a specific student or a particular resource. GISMO provides seven different visualizations: access overview, access to the course, access to resources, assignment overview, quizzes overview, access to resources overview, timeline of access to resources by student, and access to resources by student [21].

3 Method

In order to assess how the different tools work, this study uses data of 119 students from a Programming course at the Universidad Politécnica de Madrid. The course methodology aims to promote teamwork between students. The use of forums, wikis, web resources, videos, quizzes and assignments in the course is intensive, and therefore it is an adequate test bed for all the tools detailed in Sect. 2. The main results from the application of these tools are detailed next:

- Moodle Dashboard. The last version of the tool works properly for Moodle 2.5. We have tested it in a Moodle 2.6, and no results are returned from a simple query. With debugging mode activated, it is also possible to see an error, but no information is shown. The tool may be not adapted to versions of Moodle higher than 2.5.
- Moodle default reporting tool displays more than 122640 log entries (111644 are view actions, 9398 are actions to add resources and 821 are update actions). Detailed but raw information about each action is displayed in a table, and it is possible to export the results to a spreadsheet.
- Interactions. The plug-in does not work properly in Moodle versions 2.3 and higher. However, because it only processes data from the Moodle log table, it was possible to import the data directly via MySQL import and process data in Moodle 2.1. The result is a spreadsheet, where it is up to the teacher or course administrator to create graphs from the data to display information (see Fig. 1 for one example) and detect abnormal levels of different types of activity. The data may also be analyzed with statistical packages such as SPSS.

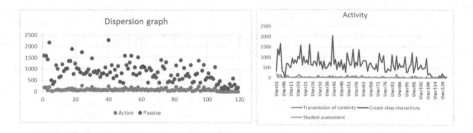

Fig. 1. Graphs created in MS Excel using data from interactions

- Teamwork assessment tool requires activation of Moodle web services. The tool provides a list of links of course forums. After selection, it is possible to see the participation in each forum, in a group, and individual participation. From this information it is possible, for instance, to know that those groups working in the mornings (there is an specific forum for them) have published 4974 posts with an average of 81,54 per user, and also who is the person with more posts (192 messages in this case). By inspecting a single group (group M9 in this case), the tool reports 990 posts,

6 users, 183 short messages (less than 140 characters) and 807 long messages, 141,43 posts per user, and how participation is distributed between students (in this case, between 13 % and 19 %) (Fig. 2). Further filtering on a per thread basis is also possible.

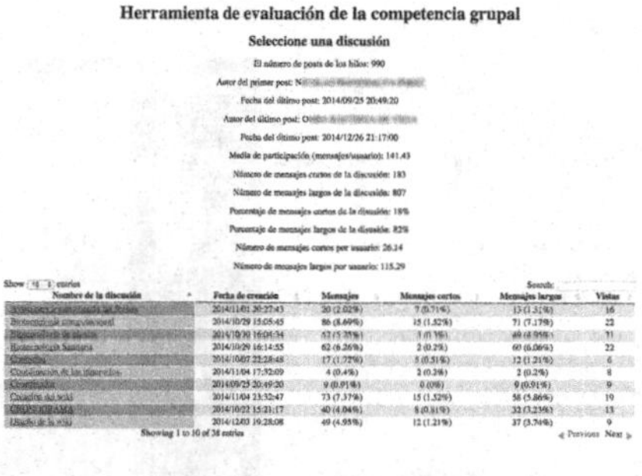

Fig. 2. Teamwork assessment tool showing information about participation of students in a forum.

- GraphFES offers a front end that requires login credentials, the platform's URL and course ID. After activation of the web service and granting user permissions in Moodle, GraphFES extracts all the information about forum activity from the Moodle data log table via the web service, and creates two lists of nodes (messages and users) and the relationships between them. The output consists of three .gefx files that can be opened and analyzed in Gephi (we refer to [18] for more information on how to use Gephi to perform social learning analytics). Figure 3 shows the three social graphs, including all users and posts (i.e., not filtered and not using node attributes), of the course.

Fig. 3. Social graphs of messages posted (9241), and read messages and replies among users (124, including teachers).

- Version 2.1 of the SNAPP applet does not work properly in any version of Moodle, and requires to configure security exceptions in Java Runtime Environment because it connects to an external source to perform the analysis. In order to build the social graph, the applet loads all threads in a forum and processes the HTML content. The problem seems to lie in the building of the social graph, and no participants are identified. Version 1.5 does not render any result for a message board either, but it allows analyzing individual threads. Unfortunately, it only works in earlier versions of Moodle (2.1), where it was not possible to restore the course data.
- Moodle Engagement Analytics aims to detect at-risk students. The setup for this study assigned equal relevance (weight) to logins, forum participation and assignments.

Figure 4a shows the results of the analysis (at-risk students are displayed in red, on the left side). The tool detected 18 students at-risk (failure probability above 65 %). Clicking on the name of the student shows a report explains why this person is considered at risk (Fig. 4a, right side).

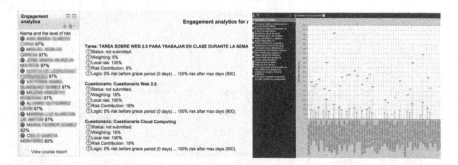

Fig. 4. Engagement block showing at-risk students, and the report of a specific student (left, 4a) and report of actions in a specific forum in GISMO (right, 4b).

- VeLA uses Moodle log data, and it revealed that the message board threads were used mainly to solve doubts, carry out the teamwork tasks, and publish news. This tool also represents users' interactions with peers and resources using force graphs. VeLA is an integrated framework, which means that filters and selections can be applied to all views at once [20].
- GISMO provides different visual representation of users' interactions. The example below presents the number of global actions in forums. Students' read and write actions are clearly distinguishable, and it is very easy to compare who has the most read actions (979) or who has published most posts (259). GISMO can also show students' actions in a specific forum (Fig. 4b) and other activities and resources.

4 Discussion

From the analysis of the tools, we can observe their strengths and shortcomings. Nevertheless, it must also be noted that the choice of tool will highly depend on the users' needs. For example, Moodle's default reporting tool offers a vast amount of information and filtering capabilities, but the information it provides consists of raw data, and therefore it offers very detailed information but it is not capable of providing meaningful aggregated information about the courses. As an example, the tool cannot answer a simple question like "How many students have not started a course yet?", or more complex questions regarding students' progress in a course.

Theoretically, Moodle Dashboard could give an answer to these questions, including visualizations of data (despite its lack of interactivity). However, this study could not test Moodle Dashboard due to its extremely difficult configuration process and its restricted compatibility with latest Moodle versions. Furthermore, Moodle Dashboard lacks flexibility for customized queries and reports, which makes it necessary to use ad hoc tools for particular purposes.

This study has explored two of these ad hoc tools. Interactions represents numerically users' interactions in a spreadsheet, allowing customization of graphs and facilitating statistical analysis, and the Teamwork assessment tool has a web interface and focuses on analysis and assessment of students' participation in message boards. Both tools solve very specific problems; however, their specificity makes it difficult to apply them in other contexts or platforms.

The study also described tools designed to address specific issues: two tools for social learning analytics (three, if we consider the social graph included in VeLA), and a tool for students' progress tracking and at-risk student detection. The main difference between the first two tools is that SNAPP includes a basic social network analysis module within the platform –note that SNAPP could not be tested with the study data due to malfunctioning– while GraphFES allows performing a complete and more detailed analysis using an external program. Regarding student tracking and at-risk student detection, Moodle Engagement Analytics relies on predefined indicators, and facilitates live monitoring of a course, which in turn allows teachers to take action when the system detects at-risk students; a major drawback is that, despite allowing customization of indicators' weights, the indicators are not intuitive and addition of new indicators requires additional coding.

Learning analytics frameworks aim to overcome the limitations of the above mentioned types of tools, and they integrate data, different functionalities and visualizations, and interactive data manipulation in one system. Obviously, learning analytics frameworks do not adapt so well to specific tasks because of their general purpose design. In a way, these frameworks could be considered some kind of advanced dashboard that integrates information but that can also provide very detailed information about courses and students.

As a conclusion, a qualitative analysis of the different tools included in the study shows that it is necessary to add some learning analytics capabilities to LMS such as Moodle within the same platform. For the sake of simplicity and compatibility, some basic dashboard and alert system would fit this task without need for further user training. Nevertheless, we show in this study how the different tools complement each other adding new functionalities, and that a more insightful analysis of educational data requires integration, complex visualizations and interactivity, for which learning analytics frameworks are suitable tools. A focus on the development, flexibility and stability of the LMS web service layer would be critical in order to facilitate implementation of these frameworks. Furthermore, a by-product of a consistent web service layer is the ability to use multiple existing external specific-purpose programs for analysis (as illustrated by the case of GraphFES and Gephi) that can provide a deeper level of analysis than some basic LMS plug-in.

Finally, we believe that the use of complex learning analytics frameworks is not oriented toward students or teachers (whose needs should be covered by basic dashboards). To reach their full potential, frameworks should also integrate institutional and academic data, and be managed and operated by experts with a role of learning platform analyst. Analysts would act then as "learning consultants" of the different agents in the learning process (course coordinators, teachers, students).

Acknowledgements. This work is partially supported by the Cátedra Telefónica of the University of León (CTULE14-4).

References

1. Macfadyen, L., Dawson, S.: Numbers are not enough. Why e-learning analytics failed to inform an institutional strategic plan. Educ. Technol. Soc. **15**, 149–163 (2012)
2. Romero, C., Ventura, S.: Educational data mining: a review of the state of the art. IEEE Trans. Syst. Man Cybern. Part C Appl. Rev. **40**, 601–618 (2010)
3. Goldstein, P.J., Katz, R.N.: Academic Analytics: The Uses of Management Information and Technology in Higher Education. Educause, Colo (2005)
4. Goldstein, P.: Academic Analytics: The Uses of Management Information and Technology in Higher Education. EDUCASE 8, (2005)
5. Ferguson, R.: The State Of Learning Analytics in 2012: A Review and Future Challenges. The Open University (2012). http://kmi.open.ac.uk/publications/techreport/kmi-12-01
6. Agudo-Peregrina, Á.F., Iglesias-Pradas, S., Conde-González, M.Á., Hernández-García, Á.: Can we predict success from log data in VLEs? Classification of interactions for learning analytics and their relation with performance in VLE-supported F2F and online learning. Comput. Hum. Behav. **31**, 542–550 (2014)
7. Hernández-García, Á., Conde, M.A.: Dealing with complexity: educational data and tools for learning analytics. In: Proceedings of the Second International Conference on Technological Ecosystems for Enhancing Multiculturality, pp. 263–268. ACM, New York (2014)
8. Leony, D., Pardo, A., de-la-Fuente-Valentín, L., Sánchez-de-Castro, D., Delgado-Kloos, C.: GLASS: a learning analytics visualization tool. In: Proceedings of the 2nd International Conference on Learning Analytics and Knowledge. ACM, New York (2012)
9. Amo, D., Casany, M.J., Alier, M.: Google analytics for time behavior measurement in moodle. Sistemas y tecnologías de la información. In: Actas de la 9ª Conferencia Ibérica de Sistemas y Tecnologías de la Información, vol. 2, pp. 383–391. AISTI/La Salle/UPM/UOLS, Barcelona, Spain (2014)
10. Mazza, R., Dimitrova, V.: CourseVis: a graphical student monitoring tool for supporting instructors in web-based distance courses. Int. J. Hum. Comput. Stud. **65**, 125–139 (2007)
11. Dashboard block. https://docs.moodle.org/27/en/Dashboard_Block. Accesed 20 February 2015
12. Fidalgo, A., Leris, D., Sein-Echaluce, M., García-Peñalvo, F.J.: Indicadores para el seguimiento e evaluación de la competencia de trabajo en equipo a través del método CTMTC. In: Fidalgo-Blanco, Á., Sein-Echaluce, M. (eds.) Congreso Internacional sobre Aprendizaje, Innovación y Competitividad CINAIC 2013. Fundación General de la Universidad Politécnica de Madrid, Madrid (2013)
13. Lerís, D., Fidalgo, Á., Sein-Echaluce, M.L.: A comprehensive training model of the teamwork competence. Int. J. Learn. Intellect. Capital **11**, 1–19 (2014)
14. Conde, M.Á., Pozo, A., García-Peñalvo, F.J.: E-learning services in moodle 2.0. CEPIS Upgrade **12**, 43–50 (2011)
15. Fidalgo-Blanco, Á., Sein-Echaluce, M., García-Peñalvo, F.J., Conde, M.Á.: Using learning analytics to improve teamwork assessment. In: Computers in Human Behavior (in press)
16. Dawson, S., Bakharia, A., Heathcote, A.: SNAPP: realising the affordances of real-time SNA within networked learning environments. In: Seventh International Conference on Networked Learning, pp. 125–134. University of Lancaster, Lancaster (2010)

17. Engagement Analytics Plugin. https://docs.moodle.org/22/en/Engagement_Analytics_Plugin. Accessed 20 February 2015
18. Hernández-García, Á.: Usare Gephi per visualizzare la partecipazione nei corsi online: un approccio di social learning analytics. Tecnologie Didattiche **22**, 148–156 (2014)
19. Hernández-García, Á., González-González, I., Jiménez-Zarco, A.I., Chaparro-Peláez, J.: Applying social learning analytics to message boards in online distance learning: a case study. In: Computers in Human Behavior (in press)
20. Gómez-Aguilar, D.A., García-Peñalvo, F.J., Therón, R.: Analítica visual en elearning. El Profesional de la Información **23**, 236–245 (2014)
21. Mazza, R., Milani, C.: GISMO: a graphical interactive student monitoring tool for course management systems. In: International Conference on Technology Enhanced Learning (TEL 2004), Milan, Italy, pp. 18–19 (2004)

Assessments of User Centered Design Framework for M-learning Application Development

Amir Dirin[1](✉) and Marko Nieminen[2]

[1] Business Information Technology (BIT),
Haaga-helia University of Applied Science, Helsinki, Finland
amir.dirin@haaga-helia.fi
[2] Sorbit IT, Aalto University, Espoo, Finland
marko.nieminen@aalto.fi

Abstract. This paper presents the evaluation criteria and process of the User Centered Design (UCD) framework for m-learning application development. Based on the proposed UCD framework we have designed and developed five mobile learning applications for various sectors. The main aim of this paper is to argue how the UCD framework as development methodology has been successful in developing robust mobile learning applications. The UCD framework for m-learning application assessments criteria is based on three evaluation processes. 1. The acceptance of the application by target group (usability assessments) 2. The user experience assessment of the target m-learning application based on education components. 3. Qualitative research e.g. semi-structured interview with developers, designers and the owner of the application. The analysis of these assessments demonstrates varies aspect of the proposed UCD framework functionalities and performance.

Keywords: User Centered Design · Usability assessments · Mobile learning application

1 Introduction

Smartphones are the popular gadget among people nowadays, the penetration is increasing with a fast pace [1]. Application development and usage for smart devices become imperative almost in all sectors. Additionally, the numbers of mobile applications such as game, social networking, entertainment, personal and professional are becoming part of our lives. These applications are however constantly competing users' time and attention [2] for sustain usage and retentions. There are many factors ensures the mobile application sustainability e.g. application usability and user experience [3]. A mobile application that needs to compete users' time e.g. students is the mobile learning application. Mobile learning application development is a complex activity as firstly, many stakeholders and role-players [4] involved who have direct and indirect impact on the application design, development and usage. Secondly, it deals with learning and learners that required extensive pedagogical considerations [5, 6] which is by nature a complex concept. Thirdly, the application is targeted for smart gadget

© Springer International Publishing Switzerland 2015
P. Zaphiris and A. Ioannou (Eds.): LCT 2015, LNCS 9192, pp. 62–74, 2015.
DOI: 10.1007/978-3-319-20609-7_7

which has many restrictions such as screen size, input and output medium etc. Fourthly, the application must attach the users emotionally from user experience perspective [2] and compete students time. As a result, we are dealing with a complex systems which required appropriate methodology to cover all the complexities. The User Centered Design (UCD) framework for m-learning application development [7] is proven successful framework to design and develop a usable mobile learning application. This framework puts intended users of the target application at the center of its design and development. It is important to validate the methodology to make sure that the method fulfilled the essential needs in addition to the usability and user experience. Over the time many approaches has been proposed to validate the software development methodology such as [8] or to select the best software engineering method to design a complex system [9].

1.1 User Centered Design Framework for M-earning Application Processes

The case studies which presented in this papers are based on the User Centred Design (UCD) framework for m-learning application development [10]. The following figure reveals the UCD for m-learning application development phases.

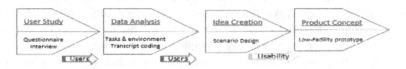

Fig. 1. User-centered *design process for m-learning application development*

- *User Study* – This is done by applying methods such as questionnaires and semi-structured interviews. In this phase, the designer aims to learn about the users' existing means to handle their work related tasks.
- *Data Analysis* – Analysis of the data gathered from the *user study* phase. This analysis consists of transcript coding of the user interviews [11], and description of users' tasks and environments [12]. The overall requirements for the target application are identified in this phase.
- *Idea Creation* – By using affinity diagrams [13], actions and requirements created in the previous phases are categorized. Use cases and scenarios are also applied as design methods to create a description of the application concept to the target users.
- *Product Concept* – Scenarios are shared with 3–5 users for their feedback. A scenario reflects the potential application concept. After the collected feedback is reviewed, the designers conduct a short, semi-structured interview to learn about users' opinions about the application concepts and functionalities. Users' feedback is analyzed to validate the feasibility of the concept and to ensure that the users and designers share the same understanding of the potential application. After validating the concept through scenarios, developers are asked to design a low-fidelity or a high-fidelity prototype based on the proposed scenarios. Finally, developers are

asked to perform usability evaluation of the prototype on users by applying Nielsen's heuristic evaluation guidelines [14].

The UCD framework for mobile learning application is an iterative design method which, mandates the users' involvement in each development phases. This minimizes the applications' failures and error rates and maximizes the application's acceptance as an educational means by target users.

2 Methodology and Research Data

The parameters of the UCD Framework evaluation comprises of the analysis of the case studies assessments' result. The analysis of these assessments demonstrates various aspect of the framework functionalities and performances. The descriptions of the utilized methods on each evaluation parameters are as follows:

1. Analysis of the Case Studies' Usability Evaluation Results. The acceptance of the application by target users group. (Usability assessments). The evaluation of the usability will be based on ISO 9241 part 11 and part 304 which recommends the measures of usability should cover: effectiveness, efficiency and Satisfaction. General metric to measure the usability as quality metric success rate (Whether users can perform the tasks at all) the measurements is based on the time a task requires to perform the tasks, the error rates, and, users' subjective satisfaction on the application performance and functionality. In this test, we ensured that the application follow the basic usability guidelines. In this phase, we often utilized the Nielsen [15] heuristic evaluation guidelines to make sure that the application is usable for the target users.

2. Metrics for Evaluating Educational Components. The usability and user experience assessment of the target m-learning application based on the education components (in press Journal). In this assessment, the m-learning application is assessed based on Brusilovsky [16] educational components layers i.e. Presentation, Activities, Communications and Administration. The assessments measures for example in each layer the Adjustability, Delightfulness, Reliability and satisfaction based on the predefined criteria. As an example of an assessment in the presentation layer we measure whether the user is able to personalize and customized the application based on his/her needs, the result of this part assessment indicates whether the application supports the adjustability factor in the learning application. In this phase, we evaluate the user experience and usability by asking users to perform predefined tasks on the application. Table 1 presents the usability criteria and guidelines [17] for M-learning application based on educational components. This acceptance criteria defines the framework performance from the educational perspective as it measures how the application performs based on educational activities.

3. Post Interview on Designers' Experiences Regarding the Applied UCD Methods. Qualitative research semi-structured interview with developers, designers and the owner of the applications. The interview pursuit to get additional information about the framework as development methodology itself. The questions like *"how did you*

Table 1. Usability criteria for m-learning application based on educational components

Components	Usability factors	Criteria
Presentation	Adjustability	Supports as a learning medium/personalization
	Delightful	Facilities and acceptance of the tool
	Reliability	Supportive for communication, and technology adequacy
	Satisfaction	Perform the required task
Activities	Adjustability	Support the learner to perform the basic learning activities
	Delightful	Support the learner to perform tasks without difficulties
	Reliability	Supports the learner to perform his task securely
	Satisfaction	Successfully performed his educational activities
Communications	Adjustability	Supports the performance of basic communication related tasks
	Delightful	Facilities and acceptance of the tool
	Reliability	Supportive for communication and technology securely
	Satisfaction	Successfully performed his/her task securely
Administration	Adjustability	Support the learners requirements
	Delightful	Supportive for communication and technology securely
	Reliability	Successfully performed his/her task securely
	Satisfaction	Successfully performed his/her tasks

find framework to help the design and development the application?" or *"how easy it was to create the concept"*, *"How many errors identified at the scenario phased"*, *"Your overall impressions of the application development?"* The analysis of the data helped greatly to get inside on developers, researcher view on the methodology.

3   Case Studies and the Measurements

The following case studies were developed and assessed during 2013−2015, except the M-learning application for Java course, which was developed during 2004.

–   **Java Application.** The aim of this case study was to analysis all phases of the UCD framework performance. With the help of this m-learning application, students were able to have access to Java course resources e.g. Lecture notes, assignments, and feedback at any time any places. In addition, students were able to submit their lab and home assignment through the m-learning application in case they had access to an internet At the elicitation phase, users study was conducted with six students (n = 6) and two staff (n = 2). Additionally, semi-structured interview and questionnaire were applied to learn how users handled the course related activities. To analysis the collected data, we applied interview transcript coding [18]

After categorizing the related task and the actions, a scenario [19] was written and shared with users for their feedback. Finally, application high fidelity prototype was designed, developed which was ready to test.

1. Usability and User Experience Assessment. Two different usability evaluation sessions were conducted, one for students (n = 6), and another for staff (n = 2) each of which had distinct sets of tasks to carry out during the given time. The main tasks that the users requested to perform were, to log in to the application, uploaded and download the lecture materials in a different format, to receive, submit and provide feedback for assignments etc. The assessment results indicated that users were able to carry all the given tasks successfully. Despite the fact that this was the first experience with the m-learning application that users ever had. They were very excited to try the application in real life, even though, the cost of the data exchange was relatively high for students. Users' initial mental models of the m-learning application were that they had to carry out all the educational activities via SMS, this however changed as soon as they tried the applications with the test devices. The users' had appreciated the simplicity of the user interface of the mobile learning application statements e.g. "I liked the application, easy to find the features, just go the categories". This had raised by several users especially during post-interview session. Users specially had complained about the input medium as the keypad were not convenient to write a long text as a result they preferred to use the application mainly for reading.

2. Educational Activities Assessment. The users carried out the given tasks according to the educational components of the criteria mentioned in Table 1, such as *presentations* e.g. users were able to download course materials such as lecture notes, audio, and video etc. despite the fact, that the technology at the time did not support many proposed functions. Similarly, as the presentation component, user were not very *delighted* to uses the provided functionalities in *activity* component because of the inconvenient input keypad. Nevertheless, users were *delighted* to receive instance feedback for the submitted assignment. Users found the *communication* functionalities very interesting, especially the capability to have direct communication capabilities with their peers and also teachers securely. Through the communication component, users were able to send/receive SMS, email to individual and group and also chat with teacher or classmate. Users find the email functionality in the communication component very interesting as they do not need to search for the course participants' email separately including the course staff. Sending an email to classmate and teachers become simple and easy with few clicks. Users also were in favor with the functionalities of *administration* component. User's had considered this service as usable in their educational activities. Through this service users were able to register for a course, register for the exam and check the credit transcript.

3. Developer Experiments. Two groups of students carried out the design and development tasks, the first group, consists of four students (n = 4) who had previously studied usability related courses, they had the designer role in the project. This group actually conducted the user studies both with students and staff.

The second group was consist of two (n = 2) students, who had previous experience in programming, they had the developers' role. These two groups interacted continuously to achieve the potential goal. The team especially appreciated the systematic approach of the framework to achieve the goal. Additionally, the role divisions were recognized as an asset in this framework by audience. Moreover, the audience believed that having the scenario as a design methodology helped both designers and developers to conceptualize the overall application themselves. They showed their wiliness to utilize the methodology in future projects "*I liked it, clear and helpful to come up with the prototype*" was heard repeatedly by developers and designers.

– **Adaptive Driving School.** With this case study, we aimed to reassess the UCD phases by applying all the steps defined in UCD framework. In this case study, we designed, developed and assessed an adaptive mobile learning application for driving license candidates. The development process and the application evaluation result was presented and published in ICCA2014 conference [20]. This application helps students to study, learn and assess the compulsory driving school theory lessons on their smart devices. Additionally, the application provides mandatory self-evaluation reports to instructors after each practical driving sessions.

1. Usability and User Experience Assessment. The prototype evaluation report indicates that the application was easy to use and provides the essential learning materials for driving school candidates. Users were especially satisfied that the driving theory lessons were accessible at anytime and anyplace even during driving sessions. The usability test was carried out at Haaga-helia UAS, with five potential users (n = 5) and two instructors (n = 2). The test users were mainly novice users meaning they have not had previous experiences on similar application for driving schools. The usability report indicates that the application provides positive user experience for our test users. Test users were able to carry the given tasks completely no savior errors appeared. The test results and the interview data revealed that the test users were founded the application helpful and easy to use.
2. Educational Activities Assessments. The test was carried out based on the educational components criteria presented in Table 1. The *presentation* component, users were able to carry their educational related tasks properly, despite the fact, that some presentation features were not implemented. The application content and UI was customizable based on students' performance on theory lessons evaluation and practical driving session reports. Moreover, the application supported multi-formatted content, e.g. audio, video etc. However, due to the technological inadequacy and lack of development time caused the usability factor e.g. *adjustability* was not able to test. The *activity* components, test users were satisfied with the clarity of the tasks and knew what to do next. We were not however able to test the *reliability* factor in this component. The *communication* component was implemented in a simple communication between student and instructor, which the test revealed, functioning properly. The *administration* component also followed the defined criteria in Table 1 accordingly.

3. Methodological Assessments. The interview that was conducted with designers and developers indicates that they were satisfied with the overall result. They show their satisfactions based on the fact that the framework reduced the application errors, before the high fidelity prototype implementation, *"We managed to find most of the errors already in scenario review phase"*. The designers were specifically happy with the continuous consultant of potential users, which helped them to come up with new features that they had not realized at the elicitation phase *"we receive nice to have features both in the scenario and in lo-fidelity"*. The stakeholders were also asked about their motivation for using the framework: *"in the beginning using the framework work was difficult, did not know what to do, but after the transcript coding everything changed"*. The main negative feedback, which we received from developers was that this methodology required extensive user consultant, which consume lots of time. The stakeholders e.g. the owners of the application were happy with the overall results, *"very surprised everything works with any errors we tested the application with students and instructors"*.

– **Customer guide game**
   In this case study, we aimed to specifically test the framework proposed design method. In this project, we developed a multi-platform mobile game application for students and staff to learn the new premises and other important locations. We applied scenario design to learn the potential user's application preferences. As the customer of the application provided us the requirements list, we mainly focused on the design. The case study development process and the usability evaluation result is submitted at CSEDU 2015 [21].

1. Usability and User Experience Assessment. As soon as the functional application prototype was developed, we conducted a usability test with five test users (n = 5). Unlike the paper prototype usability assessment, which users carried out predefined set of tasks, in this testing users had a freedom to play the games. Users were, however, asked to save the points, starts and stop different sessions. Despite receiving visual design, graphical and sound improvements recommendations, the test demonstrates that the application content and UI in general appeal users. Users believed that the game has enough challenges only two test users (n = 5) demanded that the game needs to be more demanding, these two test users were considered as expert users. The most important issues that raised by all test users were the intuitiveness and easy to use UI and the game, in general. Moreover, the final concept test results show that the scenario design and the first paper prototype identified the majority of the errors and improvement recommendations. The product concept phase the most of feedback were on the items that were not directly detectable at the paper prototype phase such as graphics improvement or the sound effect.
2. Educational Activities Assessments. The *presentation* component was not fully implemented in this prototype, even though, users were able to *adjust* the game character. Another *adjustability* feature was not seen as an appropriate for the game. Users were able, however, to create a profile, select a role image etc. The *activity*

component in this case study required users only to play and explore the game features, which all users done properly. Users demonstrated their *delightfulness* by saying "*wow, this is fun*". We did not implement the *communication* component as a result, we did not have any feature to test. The *administrations* component satisfied users as they were able to create, delete profile. Additionally, users showed their satisfaction with this component, "*I can see who played and what points they achieved*".

3. Methodological Assessments. The author act as a thesis supervisor in this project, as a result, there was constant involvement with all phases of the design and development process. In addition, we had regular Skype meetings with the application owner after each development phases e.g. scenario, lo-fi, and hi-fi evaluations. The designer viewed the framework as a good method to achieve his goal. The designer specially appreciate the scenario design "*Scenario saved lots of development time, I had plan to design an application and then check with users, now I see that users needed game and not mobile application*" or "*Scenario helped me to see the kind of game users preferred and wanted me to implement*".
   The designer was interested to apply the framework, even though, at the starting phase of the project, considered scenario design as a time-consuming step. The designer, developer, and the customer showed their satisfaction with the overall application concept. The main negative feedback that we received from developers was that this methodology required extensive user consultant which consume lots of time.

– **mhealth Application.** In this case study, we aimed to test all phases of the proposed UCD framework. There exists a variety of mHealth applications, but none of them combines essential professional tools for nursing. We tackled this problem in the Finnish elderly house. We applied the UCD framework by conducting user study. Together with 12 nurses, we first identified their profiles and their expectations on work-related mHealth application functionalities. The results were utilized in conceptual design of Context-Aware Nurse Assistant (CANA), which combines the identified functionalities and provides context-sensitive services to consolidate nurses' work activities. The result of this case study is published at the ICUM 2015 conference [22].

1. Usability and User Experience Assessment. The analysis of data indicates that hundred percent of the test users considered the application as unique and excellent. Statement such as "*I never ever thought that I can perform my work related tasks with my mobile*" was repeatedly heard from the participants. The surprising fact for the researchers was that even the expert participants, i.e. those who were familiar with smart devices, were surprised to see such an application in the field. This indicates that the user data analysis and the concept development using the UCD framework was successful.

2. Educational Activities Assessments. This case study was designed to provide services for nurses on their job related activities. As this application is not considered

as an educational application, so, the educational components cannot be fully applied in this case study. But we have identified the following findings, the *communication* component users were *delighted* to see that they have access to all those who worked in the same departments at the same time "*nice feature I don't to go to office and search for the other nurse in the department*" or "*I can see who I can contact if I need help, great*". Similarly, the assessment results demonstrated that users were able to carry their *activities* properly without any difficulties. We assessed the *administration* component ourselves and realized that we were able to see, search, print in addition to add, remove users.

3. Methodological Assessments. The discussion meeting was organized with those who were involved in this case study e.g. application designers, developers, and owner. The user study expert considered the application concept development straightforward. The overall assessment of the methodology was positive e.g. "*It is an excellent method to design and develop an application without benchmarking*". The application developers considered the methodology very effective specifically as the whole team was involved in development. The designers rather see more design guidelines on the mobile application development in the framework "*I wish we had design guidelines to help us to get the best user experience for the design*". The designers most motivation factor was the continuous feedback from users, especially the scenario design helped them very much to design the potential application look and feel. According to the designers, scenario-design helped them to conceptualize the final application. The designers promoted the scenario as a strength of the proposed framework. The discussion notes indicate that all stakeholders of the application are satisfied with the outcome "*Good model to design mobile application, I'll apply the UCD framework on my next project*".

– **Application for Tourism** In this case study, a mobile application is developed especially for outdoors' athletics. With this case study, we aimed to test the UCD framework idea creation and user study phases. The potential customer of the application was the small tourism companies in Finland. Through this application, the tourism companies were able to provide the outdoors activities maps as a web service to their potential users such as kayakers. Additionally, the portal is designed and developed for tourism companies to design content for their customers independently. The details of the application and the development process with usability test result was published at CSCEM2014 [23].

1. Usability and User Experience Assessments. The first field test happened by kayakers on the Baltic sea by Kayakers. The application usability and functional testing with kayakers had ensued that we re-design the initial product concept. The hi-fi prototype was upgraded to a new hi-fi Beta version based on the collected feedback, which was reassessed with users. The overall feedback that we received was good and optimistic, phrases such as, "*Very clear with colored arrows pointing in the right direction*". Or "*it's simple and easy to follow*". In the third round of the evaluation, we conducted additional usability test with fifty potential users (n = 50)

of four tourism companies (n = 4). The overall test results indicate that users were happy with the application performance despite the fact that several new features have proposed by users.

2. Usability and User Experience Assessments. This was not an educational application, as a result, the second assessment criteria was not directly applied. The main *activity* component tasks were that the users had to plan routes in advanced which done smoothly without difficulties. The *admiration* component also was implemented properly, the tourism companies were able to provide proper services to their customers.

3. Methodology Assessments. The overall result indicates that the UCD Framework increased the touch point from a business perspective. *"It helped us to find new business needs"*. The methodology helped very much to identify draw backs through hi-fi testing *"prototyping was good it save a lot of error fixing cost in the productions"* before developing the actual product concept. As a result, the developers and the companies shown special attention to this capability of the UCD Framework. The overall feedback on UCD was promising e.g. *"regardless of the stakeholders' divers interest in the mobile application development the methodology demonstrates that it covers all the stakeholders' interest as the application fulfil the potential users' needs, as well as the company's interest"*. The developers and designers found the methodology easy to use, and straightforward approach *"simple, and easy to follow"*. Directly jumping to design the prototype posed additional prototype design iterations in the end they realized that was not a right approach *"I wish we use scenario first it could have saved us lots of development time"*. The outcome of the application had satisfied all the stakeholders, despite the fact, that this process had taken time and extensive efforts to get the final concept *"as a tourism company owner I am very happy with the outcomes"*.

4 Discussion

UCD framework for m-learning application development helped to design and developed several case study applications for varies sectors. The nature of these applications mainly was educational, but the presentation styles were various e.g. game. We have conducted three different assessments to validate the framework 1. The application usability assessment 2. The application assessed based on educational component and finally 3. The framework assessment. The application usability assessments have carried in several iterations, such as in concept design, low-fidelity prototype, and product assessments. The framework assessment, however, carried out at the final stage of the product development.

1. Usability and User Experience Assessments. The usability assessments of these case studies revealed that in almost all cases, users were able to carry the predefined tasks. Those case studies, which were developed as a mobile learning application, we had predefined sets of tasks, so it was easy to statistically check the error rates and tasks performance rates. But, in game application we did not have any predefined tasks, but the users were asked to play the game and think aloud, the video

analysis of the test sessions indicates that users were able to explore all the features and functionalities of the game. The result of these cases studies, indicates that the UCD framework was efficient enough to produce an application that satisfy the essential needs. Additionally the tasks performance rates indicate that UCD framework has resulted in application that easy to use by all users types e.g. novice and expert. The errors rates also identified in these case studies were almost zero, this demonstrates that the UCD framework in general is efficient enough to produce effective, efficient and error free application.

2. Usability and User Experience Assessments. The actual analysis of the educational components for each of these cases is huge, which is out of the scope of this paper. The measurement and acceptance criteria are well suited to the mobile learning application, but it is also valid criteria to assess other mobile application types e.g. game. The overall assessments of the UCD framework from the educational perspective indicates that the case study applications provided *adjustable, delightfulness, reliable* with *satisfactions* to educational related components such as *presentation, activities, communications,* and *administration.* In some cases, we were not able to fully assess all components, either because of the technology did not support or the prototype had lack of proper functionalities e.g. *adjustability* in the presentation component in java application. The UCD framework promotes the m-learning application design based on educational components. This has influenced that our UI design and the development, as a result, we gained positive feedback in our m-learning application assessment.

3. Methodology Assessments. The overall results of the case studies show that the stakeholders e.g. designers and developers were skeptical with the UCD framework at beginning of each project. This trend changed after the project progressed, we received this types of feedback mainly from developers who like to code as soon as they have the project idea e.g. in outdoor application we experienced that they developed many prototypes just because they ignored the scenario design. Having waiting to collect the requirements at the beginning were also considered as a waste of time, which were not however, a valid claim e.g. in java, mhealth and adaptive driving application we followed all the UCD framework phases, which took relatively shorter time to design and develop the application high fidelity, compared with the outdoor activity app. There were also recommendations for adding the design guidelines for m-learning application development based on UCD framework. This is also not feasible to the nature of each m-learning application is different, which the design must follow the context and the content of the potential application.

5 Conclusion and Future Work

We demonstrate that the UCD framework for m-learning application is an efficient methodology for designing and developing the m-learning application. The case studies were developed for various purposes and contexts, this indicates that UCD framework support various application development contexts. The assessments criteria demonstrated that UCD framework result robust application concept, which fulfill the essential needs. These case studies, however, were not assessed from pedagogical perspective, as a result, assessing these cases from the pedagogical perspective is important to see whether the application effects the learning process?

References

1. Boulos, M.N.K., Wheeler, S., Tavares, C., Jones, R.: How smartphones are changing the face of mobile and participatory healthcare: an overview, with example from eCAALYX. Biomed. Eng. Online **10**, 24 (2011)
2. Dirin, A., Nieminen, M., Kettunen, M.: Student capabilities to utilize m-learning service in new smart devices. In: Proceeding of the 2013 International Conference on Advanced ICT (2013)
3. Mostakhdemin-Hosseini, A.: Usability considerations of mobile learning applications. Int. J. Interact. Mobile Technol. (IJIM) **3**, 29 (2009)
4. Dirin, A., Nieminen, M.: Managing m-learning application development: roles and responsibilities. In: International Conference on Advanced Information and Communication Technology for Education (ICAICTE 2014), 16–17 August 2014, Dalian, China (2014)
5. Mostakhdemin-Hosseini, A.: Analysis of pedagogical considerations of m-Learning in smart devices. Int. J. Interact. Mob. Technol. (IJIM) (2009)
6. Kearney, M., Schuck, S., Burden, K., Aubusson, P.: Viewing mobile learning from a pedagogical perspective. Res. Learn. Technol. **20**, 14406 (2012)
7. Dirin, A., Nieminen, M.: Framework for addressing usability and user experience in m-learning. J. Comput. (2014, in press)
8. Kitchenham, B., Linkman, S., Law, D.: DESMET: a methodology for evaluating software engineering methods and tools. Comput.Control Eng. J. **8**, 120 (1997)
9. Dubey, A.: Evaluating software engineering methods in the context of automation applications. In: IEEE International Conference on Industrial Informatics (INDIN), pp. 585–590 (2011)
10. Amir, D., Nieminen, M.: mLUX: Usability and user experience framework for m-Learning application. Int. J. Interact. Mob. Technol. (IJIM) (2015)
11. Saldana, J.: An Introduction to codes and coding. In: The coding Manual for Qualitative Researchers, pp. 1–31. Sage Publications, Los Angeles (2009)
12. Hackos, J.T., Redish, J.C.: User and Task Analysis for Interface Design, vol. 42. Wiley, Ann Arbor (1998)
13. Holtzblatt, K., Wendell, J.B., Wood, S.: Building an affinity diagram. In: Interactive Technologies, ch. 8, pp. 159–179 (2005)
14. Nielson, J.: Heuristic evaluation: how-to: article by Jakob Nielsen. Nielson Norman GroupNorman (1995). http://www.nngroup.com/articles/how-to-conduct-a-heuristic-evaluation/
15. Nielsen, J.: How to conduct a heuristic evaluation. http://www.nngroup.com/articles/how-to-conduct-a-heuristic-evaluation. Accessed 09, 2002
16. Brusilovsky, P. Philip, M.: Course Delivery System for Virtual University (2001)
17. Melis, E. Weber, M.: lessons for (Pedagogic) usability of elearning system. In: Elearn 2003 (2003)
18. Talja, S.: Analyzing qualitative interview data. Libr. Inf. Sci. Res. **21**, 459–477 (1999)
19. Rosson, M.B., Carroll, J.M.: Scenario-based design. In: The human-computer Interaction Handbook: Fundamentals, Evolving Technologies and Emerging Applications, pp. 1032–1050 (2002)

20. Dirin, A., Casarini, M.: Adaptive m-learning application for driving licenses candidates based on UCD framework for m-learning application development. In: 6th International Conference on Computer Supported Education (2014)
21. Dirin, A., Vainio, V.: Case Study: from requirements list to an educational game. In: Computer Supported in Education (2015)
22. Dirin, M., Dirin, A., Laine, T.H.: User-centered design of a context-aware nurse assistant (CANA) at Finnish elderly houses. In: The 9th International Conference on Ubiquitous Information Management and Communication (2015)
23. Alamäki, A., Dirin, A.: Designing mobile guide service for small tourism companies using user centered design principle. In: International Conference on Computer Science, Computer Engineering, and Social Media, Thessaloniki, Greece, pp. 47–58 (2014)

Design and Evaluation of a Learning Assistant System with Optical Head-Mounted Display (OHMD)

Xiao Du and Ali Arya[✉]

School of Information Technology, Carleton University, 1125 Colonel by Drive,
Ottawa, ON K1S 5B6, Canada
xiaodu@cmail.carleton.ca, arya@carleton.ca

Abstract. Rapid increase in the use of wearable technologies, especially Optical Head-Mounted Display (OHMD) devices (e.g. Google Glass), suggests potentials for education and requires more scientific studies investigating such potentials. The issue of information access and delivery in classrooms can be of interest where multiple screens and objects of attention exist and can cause distraction, lack of focus and reduced efficiency. This study explores the usability of a single OHMD device, as an alternative to individual and big projection screens in a classroom situation. We developed OHMD-based prototypes that allowed presentation and practice of lesson material through three displays and two control options. We conducted user studies to compare various feasible combinations of display/control mechanism using a series of evaluation criteria, including enjoyment, ability to focus, motivation, perceived efficiency, physical comfort, understandability, and relaxation. Our results suggest that improved OHMD technology will have the potential ability to be effective in classroom learning.

Keywords: Optical head-mounted display · See-through project glass · Enhanced classroom education · User experiment

1 Introduction

Traditional face-to-face education has played a primary role in human cultural heritage and development for thousands of years. Recently, emergence of wearable technologies, particularly Optical Head-Mounted Display (OHMD) devices such as Google Glass, has changed the landscape of computing for the everyday person [13]. Projects like "Mono-glass" [18], Google Glass for assisting in Parkinson's disease [7], surgeons' operation assistance [8], "Fitnamo" [10] and "Museum Guide" [15] reflect the practical value of integrating OHMD technology into relevant fields.

This study was originally motivated by existing research on classroom performance [1, 3], observation of classroom learning, and a series of informal interviews with undergraduate students about the factors that could affect their concentration during class. In a typical classroom scenario, students are provided with various visual sources of information. Among them are big screens (projection screen), personal computing devices, and face-to-face interaction with the instructor/presenter. The distraction

© Springer International Publishing Switzerland 2015
P. Zaphiris and A. Ioannou (Eds.): LCT 2015, LNCS 9192, pp. 75–86, 2015.
DOI: 10.1007/978-3-319-20609-7_8

caused by multi-orientation moving activity (switching attention to various sources) can be one of the sources of reduced effectiveness of the classroom experience. Another issue was the inefficiency caused by switching focus between the portable computer (pc) display and the teacher's projection display.

Based on the problems reported above, we focused on the usability of OHMD in classroom situations. More specifically, we aimed to investigate if the use of a single OHMD device, as an alternative to individual and big screens, can improve the learning process. Considering the need for controlling the content on this single screen, we also investigated the effect of user vs. presenter/instructor control in that process. In both cases, the effects were studied using a series of evaluation criteria such as pleasantness, ability to focus and effectiveness of learning.

Considering the research limitations and the familiarity with the learning content, the researcher chose a Chinese language class (which was easier to design the lecture material for) as the subject for the study. To make the study more pertinent, we focused on higher education students, who are studying at a college level and above.

2   Related Work

Recent products like Google Glass and Oculus Rift are responsible for popularizing the OHMD devices, but similar researches had been developed for a couple of decades. The Land Warrior system [2], developed by the U.S. army over the past decade, includes a heads-up eye display with an augmented reality visual overlay for soldier communication. In 2010, TRAVIS Callisto [19] was made for troubleshooting and training. The Motorola HC1 [4], which was released in 2014, was a fully speech controlled system, but only offering basic applications such as document viewer. Current OHMD based studies are focused in three fields: medical assistance, manufacturing and navigation.

Researchers have utilized OHMD to resolve medical problems for years. For example, to help people who have difficulty with short-range activities due to losing one eye, Toyoura et al. [18] implemented a pilot system called "mono-glass". The system is a wearable device, which has two cameras to capture images and then reconstruct them for the healthy eye. McNaney et al. [7] presented a study on investigating the feasibility of utilizing Google Glass to help people who have Parkinson's Disease (PD). Muensterer et al. [8] explored the possibility of using Google Glass to help surgeons in the operating room. Despite certain drawbacks, such as low battery endurance, data protection, poor audio quality, and long transmission latency, the authors indicated that there are benefits when integrating the device into surgery. Such benefits include: *maintaining attention, intuitive interaction, constantly accessing* related information when making decisions, and *real-time external communication* are the positive aspects that doctors reported during existing studies.

Liverani et al. [6] presented a study on utilizing an augmented reality wearable system called a Personal Active Assistant (PAA) (early prototype of OHMD) to improve the overall integration between engineering design and real prototype manufacturing, by providing features such as object recognition and operation instructions. Shen et al. [17] developed an augmented reality (AR) system to support collaborative product design among members of a multi-disciplinary team. Ong and Wang [11] presented a 3D bare-hand interaction in an augmented assembly environment to manipulate and assemble virtual components.

The "museum guide", demonstrated by Schiele et al. [15], used a see-through display. Utilizing the ability of a wearable device to perceive, recognize, and analyze objects and environments from a first-person perspective. Smart Sight, presented by Yang et al. [22], was an intelligent tourist system that made use of multimodal interaction and wireless communication by providing voice command during touring.

With ability to link virtual and real worlds, many researchers have studied utilizing augmented reality technology into education. The AR-Jam books [5] made by the British Broadcasting Corporation (BBC), for instance, combined physical pages and desktop interaction for children. The Augmented Reality Student Card, presented by El Sayed et al. [14], was designed to help students visualize different learning objects, interact with theories and deal with information in a 3D format. Moreover, Shelton and Hedley [16] presented a paper on using augmented reality for teaching Earth-Sun relationships to undergraduate students.

Nakasugi and Yamauchi designed a wearable system called Past View [9], which helped users acquire historical viewpoints. Osawa and Asai [12] designed a wearable learning support system which was focus on outdoor education. Vallurupalli [20] discussed the feasibility of using Google Glass for medical education. Wu et al. [21] found that Google Glass was able to help simulation-based training exercises without disrupting the learners' experience.

According to the above literature, the following two sets of evaluation criteria had been commonly used by existing projects, particularly in education: usability (comfort, ease of use, enjoyment) and learnability (motivation, attention, relevance, confidence, satisfaction, efficiency).

3   Experiment Design

With the intention of investigating if the use of a single OHMD device, as an alternative to individual and big screens, could improve the learning process, our main objective in this study was to find answers to two research questions; (1) the helpfulness of OHMD in classroom, and (2) identifying a suitable control mechanism for it. With options for various combinations of display or control mechanism, a series of possible scenarios existed in our study. In order to identify the potential issues and effective ways of doing the user study, a pilot study was first conducted.

3.1   Pilot Study

We considered three possible screen options: the OHMD device, projection (or large screen monitor) shared display, and personal computer (or any other common device with personal screen). To control the content on screen, three mechanisms can be considered: the teacher, the student, and a computer. The teacher-controlled method corresponds to a traditional classroom experience. The student-controlled classroom is similar to cases where students receive hand-outs to view while following a lecture or tutorial sessions where they perform actions on a computer following spoken instructions. The machine-controlled option was imagined as a possibility where a timer-based slideshow is used. Theoretically, the scenarios for user experiments should include all the combinations of screen variables (OHMD, PC screen, and projected display) and controller variables (teacher, student, and machine). Additionally, for some cases, it was possible to have more than one visual screen or controller involved in the scenario.

According to the pilot study, we found that the "machine control" scenario (app materials moving forward automatically as time goes) was not appropriate for student learning in a real classroom situation. Based on the pilot study, we decided to narrow down the 3 x 3 study plan and make it into a series of doable scenarios as presented below (Scenario D was machine-controlled and removed from the list):

- Scenario A: single projection display with teacher controlling
- Scenario B: single OHMD with teacher controlling
- Scenario C: single OHMD with student controlling
- Scenario E: projection display with teacher controlling & PC with student controlling
- Scenario F: projection display with teacher controlling & OHMD with student controlling

3.2   Hypotheses

- H1. The participants' responses will vary significantly over scenarios and criteria.
- H2. The evaluation criteria will be more positive in OHMD-based scenarios with student control.
- H3. For specific tasks, participants will prefer the use of OMHD with their own control.

3.3   Data Analysis Plan

We had the same sample group throughout the experiment, and measured the same participants 5 times (5 experimental scenarios). In each scenario, we measured the same usability criteria (enjoyment, motivation, perceived efficiency, understandability, ability to focus, physical comfort, and relaxation).

We conducted a two-way repeated measures ANOVA test to examine H1. Normality of the sample was planned to be assessed by examining histograms of the distributions, and examining the skewness and kurtosis of the distribution. Histograms were to be evaluated for evidence of central tendency and for skewness and kurtosis statistics.

We conducted one-way repeated measures ANOVA with Greenhouse-Geisser correction and Post hoc tests using the Bonferroni correction to test participants' responses on each criterion among scenarios for testing H2. Since the data was collected by Likert scales questionnaires, non-parametric ordinal methods are more appropriate. So we conducted a Friedman's ANOVA and Wilcoxon signed-rank test with Bonferroni correction for the pairwise comparison to re-examine the results. These two test method were used because Friedman's ANOVA is the related non-parametric method for repeated ANOVA, and Wilcoxon signed-rank test is the related non-parametric method for paired t-test. Even though the ANOVA test was preferred in presence of multiple variables, we added the Friedman's ANOVA and Wilcoxon sign-rank test as a measure of extra reliability of results.

We planned to collect participants' reactions and feedback towards the exercise tasks' in each experimental scenario results by self-evaluations using the survey for H3.

4   Prototype Implementation

4.1   Hardware

Our prototype uses **Epson Moverio BT-200** [19]. It is a pair of binocular digital glasses that put a micro-projection display in each transparent lens. The goal of this study is to test the applicability, particularly of a wearable device, within a language learning class. For practical purpose, the device should be easy to wear. Epson's OHMD is small and comparatively light. Unlike Google Glass, Epson's OHMD is heavier yet still acceptable.

An Apple **MacBook laptop** was prepared ahead of the experiment. Participants could view and manipulate the app which illustrated the class-related instructions on an Android emulator during the experiment.

An **Acer laptop** was used to maintain the server program, and to run class app demo which projected on the wall.

A **Samsung Galaxy S3** Android phone was used for the teacher to remotely control the content which projected on the Epson Moverio.

A **BENQ W1100 projector** was connected to the Acer laptop, and projected the class app. The content of the display was controlled by the teacher during the experiment.

4.2   Software

Epson Moverio & Mobile Phone App. Epson Moverio was originally designed for two functions: (1) allowing users to view the materials of the lecture either by manual-control or by teacher's control; (2) allowing users to do the exercise-tasks (listening, reading, writing, and speaking exercises) either by manual control or by teacher's control. We designed three modules: "Text", "Practice" and "Communication", for both Epson Moverio and Mobile control app.

The app layouts on the Epson Moverio and the mobile platform were similar. Epson Moverio, which was "Student Side", was manipulated by either participants or teacher using the mobile phone. Samsung app, which was "Teacher Side", monitored students' exercising performance.

Socket Communication Program. We used the android socket protocol to build the communication between OHMD and mobile phone. As soon as the "Student Side"

(OHMD) and "Teacher Side" (mobile phone) programs were launched, they created a socket connection to the server independently. Once certain activity was initiated on "Teacher Side", a socket stream message was sent to the "Student Side". Then "Student Side" would do a relative pre-programed activity according to the socket stream message that it read.

Desktop Simulation Apps. We used *IntuiFace* (http://www.intuilab.com/) and Android emulator to simulated apps on projection screen and personal computer, respectively.

5 User Study Results

5.1 Participants Demographic Information

15 participants (8 males, 7 females) ranging in age from 18-36 years old participated in the study. Out of 15 participants, 11 indicated they were native English speakers, and 4 were not. Majority of participants came with zero relevant background knowledge: 9 did not have much Chinese learning experience, 2 had half a year learning experience, 2 had one year of learning experience, and 2 had almost 2 years of learning experience. Moreover, 3 subjects reported they had used a Head-Mounted Display before.

On a 7-point Likert scale (1 = very low, 7 = very high), participants generally rated themselves having medium interests level in learning the main subject (M = 4.6, SD = 1.9), the majority of the participants used mobile apps often (M = 5.3, SD = 2.1), and most of them could make themselves concentrate in class (M = 5.1, SD = 1.4).

5.2 In-Study Scale Rating

We used a combination of parametric and non-parametric methods to analyze the data and verify our hypotheses. Our analysis showed that participants did in fact respond differently to changing the control mechanism or students' viewing-screen, but no significant change was observed in our evaluation criteria based on changing scenarios.

To verify the Hypothesis 1, a 5 x 7 within-subjects ANOVA was conducted on participants' agreement ratings, with scenarios and usability criteria as factors. An alpha level of 0.05 was used in our data analysis results. Overall, it was observed that scenarios and evaluation criteria did in fact have significant effect on the ratings, which indicates that the participants did change their responses based on variables. This suggests that the responses had a reasonable level of reliability and at least were not the same when variables changed.

To verify the Hypothesis 2, a combination of parametric statistic method (repeated measures ANOVA with a Greenhouse-Geisser correction and post hoc tests using the Bonferroni correction) and non-parametric statistic method (Friedman's ANOVA and Wilcoxon signed-rank test with Bonferroni correction) were conducted toward the seven evaluation criteria, respectively. We found that only physical comfort (F = 17.555, p < 0.001) showed a statistical significant difference among five scenarios, and that was not in favour of OHMD. Results summary is given in Tables 1 and 2.

Table 1. Results of repeated measures ANOVA with a Greenhouse-Geisser correction toward criteria.

Criteria	Scenarios	N	Mean	Std. Deviation	Source	F	Sig.
Enjoyment	Scenario A	15	5.33	1.113	Scenario Greenhouse-Geisser	2.370	0.079
	Scenario B	15	5.13	1.125			
	Scenario C	15	5.67	0.976			
	Scenario E	15	4.67	1.291			
	Scenario F	15	4.73	1.033			
	Total	15	5.11	1.146			
Ability to Focus	Scenario A	15	5.47	1.552	Scenario Greenhouse-Geisser	1.423	0.253
	Scenario B	15	5.20	1.568			
	Scenario C	15	5.20	1.474			
	Scenario E	15	4.73	1.438			
	Scenario F	15	4.53	1.302			
	Total	15	5.03	1.470			
Motivation	Scenario A	15	5.20	1.207	Scenario Greenhouse-Geisser	1.424	0.254
	Scenario B	15	5.53	1.125			
	Scenario C	15	5.87	0.990			
	Scenario E	15	5.20	1.082			
	Scenario F	15	5.27	1.163			
	Total	15	5.41	1.116			
Perceived Efficiency	Scenario A	15	4.93	1.100	Scenario Greenhouse-Geisser	2.123	0.117
	Scenario B	15	4.93	1.163			
	Scenario C	15	5.67	0.816			
	Scenario E	15	4.87	1.642			
	Scenario F	15	4.27	1.751			
	Total	15	4.93	1.379			
Physical Comfort	Scenario A	15	6.27	0.704	Scenario Greenhouse-Geisser	17.555	0.000001
	Scenario B	15	3.67	1.397			
	Scenario C	15	3.80	1.612			
	Scenario E	15	5.87	0.915			
	Scenario F	15	3.67	1.496			
	Total	15	4.65	1.704			
Understanda bility	Scenario A	15	5.53	1.125	Scenario Greenhouse-Geisser	0.607	0.595
	Scenario B	15	5.73	0.884			
	Scenario C	15	5.87	0.743			
	Scenario E	15	5.87	0.990			
	Scenario F	15	5.53	0.915			
	Total	15	5.71	0.927			
Relaxation	Scenario A	15	5.73	1.163	Scenario Greenhouse-Geisser	4.512	0.011
	Scenario B	15	4.53	1.187			
	Scenario C	15	4.80	1.373			
	Scenario E	15	5.00	1.254			
	Scenario F	15	3.87	1.506			
	Total	15	4.79	1.407			

These suggested that scenarios in which students wore OHMD for learning (B, C, F) elicited a statistically significant reduction on physical comfort perceptions compared with the scenarios which did not (A and E); but there were no significant difference of physical comfort among the scenarios with OHMD, or between the scenarios without OHMD.

Table 2. Results of Friedman's ANOVA and Wilcoxon signed-rank test with Bonferroni correction toward criteria.

Criteria	N	Chi-Square	df	Asymp.Sig.
Enjoyment	15	8.912	4	0.063
Ability to Focus	15	5.145	4	0.273
Motivation	15	6.070	4	0.194
Perceived Efficiency	15	7.915	4	0.095
Physical Comfort	15	37.790	4	0.00000012
Understandability	15	1.219	4	0.875
Relaxation	15	11.631	4	0.20

5.3 Post Quiz Questions

To verify the Hypothesis 3 and let participants evaluate the learning outcomes among the five scenarios, we designed listening, speaking, writing, and reading exercises based on the lecture materials.

According to results of average perceived difficulty level, helpfulness, comfort and learnability of the tasks in each scenario, we did not a find significant difference in dealing with individual tasks over the 5 scenarios. Some general observations are:

- Educational material and tasks were more suitable for listening and reading as opposed to writing and speaking, regardless of scenarios.
- Student control would result in easier reading.

5.4 Post-Study Feedback

Post-study survey was considered as an extra source of information while the research mainly relied on the analysis of the evaluation criteria. It consisted of only three open questions: (1) overall, was there anything that made you feel uncomfortable during the test? (2) which was your favourite learning scenario? (3) what would you improve about the see-through head-mounted display interaction method for studying?

Question 1. Physical feeling was mostly considered to be the main source of discomfort; and the eye-fatigue caused by wearing the OHMD for too long was another factor that caused unpleasantness for participants. Participants generally reported that looking at two screens was not an enjoyable experience, and they also reported that the virtual screen size and prescription lenses should be customized. Noticeably, providing a notes-taking option by the device was also identified as a potential need.

Question 2. We allowed participants to choose more than one scenario, most participants favoured single OHMD with student controlling. Figure 1 shows the results.

Question 3. Participants provided suggestions related to making the OHMD lighter, providing customized vision for individuals, making the virtual screen adjustable, improving the control pad, and using electronic stylus for writing practice.

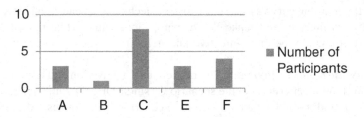

Scenario A: single projection display with teacher controlling

Scenario B: single OHMD with teacher controlling

Scenario C: single OHMD with student controlling

Scenario E: projection display with teacher controlling & PC with student controlling

Scenario F: projection display with teacher controlling & OHMD with student controlling

Fig. 1. Participants' feedback of favoured learning scenario

6 Discussion

While the study did not show a significant difference in participants' evaluation of scenarios based on the given criteria, it did provide valuable insight into the use of OHMD technology in classroom. In particular, the general comments did show that participants overall favoured the OHMD as a single replacement for all screens, and preferred a control system that provides certain level of flexibility and control by students. While this was not enough to positively verify our main hypothesis (H2), it suggests that the OHMD technology has the potential to satisfy the requirements and achieve higher ratings on our evaluation criteria provided some conditions are met. The verification of H2 showed that the only significant difference was in physical comfort, in favour of not using OHMD. This and further inspection of results offer candidates for improving the usability of OHMD, among them the comfort level and more effective control interfaces are the primary items.

Physical Comfort and Technical Difficulties. It was observed that changing the control mechanism while the display variable was constant, did not change the perception of comfort, but with the same control system, OHMD was rated less comfortable than the projection screen. One can expect that this physical discomfort had negative effect on the overall experience and could have resulted in lower ratings of other criteria due to lowered general usability. Eye fatigue in addition to technological issues such as lack of screen size-adjusting and prescription lenses, weight of the device and inconvenient controls which can be resolved in near future are likely to be the cause of OHMD-based scenarios' inability in significantly improving the experience. Improving these issues is very likely to happen in future version of OHMD devices and this will make the technology still an attractive option for research and development in education field. Participants' rating of OHMD for *ability to focus* was not higher than the projection display either, which again could be explained by the difficulties of using OHMD. Moreover, familiarity with more traditional mechanisms and the learning curve associated with new technologies can also have a potential effect on the evaluation, and make the scenarios look equal while the OHMD-based ones could potentially be more effective and helpful.

Motivation and Enjoyment. The participants' motivation and enjoyment ratings were higher than other criteria in the scenario C (single OHMD with student controlling); we did not find a similar pattern in other scenarios. This suggests that most of the participants had positive attitudes toward using OHMD by themselves for educational activities. The results of the post-study survey also verified this suggestion. Considering participants viewed and interacted with the same interface among five experimental scenarios, the reason behind this variance should be due to the novelty of OHMD and students' desire to play with new technology, rather than the design and implementation of class material software. Based on the experimental design and statistics, we could conclude that the novelty of new technology affected the participants' overall responses, but there was no evidence indicating how much novelty affected the results.

Educational Features. Contrary to our assumption, participants' responses to *ability to focus* questions were not the highest when using OHMD. According to the statistical analysis, people generally preferred scenario A (single projection display with teacher controlling) as the most satisfying scenario for concentration when learning. This suggested that participants' *ability to focus* might not only be affected by wearing an "eye-close" virtual screen at all times, but also by who controls the content or interpersonal distractions during a learning procedure. Also we found that the *ability to focus* rating was the lowest in the experimental scenario which involved projection display and OHMD screen. Most of the participants were not comfortable with switching their eye-focus between OHMD screen and teacher's projection display. This indicates that we need further research to figure out a better way for OHMD to improve user's concentration capability.

Other Considerations. Our experimental design was to have participants repeat the same learning material 5 times. Participants may have gotten bored with the tests/materials and stopped caring. So when planning the user study, we made three decisions to minimize the possible negative effects. First, the participants were informed of the experimental procedure and asked to answer the questionnaires according to the related experimental scenarios as objectively as possible. Second, participants completed the five experimental scenarios in randomized order so that potential boredom and fatigue would affect scenarios in an unbiased way. Third, we made the hypothesis H1, and conducted a two-way repeated measure ANOVA to examine participants' responses. The results for H1 verified that participants' responses varied significantly based on changes to the experimental scenarios and evaluation criteria. Therefore, we had enough reason to believe that boredom only had a slight effect on the result.

7 Conclusion

The study presented in this paper developed an OHMD-based prototype and designed a user study in order to investigate the ability of OHMD devices as a single screen in the classroom. The recent availability of wearable sensors especially OHMD devices, provides an alternative that we aimed to explore.

According to the results, there was no significant difference between participants' perceptive responses towards the enjoyment, ability to focus, motivation, perceived efficiency, understandability, and relaxation among the five feasible scenarios. This did not positively support our main hypothesis that OHMD-based approach is preferred but suggested physical comfort as a main issue. Similarly, there was no statistical significant difference between control mechanisms but over various questions participants showed a general interest toward having control over process.

However, participants' feedback showed that they favoured OHMD as a single screen, while their main complaints about it were related to physical comfort and ease of control. Our results are encouraging for the OHMD-based solutions as they show promise that by resolving some issues they can provide a more effective solution in classrooms and replace the need for multiple screens with a single see-through option with multiple control mechanisms. We believe the ergonomic design and hardware will be developed as time goes by, which will make OHMD as comfortable as normal glasses and so improve its overall usability. Although the research findings were not decisive, the lack of support for OHMD can be explained by the technical and setup issues that were discussed above. This suggests that research on usability of OHMD in classroom should continue along with advancing the technology and customized content development.

Acknowledgment. This work has been financially supported by Social Sciences and Humanities Research Council of Canada (SSHRC) through IMMERSe Research Network (http://immerse-network.com).

References

1. Bitner, N., Bitner, J.: Integrating technology into the classroom: eight keys to success. J. Technol. Teach. Educ. **10**(1), 95–100 (2002)
2. Broun, C.C., Campbell, W.M.: Force XXI land warrior: a systems approach to speech recognition. In: 2001 IEEE International Conference on Acoustics, Speech, and Signal Processing, pp. 973–976 (2001)
3. Faria, S., Weston, T., Cepeda, N.J.: Laptop multitasking hinders classroom learning for both users and nearby peers. Comput. Educ. **62**(2), 24–31 (2013)
4. H1 Headset Computer (2013). http://www.motorolasolutions.com/US-EN/Business+Product+and+Services/Mobile+Computers/Wearable+Computers/HC1?WT.mc_id=HC1
5. Hornecker, E., Dünser, A.: Of pages and paddles: children's expectations and mistaken interactions with physical- digital tools. Interact. Comput. **21**(1–2), 95–107 (2009)
6. Liverani, A., Amati, G., Caligiana, G.: A CAD-augmented reality integrated environment for assembly sequence check and interactive validation. Concurrent Eng. **12**(1), 67–77 (2004)

7. McNaney, R., Vines, J., Roggen, D., Balaam, M., Zhang, P., Poliakov, I. Olivier, P.: Exploring the acceptability of google glass as an everyday assistive device for people with parkinson's. In: Proceedings of the SIGCHI Conference on Human Factors in Computing Systems, CHI 2014, pp. 2551–2554, New York, NY, USA (2014)

8. Muensterer, O.J., Lacher, M., Zoeller, C., Bronstein, M., Kübler, J.: Google glass in pediatric surgery: an exploratory study. Int. J. Surg.(London, England) 12(4), 281–289 (2014)

9. Nakasugi, H. Yamauchi, Y.: Past viewer: development of wearable learning system for history education. In: Proceedings of the International Conference on Computers in Education, pp. 1311–1312 (2002)

10. Nguyen, E., Modak, T., Dias, E., Yu, Y., Huang, L.: Fitnamo: using bodydata to encourage exercise through google glass TM. In: Proceeding of the Extended Abstracts on Human Factors in Computing Systems, CHI 2014, pp. 239–244 (2014)

11. Ong, S.K., Wang, Z.B.: Augmented assembly technologies based on 3D bare-hand interaction. CIRP Annals Manuf. Technol. 60(1), 1–4 (2011)

12. Osawa, N., Asai, K.: A wearable learning support system with a head-mounted display and a foot-mounted RFID reader. In: 7th International Conference on Information Technology Based Higher Education and Training, ITHET 2006, pp. 523–530 (2006)

13. Pedersen, I.: Are wearables really ready to wear? IEEE Technol. Soc. Mag. 33(2), 16–18 (2014)

14. Sayed, N.A.M.El, Zayed, H.H., Sharawy, M.I.: ARSC: augmented reality student card - an augmented reality solution for the education field. Comput. Educ. 56(4), 1045–1061 (2011)

15. Schiele, B., Jebara, T., Oliver, N.: Sensory-augmented computing: wearing the museum's guide. IEEE J. Magazines. 21(3), 44–52 (2001)

16. Shelton, B.E., Hedley, N.R.: Using augmented reality for teaching earth-sun relationships to undergraduate geography students. In: The First IEEE International Workshop on Toolkit, pp. 1–14 (2002)

17. Shen, Y., Ong, S.K., Nee, A.Y.C.: Augmented reality for collaborative product design and development. Des. Stud. 31(2), 118–145 (2010)

18. Toyoura, M., Kashiwagi, K., Sugiura, A., Mao, X.: Mono-glass for providing distance information for people losing sight in one eye. In: Proceedings of the 11th ACM SIGGRAPH International Conference on Virtual-Reality Continuum and its Applications in Industry, pp. 39–42 (2012)

19. TRAVIS Callisto (2010). http://www.brueckner.com/en/brueckner-servtec/services/remote-services/remote-service-tools/

20. Vallurupalli, S., Paydak, H., Agarwal, S.K., Agrawal, M., Assad-Kottner, C.: Wearable technology to improve education and patient outcomes in a cardiology fellowship program - a feasibility study. Health Technol. 3(4), 267–270 (2013)

21. Wu, T., Dameff, C., Tully, J.: Integrating google glass into simulation-based training: experiences and future directions. J. Biomed. Graphics Comput. 4(2), 49–54 (2014)

22. Yang, J., Yang, W., Denecke, M. Waibel, A.: Smart sight: a tourist assistant system. In: The Third International Symposium on Wearable Computers, pp. 73–78 (1999)

Prediction of Learner Native Language
by Writing Error Pattern

Brendan Flanagan[1]([⊠]), Chengjiu Yin[2], Takahiko Suzuki[3],
and Sachio Hirokawa[3]

[1] Graduate School of Information Science and Electrical Engineering,
Kyushu University, Fukuoka, Japan
b.flanagan.885@s.kyushu-u.ac.jp
[2] Faculty of Arts and Science, Kyushu University, Fukuoka, Japan
yin.academic@gmail.com
[3] Research Institute for Information Technology, Kyushu University,
Fukuoka, Japan
{suzuki,hirokawa}@cc.kyushu-u.ac.jp

Abstract. The native language of a foreign language learner can have an effect on the errors they make because of similarities or differences between the two languages. In order to provide effective error prediction and correction for non-native English language learners it is important to identify their specific characteristic error patterns that are influenced by their native language. In this paper, we examine analyzing error detection scores to predict the native language of an English language learner. 15 categories of error detection scores are combined to create an error prediction score vector representation of each sentence. The native language is predicted by training an SVM classifier with the error vectors. The results are compared to an SVM classifier trained with just word representations of the learner writing sentences.

Keywords: Native language prediction · Writing errors · SVM classifier

1 Introduction

As a result of increased globalization facilitated by the Internet, the number of foreign language learners has increased. In particular, the numbers of people who speak English as a second or foreign language are increasing. Graddol [1] suggests that 80 % of communication in English is among non-native speakers. It has been estimated that there are over a billion second or foreign language speakers of English, which is the native language of only approximately 400 million people [2]. As many automated correction methods are targeted at native speakers, there is an increasing need for second or foreign language targeted tools to correct their characteristic errors.

The native language of a foreign language learner can have an effect on the errors they make because of similarities or differences between the two languages. In order to provide effective error prediction and correction for non-native English language learners it is important to identify their specific characteristic error patterns that are influenced by their native language. In our previous research into the prediction of

© Springer International Publishing Switzerland 2015
P. Zaphiris and A. Ioannou (Eds.): LCT 2015, LNCS 9192, pp. 87–96, 2015.
DOI: 10.1007/978-3-319-20609-7_9

writing errors in foreign language writing [3], we identified the differences and similarities of error co-occurrence characteristics of learners who's native language are: Chinese, Japanese, Korean, Spanish, and Taiwanese. In particular, by error clustering analysis we found that some languages were quite similar in their characteristics, such as: Japanese and Korean, while others only shared a few common characteristics.

The writing error categories used in our research are based on previous empirical studies on the writings of foreign language students in academic settings [4, 5]. A parallel corpus of original and corrected sentences was collected from the writings of learners on the popular online language learning SNS lang-8.com. A randomly selected subset of sentences from the corpus was manually categorized by hand into 15 writing error categories. This subset was then analyzed to train and evaluate SVM classifiers for each of the writing error categories [6–8]. The error category classifiers output a score for 15 error categories is a vector representation of the analyzed sentence.

In this paper, we will compare the prediction performance of two SVM models: one created by analyzing error category prediction vectors, and another created by analyzing word vectors. This can be thought of as comparing two different viewpoints: the error category prediction vector viewpoint, and the word vector viewpoint.

2 Related Work

2.1 Native Language Prediction

Wong [9] analyzed learner writing with an extension of adaptor grammars for detecting colocations not only at the word level, but also for parts-of-speech and functional words. Classification was performed at the document level by parsing individual sentences of the learner's writing to detect the native language with the final prediction based on a majority score of the sentences. Some notable characteristic features of languages extracted by this method were also discussed.

Brooke et al. [10] suggested that the International Corpus of Learner English (ICLE) corpus, which is commonly used in research into native language prediction of learner writing, has problems that can lead to misleading performance evaluation. It was argued that the problem stems from the way the corpus was built, and proposed other methods and sources to collect data that might be useful in the task of native language prediction. An evaluation was undertaken on data collected from a language learning SNS, Lang-8.com, and it was shown to be useful for the task. In this paper, we analyze data collected from Lang-8.com for the purpose of native language prediction by writing error prediction vector.

In 2013, Tetreault et al. [11] organized a shared task on native language identification of learners through analysis of their writing. A new corpus named TOEFL11, which contains essays in English by learners from 11 different native languages and was provided as the shared data set on which the participants conducted analysis. Jarvis et al. [12] was a participating group with a high identification performance. A variety of features were analyzed in the identification task, such as: word n-grams, parts-of-speech n-grams, character n-grams, and lemma n-grams. An SVM classifier was trained and the prediction performance was evaluated of several different models with varying combinations of features.

In this paper, we investigate the difference in prediction performance of an SVM classifier trained with writing error prediction vectors and an SVM classifier trained with basic word features.

2.2   Native Language Prediction by Error Analysis

Koppel et al. [13], investigated predicting a learner's native language by analyzing writing errors detected with MS Word and a Brill based parts-of-speech tagger in addition to other features, such as: function words, letter n-grams, and rare part-of-speech bigrams. They analyzed a sub-corpus of ICLE containing learner writings by learners with the following native languages: Russia, Czech Republic, Bulgaria, France and Spain. It was found that most classification errors occurred between writings from Slavic languages. An overall accuracy of 80 % was achieved using all features.

Kochmar [14], predicted the native languages of Indo-European learners through binary classification tasks preformed with linear kernel SVM. Compare to previous studies a larger set of learner native languages were examined. These native languages were divided into two main groups: Germanic and Romance, with intergroup prediction performance accuracy ranging from 68.4 % to 100 %. The features analyzed for prediction ranged from general words and n-grams, to different error types that had been manually tagged within the corpus.

Bestgen et al. [15], investigated the used of error patterns in the identification of the native languages of learners. They analyzed the manually tagged errors within the ICLE. The 46 error types that have been tagged in the corpus were used to predict the native language of 223 learner writings. Three groups of native languages were chosen: French, German, and Spanish. They identified that using just errors as a predictor of native language an accuracy of 65 % could be achieved. Discriminative error types for the three native languages were identified by comparing the mean relative frequency significance difference of each error category. They impact of proficiency on the results was also examined and resulted in improved predictive discrimination between French and German learners. In conclusion it is mentioned that it still remains to be seen if the same prediction performance can be achieved through the automatic detection of writing errors, instead of relying on manual classification by hand.

In this paper, we endeavor to investigate the prediction performance of automatic error detection as a predictor of the native language of learners.

3   Data

The data for analysis in this paper was collected from lang-8.com, a language learning SNS site. The target data was learner journals that were written in English and posted on Lang-8 during the period from Oct 9 2011 to Jan 6 2012. A total of 57,776 journals written in English were collected. Within these journals, there were 142,465 sentences that had been corrected by native English speakers who are members on the lang-8.com site. As the corrections are made at the sentence level, analysis undertaken in this paper is by sentence units. The native and target languages of the learner were also collected and each sentence was annotated with this information accordingly. An alignment algorithm was used to identify the corrected words within the sentence and were tagged as either insert or delete and also generally as an edit. Figure 1 shows the sentence distribution of the five main learner native languages who's English journals were corrected by a native English speaker. A large majority are Japanese natives who have written 100,432 corrected sentences. The other main learner native languages are in descending order: Chinese, Korean, Taiwanese, and Spanish, which each makeup more than 2 % of the total sentences.

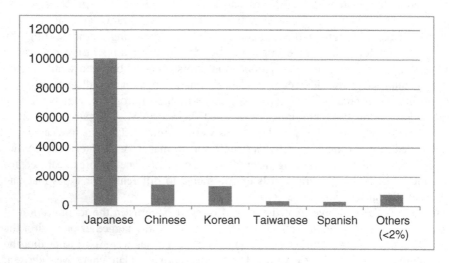

Fig. 1. Distribution of learner native languages

4 Error Prediction and Error Vector

In previous research [6–8], the authors have predicted 15 different writing error types by SVM classifier. These errors were selected from a larger list of 42 error types in [16] because of the frequency in annotated data. Table 1 lists the 15 writing error type descriptions along with the original error category number.

In this paper, we predict the errors of sentences by SVM models that were trained and evaluated using 10-fold cross validation. As a result of this evaluation there are 10 models for each writing error type. The prediction for each error type is made up of the average of the 10 scores from the models. The predictions are then combined to form an error vector representation for each sentence as seen in Fig. 2.

The distribution of predicted errors for each of the five main learner native languages is displayed in Fig. 3.

5 Trivial Biased Words

Initially an SVM model was trained to predict the native language of learners just by analyzing the words in their writings, however the prediction performance was higher than expected, so we investigated the characteristic feature words for each language.

Table 1. Predicted error categories

Category	Description
2	Subject formation
3	Verb missing
6	Dangling/misplaced modifier
11	Word order
13	Extraneous words
17	Tense
19	Verb formation
25	Ambiguous/unlocatable referent
28	Lexical/phrase choice
30	Word form
33	Singular for plural
36	Preposition
37	Genitive
38	Article
42	Spelling

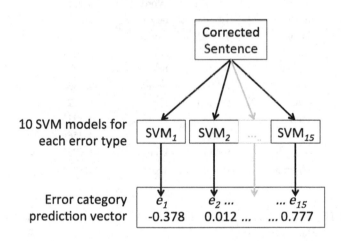

Fig. 2. The process of creating error vector representations of each sentence

An SVM model was trained for each learner native language by analyzing all of the data. These models were analyzed to calculate and rank all of the feature words by weight.

Feature words with a high positive weight are characteristic of that particular learner group. In Table 2, the top 10 positive and negative weight feature words for native Japanese learners of English are shown. Many high positive words are directly related to Japan, were as low negative words are related to other countries. Therefore, these words are trivial biased words that have been influenced by the nation or culture

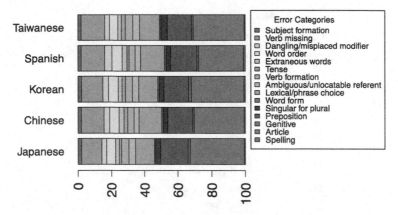

Fig. 3. Distribution of predicted errors for each language

Table 2. Top 10 positive and negative feature words by weight for native Japanese learners of English.

Top Positive 10		Top Negative 10	
Word	Weight	Word	Weight
north	1.0305	taiwan	-1.2025
japan	1.0073	campus	-1.251
tokyo	0.6735	soju	-1.26
japanese	0.572	beijing	-1.3393
peninsula	0.5502	pepero	-1.3534
jong	0.5223	korean	-1.522
kara	0.5032	kimchi	-1.5315
kyoto	0.4653	I	-1.7565
thailand	0.4447	korea	-1.7737
algerian	0.4447	seoul	-1.8214

of the learner. The characteristic feature words for each learner native language group also contained similar influences.

Other sources of trivial biased words included events that had occurred just before the collection of data from the lang-8.com website (October 2011 ~ January 2012). Table 3 contains feature words that we believe are related to the 2011 Tohoku Earthquake and Tsunami that occurred in Japan.

To reduce the influence of trivial biased words and provide a fare comparison between the proposed method of language prediction by error vector and the baseline method of prediction by words, feature words with a high frequency distribution difference between the native language groups were removed. The relative standard deviation for each word was calculated as follows:

Table 3. Biased words in the model for Japanese native language learners

Rank	Weight	word
13	0.3602	earthquake
...	...	...
24	0.3093	radiation
...	...	...
42	0.2943	nuclear

$$TDR(w, l) = \frac{TF(w, l)}{DF(l)} \tag{1}$$

$$s(w) = \sqrt{\frac{\sum_{l \in L} TDR(w, l)^2}{|L|} - \left(\frac{\sum_{l \in L} TDR(w, l)^2}{|L|}\right)^2} \tag{2}$$

$$\bar{x}(w) = \frac{\sum_{l \in L} TDR(w, l)}{|L|} \tag{3}$$

$$RSD(w) = \frac{s(w)}{\bar{x}(w)} \tag{4}$$

Where Eq. 1 is the term document ratio for the word w in language set l, and TF is the term frequency and DF with the document frequency. The standard deviation and mean of the term documents ratio between languages is calculated in Eqs. 2 and 3 respectively. Then finally the relative standard deviation is shown in Eq. 4.

A list of words ranked by RSD was manually checked for words that might identify the culture or nation of the five main groups of native languages. Through these manual checks it was estimated that words with an RSD of greater than 1.25 were trivially biased towards one or more of the native languages. Figure 4 shows a plot of all words ranked by RSD in descending order, with the horizontal line at 1.25 RSD representing the maximum threshold for non-biased words used in the analysis of this paper.

6 Method and Results

To provide a fare evaluation of the two feature sets, the same method was used for training and evaluating prediction performance of error prediction vectors and word vector features. For additional comparison, we also include the prediction performance for word vectors that contain all the words of the original learner writing, including those that were identified as trivially biased in the previous section. For the word vectors, the words of each sentence were vectorized as a bag-of-words model. The error prediction vector consists of the values of 15 error prediction scores.

Separate SVM classifiers were trained for five different native languages across all three data sets. The native language prediction performance of each of these classifiers

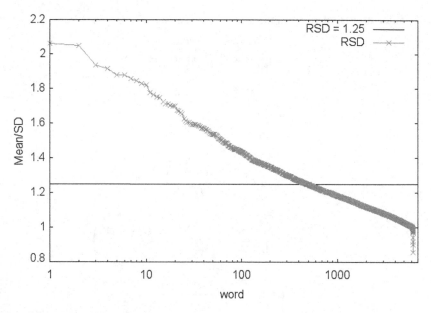

Fig. 4. The RSD distribution of word frequencies between five native languages

was evaluated by randomly sampled 10-fold cross validation, with 9:1 training to test data ratio for each of the data sets.

A comparison of the prediction performance evaluation on all three data sets for each of the five native languages is shown in Fig. 5. The prediction performance of the

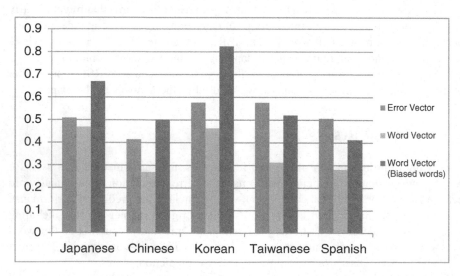

Fig. 5. Native language prediction evaluation for each vector (Accuracy, 10-fold cross validation)

word vectors that include biased words is high, especially for writings by native Korean learners. This would suggest that there are biased words that are highly characteristic of native Korean learners. The word vectors that do not contain trivial biased words have a prediction performance ranging from 36 % lower in the case of Korean, to 13 % lower for Spanish. The native language prediction performance by error prediction vector is higher than the performance of the unbiased word vector. However the prediction performance for two out of the five native languages is lower than that of the word vectors that contain all the words of the original learner writings, which we argue is influenced by biased words.

7 Conclusion

In this paper, we evaluated and compared the prediction performance of error prediction vectors and word vectors. Initial analysis indicated that the learner writing data that was collected from Lang-8.com contained trivial biases, which were in the form of differences in word use distribution due to the culture, location, and recent localized events. A method for identifying and reducing trivial biased words was proposed to alleviate the problem. SVM classifiers were then trained for three data sets: error prediction vectors, word vectors without biased words, and word vectors containing all the words from the original learner writing. The prediction performance for each data set was then evaluated with 10-fold cross validation. The prediction performance error prediction vectors were superior to the unbiased word vectors for all native languages. However, word vectors containing all words including biased words performed better in three out of five native languages.

In future work, we intend to examine in detail the results of our evaluation along with comparisons to other methods and corpora. It is also necessary to perform a search for optimal selections of error predictions to further enhance the native language prediction performance.

Acknowledgment. This work was partially supported by JSPS KAKENHI Grant Number 24500176.

References

1. Graddol, D.: English Next: Why Global English May Mean the End of English as a Foreign Language. British Council, London (2006)
2. Guo, Y., Beckett, G.H.: The hegemony of english as a global language: reclaiming local knowledge and culture in china. Convergence **40**, 117–132 (2007)
3. Flanagan, B., Yin, C., Suzuki, T., Hirokawa, S.: Classification and clustering english writing errors based on native language. In: IIAI 3rd International Conference on Advanced Applied Informatics (IIAIAAI), pp. 318-323 (2014)
4. Kroll, B.: What does time buy? ESL student performance on home versus class compositions. In: Kroll, B. (ed.) Second Language Writing: Research Insights for the Classroom, pp. 140–154. Cambridge University Press, Cambridge (1990)

5. Weltig, M.S.: Effects of language errors and importance attributed to language on language and rhetorical-level essay scoring. In: Spaan Fellow Working Papers in Second or Foreign Language Assess. vol. 2(1001), pp. 53-81 (2004)
6. Flanagan, B., Yin, C., Suzuki, T., Hirokawa, S.: Intelligent Computer Classification of English Writing Errors. In: Proceedings of the 6th International Conference on Intelligent Interactive Multimedia Systems and Services (IIMSS 2013) vol. 254, pp. 174-183, IOS Press (2013)
7. Flanagan, B., Yin, C., Hashimoto, K., Hirokawa, S.: Clustering English Writing Errors based on Error Category Prediction, ISEEE 2013, pp. 733-738 (2013)
8. Flanagan, B., Yin, C., Suzuki, T., Hirokawa, S.: Classification of english language learner writing errors using a parallel corpus with svm. Int. J. Knowl. Web Intell. 5(1), 21–35 (2014)
9. Wong, S.M.J., Dras, M., Johnson, M.: Exploring adaptor grammars for native language identification. In: Proceedings of the 2012 Joint Conference on Empirical Methods in Natural Language Processing and Computational Natural Language Learning. Association for Computational Linguistics, pp. 699-709 (2012)
10. Brooke, J., Hirst, G.: Native language detection with 'cheap' learner corpora. In Twenty Years of Learner Corpus Research. Looking Back, Moving Ahead: Proceedings of the First Learner Corpus Research Conference (LCR 2011), pp. 37-57, Presses universitaires de Louvain (2013)
11. Tetreault, J., Blanchard, D., Cahill, A.: A report on the first native language identification shared task. In: Proceedings of the Eighth Workshop on Innovative Use of NLP for Building Educational Applications, pp. 48-57 (2013)
12. Jarvis, S., Bestgen, Y., Pepper, S.: Maximizing classification accuracy in native language identification. NAACL/HLT 2013, 111–118 (2013)
13. Koppel, M., Schler, J., Zigdon, K.: Determining an author's native language by mining a text for errors. In Proceedings of the Eleventh ACM SIGKDD International Conference on Knowledge Discovery in Data Mining, pp. 624-628, ACM (2005)
14. Kochmar, E.: Identification of a writer's native language by error analysis. Master's thesis. University of Cambridge (2011)
15. Bestgen, Y., Granger, S., Thewissen, J.: Error patterns and automatic L1 identification. In: Approaching Language Transfer Through Text Classification, pp. 127-153 (2012)
16. Flanagan, B., Yin, C., Hirokawa, S., Hashimoto, K., Tabata, Y.: An automated method to generate e-learning quizzes from online language learner writing. Int. J Distance Educ. Technol. 11(4), 63–80 (2013)

An Exploration of Mobile Collaborative Writing Interface Design

Menghui Li[✉] and Young Mi Choi

346 Cumberland Way SE, Smyrna, GA 30080, USA
mli359@gatech.edu

Abstract. The Open Academic Environment (OAE) is a new platform that aims to support academic collaboration and academic networking. It allows students, researchers and faculty to create knowledge, collaborate and connect with the world.

Since authoring plays an essential part in academic activity, one of the most powerful tools OAE provides is the collaborative authoring. It enables students and faculty to create, share and collaboratively work on cloud based documents. The features provided include coworker managing, real-time collaborative text documentation, basic format editing and commenting.

The current OAE system is web based and it enables mobile accessibility through responsive web design. More and more students and research work with mobile devices these days. However the current mobile interface of for collaborative interfaces such as OAE has much room for improvement. The interface has not been optimized for mobile device usability and loses some of the essential features in both text editing and collaborative support when accessed through a mobile device. Even basic documentation may require the use of many different editing features. Collaboration support requires the availability of features that enable tracking of others' activity and that support communication.

However mobile interface design for complex tasks has always been tricky work. The smaller screen and limited input methods of the mobile device make it difficult to fit in as many features as in desktop software or a full website. Therefore, it is important to identify user needs and understand user activities so that a designer can prioritize needed features and optimize their arrangements. Better support for mobile devices will enable participation in academic collaboration whenever and wherever a person might be. This paper presents research on user needs and user activities in mobile collaborative systems, and efforts to design an alternative interface for OAE system.

Keywords: Mobile · Collaborative editing · Interface design

1 Literature Review

Writing/documentation or note taking is an important part in almost all academic activities a lot of which is done collaboratively [1]. Collaboration helps students write more efficiently and helps them improve writing skill [2]. In recent years, group wares that support online collaboration have become increasingly available and widely used [3, 4]. Several studies are investigating how well these tools support collaboration by

© Springer International Publishing Switzerland 2015
P. Zaphiris and A. Ioannou (Eds.): LCT 2015, LNCS 9192, pp. 97–105, 2015.
DOI: 10.1007/978-3-319-20609-7_10

employing different methods. Vallance, Towndrow and Wlz did evaluation and tests on several such tools, both synchronous and asynchronous, in 2010. They compared different functions that these tools provides and discussed their benefits and limitations. Whether synchronous or asynchronous these tools can connect students to work better than as individuals [4]. Another case study of an asynchronous collaborative tool showed that web based collaboration can help people communicate in a more focused and honest manner than in real life [3].

In 2014 the number of mobile device users exceeded the number of desktop users for the first time. People now spend more time on their mobile devices than desktop computers [5]. Though the use of mobile devices has not yet completely changed the way that people learn and work as it has for gaming and entertainment [6], mobile usability must be considered when providing any online service.

Current literature in collaborative learning rather sparse but has received increasing attention over the last several years. Mobility is seen as a new opportunity for academic activities since it provides more chances to personalize the collaborative process, enhance social interactions, work more effectively and more autonomously, and collaborate with other peers at anytime and from anywhere, inside and outside the formal collaborative working context [6]. Mobile devices also have the advantage of increasing environmental awareness for the collaborators [7].

As send or receive text message is already the most common mobile phone activity [8], reading and communicating on mobile devices does not appear to be a problem to users. Writing an academic paper on a smart phone may be unrealistic, but current mobile technology might definitely support activities such as note taking, group discussion, mind storming or informal collaborative writing.

There are some studies that discuss the technical approaches of collaborative editing and maintenance of the document consistency [9]. On design and usability, the problem researchers discussed most is the awareness of the group. Group awareness refers to the knowledge of each other's state and activity in a collaborative work [10]. Group awareness is a vital feature improving the usability of real-time collaborative writing systems [11]. The most common and basic features for supporting group awareness is to allow users to see coworkers' activities and simple text messaging chat tools. Color coding and work modification alert have also been suggested as other important features.

In a mobile context it is harder to support group awareness. Users can only see small parts of a document on a mobile device. More scrolling is required to move around the page making it difficult for a user to get a full view of the document [12]. It is also not possible for mobile device to provide a multitask interface as well as on a large screen [13].

2   Review Existing Products

2.1   The Open Academic Environment Collaborative Writing Tool

The Open Academic Environment (OAE) system is web based and enables mobility through responsive web design.

The desktop interface (Fig. 1) provides coworker management and color-coded authorship markings. It provides some basic format editing features and allows a user to comment on the whole document. On the mobile interface (Fig. 2), many of the features are folded or omitted.

Fig. 1. The OAE collaborative writing interface on a desktop screen

Fig. 2. The OAE collaborative writing interface on mobile device

2.2 Comparison to Other Products

Several current documentation and collaboration products were compared, focusing in particular on their mobile accessibility and usability (Table 1).

While other products don't provide mobile accessibility or mobile editing feature, Google docs and MS office online put many of the desktop features into the mobile app. Since people use tools differently in a mobile context more than simply providing

Table 1. The mobile accessibility and feature of existing products

Products	Mobile accessibility		Mobile collaborative features
OAE	Responsive web	view and edit	Share; writing; basic format edition; comment on the whole document
Google docs	Web + app	View on web and edit on app	Share; writing; format edition; comment on selected text and on whole document; real-time track co-worker activities
MS office online	app	View and edit	Share; writing; format edition; comment on selected text; need manually save and refresh for keeping synchronization
ZOHO doc	Web + app	View only on both web and app	View documents; need manually refresh to view coworkers edition
Only office	none	–	–

a redused usability app compared to the desktop version is needed. Of the products compared, none have features designed specifically for the mobile context.

3   User Needa and Design Criteria

3.1   OAE Users and Workflow Analysis

The OAE is a platform that aims to support academic collaboration and academic networking. Thus the user group are students and faculty in an on-campus context. The features of an OAE collaborative writing tool should aim at supporting on-campus group working and collaborative learning.

Users were surveyed to better understand how they do academic collaboration and what activities a collaborative writing tool should focuses on supporting. A chart of group collaboration workflow is shown in Fig. 3.

The group collaboration workflow indicated that collaborative authoring is an activity that could greatly improve group working efficiency.

3.2   Discover User Need in Mobile Context and Define Design Criteria

The user activities on collaborative writing tool on mobile device are likely to be very different to those performed on a desktop. Though mobile devices are able to provide effective reading and writing user experience, very little academic writing is done from mobile devices. Users still prefer larger screen when they do formal authoring.

However a mobile collaborative writing tool could help users keep up with group work and do informal writing such as note taking, brainstorming and commenting on group work. A mobile interface may give more space for group awareness and communication than trying to provide full feature of text format editing.

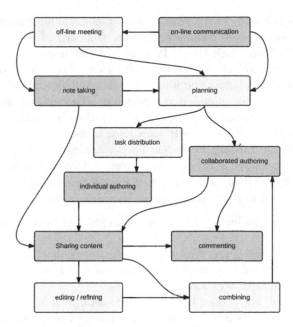

Fig. 3. Group collaboration workflow

With all of this in mind, the following design criteria were defined:

- Allow user to access and edit the shared group document on mobile device.
- Provide enhanced group awareness to allow user keep track on the group activities.
- Improve the communication between co-works when working on the collaborative document.

4   Design Schemes

Based on the design criteria, the following features are designed for the OAE collaborated writing tool:

1. **IM Tool to Allow Users to Chat and Discuss While Collaboratively Editing Documents.** Simple text messaging is both the most commonly used communication method on mobile devices and on current collaborative writing products. However on mobile devices, there is not enough space to show the chatting channel and the document at the same time.
2. **Color Coded Authorship Marking.** This feature already exists on the current OAE desktop web interface. It's an easy and efficient way to show authorship and could easily be integrated into a mobile device interface.
3. **Track Co-worker Activities by Seeing Their Cursor Synchronously.** This is the core feature used by several existing products to enhance group awareness and it also help in avoiding conflicts due to multi-user editing.

4. **Comment on Selected Text.** This feature is commonly available in existing products. It allows users to communicate on certain parts of a document.
5. **Scroll Bar to Indicate Each Users' Position in a Document.** In a mobile context, the smaller screen only allows a user to see a small part of a document. More scrolling is required and users find it harder to get a full view of the document. This makes it even more difficult understand authoring activity if they are working with others. It could be very helpful if the user had a way to be aware of others' current positions in the document and easily view those areas.
6. **Simplified Format Editing Features.** Format editing is a large component of traditional documentation software. On a mobile device such features can add too much complexity. Viewing a document on a small mobile screen makes it harder and less meaningful to focus on document style and layout.

Mobile interface mockups incorporating these features have been designed for use in future testing.

Figure 4 shows colored text background indicating authorship. The background colors can be turn on or off by tapping the icon which is how this feature currently works on the desktop OAE web tool.

A horizontal scroll bar is added above the text area, to show where other collaborators are working within the full document. The I-shaped cursor indicates the current

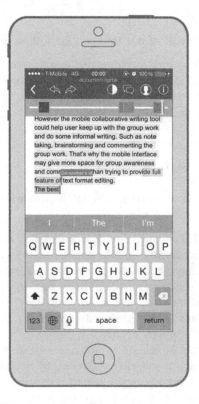

Fig. 4. The interface design with color coding off and on

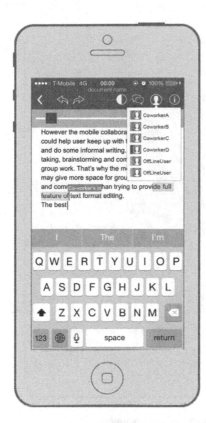

Fig. 5. The users list and the chat channel

user, and the user could tap on the bar or drag the cursor to move it. This allows easy exploration of the whole document. Tapping on the colored squares of collaborators' positions allows a way to quickly view what they are doing within the document.

Figure 5 shows the dialogue of users that are currently online working on the documents. The same colors are used in the cursor showing authorship marking, scroll bar location and chatting channel. When there is a new text message in the chatting channel, the chat icon flashes. The user can tap the icon to enter the channel and tap it again to get back to the document.

Figure 6 show the how document comments are represented in the mobile interface. The red line in the left marks that there is a comment associated with the adjacent text. Tapping the red line expands or hides the comment.

5   Discussion and Future Work

A collaborative writing tool optimized has the potential to greatly improve collaboration efficiency. The idea itself is a plus to the group synchronism, people could do less distribution and combination, and make less confliction working with it [2].

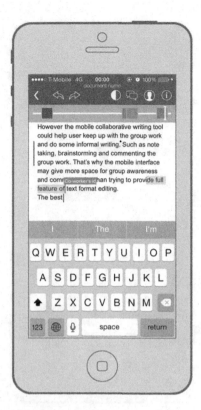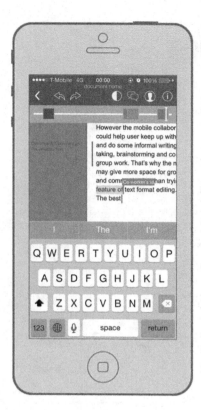

Fig. 6. Comment on selected part of the document.

In a situation where group members are together and work on a collaborative document from a desktop/laptop, collaborative editing can work well. But when people works at a distance or in a mobile context, the lack of group communication and awareness become the biggest issue. This paper presents potential features of a mobile collaborative interface designed to mitigate this issue. These features have yet to be tested and future work includes further development of the design, implementation if functional prototypes and testing with end users to measure the effectiveness of these features at improving mobile collaboration.

References

1. Calvo, R.A., et al.: Collaborative writing support tools on the cloud. IEEE Trans. Learn. Technol. **4**(1), 88–97 (2011)
2. McAllister, C.: Collaborative Writing Groups in the College Classroom. Writing in Context(s), **15**, pp. 207–227 (2005)
3. Davoli, P., Monari, M., Eklundh, K.S.: Peer activities on Web-learning platforms—Impact on collaborative writing and usability issues. Educ. Inf. Technol. **14**(3), 229–254 (2009)

4. Vallance, M., Towndrow, P., Wiz, C.: Conditions for Successful Online Document Collaboration. TechTrends **54**(1), 20–24 (2010)
5. Bosomworth, D.: *Mobile Marketing Statistics 2015 (2015)*. http://www.smartinsights.com/mobile-marketing/mobile-marketing-analytics/mobile-marketing-statistics/
6. Caballé, S., Xhafa, F., Barolli, L.: Using mobile devices to support online collaborative learning. Mobile Inf. Syst. **6**(1), 27–47 (2010)
7. Uzunboylu, H., Cavus, N., Ercag, E.: Using mobile learning to increase environmental awareness. Comput. Educ. **52**(2), 381–389 (2009)
8. PewResearch. Mobile Technology Fact Sheet (2014). http://www.pewinternet.org/fact-sheets/mobile-technology-fact-sheet/
9. Qinyi, W., Pu, C., Ferreira, J.E.: A partial persistent data structure to support consistency in real-time collaborative editing. In: IEEE 26th International Conference on Data Engineering (ICDE), 2010. (2010)
10. Khairuddin, N.N.: Interface Design for a Real-Time Collaborative Editing Tool. In: Zaphiris, P., Ioannou, A. (eds.) LCT. LNCS, vol. 8524, pp. 417–428. Springer, Heidelberg (2014)
11. Tran, M.H., Raikundalia, G.K., Yang, Y.: Split Window View and Modification Director: innovative awareness mechanisms in real-time collaborative writing. In: Proceedings of the Conference on Human Factors HF 2002 (2002)
12. Nielsen, J.: *Mobile Content Is Twice as Difficult* (2011). http://www.nngroup.com/articles/mobile-content-is-twice-as-difficult/
13. Nielsen, J., Budiu, R.: *Mobile Usability*. New Riders, Berkeley (2013)

A Tablet-Based Lego Mindstorms Programming Environment for Children

Stephanie Ludi[(✉)]

Department of Software Engineering,
Rochester Institute of Technology, Rochester, USA
`salvse@rit.edu`

Abstract. Tablets, such as the iPad and Kindle, provide a portable platform for children of all ages to explore various content through apps and interactive books. The use of gestures provides a means of interaction that is intuitive to children as a means of navigating apps or activating media-based content. The tablet as a programming platform is unique in that the gesture-based skills used in other apps are extrapolated and applied to computational thinking skills and interaction with a robot, which maneuvers based on the child's creation. This paper describes the workflow and user interface design to facilitate Lego Mindstorms NXT programming by children.

Keywords: Children · Mobile · Programming · User interface · Programming

1 Introduction

First notebook computers where viewed as a portable technology for children to use, then tablets were introduced. The advantages of tablets over notebook computers are the price, weight, and ability to use touch and gestures as the primary input mechanism over the keyboard and mouse. Touching an item as a means of the exploration of physical objects. Translating that into taps, pinches, swipes and other gestures has enabled children to explore content on the tablet.

Creating content is also another avenue of interaction. Usually artistic creations are associated with the type of content that children create, but content can also include songs, video, and even interactive content. To extent the type of content and the means of interaction, the pair of tablet-based project described in this paper are those of robotics programs that run on Lego Mindstorms NXT robots. The software line is called JBrick. JBrick for iOS enables children to create their own Lego Mindstorms NXT program by dragging and stacking blocks of programming elements or structures, an example of visual programming (as opposed to typing code).

Visual programming is a popular means of teaching programming to children. Examples include MIT's Scratch, Microsoft Kodu, and Lego Mindstorms' own programming language, NXT-G. The use of gestures, the tablet platform, and the extended metaphor of blocks for portraying program structure in Lego Mindstorms NXT programs are the focus of the JBrick for iOS project.

The use of robotics such as Lego Mindstorms as a means of engaging children in STEM (Science, Technology, Engineering, and Math) has been the subject of several

© Springer International Publishing Switzerland 2015
P. Zaphiris and A. Ioannou (Eds.): LCT 2015, LNCS 9192, pp. 106–114, 2015.
DOI: 10.1007/978-3-319-20609-7_11

classroom and outreach projects [1–3, 5]. For this work, the means of interaction using a gesture-based, tiled approach is the main focus. Cartoid has been developed to enable children to write simple programs and control devices such as Lego Minsdstorms robots, but the program construction, based on Scratch, uses simple taps to select commands that are stacked in a linear manner [7]. A tangible approach, as in Robo-Blocks [4], requires physical blocks to construct a program as well as debugging the program. The authors noted issues with some student's attention, especially with young children.

The notion of blocks as a means of building programs is also used in the Lego Mindstorms NXT-G environment. In the case of NXT-G, programs are built by connecting blocks along a horizontal line, as shown in Fig. 1.

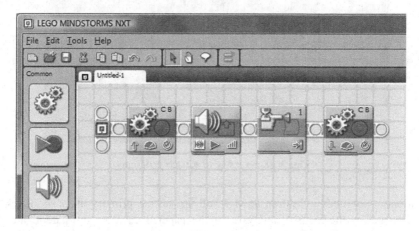

Fig. 1. Screenshot of Lego's NXT-G software (cropped)

The program, as in the case of other Lego Mindstorms programming environments, is controlled with the keyboard and mouse. In the case of NXT-G, attributes are set in a pane at the bottom of the window. The main window is often full screen, with the attribute pane being at a significant visual distance from the program. JBrick takes a vertical program building path, with attributes being visually near due to the smaller size of the screen. The vertical approach is similar to MIT's Scratch, as shown in Fig. 2.

Like NXT-G, Scratch is traditionally mouse-driven. However Scratch is used to create animations and simple games. JBrick for iOS takes a different direction with block design, as well as selection since the use of such narrow blocks in a tablet app would be difficult for a young child to accurately select. More detail will be presented in Sect. 3.

2 User and Task Analysis

2.1 User Profile

Lego Mindstorms are popular in many classrooms. However, many classrooms have a limited number of computers for children to use when programming. The smaller, portable, and low-cost tablets can be a more affordable solution.

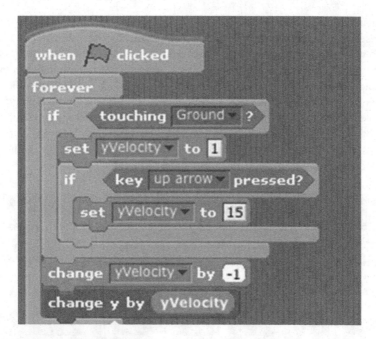

Fig. 2. Screenshot of scratch program

Students, specifically children aged 7 and up, are the primary users of JBrick for iOS. They will be the focus of analysis for this paper. Educators and parents are also stakeholders as they will set up, and in the case of the classroom environment they will oversee the use of several tablets and robots.

Based on observations from past robotics programming camp and FIRST Lego League team participants, the user profile for a child user consists of:

- Age: 7 and up
- Education level: 2nd grade (US) or above, where the child can read and comprehend 5-6 word sentences; also at minimum basic addition and subtraction
- Visual Acuity: with correction 20/20 though up to 20/200 without correction
- Motor skills: Use of a finger or stylus (if motor impaired) for taps, swipes, etc. 2-handed typing not needed
- Programming expertise: None required

Previous experience with 9-17-year old kids [8] has shown that students who are less familiar or confidant with the keyboard have more issues creating and working with their programs. Removing the keyboard and mouse hardware from the equation, as well as enabling the student to control placement of the device when programming offers more flexibility for physical and environmental differences.

The threshold for skill level is set low, as the programs created can be as simple or complex as the student can design. The user interface itself was designed to work with both younger and older students, with varying hand/finger sizes. These attributes facilitate system usability.

2.2   Programming Workflow

The goal is to make the JBrick and Lego Mindstorms NXT programming portable for kids. The previous, desktop version of JBrick as well as other robotics programming software runs on traditional desktop computers or laptops. The child's workspace and computing environment revolves around where the computer is placed.

The desktop version of JBrick's programming workflow was the basis for the tablet workflow in terms of the types of tasks to be completed (not the means of completing these tasks). The foundational programming workflow is shown in Fig. 3.

Fig. 3.   Programming workflow using JBrick

Programming involves more than entering in code, but it includes the decision as to what features or robot behaviors are desired/needed. Next, design is conducted in terms of thinking algorithmically takes place. Then the process of mapping these requirements to the language via the development environment takes over. The tasks of creating a program, compiling the program, downloading the program to the robot, running (testing) the program, then repeating the cycle as needed until the result is desired is typical regardless of which programming environment used. The differences come out in the user interface design, in order to meet user needs and support the workflow.

3   System Design

Due some external constraints, the system design has a client-server architecture. The NXC (Not eXactly C) compiler that is used for JBrick runs on the PC. As such, the compilation must be accomplished on a PC rather than the iOS device. As shown in Fig. 4, the iPad sends the NXC program to the server. The server then compiles the program and sends it to the Lego Mindstorms robot directly via Bluetooth.

In some respects, this technical limitation would be negative, but in using a Web Service approach, many iPads can be managed from a single computer. As a web service, the PC does not have to be in the same room (a feature to be developed in the future).

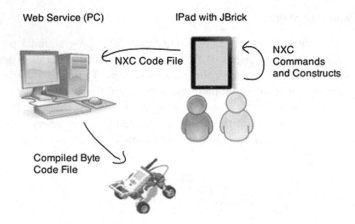

Fig. 4. Overview of JBrick for iOS

4   User Interface Design

The primary tasks associated with the user interface are those related to creating and revising a program. However the entire workflow will be presented.

Take note that the blocks have minimal text, in order to minimize cognitive and visual overload. The size of the blocks is such that small fingers or adult sized finger can interact with blocks easily. Volunteers with different hand sizes provided some initial feedback on block interaction. Since the fingertip is a small size, the outline or anywhere within the block is recognized and triggers block selection. The use of bright colors and icons helps reinforce the type of blocks (and thus concepts used to program the robot).

4.1   Creating and Editing a Program

JBrick for iOS runs on an iPad or iPad Mini as a meaningful amount of screen size is desired as the program workspace. Single finger gestures are used and the number of gestures is minimized in order to aid in ease of learning and memorability. As shown in Fig. 5, programs are built using blocks. The blocks represent constructs, variables, sensors, motors, etc. Sequential commands are laid out top to bottom in a vertical line, while constructs such as if's and repeats have blocks that are stacked within them to indicate nesting and sequence. Each type of block has an associated symbol and color to indicate the type (to help with readability and scanning the program).

Blocks are added to the program by selecting the type of block desired form the menu at the left. Selection is in the form of a long tap, where the feedback is the appearance that the block is lifted off of the screen (or floating on top of it). Upon selection, the user drags the block to the desired position. Blocks that become the body of a construct are offset in order to be distinguishable and to also to effectively use the horizontal workspace.

When a block needs to be set in between two existing blocks, the child simply places the block in between the blocks and releases their finger. After placement in the

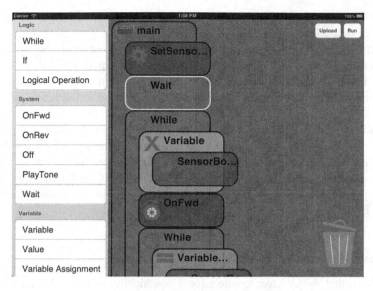

Fig. 5. Overview of JBrick for iOS user interface

program, blocks can be moved by selecting them with a long tap (which picks up the block visually) and then placing it where desired.

Deleting a block in a program occurs when a block is moved over the trashcan icon in the far side of the screen. If the child tries to place a block in a location that is not allowed such as out of the program workflow, the block will snap back to the menu pane and audio feedback is provided.

The child sets any attributes (such as which motor to use or how many seconds to move forward) by tapping the block and then selecting (and as needed entering the value) for the desired attribute. The attribute menu, shown in Fig. 6, is reveals on the right side of the screen only when a block is selected.

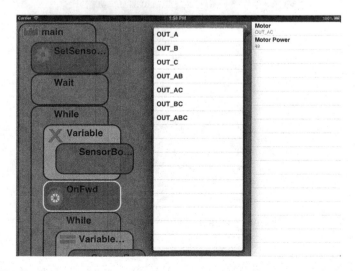

Fig. 6. Overview of JBrick for iOS screen with attribute menu displayed

As the program grows in length, the program flows down and the child scrolls the screen up or down to navigate the length of the program.

The Attribute pane and the command pane slide in and out when the task demands their presence, but the child can also swipe them in or out as desired. As needed a secondary pane will slide out if the child needs to select an item form a list such as the port for a motor. The labels used (e.g. Motor A) correspond to the labels used on the robot itself.

The attributes and command names map to those used in the NXC language. For the attributes, the use of A, B, and C are associated with the ported on the Lego Mindstorms robot. The command names such as PlayTone (to play a sound) were kept to enable students to then transition to the text-based NXC programming language. Currently programs created on the tablet can be opened in the desktop versions of JBrick or BricxCC.

4.2   Compilation and Downloading

The programs that the children create appear graphically, with the complexity of the NXC code managed in JBrick. The programs created can always be compiled, so the child can focus on computational thinking skills and problem solving.

Before the child can run their program on the Lego Mindstorms robot, the program needs to be compiled into byte code and then downloaded onto the robot.

To initiate the compilation, the child taps the Upload button, which uploads the file to the web service. The successful compilation feedback in the form of a sound and message is provided. Then the student can initiate the downloading of the program onto the robot by tapping Run. To initiate the program the child selects their program on the Lego Mindstorms robot as shown in Fig. 7.

Fig. 7. Child selecting a program on the Lego Mindstorms NXT robot

5   Evaluation

The workflow and the block design were developed incrementally, with user testing at significant checkpoints development. Due to the need to get a diverse sample of children, field tests were conducted as a public project demonstration event that was attended by about 30,000 people. The tasks tested with users included:

1. Creating a simple program to allow the robot to move forward.
2. Edit an existing program to allow the robot to move as desired by the user.

The team tested the user interface with kids of all ages over the course of the day. Children younger than 10, with little to no programming experience were of particular interest to the team. That day 22 children fit this criteria. When a child asked to use the app, a member of the team gave the child a quick overview of the software. Due to the nature of the event, each child did not necessarily complete both tasks. Observations noted the issues with identifying the purpose of the blocks (text, color, icons), how to move blocks around a program, as well as how to add/delete blocks.

Given the nature of the field test, metrics like time to complete task and number of errors were not gathered since the tasks themselves varied. The observations of the children resulted in the following findings:

- Overall the children were able to easily select and move the desired blocks, including adding blocks, moving blocks within the program (including nesting logic), and to the trash.
- The icons selected to symbolize the type of block was clear and legible to the children.
- Some of the background and text/icon color combinations need to be revised for clarity due to legibility issues, especially on a smaller tablet screen (e.g. iPad Mini)
- Some children needed a couple of attempts to move a block within a section of blocks (e.g. within a block of code in an if-then block). An additional source of confusion for some children arose when a block needed to be moved to a part of the program that scrolled down/up the screen.
- As setting variables is new to most children, that aspect of the workflow resulted in initial questions, but setting variables and understanding their intent (e.g. angle to turn) was straightforward.

6   Conclusions and Future Work

The refinement of the system and the addition of new features will move JBrick for iOS forward. Further, user evaluation will provide feedback from a more diverse set of children. Additional features desired include the use of constants to simplify the use of constructs for novice programmers and the means to create custom methods. Additional refinement of the user interface such as the simplification of parameter presentation and server-side are also needed in order to improve usability for the student and the teacher.

An Android version of JBrick is desired, though a rewrite will be needed since JBrick for iOS is a native app. Regardless, high-level design and algorithms can be reused at the conceptual level.

References

1. Johnson, J.: Children, robotics, and education. Artif. Life Robot. **7**(1), 16–21 (2003)
2. Lawhead, P., Duncan, M., Bland, C., Goldweber, M., Schep, M., Barnes, D., Hollingsworth, R.: A road map for teaching introductory programming using LEGO© mindstorms robots. In: Working Group Reports from ITiCSE on Innovation and Technology in Computer Science Education (ITiCSE-WGR 2002), pp. 191–201. ACM, New York (2002). doi:10.1145/782941. 783002. http://doi.acm.org/10.1145/782941.783002
3. Ludi, S., Reichlmayr, T.: The use of robotics to promote computing to pre-college students with visual impairments. ACM Transactions on Computing Education, 11(3). ACM New York, NY (2011). doi:10.1145/2037276.2037284
4. Sipitakiat, A., Nusen, N.: Robo-Blocks: designing debugging abilities in a tangible programming system for early primary school children. In: Proceedings of the 11th International Conference on Interaction Design and Children (IDC 2012), pp. 98–105. ACM, New York (2012). doi:10.1145/2307096.2307108. http://doi.acm.org/10.1145/2307096.2307108
5. Sklar, E., Eguchi, A., Johnson, J.: RoboCupJunior: learning with educational robotics. In: Kaminka, G.A., Lima, P.U., Rojas, R. (eds.) RoboCup 2002. LNCS (LNAI), vol. 2752, pp. 238–253. Springer, Heidelberg (2003)
6. Scratch Screenshot (2013). http://upload.wikimedia.org/wikipedia/commons/5/5e/Scratch_Screenshot_Gravity_Script.png
7. Slany, W.: Catroid: a mobile visual programming system for children. In: Proceedings of the 11th International Conference on Interaction Design and Children (IDC 2012), pp. 300–303. ACM, New York (2012). doi:10.1145/2307096.2307151. http://doi.acm.org/10.1145/2307096.2307151
8. Touretzsky, D., Marghitu, D., Ludi, S., Bernstein, D., Ni, L.: Accelerating K-12 computational thinking using scaffolding, staging, and abstraction. In: ACM Technical Symposium on Computer Science Education (SIGCSE), Denver, CO, March 2013

Voice-Based Computer Mediated Communication for Individual Practice to Increase Speaking Proficiency: Construction and Pilot Study

Yuichi Ono[1(✉)], Akio Onishi[2], Manabu Ishihara[3],
and Mitsuo Yamashiro[4]

[1] Foreign Language Center, University of Tsukuba, Ibaraki, Japan
ono.yuichi.ga@u.tsukuba.ac.jp
[2] Version 2, Sapporo, Japan
a-ohnishi@ver2.jp
[3] Electrical and Computer Engineering, Oyama National College of Technology,
Tochigi, Japan
ishihara@oyama-ct.ac.jp
[4] Electrical and Computer Engineering, Ashikaga Institute of Technology,
Tochigi, Japan
yamashiro@ashitech.ac.jp

Abstract. This paper examines the effects of an asynchronous blog system on speaking proficiency for EFL learners in Japan. The novelty of the system is its incorporation of Web Speech API, which leads to higher performance compared with the use of web applications for classroom purposes. On the basis of a questionnaire survey conducted as pilot research, we demonstrate that the system has potential to improve speaking proficiency and increases the motivation of less motivated learners.

Keywords: Computer-Mediated Communication (CMC) · Voice blog · Speech recognition · Speaking accuracy

1 Introduction

With the introduction of recent information technologies, many EFL instructors and researchers are interested in how to implement new technology-based tasks in the EFL classroom in order to have the most positive impact on language learning [1,2]. Since Computer-Mediated Communication (CMC) technologies have become widespread, there is a great potential for technology-based tasks to help learners develop their L2 oral performance [3]. Learner perceptions of how different technologies help to develop L2 skills is a topic worthy of exploration since students will undoubtedly have different reactions to such tasks [4].

This study constructs an asynchronous voice-blog system incorporating Automatic Speech Recognition (ASR) techniques and examines the usefulness of the system for English as a foreign language (EFL) learners in Japan. The choice of asynchronous

© Springer International Publishing Switzerland 2015
P. Zaphiris and A. Ioannou (Eds.): LCT 2015, LNCS 9192, pp. 115–123, 2015.
DOI: 10.1007/978-3-319-20609-7_12

CMC is methodological. It is generally agreed that synchronous CMC tools (e.g., Adobe Connect and Skype) provide opportunities for real-time interaction and negotiation of meaning [5]. On the other hand, asynchronous CMC is less face-threatening, allows students to learn at their own pace, enables self-reflection, and affords additional feedback opportunities. This paper focuses on encouraging less confident learners to speak up in more authentic communication contexts with the help of ASR.

2 Merits of Asynchronous CMC

2.1 Two Modes of CMC

An increasing number of studies have been published concerning CMC over the last two decades, and the findings of many studies support the use of CMC for language learning. Research has shown that the use of spoken CMC technologies such as chat rooms, voice blogs, and voice discussion boards can encourage student participation and foster extensive oral production in the target language (e.g., [6, 7]).

Reference [8] reviewed a number of studies and concluded that (a) learners may benefit from the practice in other contexts as well; (b) negotiation of meaning and focus on form occur in online communication; (c) syntactic, pragmatic, and intercultural competence could be developed; and (d) online communication "is potentially a transformative tool that each learner, depending on his or her own knowledge and agency, can use to construct an identity as a user of the L2 beyond the classroom" (p. 13).

There are two modes of communication: text and voice. Research on text-based CMC shows learners with speaking anxiety tend to choose text-based rather than voice-based CMC. Reference [9] conducted questionnaire research and suggested that less proficient students were more willing to choose text chat, complained when they had voice chat, and expressed frustration when they noticed they could not speak as well as they had believed. It is naturally suggested that such learners would prefer asynchronous communication, because it would allow them sufficient time for task planning in their language production. Reference [10] suggests the effects of task planning on text-based production in asynchronous CMC. In this way, learners can plan and practice what they say before uploading their recorded speech.

However, the problem is that learners cannot determine by themselves whether their speech is intelligible and appropriate in text mode. Other advancements in information technology are concerned with voice recognition. Most of the voice-application software enables learners to practice speaking and listening even in non-face-to-face environments.

2.2 Synchronous CMC

Regarding synchronicity, there are two types of CMC: synchronous CMC and asynchronous CMC. Typical examples of synchronous CMC are Skype, Video-conferencing, Adobe Connect, and so on. It is assumed that synchronous CMC promotes more equal participation than face-to-face communication in discussions in the target language [11–13]. Some of the important effects on linguistic and communication skills have been reported so far.

First, learners who have studied using synchronous CMC perform better in face-to-face conversation with regards to the amount of speech produced compared with those who have studied using asynchronous CMC and without CMC [11, 14]. Learners who were trained using synchronous CMC performed better on an oral test than those who were trained using regular classroom instruction [15]. In particular, synchronous CMC use in task-based communication is effective in promoting the use of communication strategies such as negotiation of meaning [16] and feedback for repairing lexical and syntactic errors [17]. Synchronous CMC is expected to offer the potential to develop learners´ speaking skills in communication with respect to repair moves, turn adjacency conventions, and discourse coherence structures [18].

2.3 Merits of Asynchronous CMC

However, voice-based synchronous CMC (i.e., voice-chat) is a very difficult task for less proficient EFL learners. This might be related to cognitive load. Reference [9] conducted questionnaire research on the two modes of CMC (text versus voice) and suggested that less proficient students were more willing to use text chat, complained when they had voice chat, and expressed frustration when they noticed they could not speak as well as they had believed.

It is generally agreed that the advantages of asynchronous CMC can be analyzed in two aspects: ubiquitousness and preparation. Concerning the first aspect, [19] shows the advantages of ACMC use in educational settings, such as allowing learners to study anytime and anywhere, allowing learners to study at their own pace, promoting reflective learning, and giving learners time to collect their thoughts before posting. Moreover, synchronous CMC is not flexible in terms of time [20]; since learners engage in "live" communication with their partners, they must schedule a specific time for study. On the second aspect, asynchronous CMC provides learners with sufficient time for reflection, which promotes self-correction and allows the learner to consider their ideas while being conscious of grammatical accuracy [21], which has the potential to reduce the foreign language anxiety of less-confident learners. On this point, [21] suggests that high proficiency learners utter more than low proficiency learners in synchronous CMC; in other words, learners tend to utter short sentences, which lead to inadequate output for language acquisition; and learners feel considerable pressure to utter rapidly.

2.4 Purpose of this Study

This paper assumes the merits described in the previous section and attempts to enhance the quality of planning before posting. In so doing, this paper proposes a voice-blog system that enables learners to practice pronunciation before posting with the help of the ASR application. In the experiment that follows, we would like to show that the speaking proficiency improved with regards to fluency and accuracy.

3   Construction Backgrounds

There are two approaches to the place of speech recognition engines: server operation or local operation, as illustrated in Fig. 1. Reference [22] demonstrates the difficulty and limitations of using speech recognition software in classroom settings, namely, network limitations and classroom noise. The latter factor may be solved by improving the microphone tuning and increasing users' practice.

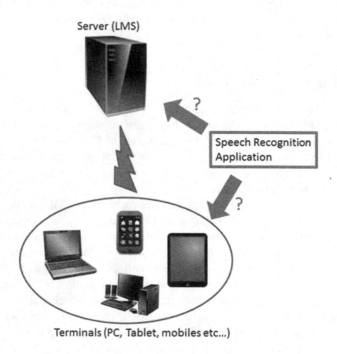

Fig. 1. Issues: local applications or web application

Generally speaking, it is preferable to employ web applications for class management. The expected merits are (a) there is no need to download or install a local application on each terminal, (b) students' scores can be stored without any additional treatment, and (c) there is no need to purchase or prepare the same number of items or licenses as the institution requires. Admitting these benefits of web application, we must bear in mind that the system is designed for use in educational settings, that is, in both the classroom and for homework. All the machines must work perfectly in the classroom, since mechanical errors discourage learners. The typical class size of a Japanese university is approximately 40 students. In our institution, we have six classrooms, each equipped with 48 wired desktop personal computers (PCs). This means that the speech recognition server would have to process all the sound data from approximately 300 terminals simultaneously if all the classes used the system at the same time. Empirically, the server does not have the capacity to deal with such a large volume of data. This paper explores the possibility of using a familiar web browser along with Web Speech API. This reduces the risk of overburden on the server operation of speech recognition and failure in processing. Moreover, this option has the potential to lead to easier congestion control in the network. In the following section, we describe the system more concretely (Fig. 2).

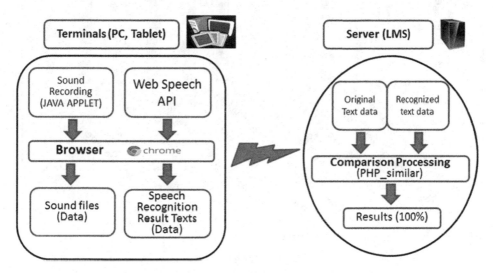

Fig. 2. System outline

Students write their comments in the textbox on the top part of the screen, as shown in Fig. 3. Then, by pressing the "record" button, they record their voice, and the recognized text appears in the box below. They can repeat this process until they feel satisfied with the results. They can then post their best recording on the blog. All the posts will appear on the instructor's screen as shown in Fig. 4.

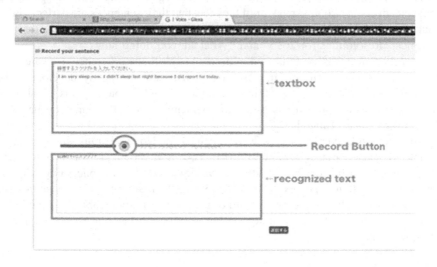

Fig. 3. Input screen

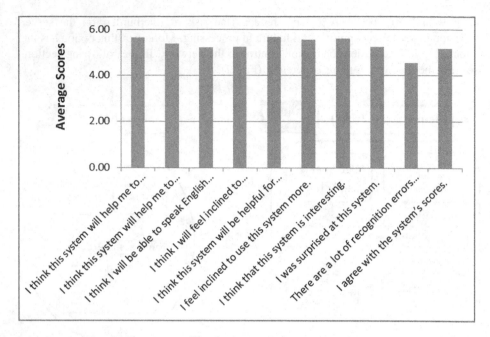

Fig. 4. Average scores

4 Experiments

4.1 Experiment 1: System Evaluation

Thirty-six first-year students at the National College of Technology in Japan participated in the study. In general, they do not like studying English, particularly speaking English. As their profiles, given in [23, 24] show, their learning styles are "bottom-up" and less communicative; they do not speak until they feel that their sentences are perfect, for fear of making a mistake. They studied English using the system for one week and discussed two topics: "Resolutions for 2015" and "What are you doing now?"

A questionnaire was administered in order to explore the difference in awareness of speaking anxiety between two modes, face to face and the newly developed CMC system. Pre- and post-tests were administered to observe how participants felt about the system. The questionnaire items asked the participants to rate their agreement on a 6-point Likert scale (Table 1).

Extremely high average scores were obtained for No. 1 "I think this system will help me to speak English accurately" (M: 5.00, SD: .96) and No. 5 "I think this system will be helpful for English study" (M: 4.92, SD: 1.08). Concerning No. 10 "I agree with the system's scores" (M: 4.25, SD: 1.40), it seems that the students were content with the system's scores, in spite of some recognition errors. This implies that they were receptive to the system despite the issue of reliability in speech recognition techniques (Fig. 4).

Table 1. Questions about the system and learner motivation

1	I think this system will help me to speak English accurately.
2	I think this system will help me to speak English fluently.
3	I think I will be able to speak English with more confidence.
4	I think I will feel inclined to communicate with others in English.
5	I think this system will be helpful for English study.
6	I feel inclined to use this system more.
7	I think that this system is interesting.
8	I was surprised at this system.
9	There are a lot of recognition errors produced by this system.
10	I agree with the system's scores.

4.2 Experiment 2: Proficiency

The second experiment is concerned with speaking proficiency. The class was conducted in February 2015 for three weeks. A total of 33 students participated in the study. They were required to repeat the sentence until the system recognized the voice completely. Some students unfortunately gave up prior to completion and uploaded incomplete sentences. Before the class, learners' speech was recorded for analysis using the recording function of the Computer-Assisted Language (CALL) classroom. After the class, another self-introduction speech was recorded for comparative analysis. The topic was "Self introduction" within 20 s.

The evaluation criteria were as follows: (i) General evaluation, (ii) Speech duration in reading compared with the average speed of the model, (iii) Deviation from native (Japanese) pronunciation, (iv) Consonant production, (v) Sharpness, and (vi) Smoothness. All the scores were calculated by the "Original Bun-Kentei," produced by Prontest, a Japanese software company. The full score is 100 for each criterion.

The result of the t-test is given in Fig. 5 below, where three out of six criteria showed significance (two-tailed). This result shows that participants' pronunciation improved with regard to the production of consonants and speaking speed, leading to an improvement in general evaluation scores.

5 Discussion

This paper demonstrated that the new type of asynchronous CMC together with ASR had an effect on motivation and proficiency. The Web SPI worked successfully on Chrome browser, reducing the burden on the network and server. This has an important implication as a more effective and economic alternative method, because this system is easily applicable to a recent trend of Chrome PC or other Tablet PC. This system makes up for the demerits of the EFL environment and helps the learners to practice their pronunciation. Needless to say, the number of participants was small, the time spent on this experiment was very short, and we cannot generalize the results to overall EFL contexts. The reliability of ASR was also an issue. Some students seemed to become bored when they could not make their speech recognizable and repeated the same

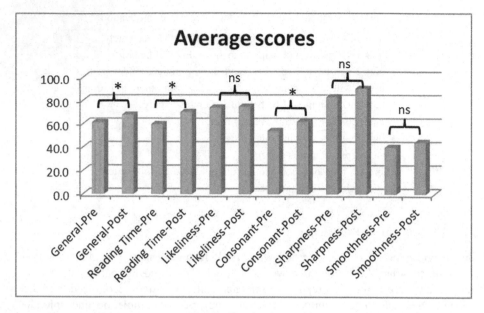

Fig. 5. Result of *t*-test

failure of certain words. Although there are some limitations of the system being properly incorporated in the class, this paper demonstrated that there are many possibilities to improve speaking proficiency using a very practical and applicable system.

References

1. Levy, M., Stockwell, G.: CALL Dimensions. Lawrence Erlbaum Associates, Mahwah (2006)
2. Hirotani, M.: Synchronous versus asynchronous CMC and transfer to Japanese oral performance. CALICO J. **26**(2), 413–438 (2003)
3. Zhao, Y.: Recent developments in technology and language learning: a literature review and meta-analysis. CALICO J. **21**(1), 7–27 (2003)
4. Gleason, J., Suvorov, R.: Learner Perceptions of Asynchronous Oral Computer-Mediated Communication Tasks Using Wimba Voice for Developing their L2 Oral Proficiency. In: Huffman, S., Hegelheimer, V. (eds.) The role of CALL in hybrid and online language courses. Iowa State University, Ames (2003)
5. Lomicka, L., Lord, G., Manzer, M.: Merging foreign language theory and practice in designing technology-based tasks. In: Cherry, C.M. (ed.) Dimension, pp. 37–52. SCOLT Publications, Valdosta State University (2003)
6. Beauvois, M.: Computer-mediated communication (cmc): technology for improving speaking and writing. In: Bush, M.D., Terry, R.M. (eds.) Technology Enhanced Language Learning, pp. 165–184. National Textbook Company, Lincolnwood (1997)
7. Rosen, L.: Reaching students: a hybrid approach to language learning. In: Oxford, R., Oxford, J. (eds.) Second Language Teaching and Learning in the Net Generation, pp. 64–84. University of Hawai'i, National Foreign Language Resource Center, Honolulu (2009)

8. Chapelle, C.: Survey on technology use for language learning (Survey). Unpublished instrument, Department of English, Iowa State University, Ames, IA, USA (2008)
9. Satar, H.M., Ozdener, N.: The effects of synchronous CMC on speaking proficiency and anxiety: text versus voice chat. Mod. Lang. J. **92**(iv), 595–613 (2008)
10. Hsu, H.-S.: Investigating the effects of planning on L2 text chat performance. CALICO J. **29** (4), 619–638 (2012)
11. Yamada, M.: The role of social presence in learner-centered communicative language learning using synchronous computer-mediated communication: Experimental study. Comput. Educ. **52**(4), 820–833 (2009)
12. Chun, D.: Using computer networking to facilitate the acquisition of interactive competence. System **22**(1), 17–31 (1994)
13. Warschauer, M.: Comparing face-to-face and electronic discussion in the second language classroom. CALICO J. **13**(2–3), 7–26 (1996)
14. Abrams, Z.I.: The effect of synchronous and asynchronous CMC on oral performance in German. Mod. Lang. J. **87**(2), 157–167 (2003)
15. Beauvois, M.H.: E-talk: Attitudes and motivation in computer-assisted classroom discussion. Comput. Humanit. **28**(1), 177–190 (1994)
16. Smith, B.: The use of communication strategies in computer-mediated communication. System **31**, 29–53 (2002)
17. Morris, F.: Child-to-child interaction and corrective feedback in a computer mediated L2 class. Lang. Learn. Technol. **9**(1), 29–45 (2005)
18. Jepson, K.: Conversations—And negotiated interaction—In text and voice chat rooms. Lang. Learn. Technol. **9**(3), 79–98 (2005)
19. Hiltz, S.R., Goldman, R.: What are asynchronous learning networks? In: Hiltz, S.R., Goldman, R. (eds.) Learning Together Online: Research on Asynchronous Learning Networks, pp. 3–18. Lawrence Erlbaum Associates, Mahwah (2005)
20. Levy, M., Stockwell, G.: CALL Dimensions: Options & Issues In Computer Assisted Language Learning. Lawrence Erlbaum Associates, Mahwah (2006)
21. Lamy, M.-N., Hampel, R.: Online Communication In Language Learning And Teaching. Palgrave Macmillan, Hampshire (2007)
22. Cox, T.L.: Using automatic speech recognition technology with elicited oral response testing. CALICO J. **29**(4), 601–618 (2012)
23. Ono, Y., Ishihara, M.: Integrating mobile-based individual activities into the Japanese EFL classroom. Int. J. Mob. Learn. Organ. **6**(2), 116–137 (2012)
24. Ono, M., Ishihara, M., Onishi, A. Yamashiro, M.: Classrooms and voice recognition applications in a foreign language teaching, In: Proceedings of 43rd International Congress on Noise Control Engineering, The Australian Acoustical Society (2014)

Supporting the Development of Computational Thinking: A Robotic Platform Controlled by Smartphone

Henrique Reinaldo Sarmento[✉], Cibele A.S. Reis, Vinicius Zaramella,
Leonelo D.A. Almeida, and Cesar A. Tacla

Federal University of Technology, Curitiba, Brazil
{hnrqer,cibele.asreis,vinicius.zaramella}@gmail.com,
{leoneloalmeida,tacla}@utfpr.edu.br

Abstract. The difficulty of students in learning logic and programming languages leads the research of technological solutions to assist in the teaching-learning process. Among these solutions, two common approaches are robotics and graphical-based programming languages. Researches indicate that these tools can aid learners to think systematically and develop computational thinking. Therefore, this work proposes the Coffee Platform, which is composed by a Web-based block programming environment and a smartphone as a robot controller unit. This platform can be expanded to work with various mobile devices and robotic kits. The Coffee Platform was applied in a classroom with the aim of assessing the tool and its effects over students' motivation. Results indicate that the proposed solution can serve as a stimulus for students and assist in understanding programming concepts.

Keywords: Teaching tool · Mobile robotics · Visual programming · Computational thinking

1 Introduction

Learning programming languages and logic in introductory disciplines of undergraduate courses are challenging for part of the students. The difficulty is attributed to several factors involving both the teaching and learning methods [4]. According to [4], learning programming languages is still tedious and difficult because lectures are usually based on an expository approach (e.g. slide presentations, diagrams, and texts) whilst studies indicate that other methods as problem solving are more effective [2,4,13].

Different approaches and artifacts were proposed aiming at attenuating the difficulty in teaching and learning programming languages and logic; among other artifacts, graphic or script-based languages and robotic applications (e.g. CALLY [12], N-Bot [1], and Lego Mindstorm[1]). Tools that use graphic

---

[1] http://education.lego.com

© Springer International Publishing Switzerland 2015
P. Zaphiris and A. Ioannou (Eds.): LCT 2015, LNCS 9192, pp. 124–135, 2015.
DOI: 10.1007/978-3-319-20609-7_13

languages as Scratch [11] assist students to think systematically and are available on the internet. On the other hand, according to [2], applications that have tangible results typically stimulate students' interests. Considering this demand, there are other teaching approaches that use concrete artifacts. One example is laboratory experiences and, in the case of computing students, experiences involving robots [2]. And a closer look in the use of robotics, [13] proposed a short course to introduce the practice of robotics in schools to provide students with a real and continuous technological experience. Zanetti et al. [13] applied Problem Based Learning (PBL) methodology, which suggests students to learn while solving problems and, consequently, performing an active role in the learning process. Furthermore, students are encouraged to study autonomously, therefore, teachers play the role of facilitators for the resolution of the problem and act as a subject consultant [7].

The application of robotics in teaching is not recent since there are well-known tools. However, acquisition cost of these tools is not always affordable. An approach that has been widely used in robotics is the replacement of the microcontroller as the main processor unity by a smartphone [3]. The direct benefits of this measure are the cost reduction and the ease to develop software extensions. Examples of projects that explore this approach are Cally [12] and N-Bot [1].

Usually, graphical languages and robotics are not applied together. In cases they are, there are few low-cost and flexible platforms available [1]. This project consists in assisting the development of the computational thinking (i.e. the ability to solve problems logically and sequentially). The project also assesses the level of motivation on students attending introductory computing classes, by presenting an extensible platform called Coffee, which articulates graphical languages and robotic platforms, controlled by a smartphone.

The evaluation of the Coffee Platform was conducted in an introductory discipline to computing in which were enrolled students from different undergraduate courses as Chemistry, Mechanical Engineering, and Electrical Engineering. We adopted PBL as our learning process and provided a series of problems that involved movement and use of sensors available in the robot. To further analyse the effects from the platform usage we considered the motivation components proposed by [9], which are: attention, relevance, confidence and satisfaction.

This paper is organized as follows: Sect. 1 presents the context of the investigation. Section 2 reviews similar studies and products. Section 3 describes the development of the Coffee Platform. Section 4 reports the field study and Sect. 5 discusses the main findings from the experiment. Finally, Sect. 6 concludes.

2   Related Work

In this section, we review projects similar to the Coffee Platform. Table 1 presents a general overview of works related to this project regarding aspects considered relevant. Table 2 compares the robots used in the approaches.

Table 1. General comparison between related work

Project name	Robot based	Smartphone based	Allows project sharing	Programming environment features	Scientific publications
Scratch	No	No	Yes	Web-based block programming environment. Game and animation programming	[8,11]
Cally	Yes	Yes	No	Lack of the user programming interface	Not found
N-Bot	Yes	Yes	No	Web-based block programming environment	[1,3]
Lego Mind-storm	Yes	No	No	Block-based. Hardware components programming	[5,6]
Romo	Yes	Yes	No	Uses a block-based sequencer. No advanced programming structures	Not found
Smartbot	Yes	Yes	No	Possibility to send commands to the robot	Not found
Coffee	Yes	Yes	Yes	Web-based block programming environment	-

Table 2. Comparison of robots between related work

Project	Cost (US$)	Main features
Cally	Not found	Robot has two mechanical arms and four wheels
N-Bot	14	Uses smartphone as the main processor. Engines controlled by the audio channel. Possibility of adding sensors
Lego Mindstorm EV3	350	Possibility to mount the robot in different ways through kit parts. Possibility of adding sensors in the robot
Romo	129	Robot has human features on the smartphone screen. Uses the smartphone camera. Possibility to control the slope where the smartphone is positioned
Smartbot	238	Robot has human features on the smartphone screen. Uses the smartphone camera
Coffee	Variable[a]	Uses the smartphone as the main processor. Engines controlled by the microcontroller. Communication between the smartphone and microcontroller through the audio channel. Possibility of adding sensors in the robot

[a]The cost depends on the robotic platform. In this project, it was used the robot from the Programa de Educação Tutorial (PET), accessed in: http://petrobo.github.io/, which costs around US$185. Others robots with microcontrollers can be find in http://www.robotshop.com costing around US$80

The review indicates that there are similar works regarding education and the use of mobile devices in robotics. However, there is not a platform that enables the use of a robot and the publication and sharing of projects simultaneously.

3   Coffee Platform

This section is organized in two parts: the project's architecture which describes the development of each computational system's component, and the aspects related to the users' interaction

3.1   Architecture

The Coffee Platform consists of a smartphone, a Web programming environment and an audio-serial adapter (as illustrated in the Fig. 1). There is also an external component to the project but necessary to its complete execution: the robotic platform, which is commanded by a smartphone.

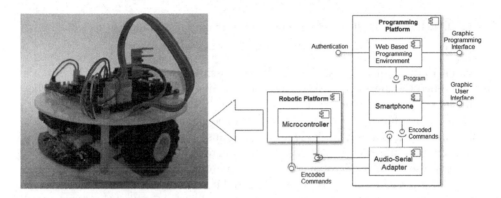

Fig. 1. The employed robotic platform and the Coffee Platform's general diagram.

The Web programming environment illustrated in the Fig. 2 is composed of three blocks including: communication, a visual programming environment based on Blockly[2], and an account and projects manager that also provides resources for users to share and publish projects. A project involves a visual programming environment which enables users to program dragging blocks. The Blockly library converts the graphical program to Javascript and the communication sends this translation to the smartphone when requested.

The Web environment was assessed using the Web usability heuristics set proposed by Rutter [10]. This assessment was held by the writers themselves, and it indicated that the website is consistent in its content and is aesthetically pleasing. Furthermore, this evaluation has shown possible problems regarding the page's compatibility for different browsers, contact information, copyright related to Blockly and the webpage's meta tags.

The smartphone presented in the Fig. 2 has its processing partitioned into five blocks, as follows: audio output, encoder, main processing, sensors, and communication with the Web environment. The communication block receives a program from the Web environment and loads it on the main processing unit, which

---

[2] https://code.google.com/p/blockly/.

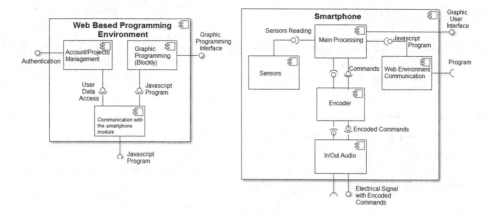

Fig. 2. Left: Web application's diagram. Right: Smartphone application's diagram.

receives data from sensors. The main processing also determines the robot's action, encodes and send them to the robot's microcontroller through the audio-serial adapter as described in Fig. 1.

The smartphone application was developed using the Cordova framework[3]. This framework is an expandable system because it enables a project's compilation without using the developer's native programming language.

The presence of a microcontroller can be observed in the Fig. 1. This microcontroller is attached in the robotic basis, and it was added to execute lower-level routines, such as generate the DC motor's control signal, control the wheel speed and read the sensors from the robotic basis.

It was necessary to develop a plug-in for carrying the audio-serial communication. The other plug-ins, such as the one for accessing sensors, used the default Cordova framework. The audio-serial adapter provides the communication between the robotic basis and the smartphone. Moreover, it uses the smartphone's P2 audio output which is the standard for current smartphones.

3.2 Users' Interaction

The Coffee Platform provides the following features: (a) user account, (b) user profile and project list, (c) create, edit, delete, share, and publish projects, (d) download project list to the smartphone, (e) attach smartphone to the robotic basis and (f) execute projects.

The need for some of the platform features were identified based on systems such as Scratch [8] for project sharing, Cally [12], N-Bot [3], Romo[4] and SmartBot[5] for the use of a smartphone attached to a robot. Other features, as the project publication in the main page, were proposed by the writers themselves.

---

[3] http://cordova.apache.org.

[4] http://www.romotive.com/.

[5] http://www.overdriverobotics.com/.

The user interaction works as follows: initially, the user creates an account and then access his or her projects through the page shown in the Fig. 3. In that page the user can save or load other projects.

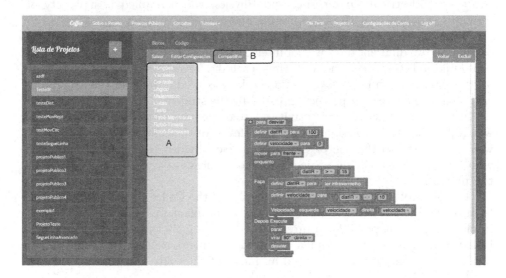

Fig. 3. Environment for block-based programming and list of projects.

In addition, in the Fig. 3 it is possible to observe a program based on the Blockly library. That program makes the robot move forward until it finds an obstacle fifteen centimetres ahead. If the robot finds it, the robot turns ninety degrees to the right. As shown in the rectangle indicated by the letter "A", there is a panel where the user can access groups of blocks, such as mathematical, conditional, and robot movements. The user can drag and fit blocks creating a top-down execution logic for the program. Another feature is the project sharing with other users or its publication in the main page through the menu indicated by the rectangle containing the letter "B".

Immediately after the user has saved a project, he/she is able to access his/her account on the smartphone and load the Javascript code on the device. Then the user can attach the smartphone to the robotic basis, connects the audio-serial adapter and executes the selected program.

4   Case Study

This section presents the case study of the Coffee Platform's and is organized as follows: the platform's presentation, an example of use, the questionnaires application, the problem solving by students and the discussion about the platform.

4.1   Dynamics

The Coffee Platform was applied in an introductory computer programming course, at the end of the semester. The students were from different graduation courses as Electrical Engineering and Physics, which implied in a variety of previous experiences with programming and interests.

The activity included the participation of seven students, and it was conducted on two different days with a interval of one week between them. Each day presented a distinct scenario and, thus, each day revealed a different behaviour on the students. On both days just one robot, located in front of the classroom, was available for testing projects created by the students.

In the first day, classroom activities lasted two hours, and concurrently there was a project delivery assigned by the professor of the course. This last activity was not related to the use of Coffee. This fact divided the class among those who had not delivered the project and those who were available to experiment the platform.

The activity started with the presentation of the Coffee Platform's goals and features to the students. Moreover, a simple problem was exposed and solved in class, making it possible to present the application's features and the block-based programming. The problem involved a simple route that the robot should perform. The researchers presented an image of the route and the step-by-step solution on the platform.

Right after the example, the students were informed that the participation would be voluntary, and there would not be any kind of reward for that. Furthermore, those who participated were invited to sign an informed consent form. After that, students filled the pre-course questionnaire. Subsequently, other problems were presented so that they tried to solve them individually or in groups. During the first day's activities, there were some technical issues with the robot that may have affected students' impressions.

In the second day, the students were able to be fully dedicated to the platform. The students who had little contact to the tool during the first day were able to solve the initial problems. The resolution of complex problems such as making the robot follow a black line or avoid obstacles was proposed for those who had solved the basic challenges during the first day course.

After one hour of activities, the students were invited to answer the post-course questionnaire and thereafter discuss about the tool. The discussion in the classroom was important to gather information that would not be collected with the questionnaires. These data aided to obtain more details of the students impressions. In the second day, there were no significant technical issues.

In both days, the Coffee Platform development team sought to act as facilitators, and they instigated the students to develop their thinking skills without giving immediate solutions to the students' questions. The researchers sought to focus on students' learning and on their computational thinking development.

The Coffee platforms also provided a tutorial that was recommended when students had some query regarding programming structures or operation of blocks. This procedure characterizes the self-taught learning encouragement.

However, some students experimented a trial and error approach. After comprehending the new knowledge, they applied it to solve the problem and finally presented the solution to the facilitator in order to reflect about the steps taken.

One of the students' knowledge deficiency noticed by the facilitators was related to sequential thinking in a block program. For example, a student had chosen all the blocks and the structures separately to solve a problem, however he was not able to integrate them to solve it. In other situation, there was a confusion about a boolean condition and the movement that the robot should do whether that condition was activated. For these situations, the facilitators identified the deficiencies and tried to correct the wrong concepts.

4.2   Questionnaires

A questionnaire inquiring about the motivational level of the students was developed based on the work of [9]. The applied questionnaire consists of two parts, one applied before and another after the course.

The first part aims to outline the students' profile, collect information about their mobile devices and analyse some motivational components when the teaching platform was introduced in the classroom.

The second part of the questionnaire captures some students' motivational components after the application of the teaching tool. The questions used the Likert's scale and covered motivational components i.e. Attention, Satisfaction, Confidence, and Relevance. The students were also asked about their future expectations involving programming and robotics courses.

4.3   Proposed Problems

For the elaboration of the problems, the features described by [7] were used. In addition, tutorial guides were also made available.

The proposed problems involved computational thinking structures, such as: sequenced instructions, control structures, and variables. The elaboration of a list of exercises in the classroom was based in other experiments held by Robô Fun![6] and [9].

The problems presented different levels of difficulty, and the most advanced was challenging and complex because it involved several programming structures. Some of them had multiple ways of solution. One of the examples used was the problem in which the robot should follow a black line on the floor for which it was found three distinct solutions before its application in the classroom.

5   Results and Discussion

This section presents the results obtained by the questionnaires the research findings and the final discussion.

---

[6] http://dainf.ct.utfpr.edu.br/peteco/2014/03/25/robo-fun/.

5.1   Questionnaire Results

The students' responses regarding the motivational components in the pre and post course are summarized in Table 3. In addition to the issues presented in the table there were other questions that aimed to identify the students' profile (i.e. age, course in which they were enrolled at the university, and their smartphone characteristics). Next, it is presented some of the findings regarding each motivational component.

Attention. In the pre-course questionnaire 14 % did not show indication of attention to the use of robots in the classroom while others varied from neutral to positive; on the other hand, in the post-course questionnaire, all questions related to attention tended to neutral and positive answers.

Relevance. In the pre-course questionnaire, there was neutrality and disagreement in the question: "I find Coffee useful in learning how to program". However, in the post-course, students answered only positively when asked about the platform aid in testing the taught concepts.

Confidence. There was dispersion regarding the confidence of students, especially when asked about the use of robots in the pre-course and the level of difficulty of the presented problems. Another relevant point is that 86 % agreed that the use of blocks in programming made the solution of the problems easier.

Attitude. Initially, the platform did not captivate all students: 43 % of the students showed indifference in relation to its use.

Satisfaction. In general, there were positive answers since 86 % did not feel bored or discouraged to use the tool, and only 14 % shown to be indifferent.

Future Expectations. As indicated, the students have divergent answers regarding their expectations of taking other robotics and programming courses.

5.2   Research Findings and Discussion

The answers regarding the motivational components, in the pre-course questionnaire, indicate that the Physics and Chemistry students showed greater indifference and even negativity when asked about the use of robots and of the Coffee Platform. However, this negativity has changed after the activity.

The Chemistry student changed his opinion about the platform between the beginning and the ending of the course. Initially, he strongly disagreed that using robots to learn how to program caught his attention. In the post course questionnaire, he turned neutral in this point. This indicates that it is possible that the Coffee Platform aids in the motivational component "Attention".

There was an overall improvement between the pre and post course for the motivational component "Relevance". That indicates that even those that shown more resistance to use the tool, could find some relevant use for it.

Initially, some students did not feel confident in using robots to learn how to program. This lack of confidence could be related to the absence of a cover for the robotic platform to omit the electronic components. This possibility was raised during the final discussion in class, and it would not be contemplated only with the questionnaires and observations of the researchers.

Table 3. Results of the questionnaires involving motivational components. E1: Strongly disagree. E2 Disagree. E3: Neutral. E4: Agree. E5: Strongly agree.

Motiv. Com	Stage	Question	E1	E2	E3	E4	E5
Attention	Pre-course	The usage of robots to learn how to program grabs my attention	14 %	0 %	14 %	14 %	57 %
	Post-course	The way Coffee was used to teach programming helped to keep me engaged	0 %	0 %	29 %	14 %	57 %
		Learning to program with a robot stimulated my creativity	0 %	0 %	43 %	29 %	29 %
		Learning to program with blocks allowed me to focus more in my learning	0 %	0 %	29 %	29 %	43 %
		The diversity of possible activities with Coffee interested me	0 %	0 %	29 %	43 %	29 %
Relevance	Pre-course	Using Coffee in class will help to learn how to program effectively	0 %	0 %	29 %	43 %	29 %
		I find Coffee useful in learning how to program	0 %	14 %	14 %	43 %	29 %
	Post-course	I could relate the programming learning with robots to my experiences and expectations	0 %	0 %	29 %	29 %	43 %
		Using Coffee helped to test the concepts taught in class	0 %	0 %	0 %	14 %	86 %
Confidence	Pre-course	I believe that at the end of this course I will have absorbed most of the taught content	0 %	14 %	0 %	43 %	43 %
		Learning to program with robots is intimidating to me	29 %	29 %	0 %	43 %	0 %
		Learning to program using blocks seems simpler	0 %	0 %	29 %	29 %	43 %
	Post-course	I could understand a little more about the programming concepts using Coffee	0 %	0 %	14 %	43 %	43 %
		The programming exercises were very difficult	29 %	14 %	14 %	29 %	14 %
		The use of programming blocks made the problem solution easier	0 %	0 %	14 %	57 %	29 %
		Learning to program and work with Coffee was easy	0 %	0 %	43 %	29 %	29 %
		Learning to program with Coffee was so abstract that it was hard to pay attention in class	71 %	29 %	0 %	0 %	0 %
Attitude and Perceptions	Pre-course	I look forward to using Coffee	0 %	0 %	43 %	29 %	29 %
Satisfaction	Post-course	The way the Coffee was used to teach programming left me bored / discouraged	71 %	14 %	14 %	0 %	0 %
Future courses and expectations	Post-course	I intend to take more programming courses	29 %	14 %	29 %	14 %	14 %
		I would not want to have to take more programming related courses	14 %	29 %	29 %	14 %	14 %
		I would not want to have to take more courses related to robotics	29 %	0 %	57 %	0 %	14 %

The lack of confidence in the pre-course was not reflected in the post-course. Some possibilities raised by the facilitators' observation and the final discussion are: the use of the PBL and the students' experience in the use of the robot.

When asked about the anxiety of using the Coffee Platform, three out of seven students remained neutral. This demonstrates that the use of robots and programming blocks do not imply curiosity and anxiety of all students. However, it is worth mentioning that despite this indifference, none of them declared to feel discouraged or disinterested while using the tool. Only one student remained neutral in both answers.

The future expectations of the students were distinct and probably not related to the use of the Coffee Platform. We hypothesize that there are two factors for that: (a) the application in the classroom was not ideal. It would be interesting that students could use the platform throughout the semester, therefore, consolidating their knowledge in programming with the aid of the platform. This observation was also raised by a student in the classroom, strengthening this hypothesis; (b) those who are indifferent to the use of the robots might not always change their perspective regarding the subject. It should be noted that the goal is not to get everyone to program professionally, given the diversity of courses, but enhance the learning through a more motivating approach.

One of the most relevant comments in the discussion was the request that platforms like Coffee to be used throughout similar courses. Students even claimed that the tool was interesting to reduce the bias against programming, and it could also aid in the comprehension of various course contents.

Another point in the evaluation of the platform is that the students did not have any doubt concerning the Web page mechanisms, in other words, they created accounts and projects prior to the presentation of these features.

The discussion held in the classroom allowed students to express their impressions of the platform. It was clear the demand for an integrated simulator in the Web page, so students could test the code before sending it to the robot. Another request was the support of other textual programming languages

Statements of enthusiasms and the general class interest indicate that the Coffee Platform has potential, and it should be applied and studied for an extended period for the verification of the reported findings.

6 Conclusion

This paper presented the Coffee Platform, an education tool which relies in block programming and robotics. The platform was applied in a classroom, and through an evaluation based on students' motivation and opinion, the platform proved to be viable to classroom activities.

The Coffee Platform, in the way it was developed, allows its components to be expanded. In the smartphone, it is possible to use other operating systems by adding specific plug-ins. Furthermore, it is possible to replace the robotic platform because of its loose coupling with the rest of the system.

In a future research, the ideal environment for the adoption of this project would be computer classes throughout the course, allowing computational thinking and, specifically, programming knowledge to be built gradually and assimilated to other programming languages. It could also be added to the platform features highlighted by the students in order to turn it more attractive.

For long-term applications, it would be interesting to analyse: the implications of the sharing and publishing of projects resources, adding periodical monitoring, collecting logs, and including teacher's evaluation since he/she has great influence in the classroom environment.

References

1. Aroca, R.V.: Plataforma robótica de baixíssimo custo para robótica educacional. Ph.D. thesis, Universidade Federal do Rio Grande do Norte (2012)
2. Aroca, R.V., Gomes, R.B., Tavares, D.M., Souza, A.A., Burlamaqui, A.M., Caurin, G.A., Goncalves, L.M.G.: Increasing students' interest with low-cost cell bots. IEEE Trans. Educ. **56**(1), 3–8 (2013)
3. Aroca, R.V., Oliveira, P.B.S., Gonçalves, L.M.G.: Towards smarter robots with smartphones. In: Robocontrol 2012 (2012)
4. Gomes, A., Henriques, J., Mendes, A.: Uma proposta para ajudar alunos com dificuldades na aprendizagem inicial de programação de computadores. Educação, Formação & Tecnologias **1**(1), 93–103 (2008). ISSN 1646–933X
5. Kato, S., Hiroyuki, T.: A style and tool for group exercise of introductory programming with LEGO robot control as pre-education event. IEEE (2010)
6. Kiss, G.: Using The lego-mindstorm kit in german computer science education. In: 8th IEEE International Symposium on Applied Machine Intelligence and Informatics. IEEE (2010)
7. Kolmos, A., Kuru, S., Hansen, H., Eskil, T., Podesta, L., Fink, F., de Graaff, E., Wolff, J.U., Soylo, A.: Problem Based Learning. TREE-Teaching and Research in Engineering in Europe (2007)
8. Maloney, J., Resnick, M., Rusk, N., Silverman, B., Eastmond, E.: The scratch programming language and environment. ACM Ttrans. Comput. Educ. **10**(4), 16 (2010)
9. McGill, M.M.: Learning to program with personal robots: influences on student motivation. ACM Trans. Comput. Educ. **12**(1), 4 (2012)
10. Rutter, J.P.: Web Heuristic Evaluation III Web Conference (2004)
11. Wang, X., Zhou, Z.: The research of situational teaching mode of programming in high school with scratch. In: 2011 6th IEEE Joint International Information Technology and Artificial Intelligence Conference, vol. 2, pp. 488–492. IEEE (2011)
12. Yim, J.D., Shaw, C.D.: CALLY: the cell-phone robot with affective expressions. In: 2009 4th ACM/IEEE International Conference on Human-Robot Interaction, pp. 319–320. IEEE (2009)
13. Zanetti, H.A.P., Souza, A.L.S.d., d'Abreu, J.V.V., Borges, M.A.F.: Uso de robótica e jogos digitais como sistema de apoio ao aprendizado. Jornada de Atualização em Informática na Educação **1**(1), 142–161 (2013)

The Use of Augmented Reality Interfaces for On-site Crisis Preparedness

Monica Sebillo[1], Genoveffa Tortora[1], Giuliana Vitiello[1(✉)],
Luca Paolino[3], and Athula Ginige[2]

[1] University of Salerno, Fisciano, Italy
{msebillo,gvitiello}@unisa.it
[2] Link Campus University, Rome, Italy
a.ginige@uws.edu.au
[3] University of Western Sydney, Sydney, Australia
l.paolino@unilink.it

Abstract. The importance of an appropriate training is widely recognized in the domain of emergency management. The goal of an efficient and effective humanitarian emergency response can be better pursued, if responders are appropriately prepared to address health, security and managerial concerns. In this paper we propose the adoption of augmented reality mobile interfaces to enhance the training efficacy for on-site crisis preparedness activities. The system we propose originated from the idea to allow trainees to exploit AR interaction and become quickly familiar with the mobile technology adopted today in emergency response activities.

Keywords: Emergency management · Mobile interfaces · AR-based training applications · Information sharing · Situation awareness

1 Introduction

Emergency management is a critical and continuously evolving research area, where each single step to improve either methods or tools make a significant contribution towards reducing human lives and resource losses. The awareness about this stimulates professionals and researchers from the crisis management field to devote much effort to define future research directions, whose results are in fact essential for drawing up an agenda by public institutions and Civil Defence agencies to identify sectors where investments could produce effective solutions.

The usage of Emergency Response Information Systems (ERIS) for the management of activities meant to reduce the number of victims and damages and restore quickly a safe situation, is largely promoted by several agencies, along with the involvement of trained personnel for their immediate deployment. Besides traditional sectors like geology, construction science, structural engineering, material science and technology, information and communication technology (ICT) represents an across-the-board sector that would contribute to enhancement in all aspects of crisis management. Currently, ICT already supports several aspects of crisis management and it is paramount in some relevant activities that require promptness. Further ICT advances

P. Zaphiris and A. Ioannou (Eds.): LCT 2015, LNCS 9192, pp. 136–147, 2015.
DOI: 10.1007/978-3-319-20609-7_14

are required anyway, which could enable teams of practitioners to quickly make the appropriate actions so as to further decrease losses both in terms of people and damages [2]. Towards that goal, several research directions have been identified, all sharing the observation that experiences of different actors and contributions from relevant domains represent the only means to achieve stable and reliable solutions for the crisis management [14].

In particular, the four phases of the emergency management process (preventing, preparing, responding and restoring) have significantly benefited from the adoption of integrated systems where procedures and standards are embedded within seamless infrastructures. Moreover, relying on efficient organizational structures and effective mechanisms for collaboration among operators represents a key factor when designing an emergency management system. In particular, the emergency preparedness and response phases include actions taken prior as well as during and after a disaster event in order to reduce human and property losses. Such actions can be performed only if an overall view of the evolving situation is available to those who make global strategic decisions from a Command and Control Center or Centro Operativo Comunale (COC), and to those who perform actions on the ground.

However, as argued by Jennex in [7], during a real situation where people are under stress, the use of emergency information systems is often hindered by the lack of familiarity with them. Unfamiliarity can notably impact the effective use of a new technology in crisis situations. In this paper we propose a solution to the general concern of training emergency responders so that they become familiar with the adopted mobile technology and hence benefit from the enhanced situation awareness. In addition to the continuous technical skill-upgrade required by the nature of the humanitarian context, the importance of an appropriate training is widely recognized by all the actors playing a role in the emergency domain. In particular, giving responders information technology skills that help them to address health, security and managerial concerns, represents a key factor to pursue the goal of an efficient and effective humanitarian emergency response. Moreover, as shown in [5], enhancing the role of the on-site operators can improve the collaboration among responders, and provide all the actors with an increased situation awareness about the crisis evolution. Situation awareness and shared mental models is gained when information is gathered from multiple perspectives, acquired from the environment, or received by voice, or encoded in artifacts [9]. Our proposal combines the pervasiveness of mobile technology, its adoption for collaboration purposes with the intuitive interaction gained through augmented reality, and its capability to engage and motivate trainees, also thanks to the impactful visual cues provided by a visualization technique named Framy [12]. In particular, in this paper we propose an AR-based training system that, through two different interactive visualization modalities leads the trainee within a scenario enriched by a virtual content where data can be aggregated and associated with visual metaphors. By performing a set of suggested activities the trainee acquires familiarity with the underlying technology both in terms of functionality and participation in the whole decision making. As a matter of fact, he/she is immediately informed about the effect of his interaction thus improving his/her situation awareness.

The remainder of the paper is organized as follows. Section 2 presents some related research on training methodologies and techniques in the domain of emergency management. Section 3 recalls the technology, which underlies the AR-based training system. In Sect. 4 we explain how the proposed training system works, describing its adoption inside a realistic scenario of use during a training session. In Sect. 5 the system architecture is described. Some conclusions are finally drawn in Sect. 6.

2 Related Work

The re-creation of realistic environments where emergency response simulations can take place is considered paramount for effective training in emergency situations [4]. Jackson et al. [6] underline the importance of training activities that rely on realistic operational or situational scenarios. They also highlight that by learning from the effects of simulation training, crisis management agencies may gain better acquaintance with respect to the preparation for actual event management. Such beliefs have greatly encouraged the use of Virtual Reality to simulate crisis management activities as a way to increase safety standards, while retaining efficiency and reducing training costs. Similar benefits coming from the adoption of VR intelligent simulators have long been experienced in the general field of education and training [8]. Compared to traditional training techniques, the trainee becomes an actor of the simulated scenario and improves his/her cognitive and spatial skills and understanding through practice.

Several systems have been proposed to assist emergency management teams during training activities within immersive environments [10]. However, one issue with the adoption of 3D virtual environments is that their construction is hard and in most cases restricted to specific emergency situations.

Aedo et al. [1] have suggested as a solution the design of emergency services training software tools for Emergency Planning, which are highly configurable, easy to use, and capable of reproducing different scenarios. With their simulation authoring system they emphasize the need to allow simulation designers to overcome problems related to the complexity of 3D virtual environments and to represent realistic situations and different action paths that can support the training processes. We fully embraced this thesis and decided to investigate the use of AR technology as a way to increase trainees' engagement and motivation. The system we propose originated from the idea to enhance the efficacy of existing training procedures allowing emergency responder trainees to exploit AR interaction and become quickly familiar with the mobile technology adopted today in response activities.

3 Background

In this section we briefly recall the technology underlying the AR-based training system we present, namely the information visualization technique Framy, the AR mobile interface Link2U and the spreadsheet-mediated collaborative system developed for the emergency management.

Framy was conceived to enhance geographic information visualization on small-sized displays through qualitative synthesis of both the on- and off-screen space [11, 12]. By displaying semi-transparent colored frames along the border of the device screen, users are provided with clues about the object and phenomena distribution. Each frame is partitioned and colored with a saturation index, whose intensity is proportional to the result of an aggregate function which summarizes a property of the objects and phenomena located in the corresponding map sector either inside or outside the screen. The higher the result, the greater the intensity.

Figure 1 illustrates a mobile device embedding Framy. The frame is partitioned into 8 yellow colored portions. The intensity of each portion is proportional to the number of POIs located around the map focus.

Fig. 1. An example of (on/off-)screen subdivision accomplished by Framy (Color figure online)

As for Link2U, it is an integrated solution for mobile devices which combines the potential of augmented reality with the ability to "communicate" of the social network [3]. It is based on two different visualization modalities, namely MapMode and LiveMode. The former is shown in Fig. 2(a), it corresponds to the classic two-dimensional map view, where paths and geographic objects of interest are drawn on the map. The latter is illustrated in Fig. 2(b), it exploits the augmented reality both to improve users' sensory perception about objects located inside the camera visual field, and to provide visual clues of those located beyond that can be visualized as aggregated data.

(a)   (b)

Fig. 2. (a) MapMode visualization of POIs and users' position. (b) LiveMode representation of a user's position.

Finally, the work described in [5] represents a solution to some relevant requirements distilled during one of the earthquake simulation events that the Italy Civil
Defence Agency periodically organizes in seismic territories. The result consists of a
spreadsheet-mediated collaborative system that combines the advantages of mobile
devices with the high potentials of spreadsheets for supporting operators acting on
a wide geographic area and requiring advanced tools for geodata collection and
management. Figure 3 shows how quantitative and qualitative aspects of a situation can
be displayed and shared on the same device. In particular, Fig. 3(a) shows a spreadsheet
shared among on-site operators about census information of a gathering area. In Fig. 3
(b) the same information is summarized and visualized through the Framy visualization
technique.

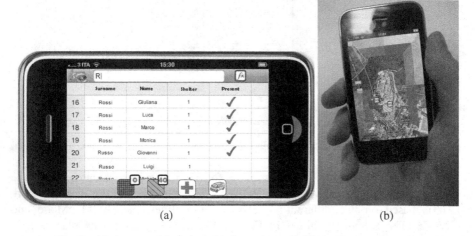

(a)   (b)

Fig. 3. (a) the spreadsheet-based information and (b) the Framy view of it

In order to achieve the goal of our present research work, the above mentioned
visualization techniques have been combined and embedded into a unique application
to allow users of more complex systems to perform training sessions and acquire
familiarity with the underlying advanced technology. In particular, the Framy capability of synthesis may help on-site responders and decision makers working in critical
situations identify more convenient solutions which may not be directly seen from
elsewhere, and evaluate constraints not detectable from remote sensors. Moreover, an
overview of the surrounding world, captured through MapMode and then LiveMode,
can help users generalize or detail the content of a given space. Finally, the integration
of AR-based functionality can enhance users' awareness about a situation and provide
them with an improved user experience.

In the next section we explain how the proposed training system works, describing
its adoption inside a realistic scenario of use during a training session.

4 The Use of Augmented Reality to Improve Trainee's Experience

In [5] we described a contextual inquiry conducted in collaboration with the Civil Defence Agency of the town of Montemiletto, in the South of Italy. We observed the emergency management activities carried out during a simulation event and were able to understand the importance of performing appropriate training activities through periodic simulations. Indeed, each emergency plan ends with a validation phase aiming at facing possible exceptions caused by both human factors and temporary objective impediments. During that phase it is relevant to schedule targeted training activities which may contribute to tune the involved parameters (residents, personnel and tools) of the underlying protocol, by taking into account both general requirements by national regulations and local availability and supply.

In the present section we depict a scenario illustrating how the system works when it is used for training sessions addressed to the emergency responders. Basically, two main categories of actors are considered, the designer of the simulation scenarios and the system stakeholders. The first category comprises people involved in the design of the simulation tasks with a deep experience in the field of the emergency management and in the conception of related evolving scenarios, for training purposes. The system stakeholder category includes people from the emergency response team, who have to learn both the system functionality and the protocols for the emergency management. The aim is to provide emergency trainers with a usable tool by which as many realistic situations as possible could be simulated.

In the following scenario, the simulation event takes place in Battipaglia (Salerno), a city in the South of Italy (Geographic coordinates 40.617 °N 14.983 °E). Basic information about the simulated situation is initially shared among participants, as follows. The territory is divided into 4 gathering area and 3 shelters. Each GA is associated with three local responders. The decision on how to distribute evacuees across the shelters is made taking into account the number of people to evacuate, information about their family composition, the number of vacancies at each shelter and the road status.

Once the simulation event is started, a configured map is deployed by on-site responders/trainees, as shown in Fig. 4. The green line identifies the involved gathering area (GA1) while the cyan area indicates the associated shelter. Red polygons highlight seven crashed buildings. Some of them are also associated with a red cross which identifies places where people have died or are injured (black and blue numbers, respectively). The configuration map contains also the coordinates where roads are interrupted and traffic must be redirected, a no-entry signal is used to illustrate those interruptions.

Figure 5 shows an example of a see-through image appearing to the trainee. Basically, in order to understand whether a building is damaged, the trainee should reach it and verify its current status. To make the status of a damaged building immediately evident, in the LiveMode modality it appears surrounded by a red line filled by a semitransparent red color. Moreover, information concerning the building and the associated GA is visualized on the left side. On the top, Building info

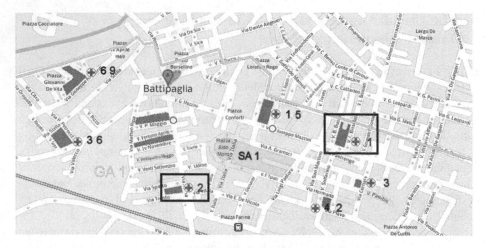

Fig. 4. The configuration map at t0 time

summaries the current situation about people living in the building, e.g., 3 families, 10 persons, the number of the currently recorded ones, the number of missing people, and finally, their health status, e.g., sane, injured or deceased. In this way, the trainee has an immediate view of the situation and can perform the appropriate operations. On the bottom, there is a general description of the gathering area he is managing, thus providing him with a complete view of the emergency management plan execution.

Fig. 5. The building as it appears to the trainee when its status is changed to crashed (Color figure online)

Once the trainee has reached the building, he has to perform the actions expected by the protocol. Each action is simulated on site and then it actually results in an interaction with the underlying system, such as notifying the building status and updating any number about the Building info. In particular, he needs to check both the status of the building and the condition of people living there (as shown on the top-left side by the training software). In this case, the trainee can interact with the other software components, namely Framy and the collaborative spreadsheet. Framy allows him to identify the building on the map through the MapMode view. Then, he has to update the new status. Moreover, he has to add information about the current status of residents starting from data shown in the AR-based LiveMode view. Figure 6(a) illustrates the spreadsheet with which the trainee can interact in order to list residents and update their status. Once he has completed the survey, his modifications immediately appear in the AR-based LiveMode view and the area surrounding the building is set to green, as shown in Fig. 6(b).

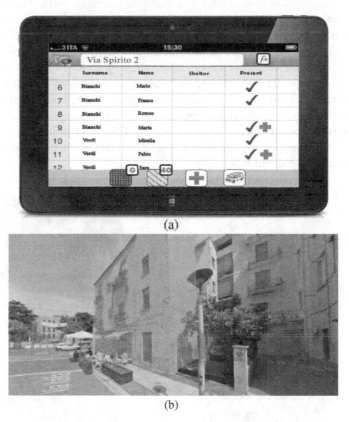

(a)

(b)

Fig. 6. (a) the spreadsheet for people status insertion, (b) the new AR-based view (Color figure online)

The usage of the AR-enriched LiveMode view along with the collaborative spreadsheet and Framy allows the trainee to immediately provide the COC with information about the current crisis evolution. Moreover, he is timely made aware of the contribution he has produced within the task thanks to the prompt update displayed on the screen. This aspect is fundamental to gain a more collaborative involvement by trainees during the training session because it generates a greater situation awareness and stimulates confidence in the new technology.

5   System Architecture

The client-server architecture on which the system is based reflects the dichotomy of
the actor categories: experts-server vs trainees-clients. In particular, this architecture
may be decomposed into several components. As shown in Fig. 7, some components,
such as SIRIO, are provided by third-party and are necessary for preserving experts'
knowledge and handling the current emergency management processes. In particular,
the server side consists of three modules fully interoperable with SIRIO. The first one is
addressed to the global management of the system, it integrates SIRIO with the other
modules in a single environment and distributes data among parts. The information
sharing is managed by the information sharing module (ISM) while the training
management is delegated to the training management module (TMM). Basically, the
ISM module captures the information generated by the SIRIO module in order to share
it with clients and, vice versa, it receives information by the clients and forwards it to
SIRIO to be computed. The TMM module works as a client even though it is located
on the server side, it is necessary to build scenarios for the trainees. It embeds a GIS
and allows to describe the evolution of the emergency in a real-time mode. In fact, the
changes applied to the emergency map are automatically sent to the ISM and then to
the clients. When they receive those updates, they manage them by using the VR
module located on the client side.

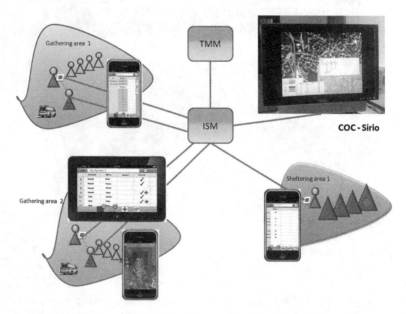

Fig. 7. The use of the collaborative system during a simulation session

As previously stated, in order to contribute to the designers' activities we developed
a GIS module (TMM) where it is possible to set a number of events for featuring
emergencies, such as the position of evacuees and the condition of some buildings.

An important characteristic of this system must be the ability to describe evolving events made up of successive sub-events. To this aim, the system embeds a temporal GIS where data consists of a spatial and a time component.

On the client side, the main components are Framy, the shared spreadsheet and the AR module. As for Framy, a fundamental requirement is that the trainee should be able to comprehend changes also in terms of temporal crisis evolution. Thus, colored frames are used to represent comparative views of the same zone. This capability is important from a training point of view to acquire a complete browsing experience useful to improve responders' familiarity with new technologies. Details about the aggregate values associated to each sector, such as the number of POIs and their distances from specified locations, may be required by tapping on the corresponding sector. The prototype featuring the present version of Framy has been developed by using Google API for the Android platform. It represents a framework specifically conceived for geographic mapping visualization and allows users both to download maps from Google Maps and to manage many typical GIS operations usually required from navigation devices. Moreover, based on tactile input and non-speech sound output as alternative interaction modalities, the prototype also offers a more appropriate interaction for users who experience difficulties due to specific environmental conditions [13].

The AR module exploits Link2U. Here, trainees can exploit both mobile devices and laptops, which are commonly provided with an integrated camera for video-image capture, a Global Position System (GPS) device to detect the position, a compass and motion sensors to detect user's point of view. In an AR-enhanced LiveMode view, visual metaphors are superimposed on the image captured by the camera phone where phenomena and objects of interest are visualized.

Finally, as explained in Sect. 3, the collaborative work is based on the shared spreadsheets, where the communication between the central application SIRIO and the mobile application exploits web services based on Apache Axis 2 and Apache Tomcat. Further details can be found in [5].

6 Conclusions

Starting from a productive field trail acquired in the domain of the emergency response, in this paper we propose an innovative approach to address the general concern of training emergency responders, which integrates some recent results from the field of information visualization, spatial data management and human-computer interaction. In particular, in this paper we show how an advanced visualization technique embedding visual summary metaphors could be integrated with AR functions in order to support responders in acquiring familiarity with new technologies and thus be well prepared to face health, security and managerial concerns in agreement with the protocol established by the Civil Defence Agency.

The proposed system aims to make the trainee with a scenario where an emergency situation is simulated. Through the interaction with a mobile device, the trainee is requested to perform some specific tasks that might result difficult to perform during a real situation where people are under stress. Such scenarios can be customized according to the skills of each trainee, thus bridging the gap between a specific technology feature and the responder who is going to use it.

An initial analysis of some demonstrator training sessions has confirmed that the AR functionality supports trainees when building their personal mobile experience with new technologies. They benefit from a shareable low cost "ubiquitous learning" thanks to the pervasiveness of the necessary hardware. Moreover, the involvement of professionals and volunteers in designing personalized training sessions reveals to be important in order to obtain a higher level of matching between a virtual content and a real emergency situation.

References

1. Bañuls, V., Aedo, I., Díaz, P., Turrof, M., Zarraonandia, T.: A scenario-based virtual environment for supporting emergency training. In: Proceedings of the 11th International ISCRAM Conference, pp. 597–601 (2014)
2. Carver, L., Turoff, M.: Human computer interaction: the human and computer as a team in emergency management information systems. Commun. ACM – Emerg. Response Inf. Syst.: Emerg. Trends Technol. 50(3), 33–38 (2007)
3. De Chiara, D., Paolino, L., Romano, M., Sebillo, M., Tortora, G., Vitiello, G.: LINK2U: connecting social network users through mobile interfaces. In: Qiu, G., Lam, K.M., Kiya, H., Xue, X.-Y., Kuo, C.-C., Lew, M.S. (eds.) PCM 2010, Part II. LNCS, vol. 6298, pp. 583–594. Springer, Heidelberg (2010)
4. Drabek, T.E.: Strategies for Coordinating Disaster Responses (Monograph No. 61, Program on Environment and Behavior, p. 242). University of Colorado, Institute of Behavioral Science, Boulder, CO (2003)
5. Ginige, A., Paolino, L., Romano, M., Sebillo, M., Tortora, G., Vitiello, G.: Information sharing among disaster responders - an interactive spreadsheet-based collaboration approach. Comput. Support. Coop. Work (CSCW) 23(4–6), 547–583 (2014)
6. Jackson, B.A., Baker, J.C., Ridgely, M.S., Bartis, J.T., Linn, H.I.: Protecting emergency responders. In: Safety Management in Disasters and Terrorism Response, vol. 3 (2004)
7. Jennex, M.E.: Emergency response systems: the utility Y2 K experience. J. Inf. Technol. Theory Appl. 6(3), 85–102 (2004)
8. Johnson, L.W., Rickel, J., Stiles, R., Munro, A.: Integrating Pedagogical Agents into Virtual Environments. Presence: Teleoperators and Virtual Environ. 7(6), 30–38 (1998)
9. Hamilton, W.A., Toups, Z.O., Kerne, A.: The team coordination game zero-fidelity simulation abstracted from fire emergency response practice. ACM Trans. Comput.-Hum. Interact 18(4), 1–37 (2011)
10. Houtkamp, J.M., Toet, A., Bos, F.A.: Task-relevant sound and user experience. Comput.-Mediated Firefighter Training. Simul. Gaming 43(6), 732–753 (2012)
11. Paolino, L., Sebillo, M., Tortora, G., Vitiello, G.: Framy - visualising geographic data on mobile interfaces. J. Location Based Serv. 2(3), 236–252 (2008)
12. Paolino, L., Romano, M., Sebillo, M., Vitiello, G.: Supporting the on site emergency management through a visualization technique for mobile devices. J. Location Based Serv. 4 (03–04), 222–239 (2010)

13. Paolino, L., Romano, M., Sebillo, M., Tortora, G., Vitiello, G.: Audio-visual information clues about geographic data on mobile interfaces. In: Muneesawang, P., Wu, F., Kumazawa, I., Roeksabutr, A., Liao, M., Tang, X. (eds.) PCM 2009. LNCS, vol. 5879, pp. 1156–1161. Springer, Heidelberg (2009)
14. Petak, W.J.: Emergency management: a challenge for public administration. Public Adm. Rev. **45**(1), 3–7 (1985)

Design and Implementation of Novel Word Learning System "Überall"

Reina Shimizu[1(✉)] and Katsuhiko Ogawa[2]

[1] Graduate School of Media and Governance, Keio University, 5322 Endo, Fujisawa, Kanagawa 252-0882, Japan
smz07@sfc.keio.ac.jp
[2] Faculty of Environment and Information Studies, Keio University, Minato, Japan
ogw@sfc.keio.ac.jp

Abstract. Previous research has found that in many cases, paper-based materials are better tools than digital-based products for learning and memorizing words. However, the advantage of digital media is that functions can be easily added. In this paper, we demonstrate a new digital system for memorizing words that is connected to the real world for each word. The use of this system is based on taking photos in daily life. The system detects the squares in the photo taken, and the square becomes the space for a word. We present a design and an evaluation using a mock-up of the system.

Keywords: Memory · Learning words · Photo · Smartphone

1 Introduction

Recently, with the development of smartphones and tablet devices, analog devices like paper are gradually being replaced by digital devices. Even in the academic sphere, tablet devices are being actively championed as notebook and pencil replacements. For example, in Saga prefecture, tablet devices are used at high schools [1], and for correspondence courses run by a major company for elementary schoolchildren, an original tablet device has been adopted [2]. However, the effectiveness of these digital devices compared with that of analog systems has not yet been widely investigated.

Some researches has compared the use of paper and digital media [3, 4]; however, only the moment at which the user was actually using one of these two media was considered. We previously researched the ability of a group of Japanese and German subjects to remember words the following day, three days after learning and a week after they first tried to memorize them [5, 6]. The results demonstrated that users who want to learn in the short term would benefit from using digital media only if they had significant experience using digital media. However, if a user wants to learn something over the long term, paper-based learning materials may be better. Our research was based on

© Springer International Publishing Switzerland 2015
P. Zaphiris and A. Ioannou (Eds.): LCT 2015, LNCS 9192, pp. 148–159, 2015.
DOI: 10.1007/978-3-319-20609-7_15

testing with the flash card method for learning and memorizing. This method is very popular among Japanese and German students.

We concluded that digital media was not so effective when the digital media product was similar to the paper product. Therefore, to effectively utilize the features of the digital media devices, the learning products need to be associated with the advanced functions. For example, the camera device in smartphones is noteworthy, because everyone has a smartphone with them, especially young people, who enjoy taking pictures in daily life.

Also, in our former research, we came to the conclusion that the feeling of the paper or the turning up of the card could contribute to memory retention. There is a mnemonic from ancient times called the "memory palace," which enhances memory by putting information in a familiar place in the brain. With this method, people are able to organize and recall information well, so, for that reason, many memory contest champions claim to use this method [7]. We believed that this method could work not only in the brain, but also in the smartphone through taking pictures. When the user takes pictures, the pictures change into vocabulary flash cards, so the user can recall words such as, "in place X there was word A."

We have developed a new digital system for memorizing words that is connected to the real world for each word. This system is based on taking photos in daily life. The system detects squares in the photo, and the square becomes the space for one word. In this paper, we talk about the design and evaluation using a prototype.

2   Überall System

2.1   Concept

Previous research has indicated that paper-based materials are better tools than digital-based media for learning and memorizing words. However, the advantage of digital media is that functions can be easily added. We developed a new digital system for memorizing words, which is connected to the real world for each new word. To use this system, users first take a photo. The system then detects squares in the photo, and this square becomes the space for a word. There have been both books and learning systems that use pictures to illustrate new words [8], but in our system, we use pictures from daily life that are not consistent with the meaning of the words (Fig. 2).

We call this system Überall, which means everywhere in German. Any location can be used to create a flash card when a photo is taken. It is speculated that users can memorize more words using this digital media system. Überall is designed to make learning fun. Most language learners these days take photos anytime and anywhere in daily life. This is especially true in Japan, where taking photos is a normal everyday behavior. People take photos of food, information on the street, or classroom shots. Therefore, because taking photos is so common, this system should be easy to use. We have chosen a German word for the name of the system, because the "Ü" from Überall resembles a smiley face.

3 Experiment

3.1 Überall Prototype

To evaluate the learning words system, we developed a prototype using POP (Fig. 3), which is an application for simulating the screen transition on smartphones. With POP, we could use many images, and users could also click on a part of the image and move to other pages.

Unfortunately, POP is unable to work with the smartphone's camera device. Because of that, we used pictures that were taken previously, but the users needed to behave as if they had taken these pictures. As Fig. 4 shows, at first the users only see the photo. Then they press the button as if they are taking a picture and the photo changes to a photo with words, which represents the mock-up of the smartphone's camera device.

We developed 81 pages for this prototype. Fourteen photos were taken on the Keio University campus in Shonanda, Japan. The developed pages were based on the 14 photos and contained photos, the same photos with words, a magnification of the words and the main Überall screen.

Until the users looked through all the words once, they were unable to look back at the previous word, so they could only go on the next word. Once all words have been studied, then users can freely browse all other words.

3.2 Experiment

Twenty students from Keio University were selected as participants, with the equal number of males and females. The average age of the subjects was 20.6 years, with the youngest being 18 years and the oldest being 26 years. None of the subjects had eyesight problems. The average duration of smartphone use was 44.1 months, with the shortest being 20 months and the longest being 104 months. The average duration of PC use was 7 years and 4.3 months, with the shortest being 3 years and the longest being 12 years. In Japan, children generally do not study English before 12 years.

3.3 Environment of Experiment

The influence of the application was investigated by testing how the students remembered the words on the following day, three days after and one week after. Therefore the test was conducted several times to verify how well the students learned. We used the iPod touch 4th generation, which has a 3.5 in. widescreen multitouch display and a 960 × 640 pixel resolution at 326 pixels/in. We used the font "MS P ゴシック" for Japanese and the font "Calibri" for English.

3.4 Flash Card Contents

In the prototype, the flash card set had 10 words in English and 10 words in Japanese. As the users were Japanese, difficult ideograms were chosen for the test. In Japan, an examination called the Japanese Aptitude Kanji Test is used to check student's knowledge of Japanese Characters. For our test, we used ideograms that had the same level of difficulty as that examination [8]. A phonetic symbol for the Japanese syllabary was added to ideograms. The English also had the same level of difficulty that a language teaching company in Japan "Alc" gives definitions [9]. The level of the Alc English words in the experiment is the advanced level over upper intermediate.

We developed a list of words with microsoft excel and randomly chose words both in Japanese and English.

3.5 Process

In former research, subjects were given 2 min to learn 20 words using two different types of media [5, 6]. However, subjects using Überall were required to do additional activities such as taking pictures, i.e., this additional work depends on the motivation and the interest of the individuals. We fixed the system so that the subjects could decide on the completion time by themselves, and they had to inform us if they thought they had learnt all the words.

On the following day, three days after the initial learning period and a week after, subjects received an email with a vocabulary test, which comprised 10 words; 2 words belonged to the group of 10 that had already been learned in the Überall prototype, with the remainder being new words (Fig. 5).

We set aside one week for the test period. We also tried a one month experiment, but there were only small differences between the results a week after and a month after memorizing the words. Psychologist Hermann Ebbinghaus did an experiment and developed a "forgetting curve." In the forgetting curve, there was only a 4 % difference between recall after a week and recall after a month.

3.6 Questionnaire

After the subjects had used the Überall prototype, they completed a questionnaire. The first part of the questionnaire collected personal data such as age, sex, and eyesight. The second part was a confirmation as to whether the Überall prototype effectively recreated the work-ings of the camera device. For that we asked two questions: one about whether the subjects had understood where the photos had been taken and the other about their impressions of the quality of the photos. Subjects answered on a scale of 1–7. The third part of the ques-tionnaire asked subjects to give a free description about the use of the system.

When the subjects took the tests, we asked them how they recalled the information, with "Only words," "Words and some photos which came with the words," "Words and photos," "Photos and some words that came with the photos" or "Only photos."

4 Results

4.1 Experiment Scores

Each word was given a score of 1 point. The number of subjects was 20 and each subject could have a maximum of 2 points. Therefore, the maximum score overall was 40 points. The graph below presents the results with the average scores (Fig. 6).

The average prototype use time was 5 min 27 s. The shortest was 1 min 42 s and the longest was 12 min 5 s.

We first tested whether subjects chose words that they already learned, and conducted an additional test to check whether they could memorize a phonetic symbol. One ideogram had been allocated an incorrect phonetic symbol, so we asked subjects how they would read the word. The word used was "玲瓏," which should be read "れいろう (reirou)," but was given as "れいせい(reisei)" in the experiment. 16 subjects answered "れいせい(reisei)" incorrectly as they had learned this using the prototype. The results demonstrated that the subjects could memorize many words using Überall and that they could recall these words well a week after memorizing them. From these results, then, we can say that the Überall learning words system was successful.

4.2 Questionnaire Results

4.2.1 Recreation of the Memory Palace
People who use the mnemonic memory palace put information in a familiar place in their brain. The subjects could recreate this type of memory system using the Überall prototype on smartphones, and in this experiment, even though the subjects could not take photos themselves, they could behave as if they had taken the photos. Therefore, we needed to confirm whether it was possible to recreate the workings of the camera device. We first asked whether subjects had understood where the photos were taken on a scale of 1–7, where level 1 was "I could understand every place" and level 7 was "I couldn't understand any of the places." All subjects answered with a 1 or 2, with the average being 1.3.

4.2.2 Connection Between the Photos and the Words
We asked the subject how impressive the photos were on a scale of 1–7, with level 1 being "the Photos were very impressive" and level 7 being "the photos do not give me any impression." The average level was 2.6, with most answers being between 1 and 5.

When the subjects took the tests on the following day, three days after and a week after memorizing the words, we asked them how they had recalled the information. The following table presents the choices and the responses. Many subjects chose the category "Only words" or "Words and some photos which came with the words," indicating that they recalled the photos from the words. None of subjects said that they recalled the words from the photos (Table 1).

Table 1. Information recall method

	1 Day	3 Days	7 Days
Only words	10	13	16
Words → photos	9	4	3
Words and photos	1	2	1
Photos → words	0	0	0
Only photos	0	1	0

4.2.3   Impressions About Überall

This part of the questionnaire was a free description. Some of the opinions given were "I felt like I was putting words in my brain when learning the words, and this system seems to put the words in a familiar place so I feel good about it," "Mapping words in daily life is interesting," "The words came up in various ways, so I could learn words enjoyably", and "I was surprised that I could remember many words after only looking at them once."

On the other hand, there were some opinions such as "It may be better if the photos were connected to the meaning of words" or "It was hard to remember when there were 2 words on a photo."

5   Discussion

5.1   Relation Between Learning Time and Results

When we reviewed the results of those subjects who only got 1 point (max. 2 point and the average point was 1.8 points) when learning Japanese, they were found to have used the prototype for 4 min 2 s on average, which was approximately 1 min shorter than the average use (5 min 27 s). We developed a table that shows the relation between the learning time and the results. Five subjects who had used the prototype for a minimum time were chosen (Table 2).

Table 2. Relation between learning time and results

		5 subjects with minimum time	Whole subjects
Japanese	1 day	1.8	1.8
	3 days	1.8	1.9
	7 days	2	1.9
English	1 day	1.6	1.7
	3 days	1.4	1.8
	7 days	1.2	1.5

From this table, it can be seen that there are only a few differences. In short, the learning time did not appear to have a large effect on the results. Firstly, the subjects did not find the learning time very long, and one subject said he could learn easily.

5.2   Relation Between Words and Places

A notable result was the way subjects recalled the information. Many subjects answered "Only words" or "Words and some photos which came with the words." When we checked with the subjects who did not recall the words well, 4 out of 5 of these subjects had chosen "Only words." On the contrary, when we checked with the subjects who had recalled the words well, almost all had chosen "Words and some photos which came with the words."

Admittedly there were some problems, for example, we did not ask them what methods they had used to recall the words and photos, but supposed that they recalled the places if they were unable to recall the photos. Nonetheless, the results suggested that those subjects who had good recall had been able to connect the words and photos well.

In addition, although we used pictures that had been taken previously, the users were required to behave as if they had taken the pictures. We believe that if the subjects had taken the photos themselves, the connection between the words and places could have been better.

5.3   Comparison with Paper Flash Cards

We compared the Überall results with the results that we had from former research [5, 6]. These two approaches had similar subjects as the subjects came from Keio University. The average age of subjects in this experiment was 20.6 years and the average age of subjects in the former experiment was 20.1 years. Subjects from this experiment had a longer experience in using smartphones, but a shorter experience in using a PC than the subjects from the former research. Consequently, there was only a small difference in experience with digital devices.

In our former research, we compared the use of paper flash cards with digital flash cards. The results demonstrated that the subjects could recall more words in Japanese or English when using the paper flash cards as a learning tool. However, when we compared the results of the English vocabulary one day after, the points scored for digital media were higher. We believe that this could happen if users had many years of experience with digital media. During the following tests, having such an experience did not appear to make any difference as the results demonstrated that the paper flash cards were more effective. We compared the results using the paper flash cards at first.

5.3.1   Comparison in Learning English

Figure 7 presents the average score for the results and the standard deviations. The average score was gradually lowered when using the paper flash cards. The differences between using the paper flash cards and using Überall were 0.6 on the following day, 0.75 after three days, and 0.8 points after a week.

We surmise that these results may be due to the additional information. The paper flash cards have additional information such as the feeling of the paper or the turning up a card, which can strengthen fixing the word in memory. However, Überall also has additional information such as places and images of the places.

5.3.2 Comparison for Learning Japanese

Figure 8 presents the average score for the results and the standard deviations. The average score increased a week after memorizing the words when using the paper flash cards. However, when using Überall, the average score increased at three days after memorizing the words and this level was maintained after a week.

While it is recognized that the data are insufficient to make sweeping conclusions, it does seem that subjects could remember not only the words itself, but also the phonetic symbols when learning Japanese, because 80 % of the subjects had answered with the wrong phonetic symbol, which they had learned as part of this experiment.

5.4 Comparison with Simply Electronic Flash Cards

The results are presented in Fig. 9. In the graph, Überall is compared with simple electronic flash cards. The appearance of the simply electronic flash cards is in Fig. 1 on page 2. This version has a similar appearance to the paper flash cards but users could only swipe the multitouch screen interface to see the next or previous words.

Fig. 1. Paper-based flash cards and its digital equivalent

Fig. 2. Scenes from using Überall

Fig. 3. Überall prototype

Fig. 4. Representation of the working of the camera device in the prototype

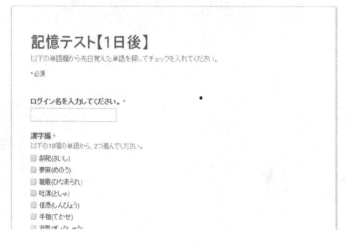

Fig. 5. Test example

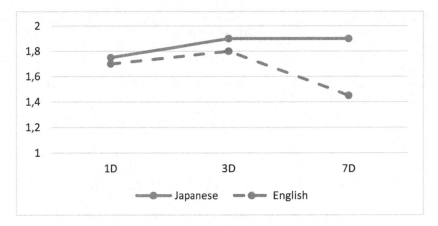

Fig. 6. Score for Japanese and English by Überall

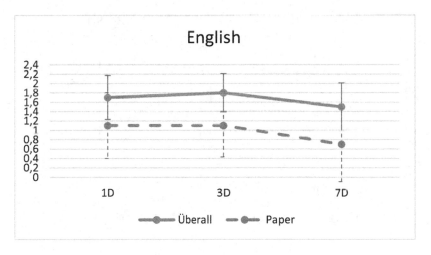

Fig. 7. Comparison for learning English

The difference on the following day was small, but it can be seen that recall three days after and one week after was significantly higher for Überall, indicating that Überall is a more effective vocabulary learning tool than simply electronic flash cards. The simply electronic flash cards have little additional information. As outlined, it appears that additional information makes it easier to recall words.

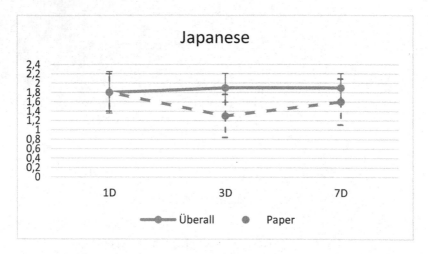

Fig. 8. Comparison for learning Japanese

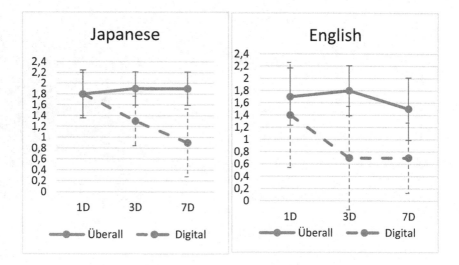

Fig. 9. Comparison with simply electronic flash cards

6   Conclusion

In this paper, we propose a new digital system, called Überall, to memorize words that are located in the real world and are associated with visual clues from the associated pictures. The prototype of Überall had been tested on 20 subjects.

When using Überall, users required more time for learning, because they had to take pictures to make the flash cards. Nonetheless, through this experiment, it can be concluded that Überall is both effective and enjoyable. The usefulness of Überall was found to be better than that of paper flash cards.

The main results and conclusions that can be taken from this experiment:

- Users could memorize and recall words when using Überall irrespective of the time they spent using it.
- When users could connect places and words well, they were found to have an effective recall.
- Überall was found to be a better tool for learning words than paper flash cards.

In the experiment, we only used a prototype of Überall. When we develop the final Überall version on the basis of the same concepts, users would be able to take their own pictures and develop their own vocabulary learning lists. It is reasonable to suppose that this real experience may be even more effective. Future work will focus on the use of the final system to assess this supposition.

Besides our research intention to test the effectiveness of the final system, we also intend to explore the following questions: "Is it better if words are related to pictures?"; "How many words should be on one picture?"; and "What kind of place is effective?".

References

1. Change Learning Method! Education with ITC in Saga (学びが変わる!佐賀県 ITC 利活用教育), January 2015. https://www.pref.saga.lg.jp/web/kurashi/_1018/ik-ict.html
2. Correspondence with Tablet Device for Schoolchildren (小学生向けタブレットで学ぶ通信教育「チャレンジタッチ」), February 2015. http://sho.benesse.co.jp/s/touch/
3. Takano, K., Omura, K., Shibata, H.: Comparison between paper books and electronic books in reading short stories. In: 2011-HCI, vol. 141, no. 4, pp. 1–8 (2011)
4. Shibata. H., Omura, K.: Comparison between paper books and electronic books in reading to answer questions. In: 2011 HCI, vol. 141, no. 5, pp. 1–8 (2011)
5. Shimizu, R., Hashiguchi, K., Ogawa, K.: Which is more effective for learning German and Japanese language, paper or digital? In: Proceedings of the 74th National Convention of IPSJ 2012, pp. 373–375 (2012)
6. Shimizu, R., Ogawa, K.: Which is more effective for learning German and Japanese language, paper or digital? Paper presented at HCI International, Greece (2014)
7. Joshua, F.: Moonwalking with Einstein. X-Knowledge, Tokyo (2011)
8. Schlecht, W.E.: German words list with illustrations (独検イラスト単語集 2・3・4 級レベル　よく出る分野をまとめて覚える). In: Kimura, H. (eds.) Sanshu-sha, Tokyo (2014)
9. The Japan Kanji Aptitude Test (日本漢字能力検定), February 2015. http://www.kanken.or.jp/kanken/
10. Words List SVL12000 Level 12 (SVL12000 Level 12 全単語リスト), February 2015. http://www.alc.co.jp/vocgram/article/svl/12.html

Design Solutions for Interactive Multi-video Multimedia Learning Objects

Caio C. Viel[1(✉)], Kamila R.H. Rodrigues[2], Cesar A.C. Teixeira[2], and Maria G.C. Pimentel[1]

[1] Institute of Mathematical and Computer Sciences (ICMC-USP),
São Carlos, Brazil
caioviel@gmail.com, mgp@icmc.usp.br
[2] Department of Computer Science, Federal University of São Carlos/UFSCar,
São Carlos, Brazil
{kamila_rodrigues,cesar}@dc.ufscar.br

Abstract. The increasing popularity of distance education courses, including Massive Open Online Courses (MOOCs), creates a demand for the production of quality video-based educational material. In order to reduce the costs involved in the production of video lectures, several researchers have investigated alternatives for capture and access systems which automatically capture lecture contents to generate corresponding video lectures. We also developed a system for this purpose; however our system generates Interactive Multimedia Learning Objects (iMLO) instead of a traditional (linear) video lecture. The iMLO's features and its interface are important issues for the development of the capture and access system. Interface aspects, such as which are proper ways to present content for users and which navigation facilities are more useful, are distinctive requirements and may impact the user experience. In this paper we present a novel design for the iMLOs which results from an evolution process supported by feedbacks from the main stakeholders: students and lecturers. The feedbacks have been acquired by analyzing the interaction of students with the iMLOs in real scenarios. Based on these feedbacks, we have identified several design implications. We present the proposed interfaces and proof-of-concepts implementations and report lessons learned during the development of the final design solution, which can guide other designers in the conception of new iMLOs. The whole process is documented by means of Design Rationale.

Keywords: Multimedia learning object · Design solution · Design rationale · Capture and access

1 Introduction

Although recording lectures is a common practice in many universities, the production of quality video lectures demands a high operational cost (cameraman, video director, editors and other audiovisual professionals). To reduce the operational cost, many tools for automatic lecture's capture were developed ([2, 4, 7, 11]). However, the majority of the capture tools only records video/audio streams and generates, as a result, a single video/audio stream, as a video lecture or a podcast.

© Springer International Publishing Switzerland 2015
P. Zaphiris and A. Ioannou (Eds.): LCT 2015, LNCS 9192, pp. 160–171, 2015.
DOI: 10.1007/978-3-319-20609-7_16

The classroom itself can be viewed as a rich multimedia environment where audiovisual information is combined with annotating activities [1]. Furthermore, the context of the class (e.g. the slide that is being presented, what the lecturer is saying, where he is looking, etc.) and how the different audiovisual contents relate to each other are also important. Such classroom experience and context are usually lost in a captured lecture. We developed a system to capture and retrieve lectures that aims to minimize such loss. Moreover, instead of a single video stream, the system produces an interactive multivideo iMLO that is made available for the students. From the iMLO, the lecture may be reconstituted and explored in dimensions not achievable in the classroom. The student may be able, for example, to get multiple synchronized audiovisual content that includes the slide presentation, the whiteboard content, video stream with focus on the lecturer, among others. The student has the option to choose what content is more important to be exhibited in full screen and may also perform semantic browsing using points of interest like slides transitions, spoken keywords, etc.

The set of features offered by the iMLO and its interface are key issues in the system developed. In this paper we present a design solution for iMLO which has undergone an evolution process supported by feedbacks from the main stakeholders: students and professors. The feedbacks have been acquired by analyzing the log of students' interactions with the iMLO and from case studies carried out in real scenarios. Based on these feedbacks, several interface elements were added to iMLO and evaluated. We report the design evolution for the iMLO, starting with a mockup interface, passing through some proof-of-concept implementations until reaching the final design solution. Thanks to experience of designing the iMLO, we are able to report some learned lessons which may guide other designers in the development of innovative learning objects. The interface evolution process is documented by means of the Design Rationale technique [8].

In the next sections we present other iMLOs' design solutions, a brief description of the system developed, the case studies carried out, the interface design evolution and learned lessons. We finish with conclusions and future work.

2 Related Work

In the work of Liu *et al.* [9], the iMLO is compound of a single video stream and a set of slides that are not synchronized with the video. Students do not have autonomy to choose the camera that gives them the best vie. Moreover, they cannot navigate by points of interest, as allowed in the iMLO generated by our system.

ClassX is a tool designed for online lecture delivery [7]. A live lecture is captured by a high definition camera split in several virtual standard resolution cameras. By using tracking techniques, the most appropriated virtual camera for a given moment is chosen. Students may choose a different stream from another virtual camera or even the original high definition stream. A synchronized slide presentation is offered.

REPLAY [12] offers similar features to the aforementioned systems. In addition it uses computer vision to recognize written words, and employs MPEG-7 to index the videos. Although REPLAY allows more navigation alternatives than the previous systems, it does not offer spatial navigation facilities.

Other authors report iMLOs with more features ([2–5]), however, the authors did not consider issues related to interface.

3 Capture and Access System

In this section we present a brief description of the system for capturing lecture-style presentations. A more detailed discussion can be found elsewhere [14].

Figure 1 depicts an overview of tools and components that compound the system. A lecturer goes to an Intrumentalized Classroom where he or she delivers a lecture. The instrumentalized classroom contains physical devices, such as video cameras, microphones, electronic whiteboard, slide projector, etc. Computers connected to the physical devices capture all data and store them as video and audio streams. Our system allows to lecturer split presentation into modules. This is useful to better organize the content of lecture. It also allows the lecturer to take breaks during the recording process and the students to navigate in the modules of the iMLO.

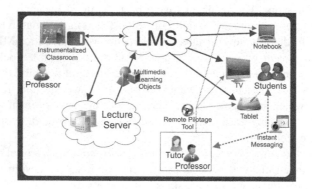

Fig. 1. System overview

When capture process is finished, captured streams are sent to the *Lecture Server*, where they will be analyzed and engineered in an iMLO. By using computational vision techniques, we extract contextual information from the streams, such as a slide transition or when the professor interacts with an electronic whiteboard. We named this contextual information as *Points of Interest* and they are used to provide semantic browsing on the iMLO. By combining the video streams with the contextual information, an interactive multi-video multimedia learning object is generated. This iMLO is stored on the Web and can be integrated with a Learning Managing System (LMS).

The iMLOs are built using Nested Context Language (NCL), a language for authory of hypermedia documents. NCL also support Lua scripts to implement features that are beyond the media synchronization domain. Since NCL is a standard for iDTV and IPTV [6], the iMLO can be presented at compatible set-top-boxes (STB). Moreover, they can be presented in HTML5-compatible browser thanks to WebNCL [10].

4 Case Studies

4.1 Pilot

This first pilot case study used an iMLO generated with the interface of the first proof-of-concept (see Fig. 5(a)). The iMLO was presented to 10 students and 3 professors which had the opportunity of interacting with the iMLO for how long they wished. Afterwards, in an informal interview, we asked them to evaluate the interface. Feedback pointed out some enhancements on the interface and missing features like the play/pause and stop buttons. Some users did not notice the possibility to view a video in full screen. Users missed information about how long is the iMLO and the playback current time. They also reported that navigation controls was taking too much space in the iMLO interface.

4.2 Students in a Real Scenario A

We captured an educational presentation for an Analyze and Design of Algorithms course. The resulting iMLO (see Fig. 5(b)) had duration of 49 min and was divided into 3 modules. The iMLO had three video streams: a camera focused in the traditional whiteboard, slide projector's output and a wide-shot camera. Users could navigate by modules, closes, slides transitions and traditional whiteboard interaction. We logged the interactions performed by the students. Sixteen students interacted with the iMLO for more than 4 min (data from students that interacted less than 4 min were ignored). Students were from presential modality of Computer Science and Computer Engineering undergraduate courses. Through analyze of interaction data, we figured out that students almost did not choose the wide-shot camera as the main video during playback. Moreover, in an informal interview, students said that missed the navigation by time slider.

4.3 Students in a Real Scenario B

One professor captured a problem solving session for a Computer Organization course in which he solved a total of 15 exercises. The presentation was organized into 12 modules, performing a total of 1 h and 18 min of content. Figure 5(c) depicts the iMLO generated from the presentation. There are four video streams: slide projector output; camera focused on the conventional whiteboard; camera focused on the slide projection; and wide-shot camera. Although the generation process allows orchestration of videos (e.g., the automatic selection of which video stream would be presented as the bigger video), we did not use this feature because the aim was to exploit the students' interaction, forcing them to choose which would be the video to be presented in the main window at each instant. Eighteen students interacted with the iMLO for more than 4 min. The average playback time was 59 min. The average number of interactions of the students was 118.55. Students are from presential modality of Computer Science and Computer Engineering undergraduate courses. We asked to the students to answer, anonymously, a survey which was organized in three parts: (i) questions about the proposal of capture lectures, (ii) about their experience in interacting with the iMLO and (iii) about iMLO's interface.

Figure 2 presents which streams were more selected as the main stream in each moment of module 1. Each line represents how many times a stream was watched in a specific moment. Figure 3(a) summarizes the number of interactions of each category performed by the students. Table 1 and Figs. 3(b), (c), and (d) present data collected from surveys.

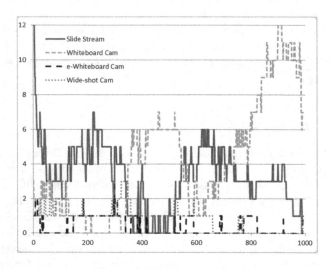

Fig. 2. Main video over time

4.4 Professors

We invited 8 professors to record presentations. Seven recorded a lecture simulation (without students); one captured a lecture with students. After a short explanation of how to use the instrumentalized classroom, all lecturers could carry out the capture alone, meeting the proposed self-service approach. Most of them did not modularize the presentation and record a single long module. The system generated iMLOs for the captured lectures using the design solution depicted in Fig. 5(c). Each generated iMLO was made accessible to the respective professor. After interacting with the iMLO, we asked to the professors to answer, anonymously, a survey. The survey was organized in five parts: (i) questions about the proposal of capture lectures; (ii) about the instrumented classroom infrastructure, (iii) about the experience of capturing a lecture; (iv) about the user interface available for control the capture process; and (iv) about the iMLO interface.

4.5 Summary of Results

Students and professor said that the generation of iMLO from the capturing of lectures is relevant. Students also said the iMLO contributed in their learning and understanding of the subject. However, Fig. 3(b) demonstrates that students think the iMLO should be used as complementary material. The case studies were carried out with students that

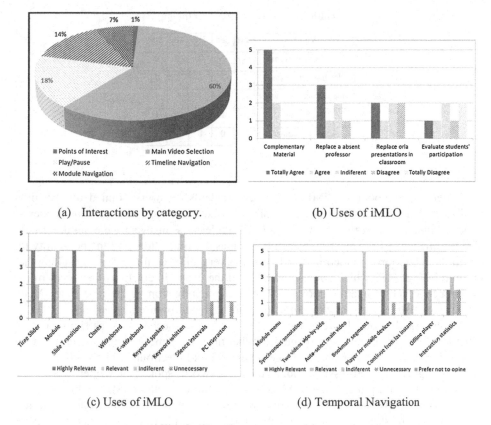

(a) Interactions by category.   (b) Uses of iMLO

(c) Uses of iMLO   (d) Temporal Navigation

Fig. 3. Data from survey and log

are used to have classroom activities with the presence of professors. Students with other educational background may have a different view about iMLO utilization.

The graphic in Fig. 3(b) also shows that students are unwilling in use interactions statistics to evaluate participation. By the other hand, professors agree that users' interactions with iMLO can be used for this purpose. A student declared: "*Some access statistics could be used to suggest the most relevant video or segments*". When asked about how they felt interacting with the iMLO instead of with a professor in a classroom, most students declared they were satisfied. This result may appear contradictory with the previous statement that iMLOs should not replace the instructors. However, even if a student, especially one that does not interact with professors in classroom, feels satisfied to be in control when interacting with the iMLO and taking advantage of its facilities, he or she still feels safer with the professor presence in classroom.

A student declared "*I really liked the multimedia lecture, especially be able to move backward and listen to an explanation again. The different videos are cool. I believe it suits to help and not to replace the professor, because it is complicated (almost impossible!) to make questions or to ask him to talk more about a subject*". Other students' answers also state that they enjoyed being in control and be able to performed both temporal and spatial navigation.

Table 1. Video importance ranking

Video	1st	2nd	3rd	4th	5th
Traditional whiteboard	4	1	2	0	0
Slide projection camera	2	3	0	2	0
Slide presentation capture	1	2	4	0	0
PC Screen	0	1	1	4	1
Wide shot camera	0	0	0	1	6

When asked about the iMLO interface, students' answers pointed out positive feedback. Among the adjectives available to characterize the interface, most students choose "*intuitive*", "*satisfactory*", "*efficient*". Professors' answers were similar. They also highlighted some interface elements, such as the time slider and the possibility to put the most important video in detail. This answer can be confirmed by consulting the graphic in Fig. 3(a), which shows that 60 % of the users' interactions were performed in order to select the main video; while 14 % were navigation by the time slider. Note that the time slider was an element of design suggested by users' feedback.

When asked about the relevance of the navigation mechanisms, as shown in the graphic of Fig. 3(c), the users pointed out that timeline (time slider), modules, slides, interaction with computer and with the traditional and electronic whiteboard are relevant. Navigation by professors' close and by keyword, spoken or written were considered indifferent by the students. Since students interact with an iMLO which did not have navigation by keywords, students may not have understood the concept. Moreover, the lecture style may not favor closes as point of interest, given that the educational presentation was focused on the traditional whiteboard and on slides. For professors, all but silent intervals options were considered relevant.

We asked to the students to classify the videos presented by the iMLO in order of importance. The most important video were the traditional whiteboard camera, followed by the slide projection capture and by the camera that frames the slide projection. The fourth position went to the PC screen and the last position went to the wide-shot camera. This result is consistent with the graphic presented in Fig. 2, in which the most watched videos were the traditional whiteboard camera and the slide projection capture. Note that students pointed out the camera that frames the slide projection as one of most important videos, but they almost did not select it as the main video. This may suggest the video is important, but as secondary video most of the time.

We listed some features that could be added to the iMLO and asked to students and professors to pointed out which are relevant. As the graphic presented in Fig. 3(d) shows, the more relevant features are the module menu, bookmark segments and the offline playback of the iMLO. The other features also had a positive acceptance, but some students considered them as indifferent, which suggest these features are secondary. Note that despite annotation was considered a secondary feature, bookmark — a type of annotation — was considered relevant. This suggests that students prefer to use simple forms of annotation. For professors, all the listed features are relevant.

5 Design Solution Evolution

Figure 4 depicts a mockup interface designed to meet both temporal and spatial navigation requirements for the first iMLO version. There are four different synchronized video streams; one of them is the main or bigger video. The other three videos (see Fig. 4(a) right) can be promoted to main video by clicking over them. In addition, clicking over the main video put it on full screen (see Fig. 4(b)). A user can navigate by modules (see Fig. 4(a) left-bottom) or by points of interest. There is also a button (see Fig. 4(c)) to open the overview interface. In the overview interface, there is a timeline representation of the iMLO with icons for each point of interest. By clicking on the icon, the presentation is moved to the instant in which the point of interest occurs.

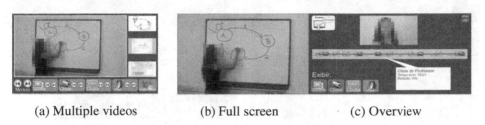

(a) Multiple videos   (b) Full screen   (c) Overview

Fig. 4. Mockup interface

We implemented a proof-of-concept for the iMLO using NCL. We have considered alternatives for NCL, such as HTML5, SMIL and flash platform, but the choice for use NCL was taken because it is a powerful language for media synchronization and it is under active development. Moreover, our previous experiences suggested that iMLO's initial requirements were covered by NCL. Figure 5(a) depicts a screenshot from a proof-of-concept implemented in NC. We noticed that are necessary three buttons for points of interest navigation: (1) move forward the next point of interest; (2) move backward the previous point of interest; and (3) return to the beginning of the current point of interest. We also found out that the overview interface is trick to be generated and implement in NCL, so we discarded this feature in this implementation.

We carried out pilot case studies (i) (detailed in Sect. 4) and used the feedback pointed to perform some enhancements in the interface. Figure 5(b) depicts a screenshot of iMLO redesigned based on these feedbacks. We added the play/pause and stop buttons which are necessary for Web environment, differently from iTV environment where these buttons are present in the remote control. We also added a button to the full screen feature. The users also pointed out the need for information about how long is an iMLO and the current time they are watching. In response, we added a timer in the interface with the current playback time and total module duration. Since NCL is a language for media synchronization, it would be complex to implement a timer in pure NCL and we opted to use a Lua script instead. We opted to favor the content rather the control interface. The different navigation indexes (module, slides transitions) share the same next, previous and return buttons. There is a control similar to radio buttons in which the user set which index she wishes to navigate by.

We carried out the case study (ii) in a real scenario. Although the iMLO offered innovative forms of navigation, the students complained about the absence of time slider. In response, we implemented another proof-of-concept prototype, depicted in Fig. 5(c). It was not trivial to implement a time slider component in NCL and Lua as reported elsewhere [13]. Moreover, note that there are indications in the time slider for the points of interest. The time slider with these indications replaces the overview interface from the mockup (Fig. 5(c)). We carried out the case studies (iii) and (iv) with professors and students in a real scenario.

(a) 1st proof-of-concept implementation.

(b) 2nd proof-of-concept implementation

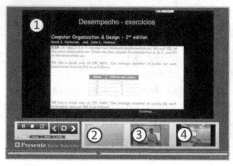

(c) 3rd proof-of-concept implementation.

(d) Final Design Solution.

Fig. 5. Design solution evolution

After analyzing the data collected from the users' interactions log and from surveys, we designed the mockup interface depicted in Fig. 5(d). The new mockup interface has a status bar (top). The title bar holds information about the iMLO' name, the current module's name and how many modules the iMLO has. The status bar also has three buttons, one for advance to the next module, one for return to the previous module and one to open the module menu. The module menu is another interface with the name and information of all modules. The user can access any module from the module menu interface. In addition to the play/pause, stop and full screen button, the new mockup interface brings annotation buttons. Via annotation buttons, a user can bookmark segments or add a time-synchronized text comments. These annotations are represented in the time slider like points of interest. There is also a button for enable or disable the main screen auto-selection based on points of interest. There is a plus button which allows users to choose other types of points of interest rather the four default types available in the interface, which are the more relevant suggested by the case studies: slides transition, traditional whiteboard interaction, electronic whiteboard interaction and computer interaction. When a user moves the mouse near a video's bottom border, a video options menu will be displayed. This menu holds buttons for put the video as main stream (however, clicking over the video does the same), for put the video side-by-side with the main video and for replace the video with other available content such as other video stream. The four default video streams are the more relevant suggested by the case studies.

The design decisions taken during the iMLO's interface project, which had as input the stakeholders' feedbacks, are summarized in the Design Rationale diagram depicted in Fig. 6. Under a white area are the solutions presented in the 1st proof-of-concept implementation. Areas shaded in light gray indicate the solutions added in the 2nd proof-of-concept prototype. Areas shaded in dark gray indicate solutions added in the 3rd proof-of-concept implementation. The solutions shown in the other areas correspond to the final design solution.

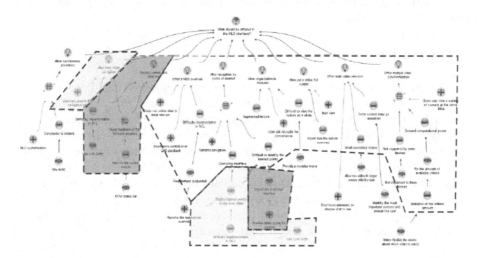

Fig. 6. Design rationale diagram - *what should be offered in the interface of an iMLO?*

6 Lessons Learned

As result of the experience shared with students and professors during the elaboration and build process of the iMLO's design solution, we present some learned lessons that may guide others designers in the conception and implementation of multimedia learning objects.

They are: (1) Students and professor enjoyed to be in control of the learning object playback. The navigation mechanisms that most promotes this control is the time slider; (2) Students and professors liked multiple videos interface proposal and highlighted the possibility of choose one video to see in more detail as the main video or in full screen; (3) Video size and position should be flexible to meet the needs of users (or the content itself); (4) The content is the more important, so the control interface must be minimalist; (5) Semantic navigation, such as by points of interest, appears to be a relevant requirement; (6) Plotting the points of interest in a timeline representation allows users to get an overview of presentation and a visual feedback of its organization (e.g. a user can see how many time the professor spent on each slide); (7) Offer information about the iMLO duration and the current playback time are important requirements to professors and students; (8) The full screen button should be visible and intuitive; (9) The points of interest pointed out as more relevant for lectures focused in whiteboard and slides presentation are: slide transition, interaction with the whiteboard and interaction with the PC; (10) Silence intervals appear not to be relevant as point of interests; (11) Students are favorable to add annotation facilities into the iMLO, but they prefer simple annotations such as bookmark; (12) The video captured by the wide-shot camera appears not to be interesting for students. However, it still can be useful in scenarios in which the lecturer needs to show interactions that the other cameras are not able to capture accordingly and; (13) Some users can consider some videos captured unnecessary. However, it is important that all captured video are present in the iMLO. A possible strategy is to occult such videos, but leave cues of their existence in the interface.

7   Conclusion

In this paper we presented the evolution of a design solution for multimedia learning objects. The evolution was guided by case studies performed with students and professors. The feedback provided several design implications in the iMLO interface, such as the most relevant videos and navigation mechanisms. The results obtained from the case studies have allowed us to report some lessons learned during the design process which can guide other professionals. The case studies also suggest that students are comfortable interacting with the iMLO instead of a professor in a classroom. However, they are unwilling to replace the classroom experience and prefer to use the iMLO as a complementary material. Students and professors also gave positive feedback about the iMLO's interface. In addition, design elements suggested by users, such as the time slider, were well evaluated. This may suggest that the design solution is on the right direction. We plan to implement a proof-of-concept for the last mockup interface and carry out new case studies which should consider other scenarios, such as distance education or middle school students. Studies about usability and accessibility of the iMLO are also of especial interest.

Acknowledgements. São Paulo Research Foundation – FAPESP (process no. 13/50469-5), CAPES and CNPQ.

References

1. Abowd, G., Pimentel, M.G., Kerimbaev, B., Ishiguro, Y., Guzdial, M.: Anchoring discussions in lecture: an approach to collaboratively extending classroom digital media. In: Proceedings of Computer Support for Collaborative Learning, CSCL 1999. International Society of the Learning Sciences (1999)
2. Brotherton, J.A., Abowd, G.D.: Lessons learned from eclass: assessing automated capture and access in the classroom. ACM Trans. Comput. Hum. Interact. **11**(2), 121–155 (2004)
3. Cattelan, R.G., Baldochi, L.A., Pimentel, M.D.G.: Experiences on building capture and access applications. In: Proceedings of Brazilian Symposium on Multimedia and Hypermidia Systems, pp. 112–127 (2003)
4. Chou, H.-P., Wang, J.-M., Fuh, C.-S., Lin, S.-C., Chen, S.-W.: Automated lecture recording system. In: Proceedings of International Conference on System Science and Engineering, pp. 167–172, July 2010
5. Dickson, P.E., Warshow, D.I., Goebel, A.C., Roache, C.C., Adrion, W.R.: Student reactions to classroom lecture capture. In: Proceedings of Innovation and Technology in Computer Science Education, ITiCSE 2012, pp. 144–149. ACM, New York (2012)
6. H.761, R. I.-T. Nested context language (NCL) and Ginga-NCL for iptv services. Technical report (2009)
7. Halawa, S., Pang, D., Cheung, N.-M., Girod, B.: Classx: an open source interactive lecture streaming system. In: Proceedings of ACM International Conference on Multimedia, MM 2011, pp. 719–722. ACM, New York (2011)
8. Lee, J., Lai, K.-Y.: What's in design rationale? Hum. Comput. Interact. **6**(3), 251–280 (1991)
9. Liu, T., Kender, J.: Lecture videos for e-learning: current research and challenges. In: Proceedings of IEEE International Symposium on Multimedia Software Engineering, pp. 574–578 (2004)
10. Melo, E.L., Viel, C.C., Teixeira, C.A.C., Rondon, A.C., Silva, D.P., Rodrigues, D.G., Silva E.C.: WebNCL: a web-based presentation machine for multimedia documents. In: Proceedings of Brazilian Symposium on Multimedia and the Web, WebMedia 2012, pp. 403–410. ACM, New York (2012)
11. Nagai, T. Automated lecture recording system with AVCHD camcorder and micro server. In: Proceedings of ACM SIGUCCS Fall Conference, SIGUCCS 2009, pp. 47–54. ACM, New York (2009)
12. Schulte, O.A., Wunden, T., Brunner, A.: Replay: an integrated and open solution to produce, handle, and distribute audio-visual (lecture) recordings. In: Proceedings of ACM SIGUCCS Fall Conference: Moving Mountains, Blazing Trails, SIGUCCS 2008, pp. 195–198. ACM, New York (2008)
13. Viel, C.C., Melo, E.L., Pimentel, M.G., Texieira, C.A.C.: Go beyond boundaries of iTV applications. In: Proceedings of ACM Symposium on Document Engineering (DocEng 2013), pp. 263–272. ACM, New York (2013)
14. Viel, C.C., Melo, E.L., Pimentel, M.G., Texieira, C.A.C.: Multimedia multi-device educational presentations preserved as interactive multi-video objects. In: Proceedings of Brazilian Symposium on Multimedia and the Web (WebMedia 2013), pp. 51–58. ACM, New York (2013)

Adaptive and Personalised Learning and Assessment

Automatic Pronunciation Error Detection and Feedback Generation for CALL Applications

Renlong Ai[✉]

DFKI GmbH, Language Technology Lab,
Alt-Moabit 91c, 10559 Berlin, Germany
renlong.ai@dfki.de

Abstract. This paper describes a new method of automatic error detection in Computer Assisted Language Learning (CAPT) system. The method combines linguistic knowledge and modern speech technology. Our HMM classifier trained from annotations of linguists is not only capable of classifying correct and wrong phonemes, but also can tell how wrong an error phoneme is pronounced. Phone errors in L2's speech, like phoneme substitution or distortion are detected with high accuracy, and at the same time, corrective feedback with multimedia support, which demonstrates how exactly error phonemes should be pronounced, is also generated.

Keywords: L2 pronunciation errors · Automatic error detection · Feedback

1 Introduction

In recent years, second language (L2) learning has become more and more popular to meet the need of communicating and integrating with a foreign community or society. However, learning a second language takes time and dedication, not only from learners, but also from teachers, hence both face-to-face and 7/24 personal online language learning are very expensive. A large and still growing number of computer assisted language learning (CALL) in the market has shown a clear trend: language learning is going to be web-based, interactive, multimedia and personalized, so that learners are flexible as to times and places for learning.

Modern technologies allow computer to beat human teacher in many aspects of language teaching like building up vocabulary and checking grammar, but not in training pronunciation, although many attempts have been made. Some industrial CALL applications are applying automatic speech recognition (ASR) on learners' speech and trying to infer existence of errors from the confidence value in recognition result. This yields results with low accuracy because no specific model is trained to deal with all possible errors, hence is far less effective than traditional classroom teaching. Researches have been made to investigate or enhance how pronunciation errors can be automatically detected, including

© Springer International Publishing Switzerland 2015
P. Zaphiris and A. Ioannou (Eds.): LCT 2015, LNCS 9192, pp. 175–186, 2015.
DOI: 10.1007/978-3-319-20609-7_17

building classifiers with Linear Discriminant Analysis or Decision Tree [1], or using Support Vector Machine(SVM) classifier based on applying transformation on Mel Frequency Cepstral coefficients (MFCC) of learners' audio data [2,3]. These methods either involve complex training process or have conditions in usage, such as targeting at a special second language, hence haven't been used in current CAPT systems yet.

We develop our method by studying the most common use case in CAPT: A learner firstly listens to the gold standard version of a sentence read by a native speaker, then tries to imitate what he/she has heard, and at last is reported how good he/she has spoken, in a comprehensive way. This means the sentence and also the correct phoneme sequence are known to the system. The system should also know all possible errors that could happen in this sentence, if such information is previously given to or continuously learned by the system. In our approach, we firstly gather learners' data and have them annotated by linguists (Sect. 2). After analyzing annotated data, we set up classifiers to distinguish not only correct and wrong phonemes, but also in which way a phoneme is false pronounced. Thus, by applying a model trained with gold standard plus learners' data, our HMM network produces fine classified results, which contain information for generating corrective feedback (Sect. 3). In our experiment, we are able to detect pronunciation error at phoneme level with 98.4 % recall and 94.6 % precision (Sect. 4). Since our method targets at the use case in CAPT, integrating it into existing CALL applications is discussed at the end.

2   Corpus and Tools

2.1   Corpus

L1 background of learners can affect the pronunciation errors they make in second language learning [4]. In order to locate the errors precisely, separate models for different L1-L2 pairs should be trained. To test our method, we target on German learning British English.

1506 sentences are chosen from LinguaTV[1]'s database, read by both native british female and male. Among these, 96 sentences, which cover most of the common pronunciation errors, like pronouncing /z/ as /s/, are then read by 14 female German learners at different English levels. 10 sets are used for training the error detection model and 4 sets are used for testing.

2.2   Annotations Tool

Pronunciation errors in speech data from learners are annotated. We extend MAT [5] as shown in Fig. 1 and focus only on phoneme errors, which are:

– Deletion: a phoneme in a word is removed while pronouncing.
– Insertion: a phoneme is inserted before or after another phoneme.

---
[1] www.linguatv.com.

- Distortion: a phoneme is pronounced is a distorted way.
- Substitution: a phoneme is replaced with another one by the learner.

In case of insertion and substitution, the phoneme, that the learner inserted or substituted with, is also annotated. Token '−' or '+' used to indicate if the phoneme written in 'spoken' column is inserted before or after the original one. By distortion, annotators are asked to mark how a phoneme is distorted. Following are summarized ways of distortion that annotators use:

- Tongue needs to be slightly further forward.
- Tongue needs to be slightly further back.
- Mouth needs to be slightly more closed.
- Mouth needs to be slightly more open.
- Lips need to be rounded.
- Lips need to be unrounded.
- Mouth needs to start slightly more open.
- Mouth needs to start slightly more closed.
- Tongue needs to start slightly further back.
- Tongue needs to start slightly further forward.
- Lips need to be rounded at the end.
- Vowel needs to be longer.
- Vowel needs to be longer and tongue needs to be slightly further back.

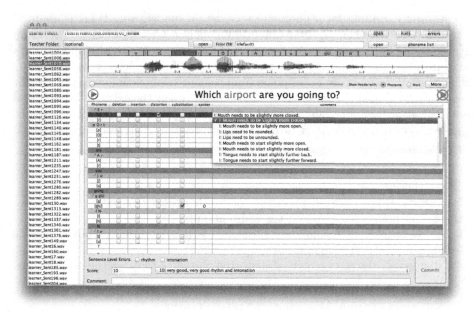

Fig. 1. With extended MAT, annotators can easily mark in which way an error phoneme is distorted.

3   Pronunciation Error Detection

The core of our method is to train a language model using HTK[2] for phoneme recognition. As a preparation of the training, errors found by annotators are classified. Then a model can be trained from correct and error phonemes. Before recognition, a grammar, which takes consideration of all possible errors that can appear in the given sentence, is generated. By passing the grammar and model, and also learner's audio to the recognizer, we can identify possible errors in learner's audio and also retrieve information for feedback from the recognizer's output.

3.1   Error Classification

After annotation, distorted phonemes are categorized by their ways of distortion and represented by new phonemes. For example, phoneme /ɑː/ in word 'are' can be distorted in two ways: either "Tongue needs to be slightly further forward." or "Tongue needs to start slightly further back.", so two new phonemes, A1 and A2, are created to represent wrongly pronounced /ɑː/. We use a database to keep track of all errors and integrate the database into MAT, so every newly annotated error is automatically classified and stored.

3.2   Language Model Training

The standard training for a phoneme recognition model using HTK is adapted to training a pronunciation error detection model, as shown in Fig. 2. The audio data contains both gold standard data and learners' data. Gold standard data are handled in the same way as a normal training for phoneme recognition. As for learner's data, in order to keep the diphone and triphone information of error phonemes, we adjust the labels to make them represent the actually pronounced phoneme sequences. The output of MARY phonemizer is modified according to what type of error the corresponding audio file contains, which can be retrieved from the annotation.

- for deletion, the removed phoneme in learner's speech is also removed from the output of the phonemizer;
- for insertion, the inserted phoneme in speech is also inserted before or after the target phoneme, based on the annotation.
- for substitution, the annotated phoneme, which is actually spoken by the learner, replaces the original one.
- for distortion, the newly created distorted phoneme replaces the original one.

For example, the sentence "I'll be in London for the whole year." should have the right labels as (in MARY phoneme representations)

I'll be in	London	for	the	whole	year.
A l b i I n l	V n d	@ n f	O r D	@ h @ U l	j I r

---

[2] http://htk.eng.cam.ac.uk/.

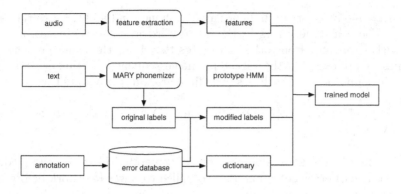

Fig. 2. Process to train a language model that detects pronunciation errors

If a learner swallows /d/ in 'London', pronounces /ɔː/ in 'for' with backward tongue and replaces /ð/ with /z/ in 'the', the following labels are generated and used for training:

I'll	be	in	London	for	the	whole	year
A l	b i	I n l	V n	@ n f O2	r z	@ h @U l	j I r

During training, distorted phonemes are treated the same as normal ones and are also added to phone dictionary. Both gold standard and learners' data are send to iterations together so the trained model has information of inserted and removed phonemes, and is also able to deal with the differences between right phonemes and distorted ones.

3.3 Grammar Generation

To run phoneme recognition, HTK needs a grammar which defines the possible phoneme sequence of an input audio file. We generate grammars from the distribution of errors stored in database and texts that learners read. Taking the sentence "I'll be in London for the whole year" as example, firstly, the correct phoneme sequence is retrieved from MARY phonemizer and surrounds with 'sil', which represents the silence at the beginning and the end of the sentence. The grammar looks like

(sil A l b i I n l V n d @ n f O r D @ h @U l j I r sil)

Next, all possible errors made by learners in the same sentence are applied to the grammar, in this case, there could be errors in words 'London', 'for', 'the' and 'year', after this step the grammar is:

(sil A l b i I n l (V |A |O) n [d] @ n f (O |O2) r (D |z) @ h @U l j (I |I1) [(r |A)] sil)

At last, we observe errors in diphones and triphones and add them to the grammar too. These include errors in the same word in other sentences, and also errors with phonemes from other sentences that have the same pre and post phonemes as appeared in the target phoneme sequence. In this case the only other error found is in word 'be', so the final grammar is adapted to:

(sil A l b (i |i1) I n l (V |A |O) n d @ n f (O |O2) r (D |z) @ h @U l j (I |I1) [(r |A)] sil)

Unlike training language model, grammar is generated based on the incoming text in runtime of error detection, and compiled to a word network before HTK can use it in recognition.

3.4   Error Detection

The process of automatic pronunciation error detection is illustrated in Fig. 3. Phoneme recognition is performed using HTK with the trained model, adapted dictionary, generated grammar and extracted features. The recognition result is a phoneme sequence, which is then compared to the correct phoneme sequence generated from MARY phonemizer. If they are identical, no error is made in learner's pronunciation; if not, possible pronunciation errors can be traced from the difference between the two sequences in a simple way:

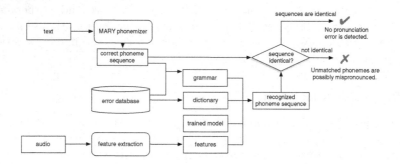

Fig. 3. Workflow of automatic error detection.

- if a distorted phoneme, e.g. I1, appears in the result, the original phoneme is distorted by the learner.
- if a phoneme from the correct sequence is missing, inserted or replaced in the result sequence, a deletion, insertion or substitution error can be inferred.

3.5   Feedback Generation

Finding out the errors is not the final destination. Intuitive feedback is needed so that learners know not only where the pronunciation errors are but also how to correct them. The advantage of our method is that these corrective information are retrieved at the same time as errors are detected. For example, if 'O2' is found in word 'for' in learner's pronunciation, we can show the annotation, from which this distorted phoneme is categorized, directly to the learner, and in this case it's "Tongue needs to be slightly further forward.". Or, if 'London' is recognized as 'l O n d @ n' instead of the correct 'l V n d @ n', we can tell the learner that he pronounces the first 'o' like /ɔː/ in 'often', but it should be like the /ʌ/ in 'cut'.

Simply displaying texts as instruction to learners is insufficient. Example of how exactly the error phoneme is pronounced, is needed. However, playing the gold standard version of the error word or sentence to learners is not enough either, because they may not be able to perceive the difference between the error phoneme and the correct one due to their L1 background [6]. In our evaluation system, we use a new way of feedback: the learner's own voice.

For each phoneme, we find out two words that are pronounced correctly from the voice data of a given learner. E.g. for /ʌ/ we have 'coming' and 'utter'. The words are chosen in the way that they have the target phoneme in different location and with different combination with other phonemes, and better represented by different letters. For /ʌ/, 'but' + 'cut' is not a good choice, neither is 'but' + 'utter'. Next, audio clips for each phoneme and its two example words are extracted. We also record some clips from native speaker. They are used for generating the final feedback. For example, if 'l O n @ n' is in the recognition result instead of 'l V n d @ n', the learner is presented with the a window as in Fig. 4. If she clicks on 'London' on the first row, the gold standard version of 'London' is played. If she clicks on the /ʌ/ on the second row, the following concatenated audio is played, where /ʌ/ and **London** are extracted from gold standard voice, other underlined text are clips from the learner and the rest are pre-recorded audio prompts. We extract audio clips of phonemes and words by using the forced alignment information from trained model (for gold standard voice) and phoneme recognition result (for learners' voice). And the text is also displayed on screen.

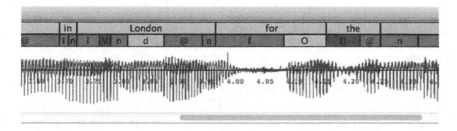

Fig. 4. A window showing learner's pronunciation error in our evaluation system. The background color of the phoneme shows what type of error the learner has made: green: no error, yellow: deletion, red: substitution, pink: distortion and purple: insertion (not presented in this example) (Color figure online).

"You pronounced /ʌ/ in **London** like /ɔː/ in *'all'* and *'door'*. It should sound like /ʌ/ in *'coming'* and *'utter'*. Please try again."

Similarly, if /d/ and /ɔː/ are clicked, the following texts are displayed and corresponding audios are played:

"You missed **/d/** in **'London'**, it should sound like /d/ in *'deny'* and *'good'*. Please try again."

"There is a little problem with the /ɔː/ in **'for'**, it should sound like /ɔː/ in *'all'* and *'door'*. Tongue needs to be slightly further forward. Please try again."

In this way, learners are explained how to pronounce a phoneme correctly, in a way they are surely able to: by recalling how they used to sound it right in other words. Learners can perceive the difference between correct and wrong phonemes better, if they compare their own voices rather than comparing their voice with the gold standard [6].

4   Evaluation

We evaluate two contributions of our method: the performance of error detection and the effect of feedback. Precision and recall of our error detection method are evaluated objectively. We also apply progress evaluation to test if and to what level the automatic feedback can help language learners.

4.1   Precision and Recall

We run automatic error detection using the trained model on 4 sets of sentence, which have the same texts as the sentences used for training but read by 4 new learners. The results are then converted to extended MARY ALLO-PHONES XML data with the same format as the annotations, so that they could be opened with the annotations tool for double-checking. Following are the results of comparing the generated data and the annotations, i.e. comparing errors detected by the system and errors found by annotators (Table 1).

Table 1. A statistic of the error detection result. True positive: actually detected errors; false positive: correct pronounced phonemes detected as errors; false negative: errors not detected.

	True positive	False positive	False negative	Total	Recall	Precision
Deletion	46	0	4	50	92 %	100 %
Insertion	17	0	1	18	94.4 %	100 %
Substitution	1264	14	2	1266	99.8 %	98.9 %
Distortion	745	102	26	771	96.6 %	88.0 %
Total	2072	116	33	2105	98.4 %	94.6 %

The result shows very high precision and recall for error types as deletion, insertion and substitution. In fact, the four deletion errors, which the system fails to detect, never appear in the training data, e.g. for the word 'central', the phoneme /r/ is removed by one of the testers. Substitutions are also detect very accurately. German tends to make the same substitution errors when speaking English, like replacing /ð/ in 'the' with /z/, and /z/ in 'was' with /s/. There are no new substitution errors in test data. Detecting distortions is not an easy task. In the 745 found errors, 114 of them are false categorized although they are successfully detected as distortion, e.g. the system returns "Tongue needs to be slightly further back." but the annotator thinks "Tongue needs to start slightly further back."

Despite a relative low accuracy at detecting distortion, we think the method is feasible for industrial CAPT applications, and we believe that the accuracy will raise if more training data is provided.

4.2 Feedback Evaluation

To use learners' own voice data as feedback, we are facing a dilemma: before a learner can pronounce a phoneme correctly, his/her correct voice data for this phoneme is not available. This problem becomes especially crucial when dealing with distortion because for some phoneme, beginners couldn't even pronounce them correctly only once, e.g. /ə/ at the end of 'number' or 'year'. In this case, we only display the annotator's hint as text, e.g. "Mouth needs to be slightly more open", to check if the learner manages to correct the pronunciation.

In our experiment, testers follow the scenario described in these steps:

1. Learner chooses a file with error and is presented with the window as in Fig. 4. But at this time, clicking on the error phoneme only displays feedback as text.
2. Learner could click on the gray words on the first row to play the gold standard as many times as she wants. When she thinks she gets the information in the feedback, she press Record and speaks the whole sentence to the microphone again. Automatic error detection process runs again and presents the learner with a new window. In this window, clicking on error phonemes not only displays text but also play audio, as described in Sect. 3.5.
3. If there are still errors shown in the new window, the learner can play the audio and check the text until she thinks she's able to correct the left errors, and then record again.
4. Another window should then show if the learner is able to correct all her errors.

Two of the four test learners took part in the experiment and the result is shown in Table 2. By deletion and insertion, it's helpful enough to display the text information to make the learners realize what they missed or inserted. The only case that require a second time was a mistake: the learner did pronounce /s/ in 'months', but in the first time correction she focused on the /s/ and didn't pronounce the /θ/ before it clearly enough.

The case with substitution is interesting. We think there are three types of substitution. The first is like replacing /z/ with /s/ in 'Please' or /v/ with /f/ in 'of',

Table 2. Statistics showing how feedback help learners correct their pronunciation errors.

	Total	Corrected after viewing text	Corrected after listening to audio
Deletion	20	19	20
Insertion	6	6	6
Substitution	641	430	608
Distortion	338	104	125

the cause of which might be that learners forget the spelling rules. If prompt texts such as "like /z/ in 'zero' " or "like /v/ in 'very' " are given to learners, they understand instantly what the right pronunciations are. In learners' first attempt, most of this kind of substitution and those that were made by mistake were corrected. Example words play here an important role. Both learners have error with replacing / əu/ with /ɔ/ in 'most'. The learner with example word 'blow' and 'over' succeeded in correcting the error by only reading the textual feedback, while the other learner with 'hotel' and 'go' had to hear her own pronunciation of these two words to make successful correction. The second type is similar with the first, only that the original phoneme does not exist in learners' mother tongue, and is replaced with an existing one, e.g. /θ/ with /d/ in 'This'. The difficulty here is that a learner may not know how to pronounce it and makes no correct pronunciation on this phoneme, and hence no correct audio template can be generated. If this happens, our feedback won't work. The learner has to be taught systematically how to pronounce it. The third type is more in the way of a distortion, the error phonemes are distorted too much that they become another phoneme, e.g. replacing /æ/ with /e/ in 'exactly' or /ʌ/ with /a/ in 'number'. These errors are hard for learners to correct but after hearing their correct version of the same phoneme in other words, a large amount of them can be fixed.

The result shows that our feedback is not so good at helping to correct distortion errors as with other error types. Learners were able to correct around a third of the errors by changing their mouth, tongue or lips according the textual instruction. Playing audio wasn't helping much. We also notice that learners could distort a phoneme in her second attempt, although the same phoneme was correct in her first try. Our conclusion with distortion is that it's caused by learners' habit or accent, and might be hard to correct at once. In fact, distortion is still acceptable as long as the error phoneme is not distorted into a new phoneme, because learners may not even be able to perceive the difference between the correct phoneme and their distorted version, and will feel confused or discouraged if they are told that they pronounce wrongly every time they try to correct.

5   Conclusion and Discussion

This paper presents a method that automatically detects pronunciation error in learners' speech and generates corrective feedback. The methods targets at a very common use case in CAPT: Learners try to imitate a sentence after they listen to the gold standard, and wait for the system to tell them if they pronounce good enough. After training with annotated data, our system is able to detect phoneme errors like deletion, insertion, substitution and distortion with high accuracy, and provides feedback that could significantly help learners to correct their errors.

The model, which we trained with only voice data from 10 learners, already has good performance. In industrial usage, if learners allow their voice data to be collected, a more capable model can be expected.

Several aspects about feedback can be adjusted or improved in industrial systems:

- For learners that just start to use the system, there is no information about which phonemes they could pronounce error-free. In this case, words from learner's mother tongue could also be used as example words, if they contain the target phonemes. This could be an option for advanced learners too because they know how to pronounce their native words better.
- Extra video tutorial can be prepared for particular difficult phonemes such like how to pronounce /æ/ and /e/, /əu/ and /ɔ/, etc. When errors with these phonemes are detected, leaners can choose to watch corresponding video to learn the pronunciation systematically.
- It might make sense to distinguish beginners and advanced learners. Distortion errors are only displayed for advanced learners. Beginners should focus on those errors they could easily recognize and fix, like deletion or substitution. If they can't perceive the difference between the right phoneme and their distorted version, they won't be able to correct them and will be discouraged at last.
- Annotators should also provide hint of articulation to some substitution errors happening between similar phonemes such as replacing /æ/ with /e/. In this case, the hint should be "Mouth needs to be slightly more open". Although the hint will not be used for categorizing distortion because no new phoneme is created, this information is helpful to the learners to correct such type of error.

Future work will seek to raise the precision of detecting distortion by studying the confidence value in HTK phoneme recognition result. The work of integrating this method into existing CALL application has already started.

Acknowledgement. This research was partially supported by the German Federal Ministry of Education and Research (BMBF) through the project Sprinter (contract 01IS12006A), Deependance (contract 01IW11003) and All Sides (contract 01IW14002).

References

1. Truong, K., Neri, A., Cucchiarini, C., Strik, H.: Automatic pronunciation error detection: an acoustic-phonetic approach. In: InSTIL/ICALL Symposium 2004 (2004)

2. Picard, S., Ananthakrishnan, G., Wik, P., Engwall, O., Abdou, S.: Detection of specific mispronunciations using audiovisual features. In: AVSP, pp. pp. 7–2 (2010)
3. Ananthakrishnan, G., Wik, P., Engwall, O., Abdou, S.: Using an ensemble of classifiers for mispronunciation feedback. In: SLaTE, pp. 49–52 (2011)
4. Jenkins, J.: Global lntelligibility and local diversity: Possibility or poroolox? English in the world: Global rules, global roles, p. 32 (2006)
5. Ai, R., Charfuelan, M.: MAT: a tool for l2 pronunciation errors annotation. In: Proceedings of the 9th International Conference on Language Resources and Evaluation (LREC-2014). European Language Resources Association (2014)
6. Flege, J.E.: Second language speech learning: theory, findings, and problems. In: Strange, W. (ed.) Speech Perception and Linguistic Experience: Theoretical and Methodological Issues, pp. 233–273. York Press Inc., Timonium (1995)

Feedback in Computer-Based Concept Mapping Tools: A Short Review

Francisco J. Álvarez-Montero[✉], Héctor Jacobo-García, and Eneyda Rocha-Ruiz

Facultad de Ciencias de la Educación, Universidad Autónoma de Sinaloa, Área de Posgrado, Ave. Cedros y Calle Sauces s/n, Fracc., los Fresnos, 80034 Culiacán, Mexico
{francisco_alvarez_montero,hmjacobo,eneyda}@uas.edu.mx

Abstract. Feedback is a core aspect of all the known psychological perspectives about cognition and learning and it has been an important aspect in machine-mediated education since the days of Sydney Pressey's teaching machines. This article reviews four computer-based concept mapping tools, that claim to provide feedback to the learners, w.r.t three research questions: (a) what type of feedback does the software use?; (b) does the feedback provided adheres to a specific model found in the literature and if so which one?; (c) are there any controlled experiments or in-class studies that give account of the efficiency of the feedback provided by the software?

1 Introduction

Concept maps [1] are the product of mapping one or more categorical propositions. These propositions are composed of two classes, known as the referent and the relatum, and a term, representing a binary or dyadic relation. Graphically, these elements take the form of nodes and labeled directed arcs, respectively. The nodes represent concepts or ideas within a subject area or domain, and the labeled directed arcs are binary relations which explain how two concepts are related. They have been applied to enhance both individual and collaborative learning, and there is strong evidence that their use is associated with increased knowledge transfer and retention across several instructional conditions, settings and methodological features [2, 3].

However, despite their graphical simplicity the construction of concept maps is complex and difficult for students, especially for newbies. Consequently, learner support or feedback is recommended. For instance, some researchers such as Cimolino et al. [4], have found that when students start out badly, with incorrect propositions, they tend to continue with further incorrect propositions until the map is grossly incorrect. In particular, feedback is a core aspect of all the known psychological perspectives about cognition and learning (see [5] for a thorough discussion of these perspectives) and it has been an important element in machine-mediated education since the days of Pressey's teaching machines [6, 7]. Moreover, from a review of 12 meta-analyses that have included specific information on feedback in classrooms (based on 196 studies and 6972 effect-sizes), Hattie [8] found that the average effect size was d = .79 which places feedback among the top 10 influences on educational achievement.

© Springer International Publishing Switzerland 2015
P. Zaphiris and A. Ioannou (Eds.): LCT 2015, LNCS 9192, pp. 187–198, 2015.
DOI: 10.1007/978-3-319-20609-7_18

From a human-computer interaction (HCI) perspective, there are three facts that under-line the importance of feedback, at least when it comes to educational software. First, an information technology savvy generation, defined by the terms digital natives, homo zappiens, Net generation, iGeneration, Google generation, etc. (see [9] for definitions and references), which really understands what they are doing with information technology and, use it effectively and efficiently does not exist. In a review of the literature, Kirschner and van Merriënboer [9] found that learners do not really have deep knowledge of tech-nology, and what knowledge they do have is often limited to basic office suite skills, e-mailing, text messaging, Facebook, Wikipedia and surfing the Internet. Social media, such as Blogs and Wikis, is used as a passive source of information and not as a tool for actively creating content, interacting with others, and sharing resources.

Second, the assumption that providing learners with control over the learning tasks they work on fosters their self-regulated learning skills and results in personalized learning trajectories [10, 11] is false. Most students do not reflect spontaneously on their learning processes [12] and consequently have difficulty in controlling and regulating their own learning. In particular, there is solid evidence, especially for computer-based learning environments, that students, particularly novices who lack prior knowledge of the learning tasks, do not apply and acquire self-regulation skills merely by engaging in self-regulated learning, but rather need additional support such as prompts or tutoring that stimulate them to reflect on their learning processes [9, 13, 14].

Third, the constructivist hypothesis that people learn best in an unguided or minimally guided environment is false. Following Kirschner et al. [15] this mini-mally guided approach has been called by various names including: discovery learning, problem-based learning (PBL), inquiry learning and constructivist learning. However, there is not a clear body of research using controlled experiments indi-cating that unguided or minimally guided instruction was more effective than guided or direct instruction. In fact, controlled experiments almost uniformly support direct, strong instructional guidance rather than constructivist-based minimal guid-ance during the instruction of novice to intermediate learners [15–17].

Several conclusions can be reached from these facts:

1. Students are not highly effective at managing their own interactions with the tech-nology and, should not be trusted to be in control of these interactions.
2. The ubiquitous presence of technology in the lives of the learners has not resulted in improved information retrieval, information seeking or evaluation skills.
3. When it comes to reflecting and regulating their learning, students need additional training or instructional support.
4. Learners should be explicitly shown what to do and how to do it, especially when dealing with novel information.

In this sense, this paper analyzes four computer-based concept mapping tools that claim to provide some form of feedback and guidance for the learners [4, 18–20] addressing the following research questions: (a) what type of feedback does the software use?; (b) does the feedback provided adheres to a specific model found in the literature and if so which one?; (c) are there any controlled experiments or in-class studies that give account of the efficiency of the feedback provided by the software?

The rest of this paper is structured as follows: In Sect. 2, some of the definitions, purposes, typologies and models of feedback are addressed. In Sect. 3, the four concept-mapping tools are analyzed. Finally, in Sect. 4, some conclusions and future work are stated.

2   Feedback: Definitions, Purposes, Typologies and Models

Although feedback is highly cited in the learning and performance literature, there is a plethora or definitions, typologies and models. For instance, Mason and Bruning [21] define feedback as any message generated in response to a learner's action, while Mory [22] states that it is information presented to the learner after any input with the purpose of shaping the perceptions of the learner or any message or display that the computer presents to the learner after a response. More recent definitions include the following: (a) information provided by an agent (e.g., teacher, peer, book, parent, self, experience, computer) regarding aspects of one's performance or understanding [23]; (b) information communicated to the learner that is intended to modify his or her thinking or behavior for the purpose of improving learning [24]; (c) post-response information which informs learners about their actual state of learning or performance in order to regulate the further process of learning in the direction of the learning standards strived for [25].

When it comes to establishing the aim, goal or purpose of feedback, the literature presents a similar scenario. Mason and Bruning [21] state that feedback should help and guide learners to identify errors, become aware of misconceptions and regulate their learning. Mory [22] asserts that feedback should help learners on the correction and analysis of errors, with a predominant focus on all the metacognitive variables (e.g., reflection) involved in this process and should also keep students motivated. Hattie and Timperley [23] claim that the main purpose of feedback is to reduce discrepancies between what is understood, what is aimed to be understood (i.e., the learning goal(s)) and performance. Shute [25] maintains that the main purpose of feedback is to direct learners in order to increase their knowledge, skills, and understanding in some content area or general skill (e.g., problem solving). Narciss [24] declares that the goal of feedback is to contribute to the regulation of a learning process in such a way that learners acquire the knowledge and competencies needed to master learning tasks.

There is not, either, a unified typology of feedback. Mason and Bruning [21] provide a typology as well as Vasilyeva et al. [26], Shute [25] and Thurlings et al. [27]. Because of the lack of space, only the typology of Shute is presented as it has several similarities with the one's of Mason & Bruning and Vasilyeva et al. In particular, Shute classifies feedback, based on its complexity, in the following way:

1. *No Feedback.* It refers to conditions where the learner is presented a question and is required to respond, but there is no indication as to the correctness of the learner's response.
2. *Verification.* It is also called "knowledge of results" or "knowledge of outcome." It informs the learners about the correctness of their responses (e.g., right–wrong, or overall percentage correct).

3. *Correct Response.* It is also known as "knowledge of correct response." Informs the learner of the correct answer to a specific problem, with no additional information.
4. *Try Again.* Also known as "repeat-until-correct" feedback. It informs the learner about an incorrect response and allows the learner one or more attempts to answer it.
5. *Error Flagging.* Also known as "location of mistakes." Error flagging highlights errors in a solution, without giving correct answer.
6. *Elaborated.* General term relating to the provision of an explanation about why a specific response was correct or not and may allow the learner to review part of the instruction. It may or may not present the correct answer.
7. *Attribute Isolation.* Elaborated feedback that presents information addressing central attributes of the target concept or skill being studied.
8. *Topic Contingent.* Elaborated feedback providing the learner with information relating to the target topic currently being studied. May entail simply reteaching the material.
9. *Response Contingent.* Elaborated feedback that focuses on the learner's specific response. It may describe why the incorrect answer is wrong and why the correct answer is correct. This does not use formal error analysis.
10. *Hints/Cues/Prompts.* Elaborated feedback guiding the learner in the right direction, e.g., strategic hint on what to do next or a worked example or demonstration. Avoids explicitly presenting the correct answer.
11. *Bugs/Misconceptions.* Elaborated feedback requiring error analysis and diagnosis. It provides information about the learner's specific errors or misconceptions (e.g., what is wrong and why).
12. *Informative Tutoring.* The most elaborated feedback, this tutoring presents verification feedback, error flagging, and strategic hints on how to proceed. The correct answer is not usually provided.

There are several models of feedback in the literature [21, 25, 27]. The most simple is the one proposed by behaviorism, where feedback acts to provide a reinforcing message that would automatically connect responses to prior stimuli—the focus being on correct responses [21, 27] and where the cognitive architecture of learners is not taken into count.

The rest of the models in the literature, as Mory [22] points out, propose a more elaborated examination of feedback that takes into account how feedback affects cognitive engagement with tasks and how engagement relates to achievement. One of the most cited models is the one proposed by Butler and Winne [28], which tries to understand the process of self-regulation as it relates to feedback. This model is shown in Fig. 1, and considers self-regulation a recursive process of interpreting information (i.e., feedback) based on beliefs and knowledge, goal setting, and strategy applications to generate both mental and behavioral products [22].

Another proposed model in the literatures is the one of Hattie and Timperley [23] depicted in Fig. 2. This model. According to these researchers, feedback must answer three major questions asked by a teacher and/or by a student: Where am I going? (What are the goals?), How am I going? (What progress is being made toward the goal?), and Where to next? (What activities need to be undertaken to make better

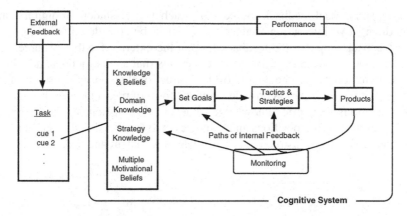

Fig. 1 Butler and Winne's model of self-regulated learning

progress?). How effectively answers to these questions serve to reduce the gap is partly dependent on the level at which the feedback operates. These include the level of task performance, the level of process of understanding how to do a task, the regulatory or metacognitive process level, and/or the self or personal level (unrelated to the specifics of the task).

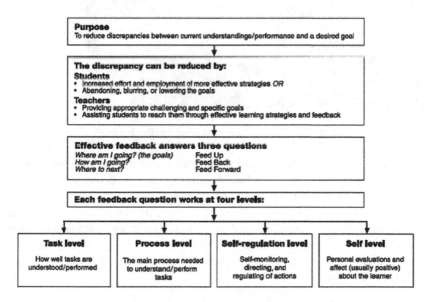

Fig. 2 Hattie & Timperley's model of feedback

Perhaps, the most recent model is the one by Narciss [24]: the Interactive Tutoring Feedback model (ITF). Narciss's model views feedback as one of several basic components of a generic feedback loop. However, when regulatory paradigms from systems theory are applied to an instructional context, in which learners are provided with feedback by an external feedback source (e.g., teacher, peer-student or digital instructional medium), two interacting feedback loops must be considered (see Fig. 3): the learner's feedback loop and the feedback loop of the external feedback source. Additionally, the model takes into account that the effects that an instructional activity can have are determined by: (a) the quality of the instructional activity (e.g. scope, nature, and structure of the information provided, and the form of presentation); (b) individual learning conditions (e.g. prior knowledge or level of competencies, meta-cognitive strategies, motivational dispositions and strategies) and (c) situational conditions of the instructional setting (e.g., instructional goals, learning content and tasks).

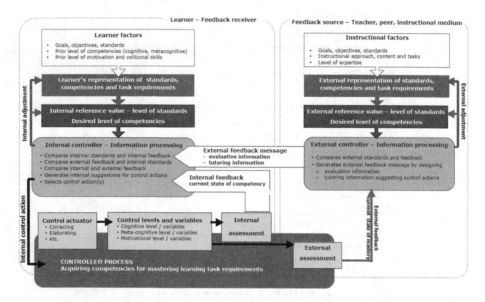

Fig. 3 Narciss' interactive tutoring feedback model

With the exception of the behaviorist model, the rest of the models in the literature, as Mory [22] points out, belong to the Information Processing perspective [5] on cognition and learning. Consequently, most studies have been carried out from this perspective. Although it is outside the scope of this paper to search and discuss these models, given that constructivist approaches tend to avoid feedback and guidance as much as possible [18, 19], the existence of such models must be scarce. In the next section, the feedback provided by the four computer-based concept mapping tools mentioned in the introductions is analyzed.

3   Computer-Based Concept Mapping Tools

Nowadays there are a lot of tools supporting different activities with concept maps. However, as Anohina and Grundspenkis underline [29], most of them only provide functions such as concept map construction, navigation and sharing, but do not analyze the learners' concept maps and do not provide appropriate learner's support in terms of feedback and help. In the following, four concept mapping tools, that claim to provide feedback for learners, are presented and analyzed in a chronological order.

3.1 Chang, Sung, and Chen's Concept Mapping Tool

The tool developed by Chang et al. [18] supports two kinds of learning strategies for students to construct concept maps. One of them is the 'construct-on-scaffold' version, which provides an incomplete expert concept map with some blank nodes and links/ relations. The students then select concepts or relations from the concept or relation list and fill in the appropriate blanks in the scaffold with these selections. In particular, the tool has a hint button, which can be used on demand, and that gives hints to students according to the comparisons between student and expert concept maps. The hints are presented in a partial proposition type, such as [Meiosis result in ???]. Additionally, there is an 'expert concept map' button which is enabled when the students have worked on constructing their maps for over 30 min.

To test their concept mapping system, the researchers carried out and experiment with forty-eight seven-grade students ($N = 48$), 23 females and 25 males, selected from three classes of one junior high school in Taipei. All the students were studying their second semester course of General Biology. Each class was randomly assigned to one of the following concept map construction groups: 'construct-by-self' using the tool, 'construct-on-scaffold' using the tool, and 'construct by paper-and-pencil' without the tool.

The experiment employed a pre-test post-test control group design. A one way ANCOVA was conducted on the post-test scores of the three groups. Pre-test scores were used as the covariate to control the potential differences in the students' biology knowledge. In particular, the ANCOVA revealed significant differences between the 3 groups: $F(2,44) = 3.79$, $p < .05$. A Post hoc analysis using Fisher's Least Significant Difference (LSD) test indicated that the 'construct-on-scaffold' method had a better learning impact on students than the 'construct-by-self' and 'paper-and-pencil' ones.

3.2 The COncept MaP ASSessment Tool (COMPASS)

COMPASS [4] is a web-based concept mapping that supports the elaboration of assessment activities employing various mapping tasks such as the construction of a concept map from scratch ("free construction" task) and the completion and evaluation of a concept map using an available list of concepts/relationships ("concept-relationship list completion/evaluation" task). In particular, after the learner has completed the assessment activity, COMPASS activates the diagnosis process for (i) the identification of errors on the learner's map according to a predefined set of errors (see [4]), based on the similarity of the learner's map to the teacher's one, and the qualitative analysis of the errors, (ii) the qualitative diagnosis of learner's knowledge, which is based on a predefined classification of errors (see [4]) which concerns the identification of unknown concepts, incomplete understanding and false beliefs, and (iii) the quantitative estimation of learner's knowledge level on the central concept of the map and subsequently on the assessment activity, which is assigned to one of several characterizations: Insufficient (Ins), Rather Insufficient (RIns), etc.

Furthermore, the tool provides a "Visual Feedback" option and an "Interactive Feedback" option. If the learner selects the "Visual Feedback" option, COMPASS graphically annotates the errors on the map, if any, following the proposed error categorization. In the student selects the "Interactive Feedback" option, COMPASS activates a process denominated "Knowledge Reconstruction + Refinement (KR + R)" which aims to provide feedback, tailored to each individual learner in order to support the reflection process, to tutor and guide the learners and subsequently to enable them enrich/reconstruct their knowledge structure.

In particular, the "KR + R" process incorporates informative and tutoring feedback components (ITRFC) and combines a stepwise presentation (see [33]) of these components with a multiple try strategy. The ITFC include (i) an initiating question (IQ) consisting of the learner's belief, and a prompt to think of the concepts included in the proposition and to write any keywords describing the concepts, (ii) specific error-task related questions (E-TRQ), (iii) tutoring feedback units (TFU) relevant to concepts/relationship included in the concept map, and (iv) the knowledge of correct response (KCR).

To evaluate the efficiency of the tool, 2 studies ($N = 6$) where carried out. The first study investigated whether the design of the E-TRQ, as the only source of feedback, helped learners to identify, reconsider and correct their error appropriately. The second study researched whether the E-TR and the TFU helped learners to identify, reconsider and correct their error appropriately. No inferential statistics and no control group where employed in these studies. The results showed that E-TRQ alone helps students, especially those with knowledge level above average, in revising their beliefs and refining their knowledge. In cases of students with low knowledge level, these improved their performance after the TFU + E-TRQ were provided and they identified and corrected a considerable number of errors.

3.3   The Verified Concept Mapping System (VCM)

VCM [19] is intended for explicit mapping tasks that have been carefully defined by an instructor or teacher. For example, the teacher might provide students with learning resources to study and then ask them to construct concept maps that capture their understanding of that material. In particular, VCM allows students to focus on the concept-mapping task as long as they need to complete it. Then, when the learner is ready for feedback, he or she moves to the analysis phase and the system displays both a learner model and some suggested elements for checking.

Feedback is provided by checking for expected propositions and, for any missing proposition, VCM produces a message intended to help the student check her or his map. The messages are previously encoded by the instructor or teacher. For instance, if an expected proposition "Concept1 link1 Concept2" is missing, the teacher might code a message asking the student to consider ways to connect "Concept1". If the teacher anticipated a misconception in the form "ConceptA linkA ConceptB", the message might ask the student to check this proposition. Examples of messages are: where should concept x be in the hierarchy? what is the definition of x? can you change the link between concept x and concept y?

A qualitative evaluation of the tool was carried out using a think aloud approach with four university level students ($N = 4$) coursing their first year of Computer Science. An experienced tutor was asked to perform the experiment so that input could be gained from one person at expert level, but independent of the design team. The mapping task involved scalability, a topic that is quite conceptual and hence suited to concept mapping.

The students spent between 1 and 2 h on the task, while the expert only spent 30 min. One student failed to complete the task and found it a frustrating experience. None of the students (or the expert) appeared to spend much time reading the supplied reading material. Nor did they make reference to it as they attempted to construct the map. Moreover, students used the analysis phase somewhat differently from what it was originally intended. Rather than wait till they had completed the map and then do the analysis, they used this facility at regular points through the mapping activity. They would do a part of the map, then stop and run the analysis to get feedback on the partially completed map.

3.4 The Intelligent Knowledge Assessment System (IKAS)

IKAS [20] is a system developed with the following goals in mind: (a) the promotion of process-oriented learning by supporting assessment focused on the process of knowledge acquisition by students; (b) to promote students' knowledge self-assessment; (c) to support teachers in improvement of study courses through systematic assessment and analysis of students' knowledge. Following Anohina-Naumeca et al. [20], the usage scenario of IKAS assumes that a teacher divides a course into several assessment stages. A stage can be any logically completed part of the course, for example, a chapter. For each stage, a map is created by specifying relevant concepts and relationships among them in such a way that a map of particular stage is nothing else than an extension of the previous one. During knowledge assessment, a student solves a task corresponding to the assessment stage and after the submission of his/her solution the system compares the student's and teacher's maps and generates feedback.

According to Lukasenko et al. [30], only one type of feedback is provided to students during the solving of a task: checking of a proposition. The idea is that a student points out his/her created proposition and the system checks its correctness. In case of incorrectness the system presents explanations of both concepts involved in the proposition. After the submission of a task a student's map and a window with quantitative and qualitative data is provided. Quantitative data is a set of numerical indicators aimed to inform a student about his or her performance and degree of achievement in a given task. They are interpreted by the student and no explanation or pedagogical remarks are provided. A qualitative description is a text summary which explains a student how well he or she has mastered concepts in a given task. A text summary points out concepts which require revision. In the student's map relationships are colored in different tones according to their correctness. The student can acquire detailed information about each relationship by clicking on it. In this case contribution of all parts of a relationship (linking phrase, type, direction and placement of concepts) to the correctness of a relationship. Lukasenko et al. [30] provide screenshots of this functionality.

Starting from 2005 all IKAS prototypes were evaluated in different courses by asking students to fill-in a questionnaire after solving a set of tasks. No other type of evaluations was carried out. In particular, these questionnaires allowed gathering student opinion about concept maps as knowledge assessment tool and the functionality of IKAS. For instance, during evaluation of the first three prototypes, students always found that it would be helpful to provide more informative feedback and to improve the system's response to user actions.

In the next section the analysis of the tools w.r.t. the research questions stated in the introduction is discussed.

4   Conclusions and Future Work

For the first research question, Chang, Sung and Chen do not declare the type of feedback they use in their tool. Nonetheless, it is clear that they use hints/cues/prompts at a basic level and do not provide the elaboration complexity considered in Shute's typology. COMPASS is in the same situation but it can be inferred that it provides: basic hints/cues/prompts (i.e., IQ and E-TRQ), correct response, topic contingent (i.e. TFU) and Bugs/misconceptions (i.e. E-TRQ). VCM only uses basic hints/cues/prompts while IKAS has correct response as well as topic and response contingent feedback.

Most of the reviewed tools do not adhere, explicitly, to a specific model of feedback. Only COMPASS proposes a feedback framework of its own: the Adaptive Feedback Framework [31]. Only Chang, Sun and Chen, and COMPASS provide evidence of the effectiveness of the feedback provided. Nevertheless, although Chang, Sung and Chen report that feedback makes a difference w.r.t to achievement, they fail to assert how important the difference is in terms of effect. The evidence provided by COMPASS is severely limited, as no control group was included in the study and only descriptive statistics were used.

In sum, with the exception of COMPASS, the feedback strategies of the rest of the analyzed tools seem to have been designed by intuition and, without taking into account the large body of literature about feedback, in the field of Educational Psychology. Nevertheless, the most important finding of this article is the lack of methodologically sound studies that prove the efficiency of the tools. There is a big software engineering effort, but without appropriate studies the effort amounts to nothing and the field does not advance. In a time where educational interventions with an effect size below .40, are deemed as not worth the effort [8], carrying methodologically sound studies, as well as including what is currently known [32] about psychological constructs such as feedback and motivation, is a necessity. More so if we consider that recent meta-analyses have shown that the impact of technology in learning has an average effect size of 0.33 [33].

References

1. Novak, J.D., Gowin, D.B.: Learning How To Learn. Cambridge University Press, New York (1984)
2. Daley, B.J., Torre, D.M.: Concept maps in medical education: an analytical literature review. Med. Educ. **44**(5), 440–448 (2010)

3. Nesbit, J.C., Adesope, O.: Learning with concept and knowledge maps: a meta-analysis. Rev. Educ. Res. **76**(3), 413–448 (2006)
4. Cimolino, L., Kay, J., Miller, A.: Concept mapping for eliciting verified personal ontologies. Int. J. Continuing Eng. Educ. Life Long Learn. **14**(3), 212–228 (2004)
5. Harris, K.R., Graham, S.E., Urdan, T.E., McCormick, C.B., Sinatra, G.M., Sweller, J.E.: APA Educational Psychology Handbook. Theories, Constructs, and Critical Issues, vol. 1. American Psychological Association, Washington, D.C. (2012)
6. Benjamin, L.T.: A history of teaching machines. Am. Psychol. **43**(9), 703 (1988)
7. Dihoff, R.E., Brosvic, G.M., Epstein, M.L.: The role of feedback during academic testing: The delay retention effect revisited. Psychol. Rec. **53**(4), 2 (2012)
8. Hattie, J.: Visible Learning: A Synthesis of Over 800 Meta-Analyses Relating to Achievement. Routledge, London (2009)
9. Kirschner, P.A., van Merriënboer, J.J.: Do learners really know best? Urban Legends Educ. Educ. Psychol. **48**(3), 169–183 (2013)
10. Hannafin, M.J.: Guidelines for using locus of instructional control in the design of computer-assisted instruction. J. Instr. Dev. **7**(3), 6–10 (1984)
11. Williams, M.: Learner control and instructional technologies. In: Jonassen, D. (ed.) Handbook of Research on Educational Communications and Technology, pp. 957–983. Simon & Schuster Macmillan, New York (1996)
12. Van den Boom, G., Paas, F., van Merriënboer, J.J.: Effects of elicited reflections combined with tutor or peer feedback on self-regulated learning and learning outcomes. Learn. Instr. **17**(5), 532–548 (2007)
13. Azevedo, R., Moos, D.C., Greene, J.A., Winters, F.I., Cromley, J.G.: Why is externally-facilitated regulated learning more effective than self-regulated learning with hypermedia? Educ. Tech. Res. Dev. **56**(1), 45–72 (2008)
14. Kostons, D., Van Gog, T., Paas, F.: Training self-assessment and task-selection skills: A cognitive approach to improving self-regulated learning. Learn. Instr. **22**(2), 121–132 (2012)
15. Kirschner, P.A., Sweller, J., Clark, R.E.: Why minimal guidance during instruction does not work: an analysis of the failure of constructivist, discovery, problem-based, experiential, and inquiry-based teaching. Eudc. Psychol. **41**(2), 75–86 (2006)
16. Sweller, J., Kirschner, P.A., Clark, R.E.: Why minimally guided teaching techniques do not work: a reply to commentaries. Eudc. Psychol. **42**(2), 115–121 (2007)
17. Rosenshine, B.: The empirical support for direct instruction. In: Tobias, S., Duffy, T.M. (eds.) Constructivist Instruction: Success or Failure?, pp. 201–220. Taylor & Francis, New York (2009)
18. Chang, K.E., Sung, Y.T., Chen, S.F.: Learning through computer-based concept mapping with scaffolding aid. J. Comput. Assist. Learn. **17**(1), 21–33 (2001)
19. Gouli, E., Gogoulou, A., Papanikolaou, K., Grigoriadou, M.: Designing an adaptive feedback scheme to support reflection in concept mapping. In: Proceedings of the Adaptive Hypermedia 2004 Workshop (2004)
20. Anohina-Naumeca, A., Grundspenkis, J., Strautmane, M.: The concept map-based assessment system: functional capabilities, evolution, and experimental results. Int. J. Continuing Eng. Educ. Life Long Learn. **21**(4), 308–327 (2011)
21. Mason, B.J., Bruning, R.: Providing feedback in computer-based instruction. What the research tells us. Center for Instructional Innovation (2001)
22. Mory, E.H.: Feedback research revisited. In: Jonassen, D.H. (ed.) Handbook of Research on Educational Communications and Technology, vol. 2, pp. 745–783. Lawrence Erlbaum Associates, Mahwah (2004)
23. Hattie, J., Timperley, H.: The power of feedback. Rev. Educ. Res. **77**(1), 81–112 (2007)

24. Narciss, S.: Designing and evaluating tutoring feedback strategies for digital learning environments on the basis of the interactive tutoring feedback model. Digit. Educ. Rev. **23**, 7–26 (2013)
25. Shute, V.J.: Focus on formative feedback. Rev. Educ. Res. **78**(1), 153–189 (2008)
26. Vasilyeva, E., Puuronen, S., Pechenizkiy, M., Rasanen, P.: Feedback adaptation in web-based learning systems. Int. J. Continuing Eng. Educ. Life Long Learn. **17**(4), 337–357 (2007)
27. Thurlings, M., Vermeulen, M., Bastiaens, T., Stijnen, S.: Understanding feedback: a learning theory perspective. Rev. Educ. Res. **9**, 1–15 (2013)
28. Butler, D.L., Winne, P.H.: Feedback and self-regulated learning: a theoretical synthesis. Rev. Educ. Res. **65**(3), 245–281 (1995)
29. Anohina, A., Grundspenkis, J.: Learner's support in the concept map based knowledge assessment system. In: Proceedings of the 7th European Conference on e-Learning, pp. 38–45. Academic Conferences Limited (2008)
30. Lukasenko, R., Anohina-Naumeca, A., Vilkelis, M., Grundspenkis, J.: Feedback in the concept map based intelligent knowledge assessment system. Sci. J. Riga Tech. Univ. Comput. Sci. **41**(1), 17–26 (2010)
31. Gouli, E., Gogoulou, A., Papanikolaou, K.A., Grigoriadou, M.: An adaptive feedback framework to support reflection, guiding and tutoring. In: Magoulas, G., Chen, S. (eds.) Advances in Web-Based Education: Personalized Learning Environments, pp. 178–202. Information Science Publishing, New York (2006)
32. Cook, B.G., Smith, G.J., Tankersley, M.: Evidence-based practices in education. In: Harris, K.R., Graham, S., Urdan, T. (eds.) APA Educational Psychology Handbook, vol. 1, pp. 495–528. American Psychological Association, Washigton, D.C. (2012)
33. Tamim, R.M., Bernard, R.M., Borokhovski, E., Abrami, P.C., Schmid, R.F.: What forty years of research says about the impact of technology on learning a second-order meta-analysis and validation study. Rev. Educ. Res. **81**(1), 4–28 (2011)

Model for Detecting Student Difficulties in Solving Formative Assessments

Camilo Castillo[1](✉), Néstor D. Duque[2], Andrés Salazar[2],
Valentina Tabares[2], and Demetrio A. Ovalle[1]

[1] Universidad Nacional de Colombia Sede Medellín, Medellín, Colombia
{cacastilloben,dovalle}@unal.edu.co
[2] Universidad Nacional de Colombia Sede Manizales, Manizales, Colombia
{ndduqueme,anfsalazarma,vtabaresm}@unal.edu.co

Abstract. From a previous review of state of art regarding to *formative e-assessment* is determined that researches are mainly addressed to learning environments and intended learning outcomes. Formative type takes advantage of both, peer review and teacher feedback. Teacher feedback when students are solving the assigned tasks has not been sufficiently explored because research has focused in contexts based on asynchronous learning technologies. Thus, in this paper is proposed a model aimed to enhance teacher feedback by means of synchronous detection of student difficulties during evaluation execution. The research experiment—composed by the model implementation and an evaluation questionnaire design—is focused on proving model capability for detecting difficulties. According to attained results is concluded that this model is able to detect early students difficulties when formative assessment is executed. The future work will be mainly addressed to propose a research for determining if the model can complement formative e-assessment environments.

Keywords: Learning technologies · Computer-assisted assessment · Formative e-assessment · Student difficulties detection · Evaluation execution · Time-assessment feedback

1 Introduction

Learning technology (LT) refers to a wide range of technologies that can be used to support learning, teaching and assessment [1–3]. In particular, the study of assessment processes taking advantage of capabilities offered by LT is known in the literature as Computer-Assisted Assessment (CAA) [4]. In this case CAA will be focused on *formative e-assessment*, i.e., the set of activities supported by LT that enable learners and teachers to monitor learning, and to use the information generated to align subsequent learning and teaching activities [5,6]. Regarding to formative e-assessment support LT arises as a powerful tool because feedback delivered by teachers may be enhanced *during* evaluation processes. However, a

© Springer International Publishing Switzerland 2015
P. Zaphiris and A. Ioannou (Eds.): LCT 2015, LNCS 9192, pp. 199–207, 2015.
DOI: 10.1007/978-3-319-20609-7_19

suitable feedback when the evaluation is being executed is subjected to capacity for fast detection of student difficulties [7].

This research is aimed to early detection of student difficulties when the assessment is performed. Early detection is important because feedback of teachers can be opportunely provided even in large groups of individuals [8]. As a result of proper feedback students speedily may correct misconceptions and thus, to be guided toward learning objectives. In this context, LT becomes an aid for detecting difficulties due to its capabilities for fast collecting and processing of evaluation information [5]. Hence, the information extraction gathered from the educational resources delivered to learners is streamlined, the fast processing lets expand feedback capacity of teachers while their workload is reduced, and assessment experience is improved by means of multimedia possibilities.

For early detection of difficulties when formative assessments are executed is necessary to take into account multidimensional issues [8,9]. We consider that among the most important of such issues are highlighted the next three: The identification of proper information to determine performance of students who are being evaluated, the methodologies definition for analyzing and processing of obtained data, and the most convenient selection of LT bearing in mind that hardware and web services are steadily lowering the price. It is also necessary to prevent difficulties caused by the inadequate task design and the usability of LT [10,11]. Although the CAA has been studied from multiple research approaches still remains a gap regarding to the opportune detection of difficulties associated to evaluation [12].

From a previous review of state of art regarding to formative e-assessment we can infer that research is mainly addressed to learning environments and intended learning outcomes [12,13]. Both, peer review and teacher feedback arise as support to reinforce the formative effects of assessment and learning. However, teacher guidance when students are solving the assigned tasks has not been sufficiently explored because research has focused in contexts based on asynchronous communications (e.g., via text or menu-driven systems). In document at hand is proposed a model aimed to detecting student difficulties within a context where feedback delivered by teacher may be supported by synchronous communications. For instance, we may refer to a context where teacher feedback is not suitable because formative task—subjected to fixed time and place—is being solved by a large number of students.

The model is divided into components that we have classified as the most relevant for evaluation development. On one hand, the component division enables to sample meaningful information throughout the evaluation process in order to detect student difficulties. On the other hand, from component-based approach can be independently dealt other key issues of the process, e.g., the requirements for establishing human computer interaction, the proper application of capabilities offered by LT, and the use of different educational resource kinds. According to attained results by means of an implementation we can infer that model is able to detect student difficulties when tasks are being solved. However, the proposed experiment in this paper is not adequate to determine if formative purposes are improved by feedback from teacher.

In previous paragraphs we have defined the research scope. The remainder of this work is organized as follows: in Sect. 2 is presented the conceptual model for detecting student difficulties when formative e-assessment is being performed. In Sect. 3 is proposed the research experiment by means of the model implementation and the questionnaire design of the test. In Sect. 4 are presented the experiment results and the work discussion. In Sect. 5 are made known the conclusions and the future research work.

2   Proposed Model

This model can be understood as a complement to traditional activities reported at formative e-assessment state of art. Bearing in mind the complexity associated to formative e-assessment process, for establishing a synergy between LT capabilities and evaluation is necessary to make use of modeling. Thus, in Fig. 1 is presented the proposed model for early detection of the learners difficulties when formative e-assessments are executed. The conceptual structure of the model is mainly constituted by three components: *teacher*, *evaluation* and *student*. Additionally, the model is complemented by including both a *module* that represents the source of educational resources and the teacher-student feedback *flow*.

Delivering of formative tasks and the continuous obtaining of apprentices responses are executed by the *student component*. When teacher assigns a new task this component handles its distribution among learners. Subsequently this part of the model must guarantee permanent interaction between the student and the assessment educational resource. From this interaction are periodically sampled each set of student responses entered to assigned tasks. Finally, answers are organized and delivered to evaluation component.

The condition of assessment is established by the *evaluation component* from the sampled student data. The performance of each student is determined by the comparison between collected answers and the task solution information. In this case the comparison term is used to allude the set of techniques implemented to determine the student performance. For example, some comparison-based algorithms are useful for reviewing closed question whereas semantic analysis algorithms are applied to open-ended questions [14]. After responses processing the obtained results are sent to the teacher component.

Summarizing, the processed data and the selection of educational resources are actions performed by the *teacher component*. On one hand, this component presents—in an understandable format for teacher—the outcomes that define the evaluation state. Therefore, based on LT capabilities, the information may be summarized by a proper interface design that would take advantage of color-based abstractions, percentages, images, among others. On the other hand, the teacher component provides the means to select the task type and the required responses for comparison process. For selecting tasks again the teacher interface is proposed as a convenient tool because it enables to set up a signal that contains the student list and the resource information.

Additionally, a representation of an educational resource source has been included in the model as a complement. A task assignment signal contains the

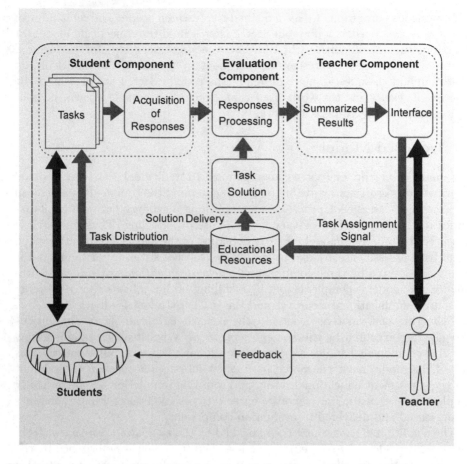

Fig. 1. Model proposed for early detection of the learner difficulties in formative e-assessments. The conceptual structure of the model is constituted by three components: *teacher*, *evaluation* and *student*.

identifiers of stored resources and the list of students tied to formative activity. In fact, when the signal is released towards the source, both the task and the task solution information are sent to the student and evaluation components, respectively. The source-based abstraction offers an advantage for implementing the model because it can be easily substituted, for example, the source may represent a repository that contains some learning objects addressed to formative e-assessment [15].

In short, the model performance is focused on maintaining a continuous information flow from the learner towards the tutor. Flow information is constructed using constant sampling of the student responses. The flow is completed when processed information is provided to the teacher for detecting and assisting of difficulties arisen from evaluation. Indeed, student attendance is improved because the teacher feedback is enriched by means of LT capabilities for processing data. In this case the feedback has been differentiated from the LT-based detection core for indicating that assistance may be applied in other contexts, e.g., face-to-face environments or virtual systems supported by synchronous tools.

3 Experiments

We have proposed an experiment aimed to prove the model capability for detecting student difficulties when formative e-assessments are performed. The experiment is mainly composed by the model implementation and the evaluation questionnaire design. Both are described below.

3.1 Model Implementation

The implementation is achieved by considering a set of technological tools that were selected bearing in mind the model components proposed. In Fig. 2 is presented the correspondence between the theoretical components and the implementation tool set. The model was initially implemented using three applications of Google: *Gmail, Drive* and *Sheets*. Additionally, an *Android mobile application* was developed by us for enabling system-teacher interaction.

In this case students use personal computers for interacting with the system, whereas teachers use a mobile device. The monitoring of assessments is initiated when application is linked to each task and then the functioning model described in Sect. 2 is followed. Regarding to the student component, questionnaires and answer acquisitions are enabled by means of spreadsheets. For comparison process the evaluation component is based on the power processing of a mobile device and the task solution information stored in a spreadsheet. Finally, the teacher component uses the application interface and a spreadsheet for representing the assessment summary by an abstraction based on color variations.

3.2 Questionnaire Development

The test consisted of ten questions. For assessment we select two types of questions: Multiple Choice Questions (MCQs) and Open-ended Questions. On one hand, we have considered the use of MCQs as a suitable assessment approach because computer capabilities can be utilized for rating the marked responses. In addition, MCQs provide a quantitative measurement regarding to student abilities and a wider scope of application for different kinds of content and objectives [16]. On the other hand, the use of open-ended questions is justified because these are excellent for measuring high level cognitive learning and overall subject understanding. These types of questions are often more applicable to real life situations.

Taking into account that feedback must improve assessment process, the evaluated concepts were interconnected by an increasingly difficulty level.

The feedback delivered during evaluation execution is aimed to correct the deficiencies and reinforce student concepts for subsequent questions. The test was carried out in a common physical place equipped with all LTs necessary for model application. In that way, when the system detects some student difficulty the teacher may deliver face to face feedback. This experiment matches with the situation mentioned in Sect. 2 where formative processes may be supported by synchronous tools.

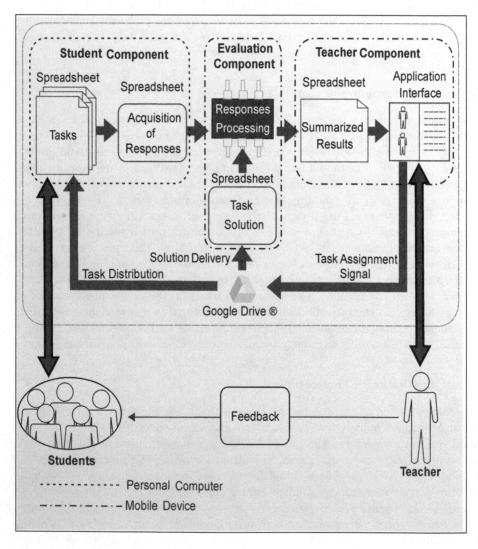

Fig. 2. Proposed model implementation. The model was implemented using three applications of Google: *Gmail*, *Drive* and *Sheets*. Additionally, an *Android mobile application* was developed for enabling system-teacher interaction.

4   Results

In Fig. 3, the results of the test are summarized. From the previously alluded questionnaire a four Colombian students group of final year of high school were evaluated. This questionnaire was designed to assess basics of differential calculus. Closed questions were formulated as quantitative response problems whereas open-ended questions were addressed to qualitative evaluation of concepts. In this case the questions 1, 2, 4 and 5 are open-ended type and the remaining ones are closed type.

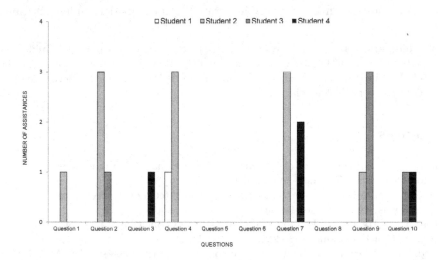

Fig. 3. Summary of the test results. Learning regarding to basics of differential calculus was evaluated in a four student group. For each question, the number of assists that required each student was counted. Questions 1, 2, 4 and 5 are open-ended type and the remaining ones are closed type.

The results show that all students needed support at least once. However, by means of model implementation it was possible to deliver the appropriate feedback during the evaluation time. The evaluated concepts interconnected by an increasingly difficulty level and the teacher feedback were useful for students who failed a question, to approve the subsequent one in almost all cases. Finally, the teacher may also use these results to identify the students who have difficulties that need to be reinforced.

5   Conclusions and Future Work

According to attained results we can conclude that model implementation is able to detect early the students difficulties when formative assessment is executed. However, determining if the model is useful as a complement to evaluation processes is beyond the scope of the posed test in document at hand. Therefore, the future work will be focused on proposing a research, aimed to determine if the model can complement formative e-assessment environments.

In addition, from multiple concepts—both theoretical and practical—concerning to the model proposed, we can explore other research fields. First of all, an inquiry field that would be worth to explore is the application of the model to enhance the group learning. Also the division by components offers an advantage for the model because the overall performance of the implementation can be enhanced by research independently performed in each of the model parts. For instance, a sophisticated semantic algorithm analysis for analysing open-ended questions may be easily integrated into the model implementation.

Acknowledgements. The research presented in this paper was partially funded by the Cyted project 513RT0481. It was also carried out under grants provided by the Ph.D. scholarship Programa Nacional de Formación de Investigadores "Becas Colciencias" 2012 funded by Colciencias.

References

1. Jonassen, D.H.: Handbook of Research on Educational Communications and Technology. Lawrence Erlbaum Associates, New Jersey (2004)
2. Liu, G.Z.: Innovating research topics in learning technology: Where are the new blue oceans? Br. J. Educ. Technol. **39**, 738–747 (2008)
3. Tsai, C.C., Hwang, G.J.: Issues and challenges of educational technology research in asia. Asia Pac. Educ. Res. **22**, 215–216 (2013)
4. Conole, G., Warburton, B.: A review of computer-assisted assessment. ALT-J. Res. Learn. Technol. **13**, 17–31 (2005)
5. Jisc: Effective Assessment in a Digital Age, UK (2010)
6. Pachler, N., Daly, C., Mor, Y., Mellar, H.: Formative e-assessment: practitioner cases. Comput. Educ. **54**, 715–721 (2010)
7. Ludwig-Hardman, S., Dunclap, J.C.: Learner support services for online students: scaffolding for success. Int. Rev. Res. Open Distance Learn. **4**, 1–15 (2003)
8. Wolsey, T.: Efficacy of instructor feedback on written work in an online program. Int. J. E-Learning **7**, 311–329 (2008)
9. Oosterhof, A., Conrad, R.M., Ely, D.P.: Assessing Learners Online. Pearson, New Jersey (2008)
10. Gaytan, J., McEwen, B.C.: Effective online instructional and assessment strategies. Am. J. Distance Educ. **21**, 117–132 (2007)
11. Hinze-Hoare, V.: The review and analysis of human computer interaction (HCI) principles. CoRR, vol. abs/0707.3638 (2007)
12. Stödberg, U.: A research review of e-assessment. Assess. Eval. Higher Educ. **37**, 591–604 (2012)
13. Gikandi, J.W., Morrow, D., Davis, N.E.: Online formative assessment in higher education: a review of the literature. Comput. Educ. **57**, 2333–2351 (2011)
14. Wang, H.C., Chang, C.-Y., Li, T.-Y.: Assessing creative problem-solving with automated text grading. Comput. Educ. **51**, 1450–1466 (2008)

15. Sánchez, S., García, E.: Haciendo Uso de Ontologías Superiores a Fomentar la Interoperabilidad Entre los Esquemas de Conceptos SKOS. Línea de Información de la opinión, pp. 263–277 (2006)
16. Centre for Teaching Excellence. https://uwaterloo.ca/centre-for-teaching-excellence/teaching-resources/teaching-tips/developing-assignments/assignment-design/designing-multiple-choice-questions

Enhancing the Learner's Performance Analysis Using SMEUS Semantic E-learning System and Business Intelligence Technologies

Fisnik Dalipi[✉], Sule Yildirim Yayilgan, and Zenun Kastrati

Faculty of Computer Science and Media Technology, Gjovik University College, Gjovik, Norway
{fisnik.dalipi,sule.yayilgan,zenun.kastrati}@hig.no

Abstract. Ontologies represent an efficient way of semantic web application on e-learning and offer great opportunity by bringing great advantages to e-learning systems. Nevertheless, despite the many advantages that we get from using ontologies, in terms of structuring the data, there are still many unresolved problems related to the difficulties about getting proper information about a learner's behavior. Consequently, there is a need of developing tools that enable analysis of the learner's interaction with the e-learning environment. In this paper, we propose a framework for the application of Business Intelligence (BI) and OLAP technologies in SMEUS e-learning environment. Hence, on one hand, the proposed framework will enable and support the decision-making by answering some questions related to learner's performance, and on the other hand, will present a case study model for implementing these technologies into a semantic e-learning environment.

Keywords: E-learning · SMEUS · Ontology · OLAP · Data analysis

1 Introduction

E-learning platforms are widely used by higher education and other research-oriented institutions to enhance the efficiency of institutional services related to teaching and learning, and to improve quality of teaching. Nowadays, many of the e-learning systems available on market lack in specific functionalities for the creation and delivery of dynamic, modular learning paths that match the knowledge needs in a contextualized (according to learner's current activities) and individualized (according to learner's experiences, competences profiles, learning history and personal preferences) way [1].

Ontologies represent an immense opportunity by bringing great advantages to e-learning systems. Their implementation is seen as a better solution for organizing and visualizing didactic knowledge, and for this knowledge to be shared and reused by different educational applications. The usage of ontology represents an efficient way of semantic web application on e-learning [2]. This is reflected on the realization of ontology-based description for the learning materials or the knowledge base. Additionally, semantic notations are added for each learning object. In terms of organizational aspect, ontology application allows the categorization of learning resources in personalized learning forms,

© Springer International Publishing Switzerland 2015
P. Zaphiris and A. Ioannou (Eds.): LCT 2015, LNCS 9192, pp. 208–217, 2015.
DOI: 10.1007/978-3-319-20609-7_20

which are being accessible to the students upon their request, depending on their profile and need to learn. In this way, the needed learning resources are easily identified, and the access time to the learning resources is reduced. Even though ontologies and semantic web can solve, among others, the process of structuring data in e-learning environments, yet there are many other problems to be addressed and solved. In order to support the innovation process in a e-learning platform on getting proper information about a learner's behavior, we extend our previous work [3] to apply business intelligence techniques to the SMEUS e-learning system. Accordingly, on one hand, the proposed framework will enable and support the decision-making by answering some questions related to learner's performance, and on the other hand, will present a case study model for implementing these technologies into a semantic e-learning environment. SMEUS is a semantic e-learning system that we have developed to focus on and address the issues of integrating ontological principles with e-learning standards, and to show how semantic concepts can bypass the problem with unstructured educational data and different techniques of knowledge representation.

The rest of the paper is organized as follows. Section 2 reviews about the related work. The process of designing the business intelligence solution and the connection with SMEUS is represented in Sect. 3. In Sect. 4 we provide some valuable results. Finally, we conclude the paper and give some future research issues in Sect. 5.

2   Related Work

The literature reports some works in order to solve mentioned problems in e-learning systems. Some tools such as MATEP [4], GISMO [5] and Sinergo/CoIAT [6] have been proposed. However, the researchers in these works are not incorporating any type of semantic aspects and BI tools to help track, measure and analyze the activities performed by learners. There are also some works performed on ontology and BI analytical applications in [7, 8] by implementing ontology to find appropriate data from different sources and semantically integrate the needed data into OLAP cube. Furthermore, tools like SBI [9], BIKM [10], SEWASIE [11] are worth mentioning.

There are also several case studies of using educational data mining in Moodle course management system to identify and analyze the learner's behavior. Authors in [12, 13] try to answer some of these questions by identifying related indicators and by offering tools that allow analysis and interpretation of results through data warehouse and OLAP technologies. To increase both efficiency of the university services related to teaching and learning and to improve its overall quality, they propose frameworks for applying business intelligence in e-learning platforms. Nevertheless, the authors provide models, which are out of the ontology based semantic web technologies scope and they lack to address the explicit definition of conceptualization on a specified domain and assembling learning objects.

3   Towards an BI Semantic Model

Semantic web supports the innovation process in a learning environment, having the property for data creation and management that are machine understandable. Semantic web also possess all the properties for creating and reusing the e-learning materials and contexts, enabling the enhancement of metadata linked with e-learning materials and expanding the current potentials of e-learning systems. The e-learning field involves many process resources, such as LOM (Learning Object Metadata), SCORM (Shareable Content Object Reference Model), RDF (Resource Description Framework), XML, OWL (Web Ontology Language), etc. LOM includes metadata for learning objects and represents a standard for educational management system and learning objects. Learning objects are digital contents or entities deliverable online, having the property of being reused in different contexts, for learning, education or training. Ontologies' usage in educational systems may be approached from various points of view: as a common vocabulary for multi-agent system, as a chain between heterogeneous educational systems, ontologies for pedagogical resources sharing or for sharing data and ontologies used to mediate the search of the learning materials on the Internet [14].

With regards to e-learning, semantic web ensures a technology where the learning object is [15]:

- *Described with metadata* – due to the distributed structure of RDF, description can be expanded and consequently new description can be added. This allows a creative use of content in a new way.
- *Annotated* – each identified resource by URI can be annotated with personal notes and links by everyone.
- *Extended* – the structured content with XML is allowing multiple versions to exist. Successive changes in the content can be executed with the help of RDF schemes, allowing private, grouped, or author versions of a certain document. The versions history is represented as a tree with known and unknown branches, which can be traversed with special version tools.
- *Shared and communicated* – to anyone who has expressed an interest in such content. Since the metadata are expressed with standard format, which is independent of basic schemes, even simpler applications can understand portions of complex RDF graphs.
- *Certified* – there is no reason why only big organizations should certify learning resources. Individuals, such as teachers, should certify learning contents as a qualitative learning resource, which is suitable for a certain educational work.

3.1   System Structure and Design

Our prototype SMEUS is developed to be used as an innovative system for knowledge retrieval and other e-learning aspects, including online testing. The system structure is presented in Fig. 1. As integral part of the system are design interface, system metadata, description of learning contents and learning methods. Within the interface design, we have developed special options for testing, online consulting and at the end, we propose a semantic representation of learning, by applying ontology. The semantic character of learning or the semantics of the learning object includes our proposal for describing learning materials within ontology domain. This provides us with a semantic representation of the content by adding semantic notation to each learning resource. The ontology is used for identifying the structure of learning module and defining the needed vocabulary for the student to conceptualize the learning modules. Another ontological approach is introduced for learning materials, which is part of the systems metadata. Here, we included also the system access alternatives, results registering and the communications.

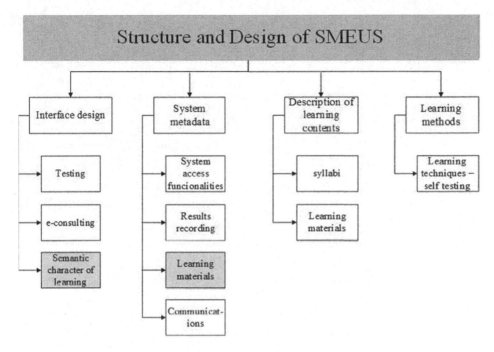

Fig. 1. System access functionalities

The section with description of learning contents includes some options where we store syllabi of subjects and learning materials. The learning method section includes self-testing for students, which is an option of preparation for them before they are subject to the real examination.

With SMEUS we aim to go beyond limitations that some e-learning application have. The semantic learning character class includes the knowledge of learning theory, language, scientific discipline, auxiliary technology, etc. Each of these can be connected in many ways with fields of ontological modeling. If we consider the scientific discipline, the content here is distinguished by type and level. In the content type, we may have: rules, processes, procedures, concepts, etc. whereas in the content level, there may appear the levels of content complexity, i.e. basic, average and advanced level.

In order to focus the learning expectations or results towards the improvement of understanding the learning material, the learning models, goals and contents should be structured or defined with an adequate pedagogical methodology. Regarding the auxiliary technologies, they support the presentation technique of learning contents with different technology, such as, ontologies, metadata and learning object warehouses (see Fig. 2).

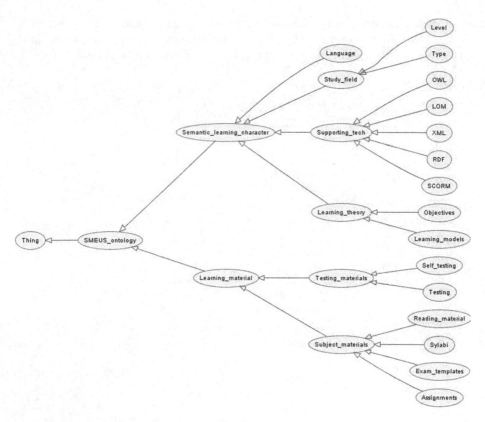

Fig. 2. SMEUS ontology

3.2 Designing the BI Solution

The objective of a business intelligence process is to refine business data and information into useful and valuable knowledge and intelligence for decision making [16, 17]. There are several proposed definitions in the literature about process steps and models in implementing BI. However, in this work we follow the idea proposed by [18], who proposes a lifecycle model as shown in Fig. 3. The first activity to create a BI solution is the requirement specifications phase. In this phase, a document is produced with example analytical questions and desired reports that would provide the needed elements for building the data warehouse schema. This document involves questions related to the time students are spending to read or view learning materials, which learning resource they like to visit and use more, how often they use collaboration tools etc. The second step or activity is dimensional modeling. This encapsulates designing a dimensional schema, which is based on the analysis of business requirements and consists of a central fact table and its related dimensions.

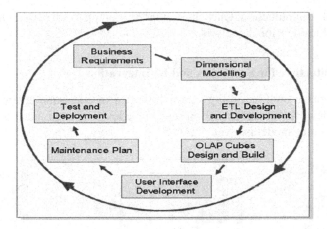

Fig. 3. BI lifecycle [18]

An example of a developed schema in our project is shown in Fig. 4, which contains details about learning activities.

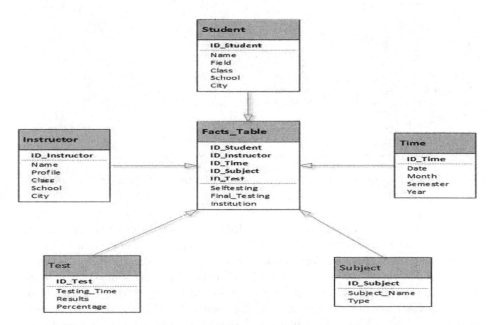

Fig. 4. Facts table schema

After the dimensional schema is designed, we start and define the development of ETL (Extract-Transform-Load) processes. During this phase, we also apply common data preprocessing tasks such as data cleaning, user identification, session identification, path completion, transaction identification, data transformation and enrichment, data integration and data reduction. Once these steps are completed, we use SQL Server BI edition for multidimensional analysis.

3.3   An Architecture for Semantics and BI Integration

In order to increase both flexibility and performance of e-learning environments, we propose a framework for applying BI in semantic e-learning environments. The workflow scenario of our model is given in Fig. 5.

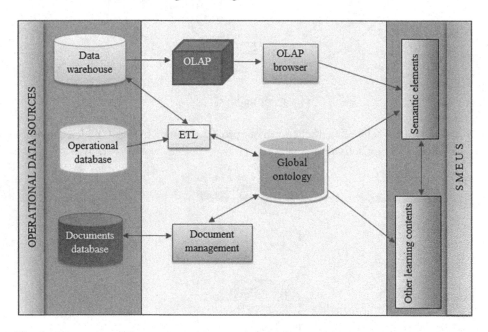

Fig. 5. Proposed workflow scenario for semantics and BI integration in e-learning environment

This model is based on the idea of web-based systems that integrate two information sources: (1) from OLAP browser, which extracts data from data warehouse, and (2) from the document management system, which enables access to the unstructured data in documents database. Considering the sensitive nature of the educational data in terms of privacy, especially those from the testing results, the heterogeneous character of the data on one hand, and to keep the global ontology updated on the other hand, we propose that ETL process to be executed two times. Firstly, for data warehouse creation and secondly, prior to integrating data into the global ontology. The process of data extraction and access control for the documents will be coordinated from the document management system, which will support RDF based metadata, thus, we use the global ontology.

The global ontology, which is an indispensable part in our model, contains the global data model and the mappings of metadata from document management system and metadata that are generated during the second process of ETL. In addition, it includes other information about learning objects. Many of the objects that are located in educational data warehouses are used for extracting various documents of the same nature. These objects can easily be created or updated; even at the first ETL process, prior to the data warehouse creation.

4   Results

Based on the suggested analytical questions that were established in the first step of the BI lifecycle, we generate several reports that would help us to answer them. We examined and analyzed the activity of 865 students over the 15 week spring semester of 2014. The conducted research provide instructors various reports related to different aspects of the learners/students behavior, by giving them the possibility of assessing learner's performance and progress. These reports using the proposed model provide information for different aspects of the student behavior, such as, the time they spend for reading or viewing learning materials online, participation in online collaborative activities and virtual classrooms, information on how frequently students do online self-testing, read and write messages, etc.

By referring to these reports, part of which are demonstrated in Fig. 6, we can conclude that 86 % of student spend their time with reading or viewing materials, but the majority of them is using this option at the end of the semester or before the exam session. Concerning the participation to collaborative activities, such as forums and messaging, on average more than 69 % are using this application, and this option is most heavily is used during weekdays. Around 14 % of students spend less than 30 min a week with online testing within the first weeks, and this percentage increased in weeks to come. During the 10th week of the semester, around 73 % use online testing, and in remaining 5 weeks this percentage grows to 87 %.

This explains the fact that as the exam session is approaching, students become more aware for their preparation and try to do online self-testing more frequently. From the teacher's perspective, by using such information, they can adopt different learning methodology of uniform distribution of teaching assignments during the semester to improve performance of students in terms of avoiding the accumulation of student's works or activities for the end of semesters.

The results of our study will give the teachers the availability to assess and track even more the student performance and to monitor the existence of certain user activity trends, for instance when to expect to have more participants in virtual classrooms, more online tests, discussions in forums, exchanged messages, etc. Hence, it is also easily to predict when to consider the system maintenance.

5   Conclusions and Future Works

In this paper, we presented an approach of application of BI tools in semantic e-learning systems to analyze and monitor the learner's behavior and performance. The ontology we presented is used to design an e-learning system and to play a significant role in representing different educational concepts. Our framework demonstrate the idea how

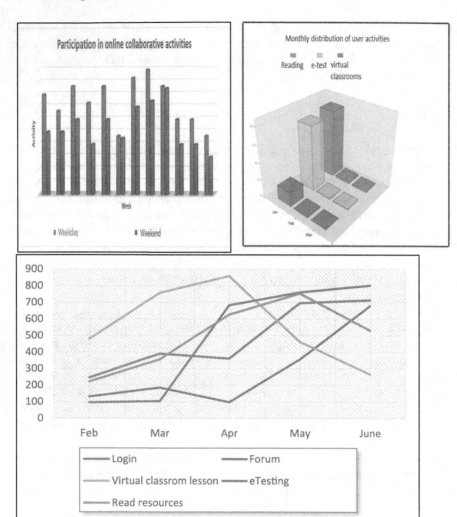

Fig. 6. Different generated reports

ontology or semantic concepts can bypass the problem with unstructured data, and different techniques of knowledge representation; and the idea of solving the lack of analytical and reporting tools in LMS, providing the instructor with detailed reports about students progression and performance.

In the future, by enlarging the number of students involved in this analytical study, we consider applying data mining techniques to extract more patterns and rules to enhance our analysis on learner's performance. In addition, having in mind that BI solutions have started to advance into the Cloud, we plan to adopt and extend SMEUS to be a semantic and cloud-based business intelligence solution.

References

1. Zilli, A., et al.: Semantic Knowledge Management: An Ontology-Based Framework. IGI Global, Hershey (2009)
2. Sanchez, M., Breis, J., Sanchez, J., Espinosa, P.: Practical experiences for the development of educational systems in the semantic web. New Approaches Educ. Res. **2**(1), 23–31 (2013)
3. Dalipi F., Idrizi F., Rufati E., Asani F.: On integration of ontologies into e-learning systems. In: Proceedings of the 6th IEEE International Conference on Computational Intelligence, Communication Systems and Networks, Tetovo, Macedonia (2014). ISBN 978-1-4799-5076-8
4. Zorilla, M.E., Alvarez, E.: MATEP: Monitoring and analysis tool for e-learning platforms. In: 8th IEEE International Conference on Advanced Learning Technologies, Santander, Spain (2008)
5. GISMO. http://sourceforge.net/directory/os:windows/freshness:recently-updated/?q=GISMO. Accessed 28 September 2014
6. Avouris, N., et al.: Logging of fingertip actions is not enough for analysis of learning activities. In: Proceedings of Workshop Usage Analysis in learning systems, Amsterdam (2005)
7. Toivonen, S., Niemi, T.: Describing data sources semantically for facilitating efficient creation of OLAP cubes. In: 3rd International Semantic Web Conference (ISWC2004), Hiroshima, Japan, November 2004
8. Priebe, T., Pernul, G.: Ontology-based integration of OLAP and information retrieval. In: The DEXA 2003 Workshop on Web Semantics, Prague, Czech Republic, September 2003
9. Sell, D., et al.: SBI: A semantic framework to support business intelligence. In: ACM Proceedings of the First International Workshop on Ontology-Supported Business Intelligence, OBI 2008, Karlsruhe, Germany (2008)
10. Cody, W.F., Kreulen, J.T., Krishna, V., Spangler, W.S.: The integration of business intelligence and knowledge management. IBM Syst. J. **41**(4), 697–713 (2002)
11. Bergamaschi, S., Quix, C., Jarke, M.: The SEWASIE EU IST project. SIG SEMIS Bull. **2**(1), 59–69 (2005)
12. Nebic, Z; Mahnic, V. Data warehouse for an e-learning platform. In: Proceedings of the 14th WSEAS International Conference on Computers: Part of the 14th WSEAS CSCC multiconference, vol. II (2010)
13. Falakmasir, M.H., Moaven, S., Abolhassani, H., Habibi, J.: Business intelligence in e-learning (case study on the Iran university of science and technology dataset). In: SEDM 2010 2nd International Conference on Software Engineering and Data Mining, Chengdu, China, June 2010
14. Cakula, Sarma, Salem, Abdel-Badeeh M.: E-learning developing using ontological engineering. WSEAS Trans. Inf. Sci. Appl. **10**(1), 1–13 (2013)
15. Naeve, A., Nilsson, M., Palmer, M.: E-learning in the semantic age. CID, Centre For User Oriented It Design, Stockhom (2001)
16. Pirttimäki, V. Business intelligence as a managerial tool in large Finnish companies. (Doctoral dissertation). TUT DPub, Tampere University of Technology, Publication 646 (2007)
17. Sangar, A.B., Iahad, N.B.A.: Critical factors that affect the success of business intelligence systems (BIS) implementation in an organization. Int. J. Sci. Technol. Res. **2**(2), 176–180 (2013)
18. Zorrilla, M.E.: Data warehouse technology for e-learning. In: Zakrzewska, D., Menasalvas, E., Byczkowska-Lipinska, L. (eds.) Methods and Supporting Technologies for Data Analysis. SCI, vol. 225, pp. 1–20. Springer, Heidelberg (2009)

Creation of Meaningful-Learning and Continuous Evaluation Education System

Habib M. Fardoun[1]([⊠]), Abdullah Albarakati[1],
and Antonio Paules Ciprés[2]

[1] Faculty of Computing and Information Technology, Information Systems
Department, King Abdulaziz University, Jeddah 21589, Saudi Arabia
{hfardoun, aaalbarakati}@kau.edu.sa
[2] EduQTech Group, Escuela Universitaria Politecnica,
University of Zaragoza, Teruel, Spain
apcipres@gmail.com

Abstract. This paper is based on the principal bases defined in the theory of communication of McLuhan and the principles of David Ausubel. We want to propose a system that allows teachers to perform a methodology based on meaningful learning and a continuous evaluation system. We take McLuhan's theory of communication as a process of creating curricular programs and turn the theory of knowledge into one based on meaningful learning. Therefore we perform a methodology to be explored by students, and teachers could develop their work through exploration within the teaching-learning process.

Keywords: Educative systems · Cloud computing · Web Services · Systems architecture · Students curriculum · Educative curricula

1 Introduction

In this paper we describe an adaptation of McLuhan [2]. So we proceed from the need of teachers for a process of evaluation and for qualification in new methods, and through the exploration of student work within a system of continuous evaluation. The following sentence is the reason we decided to start this research: *"I do not explain anything. I explore"*.

The work and ideas of Herbert Marshall McLuhan (1911–1980) obtain more force and effect in science communication and social behavior within the framework of the mass media with each passing day. His most notable works are *The Gutenberg Galaxy* (1962), *The Global Village* (1989) and essays such as "Joyce, Mallarmé and the Press" or "Laws of the Media", all included in the McLuhan anthology. *Essential Writings* (1998), and *The Gutenberg Galaxy* popularized his ideas about the media, and for McLuhan, the culture that is just based on the book has been completed.

A premise of education is that it must adapt it to its society; we hear from the media companies' terminologies such as Society 2.0 and Society 3.0, based on the definition of information systems. In this research we aim to use these societies by following McLuhan and communication technologies adapted to the educational world. Thus we have developed a specific and concrete methodology based on technological influences

© Springer International Publishing Switzerland 2015
P. Zaphiris and A. Ioannou (Eds.): LCT 2015, LNCS 9192, pp. 218–226, 2015.
DOI: 10.1007/978-3-319-20609-7_21

and the transmission of content. That is, the classroom becomes a transfer of content, and use McLuhan teaching-learning sentences:

- "The medium is the message".
- "Restructuring of the contents".
- "In a pre-alphabetic world, words are not signs."
- "We return to the acoustic space".

Also, we must consider student assessment and personalized follow-up. The teaching methodology uses these premises to improve the student's work in the classroom. Thus through the acquisition of knowledge, it can be argued that by receiving meaningful learning as taught by David Ausubel [2], meaningful learning becomes focused. For this reason we use a translation of McLuhan as the basis of self-sufficient reception learning. Thus, we will use the full potential of students and information technology.

2   State of the Art

We have to consider the creation of this platform from two points of view: (1) from the viewpoint of the teachers' work in preparing classroom activities; and (2) from the students' evaluation process of exploring the objectives achieved in the contents developed by the student through meaningful learning. According to McLuhan, the influence of communication technologies on the content they transmit is a wholly generic synthesis of thought. McLuhan's theory is based on the laws of communication [1] and patterns of communication [3]:

- The medium is the message: McLuhan adopts the concept elaborated by anthropology, according to which instruments and tools are considered to have been created as extensions of the human body. Now everything is immediate, reproducible, and combinable; there is no longer a place for everything and a time for every event. The time and space make the means for us, but also we ourselves are able to manipulate them.
- Restructuring of the Contents: Our perceptions have shaped the way we understand and think. These effects are so important that they cause distinct stages in culture. From here, McLuhan, in a historical perspective, describes three eras of humanity, which are: oral communication, written communication, and the electronic or global village.
- In a pre-alphabetic world words are not signs. This refers to the first stage of humanity, an era in which the only means for the transmission of messages is the spoken word. There are no procedures for the storage of information beyond human memory. Humans of the pre-alphabetic era had a world-view that placed great importance on the sense of hearing. The ear prevailed over vision, which created a conception of an inclusive world. With alphabetic writing came a move from a culture based on oral, direct communication, favoring an emotional type relationship, to another in which abstract rationality prevails. It is a visual activity, not only hypertrophying the sense of sight, but also distorting the harmony of the proportions

of the five senses. The written culture has unstructured relationships that kept the senses different. McLuhan wants to highlight that texts favor abstract rationality, seeing things and the world as a process, the ability to discern and classify those complex units, used first, within the group.

- We return to the acoustic space: time and space merge into the current physical on a space-time continuum, which brings us to the notion that humans cultures had in past, and still maintain communities not influenced by Western culture. Audiovisual media require the presence of transmitters and receivers in two spaces, but not in a time unit. Written communication does not require either temporary ownership or space, and fosters an enabling environment of abstraction. Broadly speaking, the main feature is that it relies on involvement, simultaneity, discontinuity, and space-time, and tends to develop at work by defragmentation and political participation by television. It should also be noted that it imposes a new electronic interdependence and a new concrete and immediate relationship, which not only detribalize, but also recreate the world in the image of a global village.
- I do not seek, I find: it is precisely the ability to see reality as multisensory that McLuhan proposed as a mechanism. The tetrad, taken as a whole, is the manifestation of how the human mind operates. This is similar to the semantic mechanism that makes the trope known as metaphor. This provides the shifting of a hidden background to the foreground of perception. The scientist, immersed in the visual world (sequential, linear, logical) asks questions concerned with reality and acts consistently. Conversely, the browser enters an area of complexity, not knowing what to find. It cannot have a logical plan of discovery. It must be delivered into the complexity with all senses alert.

Once we have described the usefulness of the media, we must first think of a teacher as a communicator. In addition, we must apply this methodology to other developing methodologies of teaching in the classroom. In this case we turn to the didactic methodology of David Ausubel, meaningful learning. In meaningful learning, ideas are substantially related to what students already know, and new knowledge is closely linked to the previous ways it is used to be performed by:

- The learning content is potentially significant, i.e. it must be able to be learned significantly.
- The student must already have the concepts used in a preformed cognitive structure. Thus, in this way the new knowledge can be linked to the previous one. Otherwise, the assimilation fails.
- The student must demonstrate a positive attitude toward meaningful learning. They must demonstrate a willingness to relate the learning material to cognitive structures that they already have.

Meaningful learning requires finding out what the students and teachers know already, which determines the working of the methodological strategy, but not the purpose, content or sequence of the curriculum.

3 Application and Adaptation of the Methodology

At this point we will try to give an overview of what type of methodology would be necessary to use McLuhan's theories for meaningful learning. On the one hand we establish the basis for a theory of knowledge and meaningful learning. The process of learning is based on information technologies. Therefore we adapt the phases and the teaching-learning process of McLuhan, as we have an amply demonstrated starting point, discussed and dealt with in the world of communications. McLuhan's phases must follow some specific steps within the child's process of learning, and must be adapted first to the educational environment and analyzed within the whole educational world. In this case, moving the steps or phases that McLuhan sets within the educational system will allow for meaningful learning. The steps we have to take into account are:

- **The medium is the message:** we need to create a system that is an extension of the classical teacher's notebook, which picks up his notes and the classroom activities, centralizes his administration, and also enables a communication channel for the teacher with parents, students, other teachers, and other members of the educational community.
- **Restructuring of Content:** The work of teachers and students towards meaningful learning leads to the creation of content. Therefore the work on the content must be allowed to modify through a system that allows the creation of content from content made before, which is a time-saver for teachers.
- **In a pre-alphabetic world, words are not signs:** At the present time and in the present educational world, educational content focused on the internet is a given; society has advanced in some points of view from the book. For years the only educational content at the disposal of both teachers and students was textbooks and teachers' notes, but now we all know this has changed.
- **We return to the acoustic space:** The transmission of the content in this case is done from three points: on one hand the teacher transmits the content, and the student learns from that content; this entails a relationship with the outside world which is implemented by the ICT and communication with other students; thus we have to emphasize improving collaborative work in the classroom and facilitate this type of work in the classroom.
- **I do not seek, I find:** In this section we understand that teachers and students develop their work to meet their needs on the internet. This is done through an initial search and easy navigation through the material. On the other hand the teacher performs an evaluation process by scanning the contents.

Adaptations or creations of methodological aspects need to be moved to ICT. That is, ICT methodologies for educational environments are necessary for the teaching-learning process, and also to present curriculum content, students' work, and integration. A methodological adaptation requires a process of previous research. As seen in the above description, we need a system that allows us to develop different parts of the required methodology, and also allows an operation in ICT environments.

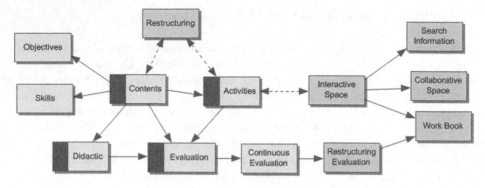

Fig. 1. Teaching-learning process diagram

In Fig. 1, the green color shows the different parts of the teaching-learning process; these parts have been worked on in previous research [5, 7, 8]. The educational contents are structured and cataloged to order achieve aims and educational skills. From these' contents, work activities are performed, correcting these teaching contents. Evaluations of activities within a continuous evaluation process are necessary elements for the teaching-learning process. That is, we need documentation of educational content and organization of the work, as done by the teacher [4]. In this way, teachers have a system that allows them to manage educational content based on the teaching-learning process.

As we can see, the process of evaluation in the teaching-learning process is performed continuously throughout the process. This requires restructuring of the evaluation process. We need to modify the teachers' workbook according to the students' work in their notebooks, and in turn restructure the students' activities in terms of their progress in achieving the objectives and the basic skills. These are evaluated in the activities of the students, and, as we have developed in other research, this is achieved by treating the educational curriculum as part of the curriculum or history of student learning [5, 6]. The curriculum and the educational curriculums of the students are fully linked, as students develop their curriculums to arising from curriculum education laws. This also involves the modification of both the activities prepared by the teacher and of the exercises and the work done by students.

4   Design Patterns

We have described the adaptation or creation of teaching methodology, justified by prestigious authors and including the use of ICT, where the method and methodology in developing a formula that allows the inclusion of ICT in the classroom-to-classroom education curriculum is implemented [7].

In this section we discuss design patterns. This is done from the point of view of the structure of these design patterns as developed in the thesis [8], where patterns are developed. In this first application of the method, we develop patterns generically, by indicating a first group and then from discussion and debate in scientific forums developing the contents thereof. This can be done because of our research background in the application of ICTs to the classroom. In this methodology we have isolated the following patterns:

- **Curricular Patterns:** These patterns are responsible for establishing the relationship between the different elements of the teaching-learning process. These are focused with the aim of establishing the evaluation of the student in the process. This pattern also includes necessary elements that are defined by the contents, activities and evaluative elements, including objectives and competencies. These elements have a relationship with each other in defining the evaluation, making it an evaluation rather than a memo. It will be well-defined according to the score of each of the parties, evaluating the students through the level of achievement of each of the objectives of each of the core competencies. These are not patterns; they are statements of curricular pattern corresponding to the evaluation. In this way we can modify the states over time, taking into account the parameters defined above for the group of students in the teacher's programming. Setting the minimum and maximum for the students to perform allows for paying attention to diversity in the case of students who do not meet the minimum or are above the maximum, thus serving students who are above or below the level of achievement of objectives.
- **Restructuring Pattern:** This pattern makes a break in the process of teaching and learning. Thus the teacher can make a modification of the process. It is a pattern that performs a state change in the curriculum pattern, and thus achieves a curriculum adaptation or modification to enhance the strengths and weaknesses of students. In addition, it allows the achievement of the objectives.
- **Interaction Pattern:** These patterns are intended for the creation and modification of activities for teachers. Additionally, this should facilitate collaborative work in the classroom and internet search information by students. As a result, this facilitates the consultation of information that teachers leave prepared for the performance of their activities. These interaction patterns are also used to edit the objects with which students and teachers work together in the classroom with patterns to share information, to add specific objects to other objects' modification, and to provide educational objects and patterns designed to share information among members of the class and the teacher.

Educational patterns are focused on areas that teachers need to do their work in the classroom. In this way we combine and integrate these patterns into an architecture that supports these features.

5 System Architecture

Cloud systems allow the integration of services and functionality in a single workspace. The users can develop their work and the system allows flexibility and growth according to the appearance of new features. These aspects make cloud systems ideal for inclusion in application platforms and educational environments, as these require a multitude of services that allow their proper functioning, and the system can develop according to new situations and the requirements of teachers.

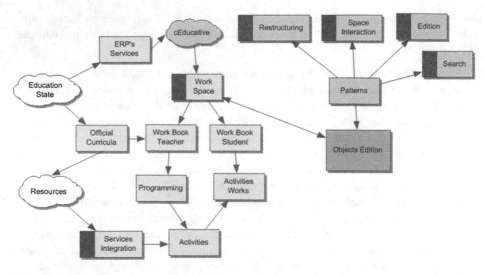

Fig. 2. System architecture

Curriculum systems in the cloud are a reality. Where some research give the integration of various systems in the cloud [8], it is possible to integrate environments defining these new services and educational methods within the systems themselves.

Figure 2 shows how the system allows integration with other systems, in this case by integration of services, which allows access to the systems that provide the resources, linked and indexed with the official curricula. From the organizational point of view, integration is important for creating users with educational ERPs within public administrations. The Web Services can perform this integration of different systems, which is by specifying a standard allowing the integration of these systems. The cloud "cEducative" is the core of this research; this cloud defines a workspace for users of the system, in this case teachers and students. Teachers conduct their activities from the workbook that includes programming, which consists of activities and curriculum elements as defined above. These activities comprise the student workbook, in which students solve problems and work with activities by editing patterns. An important aspect is the user interaction in classroom-to-classroom education. We define a space of interaction for users, in which, from patterns and editing of objects, students can perform collaborative work in the classroom, and editing these objects leads to the successful completion of the relevant activities [9, 10].

We are therefore faced with the same system, where the interaction takes place between the devices themselves that make up the micro cloud. Figure 3. Shows the different parts that make up this architecture. Figure 3 shows the different parts that compose that architecture.

We conducted a hybrid cloud on the device that consists of the following parts. On one side, there is all the logic storage, where, through a database SQL Linte for mobile devices, this database performs database operations. On the other side we have a storage repository for objects, which can store either objects in XML format or the serialized object itself, and a file system for the application where the necessary files

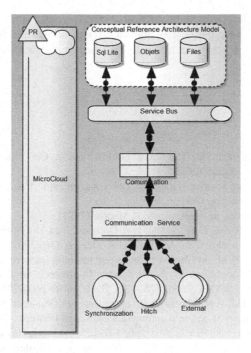

Fig. 3. System architecture in the micro-cloud

would be stored. The communication service comprises a programming package. This receives data from the device itself and tails synchronization and external engagement. These queues allow processing of information in the device asynchronously or synchronously, depending on the type of information being processed. The sternal queue receives data from other devices that make up the cloud micro, and should have a higher priority to allow interaction between devices in the micro cloud and the passing of information to each other.

These services facilitate communication device interaction in the cloud and allow its use in classroom education. The need to treat these devices independently facilitates the creation of activities by students and staff working in the classroom. It also simplifies the maintenance process and the integration with other devices, such as tablets, computers, or smart TV, which pupils and teachers may have at their fingertips.

6 Conclusions and Future Work

In this article we have adapted a method using ICT, as we have seen the necessity of adapting a method not using ICT to take ICT into account. This will allow us to further integrate these systems and also enable them to be used by members of the educational community more intuitively and to apply them more closely to the reality of their work, because sometimes teachers do not have the applications that allow certain methodologies, or that allow them to suit their own methodology.

Future work will be the creation of a distributed system interface that allows this architecture to make these patterns in the cloud, and allows the flow of information between the various objects that make up the activity regardless of which user is working on the object.

References

1. McLuhan, M., McLuhan, E.: Las leyes de los medios. CIC Cuad. de Información y Comunicación **14**, 285–316 (2009)
2. Ausubel, D.P.: Adquisición y retención del conocimiento. Una perspectiva cognitive. Editorial Paidós, Barcelona (2002)
3. Galeano, E.C.: Modelos de comunicación. Macchi (1997)
4. Díaz-Barriga, A.F., Rojas, G.H.: Estrategias Docentes Para Un Aprendizaje Significativo. Una Interpretación Constructivta. McGraw-Hill, México, DF (2002)
5. Paules, A., Fardoun, H.M., Mashat, A.: Cataloging teaching units: resources, evaluation and collaboration. In: Proceedings of the Federated Conference on Computer Science and Information Systems, SCOPUS, pp. 825–830. Thomson Reuters (2012)
6. Fardoun, H.M., Altalhi, A.H., Ciprés, A.P.: Improvement of students curricula in educational environments by means of online communities and social networks. In: Ozok, A., Zaphiris, P. (eds.) OCSC 2013. LNCS, vol. 8029, pp. 147–155. Springer, Heidelberg (2013)
7. Fardoun, H.M., Paules, A., Jambi, K.M.: Educational currículum management on rural environment. Elsevier Procedia Soc. Behav. Sci. **122**, 421–427 (2014)
8. Altalhi, A.H., Cipres, A.P.: ICT didactic system for a successful student curricula. Int. Mag. Adv. Comput. Sci. Telecommun. **4**(2), 27–35 (2013)
9. Fardoun, H.M.: eLearniXML: Towards a model-based approach for the development of e-learning systems (Doctoral dissertation, Universidad de Castilla La Mancha) (2011)
10. Paules, C.A.: TabletNet un sistema curricular en la Nube (Doctoral dissertation, Universidad Europea de Madrid) (2014)

A Computational Model to Determine Desirability of Events Based on Personality for Performance Motivational Orientation Learners

Somayeh Fatahi[1,2], Hadi Moradi[1,3(✉)], and Ali Nouri Zonoz[1]

[1] School of Electrical and Computer Engineering, University of Tehran, Tehran, Iran
{Moradih,AliNouriZonoz}@ut.ac.ir
[2] Department of Computer Science, Dalhousie University, Halifax, Canada
Somayeh.Fatahi@dal.ca
[3] Intelligent Systems Research Institute, SKKU, Seoul, South Korea

Abstract. One of the most important discussions in artificial intelligence is the modeling of human behaviors in virtual environments. The factors such as personality, emotion, and mood are important to model human behaviors. In this paper, we propose a computational model to calculate a user's desirability as one of the most important factors which in determining the user's emotions. The main purpose of this research is to find a relationship between personality and emotion in virtual learning environments. The model has been evaluated in a simulated virtual learning environment and the results show that the proposed model formulates the relationship between personality and emotions with high precision.

Keywords: Personality · Emotion · User's status · Desirability

1 Introduction

The goal of Human Computer Interaction (HCI) is to make computing systems more useful and usable. To achieve this goal, computer interfaces should be able to recognize and track users' behaviors (Zeng et al. 2009). Identifying a user's status enables machines to understand his/her needs and react to them accordingly (Trabelsi and Frasson 2010). Until now, several studies have been carried out to consider human characteristics in human computer interaction. Rosis and his colleagues (2003) implemented a 'realistic' 3D embodied agent called Greta. The affective components of personality and emotions were located in the agent's mind component. This component simulated how emotions are triggered and decayed over time based on the agent's personality. Egges and his colleagues (2004) implemented a generic model for personality, mood, and emotions in a conversational virtual humans. The model could update the emotion and mood considering the history of emotion and mood using linear regression. Also, Mehdi and his colleagues (2004) attempted to develop a model that comprises emotion, mood, and personality factors. The model considers personality as a parameter that defines the threshold of the appearance of emotions and mood as a filter for moderating the intensity of the emotions. They applied the model in a virtual reality training

© Springer International Publishing Switzerland 2015
P. Zaphiris and A. Ioannou (Eds.): LCT 2015, LNCS 9192, pp. 227–237, 2015.
DOI: 10.1007/978-3-319-20609-7_22

tool for firemen. The results show that the fireman agent can reproduce the stress emotion felt in a real emergency fire incident. Moshkina (2006) presented an integrative behavior framework for affective agent called TAME. TAME combined personality traits, attitudes, mood, and emotions to generate affective behaviors. Moshkina evaluated the TAME framework in a human-robot application. The results show that affective behavior provides many benefits such as ease of use and pleasantness of interaction. In 2008, Dang and Duhau (2008) proposed a generic model called GRACE (Generic Robotic Architecture to Create Emotions). They combined the OCC model and Lazarus-Scherer theory for its emotion component, and used MBTI for its personality component. In this model, the intensity of an emotion is related to the personality type. Fatahi and her colleague (2010) designed a model of personality and emotion that was used in an E-learning framework. The results of the model evaluation showed that the presence of the intelligent agents with same features as humans increases the learning rate. Santos and his colleagues (2011) used artificial intelligence agents that have personality, emotion, and mood in a group decision-support system. Their goal was to improve the negotiation process through argumentation using the affective characteristics of the involved participants. Kazemifard and his colleagues (2011) presented a new computational emotional model that maps the environmental events and agents' actions into emotional states to generate human like decision-making behavior. Hwang and Lee (2013) used Fuzzy Cognitive Map (FCM) to represent causal relationships between a user's personality and the target system. They ran several scenarios in which they showed that a user's personality has relation to the personality of the target system. In addition, FCM helped them to predict a human's personality but they didn't consider the human's emotion.

It could be observed that all of the recent researches focus on modeling the emotion and personality in artificial intelligence agents by using FFM as a personality model. Most of previous studies did not use computational modeling in their researches, however there was some studies which used the computational modeling, but they was not able to identify and predict user's neither the emotion nor personality.

The novel contribution of this study is in proposing a computational model to predict users' emotions based on his/her personality. We presented and evaluated this computational model, which uses the OCC and MBTI models, in a virtual E-learning environment which showed desirable performance.

2 Psychological Principles

2.1 Emotion

Many studies have proven that emotion affects reasoning, memorizing, learning and decision-making (Damasio 1994; Chaffar et al. 2007; Kort and Reilly 2001). Also, these studies show that the learner's emotional state influences his/her performance and it is an important factor in learning environments so should be considered in user modeling (Chaffar and Frasson 2004).

There are many psychological model for emotion modeling in computer science. One of the most famous of these is the OCC model (Ortony et al. 1988) that is employed in many studies. It is a computational emotion model that applied in artificial characters. The OCC model has three branches. The first branch includes the emotions which are consequences of the events faced. These consequences are obtained according to the desirability or undesirability level of the events compared to the agents' goals. The second branch includes the emotions that are results of agent actions based on approving or disapproving relative to a set of standards. The third branch consists of emotions that are the consequences of the agent's which either like or dislike his/her goals compared to the agent's position and attitude. The OCC model calculates intensity of emotions based on a set of variables. The variables are divided into two groups: global and local. One of the most important variable to calculate first branch emotions is desirability. In this research we use the OCC model and we try to calculate desirability variable based on finding its relationship with personality dimensions.

2.2 Personality

Personality comprises thoughts, feelings, desires and behavioral tendencies that exist in every person (Hartmann 2006). Each psychologist presents a different classification of personality based on his/her research. Jung's type theory specifies three dimensions: Extraversion/Introversion (E/I); Sensing/Intuition (S/N) and Thinking/Feeling (T/F). In 1920, Kathrin Briggs and Isabel Myers Briggs (Schultz and Schultz 2008) added another dimension to Jung's typological model and presented the MBTI personality model. A further fourth dimension is Judging/Perceiving (J/P) (Pittenger 1993). MBTI uses four two-dimensional functions based on Jung's theory. Sixteen personality types result from mixing four two dimensional functions. For example, people in ESTJ group are all extravert, sensing, thinking, and judging. Based on MBTI theory, every person has instinctive priorities that specify his/her behavior in different conditions (Retrieved from http://www.myersbriggs.org/my-mbti-personality-type/mbti-basics/). Although there are many models of personality in the literature, MBTI is the best-known tool used to determine personality. According to the Center for Applications of Psychological Type, MBTI is the most commonly used personality inventory in history; approximately 2,000,000 people use MBTI for their personality detection every year. Moreover, the validity of the MBTI model has been widely recognized (Kim et al. 2013). Also, MBTI is the most popular method to specify the personality type in learning environments especially in E-learning environments (Hall and Moseley 2005; Niesler and Wydmuch 2009; Haron and Salim 2006). Since we design our model in a virtual learning environment, it seems that MBTI is the best choice.

3   The Proposed Model

In this paper, our focus is on designing a computational model that identifies a user's status based on factors which include personality and emotions. It is noteworthy that people with different personalities express different emotions to deal with an event. Figure 1 shows the general view of the model showing the relationship between personality dimensions and emotion.

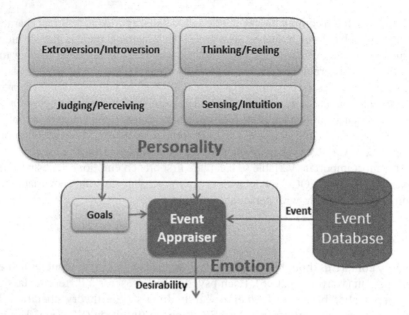

Fig. 1. General view of the proposed model

The personality module includes four dimensions of MBTI that generate sixteen personality types which influence emotions. The relationship between personal goals and personality (Reisz et al. 2013; Salmela-Aro et al. 2012) is used to model the impacts of personality on emotions. This module helps us to determine a user's personality and her/his goals based on the personality.

The emotion module is based on the OCC model in which the consequences of events are obtained according to the desirability or undesirability level of the events considering the users' goals. The event database includes many events that happen which affect users' emotions.

3.1 Calculating Desirability

To calculate desirability of an event, the following steps should be taken:

- Determine the user's personality
- Determine the user's goals based on his/her personality using the MBTI model
- Determine the importance value, i.e. the weight, of the user's goals
- Determine the relationship between personality type of the user and the event
- Determine the relationship between events and goals

In this method, the goals and their importance are shown as vectors named Goals and G, respectively (Eq. 1):

$$\text{Goals} = \begin{pmatrix} \text{Goal}_1 \\ \text{Goal}_2 \\ \cdots \\ \text{Goal}_n \end{pmatrix}, \; G = \begin{pmatrix} g_1 \\ g_2 \\ \cdots \\ g_n \end{pmatrix} \qquad \forall i \in [1, n], \; g_i \in [0, 1] \qquad (1)$$

In which, g_i is the importance of Goal_i. To show the impact of events on goals, an Impact matrix is used. Each element of the impact matrix is the impact degree of the i_{th} event on the j_{th} goal; where m is the number of events and n is the number of goals (2):

$$\text{Impact}(e_i, g_j) = \begin{pmatrix} \alpha_{11} & \alpha_{12} \cdots & \alpha_{1n} \\ \alpha_{21} & \alpha_{22} \cdots & \alpha_{2n} \\ & \cdots & \\ \alpha_{m1} & \alpha_{m2} \cdots & \alpha_{mn} \end{pmatrix} \qquad (2)$$

The desirability of each event can be computed as follows (Eq. 3):

$$\text{Desirability}(e_i) = \frac{\sum_{j=1}^{n} \alpha_{ij} g_j}{\sum_{j=1}^{n} g_j} \; \forall j \in [1, n] \; and \; \forall i \in [1, m] \; \text{Desirability}(e_i) \in [-1, 1] \qquad (3)$$

3.2 E-learning Environment Example

To show the effectiveness of the proposed model, we applied it to an E-Learning environment. A few events and goals in an E-Learning environment are considered and the model is used to predict students' desirability.

To determine the goals, we used Ames (1990) theory in which students are divided in two groups: mastery motivational orientation and performance motivational orientation. In this study, we have focused on performance motivational orientation group. When students have performance motivational orientation, they believe that performance is important and want to show that they have abilities. They feel successful when they please their teacher or do better than other students, rather than when they learn something new. When these students experience difficulty, they are not likely to increase their effort because this shows lack of ability. As they are primarily motivated by extrinsic factors (grades, parent approval, etc.), they are also called extrinsically motivated. There are three goals for performance motivational orientation students. These include: please the teacher and parents, do better than other colleagues, and show a high-level of competence.

To determine the relationship between personality and goals, we used MBTI studies to define a mapping between MBTI personality types and these goals (Durling et al. 1996; Higgs 2001; Jessee et al. 2006; Vincent and Ross 2001). In general, ENFJ, ESTP, ESFJ, ENFP and ISFP types include goals that cover the goals for performance motivational orientation in learning environments (Table 1).

Table 1. Relationship between MBTI Personality types and Goals in learning environments

Personality	Please the teacher and parents	Do better than other colleagues	Show that has a high level of competence
ESFJ	✓	-	-
ENFP	-	-	✓
ESTP	-	✓	✓
ENFJ	-	✓	-
ISFP	✓	-	-

As mentioned before, people with different personalities show different emotions in facing an event so that each event has a different degree of impact on each personality. To test our model, five events are considered. In addition, based on experts' recommendation, that the influence of each MBTI dimension on each event is defined (Table 2).

Also, based on the expert's knowledge we determined the relationships between the students' goals and personality dimensions (Table 3).

Table 2. Relationship between MBTI dimension and events in virtual learning environments

Event	E/I	T/F	S/N	J/P
Provide a correct response to the exercises	–	T	–	–
Finish the proposed activities	–	–	–	J
Receive appreciate help	E	–	–	–
Do not ask for help	I	–	–	–
Low effort	E	–	–	–

Table 3. Relationship between MBTI dimension and students' goals

Goals	E/I	T/F	S/N	J/P
Please the teacher and parents	–	F	–	–
Do better than other colleagues	–	–	N	–
Show that has a high level of competence	–	–	N	–

Finally, we designed a cognitive map to show the relationship between events, user's goals, user's personality and emotions variable in virtual learning environments (Fig. 2).

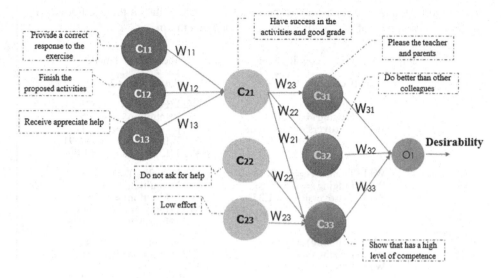

Fig. 2 The cognitive map in learning environments

Based on Fig. 2, desirability of a user is calculated according the following (4) and (5).

$$C_{21} = \sum_{i=1}^{3} C_{1i} * W_{1i}, \ C_{31} = C_{21} * W_{23}, \ C_{32} = C_{21} * W_{22}, \ C_{33} = \sum_{i=1}^{3} C_{3i} * W_{3i} \quad (4)$$

$$O_1 = \sum_{i-1}^{3} C_{3i} * W_{3i} \quad (5)$$

4   Results

To evaluate the proposed model we simulated a virtual learning environment which includes 580 agents with different personalities (ISFP, ESTP, and ESFJ with 118 agents each, 115 agents with ENFP, and 111 agents with ENFJ personality type). The agents have different goals based on their personality types and different level of knowledge which is set randomly based on a normal distribution. The five mentioned events happen randomly in the simulated environment and the agents respond to them and their emotion changes accordingly. An agent's response depends on its knowledge and personality. The simulated environment records the desirability of the agents based on Eq. 4. Also, the level of desirability for each agent is labeled by an expert. Finally, the weights of the cognitive map (Fig. 2) are learned from these data for each personality type. Weight of each layer are reported in Table 4. According to our proposed model, we expect weights with positive or negative values for each personality. For example in the ESFJ case, we expect weights which are related to E, F and J to be positive and weights which are related to T and N dimensions to be negative. Table 5 shows the accuracy of the weights for each type of personality based on our expectation.

Table 4. Weights of cognitive map for evaluating the proposed model

Personality	Weights of Layer 1	Weights of Layer 2
ESFJ	W11 (Thinking) = −1.25 W12 (Judging) = 0.24 W13 (Extroversion) = −0.68	W23 (Feeling) = −0.32 W22 (Intuition) = −1.06 W21 (Intuition) = −1.11 W22 (Introversion) = −1.91 W23 (Extroversion) = 1.89
ENFP	W11 (Thinking) = 0.50 W12 (Judging) = 0.52 W13 (Extroversion) = 1.33	W23 (Feeling) = 0.59 W22 (Intuition) = 0.34 W21 (Intuition) = 0.39 W22 (Introversion) = −0.22 W23 (Extroversion) = 0.24
ESTP	W11 (Thinking) = 0.38 W12 (Judging) = 0.18 W13 (Extroversion) = 0.60	W23 (Feeling) = −0.34 W22 (Intuition) = −0.45 W21 (Intuition) = 1.20 W22 (Introversion) = −0.42 W23 (Extroversion) = 0.18
ENFJ	W11 (Thinking) = 1.34 W12 (Judging) = −0.37 W13 (Extroversion) = 1.23	W23 (Feeling) = 0.66 W22 (Intuition) = 0.37 W21 (Intuition) = 0.69 W22 (Introversion) = −2.09 W23 (Extroversion) = 4.02
ISFP	W11 (Thinking) = −0.72 W12 (Judging) = −0.74 W13 (Extroversion) = −0.23	W23 (Feeling) = −0.52 W22 (Intuition) = −0.16 W21 (Intuition) = −0.06 W22 (Introversion) = 0.86 W23 (Extroversion) = −2.09

Table 5. Accuracy of the weights for each type of personality in train mode

Personality	Percent accuracy of weights
ESFJ	75 %
ENFP	75 %
ESTP	75 %
ENFJ	75 %
ISFP	88 %

We consider another dataset as a test dataset and evaluate the map with obtained weights. Results are reported in Table 6.

Table 6. Accuracy of the weights for each type of personality in test mode

Personality	Percent accuracy of weights
ESFJ	87.97 %
ENFP	89.16 %
ESTP	90.87 %
ENFJ	88.39 %
ISFP	87.80 %

5 Discussion

This paper aimed at modeling the relationship between emotion and personality in calculating user's desirability. Results in Table 5 show that our hypothesis in Tables 2 and 3 is correct. Based on psychology studies, we designed a cognitive map as shown in Fig. 2.

We consider a positive relationship between dimensions I in the MBTI test and "Do not ask for help" in events group. Since the introverted people are more interested in working alone, they refuse to ask for help from other people. In contrast, extroverted people have many tendencies for teamwork so we expected there is a positive relationship between "Receive appreciate help" and E dimension. Also, extroverted people, who tend to be fast in doing tasks, act quickly and sometimes without thought do not have high effort, and according to expectations, there should be a positive relationship between "low effort" and E dimension. The judging people prefer a systematized life and they care about activities which they can do on time so we expect there is a positive relationship between "Finish the proposed activities" and J dimension. Thinking people have a tendency for everything to be ideal then we expect there must be a positive relationship between "Provide a correct response to the exercises" and T dimension.

In the second layer, we expect personality type shows its effect on the user's goals. Feeling people are encouraged by others and so other people can affect their feelings. Also, feeling people cares about what others say and there should be a relationship between them. Intuitive people like to be different from other people so there should be a relationship between N dimension, and "Do better than other colleagues" and "Show that has a high level of competence".

After evaluating the proposed model with train data set, the results in Table 5 confirm our proposed model. For example for the ISFP type (Introverted Sensing Feeling Perceiving), we expected the weights related to the first layer (e.g. T, J and E) would be negative. Results in Table 5 confirm this.

In the second layer, according to ISFP type, we expected a positive value for F and I dimensions and a negative value for N and E dimensions. Results in Table 5 show the four weights are correct and just one of them is wrong.

Table 6 shows the percentage of weight correctness in the cognitive map designed for evaluating the proposed model in test mode.

It is plainly visible that there are a wide range of variables in determining user's desirability and many factors affect a user's emotion; nevertheless our results seems to be valid. The proposed model shows that we have found a significant correlation between emotions and personality using the OCC and the MBTI models.

6 Conclusions

In this paper we presented a general computational model for emotion and personality in humans. We used the MBTI model for personality and the OCC model for emotion modeling. This research focused on the personality and emotions of a user to calculate the user's desirability. We evaluated the proposed model in a virtual learning environment.

The most significant contribution of this paper is the introduction of a new computational model for determining users' desirability, based on the evaluation of events. Also, results show that our hypotheses on the relationship between emotion and personality is correct with high precision.

In future, we will add a mood module to model the relationship between mood, emotion, and personality.

Acknowledgments. This work is partially supported by the Iranian Cognitive Sciences and Technologies Council.

References

Ames, C.: Motivation: what teachers need to know. Teach. Coll. **91**(3), 409–421 (1990)

Chaffar, S., Cepeda, G., Frasson, C.: Predicting the learner's emotional reaction towards the tutor's intervention. In: Proceedings of the 7th IEEE International Conference, Japan, pp. 639–641 (2007)

Chaffar, S., Frasson, C.: Inducing optimal emotional state for learning in intelligent tutoring systems. In: Lester, J.C., Vicari, R.M., Paraguaçu, F. (eds.) ITS 2004. LNCS, vol. 3220, pp. 45–54. Springer, Heidelberg (2004)

Dang, T.H.H., Duhau, D.: GRACE – generic robotic architecture to create emotions. In: 11th International Conference on Climbing and Walking Robots and the Support Technologies for Mobile Machines - CLAWAR 2008, Coimbra, Portugal (2008)

Damasio, A.R.: Descartes' Error: Emotion, Reason, and the Human Brain. Gosset/Putnam Press, New York (1994)

Durling, D., Cross, N., Johnson, J.: Personality and learning preferences of students in design and design-related disciplines. In: Proceedings of IDATER 1996 (International Conference on Design and Technology Educational Research), pp. 88–94. Loughborough University (1996)

Egges, A., Kshirsagar, S., Magnenat-Thalmann, N.: Generic personality and emotion simulation for conversational agents. J. Comput. Anim. Virtual Worlds **15**(1), 1–13 (2004)

Fatahi, S., Ghasem-Aghaee, N.: Design and implementation of an intelligent educational model based on personality and learner's emotion. Int. J. Comput. Sci. Inf. Secur. **7** (2010)

Hall, E., Moseley, D.: Is there a role for learning styles in personalized [sic] education and training [Electronic version]? Int. J. Lifelong Educ. **24**(3), 243–255 (2005)

Haron, N.B., Salim, N.B.: Empirical evaluation of mixed approach in adaptive hypermedia learning system. In: Proceedings of the Postgraduate Annual Research Seminar, pp. 244–249 (2006)

Hartmann, P.: The five-factor model: psychometric, biological and practical perspectives. Nord. Psychol. **58**(2), 150–170 (2006)

Higgs, M.: Is there a relationship between the Myers-Briggs type indicator and emotional intelligence? J. Manag. Psychol. **16**(7), 509–533 (2001)

Hwang., J., Lee, K.C.: Exploring potentials of personality matching between users and target systems by using fuzzy cognitive map. In: 2013 46th Hawaii International Conference on System Sciences (HICSS), pp. 417–424 (2013)

Jessee, S.A., ONeill, P.N., Dosch, R.O.: Matching student personality types and learning preferences to teaching methodologies. J. Dent. Educ. **70**, 644–651 (2006)

Kazemifard, M., Ghasem-Aghaee, N., Ören, T.I.: Design and implementation of GEmA: a generic emotional agent. Expert Syst. Appl. **38**(3), 2640–2652 (2011)

Kim, J., Lee, A., Ryu, H.: Personality and its effects on learning performance: design guidelines for an adaptive e-learning system based on a user model. Int. J. Ind. Ergon. 1–12 (2013)

Kort, B., Reilly, R.: Analytical models of emotions, learning and relationships: towards an affect-sensitive cognitive machine. MIT Media Lab Tech Report, vol. 43, no. 548 (2001)

Mehdi, E.J., Nico, P., Julie, D., Bernard, P.: Modelling character emotion in an interactive virtual environment. In: Proceedings of AISB 2004 Symposium: Motion, Emotion and Cognition (2004).

http://www.myersbriggs.org/my-mbti-personality-type/mbti-basics/

Moshkina, L.: An integrative framework for time-varying affective agent behavior. Institute of Technology, Georgia (2006)

Niesler, A., Wydmuch, G.: User profiling in intelligent tutoring systems based on Myers-Briggs personality types. In: Proceedings of the International Multi Conference of Engineers and Computer Scientists, vol. I. International Association of Engineers, Hong Kong (2009)

Ortony, A., Clore, G.L., Collins, A.: The Cognitive Structure of Emotions. Cambridge University Press, Cambridge (1988)

Pittenger, D.J.: Measuring the MBTI... and coming up short. J. Career Plann. Employ. **54**(1), 48–52 (1993)

Reisz, Z., Boudreaux, M.J., Ozer, D.J.: Personality traits and the prediction of personal goals. Pers. Individ. Differ. **55**(6), 699–704 (2013)

Rosis, D.F., Pelachaud, C., Poggi, I., Carolis, N., Carofiglio, V.: From Greta's mind to her face: modeling the dynamics of affective states in a conversational agent, Embodied agent. Int. J. Hum. Comput Stud. **59**(1), 81–118 (2003)

Salmela-Aro, K., et al.: Personal goals and personality traits among young adults: genetic and environmental effects. J. Res. Pers. **46**(3), 248–257 (2012)

Santos, R., Marreiros, G., Ramos, C., Neves, J., Bulas-Cruz, J.: Personality, emotion, and mood in agent-based group decision making. J. Intell. Syst. **26**(6), 58–66 (2011)

Schultz, D.P., Schultz, S.E.: Theories of Personality. Wadsworth, Belmont (2008)

Trabelsi, A., Frasson, C.: The emotional machine: a machine learning approach to online prediction of user's emotion and intensity. In: 10th International Conference on Advanced Learning Technologies (ICALT), pp. 613–617 (2010)

Vincent, A., Ross, D.: Personalize training: determine learning styles, personality types and multiple intelligences online. Learn. Organ. **8**(1), 36–43 (2001)

Zeng, Z., Pantic, M., Roisman, G.I., Huang, T.S.: A survey of affect recognition methods: audio, visual, and spontaneous expressions. IEEE Tran. Pattern Anal. Mach. Intell. **31**, 39–58 (2009)

Recommendation Engine for an Online Drill System

Toshikazu Iitaka[✉]

Kumamoto Gakuen University, 2-5-1 Oe, Chuo-ku Kumamoto, 862-8680, Japan
iitaka2@yahoo.co.jp

Abstract. This paper presents a recommendation engine I have developed for an online drill system. The engine provides suitable quizzes for users, helping users learn effectively. The paper describes the features and effects of the recommendation engine.

Keywords: E-learning · Recommendation engine · Online drill system

1 Objective

I have developed an online examination (e-learning) system that includes practice drill functionality and a recommendation engine that recommends appropriate quizzes for each user automatically. The objective of this paper is to discuss the research background and the effects of the recommendation engine.

As shown in [2], the positive effect of an online drill system itself is confirmed. Further progress can be achieved by enabling each user to receive customized information by developing a recommendation engine that can provide appropriate quizzes for individual users. First, we aim to understand the background more precisely.

Second, the ongoing use of the online drill system in courses has prompted the implementation of a recommendation engine. We aim to prove the effect of the recommendation engine by using the data of the courses.

This paper reviews the significance and background of the research, provides the specifications of the recommendation engine, and then analyzes the recommendation engine's effects.

2 Background and Significance

This section describes the background of this research by describing the benefit of a recommendation engine's implementation in a drill system. The significance of the research derives from this benefit. Describing the use of the recommendation engine also sheds light on its significance.

People often read small paperback books of drills, while they commute to work. T. Iitaka stated that web applications for drills designed for mobile phones can be used instead of books [2]. Hence, the web application I have developed has drill functionality.

Recommendation engines recommend appropriate information based on preserved data. Some recommendation engines simply recommend popular information such as

© Springer International Publishing Switzerland 2015
P. Zaphiris and A. Ioannou (Eds.): LCT 2015, LNCS 9192, pp. 238–248, 2015.
DOI: 10.1007/978-3-319-20609-7_23

articles that many people have evaluated. However, proper recommendations must be customized for each user. Therefore, simple recommendation systems cannot provide each individual user with appropriate and personalized information. An algorithm that measures similarity is required to provide appropriate information. The proposed system recommends articles evaluated by other users with similar tendencies.

However, as shown in Fig. 1, measuring similarity often takes a significant amount of time. The requirement that recommendation data be updated periodically, e.g., once a day, interferes with real-time recommendation.

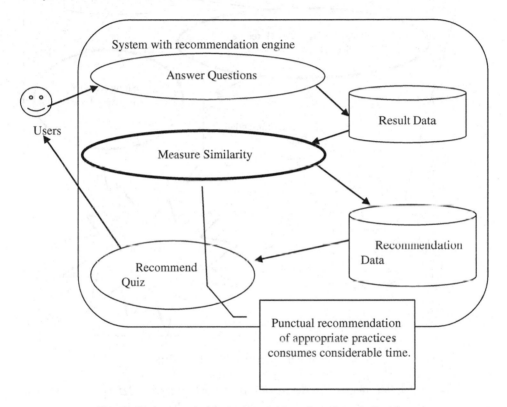

Fig. 1. Recommendation engine problems based on similarities

Consequently, recommendation engines often recommend articles that users have already read and do not need to read again. To address this problem, Iitaka has suggested the use of a "restriction list," which can be generated as quickly as a simple recommendation [3]. Both the simple recommendation data and the "restriction list" can be created using simple SQL. Here the "restriction list" is a list of quizzes that users have completed correctly; thus, these quizzes need not be attempted again.

Consequently, recommendation engines with "restriction lists" have been included in the proposed quiz system. The effects of the recommendation engines have been analyzed briefly [7] (Fig. 2).

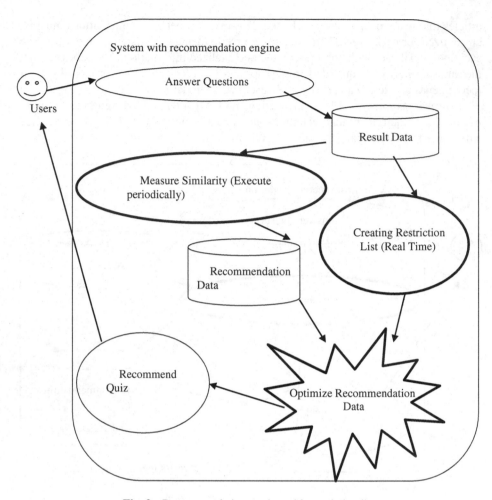

Fig. 2. Recommendation engine with restriction list

Now, the detailed features of the recommendation engine are described. As shown by [7], the basic data of the recommendation engine are the following.

(1) Data regarding evaluation on quizzes
(2) Flag data (Users can check quizzes that they want to try repeatedly)
(3) Answer data (These data tell us whether a user has given the correct answer)

The system can provide simple recommendations from (1) and (2). In other words, (1) and (2) identifies popular quizzes. Each type of data (1–3) can provide similarity based recommendations.

Similarity data are calculated periodically from data (1), (2), and (3), using Pearson's and Tanimoto's correlation coefficients. The similarity data are optimized in real time and provided as recommendation data. Recommendations from data (3), in particular, can predict which quizzes are needed for specific users to reinforce the users' learning.

Administrators of the system use the web page shown in Fig. 3 for periodical calculations.

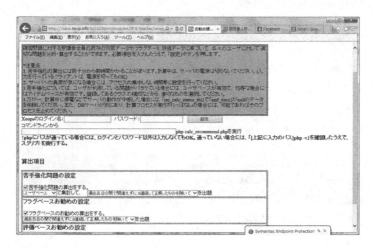

Fig. 3. Web page for creating similarity data

The program executed from this web page runs as a background program. Hence, the creation of similarity data does not interrupt normal system use.

The recommendation data (recommended quizzes) are shown on the following pages.

(1) Users' top page
(2) Special page for personalized training
(3) Page after answering a quiz

As shown in Fig. 4, two different recommendations are shown on the user's top page. One is a list of popular quizzes. The other is a list of quizzes recommended based on similarity.

There is also a special page for personalized training, shown in Fig. 5.

Furthermore, various lists of recommendations are shown on the page that appears after answering a quiz. The page shows whether the user's answer is correct. The correct answer and explanation are also shown on this page. Users can evaluate and check the quiz on this page (The system allows users to try only checked quizzes repeatedly). This page can show a list of quizzes, when the user has answered incorrectly. Users who have given incorrect answers to the quiz that has just been attempted tend to give incorrect answers to the quizzes on the list. Different lists are also shown when users check or evaluate the quiz just attempted. Users who check the quiz also tend to check the quizzes on the list displayed. Users who evaluate the quiz also tend to evaluate the quizzes on the list displayed (Fig. 6).

A recommendation engine that provides personalized information can be expected to be beneficial for higher education in general, because, as is often said, personalized education is increasingly needed for higher education [13]. Hence, this research must be significant, because such a recommendation engine can enable us

Fig. 4. User's top page

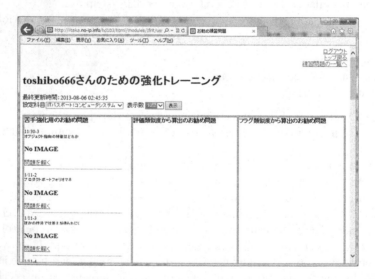

Fig. 5. Special page for personalized training

to achieve personalized education for effective e-learning. However, statistical analysis is required to prove this significance. Detailed analysis of the effects of the recommendation engine is required. The next section shows the detailed analysis.

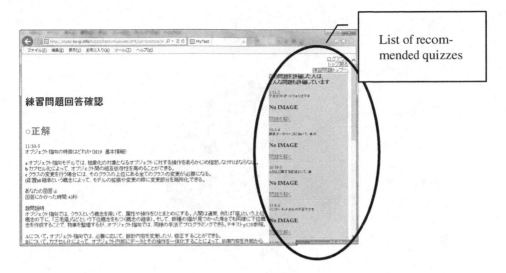

Fig. 6. Page that appears after answering a quiz

3   Methods

This section provides the statistical analysis of the recommendation engine based on the data from two courses in which the e-learning system is implemented.

The e-learning system with the recommendation engine is used in some Japanese IT classes. The classes prepare participants for a Japanese IT qualifying exam (i.e., IT passport). The effects of the recommendation engine are assessed in terms of the satisfaction and score of the periodical examinations.

Table 1 shows the course data.

Table 1. Course Data

	Participants	Participants taking exam
Course 1	144	129
Course 2	150	127

As shown in Table 1, Courses 1 and 2 have 144 and 150 participants, respectively. First, we check the satisfaction of the participants.

As shown in Fig. 7, more than 60 % of participants in both courses answered that the recommendation engine was useful. In Courses 1 and 2, 68 % and 67 % of participants, respectively, considered the recommendation engine useful.

Second, we estimate the effect of the recommendation engine using statistical analysis, with data drawn from the periodical examinations held in July 2013. Each examination consists of 40 questions previously set for the IT Passport (Fig. 8).

Now, we examine the basic data of the examination.

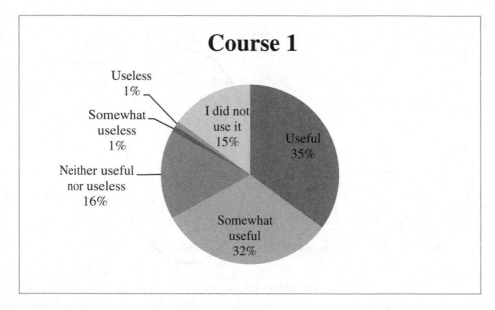

Fig. 7. Course 1 satisfaction

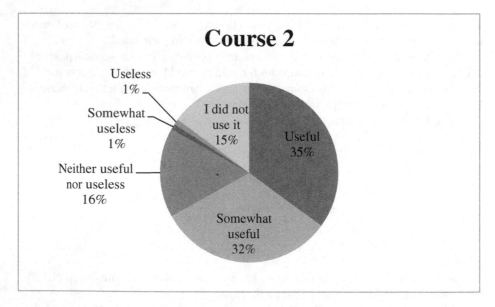

Fig. 8. Course 2 satisfaction

As shown in Table 2, skewness and kurtosis of scores in both courses are below 2.0. Hence, we can deal with the data distribution as a normal distribution. The average score of participants who used the recommendation engine is higher than that of the participants who did not. The average scores for Course 1 and 2 were 27.4 and 24.2, respectively. The users of the recommendation engine in Course 1 received 28.9 on average, while the average score of the users who did not use it was 25.8. The users in Course 2 received 25.3 on average, while the average score of users who did not use it was 23.4.

Table 2. Results of examinations

Course 1	Average score	27.4
	Standard deviation	6.6
	Skewness	−0.6
	Kurtosis	−0.1
	Number of users	69
	Average score of users	28.9
	Standard deviation of users	6.20
	Participants who did not use the recommendation engine	61
	Average score of participants who did not use the recommendation engine	25.8
	Standard deviation of participants who did not use the recommendation engine	6.80
Course 2	Average score	24.2
	Standard deviation	6.8
	Skewness	−0.1
	Kurtosis	−0.6
	Number of users	54
	Average score of users	25.3
	Standard deviation of users	6.22
	Participants who did not use the recommendation engine	73
	Average score of participants who did not use the recommendation engine	23.4
	Standard deviation of participants who did not use the recommendation engine	7.10

Users of the recommendation engine in both courses received higher average scores. However, the statistical significance of the result is not perfectly confirmed, when we check the difference between users and non-users with the t-test. Only the difference in Course 1 was statistically significant ($t(127) = 2.17$, p < 0.001). The difference in Course 2 was not statistically significant ($t(125) = 1.53$, ns). The difference is statistically significant only in the course in which the average score is relatively high. This tendency recurs in many courses.

This analysis suggests that the recommendation engine is more effective for relatively skillful users. The recommendation engine might be more effective in creating personalized recommendation data for users who use the drill system itself more often. Because the recommendation engine requires data for calculating recommendation data, users must use the drill system often. The average score is higher if the users use the drill system more frequently. Therefore, it is natural that the recommendation engine shows a clear effect only in Course 1, in which the average score is higher.

We must examine the use of the drill system to test this hypothesis. If the users in Course 1 used the system more often than the Users in Course 2 did, it is natural that the difference is statistically significant only in Course 1. First, we look at the basic data regarding drill system usage.

As shown in Table 3, there are 116 users in Course 1 out of 144 participants. More than 80 % of the participants in Course 1 used the drill system. There are 150 participants in Course 2 more than in Course 1. However, there are only 104 users in Course 2. Only 69.33 % of participants in Course 2 used the drill system. More important are the frequencies of drill system usage. Users in Course 1 used the drill system 219.8 times on average, while users in Course 2 used it only 148 times on average.

Table 3. Basic data of drill system's use

Course 1	Number of users	116
	Utilization rate	80.56 %
	Usage count	219.8
	Standard deviation	368.53
Course 2	Number of users	104
	Utilization rate	69.33 %
	Usage count	148.05
	Standard deviation	217.23

The hypothesis is confirmed to some degree. However, the assertion of this section is reinforced if the drill system was more effective in Course 1.

As shown in Table 4, the average score of users of the drill system in Course 1 was 28, while the average score of the participants who did not use the drill system was 21.92. The average score of users in Course 2 was 24.38, while the average score of the participants who did not use the drill system was 23.5. Users in both courses tend to receive higher marks than the participants who did not use the system. However, the difference between the users and the other participants is remarkable in Course 1, in which the difference was more than six points.

Table 4. Comparison of average scores

Course 1	Average score of participants who did not use the drill system	21.92
	Average score of users	28
Course 2	Average score of participants who did not use the drill system	23.5
	Average score of users	24.38

As mentioned previously, it is natural that recommendation engines based on similarity are effective only when the systems that provide data for them are used frequently. Reliable similarity data can be created, only if there are sufficient data. The analysis of the data of Table 4 might be telling us that this phenomenon is occurring. Therefore, we can conclude that the recommendation engine is effective.

4   Discussion of Results

This paper described a recommendation engine for an online drill system that I have developed. The background, the features, and the effect of the recommendation engine were explained.

The paper revealed a weakness in popular recommendation engines, which cannot provide appropriate real-time recommendations. Providing recommendations based on similarity consumes too much time. However, the recommendation engine described in this paper overcomes this weakness by using a "restriction list."

The statistical significance of using the recommendation engine was then confirmed. However, there are various algorithms that can create recommendation data. Consequently, there are many types of recommendation data, and we must consider the differences among these different types. However, there is currently insufficient data for such an analysis. In the future, we must gather more data to enable effective analysis of the difference.

References

1. Iitaka, T., Hirai, A.: CMS module for online testing. IEICE Tech. Rep. **107**(462), 25–29 (2008). Tokyo
2. Iitaka, T.: Mobile practice system using web item databank. IEICE Tech. Rep. **111**(237), 31–36 (2011). Tokyo
3. Iitaka, T.: CMS module for interactive lecture. IEICE Tech. Rep. **111**(394), 41–46 (2012). Tokyo
4. Iitaka, T.: Practice system using collective intelligence and restriction list. IEICE Tech. Rep. **111**(473), 167–172 (2012). Tokyo
5. Iitaka, T.: Introduction of the CMS module for interactive lecture. IEICE Tech. Rep. **111**(166), 35–40 (2012). Tokyo

6. Iitaka, T.: ARS module of contents management system using cell phones. In: Marcus, A. (ed.) DUXU 2013, Part IV. LNCS, vol. 8015, pp. 682–690. Springer, Heidelberg (2013)

7. Iitaka, T.: Analysis on the effect of recommendation engine for online practice system. IEICE Tech. Rep. **113**(229), 23–28 (2013). Tokyo

8. Kakitani, S., Watanabe, H.: Development of the portal site for support of programming learning. IEICE Tech. Rep. **109**(387), 7–12 (2010). Tokyo

9. Saito, Y., Hakamatsuka, A., Kuno, T., Suzuki, T., Kumazawa, H.: Development of attendance registration system using QR code and mobile phone ID. IEICE Tech. Rep. **109**(387), 13–18 (2009)

10. XoopsCube Web Page. http://xoopscube.jp/

11. Xoops Module E-frit Web Page. http://iitaka.no-ip.info

12. Xoops Module Nome Web Page. http://iitaka.no-ip.info/norm/

13. Yuan, F.: The Use of ICT in Higher Education: Media and Education, pp. 113–127. NHK Publication, Tokyo (2013)

Usability of Educational Technology APIs: Findings and Guidelines

Evangelos Kapros[(✉)] and Neil Peirce

Unit 28, Learnovate Centre, Trinity College Dublin,
Trinity Technology and Enterprise Campus, Pearse Street, Dublin 2, Ireland
{evangelos.kapros,neil.peirce}@scss.tcd.ie
http://www.learnovatecentre.org

Abstract. This paper describes a project that reviewed the usability of existing Educational Technology Application Programming Interfaces (EdTech APIs). The focus was on web-based APIs and the portals through which these are offered to developers. After analysing the state of art with regard to existing EdTech APIs and after conducting a literature review on API usability, a survey was circulated among developers and CTOs of EdTech organisations. The results of the aforementioned three steps were triangulated and resulted in usability guidelines for EdTech APIs. The contribution of this project is twofold: firstly, the production of a concrete set of EdTech API usability guidelines and, secondly, their implementation in a proof-of-concept a portal for two different EdTech offerings.

Keywords: Usability · API · Programming

1 Introduction

Application Programming Interfaces (APIs) are an important component in software development. They allow for code modularity, reuse, and separation of concerns. With the advancement of web-based applications, web-based APIs have an even more prominent role, and have even been described as "the glue of the web". While traditionally API usability has been studied in the context of development environments (IDEs) for desktop computers, research on web-based API usability is, to date, rather scarce. Moreover, APIs for Educational Technology (EdTech APIs) are even less often the subject of research with regard to their usability.

Web-based APIs are different to traditional APIs, not necessarily in structure, but primarily in the way they are offered. Dedicated portals are built to offer access to and document an API for developers. Online documentation and offering of APIs present unique usability challenges.

In addition, EdTech APIs present challenges specific to the domain of Education. For example, the variable utilisation of the hosting servers of an API is different in the case of EdTech as typically peak load will occur during a brief

© Springer International Publishing Switzerland 2015
P. Zaphiris and A. Ioannou (Eds.): LCT 2015, LNCS 9192, pp. 249–260, 2015.
DOI: 10.1007/978-3-319-20609-7_24

period of time, such as an examinations period. Other challenges include the increased need for transparency and data privacy. Another important aspect is that educational software applications are usually being developed by a combination of software *and* content developers; the case of subject-matter experts participating in the development process is not common in many fields, but in education content developers have to either prototype an application of verify its pedagogical appropriateness.

For the aforementioned reasons, it is necessary to treat EdTech API usability specially, as the domain-specific usability issues in a web context call for separate investigation.

2 EdTech APIs

In the Learnovate Centre, we partner with around 50 well-established EdTech organisations[1]. With regard to APIs that are EdTech domain-specific, we have identified the following recurring issues:

High scalability for short periods of time. Some of our partners need to scale their API usage for a brief period of time, usually during state exams. In some occasions the server utilisation has reportedly reached $200 * n$ of the required number of servers n for a period of only two days, while the utilisation during the rest of the year was ranging from n to $2 * n$.

Geo-location of cloud servers. Other Learnovate partners have a legal obligation to locate student data within the country they reside, which is not always possible with large sparsely located cloud server farms.

IP Protection. Other requirements concerning Intellectual Property and Data Protection may consist of a combination of institutional policies and legal obligations. Example of such requirements are the following:

— Universities require restriction on cloud usage.
— Requirements for ISO 27001 and other security certification.
— U.S. Safe Harbor agreement.

Overall, the aforementioned requirements consist barriers to API adoption. Moreover, the often requirement of a combination of two or all three of the above in EdTech enhances the domain-specific barriers to EdTech web-based API adoption.

3 Traditional API Usability

This section presents previous work around the usability of APIs. Since web-based APIs are a more recent advancement, most previous work assumes that developers have typically downloaded a Software Development Kit (SDK) and are using an IDE to write their code. Thus, this section describes usability issues around the use and documentation of APIs in IDE environments and not in interactive web consoles. Interactive web consoles will be discussed in the following section.

---

[1] http://www.learnovatecentre.org/membership/our-members/.

3.1   Identifying Usability Issues

Many different approaches have been taken in the study of API usability. One study [28] has correlated posts on bug-tracking systems with different API usability factors; the percentage of posts for each factor is presented below:

1. Missing feature — 43.5 %
2. Correctness — 31.1 %
3. Documentation — 27.3 %
4. Exposure of elements — 10.3 %
5. Memory management <9 %
6. Function parameter and return <9 %
7. Technical mismatch <8 %
8. ... similar smaller issues include Naming, Callers perspective, constructor parameter.

While the percentage of each category of bugs does not necessarily imply its importance, it is shown sufficiently that API usability affects the final software product. Thus, it is of concern to the developer *and* the end user alike. Apart from requests for missing features, the high percentages of bugs around the correctness and the documentation of an API show that features that are poorly communicated are causing poor development despite their usefulness.

A different approach exists in [11]. The team of this research project conducted interviews with developers about the barriers to adopting an API, in order to identify any usability issues that may occur. Since *reported* usability issues may differ from *actual* ones, workshops were conducted with developers in order to validate the reported issues while developing a piece of software. Below is an ordered list with encountered usability problems:

1. Documentation
2. Conceptual correctness
3. Callers perspective
4. Complexity
5. Data types
6. Leftovers for client code
7. Error handling/Exceptions
8. Consistency and conventions
9. Method parameters and return type
10. Factory pattern.

While results are similar in both the case of workshops and interviews, some differences exist. Specifically, interviews also mentioned Naming, but it was not encountered in workshops.

Another finding was that consistent error messages across various error types can be beneficial for developers and enhance greatly the usability of an API. Eight error types have been grouped and identified in [1,2], e.g. Structure error, Consistency error, etc.

Apart from identifying API usability factors, previous work has also investigated ways to improve the usability of APIs, and is presented below.

3.2 Improving API Usability

While the best way to design a usable API is to produce and follow guidelines that ensure its usability [12]², it is also important to provide to developers the appropriate tools that will help them understand and use an API.

A number of API classes and methods usability factors, which focus on API improvement, has been identified in [19] and is listed below.

– High number of classes is negative, re-structuring in sub-packages is beneficial
– Constructors are easier than factory methods
– Distinctive names should be used
– Parameters per method should be as low as possible
– Knowledge of domain and programming exp equally useful
– Few concepts (classes/methods) lead to high learnability.

One proposed way to improve API usability is to evaluate it automatically using Complexity Metrics and Visualizations [7]. To achieve this, a tool called `Metrix` has been built in order to evaluate Bandi *et al.* metrics, like the sum of Bandis complexity metrics for a class and the number of classes with a particular complexity.

Other approaches use text analytics to improve API usage within IDEs; for example, `Jadeite` uses a wordcloud-like experience to improve documentation by showing which calls are more frequent [22,25]. This helps identify calls that are otherwise similar. Consider for example the call `/system/student` and the call `/system/class/student`: it is highly probable that a new developer would want to use the one that has already been used the most by other developers.

Finally, other ways to make APIs more developer-friendly are colour coding, tooltips in code editors/IDEs [8,20], or diagrams [27] that help developers understand the mental model of the API.

However, while these tools improve greatly the usability of APIs that are typically part of an SDK (so that metadata to produce tooltips or diagrams are readily available), web APIs have additional challenges that need to be addressed.

4 Findings

4.1 API Usability Survey

Literature Review Findings. The table below presents a triangulated list of usability factors, compiled by combining the factors listed in the literature of the previous section. We anticipate that these issues are not specific to EdTech. Documentation, correctness, and low complexity, are the three factors that were persistent throughout (Table 1).

---

² For example, see: https://github.com/WhiteHouse/api-standards and http://guides. rubyonrails.org/api_documentation_guidelines.html.

Table 1. This table shows the difference between the *perceived* API usability issues, as described in interviews, and the *actual* ones, identified in a workshop.

Workshops	Interviews
1. Documentation	1. Documentation
2. Correctness	2. Naming
3. Complexity	3. Correctness
4. Data types	4. Complexity
5. Error handling	5. Data types
6. Factory pattern/Constructor	6. Leftovers for client code
7. ... Others, encountered <5 % of the time	

Developer Survey Results. In order to specify EdTech-specific usability issues and factors, we conducted a survey across CTOs and developers of our industry partners ($n = 11, k = 49$). The ease of integration into an organisation's existing technology stack, the API performance, and its availability, were the technical factors that were described as essential (see Fig. 1). Concerning non-technical factors (see Fig. 2), as most important were described the API meeting the organisation's needs, transparency as *how data are stored and processed*, and the *data privacy policy* of the service.

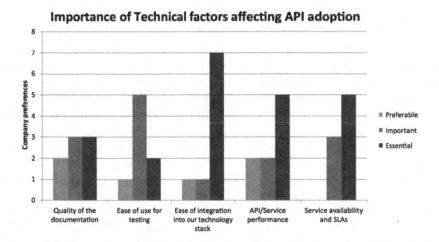

Fig. 1. The importance of technical factors that affect the adoption of APIs according to replies from CTOs and developers of EdTech industry partners of Learnovate. The survey was sent to Learnovate's k partners, and n replied ($n = 11, k = 49$).

From the results of this survey, we conclude that policy issues around Data Protection are a *sine qua non* for EdTech API adoption. As such, these policy issues should be considered as tightly coupled with API usability and

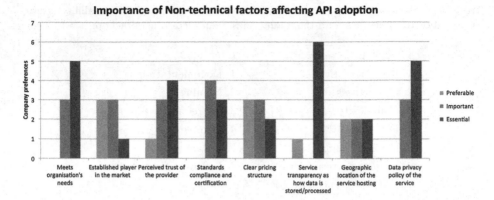

Fig. 2. The importance of non-technical factors that affect the adoption of APIs according to replies from CTOs and developers of EdTech industry partners of Learnovate. The survey was sent to Learnovate's k partners, and n replied ($n = 11, k = 49$). Policy issues around data protection are especially important in Educational Technology.

investigated under this prism during the design and development of an API. In addition, it is important that portals offering EdTech APIs are transparent in describing these policies—this and other portal-related usability issues are described in the following section.

4.2   EdTech Portal Survey

The adoption and use of new software can be positively influenced through early experimentation with the software, the internalising of structures and cultures surrounding its use, and progress validation as it is being used [5]. In scenarios where the software is not already in use within an organisation the additional factors of software discoverability and clarity in software capabilities need to be addressed. In the case of web-based APIs these challenges are addressed in part through discovery services such as the API Directory provided by `ProgrammableWeb`[3]. However, increasingly there is a growth in API or developer portals to enhance the enrolment and on-boarding of developers.

Although API portals do exist for educational technology it was found that the majority of them were either simple documentation pages (`Engrade`[4], `Khan Academy`[5]) or were only open to select partners and affiliates (`TurnItIn`[6], `Knewton`[7]). In light of this in order to understand common trends across API portals 18 portals were identified through web searches that offered web-based APIs (Table 2).

---

[3] http://www.programmableweb.com/apis/directory.
[4] https://wikis.engrade.com/engradeapi.
[5] http://api-explorer.khanacademy.org/.
[6] http://turnitin.com/en_us/integrations/overview.
[7] http://www.knewton.com/partners/.

Table 2. API Portals Surveyed.

Organisation	Industry
Aylien	Software/Text analysis
Berkeley	Education
Clever	Education
Edgar Online	Finance
Klout	Social media
Marvel	Entertainment
Mendeley	Education
MusicGraph	Entertainment
Nike+	Fitness/Clothing
Overdrive	Media/Publishing
Pearson	Education
Rovi	Software/Entertainment
Rubix	Software/Computer vision
Tomtom	Automotive/Mapping
Transport for London	Transport
USA Today	Media/News
Yellow Pages (Canada)	Advertising/Directory Services
Yummly	Nutrition

Within these portals we assessed how they facilitated early experimentation and the internalisation of structures. The assessment of progress validation has more relevance within large software teams where mentors with prior experience exist [5]. Its consideration in the context of API portals is a future direction for this research.

Early experimentation with web-based APIs requires readily available access to the functioning APIs and access to documentation. The following factors were identified as potential barriers to early experimentation:

– Access to documentation without signup
– Complexity of the signup process
– Availability of a cost-free pricing tier
– Availability of interactive documentation.

Of the portals surveyed all provided access to API documentation allowing developers to begin planning integrations without committing to a particular API. Although documentation goes part of the way to enable experimentation it still relies on the developer technically integrating with the API before realistic queries can be made and responses received. In order for this to happen in all cases except one (Clever) the developer has to signup to the portal in question.

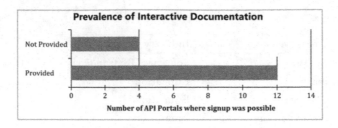

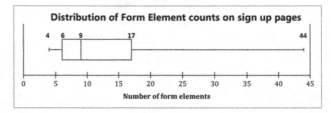

Fig. 3. Usability metrics of the surveyed API portals. Above, interactive documentation is increasingly common. Below, the number of required fields to sign up varies greatly; complexity can be a barrier to adoption.

The use of interactive documentation is increasingly common in API portals (see Fig. 3). Such documentation allows developers to make live API calls from within the portal where the submitted fields and responses are documented. By allowing developers to test real world queries to an API without the need to write any code, early experimentation is encouraged through interactive documentation. Examples of common interactive API documentation are `Swagger UI`, `Mashery IO Docs`, `3Scale Active Docs`, and `Mulesoft RAML API Console`.

The complexity of the signup process is seen as a barrier to experimentation and it is desirable to simplify the process. As a simple indicator, the complexity of signup was determined by the number of form elements (e.g. text fields, check boxes, drop downs, etc.) that had to be read and completed (see Fig. 3). The median number of form elements was nine with the minimum being four as required by `Mendeley` (first name, last name, email, password).

Four portals also provided `OAuth` sign-in for using other services, removing the need to complete a registration form and further easing signup. However, only one portal (`Marvel`) offered several service logins (`Facebook`, `Google`, `Yahoo`, `Twitter`, `Marvel`).

Two of the portals did not allow online signup as they only provided access to approved partners or affiliates (`Nike+`, `Yellow Pages` (Canada)).

5   EdTech API Usability Requirements and Guidelines

As an output of our research we produced the following guidelines, and designed a portal which incorporates these guidelines.

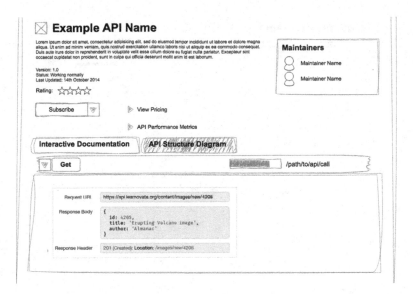

Fig. 4. (a) Colour-coding the structure of a call at an interactive console can improve the legibility of the documentation and, thus, the learnability of an API. (b) A bar that visualises the amount of calls on that method helps distinguish it from similar ones (Color figure online).

API Packaging Related. These guidelines are related to API Packaging. API designers and developers are encouraged to use them; please note that guidelines marked with an asterisk {∗} are EdTech domain specific (Fig. 4).

- ∗ Domain knowledge balances lack of programming experience
- ∗ Data Processing should be transparent
- APIs should be generic enough, that is decoupled from specific applications
- Sub-packaging is better than large categories
- Fewer method parameters is better
- Categorise error messages consistently.

API Portal Related. Other usability aspects that affect API usage and are related to the portal that offers the API are listed below. As above, guidelines marked with an asterisk {∗} are EdTech domain specific (Fig. 5).

- ∗ Explain the API's Data Protection policy (or how it may facilitate an application's policy)
- Provide an interactive console documentation system
- Visualise the popularity of a method call
- Colour code to improve learnability
- Represent visually the API's structure.

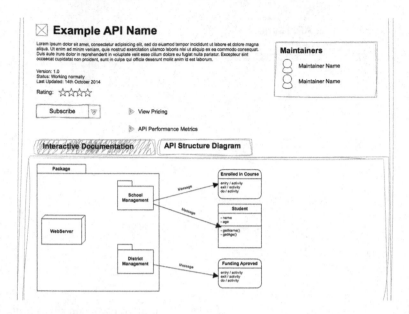

Fig. 5. A diagram that represents the structure of an API helps developers understand its mental model. Visual learners benefit especially from this representation, as API documentation is typically in text form.

6   Conclusions

In conclusion, after reviewing the API usability literature, surveying EdTech CTOs and developers, and surveying API portals, we created a concrete set of eleven guidelines that facilitate usable APIs for EdTech applications. While most of the guidelines hold for each and every API, some are specific to the EdTech field.

Moreover, we have designed and implemented a portal that offers EdTech APIs and implements the above guidelines. However, other aspects of the portal are still under development, thus public access is still not available (contact us for details).

Acknowledgments. This research is supported by the Learnovate Centre at Trinity College, the University of Dublin. The Learnovate Centre is funded under the Technology Centre Programme through the Government of Ireland's state agencies Enterprise Ireland and IDA Ireland.

References

1. Beaton, J.K., Myers, B.A., Stylos, J., Jeong, S.Y., Xie, Y.: Usability evaluation for enterprise SOA APIs. In: International Workshop on Systems Development in SOA Environments, pp. 29–34. ACM Press, New York (2008)

2. Beaton, J., Jeong, S.Y., Xie, Y., Stylos, J., Myers, B.A.: Usability challenges for enterprise service-oriented architecture APIs. In: Proceedings - 2008 IEEE Symposium on Visual Languages and Human-Centric Computing, VL/HCC 2008, pp. 193–196. IEEE (2008)
3. Burns, C., Ferreira, J., Hellmann, T.D., Maurer, F.: Usable results from the field of API usability: a systematic mapping and further analysis. In: Proceedings of IEEE Symposium on Visual Languages and Human-Centric Computing, VL/HCC, pp. 179–182. IEEE (2012)
4. Clarke, S.: Measuring API usability. Dr. Dobb's J. Windows/.NET Suppl. **9**(5), S6–S9 (2004)
5. Dagenais, B., Ossher, H., Bellamy, R.K.E., Robillard, M.P., de Vries, J.P.: Moving into a new software project landscape. In: Proceedings of the 32nd ACM/IEEE International Conference on Software Engineering - ICSE 10, vol. 1, p. 275. ACM Press (2010)
6. Daughtry, J.M., Farooq, U., Myers, B.A., Stylos, J.: API usability: report on special interest group at CHI. SIGSOFT Softw. Eng. Notes **34**, 27–29 (2009)
7. De Souza, C.R.B., Bentolila, D.L.M.: Automatic evaluation of API usability using complexity metrics and visualizations. In: 31st International Conference on Software Engineering - Companion Volume, ICSE 2009, pp. 299–302. IEEE (2009)
8. Dekel, U., Herbsleb, J.D.: Improving API documentation usability with knowledge pushing. In: Proceedings - International Conference on Software Engineering, pp. 320–330. IEEE (2009)
9. Ellis, B., Stylos, J., Myers, B.: The factory pattern in API design: a usability evaluation. In: Proceedings - International Conference on Software Engineering, pp. 302–311. IEEE (2007)
10. Farooq, U., Zirkler, D.: API peer reviews: a method for evaluating usability of application programming interfaces. In: Proceedings of the 2010 ACM Conference on Computer Supported Cooperative Work, pp. 207–210. ACM Press, New York (2010)
11. Grill, T., Polacek, O., Tscheligi, M.: Methods towards API usability: a structural analysis of usability problem categories. In: Winckler, M., Forbrig, P., Bernhaupt, R. (eds.) HCSE 2012. LNCS, vol. 7623, pp. 164–180. Springer, Heidelberg (2012)
12. Henning, M.: API design matters. Commun. ACM. **52**(5), 46–56 (2009)
13. Ko, A.J., Riche, Y.: The role of conceptual knowledge in API usability. In: Proceedings - 2011 IEEE Symposium on Visual Languages and Human Centric Computing, VL/HCC 2011, pp. 173–176. IEEE (2011)
14. Martens, A.: Usability of web services. In: 2003 Proceedings of Fourth International Conference on Web Information Systems Engineering Workshops, pp. 182–190 (2003)
15. Nelson, A.J., Dinolt, G.W., Michael, J.B., Shing, M.T.: A security and usability perspective of cloud file systems. In: Proceedings of 2011 6th International Conference on System of Systems Engineering: SoSE in Cloud Computing, Smart Grid, and Cyber Security, SoSE 2011. pp. 161–166. IEEE (2011)
16. Plunkett, L., Solow-Niederman, A., Gasser, U.: Framing the Law & Policy Picture: A Snapshot of K-12 Cloud-Based Ed Tech & Student Privacy in Early 2014 (2014)
17. Potter, T.C.: An evaluation methodology for the usability and security of cloud-based file sharing technologies (2012)
18. Robillard, M.P., Deline, R.: A field study of API learning obstacles. Empir. Softw. Eng. **16**, 703–732 (2011)

19. Scheller, T., Kuhn, E.: Influencing factors on the usability of API classes and methods. In: Proceedings - 2012 IEEE 19th International Conference and Workshops on Engineering of Computer-Based Systems, ECBS 2012, pp. 232–241. IEEE (2012)
20. Stylos, J.: Making APIs more usable with improved API designs, documentation and tools (2009)
21. Stylos, J., Clarke, S.: Usability implications of requiring parameters in objects constructors. In: Proceedings - International Conference on Software Engineering, pp. 529–538. IEEE (2007)
22. Stylos, J., Faulring, A., Yang, Z., Myers, B.A.: Improving API documentation using API usage information. In: 2009 IEEE Symposium on Visual Languages and Human-Centric Computing, VL/HCC 2009, pp. 119–126. IEEE (2009)
23. Stylos, J., Graf, B., Busse, D.K., Ziegler, C., Ehret, R., Karstens, J.: A case study of API redesign for improved usability. In: Proceedings - 2008 IEEE Symposium on Visual Languages and Human-Centric Computing, VL/HCC 2008, pp. 189–192. IEEE (2008)
24. Stylos, J., Myers, B.: Mapping the space of API design decisions (2007). http://repository.cmu.edu/hcii/169
25. Watson, R.B.: Improving software API usability through text analysis: a case study. In: 2009 IEEE International Professional Communication Conference, pp. 1–7. IEEE (2009)
26. Winckler, M., Forbrig, P., Bernhaupt, R. (eds.): Human-Centered Software Engineering. Springer, Heidelberg (2012)
27. Xiong, P.X., Fan, Y.F., Zhou, M.Z.M.: A petri net approach to analysis and composition of web services. IEEE Trans. Syst. Man Cybern. A Syst. Humans **40**, 376–387 (2010)
28. Zibran, M.F., Eishita, F.Z., Roy, C.K.: Useful, but usable? Factors affecting the usability of APIs. In: Proceedings - Working Conference on Reverse Engineering, WCRE, pp. 151–155. IEEE (2011)

Ontological Design to Support Cognitive Plasticity for Creative Immersive Experience in Computer Aided Learning

Niki Lambropoulos[1], Iosif Mporas[2,3], Habib M. Fardoun[4(✉)], and Iyad Katib[4]

[1] Department of Informatics, London South Bank University, UK and OLON Organisation, Greece LSBU, 103 Borough Road, London, SE1 0AA, UK
nikilambropoulos@gmail.com
[2] Artificial Intelligence Group, Wire Communications Laboratory, Department of Electrical and Computer Engineering, University of Patras, Patras, Greece
[3] Computer and Informatics Engineering Department, TEI of Western Greece, Antirion, Patras, Greece
imporas@upatras.gr
[4] King Abdulaziz University of Saudi Arabia, Jeddah 21589, Kingdom of Saudi Arabia
hfardouniakatib@kau.edu.sa

Abstract. This paper discusses Ontological Design (OD) to support creative and insightful thinking in the increasingly customised modern world, specialised for augmented reality interfaces. The motivation was built upon IBM's suggestion that capitalising complexity enables creativity, and the latter is the single most important leadership competency to deal with the increasing world complexity. Thus, OD simplifies the customisation processes and reduces anxiety when comes to challenging digital literacy for computer aided learning (CAL) skills. In a mixed reality modern world learners need to constantly adapt to changes into information, knowledge, signification and meaning, skills and competencies. This requires or enables cognitive plasticity bringing back the initial educational target, learning to learn. OI is based on the mediated ways the tools are used to enhance our senses and mind and the interaction as well as the influence our world view.

Keywords: HCI · Ontological design · Immersive experience · Creativity · Computer aided learning · Cognitive plasticity

1 Introduction

Our world has been changed dramatically in the ways we think, work, learn, read, communicate, play, have fun or collaborate. The Internet of Things is creating a new global network and the human perception finds hard to grasp and adjust. Education is behind the current transformations the humans and the environment is going through. As Nicolas Carr illustrates in his book [1], possibly Google makes us stupid and perhaps there is much more to say about the ways the Internet is changing us. As we enjoy the Net's bounties, we are sacrificing our ability to read and think deeply. He started a discussion about Internet's intellectual and cultural consequences as for many centuries human thought has been

© Springer International Publishing Switzerland 2015
P. Zaphiris and A. Ioannou (Eds.): LCT 2015, LNCS 9192, pp. 261–270, 2015.
DOI: 10.1007/978-3-319-20609-7_25

shaped by 'tools of the mind'; the alphabet, maps, printing press, clock, and the computer. Our brains change in response to our experiences. Neuroplasticity or brain plasticity refers to synaptic plasticity and non-synaptic plasticity, this means to changes in neural pathways and synapses which are due to changes in behaviour, environment, neural processes, thinking, emotions, as well as changes resulting from bodily injury [2]. Therefore, the technologies we use to find, store, and share information can literally reroute our neural pathways. For example, the printed book served to focus our attention, promoting deep and creative thought; however, the Internet encourages scanning and scattered small bits of information from many sources. Scanning and skimming evaporate our capacity for concentration, contemplation, and reflection. Such chronic distraction, and taking into account our brain's plasticity, aid in losing our abilities to employ a slower, more contemplative mode of thought; thus, the better we are in multitasking the less prolonged, focused concentration and in result, we are less creative in our thinking.

Currently, there are no propositions towards the continuously new capabilities needed and acquired to deal with changing complexity. Furthermore, existing working and educational models are collapsing and a need to fill the gap is urgent. ICT, the Web and open source software extend our senses and capabilities. These targets are incorporated into interface design fitting systems into the ways we function. From face-to-face conversations with more than 1,500 CEOs worldwide aiming at capitalising complexity, an IBM report [3] suggests that creativity is the single most important leadership competency to deal with the increasing world complexity. As the tools enable us to expand our perception and learning we exchange knowledge, skills and competencies by being inter-dependent and inter-collective organising ourselves into small groups, communities and social networks. A Computer Aided Learning Community is a social aggregation that emerges in online courses when enough people carry on progressive dialogues for the purpose of learning via new idea generation for the individuals and the groups. Learning occurs by containing different levels en route for members' engagement and practice whereas the group or the community evolves including the artefacts used within a cultural practice. Eventually these artefacts carry a substantial portion of our specific practices and professions heritage. Thus, users' early participation in a kind of design that enhances the immersive experience with the environment, and the learning environment in particular can be also associated with the overall cultural life.

2   On Creativity and Cognitive Plasticity for CAL

Detailed research or review of our act of perception is currently missing. One reason is that the technology is not advanced enough so that researchers can study the brain in depth. Also, instead of considering perception intact and accurate based on the ways the brain receives sensory stimuli as concrete and solid matter, we may enhance the right brain hemisphere functionality in order to receive data processed and envisaged in and delivered to our awareness differently. As the brain is our main tool for examining physical reality, in order to determine the validity of our perceptions, we need to study of our brain's physiology, and in particular the ways both parts of the brain receive and perceive sensory stimuli. The retinex (combination of retina and cortex) theory of vision posits that the brain's cortex compares the data it receives and creates an appropriate visual perception. Our visual perception requires a kind of reasoning process, not just retinal stimulation [4]. Our brain is working hard to create a classical perception that is useful mostly for practical purposes. The left-brain/right-brain dichotomy or, more accurately, processed versus unprocessed data, and the mechanism by which we form perception may provide a solution. The dichotomy suggests that classical-level perception is partly constructed by our judgmental left hemisphere. The perception of the suppressed but unbiased right hemisphere is more in line with quantum-mechanical principles. Our classical perception may be just an approximation of the actual realty out there. The left hemisphere is objective, analytical, logical or classical whereas the right one is informational, holistic, continuous, subjective or quantum mechanical. Our world has been built based mostly upon the left brain functionalities which makes our abilities and competences inadequate for the new century. Perhaps more attention, study and research to the right brain functionalities and abilities are needed, moving from the individual self-perception to a more unified perception of our world. Based on the theory of entanglement borrowed from quantum physics, both parts of our brains can function as a unity much faster providing more accurately perception of reality. This approach requires reconsidering the whole educational and corporate system as they function at the moment [5].

Insight is any sudden comprehension, realization, or problem solution that involves a reorganization of the elements of a person's mental representation of a stimulus, situation, or event to yield a nonobvious or non-dominant interpretation [6]. Insight occurs (a) when a simple solution breaks an impasse or mental block initially fixated on an incorrect solution strategy or strong but ultimately unhelpful association; (b) when the solution suddenly intrudes on a person's awareness when he or she is not focusing on any solution strategy, (c) when an insight pointing to a solution occurs while a person is actively engaged in analytic processing but has not yet reached an impasse, and (d) when a person has a spontaneous realization that does not relate to any explicitly posed problem. The neural basis of insight is anchored in the hemispheric differences. The right hemisphere contributes relatively more to insight solving than to analytic solving, whereas the left hemisphere contributes more to analytic solving than to insight solving.

A new kind of consciousness arise, a quantum total one [7]. Creativity is divided into inner creativity, the evolution and transformation of the Self, and outer creativity, the design and development of a product. Also, quantum theory can provide approaches to explain the human brain infinite trajectories to manifest perceptions of reality and suggests that creativity is an evolutionary process that requires unconscious processing. There are two realms of reality, potentiality and actuality. Collapses produce dependence co-arising of experience and creativity is a phenomenon of consciousness manifesting new possibilities anchored in brain plasticity as it chooses from quantum possibilities. It is therefore based on discontinuity, non-locality of ideas already existing in the human brain and the entanglement phenomenon; this is the holistic view that is all is part of one system. Such gestalts refer to the collections of separate fragments, the breakthrough pattern of a single significant whole. In fact, the entanglement phenomenon explains the potential for non-locality and discontinuity as non-local correlations of synapses rearrange the neuron pathways. This is idea generation, the Eureka! experience, creative insights or the quantum leap arise. As such, perception requires memory and memory requires perception, however, creativity requires changes in the brain's sub-structures responsible for memories and representations of experience. Therefore, humans' experiences intuitive insights turn into new meanings in older or newer contexts.

Learning results in the change of thinking, understanding and behaviour that can be measurable compared to specific indicators before the learning intervention. If the learning experience is enhanced, then learning is deeply experienced and thus, accelerated. To create such an immediate and rapid learning intervention, pedagogical and learning design is necessary so the coordination of both the learning activities (including associated educational content) and the group learning experience as such can occur and converge.

Based on the assumption that creativity is related to the idea generation caused by nonlocal quantum consciousness, the creativity techniques in this section are related to the broader perception of the world and the insights production in a larger community, compared to the individual and the group as in the previous sections.

In the era of the internet of Things, where all devices are going to be connected on platforms to enable communication and interaction with not only other people but also with the environment surrounding us, learners and educators are called to enable capabilities in an increasingly complex world. Humans are now participants in smaller or bigger groups, communities and networks connected with the associated and evolving tools and need to deal with complex mazes of information, communication patterns, strategic and critical thinking for information utilization and meaning making. Creativity inspires and empowers the mind with innovative ideas. For such a state to exist, a moment-by-moment awareness of our thoughts, feelings, bodily sensations, and surrounding environment is needed. Mindfulness, awareness, concentration or sentiment suspension aids in being continuously present and immerse with experience which in turn enables our brain plasticity. Such openness facilitates creativity by drawing the self away from its personality encasement and absorption, detaching from the physical, emotional and mental aspects of the personality. The development of the abstract mind and thinking makes it possible to see the broader structures underlying outer events. Life and circumstances are seen anew and not realized before developing intuitional insight to input in everyday life and production.

3   Mixed Reality in CAL

There are many different ways for people to be educated, which include classroom lectures with textbooks, computers, handheld devices, and other electronic appliances. The choice of learning innovation is dependent on an individual's access to various technologies. Virtual Reality (VR) and Augmented Reality (AR) are technologies that can dramatically shift the location and timing of education. The use of VR and AR in education can be considered as one of the natural evolutions of computer-assisted instruction (CAI) or computer-based training (CBT) [8]. Augmented Reality (AR) is a technology that allows computer-generated virtual imagery information to be overlaid onto a live direct or indirect real-world environment in real time. AR is different from

Virtual Reality (VR) in that in VR people are expected to experience a computer-generated virtual environment. In AR, the environment is real, but extended with information and imagery from the system. In other words, AR bridges the gap between the real and the virtual in a seamless way [9].

The last decade showed how production activities have been split and segments localized in some specialized countries while customers have been involved into the design processes. New technologies suggest that learners have to be creative, active innovators developing new services and products, new production and social processes. Technological waves as rapid change of technologies are becoming more frequent and shorter, so that IT expert must evaluate quickly how each wave gives opportunity for new individual, social or business applications. As an example beside may others, the Internet of things is a giant coming wave opening the web to astonishing possibilities in situation awareness as added social reality.

During the last two decades VR and AR have been experimentally applied to school environments, although not as much as classic methods of education and training [10]. Augmented Reality (AR) builds upon virtual layers that overlay superimposed on physical reality (such as for use in simulated retail and training environments), where customized messaging and applications requires positioning and orientation of visors and displays and other objects.

Moreover, the existence of mixed reality (MR) technology which is powerful and compact enough to deliver MR experiences to not only corporate settings but also academic venues through personal computers and mobile devices can make several educational approaches are more feasible [9]. Devices such as wireless mobiles, smart phones, tablet PCs, and other innovations in electronics are increasingly ushering MR into applications which offer a great deal of promise, especially in education.

Professionals and researchers have striven to apply MR to classroom-based learning within subjects like chemistry, mathematics, biology, physics, astronomy, and other K-12 education or higher, and to adopt it into augmented books and student guides [9]. However, AR has not been much adopted into academic settings due to little financial support from the government and lack of the awareness of needs for AR in academic settings [11]. It is estimated that simple AR applications in education will be realized within a few years.

Mixed reality can make education more productive, pleasurable, and interactive. MR can engage a learner in several interactive ways, which before where not possible, as well as can also provide each individual with one's unique discovery path with rich content from computer-generated 3D environments. It has been shown in previous research works that mixed reality can be focused on simplicity and ease of providing education, so that learners can accept knowledge and skills with 3D simulations generated by computers or other devices. MR can support the efficiency of education in academia by providing information at the right time and right place and offering rich content with computer-generated 3D imagery. MR may be helpful where students take control of their own learning and thus could provide opportunities for more authentic education and training styles. MR-based systems offer motivating, entertaining, and engaging environments conducive for learning. Except this, MR in education is attractive, stimulating, and exciting for students and provides effective and efficient support to the learners.

Virtual and augmented reality is not appropriate for every instructional objective. There are some teaching scenarios when VR can be used and some when it should not be used. For example the use of VR is suggested when a simulation could be used, teaching using the real thing is dangerous/impossible/inconvenient/difficult, interacting with a model is as motivating as or more motivating than interacting with the real thing, travel, cost, and/or logistics of gathering a class for training make an alternative attractive, etc. On the other hand, VR is not suggested to be used when no substitution is possible for teaching/training with the real thing, interaction with real humans, either teachers or students, is necessary, using a virtual environment could be physically or emotionally damaging.

Research on educational applications of mixed reality show the potential value of MR in the educational process. The use of MR can help the educator to enhance their courses and provide multiple perspectives for engaging learners into active learning.

4   Ontological Design for Cognitive Plasticity in Mixed Reality

Ontological Design refers to the cycle of designing and developing systems based upon the interaction between us and the tools and vice versa. Such design is not fixated but rather agile, responsive and evolving acquiring information from the surrounding environment to adjust the software to the individual user's needs. Ontological Design implementation improves the Human Computer Interaction for the human to human interaction based on existing databases as well as gathering, interpreting and integrating information via users' interaction on both individual and collective level. In this way, the design aims at serving individuals' capabilities and visions to deal with the increasing complexity of the world. OD is directed towards Computer Aided Learning (CAL) systems based upon solid educational and technical design principles for associated platforms to be designed and developed aiming at creating active participants and producers of the educational content and knowledge.

The Perception-Action Model (PAM) is a process-based suggestion on empathy made by [12]. According to PAM, attended perception activates subject's representations of the state, situation and object, and that activation of this representation automatically primes or generates the associated autonomic and somatic responses, unless inhibited. PAM suggests that levels of empathy can be associated to levels of awareness, reconciliation, vicarious learning or effortful information processing. On balance, both the neuropsychological and psychophysical data support this distinction. They claim that critical results were either statistically inconclusive (because they consisted of negative evidence) or based on a suspect "calibration" procedure. Correction ('calibration') of illusion effects is critical for comparisons across stimuli, studies, and tasks [13]. PAM proposes that vision-for-perception and vision-for-action are based on anatomically distinct and functionally independent streams within the visual cortex. It comprises a set of core contrasts between the functional properties of the two visual streams, capturing broad patterns of functional localisation suggesting that should reject the idea that, according to the two streams hypothesis, the ventral (visually guided behaviour) and dorsal (guidance of actions and recognizing where objects are in space) streams are functionally independent processing pathways. Using tools to enhance empathy and awareness of the Self and Other may lead to the next skill level of shared intentions, feelings and thoughts for common goals, desires and beliefs in CAL.

Ontological Design for CAL is applied for solutions related to complex, ill-structured, and agile, scope creep problems and situations, according to the following principles: (a) facilitating situated human cognition in an attempt to address complexity; (b) provide tools which expand the capacity of cognitive plasticity; (c) make a careful analysis of the implicit assumptions of the system and limit competing values; (d) understand social structure and context, (e) view breakdowns as creative design opportunity; (f) use digital medium to narrate a transmedia story; (g) engage features from game mechanics such as play, competition, challenge, quests, choices, surprise, curiosity, association, flow and expression; and (h) make visible the effects of interaction between the human and the world mediated by the particular tool for computer enabled mechanics, such as VR, AR and MR.

5   Creative Immersive Experience for Computer Aided Learning

Creative learning experiences are a way to think about what a learning intervention might be (i.e. – its design) in the context of desired end goals and outcomes. This can then inform our technological choices within multiples real and mixed reality contexts. Creative Immersive Experience aids in:

1. Promoting cognitive plasticity in action by activating multiple reality perceptions
2. Reducing transactive cost by enabling multiple associations in real-time to occur
3. Orchestrating learning teaching and learning pathways convergence including learning activities coordination and knowledge building for signification
4. Providing direct fit between educational tasks, methods and tools

VR, AR and MR enhance the experiential learning to develop new creativity competencies based upon the agile cognitive plasticity and rapid knowledge acquisition in such rich learning environments. HCI Education (HCI-Ed) is the design, evaluation and implementation of systems and tools from a user/learner-centred perspective and the study of major phenomena surrounding them. In HCI-Ed both inclusive and participatory User-Centred Design (UCD) and Learner-Centred Design (LCD) are utilised. UCD is that the system should have the capability in human functional terms to be used easily and effectively by the specified range of users, given specified training and user support, to fulfil the specified range of tasks, with the specified range of environmental scenarios. Whereas UCD focuses on making users more effective, LCD focuses on making learners more effective by utilising pedagogical frameworks. Pedagogical Utility is the degree to which the functionality of the system allows the learner to reach his/her learning goal. Pedagogical Usability should question whether the tools, contents, interfaces, and tasks provided within the e-learning environments can support e-learners. Pedagogical Usability utilises guidelines and principles to bring together the pedagogical and technical CAL targets. Lastly, Pedagogical Acceptability refers to the previous compatibility as well as the degree to which the system is compatible with learners' motivation, affects, culture and values. HCI-Ed works through a framework with seven iterative and non-linear stages, as follows:

1. Context & Learning Values - Hypotheses
2. (Iterative) Design – Requirements – User Modelling
3. Evaluation with user groups/experts
4. Development
5. Evaluation with user groups
6. Re-Design & Development
7. CAL Study & Research based on Final Tool Release

The process follows the suggested instructional design model ADDIE (Analysis, Design, Development, Implementation and Evaluation); however, it incorporates the initial context and learning values as initially defined before actual design.

Although user modelling has been implemented for adaptive systems, it can provide initial profiling for other systems, as it describes the process of building up and modifying a user model towards user's/earner's specific needs. The specific data needed are gathered by initial profiling questions and identifying users' preferences via observing and interpreting their interactions with the system. User modelling supports the constant evolution of technologies and services as it evolves on user abstract models that are easy to understand by systems making appropriate for multi-disciplinary educational design. The Model-Based Education System Design Environment notations (eLearniXML & eLearniCNL), which contains several and different models (Task, Domain, Platform, Environment, Context, and Presentation) and these models can be divided and classified into different ways based on multiple criteria. The Model-Driven Development specifies three models on a system, a computation independent model; a platform independent model and a platform specific model. Existing user modelling standards (e.g. IMS-LIP for eLearning) provide the learning quality assurance checklists. Model-based Distributed User Interfaces are usually anchored in the international standard ISO 9126 (ISO 9126-1, 2001) for quality assurance. The ISO 9126-1 software quality model identifies six main quality characteristics, namely: Functionality, Reliability, Usability, Efficiency, Maintainability and Portability. User modelling is taken one step further by also profiling the user based on human-human and human-computer interactions. User/Learner eXperience (U/LX) is considered to be a vital part in HCI for evaluating the Graphical User Interface as well as the Distributed User Interfaces.

Unambiguously, Adaptive VR, AR and MR have to be evaluated empirically to guarantee that the collective intelligence really works. In HCI-Ed flexibility demands are explicit for human computer interaction, including the adaptivity system capabilities for Ontological Design:

1. Evaluation of reliability and external validity of input data acquisition
2. Evaluation of the inference mechanism and accuracy of user properties
3. Appropriateness of suggestions
4. Change of system behaviour when the system adapts based on characteristics

5. Change of user behaviour when system adapts based on characteristics
6. Change and quality of total interaction to conform with characteristics
7. Triangulation for rich, valid and timely recommendations

The last evaluation step can only be interpreted correctly if all the previous steps have been completed. Especially in the case of finding no difference between an adaptive and a non-adaptive system the previous steps provide hints at shortcomings. The results of such a layered evaluation are much better to interpret and give more exact hints for failures and false inferences than a simple usability evaluation.

6 Concluding Remarks and Future Work

This paper described the need to consider both the brain cognitive plasticity and creativity when utilising Virtual or Augmented Reality in Computer Aided Learning. In order to capture users' perceptual pathways, Creative Immersive eXperience (iX) is incorporated into the common Human Computer Interaction design and development cycle. Our computer tools are used to reduce our everyday complexity. Such world increasingly complex environment, rapid adaptability is necessary. Enhancing forward thinking is therefore essential for the learners to harness this complexity to their advantage [3]. Therefore the proposed Ontological Design for Creative Immersive Experience to utilise to empowered and enabled the processes needed to achieve such engagement with the world. Furthermore, such creative engagement can exploit and catalyse such complexity with inherent power to invent new perspective and assumptions and create new models geared to an ever-changing world. A fundamental objective of HCI research is to make systems more usable, more useful, more accessible and to provide users with experiences fitting their specific background knowledge and objectives. The challenge in an information-rich world is not only to make information available to people at any time, at any place, and in any form, but specifically to say the "right" thing at the "right" time in the "right" way. User models are defined as models that systems have of users that reside inside a computational environment.

New technologies such as Adaptive VR, AR and MR tools in particular can forward and accelerate thinking and also support problem solving processes as well as creative thinking and insight functioning in complex, ill-structured, plastic and ever changing and agile contexts. Ontological Design can optimise and sustain long term user and changing needs through emotional and physiological engagement in Immersive Experience for better user engagement in the creative flow.

References

1. Carr, N.: The Shallows. W.W. Norton & Company, London (2010)
2. Pascual-Leone, A., Freitas, C., Oberman, L., Horvath, J.C., Halko, M., Eldaief, M., et al.: Characterizing brain cortical plasticity and network dynamics across the age-span in health and disease with TMS-EEG and TMS-fMRI. Brain Topogr. **24**, 302–315 (2011)
3. IBM Report: Capitalizing on Complexity: Insights from the Global Chief Executive Officer Study.http://public.dhe.ibm.com/common/ssi/ecm/en/gbe03297usen/GBE03297USEN.PDF

4. Kalat, J.W.: Biological Psychology, 8th edn. Wadsworth, Australia (2003)
5. Lambropoulos, N., Romero, M.: 21st Century Lifelong Creative Learning: A Matrix of Innovative Methods and New Technologies for Individual, Team and Community Skills and Competencies. Nova Publishers, New York (2015)
6. Kounios, J., Beeman, M.: The Eureka Factor: Aha Moments, Creative Insight, and the Brain. Random House, New York (2015)
7. Goswami, A.: Quantum Creativity, Kindle edn. Amazon, New York (2014)
8. Pantelidis, V.S.: Reasons to Use Virtual Reality in Education and Training Courses and a Model to Determine When to Use Virtual Reality.In: Themes Science And Technology Education. Klidarithmos Computer Books, Athens (2014)
9. Kangdon, L.: Augmented reality in education and training. Tech Trends 56(2), 13–21 (2012)
10. Johnson, L., Levine, A., Smith, R., Stone, S.: Simple augmented reality. The 2010 Horizon Report, pp. 21-24. The New Media Consortium, Austin (2010)
11. Shelton, B.E.: Augmented reality and education: Current projects and the potential for classroom learning. New Horizons for Learning (2002). http://www.newhorizons.org/strategies/technology/shelton.htm
12. Preston, S.D., de Waal, B.M.: Empathy: its ultimate and proximate bases. Behav. Brain Sci. 25, 1–72 (2002)
13. Norman, J.: Two visual systems and two theories of perception: An attempt to reconcile the constructivist and ecological approaches. Behav Brain Sci 25, 73–144 (2002)

The Potential Use of the Flexilevel Test in Providing Personalised Mobile E-Assessments

Andrew Pyper[(⊠)], Mariana Lilley, Paul Wernick,
and Amanda Jefferies

School of Computer Science, University of Hertfordshire, Hatfield, UK
a.r.pyper@herts.ac.uk

Abstract. Sixteen students took a test that included a Flexilevel stage and a standard Computer Based Test (CBT) stage. The results were analysed using a Spearman's Rank Order correlation and showed a significant positive correlation ($rs = 0.58$, $p <=0.05$). This was taken to provide support for the notion that it is possible to provide shorter Flexilevel objective tests that are as efficacious as CBTs. Implications that this finding may have for the use of the Flexilevel Test in mobile learning contexts is discussed.

Keywords: Flexilevel · E-assessment · Mobile assessment · Computerised adaptive testing · Mobile and/or ubiquitous learning · Personalization · Technology enhanced learning

1 Introduction

There has been increased interest in the use of the Flexilevel Test [6, 7] in Higher Education contexts [2, 3, 5] due to its potential to personalize educational experiences.

This study is part of a programme of research aimed at understanding how the Flexilevel Test may be applied in genuine educational contexts and an increasingly important part of our educational context is mobile learning and assessment. This brings new challenges to the work, particularly in terms of supporting students in attending to cognitively demanding tasks such as formative assessments in a mobile context which itself imposes significant cognitive load [8].

However, the case for supporting mobile learning and assessment is compelling, both from pedagogical and practical perspective [2, 17], for example learners are often under significant time pressure and, given appropriate opportunities, can make use of short periods of time to engage in their studies [17].

In principle, one of the possible benefits of the Flexilevel test is the ability to present fewer items in a test than a standard Computer Based Test (CBT) approach yet still obtain a comparably accurate measurement of a test-taker's proficiency [20]. This is something that the authors have also found in a simulation study [14]. The potential to provide shorter tests is of interest, since it may provide an opportunity for educationally useful experiences in a broader range of contexts as noted above [2, 17]. Further, it may provide these opportunities whilst mitigating some of the challenges to deploying formative assessments in a mobile context. As such, it is of interest to

© Springer International Publishing Switzerland 2015
P. Zaphiris and A. Ioannou (Eds.): LCT 2015, LNCS 9192, pp. 271–278, 2015.
DOI: 10.1007/978-3-319-20609-7_26

investigate whether or not this effect can be reproduced in a genuine educational context. This study is intended to investigate the extent to which shorter Flexilevel tests may provide comparably accurate measures of a test-taker's proficiency as a CBT in a summative assessment.

2 The Flexilevel Test

The Flexilevel Test was first proposed by Lord [6] as a paper-based test. One of its aims was to tailor the test difficulty level to the proficiency level of individual test-takers. This is an important difference between the Flexilevel Test and traditional CBTs as in the case of the latter, all test-takers are presented with the same set of test items.

The Flexilevel Test is a fixed branched test that supports the personalization of objective tests by presenting items to test-takers depending on their performance. It represents an approach to adapting assessment that is less resource intensive than other forms of adaptive testing, for example approaches based on other pyramidal approaches [20] or Item Response Theory (IRT) [6, 7].

A Flexilevel Test requires a set of $2n$-1 items where n is the number of items to be presented in the test. Test items are ranked in order of difficulty. There are different approaches to ranking the items; for example the use of expert calibration or calibration from an existing set of test-taker responses from preceding tests. In the work reported here, an existing set of responses from a previous test and the formula shown below, adapted from Ward [19], were used to calculate the difficulty of individual items in which n_p is the number of test-takers who answered the item correctly and n_r is the total number of test-takers answering the item.

$$D = 1 - \left(\frac{n_p}{n_r}\right) \tag{1}$$

After the difficulty of each item was calculated, items were ranked from the easiest to the most difficult.

A Flexilevel Test usually begins with the presentation of the item of median difficulty, typically an item with a difficulty of 0.5. If test-takers answer the item incorrectly, they are presented with the next available easier item. If they answer the item correctly, they are presented with the next available more difficult item (as shown in Fig. 1).

Once the true ability of a test-taker is reached, subsequent patterns will show an increasingly large range of difficulty between the items selected, as illustrated in Fig. 2.

Typical stopping conditions for the test are when the number of items to be administered have all been presented to the test-taker or the duration of the test has been reached, whichever happens first.

3 The Study

In this study, a test of 40 items was presented to 18 online distance learning students on an undergraduate Computer Science programme of study as a formative assessment.

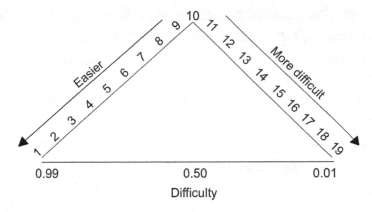

Fig. 1 The Flexilevel Test Structure (adapted from Betz and Weiss 1975)

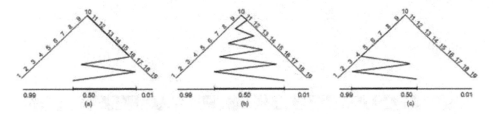

Fig. 2 Example patterns for different proficiencies (from Betz and Weiss, 1975)

3.1 The E-Assessment Application

It was necessary that the Flexilevel Test would be made available online, as the participants were geographically dispersed. A web application using HTML5, Java-Script and CSS on the client side and PHP and MySQL on the server side was purpose built for this reason.

The e-assessment application supported two different item selection algorithms: a traditional CBT and a Flexilevel Test. Test items were selected from the database and presented individually; this is consistent with the need for the Flexilevel algorithm to select an appropriate item depending on the performance of individual test-takers. Figure 3 shows how the user interface contained minimal information and gave no cues to the approach, CBT or Flexilevel, being used.

3.2 Methodology

The test presented in this study was part of the formative assessment of a group of 18 first year online distance learning Computer Science students. The test related to their knowledge and understanding of internet technologies and, in particular, ASP.NET.

The test was presented to students online via the web application introduced earlier. It was invigilated by a remote live invigilation service to ensure students were not

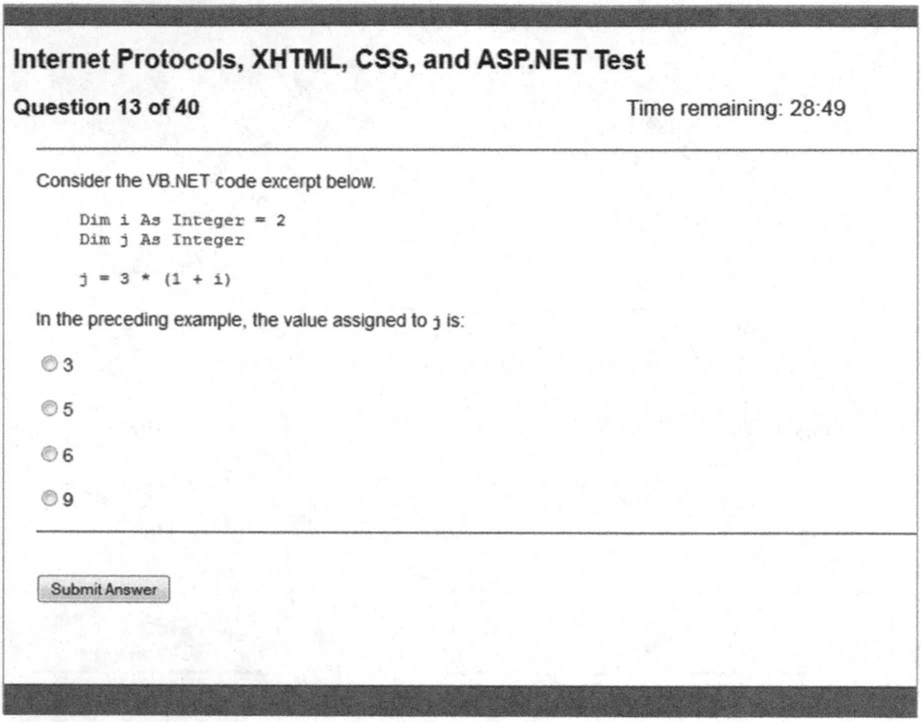

Internet Protocols, XHTML, CSS, and ASP.NET Test

Question 13 of 40   Time remaining: 28:49

Consider the VB.NET code excerpt below.

```
Dim i As Integer = 2
Dim j As Integer

j = 3 * (1 + i)
```

In the preceding example, the value assigned to j is:

◎ 3

◎ 5

◎ 6

◎ 9

Submit Answer

Fig. 3 Screenshot of the user interface of the application, showing the presentation of an item

accessing materials that were not permitted during their test. It was limited to 40 min and contained 40 items overall. The test items had gone through calibration using data from the performance of an earlier cohort of students.

An initial stage outside of the scope of the study, but relevant to the coverage of topics in the module, was presented first for every student. This stage contained 10 items. Then, the examinees were randomly assigned to one of two different groups. Half the participants were assigned to Group 1, and the second half to Group 2. Group 1 was presented with Flexilevel followed by CBT, and Group 2 was presented with CBT followed by Flexilevel. Both the Flexilevel and CBT stages covered ASP. NET and for the students there was no distinction between these two test stages. The Flexilevel and CBT stages consisted of 10 and 20 items respectively.

3.3   Results

Table 1 shows the range of the scores obtained and the mean score for each stage of the test. It can be seen that the scores for both of the stages ranged relatively widely. The responses from two participants were removed from the analysis as they did not complete one or more test stages.

Table 1 Summary of test performance (N = 16)

Test Stage	Minimum Score	Maximum Score	Mean Score
Flexilevel (out of 10)	5	9	7.625
CBT (out of 20)	5	19	12

A Spearman's Rank Order correlation was run to determine the relationship between the CBT and Flexilevel scores. It showed a significant positive correlation ($rs = 0.58$, $p <=0.05$) between the scores achieved by students in the Flexilevel and CBT test stages.

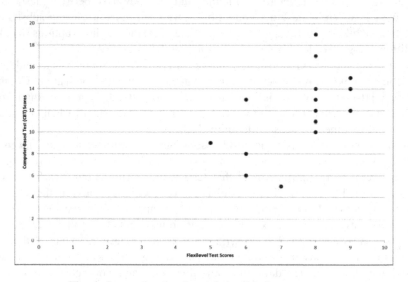

Fig. 4 Scatterplot showing relationship between scores

These results provide support for the notion that the Flexilevel approach to e-assessment can provide comparable results to a standard CBT test whilst only presenting half the items.

4 Discussion

There are practical issues to address given the application of the Flexilevel Test in mobile contexts that have not applied to the desktop and classroom contexts of studies conducted by the authors so far (for example [5, 13]). Key to the differences between desktop and mobile use of Flexilevel testing is the greater competition for limited attentional resources that mobile environments may impose.

Whilst desktop computer contexts may vary, the difference in mobile usage contexts may vary quite substantially [11] and also during a given interaction. In short, the contexts for mobile use tend to be more diverse and potentially distracting than those using desktop computers.

Oulasvirta et al. [11] used a range of tasks on a mobile device to elucidate how different contexts may impact on the attention of users. Factors that impacted upon users' attention to the tasks they had been set included the amount of social interaction that users needed to engage in, for example in managing their personal space whilst using an escalator, and the predictability of their context. Where there was much going on in the users' context, it required that users attended to their contexts for longer and more often; their attention to the task was interrupted.

These are temporary changes in the focus of attention away from a given task with a mobile device and it is worth noting that many interruptions are triggered by the user themselves [18]. Overall, an indication of the impact of such interruptions may be found in differences in the length of interaction users may have between desktop and mobile devices whereby desktop interactions have been timed as lasting substantially longer than mobile interactions [10]. Furthermore, it seems that interruptions may have an additional cognitive load in terms of switching between tasks [15].

Framing the analysis in terms of cognitive load provides a good basis to understand how mobile contexts may impact upon users' usage of a mobile application. Cognitive load theory [16] has also been influential in learning, particularly multimedia learning [8] and it seems pertinent also to mobile learning and e-assessment when considering the impact of extraneous loads on learning [12].

Clearly context of use is an important contributor to extraneous load, and in providing silent, invigilated exam conditions, extraneous load is minimized freeing cognitive resources for the intrinsic load that tests impose. This is the case for previous studies conducted by the authors. Whilst the contexts may vary in these desktop environments, the studies have previously involved environments that were controlled to some substantial extent, for example in both formative and summative assessments in computer laboratories [5, 13], or with students taking tests remotely at their own computers as in the study reported here; all were invigilated and were the focus of the students' attention. This was done for both educational and empirical reasons; but the contexts of use of the Flexilevel assessment have not varied much.

However if a Flexilevel test were deployed in a mobile context, then it could be competing for attention in a much more diverse context with a relatively high potential for interruption. As noted, this is something that impacts upon the capacity of learners to attend to a given task [10, 12].

Effectively it is more likely that there will be a higher extraneous load in the completion of tasks in a mobile context. This becomes most disruptive to the completion of tasks when the distractions occupy the same channels as the task, something that is consistent with the influential account of working memory [1]. For example, it would be expected that interruptions that require visual perception would impact more acutely on the performance of a task since the task itself involves visual perception, at least in this study.

However, it may be expected that some tasks may be attended to with greater engagement and concentration than others and an important question would be how mobile contexts may effect interactions that require greater engagement with the mobile task [11] something that seems pertinent to even relatively short mobile e-assessments. A possible implication of this is that learners may choose where and when they take formative assessments such that interruptions are less likely.

5 Conclusion and Future Work

The study reported here provides further support for the idea that the Flexilevel approach can provide shorter tests in genuine educational contexts, although this must be treated with caution given the small scale of the study. It is intended that further studies will be conducted in order to establish if this effect can be demonstrated reliably.

It has also been noted that the approach of learners to their formative assessment activities in mobile contexts is of fundamental importance. As such, future work will focus on gaining an understanding of the attitude and approach of test-takers to their mobile formative assessment. How are test-takers using the application in mobile contexts, specifically in what kinds of contexts are they taking the tests? Also, what kind of learning activities are they willing to carry out on a mobile device, and does this include formative assessment? It has been suggested that a formative assessment may motivate learners to minimize interruptions themselves, but anecdotally learners have indicated that they learn opportunistically in mobile contexts, for example the short period of time between tutorials or lectures.

It seems that future studies will need to adopt two main strands of work; establishing the reliability of the correlation between the shorter Flexilevel test and full length CBT reported in this study and investigating how this may impact upon learner attitudes to formative assessment in mobile contexts.

References

1. Baddeley, A.: Is Working Memory Still Working? Am. Psychol. **56**, 849–864 (2001)
2. Betz, N.E., Weiss, D.J.; Empirical and simulation studies of flexilevel ability testing (Research Report 75-3) University of Minnesota, Department of Psychology, Psychometric Methods Program, Minneapolis (1975)
3. Gordon, N. (2014). "Flexible Pedagogies: technology-enhanced learning." Higher Education Academy, NIACE. https://www.heacademy.ac.uk/sites/default/files/resources/TEL_report_0.pdf [last accessed 06/03/2015]
4. Herrington, J., Herrington, A., Mantei, J., Olney, I., & Ferry, B. (2009). "New technologies, new pedagogies: Using mobile technologies to develop new ways of teaching and learning." Final report to the Australian Learning and Teaching Council. Strawberry Hills, NSW: Australian Learning and Teaching Council
5. Lilley, M., & Pyper, A. (2009). "The application of the flexilevel approach for the assessment of computer science undergraduates." In Human-Computer Interaction. Interacting in Various Application Domains (pp. 140-148). Springer Berlin Heidelberg
6. Lord, F.M.: The self-scoring flexilevel test. J. Educ. Meas. **8**, 147–151 (1971)
7. Lord, F.M.: Applications of item response theory to practical testing problems. Erlbaum, Hillsdale, NJ (1980)
8. Mayer, R.E.: Applying the science of learning: evidence-based principles for the design of multimedia instruction. Am. Psychol. **63**(8), 760 (2008)
9. Mendoza, A. (2013). "Mobile user experience: patterns to make sense of it all." Morgan Kaufmann Publishers Inc
10. Monsell, S.: Task switching. Trends in cognitive sciences **7**(3), 134–140 (2003)

11. Oulasvirta, A., Tamminen, S., Roto, V. & Kuorelahti, J. (2005) "Interaction in 4-second bursts: the fragmented nature of attentional resources in mobile HCI." In Proceedings of the SIGCHI conference on Human factors in computing systems. ACM, 2005

12. Oviatt, S. (2006). "Human-centered design meets cognitive load theory: designing interfaces that help people think." In Proceedings of the 14th annual ACM international conference on Multimedia (pp. 871-880). ACM, 2006

13. Pyper, A., & Lilley, M. (2010). "A comparison between the flexilevel and conventional approaches to objective testing." In Proceedings of CAA 2010 International Conference, Southampton

14. Pyper, A., Lilley, M., Wernick, P., Jefferies. A (2014) "A simulation of a Flexilevel test." Paper presented at HEA STEM Annual Conference 2014, Edinburgh

15. Sandy J. J. Gould, Anna L. Cox, Duncan P. Brumby (2013) "Frequency and Duration of Self-Initiated Task-Switching in an Online Investigation of Interrupted Performance Human Computation and Crowdsourcing: Works in Progress and Demonstration Abstracts" AAAI Technical Report CR-13-01

16. Sweller, J. (2010). "Element interactivity and intrinsic, extraneous, and germane cognitive load." Educational psychology review, 22(2), 123-138. Multimedia learning

17. Traxler, J.: Defining, discussing and evaluating mobile learning: the moving finger writes and having writ. The International Review of Research in Open and Distributed Learning 8 (2) 2007

18. Dawood, Mohammad, Fieseler, Michael, Büther, Florian, Jiang, X., Schäfers, Klaus P.: A Multi-resolution Optical Flow Based Approach to Respiratory Motion Correction in 3D PET/CT Images. In: Zhang, David (ed.) ICMB 2008. LNCS, vol. 4901, pp. 314–322. Springer, Heidelberg (2007)

19. Ward, C.: Preparing and Using Objective Questions. Nelson Thornes Ltd, Cheltenham (1980)

20. Weiss, D.J., Betz, N.E.: Ability Measurement: Conventional or Adaptive? (Research Report 75-3). Minneapolis: University of Minnesota, Department of Psychology, Psychometric Methods Program (1973)

Supporting Golf Coaching and Swing Instruction with Computer-Based Training Systems

Maria Riveiro[1](✉), Anders Dahlbom[1], Rikard König[2], Ulf Johansson[2],
and Peter Brattberg[2,3]

[1] School of Informatics, University of Skövde, Skövde, Sweden
maria.riveiro@his.se
[2] Department of Information Technology, University of Borås, Borås, Sweden
[3] PGA Sweden, Bara, Sweden

Abstract. Golf is a popular sport around the world. Since an accomplished golf swing is essential for succeeding in this sport, golf players spend a considerable amount of time perfecting their swing. In order to guide the design of future computer-based training systems that support swing instruction, this paper analyzes the data gathered during interviews with golf instructors and participant observations of actual swing coaching sessions. Based on our field work, we describe the characteristics of a proficient swing, how the instructional sessions are normally carried out and the challenges professional instructors face. Taking into account these challenges, we outline which desirable capabilities future computer-based training systems for professional golf instructors should have.

Keywords: Golf · Swing instruction · Computer-based training systems

1 Introduction

Golf has grown exceptionally in the past decades; today it is played by over 60 million people around the world, being one of the leading sports in terms of total economic expenditure [1]. One of the crucial parts of this strategy game is the swing; an accomplished swing is key for succeeding in this sport [2]. Many amateur players spend a considerable amount of time and effort perfecting their swing, improving accuracy, precision, consistency and distance [2].

Despite the increase of golf tools available in the market and the availability of plenty of materials explaining how to carry out such sequence of movements, novice golf players still find improving their swing skills to be a challenge [3]. Normally, golfers improve their swing through sessions with professional golf instructors using verbal and gestural feedback [3]. Not withstanding the effectiveness of these traditional methods, with the rapid development of sensors, electronics and data analysis techniques, new opportunities open up for making these instructional sessions more effective, combining both guided and self assessment-based methods.

© Springer International Publishing Switzerland 2015
P. Zaphiris and A. Ioannou (Eds.): LCT 2015, LNCS 9192, pp. 279–290, 2015.
DOI: 10.1007/978-3-319-20609-7_27

Advanced computer-based training systems may support both golf instructors and players. On the one hand, golf instructors are required to make fast and accurate observations of the movement patterns and subsequently, guide the player towards a more optimal technique through appropriate coaching sessions [4]. Even if most instructors can quickly highlight the major faults and provide corrective measures, golf instructors typically lack methods to communicate guidance, follow up and administrate the learning process. In a study presented by Schempp et al. [5] regarding the major facets of professional golf instructors, several participants expressed the need to incorporate the use of technology as well as improve on its use during teaching (e.g. *"video and other technologies [could] speed the learning process"* and *"by keeping up with the latest versions of technology I feel I gain an edge in my ability to communicate with my students"* [5]).

On the other hand, coaching sessions can be expensive for amateur golfers and thus, they spend a great deal of time improving their swing movement on their own [3]. However, most of them do not know where to focus their efforts, since it is difficult to identify and modify faults in the complex combination of related movements that constitute a successful swing [3].

These aspects relate to a general area within sports, that is, performance evaluation [6]. Performance evaluation is an essential part of sports and it is concerned with domain modeling and evaluation with respect to such models [7]. Performance improvement guidance is perhaps the least investigated area of computer science within sports. Already in 2006, Barlett [8] argued for the potential of using expert systems and machine learning techniques in sports biomechanics analysis for improvement of performance. Barlett [8], however, concluded that the usage so far is very low. Owusu [7] presents a general model, recognize critique recommend, which can be used for performance improvement in sports. Owusu discusses the use of neural networks and expert systems for recognition and critique, but concludes that very little has been investigated on these topics and especially on the final step of providing recommendations for improved performance.

Both golf instructors and amateur players would benefit from feedback provided by computer-based training systems that use the analysis of sensor and historical data as a basis for their inferences. In order to guide the development of such computer-based training systems for golf instructors, this study addresses the following research questions: (RQ1) how can a good swing be characterized? (RQ2) How is the swing instruction carried out today? (RQ3) What are the challenges and difficulties regarding the instruction process? And, (RQ4) which desirable capabilities should future computer-based training systems for professional golf instructors have to overcome these challenges?

This paper is organized as follows: we first discuss related work summarizing studies describing how golf coaches carry out their instruction and which tools are used for supporting these activities. The research methods employed for answering the research questions are described in Sect. 3 while the results are presented in Sect. 4. The main capabilities of future computer-based training systems for golf instructors are outlined in Sect. 5. Finally, a brief discussion of the study's results and main conclusions are presented in Sects. 6 and 7.

2   Related Work

This section presents a summary of relevant literature related to the work of professional golf instructors, key features of an accomplished swing and tools used as aids for supporting golf training.

2.1   Professional Golf Instructors

Despite the numerous golf instructional books and materials, to the best of our knowledge, publications and formal studies regarding how professional golf instructors carry out their work and their professional practices are very scarce. However, there are three studies that can help us to understand how they assess a golf swing and provide feedback, c.f. [4], and which are the particular skills of golf instructors, c.f. [5,9].

Smith et al. [4] identify the key technical parameters that professional golf instructors associate with a "top level" swing, interviewing and observing sixteen professional coaches. The results show that many coaches determined a successful golf swing from initially observing the "ball flight". Furthermore, many coaches acknowledged that the ball flight was a result of two important parameters, the "club motion" which was affected by the player's "body motion". The descriptors used to characterize these parameters were "consistent", "powerful", "accurate", "simple" and "controlled" with the most prevalent being "repeatable". The authors also highlight that "body motion" was influenced by five intrinsically linked key parameters, i.e., "posture", "body rotation", "sequential movement", "hand and arm action" and "club parameters".

The work presented by Schempp et al. [5,9] focuses in identifying the facets of professional practice monitored by expert teachers in general, i.e. the knowledge and skills expert sport coaches normally examine in order to improve their teaching (self-monitoring). For doing so, they selected expert golf instructors, so the results presented by Schempp et al. [5,9] are relevant in the particular case of golf instructors. A paper-based questionnaire was taken by thirty-one golf teachers (ranked by the Golf Magazine as in the top 100). From the data collected, five themes were constructed that represented the activities and qualities most often monitored by golf instructors: skills (i.e., things teachers do), knowledge base (i.e., things teachers know), personal characteristics (i.e., things teachers are), philosophy (i.e., things teachers believe), and tools (i.e., things teachers use). Even if skills and knowledge were the most important components, teaching tools used in undertaking the task of teaching golf was also highlighted as an area that should be regularly monitored.

2.2   Aid Tools for Golf Coaching and Training

There are multiple systems for swing analysis, but the majority of them provide quantitative data and lack feedback that it is easy to interpret by golf amateurs [3]. In this section, we briefly review systems that not only provide sensor data but which also give some kind of guidance that can be used by the player to improve his/her skills.

Chun et al. [3] focus their analysis on the wrist movement while performing a swing. The authors describe an autonomous kinematic analysis platform, using the Microsoft Kinect camera system[1], for wrist angle measurement that is capable of evaluating a user's uncocking swing motion (i.e. downswing, see Fig. 2) and providing instructional feedback. According to the authors, the graphical user interface (GUI) provides five types of intuitive feedback: (1) verbal and (2) textual instructions for improving the user's uncocking motion based on the feedback comments and scores defined in a special module embedded in the platform (the generation module), (3) wrist angle sequence visualization using a graph, (4) 2D video and (5) 3D video based on the color and depth data streams captured by the Kinect installed in front of the golfer. A virtual coaching environment for improving the swing is presented in [10]. Using high-speed 3D motion captured data, the visualization and analysis tool identifies faults in a golf player's stroke mechanisms, aligning and comparing the player's swing with players of higher skill levels. From these comparisons explicit instructions on how the player should change their stroke mechanics are visualized in the 3D virtual environment.

There are other works that even if they do not concern golf swing, they can be used as illustrative examples. A simple GUI implemented in Matlab to improve the motor skills for performing a golf putt is presented in [11]. The video of the putt is displayed with quantitative values such as the putt tempo (ratio backswing duration:downswing duration) and score which gives an indication of how close the putt tempo is to the ideal ratio of 2/1.

There are several examples in the literature that present necessary intermediate steps to provide feedback to improve the golf swing, however, they do not present a complete system that provides feedback to players. An example is the work presented in [12], where the challenges associated with the extraction of a highly complex articulated motion from a golf swing video scene is tackled. The authors developed a markerless human motion tracking system that tracks the major body parts of an athlete straight from a sports broadcast video, using a combination of three algorithms.

Commercial solutions for analyzing golf swing are available, e.g. TrackMan, Swing Profile, Swing Smart, Swing Byte 2 or Sky Pro (a comparison of some of these solutions can be read online: http://www.mygolfspy.com/skypro-swing-analyzer-trainer-review/ [Accessed 2015-02-16]); however, to the best of our knowledge, their capabilities for providing feedback are limited.

3   Methods

In order to characterize how professional golf instructors carry out swing instructional sessions, we have conducted empirical work through two primary

---

[1] Kinect is a line of motion sensing input device (webcam-style) that enables users to interact and control their computer using gestures and voice.

qualitative methods: *participant observation* and *in-depth interviewing* (see [13] for a detailed description of these methods). Participant observation is both an overall approach to inquiry and a data gathering method, where the researcher spends a considerable amount of time in the setting, learning about the daily life there [13]. Qualitative in-depth interviews are much more like conversations, where the researcher explores a few general topics to help uncover the participant's view [13].

Three professional golf instructors participated in this study. All of them have extensive experience in golf coaching (PGA certified) and are active in the field, working at three different golf clubs in the area of Västra Götaland, Sweden. Interviews and participant observations were used to collect data, supported by visuals such as video and photographs (see Fig. 1). For consistency, the two first authors of this paper performed all the interviews and the first author carried out the participant observations.

Fig. 1. Swing instruction: video recordings and TrackMan sensors were used to collect data during the field work.

4   Results

This section presents a summary of the data collected during the field work carried out, introducing a description of the swing instruction process, the characteristics of a good swing highlighted by the instructors and a description of current tools and materials used for supporting the instruction process. Broadly, we discuss that it is not easy to provide a unique description of a "good" swing and that it varies very much from player to player. As expressed by the instructors, it is a matter of balancing power and precision, where repeatability normally is a desirable property. Historically, there has not been a unique example of the perfect swing either, and the desired properties of a good swing have evolved as well. We highlight problems associated to, for example, the communication instructor-player, the need for having a long term learning strategy, the development of repositories of exercises based on empirical evidence and the advantages of developing various types of good swing models that then can be used for providing individual feedback based on the particular characteristics off each player.

Fig. 2. Swing positions. The various illustrations show the golf swing sequence: set-up position (P1), club parallel to ground (P2), left arm parallel to ground (P3), top of the backswing (P4), left arm parallel to ground (P5), club shaft parallel to ground (P6), impact (P7), club shaft parallel to ground on through swing (P8), right arm parallel to ground on through swing (P9) and finish position (P10).

4.1   Proficient Swing and Swing Instruction (RQ1 and RQ2)

This section summarizes how the instruction of a golf swing session is carried out based on our observations. Obviously, it is a challenge to summarize a process that can have large variations from player to player, but the aim of this section is to find those leverage points were support can be provided.

The first session normally starts with a conversation where the golf instructor tries to find out as much as possible about the interests, capacities and goals of the player, a conversation that can vary largely depending on how long they have known each other. During the first training session, the coach asked the player to hit several balls. The instructor looks mainly to the ball flight and the landing positions, i.e. spread, in both length and width. Both the body motion, as well as how the ball is hit are crucial aspects of an accomplished swing. Thus, the ball flight, the body motion and the hit are the focus of the instructors' assessment. As expressed by the instructors, *repeatability* and *consistency* are both required characteristics of a good swing.

What do the instructors look at when assessing a swing? Taking into account the observations carried out and the interviews they mainly look at (1) the ball

Fig. 3. Illustrations from a swing coaching session from our field work. Figure 3(a) and (b) show the use of tools to support the performance analysis process (TrackMan, camera and computer). Figure 3(a) and (b) exhibit two examples of the traditional means, verbal and gestural, of delivering feedback for performance improvement.

flight, (2) the spread of the ball (both directions), (3) the body motion, (4) the ball hit, (5) the power and (6) the control over the whole process.

While the trainee does several swings, the instructor looks at various aspects of the swing (see Fig. 3). First, they take a look at the ball flight (does it present a similar pattern?, how is the spread of the ball?) and its connection to the ball hit (was the ball hit in the center, on its way up or on its way down?). The hit moment is crucial. If the hit is irregular (new players have larger variation), the instructor looks if the lowest point of hit is at the correct place. However, different body motions can achieve a good hit.

In general, it is desired to have a pure and similar contact with the ball every time (repeatability and consistency). Once the hit is good, the instructor will move forward to other aspects, such as e.g. achieving more power or more control of the ball flight (e.g. curvature).

Support. Broadly, the instruction process consists in observation, feedback and observation again. The trainee carries out several swings, while the instructor observes and listens (recording with the video camera). The instructor analyzes what happened with the ball and the hit. When improvements are needed, verbal and gestural feedback is provided (sometimes the feedback is provided with the support of the recorded session, showing what is necessary to change and why). After that a new trial phase starts, where the progression is assessed. We would like to note that not only repetitions of the swing were requested; the instructors also proposed several exercises to practice, for example, the body rotation, so the trainee would be aware of its own rotation motion without swinging (which part of the body should rotate around what and which part should not move during the rotation).

The support tools used by the three instructors that were interviewed and observed were mainly, video camera and TrackMan (connected to a computer). The video camera was used to record the swing. The instructor normally employed the video camera to show the trainee the rotation, highlighting the faults or improvement possibilities; the video camera was therefore normally employed as a communication means. The TrackMan radar was used to measure the club and ball parameters. It was used by the instructor for complementing and validating his analysis regarding the ball flight, the hit and the club movement. Other support tools that the instructors mentioned that could be used during the swing training sessions were pressure plates (that measure where the center of gravity is, weight pressure against ground and how does it change over time), impact tape or spray (to see the ball hit), 3D sensors to assess the body movement and several video cameras (to see the body motion from different angles).

4.2   Challenges (RQ3)

The main challenges highlighted by the instructors interviewed involve pedagogical concerns. These pedagogical concerns relate to the adjustment of the teaching situation to the particular characteristics of the player (*"which vocabulary should I use? Which metaphors? Which support tools? How do I explain how and why? How do I explain cause-effect?"*) One of the major pedagogical concerns expressed by the golf instructors was communication. Successful communication and mutual understanding instructor-player is crucial for a fruitful learning process, but not always it is easy to overcome the large age, background, interests, motivational, physiological and psychological differences among the trainees. All the instructors saw communication as a critical skill in golf training.

A clear strategy for learning and achieving training and learning outcomes was identified as problematic to establish by the instructors. The instructors lack means of structuring the learning process, the training outcomes, the content of each session, the pacing and scheduling. These challenges relate also to administrative skills and the lack of appropriate support tools; as it was mentioned, it is hard to keep record of the players, their situation, achievements and expected outcomes.

The last challenge that we frame under pedagogical concerns stressed by the interviewees relate to instructor self-assessment and self-monitoring of instructors' own practices. Instructors were concerned about their own improvement (*"how do we get better?"*), how do they critically analyze themselves and which factors can improve their performance.

Besides problems related to communication, learning strategies and self-assessment there are other challenges expressed by the instructors, such as, *"are there scientific prove that certain exercises produce certain effects? Can exercises be isolated in blocks? What is the best and fastest way of learning? Which are the most relevant exercises to achieve the desire change? How do we change movement patterns (players underestimate the amount of time that is required to change a pattern)? How do we keep players motivated? How do we ourselves keep motivated and find passion for teaching golf?"*

Regarding the support tools, instructors have expressed their desire of having an integrated platform where body motion, from different angles, images from video cameras and radar data could be analyzed. Moreover, more automatic analysis capabilities over the various types of data that can be collected are required. There are many other sensors that can be used to collect golf-related data, but it is not easy to see how to best use them in a learning context.

5   Future Computer-Based Training Systems (RQ4)

Based on the descriptions given and challenges highlighted in previous sections, we outline which key capabilities (C) future computer-based training systems should have for swing training:

C1. Semi-automatic performance evaluation: the ability of providing performance evaluation, following the model by Owusu [7]: recognize faults, criticize and recommend. Within this capability we group those methods needed to build models from historical data collected from skilled players (swing modeling), compare those models that best fit player's characteristics with actual swings and detect faults. We include here as well the capability of providing recommendations regarding which exercises should be carried out to improve performance.

C2. Interactive analysis: the ability of exploring the golf data interactively, finding patterns, clusters, anomalies, new insights, etc. For doing so, techniques from the areas of data mining (e.g. clustering, decision trees) and visual analytics (e.g. linking, brushing, parallel coordinates) need to be integrated.

C3. Visualization: effective interactive visualization methods that are able to support communication instructor–player. Visualization can be used to depict player's own swing, the swing models of high skill players, compare player's own swing with the models, illustrate improvements (if–then situations), show cause–effect relations, the swing plane, projections, etc.

C4. Data collection and sensor integration: an effective integration or fusion of the various types of data (video, radar, 3D markers, etc.) enables the construction of richer swing models and better swing assessments that take into account the relations among the interconnected characteristics of a accomplished swing. Here we include as well capabilities for solving the problems associated with the alignment of the various sensors. The integration, for example, of radar data regarding ball flight, club motion, hit with the high speed motion captures of the club and body movements seem crucial for detecting possible flaws and for providing feedback.

C5. Learning strategy: be able to build and administrate a learning and training strategy for each player. This capability should include a library of exercises and their effects based on experimental evidence, mapping training outcomes with most effective exercises. Such capability should not only focus on the individual parts of the game, e.g. swing or putting, but should take into account the complete player's game in order to allow for improvements. Naturally, such capabilities should thus not only take as input the individual parts of the game but should support gathering and analysis of data from all aspects of it.

C.6 Self-assessment: support for instructor's self-monitoring, assessment and improved performance. Furthermore, this capability should include a platform for information sharing for instructors: forums, instruction exchange, golf schools, basic instructor training, experiences, etc.

6   Discussion

This paper presents the results from interviews with golf instructors and observations of golf swing instructional sessions in order to characterize an accomplished swing, describing how the swing instruction is carried out today and which tools are used for supporting this process. The challenges highlighted relate to pedagogical concerns, and were grouped under communication, learning strategy and self-assessment. The characteristics outlined for a good swing in this study match previous research in the area. The swing descriptors *"consistent"* and *"repeatable"* expressed by the instructors interviewed for this study were also mentioned, among others, by Smith et al. in [4] (see Sect. 2.1 for more details on Smith et al.'s work). Moreover, some of the challenges highlighted in Sect. 4.2, communication and self-assessment, coincide with those found by Schempp et al. in [5].

In this paper, we have argued that rigorous scientific research that investigates the effectiveness of various swing exercises to achieve the training outcomes desired is needed. This seems to coincide with the claims by Kelly et al. [10], who state that the amount of rigorous scientific research that has been conducted into golf is surprisingly limited.

In order to compare actual swings with those "good examples" from skilled players (capability analysis outlined in Sect. 5), a set of models based on data collected from such players should be built. Even if limited, there are various examples of modeling the golf swing motion captured by, for example, the Microsoft Kinect, [14,15], where various techniques were used for modeling (Gaussian Mixture Models, Support Vector Machine and Dynamic Bayesian Networks).

Other examples that include swing modeling are presented in [16,17]; while a review of biomechanical models of the golf swing, focusing on how these models can aid the understanding of golf biomechanics and the fitting of golf clubs to individual players is presented in [18].

As highlighted by [19] the design of feedback in the motor skill domain via computer-based training systems is typically led by technology and fails to take into account pedagogical issues. The data collected during our field work showed that many of the challenges encountered in swing instruction are related to pedagogical aspects of the training process: communication, learning strategy and self-assessment. Feedback in golf should consider higher learning aims (not only particular small improvements), and the context of the learning situation. The challenge for computer-based training system's designers is to determine what constitutes effective feedback for athletes in their training [19,20].

7 Conclusions

Despite the increase of golf tools available in the market and the availability of large amounts of data, novice golf players still find improving their swing skills to be a challenge. Traditional methods are still predominant in this field, but new data and visual analysis techniques open up for making these instructional sessions more effective.

Advanced computer-based training systems may support golf instructors in their daily work. In this paper, we have presented an analysis of how the swing instruction process is carried out nowadays, highlighting which challenges are faced that can be leveraged by newly developed computer-based training systems. The major challenges highlighted by the golf instructors that participated in this study were pedagogical concerns related to communication, learning strategy and self-assessment. The results presented in this paper may guide the design and development of such future computer-based training systems for swing coaching.

Acknowledgements. This research has been supported by Region Västra Götaland (VGR) under grant RUN 612-0198-13, University of Borås and University of Skövde. We would like to thank all the participants in this study. Special thanks to Bertil Garpenholt and Andreas Ljungström for sharing their golf expertise with us.

References

1. Wheeler, K., Nauright, J.: A global perspective on the environmental impact of golf. Sport Soc. **9**(3), 427–443 (2006)
2. Jankun-Kelly, T., Ma, K.L., Gertz, M.: A model and framework for visualization exploration. IEEE Trans. Vis. Comput. Graph. **13**(2), 357–369 (2007)
3. Chun, S., Kang, D., Choi, H.R., Park, A., Lee, K.K., Kim, J.: A sensor-aided self coaching model for uncocking improvement in golf swing. Multimedia Tools Appl. **72**(1), 253–279 (2013)

4. Smith, A., Roberts, J., Wallace, E., Forrester, S.: Professional golf coaches' perceptions of the key technical parameters in the golf swing. Procedia Eng. **34**, 224–229 (2012)
5. Schempp, P., McCullick, B., Busch, C., Webster, C., Mason, I.S.: The self-monitoring of expert sport instructors. Int. J. Sports Sci. Coach. **1**(1), 25–35 (2006)
6. Dahlbom, A., Riveiro, M.: Situation modeling and visual analytics for decision support in sports. In: Proceedings of the 16th International Conference on Enterprise Information Systems, ICEIS, Lisbon, Portugal, vol. 1, pp. 539–544, 27–30 April 2004
7. Owusu, G.: AI and computer-based methods in performance evaluation of sporting feats: an overview. Artif. Intell. Rev. **27**(1), 57–70 (2007)
8. Bartlett, R.: Artificial intelligence in sports biomechanics: New dawn of false hope? J. Sports Sci. Med. **5**, 474–79 (2006)
9. Schempp, P., Webster, C., McCullick, B., Busch, C., Mason, I.: How the best get better: An analysis of the self-monitoring strategies used by expert golf instructors. Sport Educ. Soc. **12**(2), 175–192 (2007)
10. Kelly, P., Healy, A., Moran, K., O'Connor, N.E.: A virtual coaching environment for improving golf swing technique. In: SMVC 2010 - ACM Multimedia Workshop on Surreal Media and Virtual Cloning, Firenze, Italy (2010)
11. Kooyman, D.J., James, D.A., Rowlands, D.D.: A feedback system for the motor learning of skills in golf. Procedia Eng. **60**, 226–231 (2013). 6th Asia-Pacific Congress on Sports Technology (APCST)
12. Fung, S.K., Sundaraj, K., Ahamed, N.U., Kiang, L.C., Nadarajah, S., Sahayadhas, A., Ali, M.A., Islam, M.A., Palaniappan, R.: Hybrid markerless tracking of complex articulated motion in golf swings. J. Bodywork Mov. Ther. **18**(2), 220–227 (2014)
13. Marshall, C., Rossman, G.B.: Designing Qualitative Research, 3rd edn. SAGE Publications Inc., Thousand Oaks (1999)
14. Zhang, L., Stoffel, A., Behrisch, M., Mittelstadt, S., Schreck, T., Pompl, R., Weber, S., Last, H., Keim, D.: Visual analytics for the big data era: a comparative review of state-of-the-art commercial systems. In: 2012 IEEE Conference on Visual Analytics Science and Technology (VAST), pp. 173–182, October 2012
15. Lv, D., Huang, Z., Sun, L., Yu, N., Wu, J.: Model-based golf swing reconstruction. Appl. Mech. Mater. **530/531**, 919–927 (2014)
16. Kumada, K., Usui, Y., Kondo, K.: Golf swing tracking and evaluation using kinect sensor and particle filter. In: International Symposium on Intelligent Signal Processing and Communications Systems (ISPACS), pp. 698–703, November 2013
17. Huang, S.Y., Kuo, K.P., Lin, Y.H.: A golf swing analysis system using wii balance board and kinect sensors for novice players. Multimedia Tools Appl. 1–18 (2014). doi:10.1007/s11042-014-2198-5
18. Betzler, N., Monk, S., Wallace, E., Otto, S.R., Shan, G.: From the double pendulum model to full-body simulation: evolution of golf swing modeling. Sports Technol. **1**, 175–188 (2008)
19. Iskandar, Y.H., Gilbert, L., Wills, G.: Pedagogical feedback for computer-based sport training. In: International Computer Assisted Assessment (CAA) Conference: Research into E-Assessment, July 2010
20. Iskandar, Y.H., Gilbert, L., Wills, G.: The design of effective feedback in computer-based sport training. In: 7th International Symposium on Computer Science in Sport, September 2009

A Student-Centered Hybrid Recommender System to Provide Relevant Learning Objects from Repositories

Paula A. Rodríguez, Demetrio A. Ovalle[✉], and Néstor D. Duque

Universidad Nacional de Colombia, Bogotá, Colombia
{parodriguezma,dovalle,ndduqueme}@unal.edu.co

Abstract. Educational Recommender Systems aim to provide students with search relevant results adapted to their needs or preferences and delivering those educational contents such as Learning Objects (LOs) that could be closer than expected. LOs can be defined as a digital entity involving educational design characteristics. Each LO can be used, reused, or referenced during computer-supported learning processes, aiming at generating knowledge, skills, attitudes, and competences based on the student profile. The aim of this paper is to present a student-centered LO recommender system based on a hybrid recommendation technique that combines three following approaches: content-based, collaborative and knowledge-based. In addition, those LOs adapted to the student profile are retrieved from LO repositories using the stored descriptive metadata of these objects. A testing phase with a case study is performed in order to validate the proposed hybrid recommender system that demonstrates the effectiveness of using this kind of approaches in virtual learning environments.

Keywords: Student-centered hybrid recommender systems · Learning objects · Metadata · Repositories

1 Introduction

Online learning is a revolutionary way to provide virtual education in modern life, thus benefiting every day more and more people. A recommender system is a piece of software that helps users to identify interesting and relevant learning information from a large amount of educational information. Recommender systems aim to provide students with search relevant results adapted to their needs by performing predictions on their preferences and delivering those educational contents that could be closer than expected [1]. In addition, recommender systems must use different information sources such as educational databases, Learning Object Repositories (LORs), federations of LORs, among others [2].

Educational recommender systems (ERS), can be classified into several kinds as follows [3]: Content-based ERS in which recommendations are performed only by using the already created student profile. Collaborative ERS wherein recommendations are based on the similarity degree among users by applying collaborative filtering algorithms. Knowledge-based ERS, use user's browsing history to provide appropriate educational resources. Finally, hybrid ERS seek to integrate some of the recommendation techniques, in order to

© Springer International Publishing Switzerland 2015
P. Zaphiris and A. Ioannou (Eds.): LCT 2015, LNCS 9192, pp. 291–300, 2015.
DOI: 10.1007/978-3-319-20609-7_28

gather the best accurate features adapted to the user's profile hence providing better recommendations.

It is important to highlight that ERS for LOs use students' characteristics and needs in order to support their learning-teaching processes [4]. Generally, ERS are facing three important issues: sparsity, scalability, and cold-start. Using the hybrid ERS we seek to solve these problems by integrating the results of recommendation techniques.

The aim of this paper is to present a student-centered LO recommender system based on a hybrid recommendation technique that combines three following approaches: content-based, collaborative and knowledge-based. In addition, those LOs adapted to the student profile are retrieved from LO repositories using the stored descriptive metadata of these objects.

The rest of the paper is organized as follows: Sect. 2 presents the conceptual framework of this research. Section 3 reviews some related works analysis. Section 4 describes the proposed model. Section 5 explains the model validation and the results of the proposed model. Finally, the main conclusions and future research directions are shown in Sect. 6.

2   Basic Concepts

Following are the main concepts related to hybrid recommender systems, learning objects, and student profile.

2.1   Learning Objects, Repositories and Federations

According to the IEEE, a LO can be defined as a digital entity involving educational design characteristics. Each LO can be used, reused or referenced during computer-supported learning processes, aiming at generating knowledge and competences based on student's needs [5, 6]. LOs have functional requirements such as accessibility, reuse, and interoperability. The concept of LO requires understanding of how people learn, since this issue directly affects the LO design in each of its three dimensions: pedagogical, didactic, and technological. In addition, LOs have metadata that describe and identify the educational resources involved and facilitate their searching and retrieval. LORs, composed of thousands of LOs, can be defined as specialized digital libraries storing several types of resources heterogeneous, are currently being used in various e-learning environments and belong mainly to educational institutions [7].

Federation of LORs serve to provide educational applications of uniform administration in order to search, retrieve and access specific LO contents available in whatever of LOR groups [8].

2.2   Recommender Systems

Recommender Systems (RS) aim to provide users with search results close to their needs, making predictions of their preferences and delivering those items that could be closer than expected [1, 9]. In the context of LO, Educational Recommender Systems (ERS) deliver educational materials according to the student's characteristics, preferences and learning needs. In order to improve recommendations, ERS must perform feedback processes and implement mechanisms that enable them to obtain a large amount of information about users and how they use the LOs.

ERS can be classified into several kinds as follows [3, 10]:

• **Content-based ERS.** In this kind of systems, recommendations are performed based on the user's profile and created from the content analysis of the LOs that the user has already assessed in the past. The content-based systems use "item-by-item" algorithms generated through the association of correlation rules among those items.

• **Collaborative ERS.** These systems hold promise in education not only for their purposes of helping learners and educators to find useful educational resources, but also as a means of bringing together people with similar interests and beliefs, and possibly as an aid to the learning process itself.

In this case, the recommendations are based on the similarity degree among users. To achieve a good collaborative recommendation system, i.e. that provides qualified recommendations, it is necessary to use good collaborative filtering algorithms aiming at suggesting new items or predicting the utility of a certain item for a particular user profile based on the choices of other similar user profiles.

• **Knowledge-based ERS.** The knowledge-based ERS attempt to suggest LOs based on inferences about a user's needs and preferences. Knowledge-based approaches are distinguished in that they have functional knowledge: they have knowledge about how a particular item meets a particular user need, and can therefore reason about the relationship between a need and a possible recommendation. In addition, these systems are based on the user's browsing history and his/her previous LO elections.

• **Hybrid Recommender Systems.** The hybrid approach seeks to combine several ERS techniques in order to complete their best features and thus make better recommendations. The proposed hybrid filtering approach transparently creates and maintains user's preferences.

To make the hybridization of recommendation techniques – using at least two of them – Burke [11] describes the following different methods that could be applied.

Weighted: the score of different recommendation components are combined numerically.

Switching: the system chooses among recommendation components and applies the selected one.

Mixed: recommendations from different recommenders are presented together.

Cascade: recommenders are given in strict priority, with the lower priority ones breaking ties in the scoring of the higher ones.

Feature combination: features derived, from different knowledge sources, are combined together and given to a single recommendation algorithm.

Feature augmentation: one recommendation technique is used to compute a feature or set of features, which is then part of the input to the next technique.

Meta-level: one recommendation technique is applied and produces some sort of model, which is then the input used by the next technique.

2.3   Student Profile

For a SR deliver tailored results they need profiles that store the information and the preferences of each user [12]. The student profile stores information about the learner, its characteristics and preferences, which can be used to obtain search results according to its specificity. To handle a user profile can be used to support a student or a teacher in the LO selection according to its personal characteristics and preferences [13].

Some research works present the student's learning style as the most important feature for the delivery of appropriate educational resources [14, 15]. In fact, learning styles are currently used to organize collections of new information and represent different ways through which students can learn. There are different models to represent a student's learning style. For instance, Duque [16] presents a combination of VARK (Visual, Aural, Read/Write, Kinesthetic) and FSLSM (Felder and Silverman Learning Style Model) models with good results to characterize the student profiles and thus, provide students with learning materials tailored to their specific learning styles.

3   Related Works

Following some hybrid ERS research works will be described. Salehi et al., use genetic algorithms and perform two recommendation processes. The first uses explicit characteristics represented in a matrix of student's preferences. The second recommendation process assigns implicit weights to educational resources that are considered as chromosomes in the genetic algorithm for optimizing them based on historical values [17].

The authors deliver educational materials adapted to the user profile, combining several types of filtering methods with the available information about objects and users. The first method preselects the LOs from repositories, using a search based on LO metadata, then those objects passed by other filtering processes to obtain a final list which will be the best that suits the user. It is important to highlight that this research work combines several filter criteria: content-based, collaborative activity, and demographics [18].

Vekariya and Kulkami [10] perform a review of some hybrid ERS concluding that the hybrid filter obtained by integrating collaborative and content-based filtering approaches improves predictions made by the recommender. Although this research works quite well in hybrid recommender systems, however, no recommendations tests have been made on educational materials recovered from LORs.

By contrast, the research presented by Sikka et al. [19] works well on learning materials and thus some recommending activities are provided within an e-learning environment by using web mining techniques and software agents. However, authors implement just a unique collaborative recommendation filter rather than using a hybrid approach.

4   Model Proposed

The adaptive recommender model proposed consists of six modules (see Fig. 1) according to a hybrid recommendation technique that combines three following approaches: content-based, collaborative and knowledge-based. In addition, LOs are retrieved from LORs, and federations of LORs, using the stored descriptive metadata of these objects. The student profiles are also available having their personal information, preferences and learning style. Thus, there are three recommendation modules one for each of the selected techniques. A fourth module that performs the hybridization (integration) process uses intermediate recommendations results (see Fig. 1), and finally, the last two modules handle information about student profiles and LO metadata respectively.

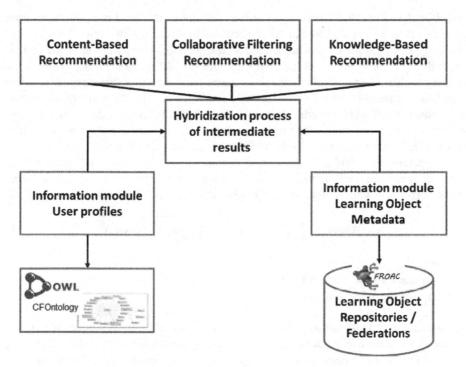

Fig. 1. Adaptive recommender model composing of six modules

Among hybridization techniques previously described in Sect. 2.2 we selected and applied the Cascade method wherein LOs recommenders are given in strict priority, consequently recommenders with lower priority affects the scoring of the higher ones.

Following the three main recommendation techniques used in the hybrid model are described.

Content-based Recommendation: this recommendation technique is based on the student profile. The LOs metadata such as Learning-Resource-Type, Interactivity-Level, Intended-End-User-Role, Context, Description, and Language are matched with the student's learning style.

This process is performed using production rules such as the following:

LearningStyle(Visual-Global) → *LearningResourceType(figure)* ∨
LearningResourceType(graph) ∨ *Learning   ResourceType(slide)* ∨
LearningResourceType(table) ∧ *InteractivityLevel(medium)* ∨
InteractivityLevel(high)

Collaborative Filtering Recommendation: the aim of this kind of recommendation technique is to deliver LOs that liked or interested to students with similar profiles. The similarity among students can be defined as the numeric representation of the coincidence degrees according to all the characteristics that define their profile. To do so, a similar profile is at first searched, and then, the cosine distance for this case was selected as similarity measure according to the study presented in [7]. The students' characteristics used are the following: education level, learning style, level of education, language preference, choice of subject, and format preference. The result of the recommendation are those LOs that users with similar profiles have positively assessed.

To perform its calculation the cosine distance is usually used along with vectors whose elements are numeric values and thus mathematical operations on such elements can be performed. This application was extended to categorical data given by formula 1.

$$\text{Cosine distance} = \sum_1^n (Pi * Qi) / \sqrt{(\sum_1^n Pi^2 * \sum_1^n Qi^2)} \tag{1}$$

where:
P_i: frequency term i on vector 1
Q_i: frequency term i on vector 2.

Knowledge-based Recommendation: This recommendation technique search for similar LOs that the user positively assessed in the past. First, the process starts searching similar LOs that have been assessed in the past, through the following metadata: title, description, and keywords. To calculate the semantic distance among LOs, we used the cosine distance, as appeared in formula 1, which measures the similarity between arrays. In this case, such arrays are the words contained in the title description and keywords of the metadata.

Hybridization process of intermediate results: As previously mentioned the selected recommendation technique is Cascade. This technique applies a filter to each result obtained by implemented recommendations. The process is applied by stages, starting with a recommendation technique to produce an initial rating for each of the candidate items and then, a second technique refines the recommendation among the set of candidates given by the first. In fact, each of the recommendations techniques refines the recommendations given by the others. Figure 2 presents the Cascade hybridization process.

Each recommendation technique executes its process at a given time and the final results appeared after applying the Cascade hybridization strategy. In this model, the

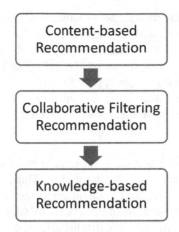

Fig. 2. Cascade hybridization process

first selected recommendation technique is the Content-based Recommendation, since this technique according to previous experiments delivers a greater number of LOs. Later, intermediate results are filtered using the Collaborative filtering technique, and finally, the Knowledge-based Recommendation technique is applied to filter again results. LOs results obtained after applying Cascade hybridization process are delivered to students.

Following the two useful external modules used by the hybrid model will be described.

User profile module: this module handles the student profile information using an ontological representation. The ontology proposed contains the student information given by the student profile such as schooling level, learning style, educational level, language, learning topics, and format preferences.

Learning Object Metadata Information module: Finally, this module handles LO metadata. This module has access to LORs and federations of LORs in order to extract the required metadata at each stage of the hybrid recommendation process.

5   Experiments and Results

The system delivers to the student a list of recommended LOs from similar profiles of students sharing learning style, historic behavior, and preferences. The recommendation process starts using a search criterion that can be expressed by keywords or educational skills wishing to be achieved.

The experiment was performed using the LOs stored in FEB (http://feb.ufrgs.br/feb/), the Brazilian Federation of LORs. Initial searches were performed with Portuguese words in order to select the LOs that would initially enter to the recommendation process. Each module executed the recommendations as follows: content-based recommendation module applies the inference rules among LO metadata and student's learning style. The collaborative recommendation module seeks similar user profiles to deliver items that have been assessed by students with similar profiles and knowledge-based recommendation module searches some LOs similar to those that the student had previously assessed. The integration module performs the hybridization process to deliver the student with the most relevant and appropriate LOs.

In addition, students of Information System Management program at National University of Colombia branch Manizales were selected to (1) use the hybrid recommender system, (2) register his/her user profile, and (3) rank the relevance of the recommendation results.

Burke [11] establishes that precision measurement helps to evaluate the results according to the relevance value given by the student. Thus, the precision measurement analyzes the quality of recovered educational materials regarding to students [20]. A LO is relevant if it supports the student learning process by adapting to his/her preferences and needs. A group of students, who qualify the relevance, determines this relevance value. Formula 2 shows the way this measurement is calculated.

$$Precision = \frac{Relevant\,LOs}{Relevant\,LOs + Retrieved\,LOs} \tag{2}$$

After executing the hybrid model proposed using the experimental group of students the results for each technique applied are the following, on average: the content-based technique recovered around 83 LOs for each student and, 42 of them were relevant. The collaborative filtering technique obtained 7 LOs since there are few students registered on the system, with similar profiles, and also, there were few LOs previously evaluated. Thus, just 5 LOs were relevant. The knowledge-based recommendation produced 19 LOs similar to those that the student evaluated previously, and relevant results are only 13 LOs.

The hybrid recommendation system proposed delivered 4 LOs, wherein 3 of them are relevant for students. Table 1 presents the results obtained by applying the precision measurement for each recommendation technique and also the hybridization technique by using the Cascade method.

Table 1. Precision measurement results

Technique	Precision measurement
Content-based	0,50
Collaborative	**0,71**
Knowledge-based	0,68
Hybrid recommendation	**0,75**

We can conclude that using hybrid recommendation techniques on learning environments might be promissory because it improves the precision measurement. The problem using the Cascade hybridization technique is the number of resulting LOs. In some cases, the recommendation result was zero, since any technique did not recover

LOs or in the process of hybridization, some LOs were lost. The collaborative recommendation technique has a high precision measurement and this result is due to the low volume of recovered LOs.

6   Conclusions and Future Work

An adaptive student-centered LO recommender model is proposed composing of six modules according to a hybrid recommendation technique that combines three following approaches: content-based, collaborative and knowledge-based. In addition, LOs are retrieved from LORs, and federations of LORs, using the stored descriptive metadata of these objects. The student profiles are also available having their personal information, preferences and learning style. Thus, there are three recommendation modules one for each of the selected techniques; a fourth module that performs the hybridization (integration) process with obtained recommendations, and finally, the last two modules handle information about student profiles and LO metadata respectively. In fact, the proposed model delivers educational materials adapted to students' needs and cognitive characteristics according to different criteria based on recommendation approaches such as content-based, collaborative and knowledge-based. During the testing phase a precision measurement was used to assess the quality of relevance of the recovered LO. By applying this precision measurement, it can be concluded that the hybrid recommendation approach enhances the results of the recommendation in terms of the relevance of the educational material to assist and hence to improve the student's learning process. The case study performed in order to validate the proposed hybrid recommender model demonstrated the effectiveness of using this kind of approaches in virtual learning environments.

As a future work, we envisage to explore and incorporate more hybridization techniques to the model and perform new case studies in order to compare their performance with previous results.

Acknowledgments. The research work presented in this paper was partially funded by the COLCIENCIAS project entitled: "RAIM: Implementación de un framework apoyado en tecnologías móviles y de realidad aumentada para entornos educativos ubicuos, adaptativos, accesibles e interactivos para todos" from the Universidad Nacional de Colombia, with code 1119-569-34172. It was also developed with the aid of the doctoral grant offered to Paula A. Rodríguez by "Programa Nacional de Formación de Investigadores – COLCIENCIAS, Colombia".

References

1. Chesani, F.: Recommendation Systems. Corso di laurea Ing. Inform. 1–32 (2007)
2. Bobadilla, J., Ortega, F., Hernando, A., Gutiérrez, A.: Recommender systems survey. Knowl. Based Syst. **46**, 109–132 (2013)
3. Burke, R.: Hybrid web recommender systems. Adapt. Web **4321**, 377–408 (2007)
4. Li, J.Z.: Quality, evaluation and recommendation for learning object. In: International Conference on Educational and Information Technology, pp. 533–537 (2010)

5. Rodríguez, P.A., Salazar, O., Duque, N.D., Ovalle, D., Moreno, J.: Using ontological modeling for multi-agent recommendation of learning objects. In: Workshop MASLE - Multiagent System Based Learning Environments, Intelligent Tutoring Systems (ITS) Conference, Hawaii, USA (2014)
6. Learning Technology Standards Committee: IEEE Standard for Learning Object Metadata. Institute of Electrical and Electronics Engineers, New York (2002)
7. Rodríguez, P.A., Moreno, J., Duque, N.D., Ovalle, D., Silveira, R.: Un modelo para la composición semiautomática de contenido educativo desde repositorios abiertos de objetos de aprendizaje a model for the semi-automatic composition of educational content from open repositories of learning objects. Rev. Electrónica Investig. Educ. (REDIE) **16** (2014)
8. Van de Sompel, H., Chute, R., Hochstenbach, P.: The aDORe federation architecture: digital repositories at scale. Int. J. Digit. Libr. **9**, 83–100 (2008)
9. Mizhquero, K., Barrera, J.: Análisis, Diseño e Implementación de un Sistema Adaptivo de Recomendación de Información Basado en Mashups. Rev. Tecnológica ESPOL-RTE (2009)
10. Vekariya, V., Kulkarni, G.R.: Hybrid recommender systems: survey and experiments. In: 2012 Second International Conference on Digital Information and Communication Technology and It's Applications (DICTAP), pp. 469–473. IEEE (2012)
11. Burke, R.: Hybrid recommender systems: survey and experiments. User Model. User-adapt. Interact. **12**, 331–370 (2002)
12. Cazella, S.C., Reategui, E.B., Nunes, M.A.: A Ciência da Opinião: Estado da arte em Sistemas de Recomendação. JAI Jorn. Atualização em Informática da SBC. Rio Janeiro, RJ PUC Rio 161–216 (2010)
13. Casali, A., Gerling, V., Deco, C., Bender, C.: Sistema Inteligente para la Recomendación de Objetos de Aprendizaje. Rev. Generación Digit. **9**, 88–95 (2011)
14. Alonso, C., Gallego, D., Honey, P.: Los Estilos de Aprendizaje. Procedimientos de diagnostico y mejora, Bilbao (1997)
15. Klašnja-Milićević, A., Vesin, B., Ivanović, M., Budimac, Z.: E-Learning personalization based on hybrid recommendation strategy and learning style identification. Comput. Educ. **56**, 885–899 (2011)
16. Duque, N.: Modelo Adaptativo Multi-Agente para la Planificación y Ejecución de Cursos Virtuales Personalizados - Tesis Doctoral. Universidad Nacional de Colombia. (2009)
17. Salehi, M., Pourzaferani, M., Razavi, S.A.: Hybrid attribute-based recommender system for learning material using genetic algorithm and a multidimensional information model. Egypt. Informatics J. **14**(1), 67–68 (2013)
18. Zapata, A., Menendez, V., Prieto, M., Romero, C.: A hybrid recommender method for learning objects. Des. Eval. Digit. Content Educ. Proc. Publ. Int. J. Comput. Appl. 1–7 (2011)
19. Sikka, R., Dhankhar, A., Rana, C.: A survey paper on E-learning recommender system. Int. J. Comput. Appl. **47**, 27–30 (2012)
20. Baeza-Yates, R., Ribeiro-Neto, B.: Modern Information Retrieval: The Concepts and Technology Behind Search. Addison-Wesley, Boston (2011)

Adaptive and Personalized Educational Ubiquitous Multi-Agent System Using Context-Awareness Services and Mobile Devices

Oscar M. Salazar[1], Demetrio A. Ovalle[1(✉)], and Néstor D. Duque[2]

[1] Universidad Nacional de Colombia, Sede Medellín, Colombia
{omsalazaro,dovalle}@unal.edu.co
[2] Universidad Nacional de Colombia, Sede Manizales, Colombia
ndduqueme@unal.edu.co

Abstract. In the last decade, some useful contributions have occurred to e-learning system development such as adaptation, ubiquity, personalization, as well as context-awareness services. The aim of this paper is to present the advantages brought by the integration of ubiquitous computing along with distributed artificial intelligence techniques in order to build an adaptive and personalized context-aware learning system by using mobile devices. Based on this model we propose a multi-agent context-aware u-learning system that offers several functionalities such as context-aware learning planning, personalized course evaluation, selection of learning objects according to student profile, search of learning objects in repository federations, search of thematic learning assistants, and access of current context-aware collaborative learning activities involved. In addition, several context awareness services are incorporated within the adaptive e-learning system that can be used from mobile devices. In order to validate the model a prototype was built and tested through a case study. Results obtained demonstrate the effectiveness of using this kind of approaches in virtual learning environments which constitutes an attempt to improve learning processes.

Keywords: Ubiquitous MAS · Adaptive and personalized virtual courses · Context-awareness services · Mobile devices

1 Introduction

The growth of digital information along with the boom in the creation of high-speed telecommunications systems and intelligent ubiquitous systems [1, 2] provide tools for the development of customized recommendation systems focused on mobile devices. This fact gives way to a new paradigm where the users have a wide range of interfaces and devices in order to communicate with information systems wherein the context plays a very important role. To do so, new technologies and innovative approaches such as intelligent software agents, wireless devices, adaptive and customized information searchers are currently been used in order to create adaptive and personalized e-learning systems.

As defined in [3] context-aware ubiquitous learning is an innovative approach that integrates wireless, mobile, and context-awareness technologies to detect the situation

P. Zaphiris and A. Ioannou (Eds.): LCT 2015, LNCS 9192, pp. 301–312, 2015.
DOI: 10.1007/978-3-319-20609-7_29

of learners in the real world and thus provide adaptive support, personalized services or guidance accordingly. In the traditional e-learning environments [4] the lack of immediate learning assistance means the learner is unable to receive learning resources in a timely manner and incorporate them based on the actual context into the learner's learning activities. The result is impaired learning efficiency. In contrast, ubiquitous computing environments enable users to easily use huge amounts of information and computing services through network connections anytime and anywhere.

Moreover, context-awareness services play a very important role within ubiquitous e-learning environments since they are useful to provide immediate alerts to students through their mobile devices when the system detects significant events such as learning tasks completed, need for student's learning re-planning, educational resource recommendation, need for learning support through assistants, etc. Using context-awareness services within an e-learning environment aims to inform students about their performance and progress during their whole learning process.

The aim of this paper is to present the advantages brought by the integration of ubiquitous computing along with distributed artificial intelligence techniques [5] in order to build an adaptive and personalized context-aware learning system by using mobile devices. Based on this model we propose a multi-agent context-aware u-learning system that offers several functionalities such as context-aware learning planning, personalized course evaluation, selection of learning objects according to student profile [6], search of learning objects in repository federations [7], search of thematic learning assistants, and access of current context-aware collaborative learning activities involved. In addition, several context-awareness services are incorporated within the adaptive e-learning system in order to inform students about their performance and progress during their learning process through mobile devices considering the students' preferences, needs, and limitations.

The rest of the paper is organized as follows: Sect. 2 presents the conceptual framework of this research. Section 3 reviews some related works analysis. Section 4 describes the proposed model. Section 5 offers the model implementation and validation of the proposed model. Finally, the main conclusions and future research directions are shown in Sect. 6.

2   Conceptual Framework

This section provides main definitions used in this research work such as learning objects, repositories, federations, student profile, multi-agent systems, context-awareness services, among others.

2.1   Learning Objects, Repositories and Federations

According to the IEEE, a LO can be defined as a digital entity involving educational design characteristics. Each LO can be used, reused or referenced during computer-supported learning processes, aiming at generating knowledge and competences based on student's needs [7, 8]. LOs have functional requirements such as accessibility, reuse, and interoperability. The concept of LO requires understanding of how people learn, since this issue directly affects the LO design in each of its three dimensions: pedagogical, didactic, and technological. In addition, LOs have metadata that describe and identify the educational resources involved and facilitate their searching and retrieval. LORs, composed of thousands of LOs, can be defined as specialized digital libraries storing several types of resources heterogeneous, are currently being used in various e-learning environments and belong mainly to educational institutions [9].

Federation of LORs serve to provide educational applications of uniform administration in order to search, retrieve and access specific LO contents available in whatever of LOR groups [10].

2.2 Student Profile

The student profile stores information about the learner, its characteristics and preferences, useful to support a student or a teacher in the LO selection according to its personal characteristics, needs and preferences. A comprehensive structure that represents the student's information into several categories is considered as the student profile model, choosing among his/her most important or the most significant issues. These categories are: personal data (e.g. name, date of birth, sex, etc.) learning styles (e.g. active, reflexive, sensorial, intuitive, visual, verbal, sequential, global), psychology profile (e.g. dominant brain hemisphere), physiology profile (hearing, vision, etc.) contextual characteristics (e.g. access device, network state, operating system, etc.), historical issues (activities developed, study times), academic achievements (learning goal approved) and group work performance [11].

2.3 Multi-agent Systems

Multi-agent systems (MAS) are composed of a set of agents that operate and interact in an environment to solve a specific and complex problem [5]. Agents are entities that have autonomy in order to perform tasks by achieving their objectives without human supervision and thus have been used for the development of virtual learning environments [7]. The desirable characteristics of the agents are as follows: reactivity, proactivity, cooperation and coordination, autonomy, deliberation, distribution of tasks, mobility, adaptation, mobility, adaptation, and parallelism.

2.4 Context-Awareness

The context-awareness concept, which is inherent to humans when performing any learning activity, becomes the main component for monitoring activities in virtual learning environments. Through context-awareness, students become conscious of all the changes produced within the learning environment by the action of their activities while performing learning tasks. Thus, it is easier for them to direct their behavior and acquire new knowledge [12]. The awareness provided by virtual learning environments allows students to generate a context of their own activity, i.e., the information regarding their learning activities is constantly updated and thus improving the performance on their learning process.

3 Related Works

Wang & Wu applied context aware technology and recommendation algorithms to develop a u-learning system to help lifelong learning learners realize personalized learning goals in a context aware manner and improve the learner's learning effectiveness [3]. In fact, they established that when integrating the relevant information technology to develop a u-learning environment, it is necessary to consider the personalization requirements of the learner to ensure that the technology achieves its intended result. The Sharable Content Object Reference Model (SCORM) platform was used as the basis and integrated with Radio Frequency Identification (RFID) technology to develop an adaptive ubiquitous learning system. Collaborative Filtering (CF) and an association rules mining model was used to develop an adaptive smart ubiquitous learning system. Adaptive learning materials are recommended to lifelong learning learners using this association rules mining model in order to improve the learning motivation and effectiveness of lifelong learning learners. Finally, the adaptive ubiquitous learning system developed in this study offers the following features: (1) Context awareness, (2) Standardized courseware, (3) Personal learning management, and (4) Adaptive course recommendation.

Zervas et al. established in [2] that in order to achieve personalized and ubiquitous learning, those tools showing characteristics of context-aware adaptive learning designs (authoring tools) and context-aware adaptive delivery of learning activities (run-time tools) should follow some design requirements at both the learning design and mobile delivery process. To attain learning design purposes, for instance, the user should be able to: (1) define appropriate content adaptation rules according to the different values of the mobile context characteristics, (2) define context-aware content adaptation rules for each individual learning activity that a learning design incorporates (3) create profiles of content adaptation rules (for certain values of mobile context characteristics), which can be used during the authoring process of a new learning design, (4) graphically design learning designs based on the interconnection of user defined learning activities, among others. Concerning mobile delivery process, for instance, the tool should: (1) be able to automatically detect contextual information such as, place, time, and in some cases physical conditions according to the user situation and it should be able also to let the user input contextual information that it is not possible to be detected automatically, (2) be client-side, so it can be installed to the mobile device and no internet connection should be required during the execution of learning activities, (3) be able to handle the adaptation rules of the delivered learning design and match them with the values of contextual information automatically detected or provided by the user, so as to enable the content adaptation mechanism and deliver adapted educational resources according to the type of user's mobile device, among others.

A context-aware learning environment was developed by Hwang et al. to guide the beginner researchers through practical experiments concerning single-crystal X-ray diffraction processes [12]. The application domain of this research regards to scientific experiments and therefore, when a student arrives at the laboratory and is in front of an instrument, sensors are able to detect the student location and thus transfer this information to server. The system performs real-time analysis using the following parameters concerning students: (1) environmental and personal context, (2) student's profile, and (3) online portfolio. The learning system is able to guide students in the laboratory, showing relevant information at the appropriate time such as processes able to be applied, the laboratory rules, as well as the emergency management procedures. Experimental results showed the benefits of applying the ubiquitous learning and context-aware approach in learning sciences as well as taking advantage of the manpower savings to assist and monitor students.

Considering the research works previously reviewed one of the improvements proposed in this paper in order to enhance current ubiquitous computing and ontological learning-teaching models is the integration of awareness services along with the personalized resources recommendation. These features regarding context-awareness and alerts offered by learning environments allow students to become conscious of the advancement status of their own learning activities and to interact with adaptive and personalized educational resources. In this way, the system gives the student the opportunity to maintain updated information that helps them to improve their performance during their learning process.

4   Model Proposed

Functional requirements of the system are initially identified along with the needs and objectives associated to current e-learning problems. From this point several use cases diagrams were built which helped understand the needs to be solved and to establish guidelines for the subsequent analysis phase.

Several functionalities were found during this stage that focus on following main axes:

a. The adaptive virtual course planning: its main objective is the educational content organization using the structure proposed for the virtual course construction. The purpose is thus to guide the students through courses, enabling new topics and proposing new contents that will help them strengthen their learning process.

b. Educational content evaluation: this functionality is intended to assess the knowledge acquired by the student in order to enable new content, so this functionality complements the planning functionality since it provides vital information relating to the progress of the student and allows to separately highlighting the shortcomings or strengths of students.

c. Customized search and selection of LO: this is an extremely important functionality within the system that provides personalized educational content, always seeking to awaken the focus and the interest of students along the AVC processing. In addition, the functionality provides the required content for the planning process. Another important feature that includes this functionality is the strengthening of knowledge throughout the adaptive virtual course, because at the time in which faults are presented in the student's learning process the system can recommend content outside of the virtual course structure in order to enrich learning as well as to address these faults. These educational contents are customized and adapted to characteristics, preferences, and limitations of students, which increases the interest of them and accelerates their learning process.

d. Search and placement of thematic learning assistants: allowing the search and allocation of learning assistants (advanced students) according to the temporal and spatial context of the student; i.e., the assistants will be assigned according to the spatial proximity that meets student, but also in agreement with the knowledge of the student's areas of interest as well as the time availability for both.

These functionalities were mapped or assigned to roles, allowing an initial division of tasks and goals. Created roles during this phase were associated with each of the functionalities. Following roles were thus considered: Planner, Content Recommender, Evaluator, and Assistants Recommender.

As the first activity in the analysis stage establishes that roles being initially identified be mapped in software agents and we decided to slightly extend the agent model adding the system's functionalities with the intention of better assign all the tasks and goals that would have associated each of system's agents. Figure 1 shows the agent model overview in which every system's functionality (being assigned to a role) is associated to a single agent. In this way all the functional requirements of the system are covered, however, during this phase new needs and non-functional requirements emerged that we have to be faced.

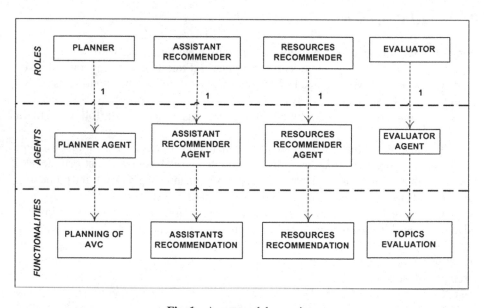

Fig. 1. Agent model overview.

System Architecture and Agent Description. Figure 2 shows the u-MAS architecture of the model proposed. This architecture was used to develop the context-aware educational multi-agent system, implemented using JADE (Java Agent Development Framework) agents [13].

- User Agent: the role of this agent, which communicates directly with the human user, is representing him within the system. This agent communicates with other agents such as Recommender and Planner. Moreover, the user agent manages the user profile, enabling the creation and modification of profile's characteristics and preferences. Most of the system's functional scenarios start and finish their execution with this agent who sends requirements and receives their corresponding answers.

- Recommender Agent: this is a kind of deliberative agent whose main role is to filter search results coming from searcher agent based on student's profile. In addition, this agent offers to students as a service support the possibility of performing searches of teaching/learning assistants for specific topics of a virtual course that have more knowledge and know-how on certain topics. Those learning assistants can give to the students with advice or answers questions on a particular sub-items or learning activities. This functionality is available from students' mobile devices.
- Searcher Agent: this is a reactive kind of agent that is in charge of performing searches of Learning Objects (LO) based on some characteristics such as LO name, educational resource, language, format, among others.
- Planner Agent: its role is to adapt learning plans to students in such a way that the student be guided by the system through a teaching-learning process in the same way as it could be performed by a real teacher.
- Evaluator Agent: this agent manages the knowledge level evaluation performed by the system to the learner taking into consideration the topics already learned and the LG attained by the student.
- Awareness Agent: The awareness agent plays an important role in the model since it is responsible of providing all the context-awareness services needed by the system either at the request of users or by effects of proactivity. The main available services provided by this agent are the following: (1) participation_level (gives the level of participation for a specific student considering the different learning activities proposed by the system), (2) graph_of_progress (gives the overview of student's status in the course and learning activities still pending), (3) assistant-student interaction_graph, (4) learning activities historical view, and finally (5) alarms and reminders.

5   Implementation and Validation

The adaptive and personalized U-MAS was implemented using JADE, a FIPA compliant framework [13]. This feature provides interoperability to the platform, what is needed for interconnect platforms and repositories. JADE was developed using JAVA language, this feature allows to integrate the ontology through JENA framework that was developed for JAVA environments as well.

Concerning the connection between the platform and user's mobile devices it was necessary to use Android platform, which allows the integration of mobile devices with the JADE Main Container hosted on the server. It is important to highlight that the platform which offers support to each AVC is self-authorship, and it was developed in the same server that deploys the U-MAS.

In order to validate the proposed model a case study is used to illustrate each of the functionalities of the adaptive and personalized U-MAS learning environment.

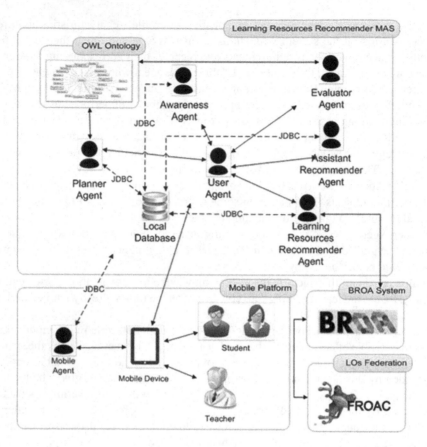

Fig. 2. Architecture of the adaptive U-MAS based on context-awareness services and mobile devices.

Functionality 1: Virtual Course Planning. As mentioned before, this scenario is handled by the Planner agent, who interacts with the Recommender agent to retrieve LO relating to the virtual course's topics. This agent then recovers the student's profile stored in the profile system database, and so it maps this retrieved information into the created ontology having semantic description of the knowledge associated to the AVC. This ontology, called PCVAOntology and specified in OWL language, was developed using Protégé and allows the system to select educational resources associated to AVC from SWRL rules. IEEE-LOM standard was used to represent the LO structure within the ontology, taking advantages of hierarchical relations and its cardinalities offered by this standard. Thinking on enhancing the selection process of LO, it was necessary also to extend the model proposed by Arias [14] for depicting the AVC structure. This model proposes a hierarchical structure where the virtual courses break down into learning basic-units which in turn are broken down into topics. Such topics have associated some educational objectives that need to accomplish certain prerequisites in order to be accessed. Finally, each topic has linked to several activities along with their respective LO for learning purposes.

Figure 3 shows the navigation interface through the student's AVC planning scenario (Fig. 3 at left) allowing the student to select the courses to be accessed as well as the current learning state of the student in the course (figure in the middle). It is important to highlight that resources selected from the planning process concerning any of topics can be proposed to the student in order to strengthen its learning process.

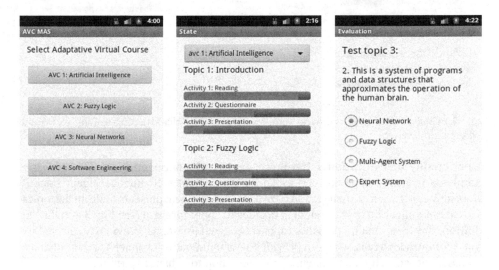

Fig. 3. Planning scenario and topic assessment functionalities.

Functionality 2: Topics Assessment. This scenario is activated at the moment in which the user concludes a topic, or wishes itself to skip it. Questions are initially selected from a question repository previously created and associated to each of the topics composing the AVC. According to the assessment structure proposed by Jimenez et al. [15] for each question there is one or may be more answers and they are validated through a 2-value field (1 when the answer is correct and 0 otherwise). One of the most important parameters is the average response time so that the student can answer the question as well as the question type that describes if the question is false, multiple choices, single choice, etc.

Functionality 3: Context-Awareness Services. This functionality allows the MAS to generate alarms at any time during the execution of the system (see Fig. 3). The aware-ness agent is in charge of performing cyclic behaviors that allow the system to contin-uously monitor the activities of the student on the database, in order to keep in real time the teacher and the student to be informed of student learning performance. These alarms can be related to activities next to expire or relevant information send to students intended to monitor and communicate their progress during learning process while they are using the virtual course platform. It is important to highlight that the information regarding students' learning activities is constantly updated and thus the fact to be aware of these changes might surely improve the performance on their learning process Fig. 4.

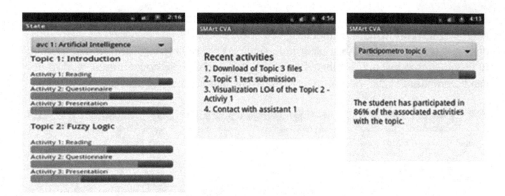

Fig. 4. Context-awareness services (progress-graph, historical-learning-activity-view and participation-level).

Functionality 4: Educational Resource Service Recommendation. This scenario includes a proactive behavior performed by the content recommender agent since it offers new educational virtual resources in case of the student presents faults in the topics assessment evaluation or if the student decides to apply for them (see Fig. 3 at right). In addition, this functionality provides topic specialized assistants, previously selected by the Recommender agent, who also provides a communication channel between students and assistants allowing them an enriched interaction to enhance learning.

The system's validation based on a case study on different functionalities shows quite satisfactory results. In addition, a ubiquitous MAS learning environment is presented where robust calculations and inferences are performed on the server while mobile devices are only in charge of generating system's interfaces. Stress tests were performed at the server by connecting a number of mobile devices (approximately 10) to see how the system behaves. This system validation demonstrates optimal advantages that supply to use a MAS approach by dividing the tasks on different nodes, hence the response times are reduced and the information is delivered in a more agile way.

6   Conclusions and Future Work

This paper presented the advantages brought by the integration of ubiquitous computing-oriented along with distributed artificial intelligence (DAI) techniques in order to build adaptive and personalized context-aware e-learning systems. Based on this model a context-aware U-MAS was developed that offers functionalities as follows: the context-aware learning planning, the course evaluation process, the selection of learning objects according to student profiles, the search of learning objects in repository federations, the search of thematic learning assistants, and the access of current context-aware group activities involved. The development of a context-awareness services module within the ubiquitous recommendation and planning MAS highlights significant contributions mainly at the level of the students' interaction within the system, since it allows them to be aware of their status and progress within the e-learning system. In addition, it allows teachers to know the interest shown by each student within the virtual course. As future work we will attempt to improve and expand context-awareness services incorporated into the U-MAS. Other context-awareness services could also be implemented such as the visual graph assistant-student interaction since in the current prototype it is described through a textual manner. Finally, it is expected to improve the experimentation of the different modules of the ubiquitous MAS using new case studies.

Acknowledgments. The research presented in this paper was partially funded by the COLCIENCIAS project entitled: "RAIM: Implementación de un framework apoyado en tecnologías móviles y de realidad aumentada para entornos educativos ubicuos, adaptativos, accesibles e interactivos para todos" from the Universidad Nacional de Colombia, with code 1119-569-34172. This research was also developed with the aid of the master grant offered to Oscar M. Salazar by COLCIENCIAS through "Convocatoria 617 de 2013. Capítulo 1 Semilleros-Jóvenes Investigadores".

References

1. Carrillo, A.: Agentes ubicuos para un acceso adaptado de usuarios nómadas en Sistemas de Información: El framework PUMAS. Tesis de Doctorado en Informática, Université Joseph Fourier, Equipe STEAMER - Laboratoire d'Informatique de Grenoble, Francia (2007)
2. Zervas, P., Gómez, S., Fabregat, R., Sampson, D.: Tools for context-aware learning de-sign and mobile delivery. In: Proceedings of the 11th IEEE International Conference on Advanced Learning Technologies (2011)
3. Wang, S., Wu, C.: Application of context-aware and personalized recommendation to implement an adaptive ubiquitous learning system. Expert Syst. Appl. **38**, 10831–10838 (2011)
4. Li, J.Z.: Quality, evaluation and recommendation for learning object. In: International Conference on Educational and Information Technology, (ICEIT), pp. 533–537 (2010)
5. Weiss, G.: Multiagent Systems: A Modern Approach to Distributed Artificial Intelligence. The MIT Press, Boston (2007). ISBN 0-262-23203-0
6. Casali, A., Gerling, V., Deco, C., Bender, C.: Sistema inteligente para la recomendación de objetos de aprendizaje. Generacion Digit. J. **9**(1), 88–95 (2011)
7. Rodriguez, P., Salazar, O., Ovalle, D., Duque, N., Moreno, J.: Using ontological modeling for multi-agent recommendation of learning objects. In: Workshop MASLE -Multiagent System Based Learning Environments, Intelligent Tutoring Systems (ITS) Conference, Hawaii, 2–9 June 2014
8. Learning Technology Standards Committee: IEEE Standard for Learning Object Metadata. Institute of Electrical and Electronics Engineering, New York (2002)
9. Rodríguez, P.A., Moreno, J., Duque, N.D., Ovalle, D., Silveira, R.: (Un modelo para la composición semiautomática de contenido educativo desde repositorios abiertos de objetos de aprendizaje) A model for the semi-automatic composition of educational content from open repositories of learning objects. Rev. Electrónica Investig. Educ. (REDIE) **16**, 123–136 (2014)
10. Van de Sompel, H., Chute, R., Hochstenbach, P.: The aDORe federation architecture: digital repositories at scale. Int. J. Digit. Libr. **9**, 83–100 (2008)
11. Duque, N.: Modelo adaptativo multi-agente para la planificación y ejecución de cursos virtuales personalizados - Tesis Doctoral, Universidad Nacional de Colombia (2009)

12. Hwang, G., Yang, T., Tsai, C., Yang, S.: A context-aware ubiquitous learning environment for conducting complex science experiments. Comput. Educ. J. **53**, 402–413 (2009)
13. Bellifemine, F., Rimessa, G., Trucco, T., Caire, G.: JADE (Java Agent Development Framework) Programmer's Guide (2005)
14. Jiménez, M., Ovalle, D., Jiménez, J.: Evaluación en línea para cursos tutoriales inteligentes adaptativos usando el modelo de sistemas multi-agente. Revista Avances en Sistemas e Informática, Universidad Nacional de Colombia. **5**(1), 20–29 (2008). ISSN 1657-7663
15. Arias, F.: Multi-agent adaptive model for adaptive virtual courses planning and LO selection. Computer Science MSc Dissertation (2010)

Math and Motion: A (Coursera) MOOC
to Rethink Math Assessment

Patricia Salinas[(✉)], Eliud Quintero, and Xavier Sánchez

Tecnologico de Monterrey, Campus Monterrey,
Eugenio Garza Sada 2501 Sur, 64849 Monterrey, Mexico
{npsalinas, eliudquintero, sax}@itesm.mx

Abstract. The Massive Open Online Course (MOOC) "Math and Motion" presents a different way for the interaction with Mathematical knowledge. In this course, digital technologies are integrated during the process of Mathematical teaching. These technologies are mixed with Mathematical contents to create a didactic scenario. In this scenario, numeric, algebraic and graphical representations are incorporated to the real-life context of linear motion. This scenario offers learning with a real meaning for the Mathematics knowledge. Assessment in this new way of interaction with Mathematics considers new challenges besides its online feature. In Math and Motion, lectures are available in weekly videos, and each week includes an assessment of multiple responses items executed in platform COURSERA. In this paper we describe the didactic design of Math and Motion MOOC and its assessment, as well as the findings during its first delivery in fall semester 2013.

Keywords: MOOC · Online assessment calculus · Online learning calculus

1 Introduction

Digital and communication technologies incorporating online access, offer new ways for delivery courses, and thus expand the autonomy of learners. Nonetheless, it is not only the access to the course content that could change, we could think in the way to present the content itself, and the way that design course could be innovative.

As all teachers, we recognize that technology allow students easy access to courses, and class material distribution and communication. But, in other hand, as education researchers, experience shows us that technology alone, does not guarantee that people learn Mathematics better.

In the Ontario Online Learning Portal for Faculty and Instructors [1], it is recognized that society demands urgent changes in education. Emphasis should be about skills and information management, as well as, how to find, analyze, evaluate and apply knowledge. Students today should learn and develop skills in a rich and complex environment where knowledge is always changing and in a constant expansion.

We believe that, as PISA in Focus [2] stated, everything is a creative problem solution. Adapt and learn from mistakes are skills that demand from students, an open-mind attitude towards unknown or uncertain situations. Having good grades in school

© Springer International Publishing Switzerland 2015
P. Zaphiris and A. Ioannou (Eds.): LCT 2015, LNCS 9192, pp. 313–324, 2015.
DOI: 10.1007/978-3-319-20609-7_30

courses does not assure, that students develop intuition to imagine new solutions for Mathematics problems.

The problems related to learn Mathematics in education institutions show the necessity to conduct education research. Our professional experience in Mathematics Education allows us to understand this reality in order to transform it. Today, digital technology creates new opportunities to change positively the learning process. That is what Math and Motion — a Massive Open Online Course (MOOC) — proposes, a free access course in which the use of technology contributes and enriches the process of learning Mathematics.

An important learning experience taking place at the MOOCs is in the process of assessment, where the learner has the opportunity to achieve the highest possible rating by performing the test many times as necessary. That means a challenge for the test design in order to evaluate Mathematical skills.

In this paper we communicate this didactic experience, showing a different way of learning Mathematics, using technology, and a different kind of assessment to evaluate learning. First, we discuss some background elements that allow us to explain our approaching to the Mathematical knowledge in the lectures of Math and Motion. Then, we deep into particular details of digital technologies, integrated in Mathematical content to foster the development of skills. After that, we discuss about the design of online assessments, taking into account, the technological features that the Coursera platform offers. Finally, we communicate assessment's results for the first MOOC experience in fall semester 2013.

Concluding remarks allow us to sum up the MOOC experience of Math and Motion, and bring to the fore how digital technology could change Mathematics education and its assessments, giving an opportunity to innovate Math curriculum.

2   The Didactic Scenario in Math and Motion

Conventionally, the teaching and learning of Mathematics takes place in a sequence of courses showing disjoint branches of this science, like Arithmetic, Algebra, Geometry, Analytic Geometry and Calculus. Each course presents contents in a logical way, and emphasizes routine procedures to solve exercises. In this kind of courses, the emission of a grade is done by an exam designed to measure the mastery for solving exercises.

In Calculus textbooks there are chapters following more or less this usual order: real numbers, functions, limits, continuity, derivatives, applications of derivative, integrals, applications of integrals. Textbooks include a lot of exercises in each chapter and it is assumed that students should practice with these exercises. Learning Calculus can then be confusing to find limits, derivatives and integrals. We find here a risk, because this kind of learning is not related with any real problem solution, it is just the performance of several routine procedures without real meaning.

Besides this common practice, it is noticeable that this textbook's structure always leaves the chapter for applications at the end, hinting that first you learn theory and then you apply the theory. However, the meaning of Calculus is in the applications. The real meaning has been an important element in Mathematical knowledge creation.

So, favoring the learning of meaning in Mathematics, should we teach Applications Chapters first? Unfortunately, it should be noted that application chapters also present the same structure than the rest, giving equal importance to applications as application exercises at the end of the chapter [3, 4].

In this landscape that we have drawn, questions related to curriculum design certainly arise, and should be taken into account for e-learning.

As part of a research group in Education, we perform a didactic innovation of Calculus restructuring the presentation of this knowledge basing on Calculus applications. "Predicting the value of a magnitude that is changing" has been our core practice. We construct an approach to Calculus notions linked to this real-life practice. In this way, notions of *derivative* and *integral* are deeply connected through their meaning as *rate of change* and *accumulation of change* in real contexts [5].

We have been disclosing this didactic through several actions. In this paper we share an experience undertaken throughout 2013 when we were invited to participate in the design of a Massive Open Online Course in Coursera.

The MOOC's design of Math and Motion involves also, an additional effort for the integration of specialized digital technology into the process of learning. The video recordings of our computer's screen include our face contact with the learner. This gives us the opportunity to perform and explain an interaction between Mathematical knowledge and specialized software. In this way, technology plays an active role in the teaching and learning process.

In Math and Motion, we introduce the study of linear motion as the scenario where three magnitudes are linked to our prediction: time, position and velocity. This everyday scenario, invites the learner to "ask questions" that will lead them back to Arithmetic, Algebra and Analytic Geometry, to combine procedures and find answers.

At the same time, being involved in this analysis of linear motion context, we have lead to an introduction to Calculus notions and procedures dealing with a real meaning. Linear motion scenario is an appropriate application of Calculus focusing in the study of change. The velocity, as rate of change of position over time, gives meaning to the derivative. The position, as the accumulation of changes (of position) over time, gives meaning to the antiderivative (or indefinite integral).

It is easy to recognize in Calculus students, some cognitive difficulties that Arcavi [6] had identified related with the flexibility of representations. It is widely known the importance of moving from a visual to an algebraic representation, and vice versa, this as part of Mathematics comprehension.

Duval [7] clarifies some cognitive aspects in the notion of representation, which become a source of difficulty in learning. Representations, he says, are signs associated in a complex manner, which meet certain rules to be produced as part of a system. Like language, they are tools that produce new knowledge as a result of their operation, and the organization of cognitive structures in our mind.

During a Mathematical activity we combine the systems of representation (algebraic, numeric, and graphical). This is key in the cognitive process involved in Mathematical thinking. Duval [8] identifies two types of transformation taking place: *treatment* and *conversion*. Treatment involves changes in the same system of representation, while conversion refers to the ability to switch between representations.

The latter also includes the transformation of everyday language statements into numeric, algebraic or graphical representations.

Even though both transformations are source of problems in learning, conversion is cognitively more complex than treatment. Difficulties reported in students, leave the impression that conversion implies a cognitive change that does not follow rules or basic associations, and as opposed of treatment, it is not possible to reduce it to a codification [9].

In Math and Motion, we focus in the graphical representation of position and velocity functions (changing over time) as an important step towards the introduction of Calculus. Linear motion led by natural language has some features that can be interpreted visually on the position and velocity graphs. It is mainly the conversion processes between language and graphical representations that make numerical and algebraic representations emerge to take part in the interpretation of the motion's features.

We finish this section referring to the Programme for International Student Assessment (PISA), which aims to evaluate education systems worldwide. PISA key findings give important information to nourish the path that Mathematics education should follow.

This international survey, taken by 15-year-old students, tests skills and knowledge not directly linked to school curriculum. PISA test for Mathematics has been applied in 2003 and 2012. Its reports declare *Mathematical literacy* as the capability of an individual to formulate, use and interpret Mathematics in a variety of contexts. *"This includes thinking Mathematically and using Mathematical concepts, procedures, facts and tools to describe, explain and predict phenomena"* [10].

The test focuses on the use of real-life contexts and tools available anywhere and anytime. This includes physical and digital equipment, also software and Calculus devices. PISA seeks to measure how well students can use what they know, and apply it in new or unfamiliar situations. Test questions involve several Mathematical procedures and contents; this forces their classification in terms of the greater source of demand for an answer. Categories named *employment*, *formulation* and *interpretation* claim different demands from Mathematics knowledge [10].

Math and Motion proposes the phenomena of linear motion as a didactic scenario for giving real meaning to Mathematics knowledge. It intends to provide a frame for cognitive action, where the learner can lead to questions involved with this real context. Video lectures invite to transfer questions in Mathematics contents, apply Mathematics procedures and finally interpret the results as useful information about the linear motion. In order to do so, digital technology takes an important place, as we propose in next section.

3   Technology Integrated in Math and Motion

Gómez [11] points out the level of interest that the academic world is having upon the integration of technology in the process of teaching and learning. Educational institutions show their concern for what is expected with recent developments, emergent technologies, and the age of the information and communication technologies (ICTs).

The direction of the educational innovation has been influenced by ICTs. But using ICTs does not guarantee any contribution to the process; instead should be based upon a scientific body that supports their application.

Del Moral and Villalustre [12] discuss the problem that faculty face, where new duties are required from them, as experts in these technologies. Teachers have to develop technological competences that let them use apps and tools didactically. Competences should include transforming the technological tool in another resource in the classroom. Teachers are also invited to develop their own teaching labor immerse in new virtual scenarios.

Our interest in digital technologies aims to favor the learning of Mathematics, creating a didactic scenario where the use of specialized software promotes the Mathematical thinking. In order to achieve this, the interaction with the software must be considered as a dialogue with a partner that knows about Math.

To understand the nature of the mediator role that digital technologies have in the learning of Mathematics, we consider the theoretical framework from Moreno-Armella and Sriraman [13]. They distinguish *tool* from *instrument* as established in the research field of cognition, where any cognitive activity is a *mediated activity*. We can use the software as a tool, in order to improve calculations or graphics plotting. But the role changes as an instrument when we make intentional actions with the software, a dialectical interaction, in order to transform our cognition.

Moreno-Armella and Hegedus [14] propose the concept of *coaction*, which helps us understand the effective integration of digital technologies in education. To think *with* a semiotic system is to use it as a cultural tool, but to think *through* the semiotic system means to use it as a cognitive instrument.

In Math and Motion, we explore this use gradually as we deepen in the analysis of the linear motion performed by a character: a Tec guy moving in Tec Campus. We use the SimCalc MathWorlds®Software (hereon SimCalc), designed at the Kaput Center for Research and Innovation in STEM Education in UMass, Dartmouth. (http://www.kaputcenter.umassd.edu/products/software/smwcomp/download/).

Salinas [15] presents a way to integrate SimCalc into the learning of Calculus in order to promote an image that includes the graphic of the position with respect to time, along with the graphic of velocity with respect to time in a linear motion case. The software allows the intentional interaction with the graphics of velocity and position. Dragging velocity graph, the software responds with the corresponding reaction in the position graph. This is possible because the software infrastructure includes the Fundamental Theorem of Calculus.

Design we produced in SimCalc gives the initial scenario for the introduction of the real-life situation of linear motion, and the core practice of predicting values for the position. Several questions arise from this scenario; some questions need a further analysis of the numeric information and the algebraic representation. The answer involves the flexibility between the different Mathematical representations. Figure 1 shows some pictures illustrating video lectures of Math and Motion with SimCalc.

Some other digital technologies for plotting and graphing are used to deepen into knowledge provided originally by SimCalc. Figure 2 shows some of those moments that involve the flexibility of representations as an important component for the learning process.

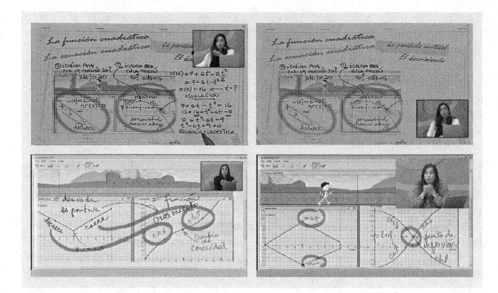

Fig. 1. Use of language, numeric, algebraic and graphical representations in videos

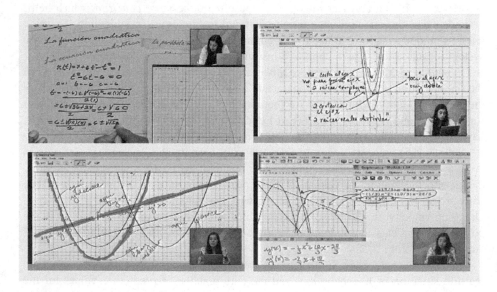

Fig. 2. Scenes showing flexibility of representations

4   The Assessment in Math and Motion

Math and Motion cares for the flexibility of representations as a Mathematical skill. This implies considering cognitive difficulties related with the conversion and treatment processes with representations, even with language. It is also important to manage in a balanced way the use of natural language with numeric, algebraic and graphical representations. Therefore, designing assessment, we focus in the Mathematical skill of transferring information between the different types of representation.

Our institution asked us to work in the design of a MOOC with six weeks long, which is a common term for this kind of courses. But finally we were asked working in a fourteen weeks design, in order to take advantage of the MOOC at our own readiness course in College. Learners had access to ten videos per week (15–20 min each) and this material is evaluated in the week assessment. The assessment, once activated, remains available during the MOOC period.

Coursera platform powers the fourteen assessments. This is the only way to have a grade for the course. Based in the concept of *Mastery Learning* that Coursera handles, each assessment could be taken as many times as the learner wants to. Each assessment contained 100 total points, and a maximum of 90 min to complete it.

Learners are informed about the policy to receive a State of Accomplishment document. The higher score obtained in each week assessment, no matter how many times done, is stated as the *effective grade* for that week. The *final grade of the course* is calculated as the average of the top 12 weekly effective grades (out of 14 total). Learners receive from Coursera the State of Accomplishment if their final grade is equal or greater than 70.

Assessments consisted of 5 questions in a *multiple-choice* format, having 5 choices each; all questions have the same score. Dealing with a multiple-choice question means that learner should understand the context of the situation posed, and take decisions about selecting or not selecting each choice, in terms of being it right or wrong as an interpretation of the situation. Partial score is assigned to each right choice selected, 20 % of the question total score. No points are given if wrong choices are selected, or right choices are *not* selected. Finally, when wrong choices are *not* selected, 20 % of the question total score is given. Table 1 shows the assigned score every time a choice is selected, or is left blank for a given question. Table 2 illustrates an example in which 2 out of 3 right choices are selected, and 1 out of 2 wrong choices are selected.

Table 1. Score assigned to the type of choice in each question

Score assigned to each choice		
	Is it selected?	
Type of choice	Yes	No
Right	0.20	0.00
Wrong	0.00	0.20

Each assessment is generated randomly and dynamically. A fixed number of questions are chosen from an available set of questions called *question group,* in the assessment source code. Each question group contains variations of the same question, and each variation contains at least a set of answers. This way, an assessment contains up to three levels of randomization: from each *question group*, i variations are randomly chosen, and from each selected variation, j answers are randomly chosen.

Table 2. Example of scoring a particular question

	Choice	Is it selected?	Score assigned
1	Right	Yes	0.20
2	Wrong	Yes	0.00
3	Right	Yes	0.20
4	Right	No	0.00
5	Wrong	No	0.20
	Score obtained in this item		0.60

All *j* answers are then shown in a random order. Randomization applies on each level; this makes a real challenge for the learner to achieve a better grade, as each try consists of another random selection of questions.

A total of 73 question groups were designed, and with the random generation considered, a total of 369 variations for them complete the assessment event. It is worth mentioning that we used *LaTex* in all Mathematics symbols in order to improve their loading and layout. The interpretation was done with *MathJax* script, which Coursera platform offers. After Mathematical expressions were interpreted, the embedded in the corresponding assessment was done as an auto-generated SVG (Scalable Vector Graphic). Figure 3 shows an example of a question.

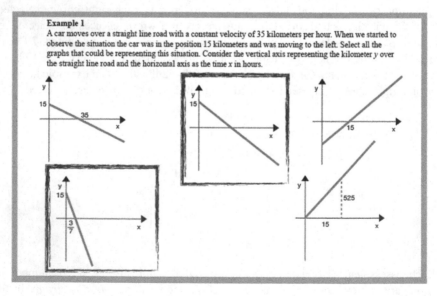

Fig. 3. Example of question, from language (and numbers) to graphical representation

5   The Assessment Experience in Math and Motion

Here we present relevant information obtained during this first experience with Math and Motion, in which 15229 users registered. From that total, only 10016 users could be considered active, which means they enter and access content from the course at least once.

In order to be fair with the findings to present here, we have to recall that many reports of low completion rates have shifted the MOOCs' narrative. In the language of the Gartner "Hype Cycle", MOOCs have gone from the "peak of inflated expectations" in 2011–2012, to the "trough of disillusionment" in 2013–2014, when they don't turn out to be the silver bullet that solves higher education's problems. Nevertheless, following the classic hype cycle we could see MOOCs now rise through a "slope of enlightenment" and their benefits could be better understood [16].

According with the information provided by the Coursera report [17], between 5 % and 10 % of the enrolled users actually passes or gets a State of Accomplishment in a MOOC. James V. Green, from the University of Maryland, during the 2013 Coursera Partners' Conference, highlighted that not all students or users intend to pass in a MOOC. Many are just interested in taking the content, probably learning the material or discussing with other students with similar interests in the forums.

For our case in Math and Motion we had that from 10016 total active users, 612 passed the course, which represents a 6.11 % approval percentage. Table 3 shows frequency of final grades in intervals, with a total population of 662 students that took at least 12 assessments in order to be graded.

Table 3. Intervals for final grades and distribution among them

Grade interval	Users
100	7
[90,100)	204
[80,90)	243
[70,80)	133
[60,70)	56
[50, 60)	18
[40, 50)	1

Table 4 offers information about the overall performance for each of the fourteen assessments, as observed, a 14 weeks long MOOC is a quite ambitious enterprise. It is noticeable the reduction of users doing the assessments as the weeks pass by. Information about the average for each assessment is around the passing grade, which is 70.

Finally we present information about the design of questions on the 14 assessments. Being interested in the skill of flexibility of representations, the design of questions should consider the conversion or treatment processes with representations. Table 5 shows some balance between the transformations.

Table 4. Participants that took assessments and average score for each week

Record of grades per week

Week	Users that took the test	Average
1	2679	79
2	1764	76
3	1354	75
4	1159	79
5	1016	74
6	898	73
7	865	73
8	833	70
9	759	75
10	747	69
11	714	68
12	688	69
13	678	69
14	652	68

Table 5. Distribution of the design of questions according to the type of treatment and conversion considered.

Design of questions considering the kind of process

	Number of questions	Percentage
Kind	Treatment	
Algebraic	28	38 %
Graphical	10	14 %
Numerical	3	4 %
	Conversion	
From real context to other	12	16 %
From graphical to other	11	15 %
From algebraic to other	7	10 %
From numerical to other	2	3 %
Totals	73	100 %

6 Concluding Remarks

In this first MOOC delivery, Math and Motion obtained the expected percentage of enrollments that get the State of Accomplishment (6.11 %) as reported from Coursera (5 %–10 %). We consider in this a positive fact, due to the 14-week-long extended format offered, and maybe also because of the Math theme, that may cause less interest to the public in general.

Low course completion has been a frequent criticism for MOOCs, and the origin of this could be an unfair comparison with courses in campi. The perspective should be that online learning is different from the traditional academic setting.

Masie [18] states that in a MOOC, the low rate completion is meaningless without any additional context. Everyone enrolled comes in a different level of understanding and expertise, not everyone needs every segment of the course. Or they just want to learn without any commitment. Numbers that really matter are the reviews and ratings, is important to understand the users perception about the value of the MOOC. Low completion rates plus negative commentaries, is not a good sign. On the other hand, low completion rates, plus whole positive feedback is a very good sign; it means they got what they wanted.

We agree with this; our experience in formal education could not compare with the one on Math and Motion. The opportunity to get in touch with so many people, of different ages, around the world, and share their enthusiasm for a different teaching and learning of Math, has been a priceless opportunity in our professional practice.

Recent research pursues clarifying the value of MOOCs. Kassabian [16] finds a partially match between the MOOC goals in the narrative playing out in press, and the MOOC goals for the universities. Common goals to public narrative and the universities are improving access to education and deriving reputational benefits. But the MOOC potential to improve College completion, or to control College costs, has been just expressed by public narrative. Those goals do not appear with universities. Instead, universities claim to pursue education research and to improve classroom education. That is our case; we have been developing research and improving our readiness course to College: Introduction to College Mathematics.

With Math and Motion we have joined the challenge to offer a better education to everyone, and at the same time, show how digital technologies can transform Mathematics learning. The complexity of the thinking processes that our society demands, have an opportunity to be experienced with the learning of Mathematics. This could be possible if we manage to change the way of interacting with this science. The integration of digital technologies can be an ally in this aim, as long as it is considered a research matter for Mathematics Education.

References

1. Ontario Online Learning Portal for Faculty and Instructors. http://contactnorth.ca/trends-directions/evolving-pedagogy-0/new-pedagogy-emergingand-online-learning-key-contributing
2. OECD.: Are 15-year-olds creative problem-solvers? PISA in Focus, pp. 4–7 (2014)
3. Salinas, P., Alanís, J.A.: Hacia un nuevo paradigma en la enseñanza del Cálculo dentro de una institución educativa. Revista Latinoamericana de Investigación en Matemática Educativa **12**, 355–382 (2009)
4. Alanís, J.A., Salinas, P.: Cálculo de una variable: acercamientos newtoniano y leibniziano integrados didácticamente. El Cálculo y su Enseñanza **2**, 1–14 (2010)
5. Salinas, P., Alanís, J.A., Pulido, R.: Cálculo de una variable: reconstrucción para el aprendizaje y la enseñanza. Didac **56–57**, 62–69 (2011)

6. Arcavi, A.: The role of visual representations in the learning of mathematics. Educ. Stud. Math. **52**, 215–241 (2003)
7. Duval, R.: A cognitive analysis of problems of comprehension in a learning of mathematics. Educ. Stud. Math. **61**, 103–131 (2006)
8. Duval, R.: Un tema crucial en la educación matemática: la habilidad para cambiar el registro de representación. La Gaceta de La Real Sociedad Matemática Española **9**, 143–168 (2006)
9. Duval, R.: A crucial issue in mathematics education: the ability to change representation register. In: Proceedings of the 10th International Congress on Mathematical Education, pp. 1–17. IMFUFA, Denmark (2008)
10. OECD.: PISA 2012 Results What Students Know and Can Do-Student Performance in Mathematics, Reading and Science, pp. 1–564 (2014)
11. Gómez, F.: Educational innovation through ICTs in the university setting: what do students think of these practices? Revista de Universidad y Sociedad del Conocimiento (RUSC) **11**, 49–60 (2014)
12. Del Moral, M.E., Villalustre Martínez, L.: Didáctica Universitaria en la era 2.0 competencias docentes en campus virtuales. Revista de Universidad y Sociedad del Conocimiento **9**(1), 36–50 (2012)
13. Moreno-Armella, L., Sriraman, B.: Symbols and mediation in mathematics education. In: Sriraman, B., English, L. (eds.) Theories of Mathematics Education: Seeking New Frontiers, pp. 213–232. Springer, Heidelberg (2010)
14. Moreno-Armella, L., Hegedus, S.: Co-action with digital technologies. ZDM **41**, 505–519 (2009)
15. Salinas, P.: Approaching calculus with SimCalc: linking derivative and antiderivative. In: Hegedus, S., Roschelle, J. (eds.) The SimCalc Vision and Contributions, pp. 383–399. Springer, Heidelberg (2013)
16. Kassabian, D.: The value of MOOCs to early adopter universities. http://www.educause.edu/ero/article/value-moocs-early-adopter-universities
17. Coursera: Consider retention in the context of student intent. https://instructor-support.desk.com/customer/portal/articles/1171946-retention
18. Masie, E.: Making a great online course, and why high drop-out rates aren't a bad thing. http://venturebeat.com/2014/08/30/understanding-the-value-of-a-massive-open-online-course-mooc/

A Notification and Recommender Mobile App for Educational Online Discussion: A Design Research Approach

Kittisak Sirisaengtaksin[1]([✉]), Lorne Olfman[1], and Nimer Alrushiedat[2]

[1] Claremont Graduate University, Claremont, USA
{kittisak.sirisaengtaksin,lorne.olfman}@cgu.edu
[2] California State University, Fullerton, Fullerton, USA
nalrushiedat@exchange.fullerton.edu

Abstract. This research presents an information system design theory (ISDT) to integrate a notification and recommendation system (NARS) into online discussion forums on mobile devices. The artifact is designed with respect to awareness and information overload as kernel theories. Furthermore, the design includes an intuitive way to improve the accuracy of short-text clustering used to extract semantic topics from posts. The paper describes a prototype of the design artifact, experiments to evaluate the proposed short-text clustering method, and a survey to evaluate the quality of the artifact prototype.

Keywords: Online discussion · Design research · Mobile · Notification · Recommender

1 Introduction

Mobile devices can enhance online discussion forums (ODFs) by allowing learners to interact with each other anywhere and anytime. Since this enables participants to access the posts as soon as they are made, the time between the posts and their replies should decrease and the participation should increase [1]. Moreover, enabling participants to check messages easily and more frequently reduces the accumulation of unread messages, which are not relevant to them anymore [1]. Additionally, if the participants are available at the same time, a critical mass can occur and the discussion can be synchronous [2]. The benefits of a synchronous ODF are immediate feedback and motivation [1].

However, just making ODFs available on mobile devices might not yet yield all of the true benefits noted above. This is because the level of activity on the ODFs still depends on participants' diligence to check their mobile devices to see new posts. Moreover, the difference of using a computer compared to a mobile device is that mobile device users cannot focus on the device and the screen for a long time, especially while they are travelling [3]. These reasons impede the participants from checking their devices frequently; as such, the effect of mobile ODFs on discussions could be similar to traditional ODFs.

© Springer International Publishing Switzerland 2015
P. Zaphiris and A. Ioannou (Eds.): LCT 2015, LNCS 9192, pp. 325–336, 2015.
DOI: 10.1007/978-3-319-20609-7_31

The current research proposes a design to integrate a notification and recommender system (NARS) into ODFs on mobile devices to address the above issues. Notification is used to inform participants that there is a new activity on the forum. Recommender systems suggest posts that might be relevant to the individual participants. Specifically, the current research focuses on ODFs that allow learners to have a discussion outside a classroom. Since the discussion is an addition to classroom time, it is difficult for the learners to know when other learners are free to discuss. With NARS, participants can check the discussion on their mobile devices when they receive prompts or when they think it is necessary.

2   Information Systems Design Theory for NARS for Educational Online Discussion

This current research uses a design science research approach to develop NARS for an educational ODF. Information system design research articulates and develops a specific class of information systems [4] or artifacts [5] in terms of an Information Systems Design Theory (ISDT) [6] in order to prescriptively guide a design of other systems in that particular class. An ISDT is design knowledge that is expressed as a theory in order to make the information system research rigorous and legitimate [6]. The design theory in this current research is described using eight components of an ISDT proposed by Gregor and Jones [6]. The remaining sections of this paper describe the eight components and evaluation of the artifact in more detail.

2.1   Purpose and Scope

The current research proposes to develop and integrate NARS into an ODF on mobile devices. Notifications are expected to increase the participants' awareness of new posts and recommendations are expected to decrease the negative effect of information overload on participants [7]. Therefore, by adding the artifact to the ODF, the effectiveness of the discussion should be improved.

2.2   Constructs

The major constructs for this research are notification, recommendation, and topic discovery. The following subsections describe each construct in more detail.

Notification. One of the benefits of an ODF is that there is no requirement to instantly reply to messages. However, long delays in responses are problematic because they tend to stifle discussion. It is possible to reduce the effect of long delays by notifying users about what is going on in the discussion [3]. Notification is a service that delivers messages to users' devices instantly or at a specific time [8]. The purpose of notification is to help users be aware of the most recent events in the current task-oriented interaction [9]. A notification system is a lightweight display of information, which is triggered by specific events and delivered to a person with a current task-oriented concern [9].

Notification is classified as push technology, which delivers "right" messages to the right users based on predefined rules or triggers [10]. One of the advantages of push technology is that it takes less time for the users to browse for their relevant information. Moreover, users are always made aware when there is an update and they can respond immediately. The disadvantages of push technology are that it can become annoying with interruptions and requires more bandwidth to deliver [10].

Recommendation. Push systems that actively deliver information to the user without a request cause information overload [11]. That is because they potentially increase the amount of useless information that a participant must handle [12]. Recommendations can help users deal with the information overload [7]. Recommender systems suggest a set of relevant posts or threads to users based on feedback such as ratings from other users and what the users post [13]. They not only mimic a person who is knowledgeable in a topic, but also take the person's tastes and preferences into account [14].

Recommender systems can be classified into three categories: content-based, collaborative-based, and hybrid [7]. Content-based recommender systems provide an item that is similar to the ones the user preferred in the past. Collaborative-based recommender systems provide a recommended item that people with similar tastes and preferences to the user liked in the past. Finally, a hybrid recommender system is the combination of content-based and collaborative-based [7]. Additionally, a recommender system provides a service to users based on explicit feedback (ratings from other users) and implicit feedback (what the other users post) [13].

Topics Discovery. The designed system needs a document clustering method to see whether a newly created post is similar to the posts that are known to be relevant to the participant. This kind of method discovers the semantic relationships between individual terms using statistical analysis on a whole dataset of documents [15] and groups the documents based on them. The research uses Latent Dirchlet Allocation (LDA) since the algorithm can discover the probability that a latent topic belongs to a document. Moreover, the model has been successfully used in order to discover topics in news articles and academic abstracts [16].

LDA is described as a generative probabilistic model that can be used with sets of discrete data such as a text dataset. The model is a three-level hierarchical Bayesian model, in which there are three levels: corpus, document, and word. The assumption of the model is that a document is a mixture of topics with each topic having different probabilities in each document [17, 18]. Moreover, in addition to words, the model is also valid for larger structure units such as n-grams or paragraphs [17]. LDA can cluster words into topics and a document into mixtures of topics [18].

Most of the methods for representing texts used by most of the clustering algorithms, including LDA, are derived from a "bag-of-words" model [15, 17]. In this model, an attribute is created to represent each word in the corpus and each document is assigned those attributes with their values corresponding to the number of times the word occurs in the document [15]. However, the bag-of-words model has a limitation when it is used with short text documents due to sparseness of data [15, 19]; it needs to measure similarity but short texts do not have sufficient terms to make them appear in more than one document [19]. Moreover, synonymy (different words that have the same meaning) and polysemy (a word that can have multiple meanings) make it even harder to analyze the texts [15].

Unfortunately, the length of ODF posts made on a mobile device tends to be short. This is because authoring a post on the forum might not be the participants' primary work or when on the move participants cannot focus their attention on writing more than a few words in a message. The small size of the screen and the on-screen keyboard of the mobile device can also impede participants from creating a long post.

2.3 Principles of Form and Function

The current research adapts the generalized architecture of an adaptive educational hypermedia systems (AEHS) model [20] to describe the implementation of NARS. The architecture is chosen because it depicts the main components of the systems and their structural interconnections. AEHS addresses the same issue as recommender systems in learning [21]. The approach deals with the problem that learners with different goals and knowledge might need different information or treatment. It overcomes this problem by adapting the presented information to an individual learner with respect to his or her information in the user model [22]. The architecture of NARS for an educational ODF is shown in Fig. 1. It defines the structure of the components of NARS, which can be used as a blueprint or framework to design the artifact.

2.4 Artifact Mutability

Courses might be different in terms of content, requirements, ontology, etc. The design of the artifact needs be adjusted to fit the course for which it is implemented. For example, the notification rules need to be defined in the way that meets the course requirements. Recommender systems can also be designed to fit the ontology of the class. The topic discovery method can be designed to utilize the structure of the content in the forum.

2.5 Testable Propositions

Three propositions are derived from the kernel theories described in the next section. As shown in Fig. 2, notification gives the participants awareness of posts, and the awareness should improve the effectiveness of the ODF. In addition, recommendation reduces the effect of participants' information overload [7]. It is expected that recommendations will manage participants' feelings of being overwhelmed, and therefore increase their confidence to contribute to the forum. Overall, the effectiveness of the discussion on the forum should be improved by NARS. The propositions are as follows:

Proposition I: Notifications can increase participants' awareness.
Proposition II: Recommendations can reduce the effects of information overload.
Proposition III: NARS can improve the effectiveness of learning.

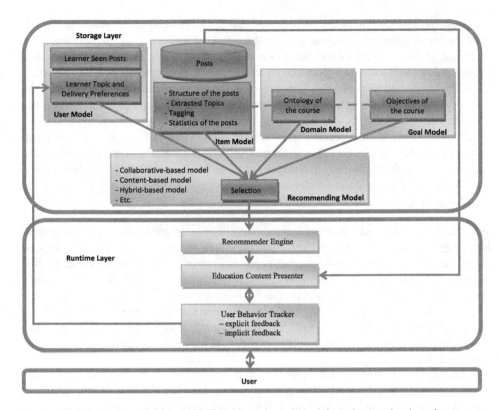

Fig. 1. NARS for an educational ODF architecture (adapted from karampiperis and sampson [20]).

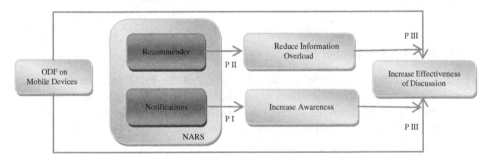

Fig. 2. Model for the effects of NARS on ODFs on mobile devices

2.6 Justificatory Knowledge

An ISDT should be based on natural and social science theories, which are referred to as kernel theories [5]. The research adopts awareness and information overload concepts and uses them as kernel theories to guide the development of the artifact.

Awareness. The current research suggests that the long delay in response in typical asynchronous online discussions is caused by lack of awareness of participants. For example, if they are not aware that a new comment is posted, they do not check the forum and respond to the new post. Awareness in computer-supported cooperative work (CSCW) is referred to as an understanding of the activities of others in order to provide a context for one's own activity. This context makes sure that the individual's actions are relevant to the group's activities and contribute toward the group's goals [23].

Awareness in the current research is defined as knowledge of existence of posts that are newly created on an ODF. This awareness is delivered to the learners via notification messages on mobile devices. It is expected to provide opportunities for learners to contribute to the discussion and allow the contribution to be relevant to the group. As a result, learning should be more effective.

Information Overload. Because learners simultaneously use knowledge in a shared knowledge space, it is highly likely that they will receive many active awareness messages at the same time. These messages can cause information overload for the learners [24]. Moreover, unlike traditional ODFs, those on mobile devices have almost constant access; therefore, participants can be overloaded with seemingly endless opportunities to learn and work [11]. In general, information overload refers to the concept of receiving too much information [12]. Having too much information can be confusing, can reduce the person's ability to set priorities, and makes it harder to recall previous information [12].

Information filtering, which refers to both looking for wanted information (filtering in) and eliminating unwanted information (filtering out) [24], can help handle information overload. The goals of knowledge awareness message filtering are to filter out irrelevant messages that might disturb the learner and to prioritize the messages with respect to their significance to the learner priority [24]. Recommender systems provide filtering.

2.7 Principles of Implementation

A prototype has been developed as an instantiation of the ISDT in order to test the propositions. Fifteen graduate students were asked to evaluate the mobile app prototype for usability. Feedback from the evaluation were used to improve the prototype system so that the undesirable or missing features were corrected.

2.8 Expository Instantiation

Enhancement Approach for the Topic Discovery Method. The current research proposes an enhancement method to improve the performance of LDA on short text documents. The proposed method is intuitive and does not require a modification of the LDA clustering algorithm. This method applies to the preparation process that creates a representation of data before feeding it to the algorithm. The proposed method starts with identifying important words from a well-organized tree structure [25] of an ODF as described in Table 1. In addition, Banerjee et al. [26] find that doubling the weight of the terms in the title of a document yields better results. The current research follows this suggestion; however, it doubles the weight of all of the important words and terms in the ontology described previously. This approach can be used with any clustering methods that are based on a bag-of-words approach.

Table 1. Proposed rules to identify important words

Rationale	Rule
All of the posts in a thread are likely to talk about the title of that thread	Important words should reside in the title of the thread
All of the posts in a thread are very likely to reply to the root (first) post of that thread [25]	Important words should be in the root post
Since a post is likely to implicitly reply to the post that is created consecutively before it [25], those two posts are likely to talk about the same topics	The common words of two consecutive posts should be important words
Most ODFs allow a participant to quote a statement from a previous post. In this case, the newly created post talks about the post from which the participant gets the quote	The common words in the post and the quoted post might be important words
Sometimes a post mentions the name of a participant in order to refer to the most recent post of that participant [25]. Those two posts talk about the same topics	Important words must be the common words in the post and the most recent post that mentions its author
Most ODFs allow a participant to explicitly reply to another post. Therefore, two posts talk about the same topic	The common words in the post and the post that is replied to are important words
A collaborative tagging system is used in an ODF to collaboratively indicate the topic of a thread	The tagging terms should be important words
The terms in the ontology of the class are the concepts discussed in the ODF	The terms in the ontology are important words

Prototype. There are three major components of the prototype: ODF, mobile application, and recommender engine. The ODF web application was adapted from an open source system called Simple Machines Forum (SMF).[1] One of the advantages

---

[1] http://www.simplemachines.org/.

of SMF is that various modifications developed by a community of SMF developers can be installed to the system. Secondly, the mobile application used to access the ODF was developed for the iPhone and Android platforms (Fig. 3). It is an interface that exchanges information with the web application. The current research adopted a technique called data scraping to extract data from the mobile forum web application and visualize it on the mobile application. Finally, the recommender engine selects relevant posts and threads for participants based on predefined rules. In addition, in order to find topics of posts, an LDA module in Mahout, which is an open source machine learning library from Apache, is used. In this research, Mahout is modified with respect to the way that the data is prepared according to the enhancement method proposed above.

3 Evaluation of the Enhancement Approach for the Topic Discovery Method

In order to evaluate the proposed enhancement to the topic discovery method, a reliable benchmark dataset of text documents with labeled topics was used. The dataset is from Travel Stack Exchange,[2] which is a Q&A site for traveling. In total, the dataset contains 1000 posts for topics that have accepted answers that more than 10 people voted as being useful. The criteria ensure that the discussions on the topics are highly active. In the dataset, the first post of each discussion thread contains tagging terms that describe the thread. These tagging terms are used as a benchmark or labeled topic.

Two versions of a topic discovery function were implemented. The first version is the baseline method that has only the LDA algorithm. The second version is the treatment method that has the LDA algorithm with the proposed enhancement method, but not all of the proposed important words identification rules are implemented because the dataset does not have some information to implement some rules. For example, the dataset does not have quotes or an ontology. Moreover, the tagging terms are not included in the rules since they are used as a benchmark.

Both versions of the method were run on the dataset 100 times. A match is made if a post is clustered into the topic that contains keywords that appear in the post's tagging terms. The total number of matched posts for each run was recorded.

An independent samples t-test showed that here was a significant difference between the mean of the treatment method ($\bar{x} = 492.57$, s = 19.29005) and the baseline method ($\bar{x} = 474.58$, s = 19.23443); $t(198) = -6.604$, $p < .001$. This result suggests that the proposed enhancement method is better than the baseline method for classifying posts. The relatively low averages of the matched scores (less than 500 out of 1000) is possibly explained by the fact that the benchmark dataset contains only 5 tagging terms. Since the purpose of the evaluation is to see whether the proposed method increases the number of matched posts, the raw averages are not important.

---

[2] http://travel.stackexchange.com/.

(a) Topic View   (b) Post View   (c) Setting View   (d) Recommender View

(e) Notification (app is not running)   (f) Notification (the app is running)   (g) Notification Center

Fig. 3. Screenshots of the application prototype

4 Evaluation of the Prototype

An experiment to evaluate the propositions was conducted with 7 students enrolled in a statistics course. The experimental subjects were asked to install the mobile application on their smartphones and participate in an ODF. The experiment lasted for two weeks and was divided equally into a control phase and a treatment phase. NARS was disabled in the control phase and was enabled in the treatment phase. At the end of the experiment, survey questions were distributed to the subjects to inquire about their experiences with the notification and recommender with respect to the ODF. Since the subject size was small and the experimental period was short, it was hardly likely that information overload would happen. Therefore, the participants were asked to imagine that they were using the artifact in a large class.

The majority of the participants thought that notification would be useful because people would be noticed right away after a reply or relevant comment has been created.

One participant mentioned that the notification features helped in finding posts; as a consequence, the person could post more. Another participant mentioned that the feature would help people follow the discussion, which is very difficult to do using a website. In addition, it was interesting that most participants automatically compared the notification on a smartphone to email. For example, one participant said that having many smartphone notifications, which take only a small space of a smartphone's screen, is not as difficult to process compared to receiving them in email. Another comment suggested that students do not check their email regularly, so a smartphone notification would be helpful. Overall, the students felt that the feature would help them to continue the discussion. However, there are some concerns that too many notification messages could disturb people and they might ignore the messages potentially leading to missing some content that is relevant to them. However, an option to turn notifications on and off would prevent the students from being overwhelmed. Two participants worried about their privacy; they thought that a smartphone was for their personal use.

Participants found that the recommendation feature would help them find other discussions that may be of interest to them. This would be true especially in a big class since nobody would read all of the posts. Two participants thought that the feature would expedite the process of looking for a post to comment on or replying to a post because the participants would know where to look. One participant suggested that the feature would allow people to respond to multiple posts in a short time. However, there were some participants who still preferred to look for a relevant post by themselves because there might be a topic aside from the one recommended in which they are interested. Another participant was concerned that the feature might discourage people from reading other posts.

Overall, the participants thought that these two features would help them contribute and be more involved in the discussion, and would make the system organized and manageable.

5   Conclusion

The current research is expected to contribute to the educational industry and the research area of technology enhanced learning (TEL). For the educational industry, the ISDT can be used as a guideline to design NARS for an ODF for learning. For researchers, the current study presents an approach to improve the performance of the LDA topic discovery method. However, the approach can also be useful for any clustering methods that are based on a bag-of-words representation. The research also proposes a conceptual model to explain how NARS can improve the quality of learning for students participating in an ODF. That is, notifications delivered by NARS can increase awareness of participants, and recommendations can reduce the effect of information overload. The results of the experiment supported the propositions, although some students expressed concerns that the notifications might disturb some participants.

References

1. Callum, K., Kinshuk, : Mobile discussion boards: an analysis on mobile collaboration. Int. J. Interact. Mob. Technol. **2**, 5–9 (2008)
2. Hill, T.R., Roldan, M.: Toward third generation threaded discussions for mobile learning: opportunities and challenges for ubiquitous collaborative environments. Inf. Syst. Front. **7**, 55–70 (2005)
3. Wojciechowski, A.: Supporting social networks by event-driven mobile notification services. In: Meersman, R., Tari, Z. (eds.) OTM-WS 2007, Part I. LNCS, vol. 4805, pp. 398–406. Springer, Heidelberg (2007)
4. Walls, J.G., Widmeyer, G.R., El Sawy, O.A.: Building an information system design theory for vigilant EIS. Inf. Syst. Res. **3**, 36–59 (1992)
5. Walls, J.G., Widmeyer, G.R., El Sawy, O.A.: Assessing information system design theory in perspective: how useful was our, initial rendition? J. Inf. Technol. Theory Appl. (JITTA) **6**(2004), 43–58 (1992)
6. Gregor, S., Jones, D.: The anatomy of a design theory. J. Assoc. Inf. Syst. **8**, 325–335 (2007)
7. Adomavicius, G., Tuzhilin, A.: Toward the next generation of recommender systems: a survey of the state-of-the-art and possible extensions. IEEE Trans. Knowl. Data Eng. **17**, 734–749 (2005)
8. Hornsby, A., Bouzazizi, I., Defee, I.: Notification service for DVB-H mobile broadcast. IEEE Wirel. Commun. **17**, 15–21 (2010)
9. Carroll, J.M., Neale, D.C., Isenhour, P.L., et al.: Notification and awareness: synchronizing task-oriented collaborative activity. Int. J. Hum. Comput. Stud. **58**, 605–632 (2003)
10. Latif, N.A., Hassan, M.F., Hasan, M.H.: Automated notification and document downloading in e-learning - development of an agent-based framework utilizing the push-pull technology interaction policy. In: ITSim 2008, vol. 1, pp. 1–7 (2008)
11. Bawden, D., Robinson, L.: The dark side of information: overload, anxiety and other paradoxes and pathologies. J. Inf. Sci. **35**, 180–191 (2009)
12. Eppler, M.J., Mengis, J.: The concept of information overload: a review of literature from organization science, accounting, marketing, MIS, and related disciplines. Inf. Soc. **20**, 325–344 (2004)
13. Abel, F., Bittencourt, I.I., Costa, E., et al.: Recommendations in online discussion forums for e-learning systems. TLT **3**, 165–176 (2010)
14. Buder, J., Schwind, C.: Learning with personalized recommender systems: a psychological view. Comput. Hum. Behav. **28**, 207–216 (2012)
15. Petersen, H., Poon, J.: Enhancing short text clustering with small external repositories. In: AusDM, pp. 79–90 (2011)
16. Mehrotra, R., Sanner, S., Buntine, W. et al.: Improving LDA topic models for microblogs via tweet pooling and automatic labeling. In: SIGIR, vol. 36, pp. 889-892 (2013)
17. Blei, D.M., Ng, A.Y., Jordan, M.I.: Latent Dirichlet allocation. J. Mach. Learn. Res. **3**, 993–1022 (2003)
18. Owen, S., Anil, R., Dunning, T., et al.: Mahout in Action. Manning Publications, New York (2011)
19. Hu, X., Sun, N., Zhang, C. et al.: Exploiting internal and external semantics for the clustering of short texts using world knowledge. In: CIKM, vol. 18, pp. 919-928 (2009)
20. Karampiperis, P., Sampson, D.: Adaptive learning resources sequencing in educational hypermedia systems. Educ. Technol. Soc. **8**, 128–147 (2005)
21. Manouselis, N., Drachsler, H., Vuorikari, R., et al.: Recommender Systems in Technology Enhanced Learning, pp. 387–415. Springer, New York (2011)

22. Brusilovsky, P.: Developing Adaptive Educational Hypermedia Systems: From Design Models to Authoring Tools, pp. 377–409. Springer, Netherlands (2003)
23. Dourish, P., Bellotti, V.: Awareness and coordination in shared workspaces. In: CSCW, pp. 107–114 (1992)
24. Ogata, H., Yano, Y.: Combining knowledge awareness and information filtering in an open-ended collaborative learning environment. Int. J. Artif. Intell. Educ. (IJAIED) 11, 33–46 (2000)
25. Wang, H., Wang, C., Zhai, C. et al.: Learning online discussion structures by conditional random fields. In: SIGIR, vol. 34, pp. 435–444 (2011)
26. Banerjee, S., Ramanathan, K., Gupta, A.: Clustering short texts using Wikipedia. In: SIGIR, vol. 30, pp. 787–788 (2007)

Generating Quizzes for History Learning Based on Wikipedia Articles

Yoshihiro Tamura[1], Yutaka Takase[2], Yuki Hayashi[3],
and Yukiko I. Nakano[2(✉)]

[1] Graduate School of Science and Technology,
Seikei University, Musashino, Japan
dml26222@cc.seikei.ac.jp
[2] Department of Computer and Information Science,
Seikei University, Musashino, Japan
{yutaka-takase,y.nakano}@st.seikei.ac.jp
[3] College of Sustainable System Sciences,
Osaka Prefecture University, Osaka, Japan
hayashi@kis.osakafu-u.ac.jp

Abstract. In intelligent tutoring systems (ITS), creating large amounts of educational content requires a large-scale and multi-domain knowledge base. However, most knowledge bases for ITSs are still manually developed. Aiming at reducing the cost of developing educational contents, this study proposes a method to generate multiple-choice history quizzes using Wikipedia articles. We also propose a method for assigning an importance measure to each relevant article based on hierarchical categories and the number of incoming links to the article. This is indispensable in generating quizzes that test basic knowledge of history. Finally, the results of evaluating these methods show that the proposed methods are useful in automatically creating quizzes for history exercise.

Keywords: ITS · Quiz generation · Wikipedia · History education

1 Introduction

In recent years, computers have become increasingly useful and popular in educational settings. Studies in intelligent tutoring systems (ITS) have attempted numerous approaches to estimate a learner's understanding and provide user-adapted, efficient learning environments. However, most knowledge bases for ITSs are still manually developed, and creating a large-scale, multi-domain knowledge base to generate educational content is costly. Therefore, in current educational systems, quizzes intended to test students' understanding of the subject matter are manually created, and their level of difficulty is manually determined.

With the aim of reducing the cost of developing education contents, this study proposes a method for generating history quizzes using Wikipedia articles. Wikipedia is a free online encyclopedia to which any users of the Internet can contribute. Since a large number of users contribute to Wikipedia, detailed information regarding a vast variety of topics is available on the site. It is customary for Internet users to refer to

© Springer International Publishing Switzerland 2015
P. Zaphiris and A. Ioannou (Eds.): LCT 2015, LNCS 9192, pp. 337–346, 2015.
DOI: 10.1007/978-3-319-20609-7_32

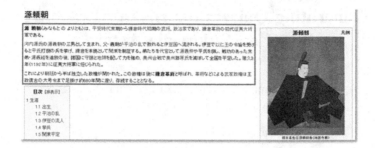

Fig. 1. Introduction part of a Wikipedia article (Color figure online)

Wikipedia. Therefore, we think Wikipedia a rich knowledge base for automatically generating quizzes.

In this study, by focusing on Japanese history, we propose a method for creating quizzes where the answer to each prompt is the title of the Wikipedia article, using which the question was generated. To this end, we address the following issues in this paper:

1. Generating interrogative expressions from introduction parts in a Wikipedia article (text enclosed by the red rectangle in Fig. 1). We propose a method to transform a sentence in introduction part into an interrogative expression.
2. Generating answer choices for each quiz. In order to reduce the difficulty and ambiguity of questions, we propose a method to generate answer choices using Wikipedia's tag information and triples in DBpedia, a project that aims to extract structured content from the information generated on Wikipedia.
3. Assigning an importance measure to each article based on the structure of the relevant category and link analysis. This is indispensable to generating quizzes that test basic knowledge of history and choosing appropriate quizzes for educational purposes.

Finally, we evaluate our proposed methods to show that they are useful for automatically creating history quizzes.

2 Related Work

As reviewed in [1], many attempts have been made in the area of question/problem generation in research on educational support tools. With regard to question generation for history education, Rus and Graesser [2] claimed that questions are categorized into two types: shallow questions (who, what, when, and where) and deep questions (why, how, what if). Since deep questions require descriptive answers, it is difficult for computer systems to judge their correctness. Thus, in this study, we address the problem of generating shallow questions regarding important people in history.

Limiting to shallow questions, this study aims to reduce the burden of manual educational content creation on educators. Previous studies on dialogue systems have contributed to this direction of research, and several methods have been proposed for automatically generating questions using Web resources as knowledge bases. Misu et al. [3] proposed a dialogue system with a question-answer function and an information recommendation function based on Wikipedia resources. Higashinaka et al. [4] proposed a dialog system that generated quizzes asking for names of a person based on Wikipedia and online newspapers. Jouault and Seta [5] proposed a system that helped students with self-directed historical learning of history in an open learning space. In order to supply questions, they used semantic Web resources by combining DBpedia and Freebase contents. However, little research has addressed the generation of multiple-choice quizzes using Web resources in Japanese history.

Therefore, focusing on Wikipedia articles as a knowledge base, this study aims at automatic generation of multiple-choice quizzes in Japanese history domain. To accomplish this goal, we propose a method of quiz generation based on the results of morphological and syntactic analysis. In addition, in order to reduce the difficulty and the ambiguity of the generated questions, we propose a method for creating answer choices using RDB triples in DBpedia.

3   Wikipedia Database

In recent years, the correctness and reliability of Wikipedia articles has improved significantly. We thus used Wikipedia articles to develop our knowledge base for our history quizzes. To this end, we extracted Wikipedia articles on famous people from the Kamakura period, the Muromachi period, Nanboku-cho, the Sengoku period, the Azuchi–Momoyama period, the Edo period and the Bakumatsu, and the Meiji period. We also extracted articles of historical Japanese battles. Figure 2 shows the structure of our database, constructed using MySQL, and Table 1 lists the contents of the information stored in the database. The tables for "era", "persons", and "battles" are related to each other through relation tables. In this manner, we extracted 3,900 Wikipedia articles to register in the "person" tables and 500 articles for the "battle" tables.

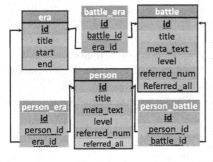

Fig. 2. The structure of history database

Table 1. Content of tables

Table name	Content
era	Era ID
person	Article about a person, difficulty level, no. of incoming links
battle	Article about a battle, difficulty level, no. of incoming links
person_era	Relation between person and era
person_battle	Relation between person and battle
battle_era	Relation between battle and era

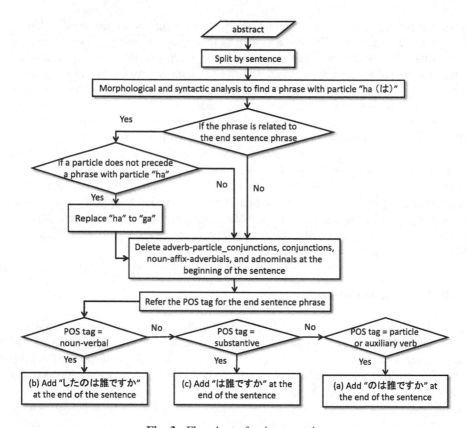

Fig. 3. Flowchart of quiz generation

4 Generating Quizzes

In this section, we detail our proposed method of generating quizzes from Wikipedia articles. The introduction parts of all Wikipedia articles are written in a very similar and consistent style. Moreover, the introduction part appears at the beginning of each page, because of which it is more likely to have been edited by many contributors, and thus is more likely to contain accurate information than other parts of the page. Based on this reasoning, we generated quizzes from the introduction part of articles.

We found two advantageous characteristics of introduction parts in generating quizzes:

1. Except for the first sentence, the subject of each subsequent sentence in the intro- duction text, which is the title of the article, is omitted.
2. Each sentence ends with either a noun or a noun phrase or with an assertive form, such as "-da" (だ), "-dearu" (である), etc.

The first observation implies that the first sentence of the introduction part of each article is suitable for generating quizzes, and the second observation suggests that generic generation rules for interrogative sentences can be defined by using simple end-of-word transformations.

The introduction part contains sentences of the form "S (subject, name of the person) + V (a be-verb) + C (some explanation)". By transforming these types of sentences, we generated a "who"-type quiz. The basic steps of the transformation are (1) deleting a noun phase that includes the answer to the question, (2) adding a wh-interrogative expression to the end of the sentence, and (3) changing particles if necessary.

The flowchart of our quiz generation method is shown in Fig. 3. The introduction part is first divided into sentences. Morphological analysis and dependency (syntactic structure) analysis are then applied to each sentence. If a noun phrase including a postpositional particle 「は」 is found and, in the dependency analysis, relates to the end-sentence phrase, the postpositional particle of the noun phrase is replaced to 「が」. This is because two 「は」 particles should not occur in one sentence. In addition, conjunctions at the beginning of sentences (e.g. noun-affixed adverbials and adnominals) detected through morphological analysis are deleted. Following this, the end-sentence expression is changed in order to convert it into an appropriate wh-question. There are three cases:

(a) if the sentence ends with a particle or an auxiliary verb, add the phrase "no (particle) + ha (particle) + dare (who) + desu (auxiliary verb) + ka (particle) [のは誰ですか]" to the end of the sentence.
(b) If the sentence ends with a noun-verbal, add a phrase "shita (verb) + no (particle) + ha (particle) + dare (who) + desu (auxiliary verb) + ka (particle) [したのは誰ですか]" to the end of the sentence.
(c) If the sentence ends with a substantive, add a phrase "ha (particle) + dare (who) + desu (auxiliary verb) + ka (particle) [は誰ですか]" to the end of the sentence.

For instance, the first sentence of the introduction part of the article on Ieyasu Tokugawa, the founder and first shogun of the Togukawa shogunate, ends with "江戸幕府の初代征夷大将軍" ("the first shogun in Edo shogunate"). Since this is a noun phrase and ends with a common noun, "征夷大将軍 (shogun)", transformation rule (c) (add "は誰ですか?" to the end of the sentence) is applied, and the generated question is "江戸幕府の初代征夷大将軍は誰ですか? (Who was the first shogun of the Edo shogunate?").

5   Choosing Important Articles for Quiz Generation

In order to generate quizzes that are appropriate as history exercises, it is necessary to select relevantly important Wikipedia articles. We assigned an article importance measure to each article using its number of referrals (incoming links) and hierarchical structure in Wikipedia.

5.1 Assigning Article Importance Using Wikipedia Hierarchical Structure

Each Wikipedia article has a list of categories that characterize its hierarchical relationships with other concepts. Therefore, these categories may be useful in estimating the importance of an article. However, while these categories are hierarchical, this structure is not entirely consistent because the categories of each article can be determined by any contributor. Because of that, we use "the main topic classification categories", which are officially defined and are composed of nine basic categories, such as Discipline, Technology, Nature, Society, Culture, and History. In this study, we used the category "History" as the route category. "History of Japan" is in the fifth hierarchical level from the top level (Main topic classification – > History – > History by region – > History of continent – > History of Asia – > History of Japan).

In the category of "History of Japan", there is an article, "Japanese history". We thus assumed that people mentioned in this article are the most important historical personages in Japanese history (level = 1). Since articles regarding eras, such as the Edo and the Kamakura eras, have direct links to the "Japanese history" article, historical personages, links to articles for whom are found within the article on the relevant historical era, are assigned the second-highest importance rating (level = 2). Other historical persons are assigned level 3.

5.2 Assigning Article Importance Based on the Number of Incoming Links

In addition to the category hierarchy in Wikipedia, the number of incoming links is used as an index of the importance of an article. These are links to the article in question from other articles in the database. We used the following two measures:

1. The number of tokens of incoming link
2. The number of types of incoming link

For example, if a person's name, which is also a link to the relevant article, say "Tokugawa Ieyasu", occurs two times in an article, the number of tokens of incoming link is 2 and the number of types is 1. In our history database, the number of tokens was registered in "referred_all" in the "person" table, and the number of types was registered in "referred_num".

6 Generating Answer Choices for History Quizzes

A major problem in our quiz generation method was that the resulting quiz contained questions regarding small details that make the quizzes too difficult. More seriously, the quiz has ambiguity, so that there may be multiple answers. By having options from which to choose, it becomes possible for the user to select one correct answer even though the question might be ambiguous. Moreover, the level of difficulty of quizzes can be controlled by changing the choices, and different levels of quizzes can be generated using the same questions.

We used DBpedia Japanese to generate answer choices. DBpedia is a community project that aims to extract information from Wikipedia and publish it as linked open data (LOD). Information in LOD is registered based on the Resource Description Framework (RDF). The RDF describes the relationship between items of information in a resource using a triple: subject, predicate, and object. This study exploits these features in DBpedia to select answer choices.

Our algorithm for selecting answers choices is shown below:

(1) Obtain a list of triples the subjects of which are matched with the title of a Wikipedia article.
(2) Obtain a predicate–object pair from each triple and create a list of predicate–object pairs (hereafter called "PO").
(3) For each PO in the list, obtain a set of subjects whose predicates and objects are identical to those of a PO by searching the database.
(4) For each PO, if either of the following conditions is satisfied, add the PO to a list of "selected" POs (hereafter caller "selected PO list").

   – More than 50 % of the subjects obtained in (3) match the title of an article in the database.
   – More than 5 % of the article titles in the database match with subjects obtained in (3).

(5) For all the combinations of two POs in the selected PO list, obtain the subjects using (3), and select those in common between the two POs.
(6) If more than one and less than 51 subjects obtained in (6) match with the title of an article about a person in the database, save the subjects and the pair of POs as candidates for answer choices.

Note that Step (3) generates a set of persons who have something in common. However, it is possible that Step (3) generates a large number of candidates. Thus, we use Steps (4)–(6) to narrow down the set of candidates by computing the intersection of the results for all combinations of two POs. Using this algorithm, a set of highly similar answer choice candidates can be obtained. However, if the candidates are too similar, multiple answer choices can be correct. In order to resolve this problem, we implemented a process to delete candidates that were too similar.

7 Evaluation

7.1 Evaluation of the Questions

In order to assess the quality of our methods, we generated 100 quizzes containing questions asking for the names of historical persons and evaluated them in terms of grammatical correctness and educational effectiveness.

We randomly selected 100 articles from our database and applied our quiz generation algorithm to each. Since a quiz is generated from each sentence in the introduction part of a given article in our method, more than one quiz was generated if the introduction part consisted of multiple sentences. We randomly selected 100 quizzes from among those generated, and asked the following questions about them:

(i) Is the quiz grammatically correct? Is the sentence transformation completely successful?

(ii) Is the quiz appropriate for learning? Is there any question with more than one correct answer choice? Is the content of the quiz educationally meaningful?

Three people attempted the 100 quizzes with regard to these two aspects. If a subject was unable to answer the quiz (because the quiz was too difficult), the quiz was determined to be educationally inappropriate. The results are shown in Table 2. The three reviewers, who were all native Japanese speakers, judged that 86.5 % of the quizzes were grammatically correct. This result suggests that our quiz generation method can generate grammatically correct quizzes. However, only 48 % of them were judged as appropriate as history exercises. Therefore, it is necessary to evaluate the content of the quizzes by professional reviewers of history and improve the method with regard to the educational appropriateness of the content.

Table 2. Evaluation of the quality of generated quizzes

	Evaluation aspects	Results
(i)	Grammatical correctness	86.5 %
(ii)	Educational appropriateness	48.0 %

7.2 Evaluating Article Importance

In order to evaluate the effectiveness of the proposed method in assigning article importance, we chose 100 historical persons using the following four methods, and compared our list with a list of historical persons who are mentioned in more than five history textbooks out of 11:

(i) Using only the number of types of incoming links

(ii) Using the levels of importance of articles in the category hierarchy and the number of types of incoming links. Under this condition, the articles are first sorted in order of category hierarchy, and articles at the same level in the hierarchy are then sorted based on the number of types of incoming links.

(iii) Using only the number of tokens of incoming links

(iv) Using the levels of importance of article in the category hierarchy and the number of tokens of incoming links. Under this condition, the articles are first sorted in order of category hierarchy, and articles at the same level in the hierarchy are then sorted based on the number of tokens of incoming links.

As shown in Table 3, 67 out of 100 historical persons selected by method (I) were found in the majority of Japanese history textbooks. On the contrary, when using the method (IV), 85 % of the selected historical persons were found in the majority of textbooks. These results suggest that our proposed method (method (IV)) can improve the accuracy of choosing important articles (historical persons) by 18 %.

Table 3. Evaluation of article importance

	Methods for assigning article importance	Result
(I)	referred_num	67 % (67/100)
(II)	referred_num + level	84 % (84/100)
(III)	referred_all	74 % (74/100)
(IV)	referred_all + level	85 % (85/100)

8 Conclusions and Future Directions

In this study, we proposed a quiz generation method using Wikipedia articles. Our method generates multiple-choice quizzes and thus generates answer choices as well as questions for quizzes. Experiments showed that our method can generate grammatically correct quizzes (more than 85 % of the generated quizzes were determined to be grammatically correct). However, more than half of the generated quizzes were determined to be educationally inappropriate. To improve the educational appropriateness of content generated by our method, we proposed a method to assign importance to articles using Wikipedia's hierarchy of categories as well as information regarding the number of incoming links for each article. The results showed that 85 % of the 100 most important historical persons ranked by our method were included in the majority of standard Japanese history textbooks. Furthermore, in order to reduce the difficulty and the ambiguity of the generated quizzes, we proposed a method to create answer choices.

In future work, we plan to integrate our quiz generation mechanism and the article importance estimation procedure into a system. We expect that by using important articles as source of quiz, the generated quizzes will be improved in the educational quality. Moreover, it is necessary to evaluate whether our multiple-choice quiz generation method can generate appropriate answer choices, and is effective in reducing the difficulty and ambiguity of the questions in the generated quizzes. With the aim of improving the answer choices, we will also develop a method for choosing words for distractors by using the categorical structure of Wikipedia and considering word similarities based on RDB triples in DBpedia.

Acknowledgements. This research was supported by CREST, JST.

References

1. Le, N.T., Kojiri, T.: Question and Problem Generation – State of The Art. In: Workshop Proceedings of the 18th International Conference on Computers in Education, pp. 47–55 (2010)
2. Rus, V., Graesser, A. (eds.) : The Question Generation Shared Task and Evaluation Challenge. ISBN: 978-0-615-27428-7 (2009)
3. Misu, T., Kawahara, T.: Speech-based interactive information guidance system using question-answering technique. In: Proceedings of IEEE-ICASSP 2007, pp. 145–148 (2007)

4. Higashinaka, R., Dohsaka, K., Isozaki, H.: Learning to rank definitions to generate quizzes for interactive information presentation. In: ACL 2007 Demo and Poster Sessions, pp. 117–120 (2007)
5. Jouault, C., Seta, K.: Content-dependent question generation for history learning in semantic open learning space. In: Trausan-Matu, S., Boyer, K.E., Crosby, M., Panourgia, K. (eds.) ITS 2014. LNCS, vol. 8474, pp. 300–305. Springer, Heidelberg (2014)

Virtual Worlds and Virtual Agents for Learning

Construction of Educative Micro-Worlds to Build Students' Creativity in Terms of Their Own Self-Learning

Habib M. Fardoun[1(✉)], Abdullah AL-Malaise AL-Ghamdi[1], and Antonio Paules Ciprés[2]

[1] Information Systems Department, Faculty of Computing and Information Technology,
King Abdulaziz University, 21589 Jeddah, Saudi Arabia
{hfardoun,aalmalaise}@kau.edu.sa

[2] EduQTech Group, Escuela Universitaria Politecnica, University of Zaragoza, Teruel, Spain
apcipres@gmail.com

Abstract. In this paper, based on Seymour Papert's learning theory, logo creator, we create a theory based on the knowledge of learning objects, which allows teachers and students a dynamic development of content and allows continuous assessment of the student. In this way, we use the cloud system and educational systems, which enables the development of learning objects as independent and modifiable elements from any location and makes it easy to integrate with other systems.

Keywords: Educative systems · Cloud computing · Web services · Systems architecture · Student curriculum · Educative curricula

1 Introduction

In his book "…Mind Challenge: Children, computers, and powerful ideas…" Seymour Papert analyzes the concept of the relationship between children and computers. In his theory, he conceives of the computer as the seed of cognitive products that transcends the presence of concrete materials [1]: "Working with computers can have a powerful influence on how people think. I directed my attention to explore how to guide this influence in positive directions". Papert bases his methodology on constructionism, where children take an active role and are constructors of their own learning, where knowledge will be the fruit of their own work and the result of all the experiences of the individual since their birth. This starting point is a good approach in the present day, primarily due to:

- Increased use of ICT in the classroom.
- Increased media use with regard to learning content developed by teachers as part of the curriculum.
- Lower economic costs.

This is possible due to the technological increase in schools and in the lives of citizens, as the school is a reflection of the social and technological situations of countries. Methodological trends are always a basis for our work, to give a theoretical basis for the creation of these methodological platforms that go beyond the content, and adapt them

© Springer International Publishing Switzerland 2015
P. Zaphiris and A. Ioannou (Eds.): LCT 2015, LNCS 9192, pp. 349–360, 2015.
DOI: 10.1007/978-3-319-20609-7_33

to the higher educational levels that we are dealing with, to be used through the platforms and software applications we are developing. For the development of methodologies using ICTs in the classroom, we must consider the curricular structure and lesson planning of the teacher in the classroom. In addition, we must bear in mind the level of achievement of objectives in terms of evaluation leading to the student's grade. From the technical point of view, we will use cloud systems as the place of location and interaction with regard to these applications. This will allow different platforms and management resources to be integrated easily with existing applications, and with the current available educational management platforms in schools.

The aim of this paper is to develop a new theory of knowledge based on Papert's methodology. This will also be supported by an application that allows the performance of these characteristics in the classroom. Another objective is to develop a system that considers the educational curricula and teachers' lesson planning with regard to the subjects, which allows the creation and construction of knowledge by students. This in turn ensures that the teacher can engage in monitoring and evaluation.

2   State of the Art

Accommodation or adjustment is a psychological concept introduced by Jean Piaget which, along with assimilation, is one of two basic processes introduced by this author as part of the process of cognitive development. Piaget's theory was that knowledge is focused on [2]:

- The construction of knowledge, not its repetition.
- Knowledge is constructed based on people's own experiences, mindsets and beliefs that are then used to interpret objects and events.
- The mind is instrumental and essential when it comes to interpreting events, objects and perspectives on a personal and individual basis.
- Our view of the outside world is different from person to person because every human being has a different set of experiences.

In his theory, Papert gives students an active role in their learning, placing them as designers of their own projects and builders of their own learning. It is within the process of learning that there are the different parts of knowledge. These affect both the process of assimilation of content and the process of reflection of that content. In turn, knowledge construction comprises two types of knowledge: (1) the construction of a public type of knowledge which can be displayed, discussed, examined and tested; (2) a natural ability that occurs when people learn through experience and create mental structures that organize and synthesize information and experiences that take in their everyday lives [3].

There are two aspects of knowledge that can be distinguished: on the one hand, mathematical knowledge that allows the resolution of a problem. On the other hand, the mathematic knowledge that is needed to solve a particular problem. This is done by the student looking for some similar mathematical construct, which he already understands, and then applying what he finds to the new problem in order to resolve it. Once some knowledge has been learned, the student can use this prior knowledge to resolve a current conflict and in this way he can construct new. Papert mentions that the difference between what is "may" and what "cannot" learn. It depends on the subject's relationship with the three concepts that we consider to be instrumental in providing students with the best opportunities for construction: objects with which to think, public entities and micro-worlds [4, 5].

The hypothesis is "objects to think", once an interaction between students and computers is complete, these objects of thought are objects that can be used by the student to think about other things. Using its own construction of the object under appropriate conditions, can allow the student to develop intellectual skills such as the acquisition of search capabilities and the problem solving skills of reasoning and formal representation, model development knowledge, thinking and learning skills, and improving cognitive, social and emotional aspects [6].

On the other hand we find public entities that allow the visual or audible representation of ideas and concepts to allow the student to experiment with them. The object once created and shared with others, a publically shared entity through which constructionist learning is powerfully reinforced [7].

Then we have micro-worlds that construct by themselves a public entity, and use it as a tool to build objects for the student to think about [8]:

"…A learning environment in which students manipulate and control various parameters to explore their relationships. The more complex micro-worlds are expandable, enabling students to use their creativity to customize and extend the micro-world environment."

The construction of micro-worlds must involve the following objectives:

- To encourage meaningful learning of content.
- To exercise skills related to the topic.
- To exercise the use of principles on which logical thinking is based.
- To develop creativity through building applications.
- To implement social methodologies.

3 Application and Adaptation of Teaching Methods

We have to establish the starting point for the implementation of a teaching methodology depending on the educational curriculum and the way in which the teacher plans to teach Currently curricula follow assumptions that are dictated by education legislation and by the different levels of specification of the curriculum. In terms of curricular programming, the teacher plans the process of teaching whereby learning is the central element of the teaching-learning process. It involves a way of planning the daily work of the classroom where the various elements of the process (level of student development, social origin, family, curriculum, resources) are contextualized. One of its most important functions is to organize the practice of the learning content, select the basic objectives, adhere to the methodological guidelines they work to, and finally to determine the teaching methods needed to improve the learning process. In this research, a system that allows the organization of a set of teaching and learning activities, presents all the elements of curriculum planning: setting goals and content, designing the lesson, the development and evaluation of the activities, the organization of space and time, and the provision of the necessary resources [9].

We must also mention that technology supports learning, and must remember that there are conceptual designs which aim to support the administration of the educational process, this can be done by applying Distributed User Interfaces (DUIs) to cloud services. CSchool [10] encourages students, teachers and parents to use new technologies in the classroom. This implementation is available across the entire proposed education sector, taking advantage of user-friendly interfaces, distributed in such a way as to facilitate learning-oriented interaction and collaboration between users [10].

In the preceding paragraphs, we have summarized previous publications regarding teaching methods and school organization. These assumptions must be taken into account when applying a particular teaching methodology in the classroom, or performing applications for differing educational environments. It is with regard to those aspects that power is given to the system, and in terms of which curricula are the basis of the daily work of the teacher. The accessibility and management of the system comes from the inclusion of these platforms in educational ERPs (Enterprise Resource Planning) and the use of these applications in the classroom is given by the DUI.

Figure 1 captures the different parts of the methodology that we are applying. These objects need feedback from different parts of the system and from outside the classroom. In addition we may modified the methodology so that an interaction occurs with the objects of knowledge. The schema of the methodology shows that its different parts, at the conceptual level, are perfectly transposable elements in the development process. Taking these elements as objectives, and seeing that they must perform specific maintenance operations for each object according to specific patterns, these objects are as described below:

- **Objects to Think:** The teacher creates an object in order to begin the task given to the students. This object is defined according to a content as defined by the teacher. These contents are introduced to the student who begins the process of building his thoughts as part of an interactive system. It should also allow pattern searching, editing, and completing the objects in terms of more specific patterns. This allows the students to complete the statement of the problem, to solve it, and to help the student build his knowledge from the questions asked.
- **Public Entities:** The teaching process is completed in this section in the discussion of the results obtained. This allows a feedback process with regard to their research, which enable them to create collaborative patterns from the proposed improvement exercise.
- **Micro-worlds:** All these learning objectives can be collected in a set of objects that define a more complex problem. Then, a system for indexing objects is created to achieve more complex objects, where students can solve complete problems by linking objects. Also the teacher can increase the level by dividing complex problems in the micro world by performing activities involving collaborative work, by creating indexed objects from the beginning.
- **Interaction Space:** The system must allow for interaction between the individuals that make up the micro-worlds, in order to allow for collaborative work. It is at this

point that the DUI are used between objects in order to perform collaborative educational patterns.

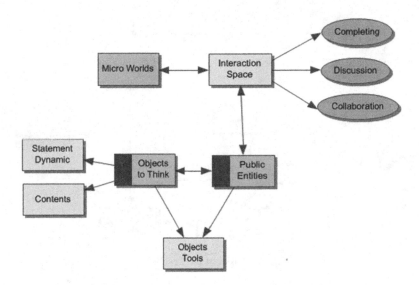

Fig. 1. Schema of the proposed methodology

The development of the methodology in the classroom should also allow the development of subject content. This is a development that enables teachers to track the achievement of the objectives of the students through the content developed by them after being mentored by the teacher. This is part of the development of the daily activities of the students. These activities can be developed over time in several working sessions. This should be taken into account in the development of this platform in order to perform the required monitoring in order to allow the evaluation and quantification of the learning associated with the subject.

In the teaching methodologies that make use of information technologies, by providing activities by which students can perform exercises with a computer or mobile device, we think that the starting point for the development of an activity must involve teacher planning as a result of which the student must complete the proposed activities. Figure 2 emphasizes the tasks that the teacher must undertake in generating objects involving thinking. These must take into account the starting point in the generation of these objects:

The different parts in this methodology are highlighted in color, in order to ensure a design that does not forget the location or the destination application, by applying concepts such as design for educational applications [11]:

- The color purple indicates the parts needed for evaluation, and represents the evaluation process. For this we need to apply the definition of educational evaluation provided by the Joint Committee on Standards for Educational Evaluation (http://www.jcsee.org/) which notes that "Evaluation is the systematic prosecution of the validity or merit of an object", so that in a study, it is important that both good

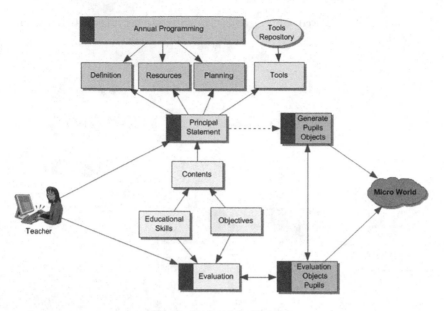

Fig. 2. Tasks of the Teacher

and bad results of an assessed situation are identified. Otherwise, it is not an assessment. From this we can see that evaluation is a complex process but also an essential one. It provides positive reinforcement which "…serves to progress and is used to identify strengths and weaknesses, and to move towards an improvement" [12]. Hence within the statements, we need, in addition to grouping them into contents, the objectives and basic educational skills that are achieved with that object. It is essential that the teacher prepare them for the students.

- The blue color highlights where to encompassed the statements that are predetermined by the annual program, which the teacher has designed for a particular subject with regard to a particular group. Here we have the planning, the precise definition of the objectives, the content and the resources needed for that academic year and for that particular group of students.

- In terms of the color yellow, the teacher has access to tools that enable the creation of the statement. Since the work is done with the computer, these tools can range from the use of text editors to educational standards, to be included in the objects that the students have to think about. This tool completes the object and allows students to perform predefined actions with this object.

- The color orange indicates generated objects as objects related to thinking. The teacher could develop a system that serves all students and allows progress for such students working at different levels. It can also be developed for collaborative work activity, in which students support each other.

When the work object is generated, we must generate an object that allows the monitoring of the work of the student. In this way we keep tabs on the steps performed during the execution of the lesson and its results. These are stored as an object that can be

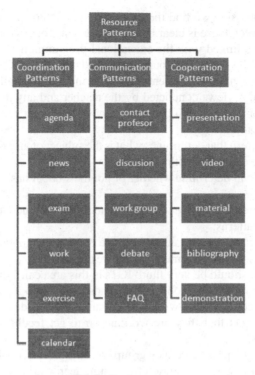

Fig. 3. Design patterns

evaluated by the teacher. The teacher may follow the progress of students throughout the teaching-learning process. In this way, the teacher can make an ongoing assessment and determine the qualifications available at the end of the course.

4 Design Patterns

Patterns are needed to develop an application of this nature and to move to a context-face work on classroom education. They can emerge from patterns of objects in e-learning [13]. See Fig. 3.

Next we describe the design patterns by adding the necessary changes in the concept in terms of its interaction. This can be done to indicate where each pattern works according to the objects of our methodology:

- Coordination Patterns:
  - Agenda: This pattern works in the micro-world as it takes the form of a school diary which the student keeps. At this point the activities undertaken in this pattern may include other coordination patterns in order to group them into objects to which the system itself can add new events.
  - Calendar: This pattern is a summary of the agenda and also indicates the level of achievement of the activities and themes undertaken. There are two types of

calendar. On one side we find the timetable of the student and the teacher. The difference between these is clear in that the student's one is not editable, and that of the teacher is linked with the educational programming in the classroom, in order to access the contents through the calendar.

- News: This pattern serves students with information internally to objects, i.e. it notifies internal reviews conducted by the teacher and any modifications. It can also be used for coordination between groups of different students when objects are treated collaboratively.
- Exam: It's a pattern that determines what is the subject of an examination. Student learning can be evaluated with this pattern.
- Exercise: This can determine whether or not the student has solved the object of an exercise.
- Work: This pattern is a homework assignment that the student must perform.
- Communication Patterns:
  - Contact teacher: It is important to facilitate communication between the teacher and the students. We must remember that we are in a classroom situation and such communication should be very fluid. ICTs in this area can facilitate communication by passing information objects that students are working on.
  - Discussion: In collaborative work is necessary for the students and the teacher to discuss the aspects that they are working on to get feedback on the teaching-learning process.
  - Work group: This pattern defines groups of objects for collaborative work and teamwork. In this way, in addition to defining teamwork, objects between them are defined.
  - Debate: You can create objects for discussion to allow discussion in the classroom with regard to these objects. Consequently, students can exchange information when the debate occurs.
  - FAQs: In our case, the FAQs is a repository of student questions. The system picks up on the contents and the teacher reviews and modifies it so that the students can have validated information on the system itself.
- Cooperation Patterns:
  - Presentation: The application allows the teacher to upload presentation material. It allows students to view content that the teacher has prepared.
  - Video: This pattern groups the multimedia content that the teacher uploads so that the students can develop the content.
  - Bibliography: This section adds the teacher's bibliographic content that may be further books, where information about the contents that they are working on can be found.
  - Demonstration: This section allows the teacher to add similar exercises in order to clarify the exercise under consideration and to allow students to see practical examples of exercises; this pattern may terminate as an object of thought developed by the teacher for part of the object.

Next we present the patterns of the editing objects of the platform where students develop the content of the exercise:

- Add: This pattern allows adding elements that allow the students to complete the activity. It is possible to add editable objects like text boxes, pictures and files.
- Delete: This pattern allows the deletion of items which the student has added.
- Check: This pattern provides access to online questions or information, which can then be added. This pattern allows the teacher to know what has been consulted so that he can add information.
- Edit: Allows the user to modify the objects added in order to correct or practice the exercise being performed.
- Question: This pattern poses a question to be solved later by the teacher or by the student group. It can also take the form of personal notes allowing the student to continue his work. This is important in collaborative work and in the methodology we are developing, since it allows feedback with regard to the problem and the mathematical solution can act as an extension of student knowledge.
- Communicate: Sometimes students need to communicate their progress to the group of students to allow feedback in terms of student knowledge, and to allow them to enter into discussion or debate. It can be used to extend the student's mathematical knowledge and improve the teaching-learning process.
- Share: Students can share the object being viewed on the screen in order to ask for help or to share their information with any of their companions.

Evaluation patterns include student assessment and the preparation processes of the activities that will subsequently be evaluated. We have determined the following patterns:

- Time distribution: This pattern makes it easier for teachers to keep to time in terms of the distribution of school activities to the students. This entails planning on the part of the teacher or an indication of the time available to the student for each activity within the overall planning for practice studies. This time distribution must include control of any lost time (idle time) and breaks allowed for the students to avoid saturation.
- Monitoring: monitoring of objects and modifications that students perform on objects are considered as part of this process. These patterns also store the goals that have been achieved.
- Correction: This pattern provides correction and scores for each of the objects.
- Rating: The rating process involves not only the final score in terms of the exercise performed by the student. It also marks the level of achievement in terms of each of the objectives and of the educational skills attained in this activity.

5 System Architecture

The system architecture is composed of a set of models, each in a different cloud, and which use Web Services to communicate between them.

Figure 4 offers a conceptual description of the system. We have discarded the operation of objects to think and public entities. Instead, we deal with this in the next section.

The process begins with the creation of objects of thought by the teacher. As we see, it has access to the patterns that will be selected, depending on the specification prepared for each of the activities. The creation of this "needs to think" object by the teacher is related to the students' curricular programs, and therefore removes the different parts of educational management (contents, objectives, powers), to extend the application to the teacher educational programming [9].

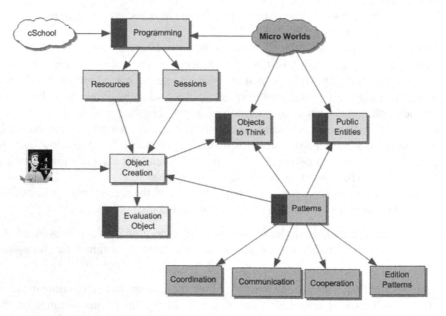

Fig. 4. Conceptual design of the system

In the process of creating the object for students, it in turn creates a system that monitors the student objects in order to perform the evaluation of such objects. Also, with regard to objects and from public entities, students have access to patterns that will work with the various objects.

Figure 5 defines a workspace [14] by DUI. This guarantees the collaboration in real time among team members or in a class [10]. Once the object changes its state, it mutates to a different status as a public entity, where students can decide to publish that part of the object outward, using Web Services posted outward from the class itself. The evaluation of the object is monitored by a system of intelligent agents with regard to the object of each student. This will continuously record student progress and allow the teacher's assessment of that particular object. It will save the result of object programming on the part of the teacher for each student.

This system facilitates the storage of information, since the objects are defined using XML language or other markup language. This will allow storage in a virtual notebook for each student. By linking these objects to each student, we can obtain an ordered list of jobs, ordered by student, with relevant information about their assessment. This can be used in the future as part of curriculum evaluation and the monitoring of the students. Such programs have been designed in previous research [15].

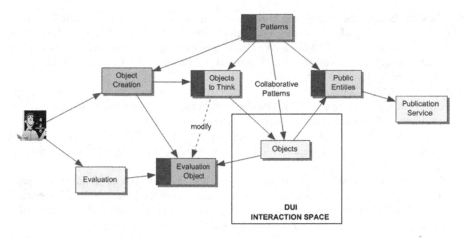

Fig. 5. List of objects to think

6 Conclusions and Future Work

This paper is the continuation of previous research in which we have presented our ideas about curricular organization and collaborative approaches in the classroom. These areas for further research have adapted teaching methods in the classroom. In this way, we have linked the curriculum methodologies. This paper differs from the others in the initial planning of a methodology that follows the ICT premises and terminology, in order to secure an ICT methodology in the field of education.

The rating system allows the control all objects made by the students by creating linked lists of objects in the database system. We believe that, over time, we can create systems that allows the monitoring of students virtually in the classroom. The system could enable new functionalities if we incorporate the process of evaluation and assessment of students in classroom using ICTs from a curricular standpoint.

References

1. Papert, S.: Mindstorms: Children, Computers, and Powerful Ideas. Basic Books Inc., New York (1980)
2. Piaget, J.: Psicología y Pedagogía. Arie, Barcelona (1969)
3. Papert, S.: Education for the Knowledge Society. Why Should Russia Not Be First the magazine. Computer Tools in Education (2001)
4. Bruera, R.: La matética: teoría de la enseñanza y ciencia de la educación. Ediciones Matética SA (1982)
5. Arellano Sánchez, B., Alfaro Rivera, J.A., Ramírez Montoya, M.S.: Uso de objetos de aprendizaje que favorecen la comprensión del conocimiento matemático: buenas prácticas en educación media (2014)
6. Nickerson, R.S., Smith, E.E.: Enseñar a pensar, pp. 87–134. Ediciones Paidós, Barcelona (1987)
7. Flake, J.L., McClintock, C.E., Turner, S.V.: Fundamentals of Computer Education. Wadsworth Publishing Company, Belmont (1985)

8. Antueno, E.A.D.: Micromundos en la escuela y simulaciones en la universidad. In I Congreso en Tecnologías de la Información y Comunicación en la Enseñanza de las Ciencias (2005)
9. Paules, A., Fardoun, H.M., Mashat, A.: Cataloging teaching units: resources, evaluation and collaboration. In: Proceedings of Federated Conference on Computer Science and Information Systems, pp. 825–830 (2012)
10. Fardoun, H.M., Ciprés, A.P., Alghazzawi, D.M.: Distributed user interfaces to enrich collaborative teaching methods. In: Proceedings of the 3rd Workshop on Distributed User Interfaces: Collaboration and Usability, pp. 37–41 (2013)
11. Fardoun, H.M., Ciprés, A.P., Alghazzawi, D.M.: CSchool - DUI for educational system using clouds. In: Proceedings of the 2nd Workshop on Distributed User Interfaces: Collaboration and Usability, pp. 35–39 (2012)
12. Stufflebeam, D., Shinkfield, A.: Evaluación sistemática - Guía teórica Y práctica. España: Centro de Publicaciones del Ministeriode Educación y Ciencia, Ediciones Paidós Ibérica
13. Fardoun, H.M.: eLearniXML: Towards a model-based approach for the development of e-learning systems. Tesis Doctoral. Universidad de Castilla La Mancha (2011)
14. Fardoun, H.M., Kateb, I.A., Ciprés, A.P., Ramírez Castillo, J.: Applying Gianni Rodari techniques to develop creative educational environments. In: Zaphiris, P., Ioannou, A. (eds.) LCT 2014, Part I. LNCS, vol. 8523, pp. 388–397. Springer, Heidelberg (2014)
15. Fardoun, H.M., Paules, A., Alghazzawi, D.M.: Centralizing students curriculums to the professional work. Elsevier Procedia – Soc. Behav. Sci. **122**, 373–380 (2012)

The Effect of Metaphoric Gestures on Schematic Understanding of Instruction Performed by a Pedagogical Conversational Agent

Dai Hasegawa[✉], Shinichi Shirakawa, Naoya Shioiri, Toshiki Hanawa,
Hiroshi Sakuta, and Kouzou Ohara

Aoyama Gakuin University, 5-10-1 Chuo-ku Fuchinobe,
Sagamihara-shi, Kanagawa, Japan
hasegawa@it.aoyama.ac.jp

Abstract. In this paper, we examine the impact of metaphoric gestures performed by Pedagogical Conversational Agent (PCA) on learners' memorization of technical terms, understanding of relationships between abstract concepts, learning experience, and perception of the PCA. The study employed a one-factor three-level between-participants design where we manipulated gesture factor (speech-gesture match vs. speech-gesture mismatch vs. no-gesture). The data of 97 students were acquired in on-line learning environment. As the results, while there was no effect found on memorization of technical terms, we found that students showed accurate schematic understanding of the relationship between abstract concepts when the PCA used metaphoric gestures matched to speech content than when used gestures mismatched, and no gesture. Contrary to the result, we also found that students judged the PCA useful, helpful, and felt the PCA looked like a teacher when performed mismatched gestures to speech content than when performed matched gesture.

Keywords: Pedagogical agent · Metaphoric gesture · Understanding · Reliability

1 Introduction

New education paradigm, as typified by the flipped classroom model, has changed the focus of education — from offering students knowledge to developing students' experience, from the teacher as a transmitter of knowledge to the teacher as a facilitator of learning. In such education process, students are often required to learn basic knowledge and skills by themselves before the classroom activity. And, the efficacy of the classroom activity depends on the initial knowledge students have. The development of effective self-education tools, therefore, becomes an important issue in modern education.

Among various computer-assisted self-education environments, a Pedagogical Conversational Agent (PCA) based environment suggests a distinct direction, introducing social relations between human and computer by utilizing

© Springer International Publishing Switzerland 2015
P. Zaphiris and A. Ioannou (Eds.): LCT 2015, LNCS 9192, pp. 361–371, 2015.
DOI: 10.1007/978-3-319-20609-7_34

human-likely embodied features [15,18]. The previous studies in the field have confirmed preferable effects of PCA on students' understanding and motivation, compared to text-based/audio-based instruction [3,13,21]. Furthermore, to better design effective PCAs, a variety of findings in human-human communication were adopted. For example, the roles of PCA as a learning partner, and the impacts of stereotyped appearances, facial expression, audio expressions, and posture has been examined so far [4,11,12,23]. Likewise, the impact of gesture are naturally of great concern [18,24,28].

In general conversation, it is confirmed that speakers' gestures help listeners to comprehend their speech content [9,16,17]. Similarly, not only recent studies in human-human educational interaction have also pointed out that gestures in scientific explanation play an important role on students' understanding and collaborative learning [2,25], but also some empirical studies have confirmed the learning efficacy of the use of gestures in education [10,26,27].

However, little studies in the field of PCA research addressed the impact of gesture and the types of gesture. Buisine et al. reported that when PCA used redundant gestures, which convey the same information included in audio instruction, the performance of verbal recall test increased, compared to when PCA used complementary gestures, which convey new information not included in audio interaction [6,7]. Also, Buisine et al. showed that the redundant use of gestures increased the perception of quality of explanation, and likability and expressiveness of PCA.

Buisine et al. examined the redundancy and complementarity of the gesture use, but they mainly employed pointing gestures which refer a certain part of a learning material and gestures which present pictorial features of concrete objects. A gesture can convey abstract meanings as well. This aspect of gesture has not addressed yet, despite the importance of conveying abstract concepts in educational instruction.

To examine the impact of gesture which presents abstract meanings in PCA based learning system, in this paper, we conduct an on-line experiment in which we evaluate learners' ability to complete a vocabulary recall test, a figure selection test, and answers to a questionnaire, when the versions of the system use gestures matched with abstract speech content, gestures mismatched with speech content, or no gesture at all. The design allows us to examine the impact of the gesture on memorization of technical terms, understanding of the abstract concepts, learning experience, and perception of the PCA.

In the following section, we will explain the specific type of gesture we aim to examine in this paper.

2   Conduit Metaphoric Gesture

Gestures, usually movements of the hands and arms, which spontaneously occur accompanying with speech are classified into four types, iconic, metaphoric, beat, deictic [19].

Iconic gestures present images of concrete objects or actions, and deictic gestures are used to indicate objects around the speaker. Iconic and deictic may be

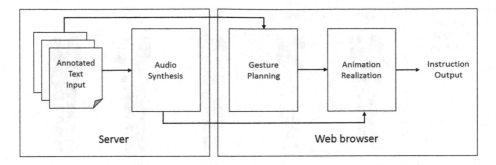

Fig. 1. System overview

called gesture of concrete. Beats are the movements with the rhythmical pulsations of speech which index the accompanied word of phrase as being significant.

Contrary to those three types, in metaphoric gestures, abstract meaning is presented as if it had form by utilizing space. For example, a speaker appears to be holding a object, meaning an abstract object, such as idea, memory, and etc. This is most often seen metaphoric gesture and it is a gestural version of the 'conduit' metaphor. The appearance of conduit metaphoric gestures are typically shown as a cup-shaped hand or hands being holding something, where the hand/hands represent as a container and word/phrase as a substance to be transfered to the listeners [8,20]. In addition, the conduit metaphoric gestures are often used to show the relationship between several concepts by being put in space.

We will examine the impact of the metaphoric gesture performed by a PCA. As the first step of our investigation, we will focus on the three types of conduit metaphoric gestures and its combinations utilizing space as described below.

Conduit Gesture: The appearance of holding an object with the both hands, indicating a single abstract concept.

Two-conduit Gesture: The movements of the object-holding hands from the right side of the speaker's upper body to the left side, synchronized with the word/phrase it accompanies in speech, indicating a schematic relationship between two abstract concepts by utilizing space.

Three-conduit Gesture: The movements of the object-holding hands from the right side of the speaker's upper body to the center, then, the left side, synchronized with the word/phrase it accompanies in speech, indicating a schematic relationship between three abstract concepts.

3 Method

In this section, we will describe our PCA based on-line learning environment, learning material, and the details of the study design.

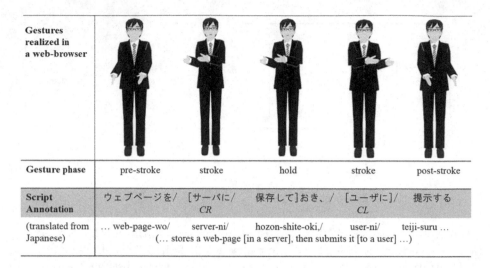

Gestures realized in a web-browser					
Gesture phase	pre-stroke	stroke	hold	stroke	post-stroke
Script Annotation	ウェブページを/	[サーバに/ *CR*	保存して]おき、/	[ユーザに]/ *CL*	提示する
(translated from Japanese)	... web-page-wo/	server-ni/	hozon-shite-oki,/	user-ni/	teiji-suru ...
		(... stores a web-page [in a server], then submits it [to a user] ...)			

Fig. 2. Metaphoric gestures representing the relationship between two abstract concepts 'server' and 'user.' ([]: stroke and hold)

3.1   E-Learning System and Materials

We developed a web-based learning environment where a PCA gives a speech instruction accompanying with gestures. The animation is processed and depicted on a web browser by using a program written in HTML5, JavaScript and WebGL (a graphic library written in JavaScript) so that participants can take part in the experiment without any special preparation of their computer. Figure 1 shows a system overview. The system processes text inputs with gesture annotation sentence by sentence. The sentence is divided into phrases (in Japanese, a phrase is consist of a content word and function words). The phrases are annotated by using the following schema: CC (a conduit gesture appears holding something with both hands in front of the speaker), CL (a conduit gesture appears holding something with both hands at the left side of the speaker), CR (a conduit gesture appears holding something with both hands at the right side of the speaker). The annotation is interpreted on a web-browser, then gesture animations are realized, synchronizing with audio. In order to synchronize gesture and speech, we estimated the timing of each gesture by indexing the order of the first character of each phrase from the top of the sentence, given that the synthesized audio's speed is constant. Lip-sync animations are also realized, synchronizing with audio.

We prepared an instruction script (4-minutes-long speech when audio synthesized) to be performed. The learning subject was the basics of web application development. The script explains the basic concepts of web application, the components of web application, and the programming languages for web application developments. A part of the instruction performed by the system is shown in Fig. 2.

3.2   Independent Variables

There is one independent variable, gesture, in the study, and we have three treatment conditions described as below.

C1. Speech-gesture Match: Two of authors who were familiar with web application development annotated the script with the schema: *CC*, *CL*, *CR*. The realized instruction included twenty-seven *conduit gestures*, twelve *two-conduit gestures*, and three *three-conduit gestures*. And overall, the number of gesture strokes was sixty.

C2. Speech-gesture Mismatch: Based on the annotation data described above, we randomly changed the tags to one of others, resulting the realized animation included forty two *conduit gestures*, fifteen *two-conduit gestures*, and five *three-conduit gestures*. The number of strokes was eighty nine. The percentages of speech-gesture mismatches in the realized animation were 25 % for *conduit gestures*, 65 % for *two-conduit gestures*, 60 % for *three-conduit gestures*.

C3. No Gesture: No gesture is performed and only audio instruction is presented with lip-sync animations.

3.3   Dependent Variables

Dependent variables included memorization of technical terms, abstract concepts understanding, learning experience, and perception of the PCA. To evaluate those dependent variables, three types of data are used: performance of a vocabulary recall test, performance of a figure selection test, and answers to a forty-six item questionnaire.

Vocabulary Recall Test: Participants were asked to answer the technical terms explained in learning material, such as "Answer three programming languages often used in server-side." In total, they were required to answer fifteen technical terms by six questions.

Figure Selection Test: Participants were asked to choose all appropriate figures which describe the relationship between abstract concepts: the interaction between components of web application (user, client, server, and database), the relationship between kinds of application program (general application program, desktop application program, web application program), and the relationship between kinds of programming languages (programming languages for general purpose, server-side development, and client-side development). Nine appropriate figures and eleven inappropriate figures were presented, we counted the number of figures correctly being selected and correctly not being selected.

Questionnaire: The forty-six item questionnaire (with a seven-point Likert scale anchored by "Strongly Disagree" and "Strongly Agree") was grouped into eight categories: learning motivation, self-efficacy, usefulness of the PCA, reliability of the PCA, human-likeness of the PCA, likability of the PCA, self-reflection of learning, and concentration on learning.

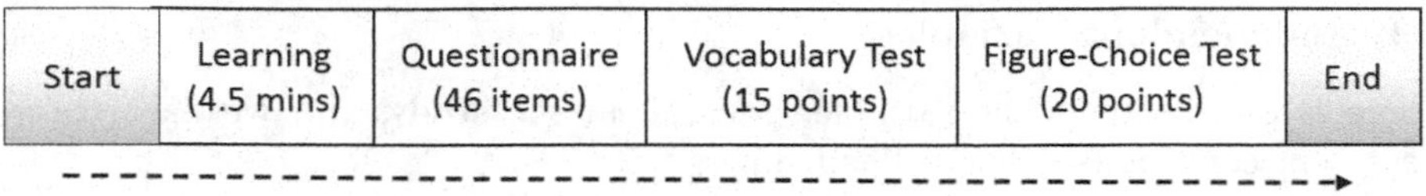

Start	Learning (4.5 mins)	Questionnaire (46 items)	Vocabulary Test (15 points)	Figure-Choice Test (20 points)	End

Fig. 3. Procedure of experiment

3.4 Participants and Procedure

The participants were 120 undergraduate students (male 84 %, female 16 %) in a web application development course held in a large private university located at Kanagawa prefecture in Japan. Students were required to participate in the experiment as a part of course activity, but they were explained that the results will not be treated as a part of their grade.

The three versions of the e-learning systems were deployed on a server, and the URL of the introduction page was announced to the students, explaining they have to prepare the latest version of FireFox and speakers/a headphone, and the URL was going to be expired in a week. The students were randomly assigned to experimental conditions when transfered from the introduction page.

Figure 3 shows the flow of learning and testing. The participants firstly watched 4.5 min long instruction, then took the questionnaire, and the tests. The questionnaire should work as a distraction task for the following tests at the same time.

3.5 Design and Hypothesis

The study employed a one-factor three-level between-participants design. The data were analyzed by one-way analysis of variance (ANOVA) with Tukey's HSD post-hoc comparisons.

We hypothesized that *conduit gestures* draw learners attentions to technical terms and help the learners remember the words, resulting in more correct vocabulary recall test results, and that *two-conduit gestures* and *three-conduit gestures* schematically convey the relationship between concepts by utilizing space, resulting in more correct figure selection test results, when the instruction speech was given with appropriate gestures than when speech was given with mismatched gestures or no gestures. In addition, we also hypothesized that learners judge learning experience and the perception of the PCA higher when the PCA performed metaphoric gestures matched with speech.

4 Results and Discussion

Of 120 students, nine did not access the URL, three did not completed the test, and one reported a web-browser error. And, the data of ten students who took longer than sixty minutes to complete the study were eliminated. Eventually, the data of 97 students were acquired. The numbers of participants assigned to each conditions were 32 for C1, 32 for C2, and 33 for C3.

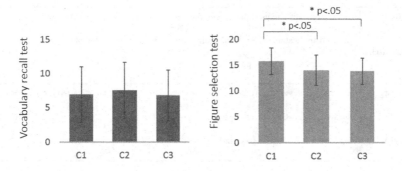

Fig. 4. Results of the vocabulary recall test and the figure selection test

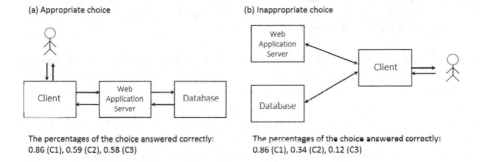

Fig. 5. Examples of appropriate choice and inappropriate choice that the participants in speech-gesture-mismatch group answered wrongly (Q. Select all appropriate figures which describe the interaction between components of web applications).

4.1 Memorization and Understanding

The results of the vocabulary recall test and the figure selection test are shown in Fig. 4. Although there was no statistically significant difference found in the results of recall test, we found a significant main effect of the gesture factor in the figure selection test $(F(2,93) = 3.09, p = .007)$. The students in speech-gesture match condition scored significantly higher $(M = 15.7, SD = 2.59)$ than the students in speech-gesture mismatch condition $(M = 13.9, SD = 2.93, t(62) = 2.61, p = .011)$, and the students in no-gesture condition $(M = 13.8, SD = 2.52, t(63) = 2.94, p = .028)$. The standardized effect sizes for these differences were Cohen's $d=0.63$ and 0.76, which indicate between medium and large effects.

Figure 5(a) shows an example of appropriate figures and Fig. 5(b) shows an example of inappropriate figures in a question, "Select all appropriate figures which describe the interaction between components of web applications." The percentages of the choice answered correctly in the speech-gesture mismatch condition decreased more than 20 % against the percentage in speech-gesture matched group, which was over 80 %. Figure 6 shows the annotated script in both

Annotated Script (Speech-gesture match)	... a user makes a request through [a client program] to [a web application server, then
	              CR CC
	the web application server dynamically produce a web page], cooperating with [a database]
	                                                                                        CL
	, then sends it to [a client program.]
	            CR

Annotated Script (Speech-gesture mismatch)	... a user makes a request through [a client program] to [a web application server, then
	                      CC CR
	the web application server dynamically produce a web page, cooperating with a database]
	, then sends it to [a client program.]
	            CL

Fig. 6. A part of the script annotated differently in speech-gesture match condition and speech-gesture mismatch condition, describing the interaction between three components of web application "client program," "web application server," and "database" ([ ]: stroke and hold, translated from Japanese).

conditions. As seen in Fig. 6, in speech-gesture match condition, conduit gestures present the appropriate layouts of abstract components of web application as described in Fig. 5 (a). In contrast, in speech-gesture mismatched group, conduit gestures were meaninglessly put in space.

These results support our hypothesis stating that spatial use of conduit metaphoric gestures help listeners' schematic understanding of the relationship between abstract concepts. However, a single conduit gesture which presents an abstract concept did not affect learners memorization of the name of the concept.

4.2   Learning Experience and Perception of the PCA

We did not found many significant differences between conditions from the results of questionnaire, but the results revealed a significant main effect of the gesture factor on perception of reliability of the PCA ($F(2,94) = 3.57$, $p = .032$).

Interestingly, despite the incoherence between speech content and gesture representation, the multiple test results showed that the students in speech-gesture mismatch condition answered the PCA was more reliable ($M = 4.45$, $SD = 0.97$) than the students in speech-gesture match condition ($M = 3.74$, $SD = 1.21$, $t(62) = 2.59$, $p = .027$). The standardized effect size for these differences were Cohen's $d = 0.65$ which indicates between medium and large effects. The results of each item in the category are shown in Table 1.

Previous psychology studies revealed that non-verbal behaviors, included gestural styles, are linked to personality [1,5]. The argument was also partially confirmed in the studies of interaction between human and animated character [14]. Neff et al. reported that the perception of extroversion increased when PCA's gesture rate was high, and when movements were produced fast [22]. In speech-gesture mismatch condition, the number of gesture strokes were larger than speech-gesture match condition, despite the length of audio speech was identical. And, strokes performed rapidly were often seen in the realized animation. This indicates that the difference of the speed of gestures caused the

Table 1. Questions asking reliability of the PCA (Cronbach's $\alpha = 0.84$)

Questions	C1 (SD)	C2 (SD)	C3 (SD)
I felt the PCA has a considerable knowledge	4.38 (1.45)	4.53 (1.19)	4.27 (1.46)
I felt the PCA was intellectual	3.88 (1.62)	4.47 (1.41)	4.15 (1.46)
I felt the PCA was useful	3.53 (1.54)	4.63 (1.31)	4.47 (1.27)
I felt the PCA was helpful	3.63 (1.48)	4.47 (1.32)	4.27 (1.13)
I felt the PCA was like a teacher	3.28 (1.63)	4.16 (1.25)	4.03 (1.31)
Overall	3.74 (1.21)	4.45 (0.97)	4.21 (1.06)

difference of the perception of extroversion of the PCA, and that caused the difference of the perception of reliability.

5   Conclusion

We examined the impact of metaphoric gestures performed by Pedagogical Conversational Agent (PCA) on learners' memorization of technical terms, understanding of relationships between abstract concepts, learning experience, and perception of the PCA. The study employed a one-factor three-level between-participants design where we manipulated gesture factor (speech-gesture match vs. speech-gesture mismatch vs. no-gesture). The data of 97 students were acquired in on-line learning environment. As the results, while there was no effect found on memorization of technical terms, we found that students showed accurate schematic understanding of the relationship between abstract concepts when the PCA used metaphoric gestures matched to speech content than when used gestures mismatched, and no gesture. Contrary to the result, we also found that students judged the PCA useful, helpful, and felt the PCA looked like a teacher when performed mismatched gestures to speech content than when performed matched gesture.

Acknowledgments. This work was partially supported by JSPS Grant-in-Aid for Young Scientists (B) Grant Number 25870698, JSPS Grant-in-Aid for Challenging Exploratory Research Grant Number 26540185, and Council for Science, Technology and Innovation(CSTI), Cross-ministerial Strategic Innovation Promotion Program (SIP), Structural Materials for Innovation (SM4I) (Funding agency:JST).

References

1. Argyle, M.: Bodily communication. Methuen, London (1975)
2. Arzarello, F., Paola, D., Robutti, O., Sabena, C.: Gestures as semiotic resources in the mathematics classroom. Educ. Stud. Math. **70**(2), 97–109 (2009)
3. Atkinson, R.K.: Optimizing learning from examples using animated pedagogical agents. J. Educ. Psychol. **94**(2), 416–427 (2002)

4. Baylor, A.L., Kim, Y.: Pedagogical agent design: the impact of agent realism, gender, ethnicity, and instructional role. In: Lester, J.C., Vicari, R.M., Paraguaçu, F. (eds.) ITS 2004. LNCS, vol. 3220, pp. 592–603. Springer, Heidelberg (2004)
5. Brebner, J.: Personality theory and movement. In: Kirkcaldy, B.D. (ed.) Individual Differences in Movement, pp. 27–41. Springer, The Netherlands (1985)
6. Buisine, S., Abrilian, S., Martin, J.C.: Evaluation of multimodal behaviour of embodied agents. In: Ruttkay, Z., Pelachaud, C. (eds.) From Brows to Trust, pp. 217–238. Springer, The Netherlands (2005)
7. Buisine, S., Martin, J.C.: The effects of speech-gesture cooperation in animated agents' behavior in multimedia presentations. Interact. Comput. 19(4), 484–493 (2007)
8. Cassell, J., McNeill, D.: Gesture and the poetics of prose. Poetics Today 12, 375–404 (1991)
9. Cassell, J., McNeill, D., McCullough, K.E.: Speech-gesture mismatches: evidence for one underlying representation of linguistic and nonlinguistic information. Pragmatics Cogn. 7(1), 1–34 (1999)
10. Cook, S.W., Duffy, R.G., Fenn, K.M.: Consolidation and transfer of learning after observing hand gesture. Child Dev. 84(6), 1863–1871 (2013)
11. Hasegawa, D., Ugurlu, Y., Sakuta, H.: A human-like embodied agent learning tour guide for e-learning systems. In: 2014 IEEE Global Engineering Education Conference (EDUCON), pp. 50–53, April 2014
12. Hayashi, Y.: Togetherness: multiple pedagogical conversational agents as companions in collaborative learning. In: Trausan-Matu, S., Boyer, K.E., Crosby, M., Panourgia, K. (eds.) ITS 2014. LNCS, vol. 8474, pp. 114–123. Springer, Heidelberg (2014)
13. Heidig, S., Clarebout, G.: Do pedagogical agents make a difference to student motivation and learning? Educ. Res. Rev. 6(1), 27–54 (2011)
14. Isbister, K., Nass, C.: Consistency of personality in interactive characters: verbal cues, non-verbal cues, and user characteristics. Int. J. Hum. Comput. Stud. 53(2), 251–267 (2000)
15. Johnson, W.L., Rickel, J.: Steve: an animated pedagogical agent for procedural training in virtual environments. SIGART Bull. 8(1–4), 16–21 (1997)
16. Kellerman, S.: 'I see what you mean': the role of kinesic behaviour in listening and implications for foreign and second language learning. Appl. Linguist. 13(3), 239–258 (1992)
17. Kelly, S.D., Barr, D.J., Church, R.B., Lynch, K.: Offering a hand to pragmatic understanding: the role of speech and gesture in comprehension and memory. J. Mem. Lang. 40(4), 577–592 (1999)
18. Lester, J.C., Voerman, J.L., Towns, S.G., Callaway, C.B.: Cosmo: A life-like animated pedagogical agent with deictic believability. In: Working Notes of the IJCAI 1997 Workshop on Animated Interface Agents: Making ThemIntelligent, pp. 61–69. Citeseer, August 1997
19. McNeil, D.: Hand and Mind. University of Chicago Press, Chicago (1992)
20. McNeill, D.: Gesture: a psycholinguistic approach. In: Brown, E., Anderson, A. (eds.) The Encyclopedia of Language and Linguistics, pp. 58–66. Elsevier, Amsterdam (2006)
21. Moreno, R., Mayer, R.E., Spires, H.A., Lester, J.C.: The case for social agency in computer-based teaching: do students learn more deeply when they interact with animated pedagogical agents? Cogn. Instr. 19(2), 177–213 (2001)

22. Neff, M., Wang, Y., Abbott, R., Walker, M.: Evaluating the effect of gesture and language on personality perception in conversational agents. In: Allbeck, J., Badler, N., Bickermore, T., Pelachcaud, C., Safonova, A. (eds.) IVA 2010. LNCS, vol. 6356, pp. 222–235. Springer, Heidelberg (2010)
23. Ogan, A., Finkelstein, S., Mayfield, E., D'Adamo, C., Matsuda, N., Cassell, J.: "Oh dear stacy!": social interaction, elaboration, and learning with teachable agents. In: Proceedings of the SIGCHI Conference on Human Factors in Computing Systems, CHI 2012, pp. 39–48. ACM, New York, NY, USA (2012)
24. Popescu, V., Adamo-Villani, N., Wu, M.L., Rajasekaran, S.D., Alibali, M.W., Nathan, M., Cook, S.W.: Animation killed the video star. In: Proceedings of Gesture-based Interaction Design: Communication and Cognition, 2014 CHI Workshop, pp. 55–59 (2014)
25. Reynolds, F.J., Reeve, R.A.: Gesture in collaborative mathematics problem-solving. J. Math. Behav. 20(4), 447–460 (2001)
26. Singer, M.A., Goldin-Meadow, S.: Children learn when their teacher's gestures and speech differ. Psychol. Sci. 16(2), 85–89 (2005)
27. Valenzeno, L., Alibali, M.W., Klatzky, R.: Teachers' gestures facilitate students' learning: a lesson in symmetry. Contemp. Educ. Psychol. 28(2), 187–204 (2003)
28. Voerman, J.L., FitzGerald, P.J.: Deictic and emotive communication in animated pedagogical agents. In: Cassell, J., Sullican, J., Prevost, S., Churchill, E. (eds.) Embodied Conversational Agents, pp. 123–154. The MIT Press, Cambridge (2000)

Designing Pedagogical Agents to Evoke Emotional States in Online Tutoring Investigating the Influence of Animated Characters

Yugo Hayashi[1](✉) and Daniel Moritz Marutschke[2]

[1] Department of Psychology, College of Letters, Ritsumeikan University,
56-1 Kitamachi, Toji-in, Kita-ku, Kyoto 603-8577, Japan
yhayashi@fc.ritsumeikan.ac.jp
[2] Department of Information and Communication Science,
College of Information Science and Engineering, Ritsumeikan University,
Noji-Higashi 1-1-1, Kusatsu 525-8577, Japan

Abstract. The affective or emotional state of the learner is known to motivate learning, and this study specifically investigated the role of pedagogical agents with animated characteristics in an online tutoring task. Previous studies indicated that sensitivity to emotion typically varies depending on the gender of the learner and the gender of the teacher; therefore, we investigated how each type of emotion is influenced by the gender of the characters. We conducted three experiments with a total of 414 Japanese students. We found that both male and female learners felt more positive toward animated characters of the same gender, and the effects became stronger with childlike characteristics, such as big eyes. We conclude that deformed characters could be incorporated into designs of web-based tutoring systems for more effective teaching.

Keywords: Web-based tutoring · Embodied agents · Affective learning · Gender

1 Introduction

One of the effective strategies to facilitate a learner's motivation during tutoring is to design effective pedagogical conversational agents (PCAs). Past studies in the learning sciences and on human-computer interaction (HCI) has taken multi disciplinary approaches in designing such PCAs [1, 2, 16]. These studies investigated the function of the agent, as well as the use of multiple agents [14]. Many studies also explored the effects of verbal communication strategies by designing effective interaction strategies, such as meta-cognitive suggestions [8, 9], linguistic strategies, such as politeness [23], and affective expressions, such as positive or negative triggers [7]. The use of multiple learning actors during teaching has also been studied [11]. Researchers are still collecting evidence on factors that contribute to the development and design of effective agents. Past studies have shown that visual design influences the learner's cognitive

© Springer International Publishing Switzerland 2015
P. Zaphiris and A. Ioannou (Eds.): LCT 2015, LNCS 9192, pp. 372–383, 2015.
DOI: 10.1007/978-3-319-20609-7_35

state and behavior during learning activities, including motivation. Learners are as sensitive to the visual appearance of an online tutorial as they are to interactions with real humans. Literature on the Media Equation [18] showed that people use the same social rules in human-agent or human-computer interactions as they do with human-human interactions. Other studies have shown that even with animally designed agent [13] and the use of a schema of human personalities [6] people still attribute human characteristics to the agents. If agents were designed to encourage emotionally satisfying human-computer interactions, we could use them as an effective tutor to keep and enhance motivation during learning activities. The question rises as to what kind of visual representation could enhance the learner's motivation to learn. In our study, we investigated the influence of the childlike designs, and how it could become an effective social cue to increase the learning motivation of the student.

1.1 The Types of Characters that Can Facilitate Motivation

Several debates discuss the design of the pedagogical agents [10]. Agents could be designed to look realistic or cartoon-like. However, even if the agent is life like and credible, a too realistic representation could distract the learners. The "uncanny valley" suggested by [17] indicates that movements and appearances that are almost realistically human-like evoke negative impressions, such as "creepiness".

A study conducted by [5] showed that female learners tend to prefer detailed stylish agents as learning companions rather than as tutoring instructors. Their study showed that the effects of the representations maybe due to the gender of the learners. Our study only focused on the type of agents that are selected prior to the learning task; it did not focus on the psychological process of how learners felt about a 3D or 2D agent. Moreover, this study did not investigate the emotional states that were caused by the motivational behaviors of the agents during learning. We studied the emotional process during a tutoring session with a 3D or 2D agent and delved into their effects.

Japanese animation is well known worldwide for its use of components that are childlike and cute (e.g., HelloKitty, Pokemon). These characters are often described as "kawaii", which is an attributive adjective in modern Japanese and is often translated into English as "cute" [19]. *Kawaii* expresses feelings, such as "can't bear to see, feel pity," that are typically elicited by human infants and toddlers and young animals. In addition, the verb "moe", which is mostly used by the Japanese subculture Otaku-culture, expresses a strong positive feeling towards a character in a Japanese animated show or game. A study indicated that, to evoke affective feelings, these characters must be designed with large eyes [4]. Based on these studies, the design of PCAs could benefit from adopting the design principles of *kawaii* and *moe*, such as the use of cartoon characters with large eyes.In this paper, we use the word "kawaii" as a collective term for "cute" and "childlike". The deformed PCA in this study was designed with large eyes and uses *moe* principles to express the childlike facial characteristics of the 2D character. In the next section, we describe how we captured the affective state during an online tutoring session. We also discuss the issue of gender differences when using these PCAs and the framework we used to investigate them.

1.2   Effects of Gender in PCA Interactions

A few cultures view women as superior to men; some cultures view women as subordinate to men; other cultures fall somewhere in between. Therefore, it is important to investigate how such social status may influence learner's affective states during interaction with a PCA. Several studies show that gender affects the interactions of the learner with the PCA [20] depending on the learner's gender and the agent's gender. [3] suggested that stereotypes could influence an individual's perception of others online. They conducted a controlled experiment to assess the accuracy of interpersonal perceptions on computer-mediated conversations. Results showed that interpersonal perceptions do not differ between computer-mediated interactions and face-to-face interactions. One possibility for this result is that social cues may be intensified in computer-mediated settings. Perhaps the gender of pedagogical agents could evoke certain stereotypes from the learners. [12] examined how positive and negative comments expressed by conversational agents affected learning performance as a function of gender. Results showed that learners had more positive impressions toward male agents with positive expressions than toward female agents. These results show that, no matter what kind of influence is detected, perhaps social stereotypes in the real world are applied to the agent-learner relationship. These studies show that the learner's gender and the agent's gender influence the learner's attitude towards the PCA. However, very few studies tried to investigate the effects of gender between the learner and the PCA; we investigated these effects using the integrated framework shown in Fig. 1. Social psychological literature has shown that gender effects are amplified with "cuteness" [22]. This indicates that gender differences may be significant when using a PCA with childlike characteristics.

Fig. 1. Interaction framework considering the learner's gender and the PCA's gender

We use Russell's two-dimensional theory of emotion as a dependent variable to discover affective states during learning activities [21], as shown in Fig. 2. Pleasure/displeasure (or valence) is a dimension of experience that refers to a hedonic tone. Activation is a dimension of experience that refers to a sense of energy. The vertical axis is a continuum ranging from sleep (at the lowest end), through drowsiness, relaxation, alertness, hyperactivity, and, finally, frenetic excitement (at the opposite end).

Our study uses this model to analyze students' affective states during learning activities. To measure the affective states of students during a learning activity with a PCA, we used emoticons (Fig. 3) to represent each emotional state in the two-dimensional model. These emoticons were presented during the online tutoring task, and learners were asked to select which emoticon best represents his/her emotional state during the task. The emoticons were selected based on a preliminary study and each represents a specific emotional state. The representations of affective states were selected through a preliminary selection task conducted with 14 participants. These participants were shown 48 random facial expressions, and they categorized the facial expressions into the emotional model shown in Fig. 2.

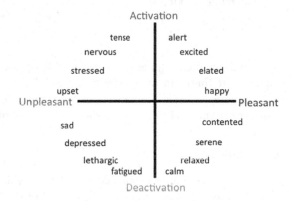

Fig. 2. Affective model based on Russell'stwo dimensions of affect

Fig. 3. Emoticons used in this study

1.3 Aim of the Study

The goal of this study is to investigate the effects of using PCAs with deformed childlike characteristics(e.g., cartooned and with big eyes). Based on the results of the previous studies, we focused on the effects of gender, which we assumed to be different based on the affective states. We also propose a new methodology on how to determine the learners' affective states by allowing them to select emoticons based on Russell's two-dimensional theory of emotions [21]. We attempt to answer the following questions using six different types of agents:

(1) How do male and female learners' emotions differ, in terms of affective sensitivity based on Russell's two-dimensional emotion model?
(2) How are male and female students' affective states influenced by the degree of childlike designed into the PCAs?

Our study aims to show the implications of the use of childlike characters in inducing affective states and motivation in a web-based tutoring activity.

2   Method

We constructed a system that guides the learner in a simple web-based tutoring system. Students in an undergraduate psychology class used the system to review key terms taught in a class. They were guided by a pedagogical agent who encouraged students by providing meta-cognitive suggestions and search results about the term on the web for further understanding. Based on Russell's emotional models [21], we collected emotional variables as dependent variables.

2.1   Participants

The participants were all undergraduate students who were taking a psychology classes part of a humanities degree program and who undertook a web-based tutoring task as part of the class work. We refer to these participants as "learners". Their task was to read about key psychological terms and to answer a short quiz based on the literature.

2.2   Materials and Conditions

We designed the agent PCA representations based on two design principles: (1) using cartoon characters, (2) using big eyes. For comparison, we developed 3 types of avatars that were different in terms of their visual appearance (Fig. 4). To represent non-childlike PCAs for the "3D condition", we used stylish 3D images of avatars that were created using Poser 8 (poser.smithmicro.com), which is a 3D image/animation design tool. In the 2D conditions, the PCAs were designed as cartoons using childlike design principles. In the 2D + eye condition, the cartoon PCA had big eyes. We compared the effects of the 3D condition and the basic 2D condition to study the differences between cartoon and non-cartoon agents. Likewise, we compared the effects of the regular 2D condition and the 2D + eyes condition to study the influence of using large eyes in affective states.

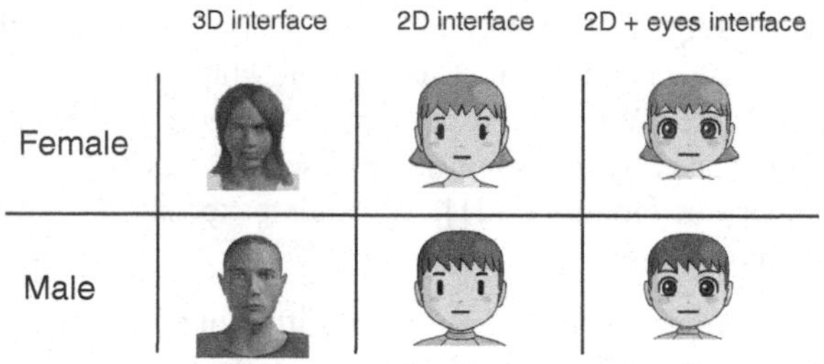

Fig. 4. Types of interfaces used in the study: left, 3D interfaces with no childlike characteristics; middle, 2D cartoon agents with childlike characteristics; right, 2D agents with more childlike characteristics, such as big eyes

2.3 Experiment Design and Participants

We examined the following three independent variables: (1) gender of the learner (male or female), (2) gender of the agent (male or female), and (3) the type of the agent (3D, 2D, and 2D + eye). Table 1 shows the combinations. The letters indicate the type of the actor ('H' for human and 'A' for the agent) and the gender ('F' for female and 'M' for male). Each combination represents an experiment condition, as follows: (a) a female learner using a female agent H(F)/A(F), (b) a male learner using a female agent H(M)/A (F), (c) a female learner using a male agent H(F)/A(M), (d) a male learner using a male agent H(M)/A(M).

Table 1. Experiment conditionsandlabels

	Female (human)	Male (human)
Female (agent)	H(F)/A(F)	H(M)/F(A)
Male (agent)	H(F)/A(M)	H(M)/A(M)

The experiment was conducted in three classes. In each class, one type (3D, 2D, or 2D + eye) of PCA was used. In Experiment 1, the 3D representations were used with 153Japanese undergraduates (71 males, 82 females, mean age = 19.50 years). In Experiment 2, the basic 2D representations were used with 132 Japanese undergraduates (59 males, 73 females, mean age = 19.45 years). In Experiment 3, the 2D + eyes representations were used with 129 undergraduates (52 males, 77 females, mean age = 19.65 years).

2.4 Tutoring System

A web-based tutoring system was developed for the class, using a web server, a database, and rule-based scripts. It was managed as a member-only system, and its main purpose was to tutor key terms taught in the class by presenting descriptive content. A total of 30 different key terms (e.g., Gestalt, long-term memory, cognitive dissonance) were extracted from an introductory psychology textbook, and its explanations were entered in the system database. Each student was assigned to work on one randomly selected key term. The tutoring sessions comprised 17 short passages, and students proceeded by clicking on to the next page/trial (Fig. 5). During the task, students were encouraged to go beyond simply reading these passages and to search through the web to further understand the terms. The average time for this activity was approximately 30 min.

Students were restricted to using specific computers in the campus at specific time periods. Learners were asked to log in to their individual page to check their progress. On the first page, the key term assigned to the student was presented, and the student was told that learning this key term was his/her task for that week. On the next page, the passage for the key term was presented with the emoticons (Fig. 6).

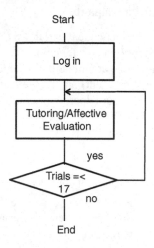

Fig. 5. Experiment procedure

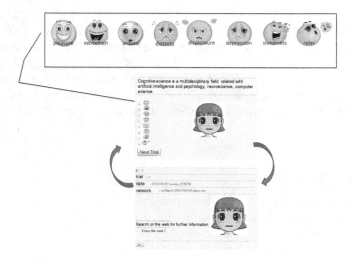

Fig. 6. Sequence of the tutoring/affective evaluation phase

The following equation calculates the ratio of each emoticon *emo*, where i is the number representing the emoticon/affective state and *total* is the total number of the trials.

$$1 = \sum\nolimits_{i=1}^{8} \frac{emo_i}{total} \tag{1}$$

3   Results

A 2 × 2 × 8 mixed factorial analysis of variance (ANOVA) was conducted on the average scores with the PCA's gender (female agent vs. male agent) and the learner's gender (female learner vs. male learner) as the between-subject factor, and affective state (pleasure vs. excitement vs. arousal vs. distress vs. displeasure vs. depression vs. sleepiness vs. relaxation) as the within-subject factor. When analyzing the results of the factorial analysis, we will only focus on the gender differences of the learner and of the PCA with each affective state.

3.1   Experiment 1: 3D Characters

Figure 7 shows the results calculated by the *emo* index. The vertical axis represents the average ratio of each individual, and the horizontal axis indicates each affective category. The ANOVA results show that the second-order interaction was not significant ($F(7,1043) = 1.740, p = .10$); however, the interaction between the learner's gender and the affective state was significant ($F(7,1043) = 2.181, p < .05$). The interaction between the PCA's gender and the affective state was also significant ($F(7,1043) = 2.405, p < .05$). However, no simple main effects were detected in each affective state. Simple main effects only show the interactions across affective states. The results of this experiment indicated no significant effects of gender on each affective state.

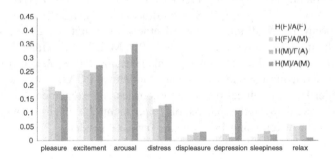

Fig. 7.   Results of Experiment 1

3.2   Experiment 2: 2D Characters

As shown in Fig. 8, ANOVA results show that the second-order interaction was significant ($F(7,896) = 4.478, p < .01$). A simple interaction exists between the agent gender and the human gender in the affective states of excitement and arousal ($F(1,1024) = 22.675, p < .01, F(1,1024) = 9.346, p < .01$). Second-order simple main effects show several differences among the conditions. Female learners rated higher excitement when using female PCAs than when using male PCAs ($p < .01$), and male learners rated higher arousal when using female PCAs than when using male PCAs ($p < .01$). Male learners also felt more excited when using male PCAs than when using female PCAs. These results indicate that same-gender PCAs induce excitement for both

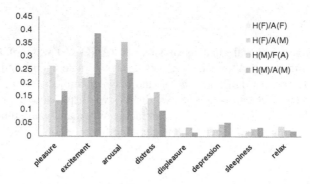

Fig. 8. Results of Experiment 2

male and female learners. However, males experienced arousal when interacting with PCAs of the opposite gender.

3.3 Experiment 3: 2D Characters with Large Eyes

Figure 9 shows the results of Experiment 3. ANOVA results show that the second-order interaction was significant ($F(7,875) = 2.565$, $p < .05$). A simple interaction existed between the agent gender and the human gender in the affective states of pleasure, excitement, and arousal ($F(1,1000) = 4.677$, $p < .05$, $F(1,1000) = 7.680$, $p < .01$, $F(1,1000) = 4.013$, $p < .05$). Second-order simple main effects showed several differences among the conditions. Female learners rated higher pleasure when using female PCAs than when using male PCAs ($p < .01$). Male learners rated higher arousal when using female PCAs than when using male PCAs ($p < .01$). Male learners also felt more excited when using male PCAs compared to female PCAs. These results indicate that same-gender PCAs produces pleasure for females and excitement for males. These results are consistent with the results of Experiment 2, which shows that males experienced arousal when using PCAs of the opposite gender.

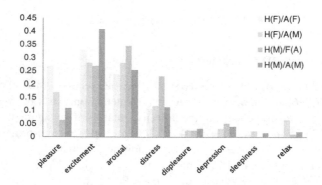

Fig. 9. Results of Experiment 3

Figure 10 shows the summary of the results of the positive affective state according to the gender of the learner and of the PCA. Male learners using a female PCA experienced more arousal, but this occurs only with 2D agents. On the other hand, female learners felt more excited when they used a female 2D PCA, and they felt more pleasure if the PCA had larger eyes.

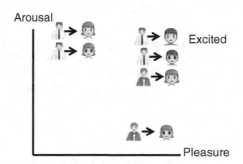

Fig. 10. Summary of results

4   Discussions and Conclusion

We investigated the effects of using PCAs that feature childlike characteristics in an online tutoring task. We studied the 8 types of a learner's affective states and processes during tutoring activities. Previous studies demonstrated that affective states are influenced by social status and gender, and we investigated how affective states change based on the gender of childlike PCAs.

Results showed that male learners using a female PCA experienced more arousal, but this occurs only with 2D agents. On the other hand, female learners felt more excited when they used a female 2D PCA, and they felt more pleasure if the PCA had large eyes. These results indicate several things. The gender interaction only occurs with the 2D cartoon character PCAs. Males feel more excited when they interact with PCAs of the same gender. Excitement includes elements of pleasure; therefore, it could mean that learners felt more positive feelings toward the agent. Based on these results, designers of PCAs should consider using 2D PCAs of the same gender for learners to induce positive emotions during online tutoring. An interesting point is that the 2D + eye interface was more successful in producing positive emotions. This also suggests that using PCAs with *kawaii* design components have a stronger effect on female learners. To understand why such characteristics have such an effect on inducing pleasure feelings, some studies investigated the social psychological structure of feelings of cuteness to explain that people perceive things as cute based on 'baby schema' [15]. Baby schema is characterized as a combination of infant-like physical traits, such as (1) a small body size with a disproportionately large head, (2) large eyes, (3) a pleasantly fair complexion, (4) a small nose, (5) dimples, and (6) round and softer body features. When people perceive humans or animals with these characteristics, they perceive cuteness. In the 2D + eye condition, we used PCAs with large eyes, which is a characteristic of the baby schema, and we focused only on the eyes of the

PCA. Further research can be done where we modify other parts to increase these characteristics to determine the ideal design for emotion-based learning systems using PCAs.

The results of our study indicate that using deformed characters as PCAs can be used to induce positive emotions and motivation in a web-based tutoring activity. In future work, we will study the different moods produced by using the tutoring systems from mobile devices, such as smart phones.

Acknowledgments. This work was supported in part by the 2012 KDDI Foundation Research Grant Program, and the Grant-in-Aid for Scientific Research (KAKENHI), and the Ministry of Education, Culture, Sports, Science, and Technology, Japan (MEXTGrant), Grant No. 25870910.

References

1. Baylor, A.L., Kim, Y.: Simulating instructional roles through pedagogical agents. Int. J. Artif. Intell. Educ. **15**(1), 95–115 (2005)
2. Baylor, A.L., Ryu, J.: The API (Agent Persona Instrument) for assessing pedagogical agent persona. In: Lassner, D., McNaught, C. (eds.) *Procedings of the World Conference on Educational Multimedia, Hypermedia and Telecommunications*, pp. 448–451 (2003)
3. Boucher, M.E., Hancock, T.J., Dunham, J.P.: Interpersonal sensitivity in computer-mediated and face-to-face conversations. Media psychol. **11**(2), 235–258 (2008)
4. Date, T., Kadomaru, T. In: Matsushita, D., Bobby, D. (eds.) How to Draw Moe Characters, Eye & Body, Japan (2010) (in Japanese)
5. Gulz, A., Haake, M.: Design of animated pedagogical agents: a look at their look. Int. J. Hum. Comput. Stud. **63**(4), 322–339 (2006)
6. Hayashi, Y., Huang, H.-H., Kryssanov, V.V., Urao, A., Miwa, K., Ogawa, H.: Source orientation in communication with a conversational agent. In: Vilhjálmsson, H.H., Kopp, S., Marsella, S., Thórisson, K.R. (eds.) IVA 2011. LNCS, vol. 6895, pp. 451–452. Springer, Heidelberg (2011)
7. Hayashi, Y.: On pedagogical effects of learner-support agents in collaborative interaction. In: Cerri, S.A., Clancey, W.J., Papadourakis, G., Panourgia, K. (eds.) ITS 2012. LNCS, vol. 7315, pp. 22–32. Springer, Heidelberg (2012)
8. Hayashi, Y.: Pedagogical conversational agents for supporting collaborative learning: effects of communication channels. In: *Proeedings of the. CHI 2013 Works-in-Progress*, pp. 655–660 (2013)
9. Hayashi, Y.: Learner-support agents for collaborative interaction: a study on affect and communication channels. *Proceedings of the 10th International Conference on Computer Supported Collaborative Learning*, pp. 232–239 *(2013)*
10. Heidig, S., Clarebout, G.: Do pedagogical agents make a difference to student motivation and learning? Educ. Res. Rev. **6**(1), 27–54 (2011)
11. Holmes, J.: Designing agents to support learning by explaining. Comput. Educ. **48**(4), 523–547 (2007)
12. Kim, Y., Baylor, A.L., Shen, E.: Pedagogical agents as learning companions: the impact of agent emotion and gender. J. Comput. Assist. Learn. **23**(3), 220–234 (2007)
13. Komatsu, T., Yamada, S.: How does the agents' appearance affect users' interpretation of the agents' attitudes - Experimental investigation on expressing the same artificial sounds from agents with different appearances. Int. J. Hum. Comput. Interact. **27**(3), 260–279 (2011)

14. Kumar, R., Rose, C.: Architecture for building conversational agents that support collaborative learning. IEEE Trans. Learn. Technol. **4**(1), 21–34 (2011)
15. Lorenz, K.: Die Angeborenen formenmoglicher erfahrung innate forms of potential experiments. Zeitschrift fur Tier-psychology **5**, 234–409 (1943)
16. Moreno, R., Mayer, E.: Role of guidance, reaction, and interactivity in an agent-based multimedia game. J. Educ. Psychol. **97**(1), 117–128 (2005)
17. Mori, M.: The uncanny valley (Mac Dorman, K.F., Kageki, N., trans.). *IEEE Rob. Autom. Mag. 19*(2), 98–100 (1970/2012)
18. Nass, C., Moon, Y.: Machines and mindlessness: social responses to computers. J. Soc. Issues **56**(1), 81–103 (2000)
19. Nittono, H., Fukushima, M., Yano, H., Moriya, H.: The power of kawaii: viewing cute images promotes careful behavior and narrows attentional focus. PLoS ONE **7**(9), 1–7 (2012)
20. Rosenberg-Kima, B.R., Plant, A.E., Doerr, E.C., Baylor, A.: The influence of computer-based model's race and gender on female students' attitudes and beliefs towards engineering. Journal of Engineering Education **99**(1), 35–44 (2010)
21. Russell, J.A.: A circumflex model of affect. J. Pers. Soc. Psychol. **39**(6), 1161–1178 (1980)
22. Sherman, G.D., Haidt, J., Coan, J.A.: Viewing cute images increases behavioral carefulness. Emotion **9**(2), 282–286 (2009)
23. Wang, N., Johnson, W.L., Mayer, R.E., Rizzo, P., Shaw, E., Collins, H.: The politeness effect: Pedagogical agents and learning outcomes. Int. J. Hum. Comput. Stud. **66**(2), 98–112 (2008)

Contextualization of Archaeological Findings Using Virtual Worlds. Issues on Design and Implementation of a Multiuser Enabled Virtual Museum

Luis Antonio Hernández Ibáñez[✉] and Viviana Barneche Naya

VideaLAB, Universidade Da Coruña, A Coruña, Spain
{luis.hernandez,viviana.barneche}@udc.es

Abstract. This paper describes the use of Virtual Worlds technology to implement a virtual museum for an interpretation center on the theme of the use of mosaics in ancient Roman villas. In order to foster the comprehension of the meaning of these archaeological remains, incomplete mosaics were completed digitally and placed in virtual rooms to recreate the atmosphere. A musealization of the virtual *domus* was then carried out. The environment was developed on an OpenSim based virtual world, which was prepared to hold groups of avatars characterized as Roman males and females, children and adults. Text chat and sound enable every visitor to share opinions with other remote users, and to perform guided tours. The system also permits to give lectures to remote audiences utilizing telepresence.

Keywords: Virtual worlds · E-learning · Virtual museums · Virtual archaeology · Roman mosaic

1 Introduction

What makes the difference between a humble piece of stone and a weapon used in a terrible fight for survival thousands of years ago? Every fragment of an archaeological remain has the power to trigger the evocation of the past in the mind of the person who contemplates it. This power resides in the object itself but the observer can release it with the knowledge needed to imagine the object in a precise space and time to recreate a situation. The deeper the understanding of the context that surrounds the existence of this object is, in terms of the different layers where the object can be inscribed e.g., material, industrial, historical, social, etc., the better the evocation may arise.

For museums and interpretation centers, especially those devoted to the fields of archaeology and historical heritage, transmitting context to their visitors is crucial in giving meaning to the exposed pieces.

Virtual worlds provide a very effective tool for the dissemination of the cultural goods of museum or interpretation center. The display and placing in context of virtual replicas allow for a better understanding of their role in history. Those virtual environments provide onsite simulation of historical reconstructions. They also have a very relevant value as a means for remote visits, gathering attention from visitors from all

© Springer International Publishing Switzerland 2015
P. Zaphiris and A. Ioannou (Eds.): LCT 2015, LNCS 9192, pp. 384–393, 2015.
DOI: 10.1007/978-3-319-20609-7_36

over the world, thus reaching people who would probably never visit the physical place. This is especially important for small institutions located a distance from touristic poles of attraction, small villages, etc., which is the case of many interpretation centers.

Computer virtual recreation of historical heritage has been a technique used in museums for the last two decades, commonly in the form of computer animation of architectural over flights, walkthroughs and depictions of virtual models displayed in video format. This is a very effective way to provide the user with an adequate knowledge of the context of the topics displayed, but implies a passive role for the visitor who is merely a spectator of things of a time past.

The user can be much more involved in this learning process by means of participation instead of merely contemplation, from looking to experiencing. In fact, the capacity of virtual worlds to make the user perceive their own presence in the simulated environment through immersion and engagement is one of the points that make them compelling [1]. In relation to the use of this technology for teaching, the feeling of presence is strongly linked with the overall satisfaction of the students with the learning activity [2]. The use of virtual worlds as a mean for joint activities between schools and museums received good results when tested [3].

In numerous cases of the use of heritage reconstruction in virtual worlds, [4–6] most appeared exclusively in the domain of virtual communities such as Second Life. Very few examples appeared that run in the context of a real museum, such as the case of the reconstruction of Villa Livia [7].

The case presented here describes the use of a virtual world as a means for contextualization of archeological findings as part of the exhibition designed for an interpretation center in Casariche (Seville, Spain). The center is dedicated to the theme of mosaics in ancient Ro-man villas, particularly those found in the archeological dig of El Alcaparral.

The virtual models had two main objectives. They should display a complete recreation of the mosaics found in the nearby excavation, allowing the visitors to contemplate the appearance of the pavements in their full size instead of just fragments. The villa model also had an objective to build an environment that could provide a context for the interpretation of the mosaics.

Designers took into account the capability of virtual worlds to act as an environment for simultaneous multiple users. The design of the virtual villa fulfilled the requirements of remote access, virtual presence, and multiuser communication via chat and voice.

2 Methodology

2.1 Background

In 1985, thirteen mosaics contained the remains of a late roman villa close to Casariche. The state of conservation of the different pieces is very dissimilar, ranging from small parts to full pavements, being specially notable the piece representing the Judgment of Paris (Fig. 1).

Fig. 1. Mosaic depicting the Judgement of Paris

Reports were made of traces of the ancient villa (Sierra 1985) (Hoz 1987). They constitute one of the bases for the virtual reconstruction described in this paper (Fig. 2).

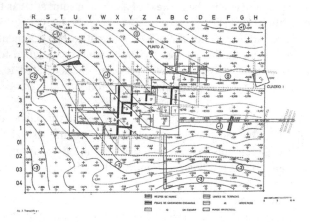

Fig. 2. Layout of the foundations and location of the mosaics at the roman villa

Taking into account all preliminary documentation, this work was carried out in two phases; the first one, consistent in the construction of the virtual model to hold the virtual exhibition and activities, and the second one included all aspects of virtual musealization.

2.2   Construction of the Virtual Model

Reconstruction of the mosaics. The mosaics displayed comprise two groups. The first one includes those only formed by geometrical motifs. Here, the modular and repetitive characteristics of the formal structure of the drawings allow one to obtain a possible full version of every original design. Patterns repeated, in search of a coherent formal structure for every case according to the dimensions and shape of every room. Apart from possible unknown irregularities or unexpected lost elements, that could break the homogeneity of the design in the original mosaic, the reconstructed versions offer an image of every mosaic that would correspond very approximately to the appearance of those ancient pavements (Fig. 3).

Fig. 3. Geometrical mosaic displayed in the atrium of the *impluvium* and reconstruction. (Photos from the intervention report – left- and from the virtual world – right).

Mosaics composed by those containing figurative drawings make up the second group. There were three mosaics on this group, with very different states of preservation. The mosaic depicting the "Judgment of Paris" was almost complete, and only needed to include a few retouches to obtain its virtual replica. The second mosaic, called "The Spring," had a big part of the face of the person represented missing, but the characteristics of the shape of the human face permitted reconstruction fairly well (Fig. 4).

Fig. 4. The mosaics of the Judgment of Paris – left- and The spring –right- in the virtual world

The third case, the mosaic that covered the bottom of the *impluvium*, was almost lost and only small parts were present. Nevertheless, those parts indicated clearly that the original drawing depicted a scene containing two Nereids riding a Triton. The detailed formal analysis of the remaining fragments displayed multiple similarities with other mosaics of the same age and similar theme found in excavations located in neighboring regions. That took the authors to consider a great influence of even a common school authorship that may induce one to think that the motif depicted in the original mosaic could be very similar. The associated descriptive panel floating over the reconstructed scene, indicate the clear character of hypothesis of such reconstruction. Nevertheless, the virtual version helps to understand the frequent use of marine scenes in *impluvia* and other hydraulic elements (Fig. 5).

Fig. 5. The *impluvium* in the virtual world with the reconstructed mosaic of two nereids riding Triton.

Finally, a generic mosaic was designed to be used in the rooms that presented more uncertainty in their layout, as a mean to remark them as the most hypothetic part of the interpretation of the house.

Reconstruction of the *villa*.

In order to facilitate a better comprehension of the late Roman architecture, the three-dimensional representation of this *villa olearia*, made for this project, tries to be as accurate as possible, based on all the data obtained from the archaeological dig, but considered the fact that the remains were neither abundant nor well preserved. Additionally, the authors interpreted the historical and ethnographical data available and the analysis of other near *villas olearias* that present a similar terrain organization based on terraces of the same period such as the *villa vinicola* of Fuente Alamo and the *villa agricola* of Villaricos.

Other reconstruction criteria for the making of the model bases design on the archaeological current of thought named Archeology of Architecture [8, 9]. This discipline provides analytical models and methodological tools that contribute significantly to the study of the different dimensions of the built space. This work used the constructive analysis to obtain the characteristics of the domestic architecture of the archaeological site, the formal analysis to construe and understand the functionality of the structures and the syntactic analysis of the space to grasp the subjacent social significance.

The virtual reconstruction mimics the constructive materials found in the dig properly described in the corresponding excavation reports [10, 11]. Those reports also give important clues about the possible distribution of spaces and how they are grouped in terraces following the slope of the terrain. Those clues were especially taken into account to obtain the hypothetical layout of the complex.

From the previous analysis, design of the model of the villa, organized in three zones followed the alignments of the terraces found in the site. The first one corresponds to the *pars urbana*, the noble area where the *dominus* and his family lived, and the area dedicated to the thermal baths *(balnea)*. The second one related to the accommodation of the servants, slaves and all personnel who worked on the crops in the surrounding fields. The third area includes the spaces for storage of farm equipment and stables. The figures display the final distribution (Fig. 6).

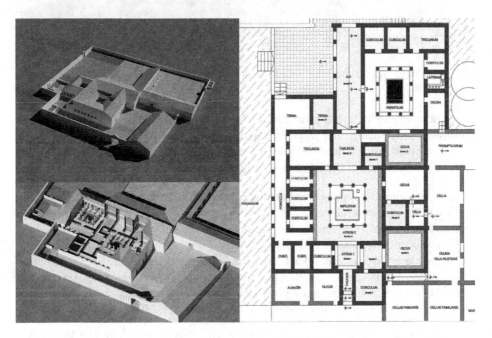

Fig. 6. General views of the villa – left- and hypothesis of distribution of the of the *pars urbana*. Pavements with mosaics are remarked –right-.

2.3   Virtual Musealization

Musealization of the model. The virtual representation of the *domus* provides one with a site fully accessible to visitors. The user, represented by his or her avatar and dressed as a Roman inhabitant of the villa, can walk freely throughout the complex. The enjoy not only the architecture of the building, but also the wall paintings, furniture, mosaics, and other ele-ments of material culture, *anphoras* for oil and wine, *tegulas*, oil lamps, etc. (Fig. 7). The setting of the different spaces (*atria, peristila, lararium, triclinium,* *tablinium*, etc.) helps to interpret the daily life in such facilities. The focus is the mosaic of the "Judgment of Paris" since this piece is unique in Hispania. It is one of the only five known cases found in all the Roman Empire depicting this theme [12].

Fig. 7. Amphoras for oil and wine and explanatory panel – left-. Maps and videos in the virtual rooms – right-.

All notable elements in the virtual villa have a descriptive panel written in Spanish and English (switchable) that gives information about every specific topic. Some rooms act as containers of descriptive elements like maps, pictures and videos related to the activities in the villa and the art of mosaic making (Fig. 7).

Implementation and support for the interpretation center. The database containing the virtual villa is implemented on an OpenSim server, accessible through the Internet using any compatible viewer such as Singularity, Kokua or Imprudence. Nevertheless, users can download a custom configured viewer from the virtual world website.

Independently from the remote access, the virtual world is usable as a local simulation of the ancient house from within the interpretation center, using a regular personal computer located in one of its ex-positive rooms. This way, this virtual museum is capable of accomplishing several objectives:

- Depiction: The virtual world displays formal aspects and characteristics of the elements to interpret, their full shape, location and use in the villa, relative importance, etc.
- Evocation: The virtual villa fosters the use of the imagination to make the visitor feel as part of the ancient world, thus helping to understand the key concepts and grasping better the knowledge that is offered.
- Experience: The visitor can perceive the villa and the mosaics located inside through a virtual, but vivid experience, feeling the relations among the spaces, contemplating the elements displayed, and experiencing the visit to the virtual villa as he or she would do it in a real museum.

Fig. 8. Some of the avatars available to visitors of the virtual villa

Fig. 9. Visitor playing the question game

2.4 Avatars and Gamification

As it was mentioned above, users enter this world using avatars that can be chosen from a small variety of male and female, adult and child, examples. Users dress their avatars in Roman garments and jewelry and personalize them. This reinforces the feeling of presence of the visitor in the virtual world (Fig. 8).

There is a quiz game implemented in the virtual world, specially designed for young visitors. The player has to face a bas-relief sculpture of Medusa that will ask them a question with an easy answer if the visitor has paid attention to the information displayed all over the villa. If the player succeeds answering the question, Medusa gives them an image of a golden apple like the one depicted in the Judgment of Paris mosaic (Fig. 9).

Fig. 10. Educational activity with remote users

2.5 Multiuser Capabilities

Finally yet importantly, the multiuser enabled remote access brings the possibility to put distant visitors in touch, allowing meeting in the virtual facility with text and voice chat enabled. This makes it possible to organize events such as lectures, guided visits to remote groups of visitors (i.e. schools) in the virtual villa, expert meetings, etc. (Fig. 10).

3 Conclusions

Virtual worlds are a very effective tool for contextualization of historical heritage remains and archaeological findings, with virtual replicas displayed in a historical referential environment, allowing for a better understanding of their cultural meaning. Those virtual environments can be used both as on-site simulation of historical reconstruction and also as a means for remote visits, gathering attention from visitors from all over the world, thus reaching people who would probably never visit the physical place. All of this makes virtual worlds a notable tool to enhance the didactic capabilities of centers. This paper describes the steps to follow in order to achieve an efficient example of such a class of virtual museum.

References

1. Carr, D.: Play and Pleasure. In: Carr, D., Buckingham, D., Burn, A., Schott, G. (eds.) Computer Games: Text Narrative and Play. Polity Press, UK, Cambridge (2006)
2. Childs, M.: Learners' Experience of Presence in Virtual Worlds. Ph.D. thesis. University of Warwick. Institute of Education (2010)
3. Barneche, V., Hernandez, L.: Evaluating user experience in joint activities between schools and museums in virtual worlds. Univers. Access Inf. Soc. 01/2014 **14**(3) (2014). doi:10.1007/s10209-014-0367-y

4. Harrison, R.: Excavating second life: cyber-archaeologies, heritage and virtual communities. J. Mat. Cult. **14**(1), 75–106 (2009)
5. Sequeira, L.: Virtual archaeology in second life and opensimulator. J. Virtual World Res. **6**, 1–16 (2013)
6. Barneche, V., Hernández, L.: Patrimonio histórico y metaversos. Estudio de caso de la recreación interactiva de la Torre de Hércules en Second Life. Virtual Archaeol. Rev. **1**(2), 59–62 (2010)
7. Forte, M.: La Villa di LiviaUn. Percorso di Ricerca di Archeologia Virtuale. L'Erma di Bretschneider, Rome (2008)
8. Steadman, S.: Recent research in the archaeology of architecture: beyond the foundations. J. Archaeol. Res. **4**(1), 51–93 (1996)
9. Azkarate, A.: Arqueología de la Arquitectura: definición disciplinar y nuevas perspectivas. Arqueología de la Arquitectura **1**, 7–10 (2002)
10. Sierra, J.: Memoria de la excavación de urgencia en El Alcaparral (Casariche, Sevilla), 1985–1987, Anuario Arqueológico de Andalucía 58 (1985)
11. Hoz, A.: Informe de la Segunda Campaña de Excavaciones en la Villa Romana de 'El Alcaparral'. Anuario Arqueológico de Andalucía, **86** vol III (1987)
12. Blázquez, J.: Mosaicos romanos del Campo de Villavidel (León) y de Casariche (Sevilla). Archivo Español de Arqueología Madrid, T III CSIC (1985)

Enhancing the Learning Success of Engineering Students by Virtual Experiments

Max Hoffmann[✉], Lana Plumanns, Laura Lenz, Katharina Schuster,
Tobias Meisen, and Sabina Jeschke

Institute of Information Management in Mechanical Engineering, Center for Learning and
Knowledge Management, RWTH Aachen University, Dennewartstrasse 27,
52068 Aachen, Germany
`max.hoffmann@ima.rwth-aachen.de`

Abstract. In a world that is characterized by highly specialized industry sectors, the demand for well-educated engineers increases significantly. Thus, the education of engineering students has become a major field of interest for universities. However, not every university is able to provide the required number of industry demonstrators to impart the needed practical knowledge to students. Our aim is to fill this gap by establishing Remote Labs. These laboratory experiments are performed in Virtual Reality environments which represent real laboratories accessible from different places. Following the implementation of such Remote Labs described within our past publications the aim of this contribution is to examine and evaluate possibilities of controlling Remote Labs from arbitrary locations. These control mechanisms are based on the virtualization of two concurrently working six-axis robots in combination with a game pad remote controller. The evaluation of the virtual demonstrator is carried out in terms of a study that is based on practical tests and questionnaires to measure the learning success.

Keywords: Virtual reality · Remote laboratories · Game-based learning · Experiential learning · Virtual theatre · Immersion

1 Introduction

The current developments within the industry and engineering sciences triggered by the Industry 4.0 pose major challenges for the education of engineering students in universities all over the world. Faster evolving technologies and rapidly changing requirements in industrial environments lead to rising demands in terms of practical education of engineering students. In the course of traditional training methods, the practical education of students is mostly performed by the attendance to laboratory experiments or the visit of factories and production sites. However, in terms of changing circumstances and dynamically performed manufacturing execution the scope of laboratory experiments and practical education has to be adopted to these novel requirements as well. It is the

© Springer International Publishing Switzerland 2015
P. Zaphiris and A. Ioannou (Eds.): LCT 2015, LNCS 9192, pp. 394–405, 2015.
DOI: 10.1007/978-3-319-20609-7_37

aim of this paper to demonstrate novel methods of imparting practical knowledge to students considering the current developments within industrial reality.

One possibility of realizing these practical experiments without neglecting the demands of the Industry 4.0 is to virtualize the experience of visiting laboratory classes or manufacturing sites. In terms of these attempts, Virtual Reality simulations can be carried out in order to create virtual environments that can be adapted according to the current demands and demonstrator configurations. Another application of the described Virtual Reality solutions is to recreate existing laboratory environments from the real world and provide these environments as virtual demonstrators.

This application of Virtual Reality is referred to as Remote Laboratories and can be integrated into the curriculum of students in order to allow engineering students from arbitrary places to visit and experience laboratory environments that are not available at their university or place of study. Prototypical implementations of these Remote Labs have been carried out and examined in previous works of the author [1–3]. In terms of these developments the suitability of creating practical learning environments for engineering students were examined in order to deliver the basis for carrying out virtual experiments of real world demonstrators.

Based on our previous work, it is the aim of the current publications to describe, examine and evaluate ways of direct interaction with real world demonstrators through their virtual representation. Doing so, we extended an existing demonstrator with control mechanisms and implemented remote control solutions for active interaction of a user who is connected to the demonstrator by Virtual Reality tools. In order to evaluate these interaction capabilities the paper is divided into several parts.

In Sect. 2 we will discuss the state of the art in Game-based Learning in connection with laboratory experiments in the form of Remote Labs. Also, we will point out techniques to examine and create the didactical concepts needed to assess the learning success of students that perform experiments in game-like virtual environments. In Sect. 3, we will describe in detail the technical solutions that have been carried out and implemented to reach full remote control of distant laboratory environments from arbitrary places. In Sect. 4, the evaluation of the remote control capabilities takes place in form of a study that have been carried out with students from different universities in Germany. Section 5 summarizes the results and takes a look at further research opportunities in the field of Remote Labs.

2   State of the Art

Based on the existing Remote Lab demonstrator that has been carried out and described within our previous publications [1] the different mechanisms for the remote control of these labs are of primary interest in this publication.

Accordingly, the state of the art section of this work deals with evaluation methods that will be selected and implemented to evaluate the learning success of students that are surrounded by virtual environments, thus in terms of a situation comparable to game-based learning/serious gaming scenarios. The evaluation part is realized on the basis of questionnaires that, on the one hand analyzes general suitability of the learning methods for each test person, and on the other hand, assesses the learning success of each individual test person from the technical point of view while taking into account their experience with digital media.

Virtuality-based learning (VBL) is a recent trend not only in engineering education. It is closely related to game-based learning (GBL), which is defined as "[...] a type of game-play that has defined outcomes. Generally, GBL is designed to balance subject matter with game-play and the ability of the player to retain and apply said subject matter to the real world" [4]. What is equal here is the digitalization of a pre-given-subject matter, which has to be learned. The difference is that digitalized places do not necessarily need gamy elements in order to be useful. There is much more about using virtual environments in education: The main advantage is that mistakes can be made without any consequences, that contents are endlessly repeatable plus that it is extremely cost saving. Thus, in terms of Remote Labs, students learn how to use a robot in a virtual environment before actually using it.

Although the advantages of VBL seem to be obvious, the measurement of learning successes presents a major challenge for the parties in charge. It is not only that the learning effect per se needs to be measured, but whether the handling is so unproblematic that users experience a sense of flow [5, 6] (a spontaneous sense of joy while performing a not too easy, not too difficult task), (tele-) presence [7] (the feeling of being enabled to act in this case in a remote lab) and finally immersion [8], the sensation of fully diving into a virtual environment. Obviously, these possible experiences are highly dependent on the user's pre-knowledge (e.g., how to use the WASD plus mouse combination) and his intrinsic technical readiness. The reason is that only users who can forget about the handling of for example a controller can experience a sense of immersion. If they need to look at it and think about the usage again and again, they will constantly be reminded that they are solely performing a virtual task, which is non-existent in reality and might thus attach less importance/meaning to it.

Another big problem in the measurement of subjective virtuality experiences is the question whether to perform the tests quantitatively or qualitatively and which influence the corresponding decision will have on the validity, transparency, causal interrelations and reliability of the results. The usage of the questionnaires on subjective user sentiments and self-assessment is a necessary step since these facts are not objectively observable. The self-assessment questions help to relate the produced results to behavior-parameters, which then lead to tentative conclusions concerning whether there is an interrelation between user preferences/habits and VBL success.

For the pre-assessment of test-persons, the BIG Five questionnaire is named as the most useful way to assess a test person's personality traits. The entailed items cover *neuroticism*, meaning emotional instabilities like fears and sadness, *extraversion*, the willingness to be in the center of attention, *openness to experience*, meaning the willingness to learn, *agreeableness*, the general need to socialize and lastly *conscientiousness*, the willingness to be disciplined [9]. For psychologists, alternative methods to assess personality traits exist; however, in the end, they all come back to the big five although they may be named differently (ibid.).

Another of the most contemporary assessment questionnaires is the MEC-SPQ on general media exposure [10]. The main advantage is that it is highly flexible and may entail eight, six or only four items per scale. It has been used in studies on mobile gaming

[11], in the realm of computer gaming [12] and serious games, thus, in the area of game-based learning [13]. So far, it is the only validated and highly consistent measurement instrument on spatial thinking [10].

In addition to this, recent studies by Witte showed that the locus for control of technology (KUT) questionnaire is a validated instrument to measure the performance of test persons while being confronted with technical problems [14]. Burde and Blankertz proved, that there is a correlation between a high score in the KUT and the performance in technical handling [15].

However, besides assessing test persons, an overall system evaluation and technical assessment of all technological devices is of utmost importance. Are software and hardware stabile? Do all components run as desired? Are there any known errors or problems and can the program run 'fluently'? [16]. Secondly, special attention must be paid to the users: how is their first reaction to the virtual robot? Did they spontaneously know what do to? Was there a lot of explanation necessary?

In sum, it must be concluded that the evaluation of virtuality-based learning is partly problematic because of subjective user assessment, talent and perception, which cannot be measured objectively. There is always the risk of users being afraid to truthfully state their abilities or that they even overestimate their capabilities. Our approach addresses this issue by creating an interplay between the estimated technical readiness of individual test persons and their actual real-time learning progress. Accordingly, the risk of falsified results due to inaccurate self-assessment of the test persons can be minimized.

3   Active Interaction for Remote Labs in Virtual Reality Environments

The creation of fully interactive virtual environments is based on the VR techniques that have been utilized by carrying out the technical and virtual environments of the remote labs. To realize a fully capable Remote Lab several steps were performed, i.e.:

1. Virtualization of machines and plants in every detail for three-dimensional representation within virtual environments.
2. Embedding of three-dimensional objects into virtual environments to create a virtual scenario, in which users can move around to exploit objects and the environment.
3. Setup and implementation of an information and communication infrastructure for data exchange between real and virtual laboratory environments.
4. Enabling one-directional communication between the real laboratory environment and its virtual representation in order to reproduce movements of the real world demonstrator within the virtual demonstrator in real-time.
5. Enabling bi-directional communication by embedding control mechanisms and devices for the real laboratory from VR experiments into the scope of the Remote Lab.

The user can interact with the Remote Lab through various interfaces, e.g. the Virtual Theatre described in [1] or other immersive technologies like the Oculus Rift. Figure 1 shows that a notebook together with a Head Mounted Display is a suitable environment.

Fig. 1. Remote lab environment – The user is immersed into the scenario via the Oculus Rift

The first step of this procedure has already been described by Hoffmann et al. [2]. The virtual demonstrator that is used within the current work consists of two cooperating six-axis robots that are placed on a table in order to perform concurrent tasks. The virtual representation of the robots has been designed using modeling tools for computer graphics and design. The modelling of the robots is performed by integrating a bone structure into the virtual representation whereas the bones of the robot are connected through joints. The meshing of this bone-joint-structure ensures the correct assignment of the single parts in terms of parent and child nodes in order to recreate physically realistic movements of the whole robot, i.e. if the root joint is moved, all subsequent child nodes of the robot (bones and joints) are moved accordingly as well.

The embedding of these robots into a virtual environment is performed by the use of a VR tool for virtual worlds, i.e. WorldViz Vizard as described in [1]. In terms of the modeling, the different components, e.g. the robot table, both robots, the objects to be treated by the robots as well as other elements like avatars or screens are included into this virtual environment to create an immersive scenario for the user experiment.

The information and communication infrastructure (ICT) for Remote Labs has been described in detail in [3] and is an integral part of the virtual laboratory experiment. The ICT consists of the two cooperating robots, which are controlled by two manual control panels and a computer that contains the Robot Operating System (ROS) environment. Over a network architecture this operating computer is connected to other computers that run the Virtual Reality simulation programs and are connected to VR simulators like the Virtual Theatre as described in [17] or the Oculus Rift in combination with a local client computer [18] as depicted in Fig. 1. The connection between the robot operating computer and the VR simulation systems is established by making use of the Protobuf Protocol interface for the exchange of robot information [19].

The ICT as described allows the one-directional communication between a robot-focused laboratory experiment and a distant representation of this laboratory in terms of a Remote Lab. Using the Protobuf interface standard the angles and joint positions of the robots can be transferred over the network in real-time. Internal tests on the real-time capabilities of such Remote Lab, which allows the observation of distant experiments, determined the maximum lag between reality and virtuality to 0.1-0.2 s.

Besides the graphical interface for the visualization of Remote Labs at distant places, e.g. by making use of the Virtual Theatre, there are also interaction devices embedded into the ICT. For our scenario we have chosen a common game pad controller, the

Nintendo Wii™, as remote control device for the interaction of the user with the real world demonstrator within the virtual environment. Using this game device, the robots of the simulation and accordingly the real robots can be successfully manipulated. The basic control functions are highlighted in Fig. 2.

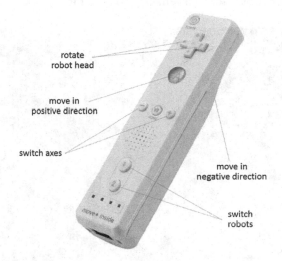

rotate
robot head

move in
positive direction

switch axes

move in
negative direction

move + inside

switch
robots

Fig. 2. Nintendo Wii™ controller and basic functions for robot control

There are two control mechanisms that have been carried out for robot control, and which are both based on the usage of the Wii™ gaming controller:

1. Direct kinematics for direct control of the joint angles for each robots.
2. Inverse kinematics for user control of the movement axis (X, Y, Z) whereas the joint angles for the current robot position or moving trajectory are dynamically calculated during the experiments.

In terms of the direct kinematics robot control method, each of the six angles of the selected robot can be individually controlled using the "A" button for positive moving direction and the "B" button on the back of the remote control for negative moving direction. Using the "+" and "–" signs the axes of the robot joints can be subsequently selected. Using the buttons "1" and "2" the according robot can be selected. For direct kinematics the cross on the top of the Wii™ is not used, as the head rotation is represented by the sixth robot joint angle.

Concerning the inverse kinematics the "A" and "B" buttons are used to move the robot claw in positive respectively negative direction of the X, Y or Z axis. The axes are switched again using the "+" and "–" signs on the controller. The "1" and "2" also change the selected robot. The rotation of the robot head for inverse kinematics is implemented using the control cross at the top of the remote control. For the dynamic calculation of the single joint angle values suitable for the goal position or trajectory, an inverse calculation method is used for determining the joint parameters. For our use-case a MATLAB™ Toolbox has been adapted to the needs of the robot demonstrator.

The scenario, in which the described robot control methods are being applied, consists of a setup, where one of the robots has to be moved along a fixed path. This path is represented by a wire. For conducting the experiment an eyelet is attached to one of the robots. The task of the controlling person is to move the eyelet attached to the robot along the wire, which forms a certain curve (see Fig. 3).

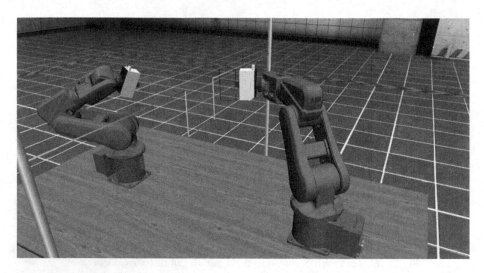

Fig. 3. The eyelet attached to the right robot has to be driven along the steel wire in the middle

The described task is performed through the Wii™ remote control either by making use of the direct kinematic mechanism or by making use of inverse kinematics. In order to assess these methods against each other, user studies were performed, which are described in the following chapter.

4   User Studies for Examination and Evaluation of Control Mechanisms for Remote Labs

4.1   Design of Experiment and Expectations

The aim of this study is to examine which of the previously described control mechanisms for six-axis robots is the most beneficial for the implementation in Remote Labs especially with regard to an intuitive control and progress of learning as well as investigating the effects of the sequent comparison of both mechanism.

We expect that students – especially those who are used to gaming – will prefer the inverse control mechanism over the direct one, because it resembles their gaming experience. Furthermore we expect that successful practice experience through the trainings session will enhance the feelings of self-confidence and thus flow.

A representative number of engineering students from different advanced information science courses at multiple sophisticated, technical universities participated in the study in order to evaluate the learning progress of the concurrent methods for remote controlling the robots. The objective of conducting the study is to assess the different methodologies of control mechanisms suitable for engineering students.

The first part of the study is performed in cooperation with the Technical University of Dortmund, where test persons were recruited. The second part of the study is carried out in the course of a lecture with engineering students at the RWTH Aachen University. The study consists of three questionnaires and two practical tests, namely the remote control of the cooperating robots using direct and inverse kinematics. The sequence of the tests (direct and inverse mechanism) is randomized, the participants are accordingly assigned to either Group A or Group B. Participants who are assigned to group A start with the inverse kinematics test whereas participants of group B start with the direct kinematics test. Both user groups conduct both experiments, however in reverse order. The intention of this approach is on the one hand to examine the learning progress of the students during the experiments and on the other hand to equalize the effects of test order. The study is implemented in six steps:

1. Theoretical input in terms of the study design and methods of examination.
2. Pre-questionnaire for general assessment concerning the personal background of the test persons in terms of video game experiences and spatial thinking abilities.
3. First experiment using either inverse kinematics (Group A) or direct kinematics (Group B).
4. Questionnaire for the assessment of the previous test.
5. Second experiment using either direct kinematics (Group A) or inverse kinematics (Group B).
6. Questionnaire for the assessment of the previous test.

The first questionnaire is given to the participants before the experiment and is used for a general classification of the test person. Whereas questions such as the frequency of confrontation with digital games, the frequency of handling a console, whether the participants are active member of a digital sodality and the amount of hours spend on computer games a week are used to assess participants experience of gaming, individuals visual-spatial imagination (in virtual surroundings) are examined by items of the FRS [20] und questions of the subscale DSI of the MEC-Spatial Presence Questionnaire (MEC-SPQ) [10] adapted to computer games. This scale was already used successfully in previous studies and is characterized by fair quality criteria [21].

Besides this scale, items of the KUT [22] are used to assess participants locus of control when confronted with technical problems. Additionally, questions of the BIG Five Inventory [23] are used to assess subjects' personality and psychological biases, to get a broad picture of the participants.

The second and third questionnaire are used to assess the students' technical evaluation of the currently performed tests as well as their experience of learning progress while working. Participants are asked to rate the feasibility, advantages and disadvantages and the control of the just practiced remote mechanism as well as adapted questions concerning the experience of absorption due to the experience of flow [24]. A mental state of operation in which the individual, who is performing the task, is fully involved and immersed by feelings of energized focus [25]. All questions are presented on a seven-point scale, ranging from 1 = *total disagree* to 7 = *total agree*.

4.2 Correlational Approach

To gain further inside of the relationship between the individual gaming experience, such as hours of gaming per week and the evaluation of the control mechanism as well as learning progress during the experiment, the correlation between the pretest data was calculated. Data were analyzed with IBM SPSS statistics software. The results are visualized in Fig. 4 in form of a graph that shows the strength of each correlation.

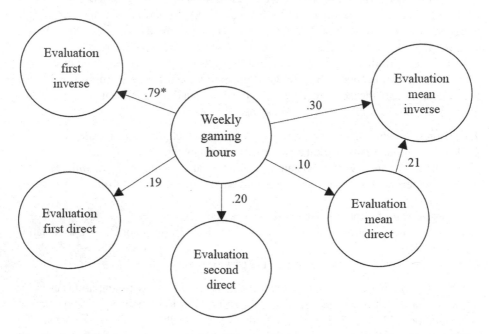

Fig. 4. Correlation between amount of weekly gaming hours and evaluation of remote control

The correlational approach shows that subjects with more playing hours per week evaluate the inverse kinematics approach better than the direct one, but only if the inverse control mechanism is the initial one. There is no significant correlation between hours played a week and an appreciation of the direct mechanism, neither as first test nor as second test.

Further differences between the two participant groups were analyzed with a multivariate ANOVA, where each group served as a between-subject factor. The assumption of homogeneity of variances is investigated with Levene's test and shows no significant violations of the assumption for the dependent variable. Inspection of histograms show no significant deviations from normality for the rating of two groups. The analysis shows no main effect of rating due to group assignment, $F(1, 12) = 1.49, p = .266$, but additional analyses of the within-subject factor task-order show significant differences ($p = < .05$) between the two tests in both groups (see Table 1).

Table 1. Results of the significance analysis of Remote Lab control mechanisms

		Group A	Group B
		inverse	direct
Test 1	M	4.44	4.20
	SD	.98	1.38
		direct	inverse
Test 2	M	4.84*	4.84*
	SD	.99	1.63

$* = p < .05$, M = Mean, SD = Standard deviation

Statistical analyses reveal that the participants show no significant differences in preference due to both remote mechanisms. In both groups, the second remote mechanism is rated significantly higher in preference than the first one, regardless of group membership. The subscale experienced learning progress is rated above the mean, in particular after the second testing session for the group that starts with the inverse mechanism $(M = 5.33; SD = 1.75)$ respectively the group that starts with the direct mechanism $(M = 4.45; SD = 2.05)$. These present findings do not confirm the hypothesis that students prefer the inverse mechanism in statistical terms, despite the fact that the mean values of the inverse mechanism are slightly higher than those of the direct mechanism. However, the results emphasize the importance of learning experience in both groups.

Thus, it can be concluded from these results, that the experience of flow and students' valuing of technical mechanism increase over time and are depending on practical experience and learning progress rather than a specific task mechanism per se.

5   Conclusion and Outlook

The aim of this work is to assess different mechanisms for the remote control of laboratory environments at arbitrary places. Based on an existing Remote Lab environment, direct and inverse kinematics control schemes have been carried out and implemented in order to enable the control of two cooperating six-axis robots.

The assessment in terms of the learning success lead to the result that there is not a significant preference for one of the two control mechanisms. However, the inverse kinematics – as expected – has been evaluated slightly better in comparison to the direct specification of joint angles. The study has also shown that the learning effect is equally good using both control methods, hence, both user groups evaluated the second test as preferable to the first one as they gained more self-confidence in controlling the robots during the progress of the study.

During the next steps in enhancing the usability and application of Remote Labs, it is our aim to enable a direct manipulation of the laboratory environment that can be located at arbitrary places. This real laboratory will be moved in real-time and accordingly to the exact digital representation, thus unexpected states of the experiment can be reached in the simulation similarly to the real-world demonstrator. In order to ensure the safety during these remote operations, a collision avoidance system based on the inverse kinematics implementation will be carried. Using this security layer, Remote Labs at arbitrary places can be independently controlled by users from Virtual Reality simulators from various locations. This will enable a holistic coverage of laboratory experiments for universities all over the world.

Acknowledgement. This work was supported by the German Research Foundation (DFG) within the project ELLI (Excellent Teaching and Learning within engineering sciences) at RWTH Aachen University in terms of investigating laboratory experiments and Remote Labs.

References

1. Hoffmann, M., Schuster, K., Schilberg, D., Meisen, T.: Next-generation teaching and learning using the virtual theatre. In: Gregory, S.; Jerry, P.; Taveres Jones, N. (eds.) At the Edge of the Rift (2014)
2. Hoffmann, M., Schuster, K., Schilberg, D., Jeschke, S.: Bridging the gap between students and laboratory experiments. In: Shumaker, R., Lackey, S. (eds.) VAMR 2014, Part II. LNCS, vol. 8526, pp. 39–50. Springer, Heidelberg (2014)
3. Hoffmann, M., Meisen, T., Jeschke, S.: Shifting virtual reality to the next level. Experiencing remote laboratories through mixed reality. In: The International Conference on Computer Science, Computer Engineering, and Education Technologies, CSCEET 2014 (2014)
4. Meier, C., Seufert, S.: Game-based learning. erfahrungen mit und perspektiven für digitale lernspiele in der betrieblichen bildung. In: Hohenstein, A., Wilbers, K. (eds.) Handbuch E-Learning. Deutscher, Köln (2005)
5. Csikszentmihalyi, M.: Finding. Flow The Psychology of Engagement with Everyday Life. Basic Books, New York (1997)
6. Csikszentmihalyi, M.: Creativity: Flow and the psychology of discovery and invention. http://books.google.de/books/about/Creativity.html?id=aci_Ea4c6woC&redir_esc=y. Accessed 12 January 2015
7. Bracken, C., Skalski, P.: Telepresence and Video Games. The Impact of Image Quality (2015). http://www.psychology.org/File/PNJ7(1)/PSYCHNOLOGY_JOURNAL_7_1_BRACKEN.pdf. Accessed 12 January 2015
8. Jennett, C., Cox, A.L., Cairns, P., Dhoparee, S., Epps, A., Tijs, T., Walton, A.: Measuring and defining the experience of immersion in games. Int. J. Hum Comput Stud. **66**(9), 641–661 (2008)
9. Matthews, G., Deary, I.J., Whiteman, M.C.: Personality Traits, 2nd edn. Cambridge, New York (2003)
10. Vorderer, P., Wirth, W., Gouveia, F. R., Biocca, F., Saari, T., Jäncke, F., Böcking, S., Schramm, H., Gysbers, A., Hartmann, T., Klimmt, C., Laarni, J., Ravaja, N., Sacau, A., Baumgartner, T., Jäncke, P.: MEC Spatial presence questionnaire (MEC-SPQ): short documentation and instructions for application. Report to the European Community, Project Presence. In: MEC (IST-2001-37661)
11. Laarni, J., Ravaja, N., Saari, T.: Presence experience in mobile gaming. In: Proceedings of DiGRA 2005 Conference: Changing Views – Worlds in Play (2005)

12. Weibel, D., Wissmath, B.: Immersion in computer games: the role of spatial presence and flow. Int. J. Comput. Games Technol. **2011**(3), 1–14 (2011)
13. Göbel, S., Müller, W., Urban, B., Wiemeyer, J. (eds.): GameDays 2012 and Edutainment 2012. LNCS, vol. 7516. Springer, Heidelberg (2012)
14. Witte, M., Kober, S.E., Ninaus, M., Neuper, C., Wood, G.: Control beliefs can predict the ability to up-regulate sensorimotor rhythm during neurofeedback training. Front. hum. neurosci. **7**, 478 (2013)
15. Burde, W., Blankertz, B.: Is the locus of control of reinforcement a predictor of brain-computer interface performance. In: Proceedings of the 3rd International Braincomputer Inferface Workshop and Training Course, Graz, pp. 76–77 (2005)
16. Wakolbinger, J., Kirchner, P.: NetAvatar – Interaktion mit einem humanoiden Roboter. www.hs-augsburg.de/~tr/prj/ss10-IP/07_WK/07_WK_NetAvatar.pdf. Accessed: 15 February 2015
17. Hoffmann, M., Schuster, K., Schilberg, D., Jeschke, S.: Next-generation teaching and learning using the virtual theatre. In: 4th Global Conference on Experiential Learning in Virtual Worlds Prague, Czech Republic (2014)
18. OculusVR. https://www.oculus.com/dk2/. Accessed 11 February 2015
19. Google: http://code.google.com/p/protobuf/wiki/ThirdPartyAddOns. Accessed 27 January 2014
20. Münzer, S., Hölscher, C.: Entwicklung und validierung eines fragebogens zu räumlichen strategien. Diagn. **57**(3), 111–125 (2011)
21. Schuster, K., Hoffmann, M., Bach, U., Richert, A., Jeschke, S.: Diving in? how users experience virtual environments using the virtual theatre. In: Marcus, A. (ed.) DUXU 2014, Part II. LNCS, vol. 8518, pp. 636–646. Springer, Heidelberg (2014)
22. Beier, G.: Kontrollüberzeugungen im Umgang mit Technik: Ein Persönlichkeitsmerkmal mit Relevanz für die Gestaltung technischer Systeme, Diss. Berlin (2004)
23. Rammstedt, B., John, O.P.: Kurzversion des big five inventory (BFI-K). Diagn. **51**(4), 195–206 (2005)
24. Rheinberg, F., Engeser, S., Vollmeyer, R.: Measuring components of flow: the flow-short-scale. In: Proceedings of the 1st International Positive Psychology Summit, Washington, D.C. (2002)
25. Rheinberg, F., Vollmeyer, R., Engeser, S.: Die Erfassung des Flow-Erlebens. In: Stiensmeier-Pelster, R., Rheinberg, F. (eds.) Diagnostik von Motivation und Selbstkonzept. Hogrefe, Göttingen (2003)

The Learning Effect of Augmented Reality Training in a Computer-Based Simulation Environment

Jung Hyup Kim[(✉)], Tiffany Chan, and Wei Du

Department of Industrial and Manufacturing Systems Engineering, University of Missouri,
Columbia, MO, USA
{kijung,tcd3b}@missouri.edu, wdgvd@mail.missouri.edu

Abstract. The purpose of this study was to investigate the learning effect of Augmented Reality (AR) in a computer-based simulation environment for training an operator to interact with a radar screen. The research team developed the AR training system for Anti-Air Warfare Coordinator (AAWC) and the training textbook for the same task. By using these, we compared the performance between a group trained by the AR method and another group trained by the textbook method. 24 undergraduate students in the Junior and Senior levels joined in this experiment. The experiment consisted of two sessions: training session and practice session. During the training session, 12 of the students completed the training lesson by using the AR training (Group A), and the other 12 students completed the training lesson using the AAWC training textbook. To evaluate the performance of AAWC task, we used Situational Awareness Global Assessment Technique (SAGAT). The ANOVA results indicate there was a significant performance difference between Group A and Group B, $F(1,12) = 12.29, p < 0.01$. Participants who were instructed by the AR training showed higher situation awareness compared to others. It supports the training, which is designed based on AR contents, can provide a positive learning effect in computer-based training simulation.

Keywords: Augmented reality · Human-in-the-loop simulation · Situation awareness

1 Introduction

Augmented Reality (AR) refers to the combination of virtual objects with the real world (Azuma, 1997). Recently, many researchers have developed applications for adapting AR into academic and industrial settings (Lee, 2012). The AR environment can improve individuals' performance significantly by reinforcing their perception and improving their contact with the real world. In this study, we investigated the learning effect of the AR training about an anti-air warfare coordinator (AAWC) task. The time window-based human-in-the-loop (HITL) simulation was used as a tool to measure participants' task performance during the experiment (See Fig. 1). This HITL simulation is a radar monitoring simulation. An operator must defend his/her ship against hostile aircraft (Kim, Rothrock, Tharanathan, & Thiruvengada, 2011; Macht, Nembhard, Kim, & Rothrock, 2014).

© Springer International Publishing Switzerland 2015
P. Zaphiris and A. Ioannou (Eds.): LCT 2015, LNCS 9192, pp. 406–414, 2015.
DOI: 10.1007/978-3-319-20609-7_38

Several Rules are embedded in the simulation so that participants must learn how to execute these task-specific rules during the training exercises.

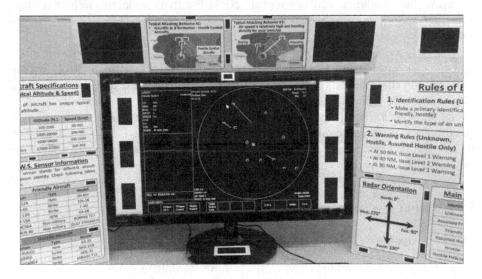

Fig. 1. Anti-Air warfare coordination human-in-the-loop training simulation

To conduct the experiment, the research team developed two different training methods: AR training system and traditional training textbook. Participants in Group A were trained on how to perform the AAWC task using the AR training, and Group B was taught with the traditional training textbook. During the experiment, the AR training system portrayed the AAWC training contents in 3D. This created a more exciting way to learn the information. To develop a collaborative AR environment and appropriate interactions between human and the AR system, the Oculus Rift goggle and Leap motion controller were used. The goggle allows participants to see the training material in 3D, such as demonstrating airplanes in 3D that fly in time with the different warning rule conditions. The motion controller provides learners an easy way to navigate the AR training system.

2   Literature Review

Many AR research studies support positive training effects of using the AR environment. First, the AR environment enables people to gain spatial relationships among complex ideas (Arvanitis et al., 2009), because the AR increases people's spatial skills (Martín-Gutiérrez et al., 2010). In addition, the AR can help learners to experience abnormal events that do not naturally occur in real life (Kaufmann, Steinbügl, Dünser, & Glück, 2005). By using 3D virtual objects, it is possible to create the abnormal events during the training session. This realistic interactive learning experience can reinforce learners' cognitive mapping regarding those events. Therefore, currently, the AR combines virtual objects or data with physical objects to create environments that allow one to think of invisible actions or ideas (Wu, Lee, Chang, & Liang, 2013). The most powerful advantage for using AR is improving performers' enthusiasm and attention and increasing their analytical skills (Wu et al., 2013). For that reason, this technology can create a novel experience, which decreases people's boredom and increases understanding during learning. (Lee, 2012, Li, 2005).

The AR environment is not only good for academic domains, but also for other industries such as medical (Kamphuis, Barsom, Schijven, & Christoph, 2014) and air traffic control environment (Hofmann, König, Bruder, & Bergner, 2012). For example, AR is used as an aid in making surgeries productive. Most surgeons normally develop mental pictures of where the surgery needs to take place. For that reason, they developed a method to find where the surgery must be performed. Shuhaiber (2004) also found that the AR of overlapping the images on a live video camera can assist surgeons to develop the desired mental pictures of the surgery.

3 Method

3.1 Participants

In this study, we have led to research efforts in AR training of AAWC task. 24 undergraduate students in the Junior and Senior levels participated in the experiment. During the training session, 12 students completed the training lesson by using the AR training (Group A), and the other 12 students completed the training lesson using the AAWC training textbook. Participants studied from one topic to the next one at their own speed. This experiment did not restrict anyone based on gender, ethnicity, or religion. Students, however, who had similar previous experience were excluded from this experiment.

3.2 Measures

To measure the performance of AAWC task, Situational Awareness Global Assessment Technique (SAGAT) was used. SAGAT is designed for the real time human-in-the-loop simulation such as an aviation monitoring or military cockpit (Endsley, 1988). This technique was used to collect objective data of SA across all the participants. Participants answered SA questionnaires after the simulation was stopped at random times. The responses were compared to the correct answers in the computer database. SA is defined as the awareness of the environment within time and space (Endsley 2012). The accuracy of situation awareness (SA Accuracy) is calculated by:

$$SA\ accuracy = \frac{Number\ of\ correct\ response}{Total\ number\ of\ SA\ probes} \times 100 \qquad (1)$$

3.3 AAWC Human-in-the-Loop Simulation

In this experiment, participants were trained on how to use the AAWC Human-In-The-Loop simulation. The participants took on the role of anti-air warfare coordinator. They were assigned to identify unknown aircraft and to apply rules of engagement (ROE).

Participants trained to take the appropriate actions on the unknown or hostile aircraft. In the AAWC simulation, the participants must focus on the radar screen to find unknown aircraft as soon as possible. They also need to perform the ROE as accurately as possible.

The ROE consists of three main tasks (see Fig. 2): identification task (Plan 1), warning task (Plan 2), and assign task (Plan 3). Figures 3, 4, and 5 show the hierarchical task analysis (HTA) charts for these respectively.

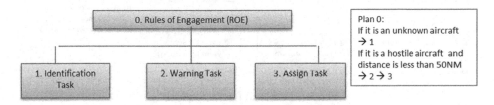

Fig. 2. Rules of engagements

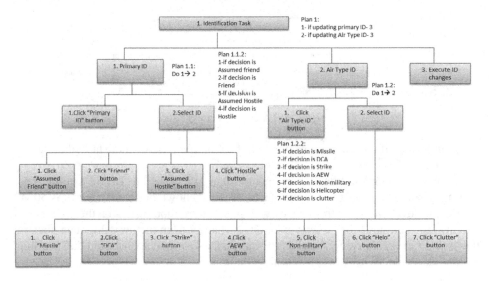

Fig. 3. HTA chart for identification task

Identification Task. The main goal of this task is to identify the unknown aircraft as soon as possible. There are two types of identification: (1) Primary ID, (2) Air Type ID (see Fig. 3).

If the participants decide to update Primary ID, they must go through Plan 1.1. First, the participants click "Primary ID" button. Then, they will select ID. If a participant chooses the unknown aircraft is a friendly aircraft, then he or she should click the "friend" button. After that, the selected aircraft will change its status from unknown to friendly aircraft.

If the participant would like to update Air type ID, he or she should follow Plan 1.2. To perform the Plan 1.2, click "Air Type ID" button. Then, select one of the Air IDs: Missile, DCA, Strike, AEW, Non-military, Helicopter, or Clutter.

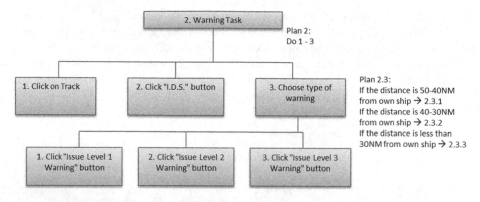

Fig. 4. HTA chart for warning task

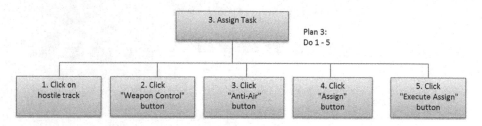

Fig. 5. HTA chart for assign task

Warning Task. If the participants would like to complete the warning task, they should follow Plan 2 (see Fig. 4).

In order to complete Plan 2, participants should click on the "I.D.S." button. After that, they should choose the warning level. If the unknown or hostile aircraft is 50–40 nautical miles (NM) away from the own ship, then they should click on the "Issue level 1 Warning" button. If the aircraft is 40–30 NM away from the own ship then click on the "Issue Level 2 Warning" button. If the aircraft is less than 30NM from the own ship, then click on the "Issue Level 3 Warning" button.

Assign Task. If the participants would like to complete the assign task, then they should follow the Plan 3 (see Fig. 5). To perform the Plan 3, the participants should execute plan 3.1, 3.2, 3.3, 3.4, and 3.5 in sequence.

3.4 Augmented Reality Training System

For the AR training, Oculus goggle and Leap Motion were used to create the AR environment (see Fig. 6). The Oculus goggle provides 3D virtual images with the real view. The Leap motion recognizes the participant's swiping gesture to turn the AR training slides. The AR training consists of 6 lessons: (1) introduction, (2) how to control the radar display, (3) how to acquire proper information, (4) how to perform the identification task, (5) how to perform the warning task, and (6) how to perform the assign task.

After each lesson, the participants will have a chance to practice what they have learned through the AR training slides.

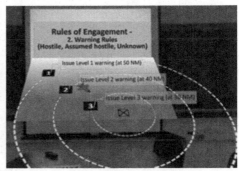

(a) AR training system   (b) AR training content

Fig. 6. Experimental setup for AR environment

3.5 Procedure

The total experimental time for each participant was about 4.5 h over a course of 3 days. Every participant executed 6 scenarios. Each scenario has 10 aircraft: 6 unknown, 3 friendly and 1 defense counter aircraft (DCA). The participants controlled the DCA to identify the unknown aircraft ID. The DCA helps them to collect a clear data about the aircraft identify. On Day 1, every participant learned how to use the AAWC simulation. However, Group A and B used different training methods. Group A learned by using the AR Training Method. Group B participants learned the information using the traditional training textbook. On Day 2, participants completed 3 scenarios. After each trial scenario, the participants asked to answer 9 SA questions. On Day 3, they completed another 3 scenarios. After each trial, they also asked answer 9 questions. So, each participant must answer 54 SA questions for two days.

4   Results

The ANOVA result shows there was a significant performance difference between Group A (M = 58.02, SD = 22.40) and Group B (M = 46.42, SD = 16.95), F $(1,12)$ = 12.29,$p < 0.01$. The Group A's SA accuracy was higher than Group B's (see Fig. 7). In addition, the learning curves in Fig. 8 support that the AR training can give a positive learning effect in the computer-based military training simulation.

5   Discussion and Conclusion

In this study, we found the performers who were trained by the AR training showed higher SA scores compared to those who used the textbook. One explanation of this is the

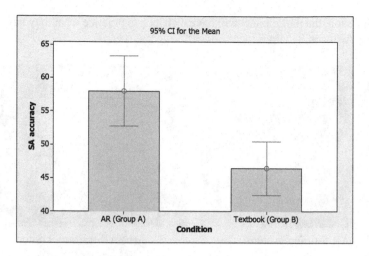

Fig. 7. Interval plot of SA accuracy between group A and B

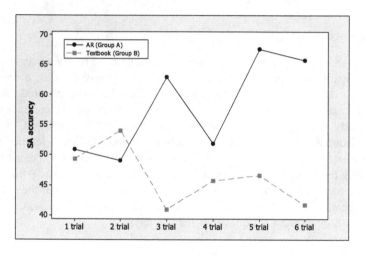

Fig. 8. Line plot for SA accuracy by trials

AR environment provides the participant an improved connection between declarative knowledge of AAWC rules and cognitive mapping of ROE. According to the research done by Kaufmann (2002), viewing objects in 3D and having the ability to interact with those objects can improve a learner's understanding of three-dimensional geometry. Another study also shows the students could effortlessly view not only the desired catalyst, but also its spatial structure when it reacts with another molecule (Maier, Tönnis, & Klinker, 2009). In the experiment, the radar monitoring screen displays all tracks in a 2D environment (see Fig. 1). However, the flight path of an aircraft is in a 3D environment. To be aware the accurate flying pattern of all aircraft, the learners need to develop an ability to draw the detailed 3D map of space in their heads. By using the AR training, participants learn effectively, how to interpret the 2D information as the 3D information.

Another explanation is the AR environment stimulates the motivation to learn about AAWC rules. The Group B less paid attention to the materials being taught compared to the participants in Group A, because the AR contents created an interactive environment to boost participant's interest in learning. Many research studies have found a similar positive effect on learner's motivation because of AR (Di Serio, Ibáñez, & Kloos, 2013; Liu, Tan, & Chu, 2007; Medicherla, Chang, & Morreale, 2010).

In this study, we have found the AR training method is better than the traditional textbook method to improve learners' situation awareness during the AAWC training. This result tells us the AR environment is helpful to train developing a cognitive map of 3D space. Moreover, the participants expressed higher interest in the AR training through learning. One limitation of this study is the each participant had only experienced 1.5-hour a day training and 6 trials for the HITL simulation. In order to understand the long-term learning effect of AR training, the experiment should last longer.

References

Arvanitis, T., Petrou, A., Knight, J., Savas, S., Sotiriou, S., Gargalakos, M., Gialouri, E.: Human factors and qualitative pedagogical evaluation of a mobile augmented reality system for science education used by learners with physical disabilities. Pers. Ubiquit. Comput. **13**(3), 243–250 (2009). doi:10.1007/s00779-007-0187-7

Azuma, R.T.: A survey of augmented reality. Presence **6**(4), 355–385 (1997)

Di Serio, Á., Ibáñez, M.B., Kloos, C.D.: Impact of an augmented reality system on students' motivation for a visual art course. Comput. Educ. **68**, 586–596 (2013). doi:10.1016/j.compedu.2012.03.002

Endsley, M.R.: Situation awareness global assessment technique (SAGAT). In: Paper Presented at the Aerospace and Electronics Conference, Proceedings of the IEEE 1988 National, NAECON 1988 (1988)

Endsley, M.R.: Designing for situation awareness: An approach to user-centered design. CRC Press, Boca Raton (2012)

Hofmann, T., König, C., Bruder, R., Bergner, J.: How to reduce workload–augmented reality to ease the work of air traffic controllers. Work: A Journal of Prevention. Assess. Rehabil. **41**, 1168–1173 (2012)

Kamphuis, C., Barsom, E., Schijven, M., & Christoph, N.: Augmented reality in medical education? Perspectives on medical education, pp. 1–12 (2014)

Kaufmann, H.: Construct3D: an augmented reality application for mathematics and geometry education. In: Paper Presented at the Proceedings of the tenth ACM international conference on Multimedia (2002)

Kaufmann, H., Steinbügl, K., Dünser, A., Glück, J.: General training of spatial abilities by geometry education in augmented reality. Annu. Rev. CyberTherapy Telemedicine: A Decade of VR **3**, 65–76 (2005)

Kim, J.H., Rothrock, L., Tharanathan, A., Thiruvengada, H.: Investigating the Effects of Metacognition in Dynamic Control Tasks. In: Jacko, J.A. (ed.) Human-Computer Interaction, Part I, HCII 2011. LNCS, vol. 6761, pp. 378–387. Springer, Heidelberg (2011)

Lee, K.: Augmented reality in education and training. TechTrends **56**(2), 13–21 (2012)

Li, C.: Augmented Reality in Medical. Advanced Interface Design, p. 49 (2005)

Liu, T.-Y., Tan, T.-H., Chu, Y.-L.: 2D barcode and augmented reality supported english learning system. In: Paper presented at the 6th IEEE/ACIS International Conference on Computer and Information Science, 2007. ICIS 2007 (2007)

Macht, G.A., Nembhard, D.A., Kim, J.H., Rothrock, L.: Structural models of extraversion, communication, and team performance. Int. J. Ind. Ergon. **44**(1), 82–91 (2014)

Maier, P., Tönnis, M., Klinker, G.: Augmented Reality for teaching spatial relations. In: Paper Presented at the Conference of the International Journal of Arts & Sciences, Toronto (2009)

Martín-Gutiérrez, J., Luís Saorín, J., Contero, M., Alcañiz, M., Pérez-López, D.C., Ortega, M.: Design and validation of an augmented book for spatial abilities development in engineering students. Comput. Graph. **34**(1), 77–91 (2010)

Medicherla, P. S., Chang, G., Morreale, P.: Visualization for increased understanding and learning using augmented reality. In: Paper Presented at the Proceedings of the international conference on Multimedia information retrieval (2010)

Shuhaiber, J.H.: Augmented reality in surgery. Arch. Surg. **139**(2), 170–174 (2004)

Wu, H.-K., Lee, S.W.-Y., Chang, H.-Y., Liang, J.-C.: Current status, opportunities and challenges of augmented reality in education. Comput. Educ. **62**, 41–49 (2013)

Virtual Music Teacher for New Music Learners with Optical Music Recognition

Viet-Khoi Pham[✉], Hai-Dang Nguyen, and Minh-Triet Tran

Faculty of Information Technology, University of Science, VNU-HCM, Hồ Chí Minh, Vietnam
(pvkhoi,nhdang12)@apcs.vn, tmtriet@fit.hcmus.edu.vn

Abstract. Learn to read and understand a music sheet, then play it on a musical instrument are difficult tasks to most beginner music learners. This motivates the authors to propose Virtual Music Teacher, a system to assist beginner music learners in their learning process. By applying our proposed lightweight Optical Music Recognition algorithm to scan and recognize a music sheet, then combine with sound classifying technique, the proposed system can learn what note to be played next, then help a music learner to play it correctly. The experimental results on the dataset consisting of 15 musical scores for beginners show that the proposed system can classify with precision up to 99.9 % using multiple SVM classifiers approach, whereas the sound classifying technique using Fast Fourier Transform can classify note's pitch recorded from a piano with precision up to 95.71 %. The system is implemented as an application on mobile devices and can be used to assist a music learner to play not only piano but other musical instruments as well.

Keywords: Optical music recognition · Note's pitch recognition · Virtual music teacher

1 Introduction

It is difficult for a beginner music learner to read a musical score sheet, then to recognize a musical note, i.e. its pitch according to its position on staff lines and its duration established by its note head, stem, and flag. In class, a teacher helps new learners to identify and to play notes in a musical score sheet. However when music learners practice at home, there is no one to warn them when they read or play wrong notes. Therefore, it is necessary to have helpers to notify learners when they make mistakes and assist them in recognizing what musical notes to play next, even when they are practicing by themselves at home, without any teachers.

Although there are different games and utilities in computers or mobile devices to teach or support users to learn playing music, these applications mainly provide lessons, games, or exercises with fixed contents or scenarios. Thus, it would be more efficient for users to have real-time guidance adapting to their current practice on real musical instruments. This motivates us to propose Virtual Music Teacher, a system to assist beginner pianists in their learning process to play piano. Our proposed system can also be adapted to assist music learners to play other instruments.

© Springer International Publishing Switzerland 2015
P. Zaphiris and A. Ioannou (Eds.): LCT 2015, LNCS 9192, pp. 415–426, 2015.
DOI: 10.1007/978-3-319-20609-7_39

Our proposed Virtual Music Teacher system has two main useful features for new music learners. First, it can recognize musical notations from regular printed musical score sheets, then speaks out which note to be performed next. Second, it records sound performed by the learner in real-time, recognizes which note is played, checks with the recognized note in the musical score sheet, and give warnings to the learner if he or she plays a wrong note.

The main contribution of this paper is that we propose our idea to apply optical music recognition (OMR [1]) and sound recognition to develop a Virtual Music Teacher system to assist new music learners. We propose an improved version of our light-weight method for optical music recognition [2] to recognize musical notations in musical score sheets with high accuracy and low computational cost. Besides, we also utilize a simple method based on Fast Fourier Transform (FFT) to efficiently recognize musical notes from audio recorded in real-time from a piano at difference distances.

We conduct experiments for our proposed OMR algorithm with 15 musical scores for beginners to play piano and our method achieves precision up to 99.9 % using multiple SVM classifiers approach. Then we also conduct experiments for musical note classification from audio recorded in real-time from a piano and the precision is up to 95.71 %. With these promising experimental results, our method and its implementation on mobile devices can be used to assist new music learners in their studying and practice to play piano as well as other musical instruments.

The content of this paper is as follows. In Sect. 2, we briefly review related methods of optical music recognition. Section 3 presents the overview of our proposed Virtual Music Teacher for new music learners. The detailed information of our proposed method to recognize a music sheet is presented in Sect. 4 whereas our method to recognize musical notes based on audio is discussed in Sect. 5. Section 6 shows experimental results for optical music recognition and musical note recognition from audio. Conclusions and future work are discussed in Sect. 7.

2   Background & Related Works

There are various applications on computers or mobile devices to help users to learn how to play musical instruments. These applications usually provide lessons or games to assist users in learning to play music. Several applications also allow a user to practice with audio or visual hints on a virtual musical instrument, such as a virtual keyboard of a piano. However, existing applications do not provide real-time warnings or hints corresponding to the real context when a music learner is practicing on a real musical instrument.

To realize our idea of a virtual music teacher with useful warnings and hints in real-time, the first task is Optical Music Recognition (OMR), i.e. to recognize all music symbols in a score sheet. In late 1960 s, Pruslin [3] and Prerau [4] initiated the first steps into the field of OMR. Initially the main objective of OMR is to preserve musical scores and to help music composers to digitalize music sheets into machine-readable format. However, OMR can also be applied to develop a system that can automatically perform a song directly from a musical score sheet [5].

Although there are different OMR methods, they usually follow a common process. After necessary pre-processing steps, staff lines should be removed before music symbols are extracted and classified with a particular classification method. We inherit this common process in our proposed method [2] and its enhanced version in this paper.

Various classification methods have been proposed to recognize music symbols extracted from a musical score. Template matching is among the first and simple approaches for music symbol recognition [6,7]. Other techniques in machine learning are also used to process music symbols, such as Hidden Markov Model [8], Support Vector Machine [9], or Neural Network [9]. In our proposed method [2] and its enhanced version, we also use Support Vector Machine (SVM) as the main tool to classify a musical notation. However, we do not use a single SVM classifier but we train multiple classifiers and combine the outputs of them to determine which class a musical notation belongs to. By this way, we can boost the overall accuracy of our method.

3   Proposed System

Figures 1 and 2 illustrate the overview of the two main processes in our proposed Virtual Music Teacher, including the musical score recognition process to give hints and the sound recognition process to give warnings to music learners, respectively.

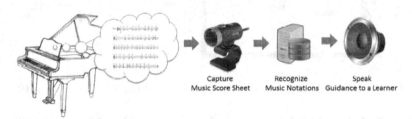

Capture   Recognize   Speak
Music Score Sheet   Music Notations   Guidance to a Learner

Fig. 1. Overview of musical score recognition process to give hints to music learners

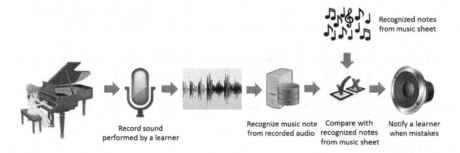

Fig. 2. Overview of sound recognition process to give warnings to music learners

In Fig. 1, a regular printed musical score sheet is captured by a regular camera. Musical notes and notations are recognized by our proposed light-weight OMR algorithm. Hints are spoken out by a speaker corresponding to a recognized note so that a learner knows which note to play next.

In Fig. 2, when a learner is playing a music lesson, his or her performance is recorded and processed in real-time to recognize which note is performed. The note recognized from recorded audio is compared with the expected note recognized from music sheet to verify if the learner plays the correct note. If the learner plays a wrong note, a warning is generated and notified to the learner via a speaker.

4   Light-Weight Optical Music Recognition Method

We follow the common framework for recognizing musical notes to propose our light-weight OMR method [10]. Figure 3 shows the preprocessing and recognition phases of our OMR method.

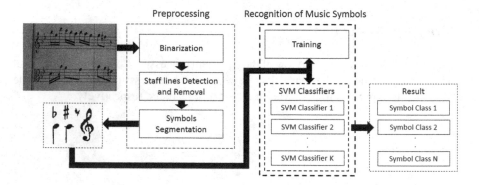

Fig. 3. Proposed framework for preprocessing and recognition phases in OMR

In the first phase, staff lines are removed after the binarization step. We simplify and apply the Stable Paths approach for this step [11]. We also suggest a method to simplify the complexity of the symbol segmentation step based on the idea in [11]. In the music symbol recognition stage, we suggest a new way for representing music symbols by using grids of $M * N$ cells and apply multi-lightweight SVM classifiers for classification of this type of features.

The system is the enhanced version of our method in [2]. In the enhanced version, staff lines detected are used for filtering out the noise symbols. The removing staff lines process is also improved with a method to avoid breaking the symbols apart. One other improvement is to use the symbol beams detected to deduce the note's type.

4.1   Preprocessing

Binarization.

The binarization algorithm proposed by Otsu [12] is suggested to separate the image of the score into foreground and background. Otsu's method is a global binarization algorithm, thus for image with dark and white areas, the algorithm is likely to fail.

However, music learners who use the system for their training, is required to take a clear picture of the musical score. Hence the score's image is always expected to be clear without dark areas. As a result, only using Otsu's global binarization algorithm still brings satisfactory results in this step.

Staff Lines Detection and Removal:

Staff lines detection:

It is necessary to detect and remove staff lines from music sheets, since they overlap with music symbols and make the segmentation and classification step become difficult. By detecting staff lines' positions, the results can be used to determine the pitch of any musical notes. Moreover, staff lines' positions can also be used for validating the presence of other music symbols (i.e. any symbols that are far from the staff lines will be ignored as there is a high possibility that they are the lyrics, titles… or any unused data in the score).

One existing algorithm to detect staff lines is using Hough Line transformation [13] to detect all lines in the image. However, the authors suggest using a simplified method based on the Stable Paths approach [11]. The approach's idea is to build a graph for the musical score. Every pixel in the score is represented by a vertex; and if 2 pixels in 2 consecutive columns are adjacent to each other, then there exists an edge connecting the 2 vertices. Every edge in the graph is assigned with weight based on the following rule: initially, each edge is given with weight equal to 2; if the 2 pixels of the edge are diagonally adjacent, the weight is incremented by 1; after that, the edge's weight is incremented by a value equal to the number of white pixels in the 2 of them. The graph is successfully built, and staff lines' position can be detected by finding the shortest paths from the first to the last column of the image.

The problem of finding the shortest paths from the first to the last column can be solved using dynamic programming. Let $pixel_{i,j}$ be the pixel on row i and column j of the image, $F_{i,j}$ be the cost of the shortest path that starts from a pixel in column 1 and stops at $pixel_{i,j}$, and $w_{x,y}$ be the weight of the edge connecting $pixel_x$ and $pixel_y$. $F_{i,j}$ is calculated using the following recurrence:

$$F_{i,j} = \min \begin{cases} F_{i-1,j-1} + w_{(i-1,j-1),(i,j)} \\ F_{i,j-1} + w_{(i,j-1),(i,j)} \\ F_{i,j+1} + w_{(i,j+1),(i,j)} \end{cases}$$

The value of the shortest path is the minimum value in the last column of F, and the shortest path itself is the staff line.

The algorithm's time complexity is high, since after one path is found, that staff line is removed from the score and the graph is rebuilt to find the next staff line. For instance, there is a large computational cost to run the algorithm 20 times to find 20 staff lines in a 1000 by 2000 music sheet. Hence, this problem leads to the idea of the Stable Paths approach [11]. The idea is as follows: let *cols* be the number of columns in the image; let the end pixel of the shortest path starting from $pixel_{i1,1}$ (an arbitrary pixel in column 1) be $pixel_{i2,cols}$, then if the start pixel of the shortest path ending at $pixel_{i2,cols}$ is $pixel_{i1,1}$, we say the path from $pixel_{i1,1}$ to $pixel_{i2,cols}$ is a stable path.

Thus, it is possible to find all staff lines at once by finding all stable paths in the graph. However, it is necessary to validate the staff lines by calculating the percent of black pixels lie on the paths (the threshold value is taken as 70 % by the authors).

Staff lines removal:

After detecting all staff lines in the musical score, it is not obvious to simply remove them by assigning them with white pixels, because this will cut through the music symbols and divide them into smaller different parts. Thus, the authors propose a simple idea: for every black pixel p belongs to a staff line, we find the 2 nearest white pixels above and below it on its column; if the distance between the 2 pixels is less than a threshold value (taken as *staffLineHeight* + *1* by the authors), then the pixel is assigned with white pixels to remove it from the score. This method is to prevent removing pixels that both lie on staff lines and music symbols (Fig. 4).

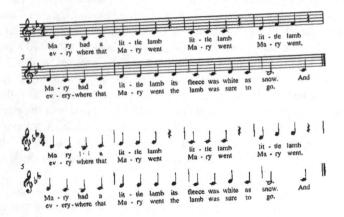

Fig. 4.   Successfully remove staff lines when the musical score is inclined

Symbols Segmentation:

It is possible to collect all connected components of black pixels in the image after removing staff lines, then treat them as each individual music symbol for classifying in the next step. However, there is a case when multiple quarter notes are connected by beams, leading to a component consisting of several notes. Thus, beams need to be detected to split the component into different notes, and to convert the notes into appropriate notes (i.e. quarter note connected with 2 beams becomes sixteenth note, etc.).

The authors suggest using the idea of beam detection from [11]. Firstly, stems connecting beams and noteheads are removed from the component. The stems are detected by finding long vertical run-length of blacks pixels with length larger than a threshold ($2 * staffSpaceHeight$). After that, connected components are found again on the component. The beams will be the components with height less than $4 * staffSpaceHeight$, width over $2 * staffSpaceHeight + 2.5 * staffLineHeight$, and are connected with stems (the values are taken experimentally).

The remaining connected components are extracted out after the beams are removed. The components are considered as music symbols to go through the next step of classification (Fig. 5).

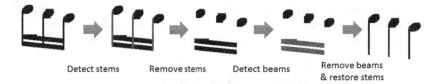

Detect stems   Remove stems   Detect beams   Remove beams
& restore stems

Fig. 5. Process of detecting and removing beams

4.2 Music Symbol Recognition

For each music symbol segmented, the objective is to classify it into the correct class of symbol. Support vector machines algorithm is used as the classifier for this step. The approach of using SVM classifiers is based on the method that is applied in [2]. There are 2 processes in the classification step, the training phase and the classification phase (Fig. 6).

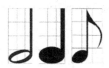

Fig. 6. Examples of representing music symbols by grids of $M * N$ cells

Before working on the training and the classification phase, it is necessary to convert music symbols into feature vectors. As each symbol has different height and width compared with the others, the next step is to represent music symbols by grids of the same size $M * N$. For each symbol of size $W * H$ (W – width, H – height), the image of the symbol is divided into grid of size $M * N$. For each cell (i, j) in the $M * N$ grid, the cell is assigned with color black or white depending on the higher number of black or white pixels in the corresponding cell (i,j). The grid is then converted into a 1-dimensional feature vector with size $1 * (M * N)$. The feature vectors of all music symbols are then used as training and testing data for the SVM classifier.

Given an image of a music symbol, the SVM classifier will find the class with the highest probability that the music symbol belongs to. However, the precision result achieved using one SVM classifier is not high as expected. Thus, the authors propose to apply a new method of using multiple SVM classifiers to train and classify in order to improve the accuracy on the classification problem. In general, a number of k SVM classifiers are trained with only a proportion of samples data (instead of all of the data for a single classifier). When classifying a music symbol, the class that the majority of SVM classifiers predict is chosen to be the result class.

Several connected components extracted from the previous step are not music symbols but noise. The noise can be filtered out by finding the distance between each component to the nearest staff line. If the distance is larger than $2.5 * staffSpaceHeight$, then the component is considered as noise and it is removed.

After recognizing all music symbols in the score, the notes are sorted by their coordinates to figure out the order to play the notes. The coordinates of the symbols combined with the positions of the staff lines help to deduce the pitch of the symbols.

5   Recognize Music Notes Based on Audio

The authors aim to serve and help beginner music learners to lean and practice music, thus the system is only developed for using with music sheets consist of the following fundamental music symbols: quarter note, eighth note, half note, whole note, flat, sharp, and natural. As beginner music learners usually practice with one hand, the authors only conduct experiment on notes belonging to 2 octaves C4 and C5.

In order to recognize the musical note's pitch from a given audio file, the authors conduct recording sound of each note's pitch. Each note's pitch is recorded 5 times, as there are 2 octaves with 12 pitches per octave, we have 120 recording files in total. After having recorded, the authors reduce the noise and use Fourier Transform algorithm to convert sound waves into frequency [14]. Then, the authors base on the highest peak of frequency in order to distinguish and identify the note's pitch (Fig. 7).

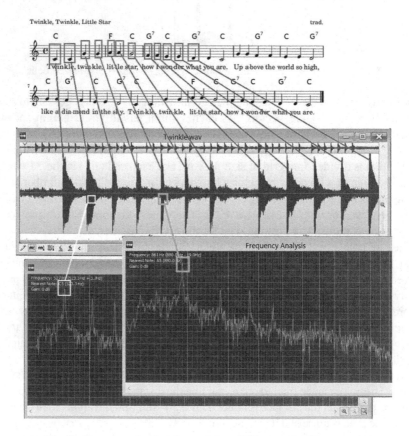

Fig. 7. Every note's pitch has a unique highest peak of frequency

The authors decide to use Fourier Transform because the experimental results show that 100 % notes that have the same pitch will produce the same highest peak of frequency, and the highest peak of frequency is distinguishable between different note's pitch. This dataset is used for the system to recognize new input note's audio (Fig. 8).

	C	C#	D	Eb	E	F	F#	G	G#	A	Bb	B
0	16.35	17.32	18.35	19.45	20.60	21.83	23.12	24.50	25.96	27.50	29.14	30.87
1	32.70	34.65	36.71	38.89	41.20	43.65	46.25	49.00	51.91	55.00	58.27	61.74
2	65.41	69.30	73.42	77.78	82.41	87.31	92.50	98.00	103.8	110.0	116.5	123.5
3	130.8	138.6	146.8	155.6	164.8	174.6	185.0	196.0	207.7	220.0	233.1	246.9
4	261.6	277.2	293.7	311.1	329.6	349.2	370.0	392.0	415.3	440.0	466.2	493.9
5	523.3	554.4	587.3	622.3	659.3	698.5	740.0	784.0	830.6	880.0	932.3	987.8
6	1047	1109	1175	1245	1319	1397	1480	1568	1661	1760	1865	1976
7	2093	2217	2349	2489	2637	2794	2960	3136	3322	3520	3729	3951
8	4186	4435	4699	4978	5274	5588	5920	6272	6645	7040	7459	7902

Fig. 8. Frequency of pitches [15]

6 Experiments and Implementations

6.1 OMR

Experimental results on the dataset consisting of 4929 music symbols taken from 18 modern music sheets in the Synthetic Score Database [16] show that our proposed method is able to classify printed musical scores with accuracy up to 99.56 % using 11 SVM classifiers trained on 80 % sample images [2]. However, as the authors only aim to develop the system for beginner music learners, the system is tested on a new dataset consist of 15 simple music sheets for beginners using the same number of SVM classifiers and proportion of samples data (11 SVM classifiers and 80 % samples). As the new dataset is more simple compared to the Synthetic Score Database, the accurarcy acquired becomes higher: 99.9 % precision and 98.34 % recall.

6.2 Recognize Note's Pitch Based on Audio

The authors propose experiments to test the accuracy of the recognition step in the case the recording environment has noise and the recorder is placed far from the player.

Our experiment is conducted by recording multiple times the performance of a music learner. The records are taken from different angles, distances, relative to the position of the player (the record even has noise and errors made by the player when he/she mistakenly plays 2 notes at the same time). After that, the authors test the accuracy of the system by playing each record and take note of the result returning from the system everytime it listens to the sound of a note. More specifically, when the system hears the sound of a note, the system will analyze the sound wave and use Fourier Transform algorithm to get the sound frequency and compare it with its dataset. The frequency data in the dataset that looks closest to the new input audio is returned as the result from the system.

There is one problem in the case that the player plays 2 notes at the same time. This leads to the frequency graph having 2 peaks with the same height (each peak for one note's pitch). However, the algorithm only chooses the highest one, because the system is unable to know when the player makes mistakes. Hence, the system may output the wrong note in this case. The problem is illustrated in Fig. 9.

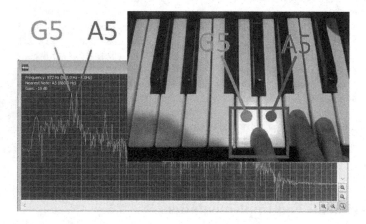

Fig. 9. There are 2 highest peaks when the player plays 2 notes at the same time

The experiment is conducted on a musical score consists of 42 musical notes, including 36 quarter notes and 6 half notes. The performance of the player on this musical score is recorded five times with the distance between the recorder and the player as follows: two times on the left and two times on the right, with the distance of 0.25 m and 0.5 m, one time in the middle with the distance 0.25 m. In 210 notes played by different beginner piano players, only 9 notes are recognized incorrectly, yielding the accuracy of the experiment to be 95.71 %. All the incorrect cases are due to a player presses on two or more keys on the keyboard at the same time.

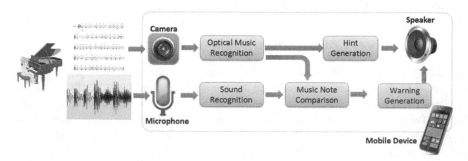

Fig. 10. System implementation on mobile devices

6.3 Implementation

We implement our proposed Virtual Music Teacher in two versions. Beside the initial prototype with a regular laptop with a webcam and a speaker, we also develop our system on mobile devices. Figure 10 shows the main processing components of Virtual Music Teacher implemented on a mobile device. A new music learner can simply use a mobile device to capture a regular printed music lesson via the built-in camera, then our system recognizes music notes, generates hints via the built-in speaker, records sound via the built-in microphone, recognizes notes in recorded sound, and generates warnings via the built-in speaker.

7   Conclusion

Our Virtual Music Teacher system is appropriate to assist new music learners in the very first step to study music and play musical instruments. Lessons for beginners are usually easy with simple notes and notations. This ensures that our proposed method OMR can provide high accuracy to give hints for a music learner to play. Furthermore, such lessons are usually in nearly monotonous rhythms with slow tempo. Thus, the sound recognition process to give warnings to music learners can perform well in audio segmentation and note recognition.

We will continue to integrate the augmented reality feature for smart eyewares to show hints as real-time highlights on the keyboard of a piano to further support to a music learner on playing correct keys.

References

1. Optical Music Recognition Bibliography, a list of works done on OMR. http://ddmal.music.mcgill.ca/wiki/Optical_Music_Recognition_Bibliography Accessed on 25 February 2014
2. Pham, V.K, Nguyen, H.D., Nguyen-Khac, T.A., Tran, M.T.: Apply Lightweight Recognition Algorithms in Optical Music Recognition. In: Seventh International Conference on Machine Vision (ICMV 2014). Proceedings of SPIE vol. 9445 (2015)
3. Pruslin, D.: Automatic recognition of sheet music. PhD thesis, Massachusetts Institute of Technology (1966)
4. Prerau, D.: Computer pattern recognition of standard engraved music notation. PhD thesis, Massachusetts Institute of Technology (1970)
5. Byrd, D.: Optical Music Recognition Systems survey. Indiana University (rev, School of Informatics and School of Music (2007)
6. Rossant, F., Bloch, I.: Robust and adaptive OMR system including fuzzy modeling, fusion of musical rules, and possible error detection. EURASIP J. Appl. Sig. Process. **2007**(1), 160 (2007)
7. Toyama, F., Shoji, K., Miyamichi, J.: Symbol recognition of printed piano scores with touching symbols. In: Proceedings of the International Conference on Pattern Recognition, pp. 480–483 (2006)

8. Pugin, L.: Optical music recognition of early typographic prints using Hidden Markov Models. In: Proceedings of the International Society for Music Information Retrieval, pp. 53–56 (2006)
9. Rebelo, A., Capela, G., Cardoso, J.S.: Optical recognition of music symbols: A comparative study. Int. J. Doc. Anal. Recogn. **13**, 19–31 (2010)
10. Rebelo, A., Fujinaga, I., Paszkiewicz, F., Marcal, A.R.S., Guedes, C., Cardoso, J.S.: Optical music recognition: state-of the-art and open issues. Int. J. Multimedia Inf. Retrieval **1**(3), 173–190 (2012)
11. Rebelo, A.: New methodologies towards an automatic optical recognition of handwritten musical scores. Master of Science thesis, University of Porto, Portugal (2008)
12. Otsu, N.: A Threshold Selection Method from Gray-Level Histograms. IEEE Trans. Syst. Man Cybern. **9**(1), 62–66 (1979)
13. Duda, R.O., Hart, P.E.: Use of the Hough Transformation to Detect Lines and Curves in Pictures. Commun. ACM **15**(1), 11–15 (1972)
14. Marchand, S.: An efficient pitch-tracking algorithm using a combination of Fourier Transforms. In: Proceedings of the Conference on Digital Audio Effects (DAFX 2001), pp. 170–174 (2001)
15. Frequency of pitches: http://www.seventhstring.com/resources/notefrequencies.html Accessed on 8 March 2015
16. Synthetic Score Database. http://gamera.informatik.hsnr.de/addons/musicstaves/ testsetmusicstaves.tar.gz Accessed on 25 February 2014

The Visual Design and Implementation of an Embodied Conversational Agent in a Shared Decision-Making Context (eCoach)

Scott Robertson[1(✉)], Rob Solomon[1], Mark Riedl[2],
Theresa Wicklin Gillespie[3], Toni Chociemski[4], Viraj Master[3],
and Arun Mohan[5]

[1] Interactive Media Technology Center,
Georgia Institute of Technology, Atlanta, GA, USA
{scott,rob}@imtc.gatech.edu
[2] School of Interactive Computing,
Georgia Institute of Technology, Atlanta, GA, USA
riedl@cc.gatech.edu
[3] School of Medicine, Emory University, Atlanta, GA, USA
{tgilles,vmaster}@emory.edu
[4] School of Public Health, Emory University, Atlanta, GA, USA
tchocie@emory.edu
[5] ApolloMD, Atlanta, GA, USA
arun.mohan@emory.edu

Abstract. This paper outlines the design process and challenges of creating a character for our implementation of an embodied conversational agent (ECA), specifically integrating diverse views from focus groups consisting of individuals representing different levels of socio-economic status and health literacy. Initial focus groups consisting of members from both higher and lower socio-economic status and health literacy found the stylized ECA to be unappealing. Later focus groups conducted after completion of the educational intervention better accepted the ECA, reporting it to be acceptable.

Keywords: Computer supported collaborative learning · Design and evaluation of collaboration technology · Interdisciplinary studies on collaboration technology and learning · Methodologies for the study of computer supported collaborative learning and /or technology-enhanced learning

1 Introduction

In many health care situations, patients and their providers must choose a course of treatment from among many viable options. When there is not a clearly superior course of treatment, there are often major discrepancies between patient preferences and care received and these discrepancies can challenge patient autonomy, quality of care and can result in costly and unnecessary treatments. Shared decision-making (SDM) can help to better align patient preferences, values and health care goals with the care they receive [1].

© Springer International Publishing Switzerland 2015
P. Zaphiris and A. Ioannou (Eds.): LCT 2015, LNCS 9192, pp. 427–437, 2015.
DOI: 10.1007/978-3-319-20609-7_40

Shared Decision-Making (SDM) is a collaborative process of interaction and communication between patients and their providers allowing them to make health care decisions together. SDM takes into account the clinician's knowledge and experience, the best scientific evidence available as well as the patient's goals, preferences and values. Research demonstrates that SDM can increase patients' knowledge, reduce uncertainty, improve quality of care and reduce costs, often by limiting overuse of treatments that patients do not value [1].

Implementation of SDM has been limited by the available time for patients to explore treatment options with their physicians. This process is further complicated by the presence of low health literacy. Patient decision aids can help foster SDM, however, decision aids often do not address low health literacy users [2]. The usage of ECAs has been identified as a possible solution to facilitate shared and knowledge transfer to patients with low health literacy [3].

The primary goal of this study was to identify the characteristics of an ECA to help patients understand the benefits and drawbacks of different treatment choices in response to prostate cancer using a user-centered design process. Through this process, an African-American character was created in a stylized, two-dimensional animation style and with facial, hand and body gestures intended to convey empathetic emotions such as optimism and concern. Facial expressions and body poses and gestures were authored to display in conjunction with a physician-authored patient dialogue between the ECA and patient.

This paper outlines the design process and challenges of creating this character for our implementation of an ECA (eCoach), specifically the diverse views of focus groups consisting of different socio-economic groups and levels of health literacy. Initial focus groups consisting of members representing both higher and lower socio-economic status and levels of health literacy found the stylized ECA to be unappealing. Later input after completion of the educational intervention accepted the portrayal of the ECA, reporting it to be acceptable.

We also present the qualitative and quantitative findings of a series of user focus groups conducted during the development of the eCoach ECA and the design implications and lessons learned for future work using ECAs within a shared decision-making context, particularly when designing to accommodate differing health literacy and socio-economic backgrounds.

2 Health Literacy and Shared Decision-Making

Numerous decision aids have been developed to foster shared decision-making, but most fail to address the needs of patients with low health literacy, which is particularly prevalent among racial and ethnic minorities. Health literacy is an individual's ability to read and comprehend a range of health-related materials required to successfully function in the healthcare environment [4]. Health literacy includes the ability to perform both basic reading and numerical tasks and requires a complex combination of analytical and decision-making skills to be applied to health situations.

Low health literacy disproportionately affects minorities – more than half of African American adults and two-thirds of Hispanic adults have low health literacy compared to less than one-third of white adults [5]. Decision aids utilizing embodied conversational agents have shown promise at addressing health disparities due to low health literacy [3, 6].

3   Embodied Conversational Agents for Health Decision Aids

There is evidence to consider face-to-face consultation with a health provider, coupled with well designed, written instructional materials, a health care best practice, especially when communicating health information to patients with low health literacy [7]. The many affordances of face-to-face consultation include the use of verbal and non-verbal cues and behaviors, such as empathy and immediacy, which can foster patient trust and satisfaction and enable better health communication and understanding. Because they simulate face-to-face communication, embodied conversational agents have shown promise for delivering health information in decision aids [3, 6].

An embodied conversational agent is a user interface which simulates face-to-face conversation, typically by presenting the user with an animated, human character who talks to the user and often also uses other naturalistic modes of communication such as facial expressions and hand, head and body gestures [8]. The use of an ECA in a health decision aid offers many potential advantages:

1. Patients can learn essential health information without requiring time from their provider.
2. The interactive, conversational modes of communication used by ECAs can overcome passivity limitations of traditional health decision aids and can promote active learning and decision-making.
3. ECAs can allow patients to take adequate time to understand important information, repeating content or explaining content in simpler terms as necessary, all critical features for patients with low health literacy.

4   Decision Aids for Prostate Cancer

Prostate cancer is an ideal candidate to test interventions intended to increase shared decision-making and decrease decisional regret. Prostate cancer is a leading cause of morbidity and mortality in men. Its direct treatment costs alone are estimated to be $11.9 billion annually [9]. There are several different treatment options for prostate cancer patients that do not differ greatly in efficacy. However, the potential side effects and possibilities for adverse events vary significantly among the various treatment options. Patients can have difficulty understanding the large range of treatment options and each option's adverse event and possible side effects profile, often leading to distress and decisional regret. SDM can address these issues by seeking to better match patients' preferences to the treatment option ultimately chosen.

Although decision aids and educational materials can reduce some of the time and cost burdens to physicians for SDM, research shows that those for localized prostate cancer are inadequate [10]. We have chosen to explore the use of an ECA-based decision aid for localized prostate cancer as a possible better alternative.

5   Effects of Appearance in Embodied Conversational Agents

The physical appearance of an ECA and the use of embodied, non-verbal cues has been shown to impact patients' perceived trust and understanding [11].

5.1   Agent Realism

McDonnell, et al. investigated how different rendering styles, ranging from abstract to realistic, affect users' perception of a virtual human character, finding that more abstractly depicted, cartoon characters were often considered highly appealing and more pleasant than realistically rendered characters and that they were rated as more friendly and trustworthy and therefore may be more appropriate for certain virtual interactions (e.g. health care decision aids, motivational agents, etc.) [12]. These findings also confirm the Uncanny Valley hypothesis [13] that as realism is increased in rendering and animating a virtual human character, at some point, the character begins to trigger increasingly negative reactions: Study participants experienced relatively negative reactions to several versions of a moderately realistic character compared to highly realistic characters or cartoon characters.

5.2   Agent Gender, Race and Age

Other studies have shown that gender, race and age of pedagogical agents can have significant effects on a learner's motivation, self-efficacy, engagement and satisfaction [14, 15]. Social psychology research suggests that people are more persuaded by members of their in-group and research with ECAs generally confirms this finding, though with some context and task-dependent caveats [14–16].

For example, Baylor et al. found that Caucasian students who were assigned an African-American virtual agent "expert" in an education task had greater self-efficacy (confidence) and interest towards the topic than those who were assigned a Caucasian agent, perhaps because their expectations of what a domain expert should look like were challenged. In contrast, they found that African-American students have strong affiliations with same-race agents, performed better and were more satisfied with an African-American agent [16].

5.3   Interactions Between Agent Appearance and Task Domain

A series of experiments by Ring, et al. demonstrate an interaction between virtual agent appearance and task domain [17]. A cartoon-rendered character was rated as more likeable and caring for a social dialogue task and more friendly for a health counseling task, but a realistic rendering of the character was rated higher for appropriateness, trustworthiness and familiarity for the health counseling task. The effects of character proportions (i.e. realistic cartoon rendering vs. exaggerated, stylized cartoon rendering) were also explored, showing similar results: a highly exaggerated cartoon character was rated as being more friendly regardless of task, but a more realistic cartoon rendering was rated as being more appropriate for a health counseling task.

Studies by Gulz and Haake demonstrate that when learners are given a choice between a more realistic versus stylized visual appearance of virtual pedagogical agents and also a choice between engaging with an agent via a strictly task oriented communication style versus a more socially oriented communication style, there was a significant correlation between preferences for agents with a social communication style and a more stylized visual appearance [18, 19].

6 eCoach: An ECA-Based Prostate Cancer Decision Aid

In order to investigate the feasibility and acceptability of an ECA as a health decision aid, we developed a prototype system consisting of a brief conversation with a virtual agent health advisor (eCoach) to inform and advise prostate cancer patients of the range of treatment options available to them as well as the risk factors and possible side effects associated with each option. We developed an animated, 2D character using the Unity game engine (see Fig. 1). The agent interacts with the user via a turn-based conversation driven by a branching dialogue tree and state-machine-based dialogue engine. Recorded voice-over audio clips were used for the agent's speech rather than speech synthesis, since we hypothesized that more realistic speech reproduction would enhance users' affinity with the agent. The agent's mouth motions were synchronized to the speech recordings by sampling the audio amplitude (not viseme/phoneme synching).

A range of non-verbal, embodied cues were also incorporated, such as mouth movements and eyebrow raises synchronized to speech, head nods, facial displays of emotion (concern, empathy, hope, etc.), posture changes, deictic gestures (attention-directing), and idle behavior (blinking, etc.). Various supplemental illustrations and animations were included, such as mortality and side effect risk probabilities, animated visualization of procedures, etc. User participation in the conversation is achieved by selecting from multiple-choice responses and questions. The dialogue, both the agent's speech and the users' responses, was authored to closely model the conversational style of a face-to-face, patient-provider encounter, with the intention of establishing rapport, trust and affinity with the agent.

Synthesizing the findings of previous research on agent appearance, and considering that our ECA would be designed to both explain health information (task oriented communication style) as well as engage in social dialogue and present an empathetic demeanor (social oriented communication style), we hypothesized that a moderately realistic, stylized agent with African-American appearance would appeal to our target demographic. eCoach was designed as a decision aid to facilitate shared decision-making for prostate cancer patients with low health literacy, which disproportionately affects minorities.

Fig. 1. Screenshots from the eCoach prostate cancer decision aid

6.1   User-Centered Design Process for Creating an ECA

We utilized a user-centered design process during the development of the prototype prostate cancer decision aid (eCoach). This process included:

1. *Requirements gathering and functional specifications:* utilized input from stakeholders, including patients, providers and domain experts (medical experts and ECA experts).
2. *Design and development:* iterative design of ECA, dialogue script, medical and risk visuals with input and feedback from a series of user focus groups and key informant interviews.

   During the design and development phase of our study, we created several versions of the eCoach agent in response to feedback and ratings by our user focus groups. We tested a number of different agent designs, including highly realistic (photographic) to highly stylized renderings, younger and older looking agents, different racial appearances, etc. Figures 2 and 3 illustrate some of the variants of the eCoach agent visual design that we evaluated.

Fig. 2. Early design sketches and ECA design alternatives showing a range of facial, hair and clothing features, some more stylized than others, and a range of skin tones indicating ethnicity.

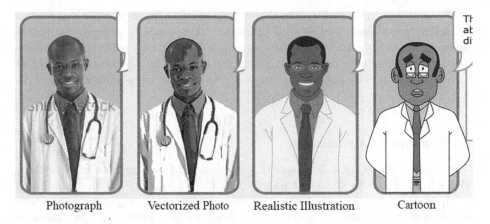

Th
at
di

| Photograph | Vectorized Photo | Realistic Illustration | Cartoon |

Fig. 3. Four rendering styles presented in our focus groups, ranging from photorealistic to abstract. Based on prior research findings and interviews and focus group feedback (with greater weight given to focus groups meeting our target demographic composition), the cartoon option was chosen for the prototype decision aid implementation.

Early focus groups were conducted at the Emory Clinic and were largely composed of Caucasian men diagnosed with prostate cancer, with increasing participation by African American men in later groups. A few women, wives of patients, also participated in these focus groups. Participants in the Emory groups also tended to have higher health literacy, education level and socio-economic status than our target demographic. Contrary to our expectations, these participants uniformly expressed a negative reaction to the stylized versions of the eCoach agent. Some participants even expressed anger about the "cartoon" versions of the agent. Anecdotes collected from these groups include:

- *"Prostate cancer is not like a cartoon."*
- *"This is a serious matter and having a cartoon seems to minimize it."*
- *"The cartoon character is very brown."*

Focus groups were also conducted at Grady Memorial Hospital and in these groups participants were more racially diverse and tended to better match our target demographic (lower health literacy and socio-economic status). The final focus group at Grady, in fact, was the only all-male, all African-American group convened. While the Grady groups also largely expressed dislike for the stylized, "cartoon" agent, the final Grady focus group bucked this trend and collectively expressed approval for this version of the agent. Many participants said the agent was "good" and comments on the visual appearance of the stylized agent included:

- *"The cartoon character is good."*
- *"[He] looks professional and has an agreeable look."*
- *"[He] looks like a comic strip, but he is alright."*

This group was also asked for their reactions to more realistic renderings of the agent, as seen in Fig. 2. The group agreed that the vectorized photo version looked "fake", a reaction shared by all of the Grady focus groups. The photographic agent was considered "good" and "looked cool", however, when asked to compare the photographic agent with the most stylized, cartoon agent, the group preferred the cartoon version of the agent with participants saying that this version *"drew you in"* and that *"he was softer; he was not serious so, in a sense, you're more willing to listen [to him]."*

6.2   Prototype ECA Evaluation

A prototype of the eCoach decision aid was developed based on prior ECA research and feedback from our focus groups. Though only a minority of our focus group participants had a positive assessment of the stylized, cartoon agent rendering, with some Emory participants even expressing dislike for any ECA at all, we chose to continue development of a prototype decision aid using this version of the ECA in order to test our original hypothesis that it would be appealing to our target demographic. To evaluate the eCoach decision aid prototype, focus groups were held at both Grady Memorial Hospital and Emory Clinic, composed of men diagnosed with prostate cancer who had previously served in the earlier focus groups to provide input on the design and content of the decision aid. The eCoach prototype was developed based on initial clinical and patient feedback in order to test the algorithms, animation, content and usability by patients as well as their satisfaction and affinity for the ECA. The prototype consisted of an animated ECA with recorded voice-over and closed-captioned dialogue presented in a conversational style intended to simulate a typical face-to-face consultation with a doctor.

Focus group participants were shown, as a group, an example walk-through of the decision aid dialogue. A computer running the eCoach decision aid was connected to a video projector and speakers and a focus group facilitator demonstrated a typical user session with the tool. Satisfaction with the eCoach decision aid was measured by single items on seven-point scales and feasibility and acceptability of the tool was measured on 7.5-point scales. In addition, semi-structured interview questions were asked of the participants and their responses were manually transcribed.

6.3   Results

Table 1 summarizes quantitative results of questions related to their level of satisfaction with the ECA decision aid as well as their assessment of its feasibility and acceptability as a prostate cancer decision aid.

The quantitative results reveal that the Grady participants, who better matched our target demographic, had a higher level of satisfaction with eCoach. In general, statements regarding the feasibility and acceptability of eCoach as a prostate cancer decision aid were rated somewhat lower, however, when asked how effective eCoach would be as a patient decision aid, both Grady and Emory participants gave a significantly lower rating (2.5 for Grady, 3.2 for Emory).

Table 1. Quantitative results for prototype focus groups

Satisfaction with eCoach [0 – 6 Scale, 6 = Strongly Agree]	Grady (mean)	Emory (mean)	Overall (mean)
Easy to use	6	5.8	5.9
Answered questions about prostate cancer	6	4.2	5.1
Easy to understand	6	5.8	5.9
Important for treatment decisions	6	4.6	5.3
Important for quality of Prostate cancer care	5.8	5.4	5.6
Being well informed is important	6	6	6
Prostate cancer care at this institution is highest possible	6	4.8	5.4
Satisfied with way could use eCoach	6	5	5.5
Quality of eCoach as tool is best possible	4.16	5	4.58
Satisfied with eCoach as means to improve quality of prostate cancer care	6	5.2	5.6
Feasibility & Acceptability of eCoach Tool [0-6.5 Scale]			
How well liked tool overall	4.6	4.2	4.4
Would recommend to other institutions to use	4.75	5.3	5.02
Would recommend to other patients to use	4.75	5.5	5.6
How effective eCoach would be as patient decision aid	2.5	3.2	2.8
How helpful was communication with providers about prostate cancer decision making	4.1	3.8	3.95
How likely eCoach might be to affect decisions	3.9	3.7	3.8
How effective eCoach might be compared to usual care	4.0	5.5	4.75

Focus group participants were also asked to comment on their impressions of eCoach, including its usability, how a tool like eCoach might augment usual care for patients with newly diagnosed prostate cancer and how eCoach might be changed to be more usable or acceptable. Grady participants found the stylized ECA character to be "OK" in contrast to the Emory participants who disliked the ECA's cartoon appearance and stated a preference for a "real person", a difference of opinion that was not surprising considering feedback from prior focus groups.

When asked to comment on their impressions of the eCoach tool, the Grady group offered the following:

- The program helped focus information for them.
- They would rather use eCoach than explore information on their own.
- eCoach took fear out of decision making.

7   Conclusion

Designing an embodied conversational agent as a health decision aid for patients with low health literacy requires careful consideration of visual design parameters. Our findings suggest that, when designing an ECA for a health decision aid, there is no optimal set of appearance parameters that will be appealing and acceptable to every user. Rather, we find that the ECA's demographic appearance (e.g. gender, race, age) should align with the target user population's demographics and further, that additional demographic factors, such as socioeconomic status and level of health literacy should often be considered. The most appropriate rendering style of an ECA is also challenging to determine, especially in the context of a health decision aid. Though prior research on ECAs suggested that we utilize a stylized ECA, given our intention of presenting a health counseling task but using a social dialogue style of communication, we encountered considerable resistance to stylized versions of the ECA among the majority of design-phase and prototype focus groups. Many of the Emory focus group participants, in fact, did not like having an ECA at all, whether realistic or stylized.

Our findings provide evidence that, in certain contexts, such as advising newly diagnosed cancer patients on treatment options and associated risks, presenting a cartoon or stylized avatar in an attempt to appear friendly, empathetic, trustworthy, etc. may actually backfire due to users' sense of the extreme seriousness of the subject. It may be the case that a stylized, cartoon ECA would be better accepted in a less serious health context.

8   Future Work

Our study has a number of limitations, including exploring a small subset of the design space for ECAs used for health decision aids. Our study was limited to a series of focus groups as part of a user-centered design process and we did not test the completed eCoach decision aid as an intervention to promote shared decision-making. Future work should evaluate the eCoach decision aid against currently available decision aids for prostate cancer with outcome measures to include validated measures of decisional conflict.

References

1. Oshima, L.E., Emanuel, E.J.: Shared decision making to improve care and reduce costs. N. Engl. J. Med. **368**(1), 6–8 (2013)
2. McCaffery, K.J., Holmes-Rovner, M., Smith, S.K., Rovner, D., Nutbeam, D., Clayman, M.L., Kelly-Blake, K., Wolf, M.S., Sheridan, S.L.: Addressing health literacy in patient decision aids. BMC Med. Inform. Decis. Mak. **13**, S10 (2013)
3. Bickmore, T.W., Pfeifer, L.M., Jack, B.W.: Taking the time to care: empowering low health literacy hospital patients with virtual nurse agents. In: CHI 2009, pp. 1265–1274 (2009)
4. Health literacy: report of the council on scientific affairs. Ad hoc committee on health literacy for the council on scientific affairs, american medical association. JAMA **281**(6), 552–557 (1999)
5. Kutner, M., Greenberg, E., Jin, Y., Paulsen, C.: The Health Literacy of America's Adults: Results From the 2003 National Assessment of Adult Literacy, pp. 1–76 (2015)
6. Bickmore, T.W., Pfeifer, L.M., Byron, D., Forsythe, S., Henault, L.E., Jack, B.W., Silliman, R., Paasche-Orlow, M.K.: Usability of conversational agents by patients with inadequate health literacy: evidence from two clinical trials. J. Health Commun. **15**, 197–210 (2010)

7. Westpheling, B.P.: Health Literacy Practices in Primary Care Settings: Examples from the Field. The Commonwealth Fund, New York (2008)
8. Cassell, J.: Embodied Conversational Agents. MIT Press, Cambridge (2000)
9. Cancer trends progress report - 2011/2012 update. National Cancer Institute, Bethesda, MD (2012)
10. Lin, G.A., Aaronson, D.S., Knight, S.J., Carroll, P.R., Dudley, R.A.: Patient decision aids for prostate cancer treatment: a systematic review of the literature. CA Cancer J. Clin. **59**, 379–390 (2009)
11. Bickmore, T., Gruber, A., Picard, R.: Establishing the computer-patient working alliance in automated health behavior change interventions. Patient Educ. Couns. **59**, 21–30 (2005)
12. McDonnell, R., Breidt, M., Bülthoff, H.H.: Render me real?: investigating the effect of render style on the perception of animated virtual humans. Trans. Graph. (TOG) **31**(4), 1–11 (2012)
13. Mori, M., MacDorman, K.F., Kageki, N.: The uncanny valley [from the field]. IEEE Robot. Autom. Mag. **19**(3), 98–100 (2012)
14. Baylor, A.L.: The design of motivational agents and avatars. Educ. Tech. Res. Dev. **59**, 291–300 (2011)
15. Baylor, A., Kim, Y.: The role of gender and ethnicity in pedagogical agent perception (2003)
16. Baylor, A.L.: Promoting motivation with virtual agents and avatars: role of visual presence and appearance. Philos. Trans. R. Soc. B: Biol. Sci. **364**, 3559–3565 (2009)
17. Ring, L., Utami, D., Bickmore, T.: The right agent for the job? In: Bickmore, Timothy, Marsella, Stacy, Sidner, Candace (eds.) IVA 2014. LNCS, vol. 8637, pp. 374–384. Springer, Heidelberg (2014)
18. Gulz, A., Haake, M.: Social and visual style in virtual pedagogical agents. In: Proceedings of the Workshop on Adapting the Interaction Style to Affective Factors, 10th International Conference on User Modelling (UM 2005) (2005)
19. Haake, M., Gulz, A.: Visual realism and virtual pedagogical agents. In: Proceedings of the 3rd International Design and Engagability Conference @ NordiChi 2006 (iDec3) (2006)

CyberPLAYce, A Cyber-Physical-Spatial Storytelling Tool: Results from an Empirical Study with 8-10-Year-Old Storytellers

Arash Soleimani[1]([⊠]), Keith Evan Green[1], Danielle C. Herro[1], Ian D. Walker[1], and Christina Gardner-McCune[2]

[1] Institute for Intelligent Materials, Systems and Environments [CU-iMSE], Clemson University, Clemson, SC 29634, USA
{asoleim,kegreen,dherro,iwalker}@clemson.edu
[2] Department of Computer and Information Science and Engineering, University of Florida, Gainesville, FL 32611, USA
gmccune@ufl.edu

Abstract. The product of a multidisciplinary and iterative process, Cyber-PLAYce is an interactive, portable learning tool for children enhancing personal and computational expression, and particularly, playful storytelling. Cyber-PLAYce finds inspiration in the concept of embodied child-computer interaction, where meaning is constructed through spatially reconfiguring the physical environment. This paper briefly outlines the motivations for CyberPLAYce, and focuses on an iterative design, mixed-methodology and usability studies involving 8-10-year-old storytellers. The kinds of digital-physical-spatial activity afforded by CyberPLAYce promise to scaffold thinking, imagining, creating, and sharing in children. Lessons learned from this *research-through-design* case will aid members of the HCI International community as they design and test tools for our youngest learners.

Keywords: Computer support tools · Play · Childhood education · Storytelling · Interactive environments · Architecture · Usability evaluation · User-Centered design · Tangible computing · Prototyping

1 Introduction

We describe the design and evaluation of CyberPLAYce, (Fig. 1), a novel, interactive, computational learning tool for children and their teachers. CyberPLAYce aims to bridge physical and digital worlds, allowing children to make storytelling tangible through the spatial manipulation of cyber-physical elements.

CyberPLAYce was designed as a 21st century version of House of Cards (Fig. 2) designed by famed American designers Charles and Ray Eames in 1953. House of Cards is an oversized deck of cards featuring imaginative patterns and pictures on their surfaces

© Springer International Publishing Switzerland 2015
P. Zaphiris and A. Ioannou (Eds.): LCT 2015, LNCS 9192, pp. 438–446, 2015.
DOI: 10.1007/978-3-319-20609-7_41

that children join together to give form to their thoughts through spatial construction. CyberPLAYce also builds upon the concept of embodied, child-computer interaction [1], where "meaning is created through restructuring the spatial configuration of digital-physical elements in the environment" [2]. With CyberPLAYce, "an object-to-think with" [3], children explore concepts through bodily, cyber-physical interaction. Cyber-PLAYce was introduced at the CHI'14 Video Showcase [4]; but this paper is the first to present the usability results of the empirical study.

Fig. 1. *CyberPLAYce*, LEFT: children engaged in our cyber-physical storytelling study; RIGHT: children completing the study's questionnaire.

Fig. 2. Children giving form to their thoughts and ideas through the spatial reconfiguring afforded by *House of Cards* (1953) and the *CyberPLAYce* prototype.

1.1 Play and Storytelling

Research shows that well-developed play has positive impacts on the development of children [5]. The concept of play has extensively been considered and cultivated within the HCI community [6–9]. CyberPLAYce is particularly targeted at developing children's personal and computational expression. CyberPLAYce promotes children's active involvement and imagination in creating their own play activity which is in alignment with Caillois's paidia play [6, 7], where play is open and affords uncontrollable imagination while giving life to fantasy worlds using physical-digital elements (see, e.g., [10, 11]). CyberPLAYce takes inspiration from research on storytelling in the field of HCI [12, 13] that specifically highlights storytelling as a creative activity: in PETS [14], child-assembled, augmented toys support emotional expression as children create and tell stories; in StoryMat [15], children move around a blanket while they make stories with tangible objects; and in StoryRoom [16] and POGO [12] children play with tangibles offering visual and sound effects that guide the storytelling activity. Collectively, this prior research suggests the promise of tangibles as tools for children to creatively express themselves, to construct meaning, to learn new knowledge, and to communicate during storytelling activities. Our tangible learning tool, CyberPLAYce, novel for expanding tangibles into the dimension of space, aims to merge play and learning in the physical world while transitioning children from consumers of virtual and digital-centric technologies into technological innovators and cyber-playful storytellers.

2   Design Process

Our design-research team initially explored the potential of linking tangible tools, playful storytelling and theoretical frameworks for childhood meaning-making. Our multi-disciplinary team (two architects, an education specialist, a computer scientist, a robotics engineer, and six interaction designers) developed a common framework for designing an interactive learning tool that would engage children in playful activity while enhancing their learning and storytelling experience. After pondering and debating the different aspects of the tool, including its physicality and its user experience, as well as considering digital media and learning theory, the design team developed alternative prototypes, which converged during a follow-up design phase as CyberPLAYce (Fig. 1). The following scenario, developed with the education specialist leading the effort, envisions how CyberPLAYce operates in the classroom setting:

> One day, in a classroom of 8 year olds, Mr. Smith asks the students to think of the routine tasks the students perform each morning at home. Then he tells his story of "Jane": The sun rises just before Jane's alarm goes off. When Jane hears the sound of the alarm, she pushes a button to turn it off. She turns on her bedroom light and her room becomes yellow. Jane walks to the bathroom to take a shower, but first she tests the water to make sure it isn't too hot....

When children break down a story or problem into smaller and more manageable segments, they better understand, interpret and construct knowledge (i.e., they think computationally) [17]. Jane's story was broken down in this way (Table 1), and each story segment was defined by concepts and actions.

CyberPLAYce icon and action cards (Fig. 3) were designed to help children create pattern sequences and map-out story ideas of their own.

Table 1. The break-down of Jane's story into segments, as a vehicle to thinking algorithmically and computationally

> *1. The sun rises just before Jane's alarm goes off.*
> ➔Peel off the cover of the light sensor (input) to activate LED and Buzzer Module (output).
> *2. When Jane hears the sound of the alarm, she pushes a button to turn it off.*
> ➔Push the button on the Buzzer Module (input) to turn it off (output).
> *3. Jane turns on her bedroom light and her room becomes yellow.*
> ➔Push a button on the 2x2 Button-Light Module (input) to turn on the yellow light (output).
> *4. Jane walks to the bathroom to take a shower, but first she tests the water to make sure it isn't too hot.*
> ➔Display the distance on LCD Module (output) using the distance sensor. Use the LED Module (outputs) to indicate if the water is too hot (input) using the Temperature Module.

Fig. 3. CyberPLAYce icon and action cards

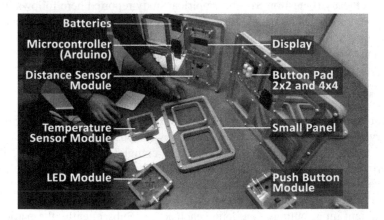

Fig. 4. CyberPLAYce components. The system is wireless and the panels link by neodymium magnets.

In a ten week period, the first-functioning CyberPLAYce prototype was designed and built by our design-research team employing the open – source Arduino [4] platform, and containing magnetic panels and modules of electronic components, such as push buttons, LEDs, temperature sensors, light sensors and LCDs (Fig. 4). Etched into the electronic modules were the images of the icon cards, providing real-time feedback when children plug the modules into the panels, and assemble the magnetic panels into spatial constructions.

As an early test of CyberPLAYce's capacity, the segments from the CyberPLAYce scenario were matched to various input-output activities (Table 1) – a linkage of cards, modules and ideas that suggests how CyberPLAYce might provide children the means to think, understand, learn and share through a multi-modal, interactive and tangible experience. The different physical, digital and spatial dimensions of the CyberPLAYce tool offer children a variety of story-making elements to choose from which and create their own story of interest.

3   Empirical Study

The CyberPLAYce study posits three research questions for this mixed-technology learning tool: (1) Can children comfortably use the technology during storytelling?; (2) To what extent is a modular, multi-sensor design-kit usable?; and (3) How does Cyber-PLAYce support children's storytelling experience and enhance their personal and computational expression? To test the CyberPLAYce experience, an initial evaluation of the CyberPLAYce prototype was conducted in our lab prior to the empirical study assuring that the children (two 4th grade students) can comfortably use the technology. This initial study informed a few minor fixes and refinements including both visual and technical enhancement.

The empirical study was conducted over three days. Each day, one pair of children, ages 8–10, participated in a 2.5-h evaluative session. Relative to the research questions posed, the sessions were designed to elicit data on the system's usability (Questions 1 and 2), and efficacy (Question 3). The empirical study reported here follows from the recorded observations and feedback received from children and the research team in the evaluation of our full-functioning CyberPLAYce, carried out with 8 and 10 year old children, and mostly focuses on the usability studies (Questions 1 and 2).

3.1   Research Activity

To collect data on whether children could comfortably use CyberPLAYce during inter-active storytelling, the research team was guided by established protocols for evaluating interactive technology for children [18]. Children completed two main tasks, Tasks 1 and 2, during each session. In Task-1, children listened to a given story (Jane's story), and then were asked to retell the story through the icon and action cards (Fig. 3). Children began by: 1. matching the story segments to the action cards, and 2. using the icon cards, finding different input-outputs that define each action. Subsequently, the participating children were asked to retell the story by plugging-in the associated CyberPLAYce modules into the panels according to the order of the icon cards that they had previously organized. In Task-2, the children were asked to choose at least six action cards out of ten provided them, and to match these action cards with the relevant icon cards. The action cards provided the children pictured different phenomena (e.g., a jungle, a GPS device, a car, a lion, and a thunderstorm). Children then wrote on paper their own stories following from the prompts pictured on their selected action cards. Lastly, each group presented their composed story through a creative combination of the CyberPLAYce cards and modules. Children completed Tasks 1 and 2 collaboratively while sharing ideas and communicating through the tangible tool. During each session, the research team observed the storytelling activity, and made notes on how participants engaged with the cards, module and panel interfaces, and reacted to the tool overall. Immediately after the storytelling and story creation activities, the research team asked the children

1. How much did you like the way CyberPLAYce looked? (Was it attractive?)

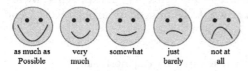

2. How easy was it to use the plug and play modules?

3. How easy was it to form a space with the panels of CyberPLAYce?

4. How easy would it be to explain how to use CyberPLAYce to one of your friends?

5. How much did CyberPLAYce make creating stories fun?

Fig. 5. "Smileyometer" [18] sample of questionnaire that children completed at the end of the empirical study.

for feedback about their experience of telling stories through CyberPLAYce. The sessions were videotaped (see http://youtu.be/uZpGh-_KXQY) and the discourse transcribed.

Furthermore, at the end of the session, each child completed a facilitated questionnaire (employing *Smileyometer* [18] on a 5-point Likert scale) that evaluated CyberPLAYce on measures of usability, aesthetic design and storytelling engagement.

Figure 5 illustrates samples of questions included in the questionnaire. To offset any potential limitations of the "Smileyometer" instrument, such as inclusion of leading or confusing questions, the results of the questionnaire were confirmed against documented observations of usability errors exhibited by the children.

The results of the questionnaire (Table 2) indicate that most of the children enjoyed the process of creation, discovery and storytelling, and found the tangible tool fun and engaging. High rating on "storytelling motivation" suggests that the children surveyed would use CyberPLAYce again to create and tell other stories, and this tangible may have helped them understand story concepts through a playful experience. Meanwhile, children reported that they thought it would be difficult to explain to a friend how CyberPLAYce works – something to consider.

Table 2. Questionnaire results of the empirical study

Variable	Mean	Graph
How **attractive** …?	4.5	
How easy to **plug-n-play** modules …?	3.83	
How easy to **form space** …?	3.6	
How easy to **explain to friend** …?	**2.5**	
How **fun** …?	**4.83**	
How much learned **electronics** …?	4	
How much helped to **tell a given story** …?	3.5	
How much helped to **create your story** …?	4.5	
How much want to **tell stories** …?	**4.83**	
How much **icon cards** helped …?	3.5	
How much **modules** helped …?	3.5	

4   Four Things Learned

1. Most children found the plug-and-play activity frustrating when they were plugging electronic modules into the large panels. Friction must be reduced.
2. Some children had difficulty matching the icon cards to the associated modules; they suggested we color-code and name the cards and modules appropriately.
3. Most children wanted more electronic modules, including ones with a sound recorder, a camera, and a large LCD screen to show pictures and hand drawings of visual representations of their stories.
4. All participants preferred to see more color in everything.

5   Future Work

Our next experiment will focus on advancing the spatial dimension of CyberPLAYce and answering the third CyberPLAYce research question: How does CyberPLAYce support children's storytelling experience and enhance their personal and computational expression? A new CyberPLAYce prototype was designed and built following the feedback received from the children, educators and our research team participated in the empirical study reported here.

The next empirical study with children is currently being conducted in S. Carolina middle schools. The most recent prototype is being used for the new empirical study which contains triangular-shaped panels (Fig. 6) employing friction joints on the edges of the panels providing temporary connections between the panels. The current study seeks to answer how spatial and computational thinking [17] can help students grasp and construct knowledge. Results of this study, combined with the study reported here, will be presented at the HCI International Conference.

Fig. 6. Most recent CyberPLAYce prototype, RIGHT: Children collectively giving form to their thoughts through the spatial construction of the CyberPLAYce panels –friction joints were designed to make temporary connections between the panels.

6   Import for HCI International Community

For the larger HCI International community, CyberPLAYce is a case of research through design focused on cyber-physical learning tools, and tangibles extending into the spatial dimension. As computing becomes ever-more ubiquitous in our everyday lives, it will inevitably occupy the physical spaces we live in, and increasingly converges with it to construct a tangible environment – a next frontier for HCII.

References

1. Dourish, P.: Where the Action is: The Foundations of Embodied Interaction. MIT Press, Cambridge (2001)
2. Antle, A.N.: Embodied child computer interaction: why embodiment matters. Interactions **16**(2), 27–30 (2009)
3. Papert, S.: Mindstorms Children, Computers, and Powerful Ideas, p. 23. Basic Books, New York (1993)
4. Soleimani, A., Green, K. E., Herro, D., Walker, I., Garder-McCune, C.: Design Team: Learning with CyberPLAYce. In: Proceedings of the CHI 2014, p. 165. ACM (2014)
5. Leong, D.J., Bordrova, E.: Assessing and scaffolding: make-believe play. Natl. Assoc. Educ. Young Child. **67**(1), 28–34 (2012)
6. Gaver, B.: Designing for homo ludens, still. In: Binder, T., et al. (eds.) (Re)searching the Digital Bauhaus, pp. 163–178. Springer, London (2009)
7. Lindley, E. S., Harper, R., Sellen, A.: Designing a technological playground: a field study of the emergence of play in household messaging. In: Proceedings of the CHI 2010, pp. 2351–2360. ACM (2010)
8. Monk, A., Hassenzahl, M., Blythe, M., Reed, D.: Funology: designing enjoyment. Interactions **2002**, 11 (2002)
9. National Literacy Trust: Literacy Guide for Secondary Schools. National Literary Trust, London (2012)
10. Åkerman, P., Puikkonen, A.: Prochinima: using pico projector to tell situated stories. In: Proceedings of the Mobile HCI 2011, pp. 337–346. ACM (2011)
11. Garzotto, F., Forfori, M.: Hyperstories and social interaction in 2D and 3D edutainment spaces for children. In: Proceedings of the HYPERTEXT 2006, pp. 57–68. ACM (2006)
12. Decortis, F., Rizzo, A.: New active tools for supporting narrative structures. Pers. Ubiq. Comput. **6**(5–6), 416–429 (2002)
13. Hourcade, J., et al.: KidPad: collaborative storytelling for children. In: Proceedings of the CHI EA 2002, p. 500. ACM (2002)
14. Druin, A., Hendler, J.: Robtos for Kids: Exploring New Technologies for Learning, pp. 75–84. Academic Press, San Diego (2000)
15. Cassell, J., Ryokai, K.: Making space for voice: technologies to support children's fantasy and storytelling. Pers. Ubiq. Comput. **5**(3), 169–190 (2001)
16. Montemayor, J., et al.: Tools for children to create physical interactive storyrooms. J. Comput. Entertain. **2**(1), 1–24 (2004)
17. Wing, J.M.: Computational thinking. Commun. ACM **49**(3), 33–35 (2006)
18. Read, J., Markopoulos, P.: C15: evaluating children's interactive technology. In: Course Notes SIGCHI Conference on Human Factors in Computing Systems, Vancouver, 7–12 May 2011

Collaboration and Learning

What Do My Colleagues Know?
Dealing with Cognitive Complexity
in Organizations Through Visualizations

André Calero Valdez[1](✉), Simon Bruns[1], Christoph Greven[2],
Ulrik Schroeder[2], and Martina Ziefle[1]

[1] Human-Computer Interaction Center, RWTH Aachen University,
Campus-Boulevard 57, Aachen, Germany
{calero-valdez,bruns,ziefle}@comm.rwth-aachen.de
[2] Learning Technologies Research Group, RWTH Aachen University,
Ahornstr. 55, Aachen, Germany
{greven,schroeder}@cs.rwth-aachen.de

Abstract. In order to cope with the growth of information complexity, organizations have started to implement various forms of knowledge management applications. Approaches range from file-, data-, information-centric software to information retrieval, search engines, and decision support systems. Thereby, the data presentation plays often a crucial part in making knowledge available in organizational settings. We examine two visualizations and investigate their capabilities to support organizational knowledge and their usability. One is a document-keyword centric graph-based visualization, while the other is person-institute centric. Both were evaluated positively in supporting improvement of organizational knowledge.

Keywords: Social portals · Knowledge discovery · Recommender systems · Visualization · User-study · Trust

1 Introduction

Knowledge grows. The growth of knowledge has continued to accelerate over the recent years and is expected to do so in the future [1]. As a result, it becomes more and more difficult to extract meaningful data from the available knowledge. For this extraction, it is necessary to turn knowledge into information and the information into data [2]. The field of information science and information management has developed a copious amount of research on how to store data effectively as information (e.g. meta-data). Nevertheless, the amount of information and data is growing rapidly, therefore hindering the user from acquiring his desired knowledge from data and information.

Coping with this ever increasing amount of information and data is the central challenge of big data and knowledge discovery. The challenge shifts from

© Springer International Publishing Switzerland 2015
P. Zaphiris and A. Ioannou (Eds.): LCT 2015, LNCS 9192, pp. 449–459, 2015.
DOI: 10.1007/978-3-319-20609-7_42

organizing information to finding information that is both relevant [3] and helpful to the user in order to create knowledge. This search process becomes increasingly important in the organizational context.

Organizations are becoming ever more complex and employee fluctuation makes knowledge management increasingly harder to do [4]. To prevent knowledge loss, knowledge management systems are increasingly used. However, these address mainly explicit knowledge and fail to capture tacit knowledge. Social software solutions have tried to address this topic by capturing communication processes as they happen and storing this data for later evaluation.

Nonetheless retrieval of this knowledge from the stored data is still a great challenge. Whenever information is connected and complex, it becomes necessary to not only transfer the information from system to user, but also to shape the mental model [5] the user has of the information. It is furthermore necessary to take into account what the model of the technology behind knowledge management software is, due its strong effect on acceptance [6]. The composition of the software must be clearly communicated. Here various forms of systems come into play that address different aspects of knowledge management and knowledge transfer. Still, if the mental model of both system and content are clear, success of such a system can not be guaranteed. Often the creator of information and the benefactor are different persons [7] thus a sense of community or even locality [8] are important criteria for their success.

2   Related Work

In this paper we look at various forms of knowledge management and discovery systems and address their applicability in an organizational setting. Typical forms of knowledge management systems that deal with big data are the following [9]:

1. *Intranet and Groupware* software [10] are designed to support organizational collaboration and integrate a network of clients. Typically summarized under the term CSCW they are designed with work tasks in mind and often based on well known protocols like HTTP, SMTP and FTP. They are most of the time file-centric.

2. *Data Warehousing & OLAP* [11] are data centered solutions. Transaction and Process data [12] is integrated and stored in data cubes, which can later be analyzed for reporting purposes. Data warehouses implement a single-source of truth policy and keep track of data history. Tools are required for extraction, cleaning and loading data into the Online Analytical Processing (OLAP) system. Afterwards, the OLAP system analyzes the given data cubes to find patterns or possible trend candidates. Since queries are often multidimensional, meta-data management and query management is important and often tool-assisted.

3. *Content Management Systems* are content-centric and focus on publishing processes. Content can be created, updated, published and deleted. In addition, editing workflows are implemented to address publishing responsibilities.

Generally versioning and authorship meta data is maintained. Recently CMS have been used in enterprise content management, as internal documents often follow similar procedures as publishing.

4. *(Collaborative) Search engines* [13,14] or enterprise search engines merge the joint efforts of users in locating and tagging information. This allows the retrieval of more relevant information by learning from user input and the relations of users interests.

5. *Recommender Systems* [15] are used to actively suggest interesting content to the user. Often used in Internet sales to suggest other products that are of interest. Furthermore, they are used to recommend documents, books [16], scientific literature [17] or even teams [18]. Recommender System often learn from users previous choices [19] but may also rely on multi-criteria filtering [20]. How suggestions are generated, should be clearly explained. [21] This is especially important in the case of hybrid systems [22] that integrate collaborative filtering and machine learning approaches.

6. *Decision Support Systems (DSS)* [23] derive significant information and possible emerging patterns from raw data. By considering the extracted information, the system assists the decision making process. DSS often incorporate visualizations and can be fully automatic, fully human dependent or combine both efforts.

Still all of these systems rely on various forms of information presentation to allow the user to acquire knowledge from the information or data presented. In all cases the type of visualization is critical to improve the transfer of deep structure from machine to user [24]. The concept "overview, zoom, detail on demand" [25] summarizes a core paradigm of visualizations that are based on full information display. The field of *HCI-KDD* [26] addresses the need for research of the interaction of Human-Computer Interaction and Knowledge Discovery in Databases.

For the case of organizational knowledge it is also important to understand the complexity of knowledge available in an organization that is shared between employees. Finding an employee or a document with critical knowledge or information is a challenge when organizational structures are not well understood. Users must learn the intricacies of overview, structure, and detail along the hierarchy of an organization.

2.1   Visual Recommender Systems

In order to ease the understanding of information, visual approaches can be used. In our case we focus on visual recommender systems. The recommender component, serves the purpose of increasing the transparency of the underlying system. The only similar solution that we could find to our prototypes is proposed by O'Donovan et al. [27]. They propose a graph-based visual collaborative filtering tool called PeerChooser that uses multiple criteria to allow users to find movie suggestions. Montaner et al. [28] propose a taxonomy of recommender systems spanning seven criteria. These should be used in order help in designing a recommender system. The instances are task dependent but are for most cases interchangeable.

- *Representation* describes how data is represented (e.g. historical, feature vector, etc.)
- *Initial Information* describes how data is preloaded into the algorithm before the user interacts with it (e.g. none, manual, training set)
- *Learning* refers to how the algorithm improves on usage (e.g. TF-IDF, ID3, etc.)
- *Feedback* describes how the user can give feedback to the algorithm (e.g. rating systems, choice).
- *Adaptation* refers to how the algorithm adapts to the feedback (e.g. add new, natural selection, GFF).
- *Filtering* indicates how data is filtered before used in the algorithm (e.g. collaborative, hybrid, demographic)
- *Matching* describes how items are matched with the users requests or feedback (e.g. nearest neighbour, cosine similarity, etc.)

3   Visualization Prototypes

By considering Montaner et al. criteries, we investigate two different types of knowledge discovery systems in a research setting addressing these topics. We present a user evaluation of these systems and their particular visualizations. The first system is a visual recommender system that recommends documents to read that are relevant to the research interest of the user. The second system presents a visual collaboration support system that allows finding collaborators in a research organization that can contribute to the user's topic. Both systems are integrated in a social portal that is used within the research organization.

Graph-Based Document Recommender System. The graph-based publication recommender system TIGRS uses a mixed-node graph [29] connecting publications with their keywords, with respect to their relative relevance (see Fig. 1 and [30]). Users can now filter for keywords and their relative relevance in order to find relevant documents. The system uses the users previous keywords to suggest only documents that are relevant to the user. It allows to browse through content, while at the same time seeing connections between documents sharing mutual keywords.

Collaborator Suggestion System. The collaborator suggestion system proposed by Yazdi et al. [31] is used to suggest fruitful collaboration in a research cluster by analyzing previous collaboration and mutual keywords. By using social network analysis possible coauthors are visually suggested when hovering over a bubble-based graph. Using a bubble-bag layout (see Fig. 2) it additionally conveys information about where a suggested collaborator works. This further conveys organizational structure information, allowing users to understand who is who in their organization and what they work on.

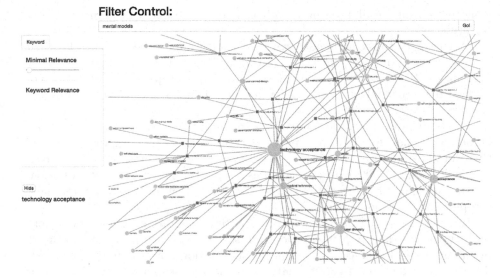

Fig. 1. Publication and keyword centric visualization of collaboration [30]

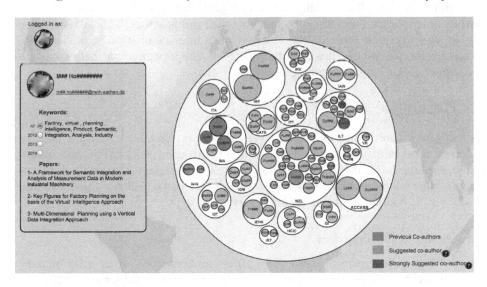

Fig. 2. Author and institute centric visualization of collaboration [31]

4   Method

We tested both systems in a large research facility (i.e. over 180 researchers) with a sample of 16 and 20 members from different fields for each system. Both prototypes were used in a user-studies ($N = 16$, $N = 20$) determining both the overall usability (SUS [32]) and the likelihood of being recommended to a fried (NPS [33]). We investigated user factors (e.g. age, discipline, research expertise, track record) and evaluated how both prototypes complement each other in a scientific setting.

With regard to recommender systems, finding appropriate metrics for their evaluation is critical [34] in order gain an understanding of what needs to be optimized. Here we only look at general usability and qualitative insights. For further detailed analysis please refer to the original works of the prototypes (cf. [30,31]).

For both prototypes users were invited to take part in a user study in our laboratory. They were given time to get accustomed to the prototypes and their handling and were then given tasks to complete (i.e. find suitable publication/collaborator). The whole process was recorded and then analyzed. Additionally further quantitative analyses were performed derived from a questionnaire completed by the participants.

In this paper we want to focus on reporting qualitative findings from both prototypes and their implementation in a social portal. Both prototypes are to be integrated in the so-called "Scientific Cooperation Portal" (SCP). [35] a tool devised to tackle the high staff volatility in a large research cluster. The SCP is a social portal which centralizes communication, file-exchange, member profiles, and offers interdisciplinary collaboration support. Additionally, it tracks research output of individual researchers by tracking their publications. This latter feature is also used to enable steering the cluster from a management point of view [29]. In the prototypes we use this data to construct visualizations that help facilitate collaboration and understanding the organization.

5   Results

Our analyses (univariate analysis of variance) show that both systems address different aspects of understanding how an organization works. The first allows understanding how different departments work on various topics, while overlapping in their content and methodology. The second system allows understanding the scientific content that researchers work on in depth.

5.1   Sample Description

For the first prototype we asked $N = 16$ researchers from an interdisciplinary research facility whose average age was $\bar{x} = 33.6$ years ($\sigma = 6.14$, range= $23-52$) and 56% of whom were female to take part in our study. Ten had finished their undergraduate training (Masters) while five already had graduate training (PhD or Professor). Most researchers came from the fields of linguistics or communication science (see Table 1). Most researchers had published about 5-6 papers in their careers with some outliers of over 150 (i.e. a professor) and some none (new colleagues). The facility has a total of 25 researchers.

The second prototype was testes with $N = 20$ researchers from an interdisciplinary research cluster (out of 180 employees). Forty participants were approached at seven different institutes mostly from engineering sciences, but also including communication science and computer science.

Table 1. Research fields in sample for the first prototype (multiple selections allowed)

Field	Count
Linguistics and communication science	6
Psychology	5
Computer science	4
Sociology	3
Architecture	1

5.2   Quantitative Results

The first prototype received very high ratings in usability. Overall SUS was high ($\bar{x} = 81.5$, $\sigma = 2.17$) indicating a good usability of the system. Nonetheless the NPS was relatively low (-7). We got 4 detractors, 8 passives, and 4 promoters. This means further development of the system needs to be performed to align with user requirements.

Quantitatively the SUS showed a mean of $\bar{x} = 82.5$ ($\sigma = 24.4$) indicating a high acceptance of the prototype. The NPS analysis yields 4 Promoters, 6 Passives and 0 Detractors. The overall NPS is 40 indicating good usability [32,33].

5.3   Qualitative Results

In addition to the quantitative evaluation we screened the user study recordings for mentions of various categories. We also analyzed the behavior how users were using the prototypes and in particular how surprised they were. Furthermore we asked users what they learnt about their organization and how much the visualization improved their knowledge of the organization.

Looking for Relevant Publications. An interesting observation during the usage of the first prototype was the different styles of how it was used. We identified three different approaches how users used the filtering mechanism.

The first style was a *drill down* approach. Users that applied this approach first looked at the full graph including all publications from their institute, resetting all filters before looking for a recommendation. They then used generic terms that were of interest to them and played with the relevance sliders to further drill down on interesting suggestions. Then more experienced users were trying to look for items they did not know yet while keeping their focus on the center of the graph were items are that are connected to all relevant filter terms.

The second style was an *incremental bag* approach. They started with a very specific term that was of current interest to them often dissatisfied with the few results they gradually increased the bag of filters with specific terms. Interestingly these users reported to find very relevant suggestions albeit often previously known suggestions.

The third style was a *traverse related work* approach. Users applying this style looked for single items that they found interesting and sequentially added keywords that were relevant to that single item, repeating this process several times. This can be seen as a traversal along keywords approach often leading to utterances like "we have someone writing about this, I was looking for something like that", indicating very serendipitous finds.

Finding Fruitful Collaborators. When using the second prototype most users were astonished with how much the visualization revealed about the organizational structure. Users were surprised to see that others in the organization (out of 180 researchers) were working on similar topics that they were. In particular seeing the who has worked with whom was interesting as this information was somewhat opaque to find from publication lists.

Discovering New Knowledge About the Organization. Both prototypes were able to reveal new knowledge by visualizing publicly available information in a new fashion. Both prototypes caused users to have serendipitous finds either as publications or possible collaborators from a pool that was theoretically available to them. Nevertheless, the effort to manually look for this information had been a barrier to do so (both organizations existed for more than 5 years).

In both cases the head of the organization was asked to use the prototypes and talk about the benefits of the visualization for managing purposes. Both mentioned the benefits of getting overview knowledge about their organization. They were also surprised to see how much publications had been written since the funding of the organization and realized the scope of their organization. Interestingly, a need to communicate publications to teams arose during these experiments.

6   Conclusion

In this paper, we have examined two knowledge systems. The first system recommended relevant documents to the user in the form of a visual recommender system. Thereby, the system provides the user with the means to directly influence the recommender algorithm and the recommender visualization. Whereas the second system, supports the user in finding suitable future collaborators, who can contribute to the user's topic.

In conjunction both systems provide insights into what the colleagues do and how their work can be useful in respect to the user's own work. This knowledge can be used either for collaboration or as a basis for one's own work. The systems help in creating knowledge from data and information through their specifically adapted visualizations.

During the use various types of new applications arose. The need to extend the visualization to other types of documents was seen. In particular seeing not only publications but also grant proposals for a whole university and collaboration suggestion within the university was mentioned as a possible application.

6.1 Limitations

Both tools require PDFs and Full-Texts with meta information to work properly. The conducted studies were done with relatively small user groups because of the intensive analysis required after the test. Therefore, the experiment is not able not reveal any effects between user-factors and usage behavior. Differences are too small to be statistically significant, thus they must be assumed non-existent. Inspite of that the experimenter felt the need to report, that less experienced researchers were using the tool differently than experienced researchers. Further analysis of the videos might reveal these differences at a later point in time.

6.2 Outlook

The user studies indicate that both prototypes can be used not only to assist scientific collaboration but also in organizational knowledge management. Here they can be used to interlink documents from an enterprise content management system in order to find relevant documents when working on another. The aim of our prototypes is to bring the various levels of collaboration support together. Documents can be served from the intranet or CMS and be connected with col laborative search and tagging from a social portal. The publication recommender system TIGRS brings these together by providing relevant documents to the user integrated into the social portal. The collaboration suggestion system even goes a step further as it actively recommends suitable collaborators for the users of the social portal. Nonetheless, only in conjunction can they help in understanding the organizational structure, the employees and the topics that are being worked on collaboratively.

Acknowledgments. We would like to thank the anonymous reviewers for their constructive comments on an earlier version of this manuscript. The authors thank the German Research Council DFG for the friendly support of the research in the excellence cluster "Integrative Production Technology in High Wage Countries".

References

1. Metcalfe, J.S.: Knowledge of growth and the growth of knowledge. J. Evol. Econ. **12**(1–2), 3–15 (2002)
2. Bellinger, G., Castro, D., Mills, A.: Data, information, knowledge, and wisdom (2004). http://www.systems-thinking.org/dikw/dikw.htm
3. Wang, J., De Vries, A.P., Reinders, M.J.: Unified relevance models for rating prediction in collaborative filtering. ACM Trans. Inf. Syst. (TOIS) **26**(3), 16 (2008)
4. Holsapple, C.W., Whinston, A.B.: Knowledge-based organizations. Inf. Soc. **5**(2), 77–90 (1987)
5. Calero Valdez, A., Ziefle, M., Alagöz, F., Holzinger, A.: Mental models of menu structures in diabetes assistants. In: Miesenberger, K., Klaus, J., Zagler, W., Karshmer, A. (eds.) ICCHP 2010, Part II. LNCS, vol. 6180, pp. 584–591. Springer, Heidelberg (2010)

6. Orlikowski, W.J., Gash, D.C.: Technological frames: making sense of information technology in organizations. ACM Trans. Inf. Syst. (TOIS) **12**(2), 174–207 (1994)
7. Grudin, J.: Groupware and social dynamics: eight challenges for developers. Commun. ACM **37**(1), 92–105 (1994)
8. Olson, G.M., Olson, J.S.: Distance matters. Hum.-Comput. Interact. **15**(2), 139–178 (2000)
9. Sharma, S.K., Gupta, J.N., Wickramasinghe, N.: A framework for building a learning organisation in the 21st century. Int. J. Innovation Learn. **2**(3), 261–273 (2005)
10. Ellis, C.A., Gibbs, S.J., Rein, G.: Groupware: some issues and experiences. Commun. ACM **34**(1), 39–58 (1991)
11. Chaudhuri, S., Dayal, U.: An overview of data warehousing and olap technology. ACM Sigmod Rec. **26**(1), 65–74 (1997)
12. Dumas, M., Van der Aalst, W.M., Ter Hofstede, A.H.: Process-Aware Information systems: Bridging People and Software through Process Technology. Wiley, New York (2005)
13. Sugiyama, K., Hatano, K., Yoshikawa, M.: Adaptive web search based on user profile constructed without any effort from users. In: Proceedings of the 13th international conference on World Wide Web, pp. 675–684. ACM (2004)
14. Morris, M.R., Horvitz, E.: Searchtogether: an interface for collaborative web search. In: Proceedings of the 20th annual ACM symposium on User Interface Software and Technology, pp. 3–12. ACM (2007)
15. Burke, R.: Hybrid recommender systems: survey and experiments. User Model. User-Adap. Inter. **12**(4), 331–370 (2002)
16. Thudt, A., Hinrichs, U., Carpendale, S.: The bohemian bookshelf: supporting serendipitous book discoveries through information visualization. In: Proceedings of the SIGCHI Conference on Human Factors in Computing Systems, CHI 2012, pp. 1461–1470. ACM, New York (2012)
17. Miller, L.J., Gazan, R., Still, S.: Unsupervised classification and visualization of unstructured text for the support of interdisciplinary collaboration. In: Proceedings of the 17th ACM Conference on Computer Supported Cooperative Work & #38; Social Computing. CSCW 2014, pp. 1033–1042. ACM, New York (2014)
18. Datta, A., Tan Teck Yong, J., Ventresque, A.: T-recs: team recommendation system through expertise and cohesiveness. In: Proceedings of the 20th International Conference Companion on WWW, WWW 2011, pp. 201–204. ACM, New York (2011)
19. Loepp, B., Hussein, T., Ziegler, J.: Choice-based preference elicitation for collaborative filtering recommender systems. In: Proceedings of the 32nd Annual ACM Conference on Human Factors in Computing Systems, pp. 3085–3094. ACM (2014)
20. Adomavicius, G., Tuzhilin, A.: Toward the next generation of recommender systems: a survey of the state-of-the-art and possible extensions. IEEE Trans. Knowl. Data Eng. **17**(6), 734–749 (2005)
21. Herlocker, J.L., Konstan, J.A., Riedl, J.: Explaining collaborative filtering recommendations. In: Proceedings of the 2000 ACM Conference on Computer Supported Cooperative Work, pp. 241–250. ACM (2000)
22. Gunawardana, A., Meek, C.: A unified approach to building hybrid recommender systems. In: Proceedings of the Third ACM Conference on Recommender Systems, pp. 117–124. ACM (2009)
23. Shim, J.P., Warkentin, M., Courtney, J.F., Power, D.J., Sharda, R., Carlsson, C.: Past, present, and future of decision support technology. Decis. Support Syst. **33**(2), 111–126 (2002)

24. Gretarsson, B., O'Donovan, J., Bostandjiev, S., Hall, C., Höllerer, T.: Small-worlds: visualizing social recommendations. In: Computer Graphics Forum, vol. 29, pp. 833–842. Wiley Online Library (2010)
25. Shneiderman, B.: The eyes have it: a task by data type taxonomy for information visualizations. In: Proceedings of the IEEE Symposium on Information Visualization, pp. 336–343. IEEE (1996)
26. Holzinger, A.: Human-Computer Interaction and Knowledge Discovery (HCI-KDD): what is the benefit of bringing those two fields to work together? In: Cuzzocrea, A., Kittl, C., Simos, D.E., Weippl, E., Xu, L. (eds.) CD-ARES 2013. LNCS, vol. 8127, pp. 319–328. Springer, Heidelberg (2013)
27. O'Donovan, J., Smyth, B., Gretarsson, B., Bostandjiev, S., Höllerer, T.: Peer-chooser: visual interactive recommendation. In: Proceedings of the SIGCHI Conference on Human Factors in Computing Systems, pp. 1085–1088. ACM (2008)
28. Montaner, M., López, B., De La Rosa, J.L.: A taxonomy of recommender agents on the internet. Artif. Intell. Rev. **19**(4), 285–330 (2003)
29. Calero Valdez, A., Schaar, A.K., Ziefle, M., Holzinger, A., Jeschke, S., Brecher, C.: Using mixed node publication network graphs for analyzing success in interdisciplinary teams. In: Huang, R., Ghorbani, A.A., Pasi, G., Yamaguchi, T., Yen, N.Y., Jin, B. (eds.) AMT 2012. LNCS, vol. 7669, pp. 606–617. Springer, Heidelberg (2012)
30. Bruns, S., Calero Valdez, A., Greven, C., Ziefle, M., Schroeder, U.: What should i read next? a personalized visual publication recommender system. In: Proceedings of the HCI International 2015 (2015)
31. Yazdi, M.A., Calero Valdez, A., Lichtschlag, L., Ziefle, M., Borchers, J.: Visualizing opportunities of collaboration in large organizations. In: Manuscript Submitted for Publication (submitted)
32. Brooke, J.: SUS - a quick and dirty usability scale. Usability Eval. Ind. **189**, 194 (1996)
33. Reichheld, F.F.: The one number you need to grow. Harvard Bus. Rev. **81**(12), 46–55 (2003)
34. Herlocker, J.L., Konstan, J.A., Terveen, L.G., Riedl, J.T.: Evaluating collaborative filtering recommender systems. ACM Trans. Inf. Syst. (TOIS) **22**(1), 5–53 (2004)
35. Calero Valdez, A., Schaar, A.K., Ziefle, M., Holzinger, A.: Enhancing interdisciplinary cooperation by social platforms. In: Yamamoto, S. (ed.) HCI 2014, Part I. LNCS, vol. 8521, pp. 298–309. Springer, Heidelberg (2014)

From Formal to Informal 3D Learning. Assesment of Users in the Education

David Fonseca[1(✉)], Ernest Redondo[2], Francesc Valls[2], and Oswaldo Daviel Gutiérrez[3]

[1] Architecture School - La Salle, Universitat Ramon Llull, Barcelona, Spain
fonsi@salle.url.edu
[2] Universidad Politécnica de Cataluña-Barcelona Tech, Barcelona, Spain
{ernesto.redondo,francesc.valls}@upc.edu
[3] Universidad de Guadalajara, Jalisco, México
arq.odgb@gmail.com

Abstract. This work is focused on the design of an educational experience involving the implementation of virtual and augmented 3D information in the architectural and urban design precesses. This process has two distinct educational parts: the first within a formal framework (regulated course where the student gets a qualification within their studies), and the second in an informal environment with the end-users feeback. The responses of the end-users are obtained using 3D visualization with mobile devices and in situ assessment using QR codes (Quick-Response) of the proposals. This social interaction contributes indirectly and unconsciously in a crucial training of students, validating environments and real situation proposals and providing them with experiences and professional skills.

Keywords: 3D learning · E-Learning · Formal and informal learning · Urban planning · Educational research

1 Introduction

New technology implementations in the teaching field have been largely extended to all types of levels and educational frameworks. In recent years, in addition to technology use in the classroom, new areas of research are opening to assess and recognize more effective and satisfactory teaching methods, such as: gamification strategies, Project Based Learning (PBL), Scenario Centered Curriculum (SCC), and the recognition of capabilities that provide the non-formal and informal education.

The current paper is based on four main pillars: The first pillar focuses on teaching innovations within different educational frameworks that promote higher motivation and satisfaction in students (especially at High School and University levels). The second pillar concerns how to implement such an innovation; we propose the utilization of different Information Technologies (IT) like Virtual and Augmented Reality (VR/AR), Digital Sketching (DS), and hybrid models, based on which students, as "digital natives", will be more comfortable in the learning experience. The third main idea is to employ a mixed analysis method to obtain the most relevant aspects of the experience that should

© Springer International Publishing Switzerland 2015
P. Zaphiris and A. Ioannou (Eds.): LCT 2015, LNCS 9192, pp. 460–469, 2015.
DOI: 10.1007/978-3-319-20609-7_43

be improved both in future interactions and in any new technological implementations within a teaching framework. And finally, the incorporation and analysis of users informal interaction of the implemented 3D proposal.

These interactions, as it pursues to demonstrate, provide an informal teaching to students, creating a link with formal systems through a central axis: the user and the assessments of both the experiment and its results. These relationships are vital in the field of architecture, where proposals of students and professionals have particular repercussions to the end-users of the proposal.

2 Background

2.1 Informal Education: The Citizenship Background in Architectural Education

The users experience (UX) and the usability have been handled normally as tools for the final product or system [1, 2]. Based on the results that the product obtained of the interaction with end-users, developers get value information. This feedback allows a better adaptation, redesigning and improving a system based on the opinion and typology of the end users. Historically this process has been used in the design of web environments, consumer products such as appliances and all kinds of technology especially those targeted areas such as leisure and social relations [3]. However we can affirm that it has great potential if adapted appropriately to education. As based on the behavior and emotions of end users of a proposal, the designers of the same (students) may improve in future projects.

Usually most studies are designed in a regulated manner, i.e. within an educational environment and a formal student training. However, in recent decades, there have been studies and research that emphasize the importance of other forms of education away from schools (regardless of the level) [4]. Learning processes are not only confined in regulated areas but also non-formal or informal are present throughout a person's lifetime [5]. To do so initially we must clearly differentiate between all types of education currently defined [6–8]:

- Formal Education: Learning typically provided by an education or training institution, structured and leading to certification. Formal learning is intentional from the learner's perspective: the hierarchically structured, chronologically graded 'education system', running from primary school through university and including, in addition to general academic studies, a variety of specialized programs and institution for full-time technical and professional training.
- Non Formal: Any organized educational activity outside the established formal system – either operating separately or as an important feature of some broader activity – that is intended to serve identifiable learning users and learning objectives.
- Informal: Learning resulting from daily life activities related to work, family or leisure. It is not structured (in terms of learning objectives, learning time or learning support) and typically does not lead to certification. In this case, each individual acquires attitudes, values, skills and knowledge from daily experience and the educational influence and resources in his or hers environment.

In base of these definitions, the architectural edication allows incorporationg (in a complementary way) non-formal educational elements, such as specialized courses, as well as informal education. In the education of a future architect or of a similar profession (such as a building engineer, civil engineer, interior design), the acquisition of knowledge informally is vital, because the development of a professional project always has a huge based on experience. Along this line, one of the great forgotten issues in urban design has been the project perception of the end-users. This review not only determines the success or failure of a project, but also informally influences the education of both future architects and active professionals.

It would be difficult to compile the number of functional projects in the design phases that have become architectural failures or that have generated controversy once finished because of the number of possible examples [9–11]. As we see below, not even the great architects and their works have been free of bad user experiences, from structural problems or other minimum problems that affect the end user. The perception and assimilation of the criticism continues to be an example of informal education, better or worse incorporated into new professional projects:

- 7 buildings with structural problems that cause problems in the environment or in its habitability [12].
- Examples of dangerous construction for users and /or with building problems [13]:
- Constitution Bridge, Venice. Santiago Calatrava.
- Zubizuri Bridge, Bilbao. Santiago Calatrava.
- City of Culture, Santiago de Compostela, Peter Eisenman.
- Nous Encants, Barcelona, Fermín Vázquez.
- Farnsworth House, Mies van der Rohe. This weekend retreat was never inhabited apart from the budget problems between client and architect; it is remarkable due to environmental confort issues [14].
- Ville Savoye, Le Corbusier [15]. From the outset of this construction, the building had severe problems with the weather, both from water and wind, being widely documented in the correspondence between the residents and the architect [16, 17]:
- Paving tiles in Paseo de Gracia, Esteve Terradas. The design of the new pavement meets aesthetic, a comprehensive study of materials and their adaptation to the Mediterranean climate, but has also been criticized for its roughness and possible problems that can cause treading with heels [18].
- The disease of modern buildings: the semicircular lipoatrophy. Referenced and related buildings for the first time in 1974 [19–21].

This does not only happen in the professional field, the same thing happens in educational fields for example: Designing an educational experiment does not always work successfully. Involving new technologies and the use of various devices is not always synonym of an effective user experience [22, 23]. A good design to motivate and improve students' learning can be transformed into just the opposite. Any "Good Educational Practice" must have different parameters for monitoring and evaluating each exercise, environment and student [24, 25].

And on the opposite side is the student's work. As a practical exercise it can perfectly meet all evaluable and pre-established criteria in technology and performance. But it would be necessary to check whether the proposal is also functional and usable [26]. This step is an essential step which is usually forgotten in the teaching faculties, mainly due to lack of time [27], and where we focus our case study.

2.2   Improving the Student's Motivation: Assessment of IT in Education

In recent years, various technologies are proving useful in all kinds of educational areas, noted for its flexibility, spatial ability and adaptability to all educational levels. AR has emerged from research in VR. VR environments make possible total immersion in an artificial three-dimensional (3D) world. The involvement of VR techniques and models in the development of educational applications brings new perspectives to engineering and architectural (civil, building and urban) degrees. For example, through interaction with 3D models of the environment, the whole construction sequence in time and space of a bridge deck can be simulated for students' better understanding [28]. We can also explore hidden structure through ghosted views overlaid on the real-world scenes [29] or find several examples of AR and VR applied to monitoring the maintenance of new buildings and to preserve cultural heritage [30–32].

In a way, the new digital systems, devices and users (*based on the role of the students as "digital native" users*), enable new workflows that allow testing of more interactive, collaborative and generally misplaced progress and student skills. The 3D modeling and computer simulations (using both CAD and BIM models, Computer Assisted Design / Building Information Modelling), provide new ways for architecture students to study the relationship between the design, the space and the construction of buildings. Digital media helps integrating and expanding the content of courses in drafting, construction and design using for example *digital sketching (DS), and hybrid models* [33].

However, there is a fundamental problem: the evaluation. And when we do, we evaluate at different levels:

- The Teacher evaluation. In this field, we are migrating from traditional systems based on tests to testing new models that assess the degree of acquisition of competencies and skills described in each case. The evaluation through rubrics and their adaptation to the student tracking systems are currently a challenge for its implementation.
- The evaluation of the technological proposals and their adaptation to students. For any given assessment of both technological or not, discussions arise whether the best approach is quantitative work, qualitative or mixed (that fuses both), the generation of statistical analysis of responses, indicators, correlation studies, etc.
- The evaluation of the informal feedback from users. The study by SCC and PBL generates a huge amount of subjective and difficult to parameterize information, but nevertheless provides a quality assessment on the work done by the student.

For the experiment described in this paper we propose the use of AR and DS as working platforms and presentation of planning proposals. To this objective we will design various assessment tasks in order to parameterize the experience at the highest level possible. This process is necessary for future iterations to more clearly define in a teaching methodology that integrates formal and informal aspects. Initially students will do a quantitative test to assess their technological profile. After the practical part, we have generated rubrics for teacher evaluation, a quantitative test for the evaluation of the usability of the technology used and a qualitative assessment interview the proposed method. Finally (and in order to incorporate the informal evaluation of the project), we have interviewed a number of random users about whether their valuations affect the educational experience of students, but this first proposal without being quantified formally.

3   Case of Study

The city of Tonalá is located a few kilometers from Guadalajara and is part of its urban area. It is an urban area whose traditional activity has been the industry and handicraft of pottery and its street markets, called "Tianguis", having ones taking place on Sundays and Wednesday an industrial fame because of its size and the variety of products sold. This market chaotically occupies much of the streets of the city and the Municipality of Tonalá is trying to regulate them while at the same time improving the infrastructure of the city, especially the streets, sidewalks and signage. These objectives not only aim to improve the urban landscape but also remove architectural barriers (Fig. 1). Citizen participation in those processes is not common practice in Mexico. In this occasion, in addition to evaluating the use of ICT in the design phase and the visualization of new proposals in an education environment, we aimed to harness the structure of the University of Guadalajara to engage the students in the Tonalá High School, with whom several collaboration links had been established.

The objective to be developed throughout 2014 was the usage of QR (Quick Response) codes to perform an experiment on citizen participation that allowed the evaluation of proposals in its location. The final presentation of the course was the creation of a panel, triptych or report that explained the urban design project and point of sale proposal that at the same time described the creative process. For this purpose, the students had to illustrate their work and the design process through DS, AR and VR-Objects, including an explanation of the process [34]. All the information had to be stored in a link identified with a QR code. This code would be the one which, attached to all places in Tonalá where the project would be built (in the second phase of the work to be developed over 2014–2015), would allow the students of the High School of Tonalá of the UDG that wished to access the studies of CUAAD to participate in the evaluation of the projects (see sample panel in Fig. 2).

4   Informal Feedback. Main Results

As stated previously, to evaluate theend-users' feedback based on their subjective criteria visualizing the student's proposals, a qualitative approach was used. The users were invited to voluntarily participate in the study and share their opinion. The first set of users who tested the display was composed of a total of 24 people. We have identified four main subgroups, users related to architecture (students and professionals N1: 6), commercials (N2: 4), workers with no architecture skills (N3: 7), students and teachers from high school (N4: 7). Asked about two proposals made by the students, the most

Fig. 1. Urban-rehabilitation project: "Tianguis", the new street markets

talked about aspects (positive and negative) mentioned were:

- Mention Index 45.83 % (+, positive aspect): Users who first saw operation of RA and were highly impressed. Highlights included citations of 71.4 % of students and 57.1 % of employed persons, and that none of the merchants in the market discussed the technology used.
- 29.16 % (-, negative aspect): The users understood that these proposal would be best suited to a wider environment (like a square) and for stationary use (static, without displacement). The mobile tianguis proposed do not adapt to the urbanization of Tonalá and produce serious problems of its installation and displacement. This has been cited by 75 % of traders, reflecting the understanding of the problem as something close to their daily work. The other subgroups have cited this aspect below average, highlighting the 28.5 % of students.
- 29.16 % (-): Selection of materials used in the proposals was criticized, considering that the more traditional wood be better adapted to the market rate, instead of other cutting edge materials. The group with a higher rate in this commentary was the people related to architecture (50 %).
- 24.33 % (+): Users understood the AR as a very useful and applicable technology in other areas especially on issues related to architecture, leisure, tourism and generally

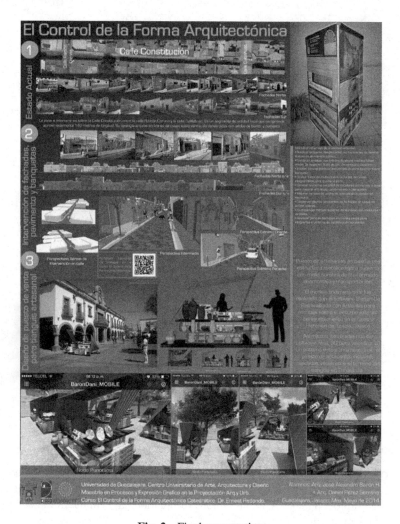

Fig. 2. Final presentation

displaying heritage. In this section, the group that has commented on this aspect was those related to the field of architecture with a total of 33.3 %.

- 16.6 % (-): Little display space for products and /or too much unexploited volume. 75 % of traders have criticized the proposals due to a reduction in the useful area of commercial stands compare to the current system, something that directly affects their operation.

5 Conclusions

The first results of the education designed experiment show as we had previously hypothesized the importance of informal education. Of the students who conducted the workshop for the proposed exercise, 95 % got the job done in time and fulfilling their objectives, with success rates of exercises presented all of them with passing grades and 85 % of them with distinction. However, as a result of informal surveys conducted for users who viewed and interacted with their proposals, we can conclude that they would not adapt successfully to the main objectives of the experiment: a new reformulation and urban restructuring of street trading in Tonalá. We discover 1 in 3 people (about 30 %) questioned the proposals, just the kind of information that allows to informally educate students in areas not covered by the proposed practices.

Note also that the AR is a technology that adapts very well to the actual visualization needs both architectural and urban 3D models. This adaptability and ease of use allows us to state that to the extent that they can optimally control aspects such as display materials, casting shadows and the ability to make changes and queries directly on the models, it is a system that perfectly complements one of the key aspects in architectural education: project presentation.

Nowadays, the project continues with the next phase of collectiong the opinions of users viewing ths site proposals. It is anticipated that this phase of informal assessment and wide sample of comments performed in this article will be closed throughout the month of January 2015. With the final results a new workshop is proposed disaggregating comments by user gropus as the main desing principle so that students effectively incorporate the information received informally in their proposals.

Acknowledgements. Project funded by the VI National Plan for Scientific Research, Development and Technological Innovation, 2008–2011, Government of Spain. No EDU-2012-37247/EDUC.

References

1. International Organization for Standardization: Ergonomics of human system interaction - Part 210: human-centered design for interactive systems (formerly known as 13407). ISO FDIS **9241**(210), 2009 (2009)
2. Nielsen, J.: Usability 101: Introduction to Usability. Jakob Nielsen's Alertbox, Accessed 01 June 2010
3. Nielsen, J., Norman, D.A: Web-Site Usability: Usability On The Web Isn't A Luxury. InformationWeek (2000)
4. La Belle, T.J.: Formal, nonformal and informal education: a holistic perspective on lifelong learning. Int. Rev. Educ. **28**(2), 159–175 (1982). doi:10.1007/BF00598444
5. OECD-Better Policies for Better Lives: Recognition of Non-formal and Informal Learning. Skills beyond school. http://www.oecd.org/education/skills-beyond-school/recognition ofnon-formalandinformallearning-home.htm. Accessed 01 December 2014
6. Cedefop Glossary:http://www.cedefop.europa.eu/EN/about-cedefop/projects/validation-of-non-formal-and-informal-learning/european-inventory-glossary.aspx.   Accessed   01 December 2014
7. Faure, E.: Learning to Be. UNESCO, Paris (1972)
8. Coombs, P.H., Prosser, C., Ahmed, M.: New Paths to Learning for Rural Children and Youth. International Council for Educational Development, John Hopkins Press, New York (1973)
9. Benévolo, L.: Historia de la Arquitectura moderna. Gustavo Gili, Barcelona (1997)

10. Pampinella, S.: Arquitecturas de autor o Arquitecturas de mecenas, en Revista Block, n. 5, Buenos Aires (2000)
11. Frampton, K.: Historia crítica de la Arquitectura moderna. Editorial GG, Barcelona (1981)
12. Taylor-Foster, J.: Los siete pecados arquitectónicos cometidos alrededor del mundo (2013). http://www.plataformaarquitectura.cl/cl/02-291775/siete-errores-arquitectonicos-cometidos-alrededor-del-mundo. Accessed 15 December 2014
13. Corento, J.L.: Fiascos arquitectónicos: los peligros del efecto Guggenheim (2013). http://elarquitectohamuerto.blogspot.com.es/2013/12/fiascos-arquitectonicos-efecto-guggenheim.html. Accessed 15 December 2014
14. Craven, J.: Trouble in Paradise. The troubled story of the glass wallwd Farnsworth House (2013). http://tweedlandthegentlemansclub.blogspot.com.es/2013/05/trouble-in-paradise-troubled-story-of.html. Accessed 15 December 2014
15. Bobhate, P.: Villa Savoye – An architectural wonder or a thermal disaster. In: Proceedings of Conference: People and Buildings held at the offices of Arup, London, UK, 23 September 2011. http://nceub.commoncense.info/uploads/MC2011_MC22.pdf. Accessed 10 December 2014
16. Al Shawa, B.: The Darker Side of Villa Savoye. Misfits' Architecture (2011). http://misfitsarchitecture.com/2011/09/03/the-darker-side-of-villa-savoye/.   Accessed   10 December 2014
17. Sully, N.: Moder architecture and complaints about the weather, or, dear monsieur le corbusier, it is still raining in our garage. M/C J. 12(4), 1–10 (2009). http://journal.media-culture.org.au/index.php/mcjournal/article/viewArticle/172. Accessed 10 December 2014
18. Mateos, R., Quelart, R.: La nueva baldosa de Barcelona, un suplicio para ir con tacones (2014). http://videos.lavanguardia.com/local/barcelona/20141119/54419992257/la-nueva-baldosa-de-barcelona-un-suplicio-para-ir-con-tacones.html. Accessed 19 November 2014
19. Gschwandtner, W.R., Münzberger, H.: Lipoatrophia semicircularis. ein beitrag zu bandförmig-circulären atrophien des subcutanen fettgewebes im extremitätenbereich. Der Hautartz 25, 222–227 (1974)
20. Lipoatrofia semicircular, la enfermedad de los edificios modernso. Taringa Post (2011). http://www.taringa.net/posts/salud-bienestar/1886145/Lipoatrofia-semicircular-la-enfermedad-de-los-edificios-mod.html. Accessed 12 December 2014
21. Romanillos, T.: Lipoatrodia semicircular. La enfermedad de los nuevos edificios de oficinas   (2007).   http://www.consumer.es/web/es/salud/problemas_de_salud/2007/04/27/162011.php. Accessed 12 December 2014
22. Rodriguez-Izquierdo, R.M.: El impacto de las TIC en la transformación de la enseñanza universitaria: repensar los modelos de enseñanza y aprendizaje. Teoría de la Educación, Educación y Cultura en la Sociedad de la Información 11(3), 32–68 (2010)
23. Fonseca, D., Redondo, E., Villagrasa, S.: Mixed-methods research: a new approach to evaluating the motivation and satisfaction of university students using advanced visual technologies. Univ. Access Inf. Soc. (2014). doi:10.1007/s10209-014-0361-4
24. Fonseca, D., Martí, N., Redondo, E., Navarro, I., Sánchez, A.: Relationship between student profile, tool use, participation, and academic performance with the use of augmented reality technology for visualized architecture models. Comput. Hum. Behav. 31, 434–445 (2014). doi:10.1016/j.chb.2013.03.006
25. Fonseca, D., Villagrasa, S., Valls, F., Redondo, E.: August climent, lluís vicent: motivation assessment in engineering students using hybrid technologies for 3D Visualization. In: XVI Simposio Internacional de Informática Educativa. Logroño, Spain, pp. 157–164, 12–14 November 2014

26. Sánchez, A., Redondo, E., Fonseca, D.: developing an augmented reality application in the framework of architecture degree. In: Proceedings of the ACM workshop on User experience in e-learning and augmented technologies in education (UXeLATE 2012), pp. 37–42. ACM, New York, USA (2012). doi:10.1145/2390895.2390905

27. Fonseca, D., Villagrasa, S., Valls, F., Redondo, E.: August climent, lluís vicent: engineering teaching methods using hybrid technologies based on the motivation and assessment of student's profiles. In: 44th Annual Frontiers in Education Conference (FIE 2014), pp. 1356–1363, Madrid, Spain, 22–25 October 2014

28. Sampaio, A.Z., Viana, L.: Virtual reality used as a learning technology: visual simulation of the construction of a bridge deck. In: Rocha, A. et al. (eds.) Proceedings Of Information Systems and Technologies (CISTI), vol. 1, pp. 19–22 (2013)

29. Kalkofen, D., Veas, E., Zollmann, S., Steinberger, M., Schmalstieg, D.: Adaptive ghosted views for augmented reality. In: IEEE International Symposium on Mixed and Augmented Reality (ISMAR), pp. 1–9, (2013). doi:10.1109/ISMAR.2013.6671758

30. Sampaio, A.Z., Rosário, D.P.: Maintenance planning of building walls supported on virtual reality technology. In: Rocha, A., et al. (eds.) Proceedings Of Information Systems and Technologies (CISTI), vol. 1, pp. 1–7 (2013)

31. Redondo, E., Riera, A.S., Puig, J.: Gironella tower in Gerunda, teaching roman architecture, using 3D model-ing and augmented reality. In: A case study. S.A.V.E. Heritage - International Forum S.A.V.E. Heritage Safeguard of Architectural, Visual, Environmental Heritage, pp. 102(1)–102(9), Capri (2011)

32. Perrone, F.R., Heidrich, F.E., Gomes, H.M., da Silva, A.B.A.: Desenvolvimento de Aplicativo para Visualização de Patrimônio Histórico-Arquitetônico em Realidade Aumentada (Development of an Application for Visualization of historical and Architectural heritage in Augmented Reality) SIGRADI, vol. 1, pp. 366–368 (2012)

33. Clayton, M.J., Warden, R.B., Parker, T.W.: Virtual construction of architecture using 3D CAD and simulation. Autom. Constr. 11(2), 227–235 (2002). doi:10.1016/S0926-5805(00)00100-X

34. Redondo, E., Valls, F., Fonseca, D., Navarro, I., Villagrasa, S., Olivares, A., Peredo, A.: Educational qualitative assessment of augmented reality models and digital sketching applied to urban planning. In: Proceedings of the Second International Conference on Technological Ecosystems for Enhancing Multiculturality (TEEM 2014), pp. 447–454. ACM, New York, NY, USA (2014). doi:10.1145/2669711.2669938

Evolution of the Conversation and Knowledge Acquisition in Social Networks Related to a MOOC Course

Francisco J. García-Peñalvo[1(✉)], Juan Cruz-Benito[1],
Oriol Borrás-Gené[2], and Ángel Fidalgo Blanco[3]

[1] GRIAL Research Group, Department of Computers and Automatics,
Research Institute for Educational Sciences,
University of Salamanca, Salamanca, Spain
{fgarcia, juancb}@usal.es
[2] GATE, Technical University of Madrid, Madrid, Spain
oriol.borras@upm.es
[3] Technical University of Madrid, Madrid, Spain
afidalgo@dmami.upm.es

Abstract. This paper presents a real case of tracking conversations and participation in social networks like Twitter and Google+ from students enrolled in a MOOC course. This real case presented is related to a MOOC course developed between January 12 and February 8, 2015, in the iMOOC platform, created as result of the collaboration by Technical University of Madrid, University of Za-ragoza and University of Salamanca. The course had more than 400 students and more than 700 interactions (publications, replies, likes, reshares, etc.) retrieved from the social both social networks (about 200 interactions in Twitter and 500 in Google+). This tracking process of students' conversations and students' participation in the social networks allows the MOOC managers and teachers to understand the students' knowledge sharing and knowledge acquisition within the social networks, allowing them to unlock the possibility of use this knowledge in order to enhance the MOOC contents and results, or even close the loop between the students' participation in a MOOC course and the parallel students´ usage of social networks to learn, by the combination of both tools using adaptive layers (and other layers like the cooperation or gamification like in the iMOOC platform) in the eLearning platforms, that could lead the students to achieve better results in the Learning process.

Keywords: MOOCs · iMOOC · Conversation · Knowledge acquisition · Social networks · Informal learning · Twitter · Google+

1 Introduction

The informal conversations through social networks are one of the most successful ways to get extra knowledge and enhance the Learning experience in many online courses [1–4]. Many authors have pointed that the conversations and interactions in the social networks could reveal some real characteristics and results of different Learning

© Springer International Publishing Switzerland 2015
P. Zaphiris and A. Ioannou (Eds.): LCT 2015, LNCS 9192, pp. 470–481, 2015.
DOI: 10.1007/978-3-319-20609-7_44

activities, offline activities, etc. [5]. For example, it is possible to highlight the theory of Connectivism [6, 7], where the Learning process is enhanced by the connections between students and teachers and online resources [8], refers to the elements of social networks that encourage such relationships or interactions, so these will offer an ideal space for creating Learning communities. According to Siemens [6] from ICTs the importance of individual knows what an shift to what an individual knows how to find out.

According to the literature [3, 9–12], it is possible to identify three types of Learning:

- Formal Learning: "Learning that occurs in an organized and structured environment (in an education or training institution or on-the-job) and is explicitly designated as Learning (in terms of objectives, time or resources). It typically leads to validation and certification".
- Non-formal Learning: "Learning which is embedded in planned activities not explicitly as Learning. Non-formal Learning outcomes may be validated and lead to certification".
- Informal Learning: "Learning resulting from daily activities related to work, family or leisure. It is not organized or structured in terms of objectives, time or Learning support".

In the case of a MOOC, the informal Learning emerges from connections between students in a spontaneous way against non-formal, than even being also a kind of in formal Learning is a pedagogical focus directed by the course team, as it would be the case where specific tags in social networks (*hashtags* [13] in Twitter [14] or Google+) are proposed by teachers to start a discussion or conversation out of the MOOC [15, 16]. These kinds of Learning out of the MOOC (informal and non-formal) can influence the results and achievements of the students within the MOOC [17], also it can allow to MOOC teachers, from the study of the conversations of the students, to discover their shortcomings, their major problems faced in the course or even what or how to find solutions to community faced such problems. On the other side it could be a used to reuse in future editions and improve the Learning platform (using the gained knowledge about those subjects that are more interesting for students, those that enhance the informal Learning around the MOOC course, etc.).

The main goal of this research work, based on previous considerations and other that will be discussed below, is to discover the knowledge acquisition and to track the conversations related to the MOOC content courses in environments non-designed for Learning like the social networks [18] to allow MOOC teachers and managers to improve the Learning process in this kind of platforms in future editions of the MOOC courses.

The manuscript is divided into the following sections: Sect. 1 (Introduction) introduces the problem and main concepts that will be used and discussed in the manuscript. Section 2 (Materials and Methods) presents the resources used to perform the analysis, which are basically the MOOC course, and the social networks where students and course teachers had performed the conversations and where the informal Learning take place. Section 3 (Results) describes the analysis results, presenting also the data retrieved within the analysis and showing the main trends in conversations, the most used tags for discussions, main users that participated, etc. Section 4 (Discussion) discusses the data presented in the previous section include also considerations regarding also the Learning community features and issues. Finally, the Sect. 5 (Conclusions) presents several conclusions about the research work and potential work for the future.

2 Materials and Methods

2.1 Materials

iMOOC and the Course "Social Networking and Learning". The intelligent platform MOOC (iMOOC) is the outcome of an agreement of collaboration in 2013 among the Technical University of Madrid, the University of Zaragoza and the University of Salamanca. It is based on the eLearning platform Moodle 2.6.5. Its principal distinguishing features are the adaptability and the promotion of cooperative informal Learning. One of the main features is the use of Cooperative MOOC model proposed by Fidalgo et al. [19] part of a xMOOC (eLearning platforms) combining connectivist characteristics typical of cMOOCs based on Learning communities. In this model, which integrates three layers, we have added a fourth one with gamification elements [20] involving the others. These layers represent the eLearning platform and social networking (technological layer), the instructional design of the course (training layer), the results and generated content from cooperation between students and teachers (cooperative layer). Eventually associated elements are added to the three layers to improve motivation (gamification layer).

Within a single course we find a set of educational itineraries based on three variables: the general user's profile, preferences and choices of the users or students and progress in the Learning process within the course. To configure these features we have used Moodle platform features such as conditional or groups, supported by external plugins to create groupings, obtain statistics or offer certificates automatically. On the other hand the promotion of informal Learning through collaboration has been implemented using tools offered by the platform such as profiles, forums, workshops and external tools like social networks.

The MOOC course "Social Networking and Learning" [21] is an adapted version of the course "Application of social networking to education: virtual communities" version given on the platform Miriada X. The course duration was 1 month, starting on January 12 and ending on February 8, 2015. Regarding the participation, 793 students were enrolled for the course, more than 400 started it, and 183 students finally accomplish the goal. This course aims to teach students to create virtual Learning communities using social networks. Over four modules an overview of the social web, exploring two of the most extended social networks such as Facebook and Twitter is given. In the last module other social networks are studied, without going into too much detail, highlighting those characteristics that define them and can serve for educational purposes. The course takes advantage of features of the platform like is adaptability [22, 23], offering students the possibility of choosing various educational itineraries based on the topics covered in the course. The student can choose from 5 itineraries: Full course for teachers (offers two additional lessons from implementation of Twitter and Facebook to teaching), complete course for non-teachers, Twitter (only one module on the network), Facebook (only one module this network) and special itinerary. The special itinerary was addressed to students who had participated in the course in a previous edition, featuring a new module focused on Learning communities with a more practical approach. This itinerary allowed access to the rest of the course.

Hahstags and Social Networks. Regarding the social part with a non-formal Learning approach, where the connections between the members and the content is generated, it was decided to use a Learning community for the course. To develop the community the course managers chose the Google+ and its "Communities" tool, where members could publish using classification categories proposed by the course team. Thereby they could interact, ask questions or discussions and share resources (links, application examples and exercises or activities raised in the course). This community consists of more than 5000 members having students from previous editions of the course and professionals interested in the subject.

To encourage community use throughout the course, different exercises have been proposed to the enrolled students that must be resolved publishing the solutions in this community or in their Twitter accounts, using specific *hashtags* included in the statement of each exercise. Although the discussion of the solution in the social media helped to generate more interaction among students [24]. Both debates as the exercises were associated with a specific category ("discussions" and "activities and exercises"). These relations will also be enhanced off the platform by community discussions or videoconferences a group of students can submit projects related to course topics after voted in the community for the other fellow. These are broadcast live video from YouTube by Google Hangout tool and using *hashtags* students pose their questions to the speakers, both Twitter and from the community in Google+.

As a result of use of *hashtags* within the course, one can distinguish among several types depending on its origin and its use over time:

- Course *Hashtags,* proposed by the teaching staff, would be framed within what is non-formal Learning. There are two types, generic for the entire course or specific for a module, which students could use in their related publications, even in specific activities or exercises for the course.
- *Hashtags* different to those proposed in the course depending on the needs and according to the students' publication. This use would be more associated with informal Learning.
- *Hashtags* used synchronously by participants at specific times of the course, for example *#RSEHangout* for hangouts sessions.
- *Hashtags* proposed in the course and used asynchronously, as the need arises them.

The goal of using these kinds of tags and resources seeks to improve dropout rates due to the heterogeneity of students in the course. Within the MOOC course ecosystem it is also possible to distinguish the three types of Learning explained previously, with the theoretical part in the iMOOC platform corresponding to formal Learning, community Google+ created by teachers or *hashtags* proposed by them corresponds to the non-formal Learning and those conversations initiated by students parallel to the course so through social networks or community contributions in periods the course is not taught as informal Learning in the course.

2.2 Methods

To get insight about the usage of social networks and use of conversations and interactions in order to gain knowledge around the MOOC topics, it is necessary to develop a strategy to retrieve, save and use the information that users share on social networks. In this strategy, the authors have developed some crawlers and automatized systems that search in Twitter the usage of some previously-defined *hashtags* related to the MOOC course, determining the amount of users who use it, identifying, if it is possible, the users who are already enrolled in the MOOC course and the users that are only participating in the informal conversation (and without participating in the MOOC), and even those *hashtags* created *ad hoc* by the students to start new conversations or tag the publications with other extra search. In the case of Google+ the researchers did not develop any crawler due the API restrictions of the social network, but they used third-party tools like AllmyPlus (http://www.allmyplus.com/) that allow them to retrieve social interaction related to each *hashtag*.

The analysis in the first stage was not intended to dig inside the real conversations (was not intended to make text mining or other text analysis techniques), but it intend to reveal the use of some *hashtags*, the interaction among users, etc. that will serve as basis for later analysis that could reveal the URLs that users share, the identification of leaders and influencers in the conversations, determining coincidences between the students or users of the social network, their usage rates of some resources, etc. in order to get a full insight about the MOOC community that could be used to improve it for later editions of courses. This full insight will reveal some aspects like the students' interaction and conversations, and what kind of informal or non-formal Learning happens in detail in these social networks (which are not specialized in academic content but intended for general purpose).

Once the analysts have retrieved and saved the information, it is needed to define how can be possible to extract true knowledge from the raw data, and how the system could reveal and show this knowledge to the analyst, MOOC managers, etc. In this first approach of the analysis, the representation is performed mainly by through tables and structured data, also some basic graphs were implemented to help the analysts to understand the information presented.

3 Results

The application of the previously described information tracking strategy in the social networks led the authors to discover some relevant information. This information help to understand the scope of the social interactions between MOOC course users, and MOOC course contents. As previously stated, the course teachers proposed several *hashtags* to help the conversation tagging and tracing its evolution, or simply to tag the common conversations about the MOOC contents (*hashtags* related to non-formal Learning). These *hashtags* were the following: *#DebatesRSE, #ActividadesRSE,*

#DudasRSE, #AvisosRSE, #EjerciciosRSE, #modulo1RSE, #modulo2RSE, #modulo3RSE, #modulo4RSE, #RSEMOOC, #RSEHangout, #RSEEjemplosRRSS, #RSEMalasPracticas, #RSEmiKlout, #UsosTwitterEnseñanza, #RSEMoodleTwitter.

The analysis of these *hashtags* revealed the following amount of interactions (publications, replies and comments to the publications, retweets and reshares of publications, and favorites or +1 in Google+) and its distribution over both social networks (Table 1, Fig. 1)

Table 1. Total interactions in Twitter and Google+ with teachers' proposed *hashtags*

Total interactions	Twitter	Google+	Total
Publications	108	119	227
Replies/Comments	17	76	93
Retweets/Reshares	42	17	59
Favorite /+1	45	315	360
Total	212	527	739

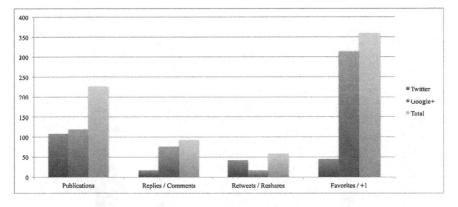

Fig. 1. Total interactions versus interactions in each social network related to the MOOC course

Among these global data per social network, it is possible to filter the information depending the type of interaction and each *hashtag* so it is possible to know the real interactions with the contents related to the MOOC course (through its tagging by *hashtags*). Following are presented the data of the most used *hashtags* proposed by teachers (Table 2, Fig. 2).

Also, the teachers proposed some debates (non-formal Learning) in the social networks (mainly in Google+) to discuss some concepts near to the MOOC contents. In the case of this course, the teachers used one debate started in the previous course, obtaining in this edition 28 comments and 5 +1's on Google+ .

Regarding the informal Learning component of the social networks usage, the analysis revealed some interesting data about the trends in informal conversations and learners' knowledge sharing preferences. These data, as the previously explanation

Table 2. Official *hashtags* interactions in each social network (*hashtags* most used)

Interactions/ Hashtag	#RSEMOOC	#RSEHangout	#RSEEjemplosRRSS	#RSEMalasPracticas	#RSEmiKlout	#RSEMoodleTwitter	Total interactions per type
Twitter Tweets	9	19	4	5	8	59	104
Google+ Publications	16	4	35	27	20	0	102
Twitter Replies	2	4	1	0	1	9	17
Google+ Comments	33	15	9	2	8	0	67
Twitter Retweets	5	16	0	1	5	9	36
Google+ Reshares	3	2	6	5	1	0	17
Twitter Favorites	5	15	0	2	6	11	39
Google+ + 1's	57	25	84	47	51	0	264
Total Hashtag Interactions	130	100	139	89	100	88	

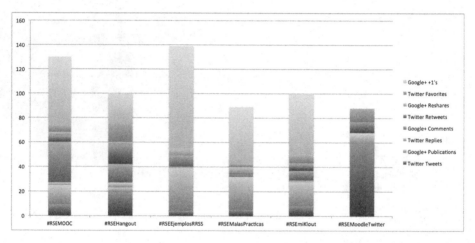

Fig. 2. Distribution of interactions in each proposed *official hashtag* in the social networks

about the teachers' proposed *hashtags*, can be showed filtered by social networks interactions with *hashtags* and debates started (by the students in this case). As example, in the case of *hashtags* used by students, not proposed by the teaching staff, it is possible to find, in Google+ 169 publications started by students. In these publications, the *tags* most used (and most interacted) by them are the following (Table 3, Fig. 3): *#facebookeducacionrse*, *#twitter*, *#educación* (education in Spanish language), *#facebook*, *#aprendizaje* (Learning in Spanish), *#infografía* (infographics in Spanish), *#aula* (classroom in Spanish).

Table 3. Unofficial *hashtags* most used by the students within the MOOC course (related to informal Learning) in Google+

	#facebookeducacionarse	#twitter	#educación	#facebook	#aprendizaje	#infografía	#aula
Number of publications	26	12	10	9	7	6	4
Comments	7	18	14	7	4	13	0
Reshares	5	21	20	6	8	7	0
+1's	61	94	65	54	55	35	4
Total Interactions /Hastags	99	145	109	76	74	61	8

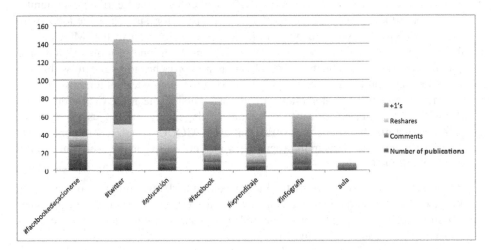

Fig. 3. Distribution of interaction with unofficial most used *hashtags* proposed by students in Google+

Also, about *unofficial* and *informal* debates started by the students, the analysis raised 10 different discussions with 14 publications and 45 +1's also on Google+ community.

4   Discussion

Regarding the results, the authors want to discuss two main questions about the utility of the study and its application. These questions are: Is it possible to identify the *trending topics* (subjects that interested more to the MOOC and social networks audience) in this Learning community through this analysis approach? Is it useful to know these data to improve the MOOC or the Learning community?

From the authors' point of view, the answer to both questions is yes:

- Yes, it is possible to identify in the social networks the trending concepts and contents most discussed and probably more interesting for the students in both ways, through *official hashtags* and through *unofficial hashtags*. Regarding the data, it is possible to identify what are the most used tags, what contents reflect more users' interactions, etc., so it is possible to assert that retrieving information about the interaction with the tags, the teachers and MOOC managers could identify what subjects and concepts are more interesting for the users and apply this knowledge to improve the experience within the MOOC and its results. Also, it should be remarked that if this analysis approach is enriched, for example with basic text mining techniques, the teachers and managers could filter the interactions and comments using extra information that learners use, like URL, news posted, content feeds, etc., and this can open new advanced possibilities even helping the personalization and adaptation to users that iMOOC approach performs.

- Yes, the data is useful to improve the MOOC and enhance the Learning community. The retrieved knowledge can be used, as stated just before, to "close the loop" with the adaptativity, cooperation or gamification features present in the iMOOC platform, or even closing the loop in other way, using both kind of tools (MOOC and social networks) to establish tools collaboration approaches to use them within the same Learning processes. For example, knowing the main interests for a user (based on the comments and interactions inside and outside the MOOC platform), the iMOOC could present contents or resources depending on the user's interests detected within the social networks, or even MOOC could recommend some debates and conversations in the social networks, etc. based on the users' interaction inside the MOOC course.

There are another two issues that authors would remark regarding the conversations tracking; one is the limitation retrieving data from the social networks, and the other main issue is related to the previous students' skills using social networks and the errors and mistakes they can make using the systems, the *hashtags*, etc.

In the case of the limitations retrieving information, there are many problems with Twitter and Google+.

- In the case of Twitter, the API only allows to search tweets in a 7-day window before the moment of the search, so it difficult too much to perform the analysis post-course. Instead of this search methods, the Twitter's API allows to *live stream* the tweets under some *hashtags*, but it requires that the analysts know previously all the possible *hashtags* that would be used, or another techniques that make possible to include new *hashtags* within the live tweet stream.
- In the case of Google+, Google APIs limits the access to retrieve data, so if analysts want to retrieve the interactions and data about the activity on Google+ without restrictions, they should perform manual analysis tasks, use web scrapping techniques, or utilize third-party tools like those used in this research work (http://www.allmyplus.com/ for example).

Other relevant issue regarded in the analysis, is the importance of the students' previous skills using these kinds of systems like the social networks. During the analysis, the researchers have observed many errors using tags in publications, error commenting other activities performed purely in the social networks, etc. These skills and the performed mistakes are relevant in the analysis because they could introduce noise and errors in the results. Thus, the researchers would develop strategies in the future to avoid this kind of noise and possible errors during the analysis phase.

5   Conclusions

This paper explains the authors' way to track the conversations in social networks related to a MOOC course and how they make basic analysis in order to review the knowledge sharing and knowledge acquisition through these social networks. The paper also reveals how this kind of data retrieval and basic analysis empowers the MOOC managers and teachers to understand and track the conversations in social networks like Twitter and Google+ around MOOC concepts and subjects, so they can measure the Learning process in these social networks regarding three kinds of Learning, formal, informal and non-formal Learning. The data presented in this paper can serve as a basic example of this usage, and the authors present some other applications and future work to enhance and improve this analysis to make it more powerful.

Regarding the results of this preliminary study about the students' conversations in social networks and its reflection on their knowledge acquisition and Learning, the authors agree that it is possible to enhance the retrieval and analytics process, achieving a clear process with great outcomes regarding the detection of interests, desires and concepts and subjects that the students want to discuss with others.

The improvement of this process, would allow achieve the combination of both Learning tools, the MOOC platform or eLearning platform that the students use to learn in a formal or non-formal ways, and the social networks that the students use to learn in non-formal or informal ways. This combination could produce a loop process where the MOOC and social networks can feedback themselves, detecting students' behaviors, desires and interest, to use them later by the integration with adaptive Learning platforms, like the iMOOC platform or many others, improving by this way the Learning processes through the use of personalization layers that use interests detected and the insights retrieved from users' interaction in social networks, to present personalized contents to the students that could encourage them to improve their Learning, to obtain better outcomes from this process, and better performance in the Learning experience.

Acknowledgments.   We'd like to thank to the GRIAL and LITI research groups by their support in this research and also we'd like to thank to the UPM by its financial support throughout the "Diseño y desarrollo de MOOC universitarios" (Ref. PT1415-05000) Project.

References

1. Mackness, J., Mak, S., Williams, R.: The ideals and reality of participating in a MOOC. In: 7th International Conference on Networked Learning, pp. 266–275 (2010)
2. McAuley, A., Stewart, B., Siemens, G., Cormier, D.: The MOOC model for digital practice. In: SSHRC Knowledge Synthesis Grant on the Digital Economy (2010)

3. Vanbaelen, R., Harrison, J., van Dongen, G.: Lifelong learning in a fourth world setting. In: IEEE international professional communication conference (IPCC) 2014, pp. 1–9 (2014)

4. García-Peñalvo, F.J., Johnson, M., Ribeiro Alves, G., Minovic, M., Conde-González, M.A.: Informal learning recognition through a cloud ecosystem. Future Gener. Comput. Syst. **32**, 282–294 (2014)

5. Aramo-Immonen, H., Jussila, J., Huhtamäki, J.: Visualizing informal learning behavior from conference participants Twitter data. In: Proceedings of the Second International Conference on Technological Ecosystems for Enhancing Multiculturality, pp. 603–610. ACM, Salamanca, Spain (2014)

6. Siemens, G.: Connectivism: a learning theory for the digital age. Int. J. Instr. Technol. Distance Learn. **2**, 3–10 (2005)

7. Zapata-Ros, M.: Teorías y modelos sobre el aprendizaje en entornos conectados y ubicuos. Education in the Knowledge Society 16, 69–102 (2015)

8. Evans, C.: Twitter for teaching: Can social media be used to enhance the process of learning? Br. J. Educ. Technol. **45**, 902–915 (2014)

9. Marsick, V.J., Watkins, K.E.: Informal and incidental learning. New Directions Adult Contin. Educ. **2001**, 25–34 (2001)

10. García-Peñalvo, F.J., García-Holgado, A., Cruz-Benito, J.: Formal and informal learning experiences in multicultural scopes. In: Proceedings of the First International Conference on Technological Ecosystem for Enhancing Multiculturality, pp. 523–527. ACM, Salamanca, Spain (2013)

11. Bjornavold, J.: Training, E.C.f.t.D.o.V.: Validation of non-formal and informal learning in Europe: a snapshot 2007. Office for Official Publications of the European Communities, Luxembourg (2008)

12. García-Peñalvo, F.J., Colomo-Palacios, R., Lytras, M.D.: Informal learning in work environments: training with the Social Web in the workplace. Behav. & Inf. Technol. **31**, 753–755 (2012)

13. Ghenname, M., Abik, M., Ajhoun, R., Subercaze, J., Gravier, C., Laforest, F.: Personalized recommendation based hashtags on e-learning systems. In: ISKO-Maghreb 2013 Concepts and Tools for Knowledge Management (KM), pp. NA, Tunisia (2013)

14. Twitter Inc, https://support.twitter.com/articles/49309

15. West, J.: Recognition of non-formal and informal learning: the Case Against. Study prepared for the meeting of the OECD Group of Experts (2007)

16. Vosecky, J., Jiang, D., Leung, K.W.-T., Xing, K., Ng, W.: Integrating social and auxiliary semantics for multifaceted topic modeling in twitter. ACM Trans. Internet Technol. **14**, 1–24 (2014)

17. Fidalgo-Blanco, Á., Sein-Echaluce, M.L., García-Peñalvo, F.J., Esteban Escaño, J.: Improving the MOOC learning outcomes throughout informal learning activities. In: Proceedings of the Second International Conference on Technological Ecosystems for Enhancing Multiculturality, pp. 611–617. ACM, Salamanca, Spain (2014)

18. Alario-Hoyos, C., Pérez-Sanagustín, M., Delgado-Kloos, C., Parada G., H.A., Muñoz-Organero, M., Rodríguez-de-las-Heras, A.: Analysing the impact of built-in and external social tools in a MOOC on educational technologies. In: Hernández-Leo, D., Ley, T., Klamma, R., Harrer, A. (eds.) EC-TEL 2013. LNCS, vol. 8095, pp. 5–18. Springer, Heidelberg (2013)

19. Fidalgo, Á., Sein-Echaluce Lacleta, M.L., García-Peñalvo, F.J.: MOOC cooperativo. Una integración entre cMOOC y xMOOC. In: Fidalgo Blanco, Á., Sein-Echaluce Lacleta, M.L. (eds.) Actas del II Congreso Internacional sobre Aprendizaje, Innovación y Competitividad, CINAIC, Madrid, 6–8 de noviembre de 2013, pp. 481–486. Fundación General de la Universidad Politécnica de Madrid, Madrid, España (2013)

20. Borrás Gené, O., Martínez Núñez, M., Fidalgo Blanco, Á.: Gamification in MOOC: challenges, opportunities and proposals for advancing MOOC model. In: Proceedings of the Second International Conference on Technological Ecosystems for Enhancing Multiculturality, pp. 215–220. ACM, Salamanca, Spain (2014)
21. Technical University of Madrid (Spain), University of Zaragoza (Spain), http://gridlab.upm.es/imooc/course/view.php?id=2
22. Fidalgo Blanco, Á., Sein-Echaluce Lacleta, M.L., García-Peñalvo, F.J.: Methodological Approach and Technological Framework to break the current limitations of MOOC model. Journal of Universal Computer Science. In Press (2015)
23. Fidalgo Blanco, Á., García-Peñalvo, F.J., Sein-Echaluce Lacleta, M.L.: A methodology proposal for developing adaptive cMOOC. In: García-Peñalvo, F.J. (ed.) Proceedings of the First International Conference on Technological Ecosystem for Enhancing Multiculturality (TEEM 2013), pp. 553–558. ACM, New York, USA (2013)
24. Karaoglan, B., Candemir, C., Haytaoglu, E., Algin, G.B., Demirci, S.: Using Twitter as a diagnostic teaching and learning assessment tool. In: 25th Annual Conference EAEEIE 2014, pp. 73–76 (2014)

CATALYST: Technology-Assisted Collaborative and Experiential Learning for School Students

Vikas Goel[1(✉)], Utkarsh Mishra[1], Soumya Tiwari[1], Ravi Mokashi Punekar[1],
Keyur Sorathia[1], Kuldeep Yadav[2], and Om Deshmukh[2]

[1] Indian Institute of Technology, Guwahati, Assam, India
{v.goel,m.utkarsh,t.soumya,mokashi,keyur}@iitg.ernet.in
[2] Xerox Research Centre, Bangalore, India
{Kuldeep.R,Om.Deshmukh}@Xerox.com

Abstract. Advent of technology in the education domain has led to the emergence of new pedagogical models. However, there is very little study on the relevance of these models in developing regions. In this paper, we present a technology-enabled learning framework called CATALYST, which caters to technology-lean classroom environments particularly in developing regions such as India. The CATALYST framework combines concepts from experiential learning, collaborative and cooperative learning in education. The CATALYST framework is compared with the traditional classroom teaching in the context of teaching a 10th grade science concept of the Doppler Effect. Our user study on a set of 30 students demonstrates that CATALYST is more effective in improving students' understanding while generating higher student engagement as compared to the traditional approach. Additionally, the unique design of group activities in CATALYST leads to higher interaction among low and high performers as well as across the genders.

Keywords: Technology-lean environment · Experiential learning · Peer learning · Doppler Effect · Technology Enabled Learning (TEL)

1 Introduction

Education system in several developing economies faces acute shortage of qualified teachers [1, 2]. For instance, India currently needs 1.2 million additional school teachers [3], which is likely to grow to 5 million by 2020. Further, 20 % of currently employed teachers are untrained. Due to these problems, students often feel disengaged in the classrooms and often are not able to learn appropriately [2]. Extensive usage of technology in the educational domain in a past few years has led to the emergence of new methods of learning and some of these methods are being experimented in real-world. Massive Open Online Courses (MOOCs) is one such method that aims to broadcast video lectures on the Internet to a wide student audience [4]. MOOCs assume easy access to a personal computing device, high speed Internet connectivity for anytime anywhere access to e-learning content. However, most of the classrooms in developing countries do not have access to these technologies due to cost-constraints. There have been many efforts

© Springer International Publishing Switzerland 2015
P. Zaphiris and A. Ioannou (Eds.): LCT 2015, LNCS 9192, pp. 482–491, 2015.
DOI: 10.1007/978-3-319-20609-7_45

recently, which use MOOC content with classroom teaching in a blended learning environment [5]. Flipped Classrooms [6] and Blended Learning [7] methods which combine classroom learning with anytime anywhere learning are also being explored extensively.

Our team has been working to identify synergies between the various methods of technology-enabled learning and classroom teaching, particularly for technology-lean schools, which are typical of a developing region such as India. Technology-lean school refers to a school, which has only a select few 'lab rooms' that have computers and/or projector facilities to augment the traditional classrooms, which have no technology presence. Moreover, the computer in the 'lab rooms' is typically shared by 3-5 students. We are trying to identify the methods and frameworks promoting better learning environments in technology lean environments with additional challenges associated with inaccessibility to the well trained teachers.

The fact that lab rooms in our schools require 4-5 students to share a single computer also opens up opportunities for peer learning. Design methodologies for technology-enabled peer interactions and their impact on student performance and retention is an active area of research [8]. Authors in [9] show that peer learning also plays a key role in developing students' social interactions and communication skills. Authors in [10] show that collaborative computer-game-based learning approach leads to improved learning, motivation, and achievements as compared to learning approaches based on either conventional collaborative learning or individual game-based learning. However, there is limited exploration of using online video content in classrooms in developing economies such as India. Moreover, by using video content in the classroom also opens up opportunity of enhancing the learning process by using concepts like gamification [11], adaptive learning [12], game based learning [13], experiential learning [14] and many more. We primarily focused on experiential learning where new concepts are learnt in relevance to the activities of everyday life by reflecting on our experiences. There are many questions surrounding the effectiveness of video based learning frameworks with limited no. of computers and technology-assisted experiential learning experience in classrooms in such technology-lean environments.

In this paper, we propose a learning framework called CATALYST that combines technology enhanced learning, peer learning, and classroom-based teaching in the context of teaching a tenth grade science concept of the Doppler Effect. We designed an experiential application, which uses real-world artifacts to create curiosity among students just before the actual classroom teaching. These applications are interactive and exploratory in nature and give the students an opportunity to try and understand new concepts themselves. We present our initial findings from an on-going user study where we compare the efficacy of the proposed CATALYST framework with the traditional classroom teaching. Specifically, we aim to answer following questions:

1. What is the impact of the CATALYST approach on students' learning when compared to the traditional teaching, especially on the low performing students?
2. How does student engagement and curiosity vary across the two approaches?
3. What are the observed barriers in peer learning in an Indian classroom scenario and does the proposed CATALYST framework help in enhancing peer collaboration as well as learning?

2 Catalyst Framework

We present a technology-enabled learning framework called CATALYST, which caters to the technology-lean classroom environments predominantly present in developing regions such as India. CATALYST adheres to the following theoretical methods of learning: provide experiential learning where students can relate the learning to real life experiences [14]; adheres to the 'cycle of learning' which combines the three stages of situative, cognitive and associative learning [15]; provides peer-learning opportunity where collaboration and cooperation are combined (please refer [16] for details). It aims to enhance the learnability of the students, keeping them engaged and promoting them to interact among themselves. It also emphasizes on making students inquisitive in order to retain their interest in what they are learning.

An interactive and explorative application is a part of the proposed framework that gives the students an opportunity to explore and learn the concept themselves. For example: an experiential learning application for the Doppler Effect (Fig-2), left) gives the students flexibility to change the various parameters like velocity, frequency, wavelength and amplitude of the source, the velocity of the source and observer to get appropriate audio-visual feedback. CATALYST has following four important stages: (a) explore and learn: A group of three students explore the application collectively on a single device and change various parameters to get audio-visual feedback; (b) documentation: students discuss and write what they observe, this phase also help students to channelize their exploration of the application with clearly stated objectives. (c) Teaching: the teacher explains the scientific reasoning behind the concept, and (d) group activity: students perform a group activity with clearly stated individual subtasks and a final collaborative task.

3 Experiment Design

The experiment was designed to compare traditional and CATALYST approaches by teaching the Doppler Effect to two different groups of students. The Doppler Effect is a physics concept, which deals with the perceived change in frequency when either the sound source or the observer or both are in motion.

3.1 Participants

30 students of 9th grade from a public school in Delhi (India) participated in the study. The participants age range between 12-15 years. For the study, it was ensured that there is equal participation of high, average and low performing students (HP, AP and LP respectively) i.e. 10 students from each category. The categorization of HP, AP and LP students was based on cumulative grade achieved by them in their 8th grade. The HP students' cumulative grade is either A1 or A2, similarly for AP students it is B1 or B2, and for LP students it is C1 or C2. The study also had an equal participation of boys and girls. 30 students were randomly divided into two equal groups of 15 students each, the control and the experimental group. Each control and experimental group had equal

share of HP, AP and LP students. The control group had 7 girls and 8 boys, whereas experimental group had 8 girls and 7 boys.

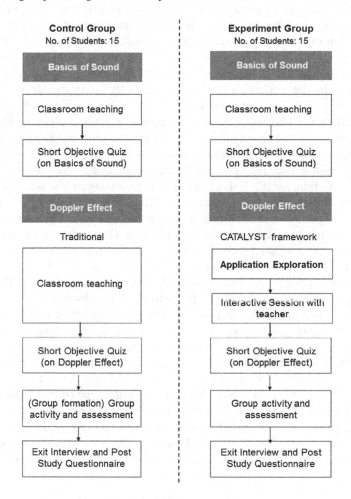

Fig. 1. Experiment design - Activities conducted in control and experimental group

3.2 Experimental Process

Thirty students participated in (a) pre-study discussion and questionnaire, (b) the actual learning experiment, and (c) post-study discussion and questionnaire. Students in control and experimental group were taught the Doppler Effect through traditional and CATALYST approaches respectively. In CATALYST, 15 students were further divided into 5 teams, each team having one HP, AP and LP student. Each team also had at least one girl and a boy. Each team in CATALYST framework was sharing a common laptop sitting together around it (Fig. 2). In the traditional approach, students were sitting like how they sit in their normal classes.

Figure 1 present the flow of the various activities conducted during the two approaches. 'Basics of Sound' a prerequisite to understand Doppler Effect was taught through traditional method, i.e. a lecture of approximately 15 min in both control and experiment groups. The lecture was followed by a short objective quiz (refer Fig. 1) of duration 15 min in both the approaches. The teacher and the material across both the approaches were also kept same. After the quiz a break of 10 min was given to the participants. After the break, students in the control group were given a lecture of duration 30-35 min by the teacher on the basics of Doppler Effect similar on the lines of traditional approach followed in normal classrooms. Where as in CATALYST framework, students started with exploring an application on a laptop in a team of 3 for 10 min. There were no pre stated objectives for the exploration and student took notes. After 10 min of exploration each student was given a documentation sheet to further help them in exploration and self-learning process. In the documentation students were asked to answer a few question, for ex. "Is there a change in the sound you hear when the observer starts to move towards or away from the source. How does it change?" After 10-15 min of objectified exploration of the application and documentation a short lecture was delivered by the teacher for approximately 10-15 min. The teacher also took the doubts of the students and discussed their observations. In both the approaches activities to teach Doppler Effect lasted for 30-35 min.

The application in CATALYST framework allowed student to control the velocity and frequency of the source (train), and the velocity of the observer (animated person) to receive live audio-visual feedback as shown in Fig. 2, thereby facilitating the experiential and explorative learning. Our hypothesis is that this kind of feedback would help them experience and understand the Doppler Effect in a much better way. After teaching the Doppler Effect, in both the approaches students were asked to solve an objective quiz (comprised of 10 questions) individually within 15 min. A short break of 10 min was given to all the participants. After the break students in the control group were also made to form teams of 3 comprising of one HP, AP and LP student similar to that in the experimental group. This change in the sitting arrangement of the students in the control group was done to conduct group activity. Under this group activity, a complex objective question was given in both the approaches to be solved in a team together. This group activity was followed by post study questionnaire and exit interviews.

3.3 Measuring Tools

A pre - study questionnaire was conducted before participants were finalized for the study and helped in ensuring that the students had no knowledge of the Doppler Effect. We conducted two different kinds of assessments: an individual-based short objective quiz on understanding of the basics of sound and Doppler Effect concepts and a group-based objective assessment on the Doppler Effect. Post-study questionnaire and an exit interview were also conducted for all the participants to understand their experience and preferences. Additionally, we observed and video recorded the in-class dynamics in both the approaches.

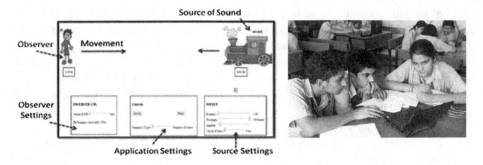

Fig. 2. Left – Screenshot of application used in CATALYST framework; Right – Student exploring application in a group.

4 Experimental Evaluation

The two approaches were compared quantitatively (using student performance on the assessments) and qualitatively (using student feedback and in-class observations).

4.1 Quantitative Comparison

Based on participants' performance in two individual short objective quizzes containing questions of basics of sound and the Doppler Effect, we try to answer some of the research questions raised above. We first wanted to determine whether there was any major bias in the results due to difference in participating students in two different approaches. It is important to note that participants in both the approaches were taught 'the basics of sound' in a similar manner and were subjected to almost identical experimental conditions. The teacher responsible for delivering the lecture component in both the approaches was also kept same. Participants in both the approaches were also assessed by the same objective quiz. Two tailed t-Test with 5 % alpha-level revealed that average marks of all participants in control group (traditional approach) was not significantly different from average marks of all participants in experiment group (CATALYST approach) (p = 0.71) (Table 1).

Table 1. Average score of students in Objective quiz 1 based on the basics of sound for both control and experimental group.

	$\bar{x}$ (Mean)	SD (Standard Deviation)	N (Sample Size)
Control Group (Traditional)	$\bar{x}_1 = 3.93$ (μ_1)	$S_1 = 1.43$	15
CATALYST (Experimental group)	$\bar{x}_2 = 4.00$ (μ_2)	$S_2 = 1.41$	15

The second question to answer is whether CATALYST framework helps in improving the learnability of the students as compared to traditional classroom teaching. To determine this average score of participants in objective quiz based on Doppler Effect was compared for both the approaches. Two tailed t-Test with 5 % alpha level revealed that the average scores of participants taught through CATALYST framework was significantly higher than average score of participants taught through traditional approach ($p = 0.013$) (Table 2).

Table 2. Average score of students in Objective quiz 2 based on the Doppler Effect for both control and experimental group.

	$\bar{x}$ (Mean)	S (Standard Deviation)	N (Sample Size)
Control Group (Traditional)	$\bar{x}_3 = 6.40$ (μ_3)	$S_3 = 1.88$	15
CATALYST (Experimental group)	$\bar{x}_4 = 8.06$ (μ_4)	$S_4 = 1.57$	15

The third question we would like to answer is whether the proposed CATALYST approach leads to uniform change in performance across all the students or if the change is dependent on the grade performance of the students. To answer this, Fig. 3 compares the average performance of HP, AP and LP students using the traditional classroom setup and the CATALYST set up on the basic of sound concept as well as to the Doppler Effect. Several interesting inferences can be drawn from this figure:

- The high-performers perform better than the low and average performers in both the approaches
- On the bases of the marks obtained by the students in the quiz the proposed CATALYST approach outperforms the traditional classroom setup
- The improvement in performance due to the proposed CATALYST approach is more pronounced for low-performers.
- This observation is consistent with the finding in [17] where the authors show that peer learning is most beneficial for complex cognitive tasks.

4.2 Qualitative Comparison

We use students' written feedback, oral feedback, and our in-class observations to qualitatively compare the two approaches in terms of student engagement and group dynamics. The 'explore and learn' phase of the CATALYST approach worked as an ice-breaker and got the students to talk to each other. Specifically, we observed that in the traditional approach, girls and boys within a team would largely work separately on the group problem, whereas in the CATALYST approach by the time the exploration phase was over, the group was already talking to each other. To quote one of the students: *"Group activity was good we would clear our doubts with others and helped each other"*. The structured group tasks in the CATALYST approach led to a clear division of labor, a sense of ownership, but at the same time encouraged each student to put forward his/her view in order to solve the group activity. This was also evident from the post-study survey, about 86.6 % of the CATALYST students agreed or strongly-agreed that they would be able to properly explain the Doppler Effect to their friend, whereas the corresponding number in the traditional approach was 46.6 %. Moreover, 91 % of CATALYST students agreed that the group task was helpful in understanding the Doppler Effect whereas the corresponding numbers for the other traditional approach were 42 %. The experiential aspect of the proposed CATALYST framework also triggered student engagement and enthusiasm and resulted in significantly improved classroom participation as observed by the researchers. In post study questionnaire, most of the students commented that the connection of the experiential web-application with the real life scenario helped them understand the concept and the underlying science in a better way. Also, in case of the CATALYST approach, students in a group interacted more frequently, irrespective of the gender or academic performance due to the collective exploration of an application on a single device. However, such interactions were missing in the conventional classroom teaching. In addition to the results above, 12/15 participants stated that CATALASY framework helped them learn the concept in a better way than traditional classroom approach.

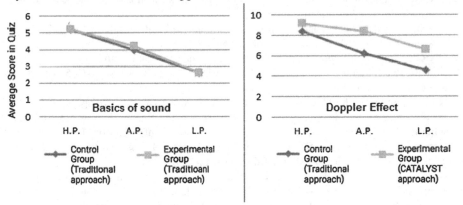

Fig. 3. For both control and experimental group, average score of high performing (HP), average performing (AP) and low performing (LP) students in quizzes based on the basics of sound (Left) and the Doppler Effect is compared.

5 Conclusion

In this work, we present our framework, called CATALYST, to create a learning environment, which combines concepts from experiential learning, collaborative and cooperative learning in education. In technology-lean learning environments, a single computing device is often simultaneously shared by multiple students. We use this constraint to our advantage by incorporating aspects of cooperative and collaborative learning in CATALYST to enhance peer-learning. We demonstrate the efficacy of the proposed framework in improving student understanding and engagement in the context of teaching the tenth grade science concept of the Doppler Effect. We are currently in discussions with the school to seek help from more teachers in better formulation of the framework and to recruit more students to conduct large scale experimentations. We have also formulated ways in which the proposed CATALYST design framework can be extended to other basic concepts such as 'resonance frequency' and 'constructive and destructive interference'. Our broad goal is to provide a stimulating environment in a typical technology-lean classroom so that learning is more experiential and loosely structured, which in turn will provide flexibility to the students on learning different concepts. We believe the proposed strategy will not only lead to increased learning outcomes along with sustained student engagement, but will also extend the recall duration. We are currently working on lesson planning strategies for an entire semester-long module of a tenth grade science course and subsequently measure its impact at a larger scale.

References

1. UNESCO Education for All. http://www.unesco.org/new/en/education/themes/leading-the-international-agenda/efareport/reports/
2. Teachers and educational quality: Monitoring global needs of 2015. http://www.uis.unesco.org/Library/Documents/teachers06-en.pdf
3. UNICEF Education Report. http://www.unicef.org/india/education.html
4. MOOCs in K-12 Education. http://edtechreview.in/trends-insights/insights/565-how-to-use-moocs-in-k-12-education
5. Kilde, J., Bennett, J.K., Gonzales, L., Sterling, S.: A connective massive open online course for K-12 science, technology, engineering, and mathematics teachers in New Mexico Pueblo schools. In: Proceedings of the Sixth International Conference on Information and Communications Technologies and Development: Notes-vol. 2, pp. 61–64. ACM (2013)
6. Tucker, Bill: The flipped classroom. Educ. Next 12(1), 82–83 (2012)
7. Horn, M.B., Staker, H.: The rise of K-12 blended learning. Innosight Institute (2011)
8. Topping, K.J.: Trends in peer learning. Educ. Psychol. 25(6), 631–645 (2005)
9. Lau, C.C.Y.: What effects does peer group study have on students's learning in commerce mathematics? A case study of diverse ethnic learning (2006)
10. de Freitas, S., Neumann, T.: The use of exploratory learning for supporting immersive learning in virtual environments. J. Comput. Educ. 52(2), 343–352 (2009)
11. Lee, J.J., Hammer, J.: Gamification in Education: What, How, Why Bother? Academic Exchange Quarterly 15(2) (2011)
12. Rethinking Higher Ed: A Case for Adaptive Learning. http://www.forbes.com/sites/ccap/2014/10/22/rethinking-higher-ed-a-case-for-adaptive-learning/
13. Kiili, K.: Digital game-based learning: Towards an experiential gaming model
14. Moon, J.A.: A handbook of reflective and experiential learning: Theory and practice. Routledge, London (2013)
15. Mayes, T., de Freitas, S.: Learning and e-learning. In: Beetham, H., Sharpe, R. (eds.) Rethinking Pedagogy for a Digital Age, pp. 13–25. Routledge, London (2007)

16. Lehtinen, E., Hakkarainen, K., Lipponen, L., Rahikainen, M., Muukkonen, H.: Computer supported collaborative learning: A review. The JHGI Giesbers reports on education 10 (1999)
17. Kirschner, F., Paas, F., Kirschner, P.A.: Individual and group-based learning from complex cognitive tasks: Effects on retention and transfer efficiency. Comput. Hum. Behav. **25**, 306–314 (2009)

A Study to Activate Communication by Using SNS on Mobile Phone

An Essay Lesson at the Elementary School

Yuko Hiramatsu[1], Atsushi Ito[2(✉)], Koutaro Inagaki[3], Fumie Shimada[3], and Fumihiro Sato[1]

[1] Chuo University, 742-1 Higashinakano, Hachioji, Tokyo 192-0393, Japan
{susana_y,fsato}@tamacc.chuo-u.ac.jp
[2] Utsunomiya University, 7-1-2 Yoyo, Utsunomiya, Tochigi 321-8505, Japan
at.ito@is.utsunomiya-u.ac.jp
[3] Honmachidahigashi Elementary School, 3150 Honmachita, Machida, Tokyo 194-0032, Japan
e-honmachida-e-vp@machida-tky.ed.jp

Abstract. Living in the ICT society, not only adults but also children use ICT instruments. However, children usually cannot recognize what happens beyond the screen of ICT devices indeed. It is effective for such children to learn well designed concrete tasks in the classroom step by step. Using our original SNS that designed as closed system in a school, children can share information on the SNS and check classmates' screen each other without considering danger in the real world. They can know what happened beyond the instruments and many people can look the same massage at the same time. It cultivates ICT literacy and critical thinking skill for children. In this paper, we will explain the result of one of our trials using our learning methods: an essay lesson with SNS.

Keywords: SNS · Smartphone · ICT literacy · Essay · Primary education · Critical thinking

1 Introduction

Mobile phone is the most popular ICT instrument now. 7.1 Billion mobile phone accounts in use worldwide [1]. People including children use this little convenient instrument whenever and wherever they want. Now we are at 100 % Mobile Subscription Penetration Rate Per Capita Globally. However, such convenient functions sometimes bring us serious troubles.

In addition to Internet crimes, Net addiction by smartphone [2] has become a big problem for young students in Japan. They cannot stop using SNS.

Because smart phone is the Ubiquitous instrument and they cannot excuse some scenes of disturbing them from smart phone use. According to research of Ministry of Internal Affairs and Communications in Japan [3], operating time of smartphone is increasing rapidly. The results of the research revealed that high school students tend to use Internet endlessly by the criterion of Young 20 [4].

© Springer International Publishing Switzerland 2015
P. Zaphiris and A. Ioannou (Eds.): LCT 2015, LNCS 9192, pp. 492–502, 2015.
DOI: 10.1007/978-3-319-20609-7_46

The average smartphone using time for teenagers is 26.9 min per day in 2012. In 2013, it became 48.1 min per day. Especially the rate of using SNS is increasing. The tendency is expending to younger children.

Communication without spatiotemporal restraints is also useful and convenient for primary education. However, it creates many problems. Children of the concrete operational stage (from seven to eleven years old) have difficulty to understand abstract or hypothetical concepts. They are used to recognizing new objects step by step, from closely concrete ones to invisible abstract steps. ICT communication doesn't have such steps. Though children can use mobile devices easily, they cannot understand the results and influences of their own operations.

To solve this problem, we have been working on several experiments at elementary schools [5–8].

This paper examines our learning model for primary education. After addressing the related works and our leaning model at the second chapter, we will explain our original system; PNS (Pupil Network System), and will mention one example of our methods: a lesson of essay.

2 Related Works and Our Method

2.1 Related Works About Mobile Learning

In 2009 the Ministry of Education, Culture, Sports, Science and Technology (MEXT) issued a notification forbidding school children to take mobile phones to elementary schools in Japan. Prior to the notification several studies were made and reports such as, "Development and Evaluation of a System Supporting Collaborative Learning Using Camera-Equipped Mobile Phones" (Ohkubo, 2010), and "Research on the Function of Mobile Communication System to Support Outdoor Study" (Ito K, 2005) were published. However, increasing cybercrimes, especially using mobile phones, have led to the abovementioned notification by MEXT. Most school principals are inclined to abide by such notifications from MEXT, and as a consequence active research in this field has not made substantial progress. However, there are over 1 million subscribers in Japan. It means 94.5 % of the households in Japan have mobile phones and 49.5 % of the households have smartphone according to the Internal Affairs Ministry of research (2012) [9].

The viewpoint of protecting children in cyberspace, International Telecommunication Union (ITU) published leaflets "Child Online Protection", "Guidelines for Child Online Protection", "Guidelines for Industry on Child online Protection" and "Guidelines for Parents, Guardians and Educators on Child Online Protection" in 2009.

Many methods and concrete examples were told in those leaflets. In 2014 the updated guidelines for Industry on Child Online Protection provide advice on how the ICT industry can help promote safety for children using the Internet or any technologies or devices that can connect to it by ITU and UNICEF [10].

On the other hand, there is a working paper written about the effectiveness of mobile phone learning in Africa. Not only the result of the experiment, but also the price and mobility of mobile phone that are focused in the same paper. Jenny Aker and co-authors report on the results from a randomized evaluation of a mobile phone education program (Project ABC) in Niger [11].

The results suggested that simple and relatively information using mobile phones could serve as an effective and sustainable learning tool. However, the users were not children. Adult students used mobile phone at the experiment.

From the viewpoint of lesson for creating compositions, the effects of creating sentences with others were mentioned in "Knowledge building", (Scarmalia & Bereiter) [12]. Using SNS at the lesson of essay, we have such new creative class at the elementary school.

2.2   21st Century Learning

For the purpose of cultivating Mobile literacy, we specifically try to use mobile phone at schools. In the course of these lessons, we found such mobile literacy lesson would lead children to the 21st century learning. The concept of Key Competency is introduced in the DeSeCo Project of OECD (1997-2003) and mobile learning seems to implement this concept. The international research conducted by PISA and PIAAC also mention their concept [13].

Meanwhile, USA had another project named "The Partnership for 21st Century Skills" [14].

"There is a profound gap between the knowledge and skills most students learn in school and the knowledge and skills they need in typical 21st century communities and workplaces. It is said that schools must align classroom environments with real world environments by fusing multi subjects including critical thinking and problem solving; communication, collaboration; and creativity and innovation."

It is said that students need to think deeply about resolving issues, solving problems creatively, working in teams, communicating clearly in many media, learning ever-changing technologies, and deal with a flood of information to hold information-age jobs. The rapid changes in our world require students to be flexible, to take the initiative and lead when necessary, and to produce something new and useful. In Japan we have a research named "National Institute for Educational Policy Research" [13]. In the research the 21st Century skill was mentioned.

It is said that students need to think deeply about resolving issues, solving problems creatively, working in teams, communicating clearly in many media, learning ever-changing technologies, and deal with a flood of information to hold information-age jobs. The rapid changes in our world require students to be flexible, to take the initiative and lead when necessary, and to produce something new and useful. In Japan we have a research named "National Institute for Educational Policy Research" [13]. In the research the 21st Century skill was mentioned.

We suggest one of the concrete methods to obtain this skill as following using mobile phones which is the most popular instrument at this information age.

3   Our Original System, PNS (Pupils Network System)

3.1   Our Method to Teach Mobile Literacy

In order to teach ICT literacy, we have had trial lessons with 3rd to 6th grade pupils in Tokyo. Children have opportunity to use PCs in their school. However, they tended to investigate some bookish information or simply learned how to operate PCs. We suggest that it was important for children to learn basic information flow recognizing human persons beyond the PC screen, in order to live actively in today's ICT society where abundant information is circulated.

We will explain our method for ICT literacy at the elementary school using mobile phone. (Refer to Fig. 1).

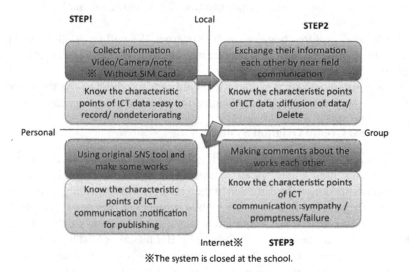

Fig. 1. Our method to teach ICT literacy step by step

The goal of this study is producing feelings of reality beyond the mobile screen and learning how to digest information to live actively in the information society.

At the first step, children use mobile phone without SIM card. They can use note, photo and video. For example they took continuous shooting photos in order to correct jumping form of vaulting horse in order to check their own forms and improve them. They checked their form as soon as they jumped and this rapidly checks were useful to improve their forms. In addition, after the lesson, pupils had to delete those photos. The mobile phones were common property at the school. So if they didn't delete them, someone they didn't know might have chance to look at their jumping forms: some of their forms were not so cool. Pupils learned not only one useful functions of mobile phone, but also a caution when they use the instrument. In other case, pupils brought mobile phones to the outdoor studying at the market. They made their own newspapers by taking photos. They became to know the easy usage of mobile phone and to record information soon. In addition they learned manners to take photos of some other persons or objects. They had to ask permission before taking photos.

At the second step, they used near field communication (Bluetooth and infrared) of mobile phone. They saw with their own eyes how information spread widely and knew how difficult to delete information diffused. Teacher sent his photo to a pupil and then the pupil sent it to other classmates. He or she can sent it any number of times. It took only 3 min to spread it all over the class. However, when the teacher asked the first pupil to delete the photo all over the classroom, it was troublesome. When someone refused to delete it, not only his/her data but also following date would not delete. Pupils figured out that after they spread some data, it was difficult to delete it thoroughly.

We also used near field communication for creation in several subjects. For example, taking photos of the trees in the schoolyard, they made a pictorial book. Pupils sent their photos each other by near field communication. They learned some kinds of pictures were useful to store.

At the 3rd step, children began to use the Internet. We will report about it at the 4th chapter. Using mobile phones, children created literature not only in the classroom but also outside of the classroom.

Those experiments suggested that we should care for children. As the outcome of the actual trials, we created a new application for children's communication education.

3.2 Purpose to Create Original System

Mobile phone is easy to treat for children. It is light, small and portable. In addition there are many contents; mail, photo, video, Internet applications etc. Pupils learn how to use ICT instruments and know the diffusion of their information concretely in the classroom step by step. They can look at the other mobile phone after they send a message. They feel they have to process the information carefully. However, children have many mistakes to send their massages. It is dangerous. But mistakes lead them new stages to use the ICT instrument with their thoughtful usage. So we create original system named PNS (Pupils Network System) for ethic education of mobile phone literacy.

3.3 Characteristic Points of Our Original System, PNS

It is not only closed system in the school but also several original points. On this system pupils upload information and communicate with others. The most remarkable point is that this system will provide a place for pupils to evaluate a posted article from other pupils with autonomy and check each other. When a pupil sends an article, the other one in his group checks the posted articles and sends back evaluation reports. If two or more pupils agree, the article will be uploaded on the site. Pupils from 3rd to 6th grade can vote for good articles. The pupil who gets good feedback might be satisfied and would like to be the new leader of a group. Teachers and parents can peruse these articles. Figure 2 displays a typical behavior and information flow of the submission to PSN.

Step 1: A pupil inputs an article, texts and photos, from smartphone.

Step 2: Two or three pupils should check the article before it is opened to people in a school. They evaluate that the article is appropriate to submit to PNS about the theme, and check and correct grammatical mistakes. Also, they check there are no prohibited words in the articles. At this step, pupils learn ethics of using mobile phone and SNS as a typical Internet services.

Step 3: Then the article is opened to other pupils. They can add comments on that article.

Step 4: The teacher checks the article and he/she uploads the article to the website of the school.

Step 5: Parents can see the article, teachers can choose some or full steps of them. For example if it is no time to check each other, teacher can check pupils' works and upload them the site directly.

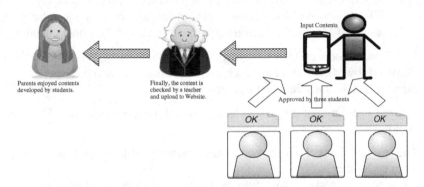

Fig. 2. Typical behavior flow of permission to PSN

Figure 3 is our SNS system. Using this system in the classroom, pupils learn the characteristic points of Internet information step by step, using Smart phone.

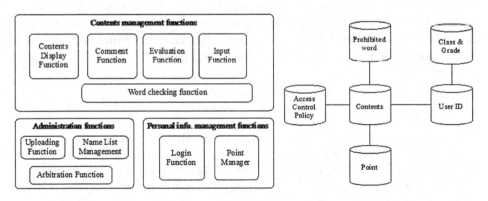

Fig. 3. Our original SNS system (PNS)

4   The Characteristic Points of Mobile Phone and Our Experiment

We will mention one of our experiments. That is an example of pluralistic works and lesson for developing a sense of exact determination of the situation by oneself. Mobile phone is used at the classroom and in the schoolyard. It connects one pupil to others in the classroom.

4.1   Purpose of the Experiment

Using mobile phones aren't written about in the guidance of MEXT in Japan, however, we used mobile phones in order to achieve the concrete aim of the subject that is aimed at by the guidance of MEXT. So there are 2 purposes to use mobile phones in our lesson.

(A)   Based on subjects of THE COURSE OF STUDY FOR LOWER SECONDARY SCHOOL by MEXT and have each purpose to learn about the subject
(B)   Educate ICT literacy and 21st Century Skills

We made a research of a Japanese lesson by mobile phone this time. The purposes are as below.

(A)   The study of Essay: Learn famous essays and try to make original ones. Then read them each other.
(B)   Using SNS: Experience to diffuse and share information by Internet. Matters to be attended to open information.

4.2   Essay Lesson Using SNS System

Pupils had Essay lesson at an elementary school in Tokyo on February 2014 after the 2nd step (Refer to Fig. 1). At this lesson, we used PSN Step1 and Step 3 and Step 4. Because teachers figured there were no time for pupils to check each other and the most important point for essay writing lesson was not such checking. Instead of Step 2 as a checking function, teachers could add comments to pupils if they found some inappropriate sentences.

Pupils at the 6th grade (n = 90) made essays using smartphone.

(1)   Taking photos

They took photos for their essays at the schoolyards with smartphone.

Most children were not good at writing essays. Because there are no special styles and it is difficult for them to become confident in their own sentences. In addition they had to think about abstract words. The theme is "Coldness". However, it became easily by taking concrete photos. Photos have some images of their feeling of "Coldness".

(2)   Making an essay with the photos using PNS

After going back to the classroom, they wrote down essays with the photos they have chosen. One sample of their essays is as follows.

Fig. 4. A photo for pupil's essay named "Winter at the hallway".

"Winter at the hallway" (Refer to Fig. 4)

Such a hallway at school makes me cold. When we have lessons in the classroom, the hallway looks so cold in winter. After the class, that becomes a place for us. Some talk each other. I feel the passage become warmer with voices of my classmates.

(3) Reading classmates' essay and sending comments each other

All children wrote their own essays. Then children put comments to their classmates by PNS. They were encouraged by each other, using our original PNS system (Refer to Fig. 3). The system is closed in the school. Using SNS, 184 comments were written. If they didn't use SNS, the teacher would ask them some comments and then one child raised a hand and spoke a comment. If it takes 5 min for this real motion, only 9 children speak to others in one lesson (45 min). The lesson with mobile phone made children active.

This lesson showed us children have their own messages to other classmates. Most of them encouraged the essay with praise. Pupils seemed to become positive. The viewpoint of 21st Century skill, using SNS, children can make collaboration and communication actively. It is possible not to be led by teacher but by children themselves. In this lesson teacher had different standpoint from usual ones. Children used the SNS proactively and were working together to share feeling of "Coldness". Teachers checked their writing after children wrote down and communicate with each other. Children sometimes made mistakes. They had promised some prohibited matters　in order to use SNS at the Internet. They had promised not to take picture of someone's face and not to write some name of classmates. They used student number in the class then. However, they sometimes wrote real names, especially to friends. Teacher noticed them and drew their attention using SNS comments. We found one characteristic point: After some child wrote down real name to others, the follower tended to use real name without awareness. When one child started to use informal words, the comments followed with informal ones. Children and teachers recognized this problem.

In addition the mobile literacy was improved. They enjoyed using the new instrument, Smartphone, and had succeeded creating essays. On the other hand they experienced some faults or some difficulties using SNS communication with smartphone.

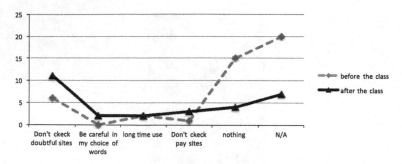

Fig. 5. "What do you have attention to use mobile phone?"

4.3 Questionnaires Before and After the Essay Lesson

We had questionnaires before and after the essay class (n = 90).

Before the essay class, 15 children answered there were no dangerous points to use mobile phones and 20 children wrote nothing to this question (Refer to Fig. 5). Answers are free writing and many children wrote their attention though those comments were not mention in Fig. 3. However, after the essay class, the answer "no dangerous points" and no answer were decreased clearly.

According to Fig. 6, children are interested in using SNS (LINE). After the essay lesson, teachers explained the dangerousness of using SNS. Pupils noticed they tended to make mistakes or some impertinent comments and listened to the lecture carefully.

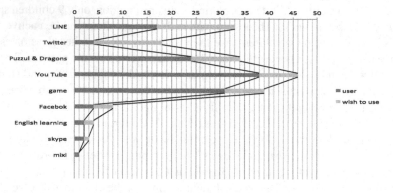

Fig. 6. Functions pupils use now and wish to use

5 Conclusion

Our SNS system, PNS is effective for following point.

(1) Essay lesson

Pupils made essays and sent comments to each other. SNS clarified what they were thinking about. They could communicate directly without talking process. It brought them many chances to communicate in the classroom.

(2) ICT literacy and 21st Skill

Using smartphone, children had to judge by themselves. They choose words to others and were careful not to put wrong letter. If they send some wrong messages, everybody in the classroom would know it on PNS (SNS). They imagined real Internet communication and knew necessity of ICT literacy. The total skill to live in the ICT society at the 21st century, such competency will be necessary for children.

Using SNS Pupils studied in the new field. They encouraged creating essays each other. Teachers looked on them in principle instead of leading in front of the classroom.

(3) To figure out what happen beyond the screen of Mobile device.

Using smartphone in the classroom, pupils sometimes confirmed the other screen of their classmates. It is important for pupils to figure out diffusion of information. When they use PC at the PC room in the school, they always sat down. They are just looking at the screen in front of them. Mobile phone is so small that they naturally notice other users in the class. So they cannot help checking what is happening beyond their own screens.

PNS has many functions and our experiment will be continued. Especially the function of checking comments by 2 or 3 pupils will bring up the skill of critical thinking.

Schools have to align classroom environments with real world environments now. Using mobile phone: the most popular ICT instrument, in the classroom for concrete subject, pupils can feel and understand the characteristic points of ICT communication. It will bring them to have new skills of critical thinking and problem solving; communication, collaboration; and creativity and innovation.

Mobile phones are increasing in the world and are low price instruments. It will be useful for children to cultivate Competency by mobile phone. Our method will be useful for another countries.

Acknowledgments. We would like to express our gratitude to Ms. Katayama. She assisted us and edited data of PNS at Honmachida-higasihi Elementary School.

References

1. Tomi Ahonen Almanac (2014). http://communitiesdominate.blogs.com/brands/2014/05/lets-do-the-big-mobile-numbers-blog-where-are-we-in-mobile-stats-in-2014the-mobile-subscription-rate-is-at-or-very-very-nea.html
2. Young, K.S.: INTERNET ADDICTION: THE EMERGENCE OF A NEW CLINICAL DISORDER, University of Pittsburgh at Bradford (1998)
3. Ministry of Internal Affairs and Communications: Usage of Smart phone application and the tendency of Internet Addiction Disorder at the high school students (2014)
4. Young, K.: CAUGHT IN THE NET -How to Recognize the Signs of Internet Addiction. And a Winning Strategy for Recovery, p. 256 (1998)

5. Hiramatsu, Y., Ito, A., Sato, F.: Study of ICT Literacy Education by Mobile Phone for Children of Elementary School. In: E-learning 2011, vol. 2, pp. 204–208. IADIS (International Association for Development of the Information Society), Freiburg (2010)

6. Ito, A., Hiramatsu, Y., Shimada, F., Sato, F.: Designing PNS (Pupils Network System) for ethic education of mobile phone literacy: Broadband and Biomedical Communications (IB2Com). In: 6th International Conference, pp. 97–102, Melbourne (2011)

7. Hiramatsu, Y., Ito, A., Sato, F., Shimada, F., Tanaka, N.: A Study of Mobile Application for Children's Learning -Based on Study of Japanese Old Poetry. In: E-learning 2012, pp. 161–168. IADIS (International Association for Development of the Information Society), Lisbon (2012)

8. Ito, A., Hiramatsu, Y., Shimada, F., Sato, F.: Designing education process in an elementary school for mobile phone literacy. J. Green Eng. **3**, 307–324 (2013)

9. Ministry of Internal Affairs and Communications: 2014 WHITE PAPER Information and Communications in Japan. http://www.soumu.go.jp/johotsusintokei/whitepaper/ja/h25/html/nc243110.html

10. ITU: Child Online Protection. http://www.itu.int/en/cop/Pages/guidelines.aspx#industry

11. Aker, J., Ksoll, C., Lybbert, T.J.: ABC, 123: The Impact of a Mobile Phone Literacy Program on Educational Outcomes - Working Paper (2010). http://www.cgdev.org/publication/abc-123-impact-mobile-phone-literacy-program-educational-outcomes-working-paper-223

12. Scardamalia, M., Bereiter, C.: Knowledge building: Theory, pedagogy, and technology. In: Sawyer, K. (ed.) Cambridge Handbook of the Learning Sciences, pp. 97–118. Cambridge University Press, New York (2006)

13. Katsuno. Y (eds.): National Institute for Educational Policy Research (2013)

14. The Partnership for 21st Century Skills. http://www.p21.org

Collaborative Tablet PC the System for Self-Active Awareness in a Dormitory Environment

Hironobu Satoh, Shigenori Akamatsu, Masanobu Yoshida,
Takumi Yamaguchi[✉], Fuyuko Eguchi, and Yuriko Higashioka

National Institute of Technology, Kochi College, 200–1 Monobe,
Nankoku, Kochi 783–8508, Japan
{satoh,myoshida,yama}@ee.kochi-ct.ac.jp,
aka@me.kochi-ct.ac.jp,
feguchi@ge.kochi-ct.ac.jp,
higashioka@ms.kochi-ct.ac.jp

Abstract. We describe a new interactive system using a social learning platform to provide dormitory students with the ability to communicate with teachers/advisors in a timely manner to promote self-active awareness in the dormitory environment. Our system comprises tablet PCs, cloud computing services, and application and server software to enable collaboration over a high-speed wireless local area network (WLAN) that covers the campus, dormitory, and teachers' homes.

To enable students to review their behavior in the dormitory, the dormitory staff records the evaluations of student activities related to acceptable and unacceptable behavior based on dormitory room inspections as objective information by capturing an image on a tablet computer. The information is stored as centralized time-series data on a cloud server using several front-end graphical user interface (GUI) tools via the WLAN in the dormitory. The students can access the high-speed WLAN with multipurpose pocket sized electronic devices provided to all students.

The purpose of this system is to facilitate the self-recognition of behavioral problems, raise awareness, and encourage student initiative in a natural manner.

Keywords: Advanced educational environment · Mental health · Distance education

1 Introduction

In contemporary society, promoting the use of computers in schools is very important. It has been suggested that the primary challenge in our information-rich world is to use information specifically to say the right thing at the right time and in the right manner [1]. In particular, the fundamental pedagogical concern regarding information use is to provide learners with the right information at the right time and place in the right manner rather than merely enabling them to learn at any time and any place [2]. Moreover, to facilitate the task of learning at the right time and place, educators should

© Springer International Publishing Switzerland 2015
P. Zaphiris and A. Ioannou (Eds.): LCT 2015, LNCS 9192, pp. 503–509, 2015.
DOI: 10.1007/978-3-319-20609-7_47

employ transparent methods that allow students to access lessons flexibly and seamlessly [3]. Such an approach involves the use of calm technology for ubiquitous computing environments that can adapt to student needs by supporting specific practices. Information and communication technology for education is expected to increase student motivation to study.

In our present study, we have developed a new collaborative learning system called Terakoya [4–6] for remedial education, which helps students actively study anywhere on a high-speed wireless local area network (WLAN) that is linked to multipoint remote users and covers the campus, dormitory, and student and teacher homes. Terakoya provides interactive lessons and a small private school environment similar to the 18th-century Japanese basic schools called Terakoya.

The system consists of 50 client PC tablets with 12-inch extended graphics array (XGA) monitors in conjunction with a server machine, and software to enable collaboration among the tablets over WLAN. The network speed was maintained at 500 kbps or less for each connection. Furthermore, this system interconnects via a Gbit LAN for the server on our campus and via an IEEE 802.11a/g/b WLAN for the target hosts in our dormitory and via an IP virtual private network (VPN) for a teacher in his/her home.

A one-year study of Terakoya was implemented using the tablet computers in a prototype application to provide real-time counseling to students in a girl's dormitory with a teacher at home or in a teacher's room on campus. The test verified the effectiveness of Terakoya for helping the students study actively and willingly. Although Terakoya can be used to collaborative learn up to 50 students simultaneously, it cannot be applied to promote self-active awareness for over 400 all students in the dormitory.

We propose a new interactive communication system with the use of a social learning platform to provide students housed in dormitories with the ability to communicate with teachers/advisors in a timely manner for promoting self-active awareness in the dormitory environment. The target dormitory houses over 400 students and is supported by 11 staff members. At least one staff member is present in the dormitory at all times when it is occupied by students. Regularly scheduled transition briefings allow information sharing among staff members. However, the staff members are a small group, and it is difficult to provide instantaneous services for real-time information sharing.

Under such conditions, it is necessary to design and implement a new communication system for the students to create the environment required to build self-discipline by reflecting on their behavior. To enable the students to review their behavior in the dormitory, the staff records student activities, i.e., the five W's and the one H (who, where, when, why, what, and how), related to acceptable and unacceptable behavior using a tablet PC. Information that is difficult to quantify is recorded as objective information by capturing an image on a tablet computer.

This information is stored as centralized time-series data on a cloud server using several front-end graphical user interface (GUI) tools via the dormitory WLAN. Thus, students can review their behavior in chronological order. The dormitory WLAN connects seamlessly to the campus WLAN. Multipurpose pocket size electronic devices are provided to all students; thus, each student can access the high-speed WLAN anytime and anywhere.

The purpose of this system is to facilitate the self-recognition of behavioral problems, raise awareness, and encourage student initiative in a natural manner.

This paper describes how the proposed new interactive communication system assisted in student dormitory life, and the implementation of a prototype framework and its practical application. The test verified the feasibility of the system for helping the students to obtain advice actively and willingly. The feasibility of the system indicates that the proposed new interactive communication system has the ability to create an environment that facilitates the development of student socializing skills. Enhancing student sociality through dormitory life is an educational policy of our school.

2   Basic Configuration

Our prototype system comprised 10 iPad tablet PCs, cloud computing services, and application and server software to enable collaboration over the WLAN. In Fig. 1 we display a framework of the proposed interactive communication system. The prototype system was applied to facilitate real-time counseling for a group of students in a dormitory. The tablets were used to record the evaluations of the acceptable and unacceptable behaviors of the students based on dormitory room inspections, which are then stored as secure centralized time-series data on a cloud server. Students can review their behavior by accessing the data on the cloud server using a multipurpose pocket-sized electronic device provided to each student. Individual data of the students on the cloud server is backed-up in order to secure data. Furthermore, the parent of a student can access that student's behavior data on the cloud server via the Internet to monitor his/her child's activity.

As the cloud server, we adopted Edmodo, which is a social learning platform website for teachers and students, and a customized version of OpenMeetings running on Ubuntu Linux. OpenMeetings is an open source web conferencing system developed for distance education, which supports multiple audio and video sharing as well as presentations with extended whiteboard capabilities. Edmodo provides a user ID for parents. Parents receive their own unique parent code from their child, which is used to create an account that can be used to interact only with the teacher and their child. Edmodo supports the Japanese language on the login screen—a part of the "Invitations" page—and some menus and buttons. As such, it is accessible for teachers and schools in Japan.

However, it is difficult to introduce a learning management system in the field of education in Japan due to school regulations that do not permit students to use cellular phones and/or smartphones in the classroom. According to the latest survey of elementary and junior high schools by the Japan Association for Promotion of Educational Technology (JAPET), the penetration rate of tablet PCs is less than 10 % [7]. The penetration rate of tablet PCs for each individual student is no more than 0.7 %.

A four-year environmental improvement project for the introduction of educational information technology (IT) was begun in 2014 by the Ministry of Education, Culture, Sports, Science and Technology in Japan, which indicates that a great deal of time is required to increase the prevalence of educational IT environments in elementary and junior high schools. Therefore, especially in elementary and junior high schools, owing to the low penetration rate of the electronic devices in Japanese schools and students, it is necessary for the schools to provide electronic devices such as tablet PCs.

Our school provides multipurpose pocket-sized electronic devices to all students. A team in our school has developed some software enabling the electronic devices to be used for learning English with online software, receiving assignments, research purposes, checking the attendance book, and so on.

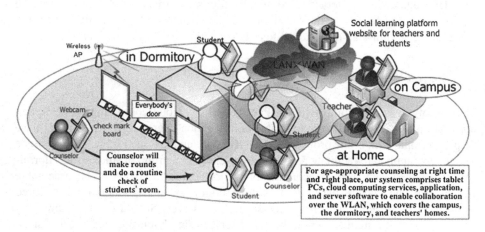

Fig. 1. Framework of the proposed interactive communication system

3   Practice and Evaluation

The proposed prototype system was implemented experimentally in a women's evening dormitory. After implementing the prototype system in this environment, the feasibility and practicality of the system in helping the students get advice actively and willingly was verified through the observation and evaluation of the assistance provided. Using this system, a teacher was able to send instructions or age-appropriate counseling from their office to the electronic devices of all students via the network. Consequently, it became easier for students to ask questions to teachers via face-to-face and/or online interaction. In addition, student queries could be answered immediately, and therefore their work could be adjusted appropriately in a timely manner.

The conventional procedure employed in our dormitory required an inspection of each student room every weekday morning by a dormitory matron to ensure that the door and the window were locked, the bedding was put away, and the curtains were opened. The inspection results were recorded on a checking list, and later manually entered into a computer. The dormitory staff provided only verbal commentary to a student in accordance with the records. It seems that it is difficult for many students to heed the staff's advice due to verbal advice alone. We have come to embrace the idea that to facilitate self-recognition, raise awareness, and encourage student initiative in a natural manner, it is necessary for students to review their actual behavior in the dormitory.

We required the new procedure incorporating the interactive communication system that additional procedures be kept down to the minimum necessary, and the conventional procedure used by the dormitory matrons employing non-exclusive equipment such as pens and paper were retained as much as possible. Doing so alleviated the need to require individuals unfamiliar with the use of electronic devices such as smartphones, tablet PCs, and laptops to adopt complicated and non-intuitive procedures in order to provide digital records of inspection results. This also allowed students to obtain feedback easily and timely from the written record on the checking list, and the communication is recorded for students' subsequent use.

(a) The inspection results are entered on the appraisal list as check marks.

(b) The written record is captured by the camera on the tablet PC.

Fig. 2. Snapshots of the daily inspection and the recording of written records

Figure 2 illustrates the actual inspection recording procedures. After the dormitory matron inspects the condition of the room, the results are entered on the appraisal list as check marks for each condition, and the written record is then captured by the camera on the tablet PC and stored electronically. The written record remains on the wall outside the room as a message to students. The students are therefore provided timely information regarding their behavior when they return to their rooms.

The captured images were placed on Edmodo to share with the dormitory staff. The on-campus teacher was able to access Edmodo to clarify the conditions of each student's dormitory room, and the teachers were able to engage in face-to-face and/or online contact with students as needed. The student's parent was also able to examine their child's behavior in the dormitory via Edmodo.

The proposed system can provide the necessary counseling and a perspective to provide relief from study stress, relationship difficulties, social network site (SNS) addiction, and serious mental health problems. Because of experience with the system, teachers will be better informed, provide sound counseling, and recommend appropriate treatment or actions to help students overcome traumatic events and other difficult periods of their lives.

4   Conclusions

In this paper, we detailed how the proposed new interactive communication system assisted in student dormitory life. A prototype system was implemented experimentally in a women's evening dormitory as a social learning platform to provide dormitory students with the ability to communicate with teachers/advisors in a timely manner for self-active awareness of the dormitory environment. The staff members, including student advisors, record acceptable and unacceptable behaviors using a tablet PC. This information is stored as centralized time-series data on a cloud server using several front-end GUI tools via high-speed WLAN in the dormitory in order to enable students review their behavior in the dormitory. The feasibility and practicality of the system in helping students to obtain advice actively and willingly was verified through observation and by evaluation of the assistance provided.

For our system, we considered the benefit of continuing the use of conventional methods employing paper and pens owing to its simplicity and requirements for no exclusive equipment. The written records can be used by students to review their behavior. Consequently, the new communication method requires no additional procedures, no complicated and non-intuitive actions, and no exclusive equipment. The captured images are placed on Edmodo to share with the dormitory staff. The campus teacher is able to access Edmodo to clarify the conditions in a student's room. The teachers can engage in face-to-face and/or online contact with the students as needed. The proposed system can provide the necessary counseling and a perspective to provide relief from study stress, relationship difficulties, SNS-addiction, and serious mental health problems.

In conclusion, experience indicates that a more effective system is required for student self-active awareness of the dormitory environment and to reduce dormitory staff workload. In the future, we would like to further evaluate the impact of this system on student motivation. We would also like to study various configurations of our proposed system under various dormitory life conditions and procedures, including the development of increased interaction with parents. Our ultimate goal is to work toward realizing a ubiquitous user-oriented human interface system.

Acknowledgments. This study was partially supported by a Grant-in-Aid for Scientific Research (C, Area #1602, Project No. 24501236).

References

1. Fischer, G.: User modeling in human-computer interaction. J. User Model. User-Adap. Inter. (UMUAI) **11**(1–2), 65–86 (2001)
2. Ogata, H., El-Bishouty, M.M., Yano, Y.: Knowledge awareness map in mobile language-learning. In: Proceedings of the Sixth IEEE International Conference on Advanced Learning Technologies (ICALT), pp. 1180-1181 (2006)
3. Jones, V., Jo, J.H.: Ubiquitous learning environment: an adaptive teaching system using ubiquitous technology. In: Proceedings of the 21st ASCILITE Conference, pp. 468-474 (2004)
4. Matsuuchi, N., Shiba, H., Yamaguchi, T., Fujiwara, K.: The practice and the evaluation of a new campus wide collaborative active learning system. IPSJ J. **49**(10), 3439–3449 (2008)
5. Nishiuchi, Y., Matsuuchi, N., Shiba, H., Fujiwara, K., Yamaguchi, T., Mendori, T.: Evaluation of TERAKOYA learning system linking multipoint remote users as supplementary lessons. In: Proceedings of the 18th International Conference on Computers in Education (ICCE), pp. 486-488 (2010)
6. Yamaguchi, T., Shiba, H., Yoshida, M., Nishiuchi, Y., Satoh, H., Mendori, T.: Posture and face detection with dynamic thumbnail views for collaborative distance learning. In: Zaphiris, P., Ioannou, A. (eds.) LCT. LNCS, vol. 8524, pp. 227–236. Springer, Heidelberg (2014)
7. Japan Association for Promotion of Educational Technology: The 9th questionnaire survey on instructional computer, May (2014). http://www2.japet.or.jp/info/japet/report/ICTReport9.pdf

A Knowledge Management System to Classify Social Educational Resources Within a Subject Using Teamwork Techniques

María Luisa Séin-Echaluce[1(✉)], Ángel Fidalgo Blanco[2], Francisco J. García-Peñalvo[3], and Miguel Ángel Conde[4]

[1] University of Zaragoza, Zaragoza, Spain
mlsein@unizar.es
[2] Technical University of Madrid, Madrid, Spain
angel.fidalgo@upm.es
[3] University of Salamanca, Salamanca, Spain
fgarcia@usal.es
[4] University of León, León, Spain
miguel.conde@unileon.es

Abstract. The traditional way to develop contents for a subject is based on the faculty perception and experience, however students should be taken into account. This work proposes a methodology that promotes the creation, classification and organization both teachers' and students' learning resources within the same subject scope in a timeless manner. Teamwork process is monitored by a proactive method that makes possible the generation of resources collaboratively. A knowledge management system allows to Classify, Search, Organize, Relate and Adapt the generated resources and includes a semantic search engine, based on ontologies, which provides a final product for users' needs. A first iteration of an action-research allows answering questions such as the types of resources created during the teamwork (with academic, social and service orientation), how to stablish a common organization of the created knowledge for all potential users and improve educational resources of an academic subject with these collaborative resources.

Keywords: Knowledge management system · Educational repositories · Teamwork competence · E-learning · Service learning

1 Introduction

Before Internet became as permanent tool in education, teachers used to use books or notes as learning resources. Students got those books, the teacher's notes or the notes taken by them. Current proliferation of online systems and the social media make extremely easy and quick to achieve different learning resources and share them among peers.

On the one hand, teachers often provide learning contents through the Learning Management Systems (hereinafter LMS), usually structured according the syllabus of

© Springer International Publishing Switzerland 2015
P. Zaphiris and A. Ioannou (Eds.): LCT 2015, LNCS 9192, pp. 510–519, 2015.
DOI: 10.1007/978-3-319-20609-7_48

the subject. The organizational structure depends on the specific technology. Teachers select the sequencing and timing for the resources availability, and students can access to them through the platform as a simple consumer.

On the other hand, the use of teamwork methodologies has increased exponentially in higher education, specially demanded from professional fields. Among the teamwork benefits, Boundless [1] emphasizes the following: increased efficiency, greater effectiveness and faster speed (by the combination of individual efforts), more thoughtful ideas (from the ability to focus different minds on the same problem) and mutual support and outcomes, that make better use of resources. In this sense, Collaborative information created by students during an official subject enriches student learning and experience of teachers. Schuster [2] also says that "Collaborative document creation enables humans to solve complex problems in a team, to exchange ideas, and to benefit from synergistic effects."

Moreover, teamwork increasingly converges to the knowledge management fields [3] and Nonaka and Takeuchi [4] stress the importance of teamwork in the conversion of tacit knowledge into organizational knowledge. In educational organizations the knowledge created by the work teams and related with the topics of a specific subject, can improve its resources (academic contents) if they are accessible to the next subject's edition students. In particular, academic contents related to social and service aspects increase student motivation and improve student learning. Astin et al. [5] show, in a study of 22,236 students, that service learning influences positively on different dependent measures such as writing skills, critical thinking skills, values, self-efficacy, leadership, etc.

In that sense, the information generated by students is only usually used during the period of subject teaching (increasingly smaller with biannual subjects) and has a very limited impact. But if resources created by students can be used outside the spatial and temporal subject's context, this fact produces an experience's enrichment to all stakeholders (creator students, prospective students and teachers). Some authors pose that thinking and creating resources has a big impact on the students' learning but using repositories, with contents created by other authors, encourages critical thinking and avoid "reinventing the wheel" [6].

This work proposes a methodology that promotes, classifies and organizes both teachers' and students' learning resources within the same subject scope in a timeless way, allowing students from different classes to introduce new resources. Students generate new resources by means of collaborative and reflective teamwork methodology. The academic contents, generated in a specific subject, are integrated with social and service motivations (explaining academic contents to the course fellows, motivating to start to future degree freshmen or showing opportunities to future graduates). Both collaborative and service learning offer obvious benefits to students [7, 8].

Also a knowledge management system (hereinafter KMS) is used. It makes possible to classify the resources created by the teams during a subject edition. This provides access to authors, prospective students and faculty, the access to the resources created. Moreover the KMS provide adapted searches to students based on their particular needs so the resources can be really useful to them [9].

In order to carry out this work an action-research methodology is used, which has the following features: (1) It takes the context into account,which means that may some problems of a specific context; (2) It is *collaborative*, addressing collective concerns of the agents included in the present context that, grouped in teams, are based on review and reflection; (3) It facilitates self-evaluation, the discussion and reflection process produces a permanent assessment of the practice and its results directly affect their improvement [10, 11]. In this case the context is a specific academic subject and the aims are: categorizing, organizing and accessing to resources created collaboratively (during TW) and studying its impact on improving learning. This paper is the first iteration of action-research and provides the basis for optimizing the classification, organization and access to content created collaboratively. The assessment and improvement of resources and of the impact on the learning of the users of these contents is the objective of other work already underway.

Therefore, the following questions arise here:

- What kind of knowledge, based on student experience, can be generated by themselves to help prospective students of the same subject/degree?
- Can the knowledge, based on the students experience in a subject, be organized and published in a common way to all of students?
- Is it possible to create educational resources from the knowledge generated by students?

In order to achieve the objective of this work it is essential that students were motivated, active and organized; and what it is still more important is that they explain their experience to help their peers. This experience exchange process is facilitated by the proactive method *Comprehensive Training Model of the Teamwork Competence* (hereinafter CTMTC) [12, 13]. This method has been used to promote dynamic cooperative work teams to form and assess the teamwork competence.

But the knowledge generated collaboratively must be managed flexibly and dynamically. This will generate new relationships between knowledge, that allows finding useful information for a further application in different contexts. To manage knowledge the CSORA system (Classify, Search, Organize, Relate, Adapt) [14] is applied. This system contains, among other features, a semantic search engine which allows searches based on ontologies, logically connected, which define the search target. Categorizing the generated contents is a key element of its management and subsequent search.

In the following sections the context of action research is exposed, the proactive method CTMTC for the students to create contents based on their experience is described, as well as the CSORA system. Finally the main results obtained in this first iteration of action-research and the conclusions of this work are presented.

2   Research Context and Teamwork Methodology

This study involves 107 students (grouped into 18 teams) of the subject "Programming Fundamentals" of the Biotechnology degree, taught at the Technical University of Madrid. The topics included in the teamwork process are Web 2.0 and Cloud Computing.

These teamwork topics are the 25 % of the total subject's contents and they are associated to a 25 % of the final grade. The remaining 75 % of the subject is based on traditional taught (lectures and labs).

Teamwork monitoring and individual and group teamwork assessment are done with the method CTMTC [12, 13]. It is a proactive method based on three aspects: teamwork phases (mission and goals, map of responsibility, planning, implementation and organization of documentation), collaborative creation of knowledge and cloud computing technologies (wikis, forums, social networks and cloud storage systems). Team members collaboration and individual evidences are continuously monitored by faculty along the teamwork phases and through this cloud technology. This monitoring carries out training assessment by teachers to guide students' individual learning. At the same time, this method allows teacher to do partial summative assessments in order to compose the final summative evaluation of TW. The work [7] shows the potential of this method.

Team members, team coordinator and works topic are all chosen freely. This last one has to fulfill two conditions: current subject students must be the target audience and knowledge must be generated from the personal academic experience (in the subject, other subjects or as a result of the academic life).

Teamwork is developed online along the course (forums and wikis/Dropbox are used to communicate and store contents respectively). Every four weeks a classroom session is carried out in order the teams can present their partial results. Faculty use these presentations to teach and stimulate discussion and reflection.

During teamwork process, team members interact with the systems used (the LMS and Dropbox). These interactions are individual evidences of students' activity. Specifically the evidences taken into account are: interventions in forums or usual mobile communication applications (mainly WhatsApp messages), group evidences (on the achievement of the TW phases, mission and goals, map of responsibility, planning, etc.) and outcomes (final resources of teamwork). Individual and group evidences of a team are accessible only by faculty and team members. However, the final result should be accessible via the Internet and the teams can choose an online tool (wikis are recommended, but other systems such as web pages are used).

Work teams optionally make a video (10 min maximum) to present the final result, describe how the team is organized and partially show individual and group work evidences.

3   Results

In this section the typology of contents, generated by work teams, and their inclusion in a KMS are presented. It is important to point out that the high cooperation among team members made possible the creation of resources with high quality and usefulness. Regarding the cooperation between team members during the teamwork development, the average number of messages per member was 83,94, only in the official forum. All messages were grouped in thematic threads to describe the different phases (that were created for different issues of phases). Work teams have an average of 29,33 thematic threads.

3.1 Types of Generated Knowledge

All teams finished the work and organized their resources (texts, videos, presentations, etc.) through online systems. 66,34 % of total teams organized the work result in a wiki, while 33,33 % did it in a website. Each final work (wiki/website) had an average of 25,16 individual content pages.

Regarding the format of the created resources, the 88,89 % of total teams made a video to present briefly their final work. All these videos also include a description of how the forum was used to facilitate the communication between team members and the team's organization with the aim to produce collaborative knowledge.

Regarding the source of knowledge generated by teams, it can be grouped in: Knowledge generated by students of a specific subject, knowledge generated by students of other subjects and knowledge generated by graduates integrated into professional environment.

Each team members identified previously the type of contents to be created and its usefulness for the rest of subject's students. Table 1 includes the specific type of knowledge observed in the results, grouped by their source.

Table 1. Types of generated contents from their sources

Subject's students
Academical support (organization, subjects, competences, teamwork, etc.)
Wellcome pack
Biotechnology degree information in Technical University of Madrid
Information about other universities with Biotechnology degree
Subjects' information
Faculty's information
Students and faculty poll on the first bi-annual subjects
Center spaces (classrooms, labs, etc.)
Center Associations
Freetime, transport, events, courses, etc.
Subject's external students
Grants, financial support
Academical itineraries
Advices
Interchanges
Graduates
Professional opportunities
Companies
Research institutions

3.2 Knowledge Organization

The work teams organized their experience with their own criteria and without a common organization of resources. Finding a particular resource means that the user needs to access to 18 websites and browse in more than 453 specific web pages. But web search engines are not suitable to only search on specific websites as a set. The number of websites will increase each academic year and, consequently, the organization of knowledge generated by students will be much more complicated.

In this paper a KMS is used to solve the mentioned difficulties. Once the typology of resources has been analyzed in the previous section, they are classified by means of ontologies in the KMS which includes a semantic search engine. The system is called CSORA (Classify, Search, Organize, Relate, Adapt) and was developed by one of the authors in the "Laboratory of information technologies' innovation", Technical University of Madrid [14]. This system is being successfully used in the "Information Points Network on Research Development and innovation activities". It has shown its effectiveness to search R&D&i projects because the user's searching is based on generic search targets, without knowing the specific nature of what is searched [15].

An ontology (set of tags) is proposed for this educational environment. It is based on the traditional models used in innovation [16], which have been already tested in educational innovation contexts [17]. The proposed tags are grouped in categories following the classification: input, process and output. Input includes categories referred to the knowledge source. Process refers to academic activities related with the knowledge. Output refer to the type of created knowledge: academic support, welcome pack, professional opportunities, etc. See Table 2 for more details about example tags included in the categories.

Table 2. Proposed ontology

	Category (tags)
INPUT (knowledge source)	**Author** (Students, Faculty) **Academic Course** (2013-2014, 2014-2015) **Degree** (Biotechnology, Energy, Mining) **Subject** (Computing and Programming, Programming fundamentals) **Topic** (Numeric, Computing, Algorithms, Matlab)
PROCESS (usefulness and activity related to resource)	**Learning** (Theory, Laboratory, Examples, General description, Notes, etc....) **Activity** (Exam, Practical session, Theoretical session, Teamwork) **Teamwork competence** (Mission and objectives, Chronogram, Results, etc.) **Technology** (Wiki, Dropbox, Website, Forum)
OUTPUT (type of knowledge)	**Type of knowledge** (Professional opportunities, Welcome pack, Degree information, Academic support, Leisure, Students' Associations, etc.)

The search engine included in CSORA system allows defining a search based on logical expressions, with connectors (and, or), between different ontologies and by means of text.

Also, CSORA allows several ways of selecting and organizing the contents. Any user of this search engine (current students that create the contents and contribute to the repository, future students that will use the search engine and teachers) can generate a portfolio (file with editable text) with a selection of resources obtained during the search. Faculty also can organize the search outcomes as a personalized webpage with their own selection. See Fig. 1. An example of a search with the following tags: "Example" and "Teamwork" and ("Chronogram" or "Planning") and "Professional opportunities". This search generates examples and chronograms (or planning) during teamwork process about professional opportunities.

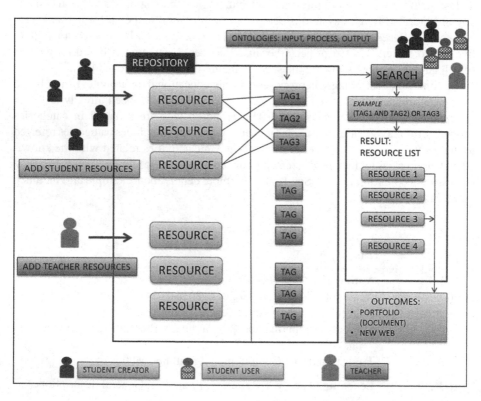

Fig. 1. Design of search methodology

4   Discussion

The previous considerations try to answer the questions proposed in the introduction.

What kind of knowledge, based on experience, can be generated by students to be helpful for prospective students of the same subject/degree? The authors have carried out an analysis of of the types of resources generated collaboratively. Students have been interested in the creation of academic knowledge included in the subject and also in the knowledge as a service to academic life (helping present and future students). Both types of knowledge improve students learning [8]. This knowledge has been obtained through the interaction with other people in the same school of engineering (students of higher courses and faculty external to subject) and outside the school (external professionals and research organizations). The analysis shows the typology of knowledge generated by students: academic support for current subjects, information about their own experience to choose the Biotechnology degree, information about services and necessary places to carry out academic and learning activities, information about different formative itineraries, scholarships, grants and professional opportunities.

Can the knowledge, based on the students experience in a subject, be arranged in a common way to all of students? Students have chosen wikis and website builders to organize their generated contents and publish the evidences of the teamwork. However, it is necessary to organize the learning contents under a common point of view to give service to both current and future faculty and students. In this proposal the tacit knowledge (informal, personal and social) becomes organizational knowledge [4] and the common point of view of its management is based on both the nature of the generated contents and their applications. The considered KMS (CSORA) allows classifying, organizing and searching the contents regarding to indicators common to all students and covering different search objectives.

Is it possible to create educational resources from the knowledge generated by students? In this research students have generated resources from the reflection inside the team, but also with the rest of students during the sessions oriented by the subject's teachers. In addition each team has chosen freely the topic of the generated resources and has linked academic topics with social and service motivation. All of this provides educational features to the resources which help authors to learn [2]. Besides the resources, educational examples and good practices are included to the subjects for future students.

5   Conclusions

Students generate learning contents from their own experience acquired from: subjects they are studying, interaction with their own context (degree, school) and from the interaction with their peers, as for instance students in upper courses.

CSORA searches allow the definition of new resources by identifying and joining learning contents created by the different teams. Initial expectations of this work have gone further away. From the traditional contents based on specific contents of the subject, students have generated social and helpful learning contents. For this reason it is possible to develop learning resources, assessment resources and even services both for past, present and future students (for example, degree orientations or professional opportunities). The generated resources can also be helpful for the mentorship planning that most of universities carry out, because mentors could make use of these resources to orientate students in lower courses.

Regarding the teamwork, students have generated resources to explain how they have interacted, how they have used cloud computing tools (forums, wikis and online storage) and to show the final work.

The analysis of the generated learning contents in this work highlights that this is the first step for freshmen to initiate a reflexive path into service learning, which will report great benefits in their academic learning and the future professional life. Astin et al. [5] shows that reflexive service learning provides improvements and says "the power of reflection as a means of connecting the service experience to the academic course material".

For future studies the starting point will be the current repository of contents generated by teams. The following stages of the action-research will be carried out by means of: studying the impact on the learning process of new subject's students and students with the same needs in other subjects, the evaluation of resources already created regarding to their usefulness to improve them and orientate the creation of new ones, the integration with the educational resources generated by faculty and the future access to the repository's resources by their own authors.

With respect to the applicability of the generated resources, the start up of the mentors' usage is another future work line. In that sense, mentors could identify the students' needs (symptoms), establish a training plan (diagnostic), use the learning resources available in the system (rehabilitation plan), generate a document with these resources using the search engine and monitor the results (check the effectiveness of the training plan in order to maintain it or change it, introducing useful comments about the process inside the generated document). The final generated document will be stored in the KMS to help other mentors. This way the generated knowledge jointly with learning resources will help students with similar needs.

Acknowledgements. We would like to thank the Educational Innovation Service of the Technological University of Madrid by its support to the educational innovation projects IE415-06002, PT415-05000, the Centre for Industrial Technological Development (CDTI), the Government of Aragón, the European Social Fund and the Ministry of Education of the Region of Castilla-León for their support. Finally, the authors would like to express their gratitude to the research groups (LITI, http://www.liti.es; GIDTIC, http://gidtic.com and GRIAL, http://grial.usal.es).

References

1. Boundless: Advantages of Teamwork. Boundless (2014). https://www.boundless.com/management/textbooks/boundless-management-textbook/groups-teams-and-teamwork-6/defining-teams-and-teamwork-51/advantages-of-teamwork-259-4562/
2. Schuster, N.: Coordinating Service Compositions: Model and Infrastructure for Collaborative Creation of Electronic Documents. KIT Scientific Publishing, Karlsruhe (2013)
3. Sapsed, J., Bessant, J., Partington, D., Tranfield, D., Young, M.: Teamworking and knowledge management: a review of converging themes. Int. J. Manage. Rev. **4**, 71–85 (2002)
4. Nonaka, I., Takeuchi, H.: The Knowledge Creating Company: How Japanese Companies Create the Dynamics of Innovation. Oxford University Press, Oxford (1995)

5. Astin, A.W., Vogelgesang, L.J., Ikeda, E.K., Yee, J.A.: How service learning affects students. Higher Education Research Institute, University of California Los Angeles (2000). http://epic.cuir.uwm.edu/ISL/pdfs/asthow.pdf
6. Daud, S., Eladwiah, R., Rahim, A., Alimun, R.: Knowledge creation and innovation in classroom. Int. J. Hum. Soc. Sci. **3**, 75–79 (2008)
7. Fidalgo-Blanco, Á., Sein-Echaluce, M.L., García-Peñalvo, F.J., Conde, M.Á.: Using learning analytics to improve teamwork assessment. Computers in Human Behavior (2015) doi: 10.1016/j.chb.2014.11.050
8. Simonet, D.: Service-learning and academic success: the links to retention research. Minnesota Campus Compact, pp. 1–13 (2008)
9. Fidalgo, A., Balbin, A.M., Leris, D., Sein-Echaluce, M.S.: Repository of good practices applied to higher education in engineering, p.1–7. IEEE (2011)
10. Carro-Sancristobal, L.: Estrategias de Investigación Acción para la Educación Especial en Centros Específicos. Rvta Interuniversitaria de Formación del Profesorado **17**, 117–124 (1993)
11. Munarriz, B.: Técnicas y métodos en Investigación cualitativa. (Universidade da Coruña, 1992) http://ruc.udc.es/dspace/handle/2183/8533
12. Lerís, D., Fidalgo, Á., Sein-Echaluce, M.L.: A comprehensive training model of the teamwork competence. Int. J. Learn. Intellect. Capital **11**, 1–19 (2014)
13. Fidalgo, A., Lerís, D., Sein-Echaluce, F.J., García-Peñalvo, F.J.: Monitoring indicators for CTMTC: comprehensive training model of the teamwork competence. Int. J. Eng. Educ. (2015, in press)
14. Fidalgo, Á., Ponce, J.: CSORA method: the search for knowledge. Método CSORA: La búsqueda de conocimiento. Arbor **187**, 51–66 (2011)
15. García, M.A., Fidalgo, A., Valle, M.: Design of a continuos training system based on X & C MOOC models: corporate MOOC of the PI + D+i network. Fundación General de la Universidad Politécnica de Madrid, Proceedings II Congreso Internacional sobre Aprendizaje, Innovación y Competitividad, CINAIC 2013, pp. 487–492 (2013)
16. Oslo Manual: Guidelines for collecting and interpreting innovation data. OECD Publishing European Commission, 3rd Edition (2005)
17. Fidalgo Blanco, Á., Sein-Echaluce, Mª L., Lerís, D., García-Peñalvo, F.J.: Sistema de Gestión de Conocimiento para la aplicación de experiencias de innovación educativa en la formación. Fundación General de la Universidad Politécnica de Madrid, Proceedings II Congreso Internacional sobre Aprendizaje, Innovación y Competitividad, CINAIC 2013, pp.750–755 (2013)

Let's Play, Video Streams, and the Evolution of New Digital Literacy

Peter A. Smith[1(✉)] and Alicia D. Sanchez[2]

[1] University of Central Florida, Orlando, FL, USA
Peter.smith@ucf.edu
[2] Defense Acquisition University, Ft. Belvoir, VA, USA
Alicia.Sanchez@dau.mil

Abstract. The use of videos, video streams, and user created videos has recently surged as consumer based websites are allowing increased access to high quality learning assets. You Tube, Let's Play, MOOCs, and the Khan Academy are discussed in order to understand how they differ in their offerings of multi-media based assets. As these assets evolve, a new digital literacy in which a learner transforms into a reviewer, a commentator, a curator, and possibly a creator of new content emerges.

Keywords: Digital literacy · Video based learning · User created content · Let's Play · You Tube · Informal learning · Curation

1 Introduction

Educators have used video in classrooms for years, and the flipped classroom has brought video based education home, however, the rise of learning through participatory video streams and Let's Plays has gone largely overlooked. While previous generations have engaged with websites, blogs and social media based learning channels, the current generation is quietly learning more through YouTube Let's Plays, and Twitch based video streams than they do with books, webpages, or any of the technologies adults have traditionally used. The new digital literacy required to participate in these largely ad hoc learning environments are the ability to record and edit video, capture and stream gameplay and other on screen actions, high levels of technical communication, and the ability to inform and educate others while accomplishing complex tasks. At the same time the participants feel like they are playing and being part of a community, not learning or teaching.

The learning process is similar to the tried and true 'see one, do one, teach one' methodology.

1. Observe Let's Plays and Streams
2. Develop new skills based on applying what was learned and personal experiences
3. Create streams and recordings, and answer questions

© Springer International Publishing Switzerland 2015
P. Zaphiris and A. Ioannou (Eds.): LCT 2015, LNCS 9192, pp. 520–527, 2015.
DOI: 10.1007/978-3-319-20609-7_49

By engaging through video streams learners are feeling like they are part of a community. They strive to help each other in an effort to build up their own viewership, and gain status in the community. They also learn important skills in video editing, public speaking, teaching, and sharing their knowledge. As the new generation grows they will be expecting this level of engagement and participation in their learning. This paper will explore how Let's Plays and video streams are being integrated into a classroom setting and how students are engaged in both learning and teaching each other.

2   The Minecraft Example

While it may superficially appear that the current generation is spending most of its time playing games like Minecraft together online, much of their time is being occupied by watching other people play and learning new techniques and secrets about the game and its world. Minecraft has sold over 18.5 Million copies on PC alone [1]. It is widely considered the best selling game of all time [2]. It has also been acquired by Microsoft for 2.5 billion dollars [3]. The obvious conclusion is that there is a huge group of people actively playing Minecraft.

This is of course true. Yet, the community that plays Minecraft doesn't spend all of their time interacting with the community in the game. A quick search of the game Minecraft yields 94,200,000 results on YouTube. This is more than 5 videos per copy of the game sold. Granted it cannot be concluded that every Minecraft owner makes 5 videos, it is clear that there is more to this game than the game world alone.

More to the point is the actual content of these videos. Many of these results are fun videos made to entertain other players, but large numbers are actually video based training disguised as entertainment. A search for Minecraft tutorial yields 6,300,000 results, explaining simple things like how to get started in the game, to complex building tasks and programming skills.

This is not a phenomenon isolated to Minecraft. The game League of Legends is a Multiplayer Online Battle Arena (MOBA) that has over 27 million players a day [4]. It is arguably the largest massively online game in the world right now. There are hundreds of thousands of videos explaining in detail how to play as every character in the game. Minecraft, however, has somehow captured the ethos of our youth, replacing Lego as the building blocks of choice among American boys. At MineCon 2013, a convention celebrating Minecraft, Devon Loffreto presented the results of a study in which 95 % of boys and 45 % of girls reported that they would learn anything, regardless of subject matter, as long as it was presented in Minecraft [5]. The potential educational power of this one game may never be fully tapped.

3   The New Use of Videos in Education

The use of videos in education has been reinvigorated through the availability of high quality learning programs like the Khan Academy [6] and the surge in popularity of Massively Open Online Courses (MOOCs). The Khan Academy makes thousands of videos available free online in areas that include math, science and test preparations.

The Khan Academy is primarily geared towards K-12 learners, but parents and teachers may also use these videos as resources. Historically, videos were used to replace traditional classroom models by providing increased access to standardized learning assets. Now however, videos are often used in single serving chunks of just in time learning and performance support. The instructors of the videos hosted by the Khan Academy are teachers and lecturers as well as subject matter experts.

MOOCs follow a similar model of increased accessibility by using videotaped lectures for an entire semester of college or graduate level course topics often hosted by a single instructor or professor for an entire semester. In these examples homework and assignments are handled using learning and content management systems and online discussions hosted synchronously whenever possible. They will often leverage existing or previous students as instructors or lab assistants. By making educational content universally available, these examples are creating new possibilities for those who are not able to access traditional classroom experiences for a variety of reasons, one reason being a preference to not be in a classroom.

To conventional learning scientists these forms of course structure seem new, but YouTube has provided a similar experience in a less formalized fashion each day. Where individual videos are providing small chunks of authentic learning, channels and collections are acting as courses and classes where students are learning through informal means.

3.1 Providers

One of the key components to informal video based education is access to large providers of video content. One of the most prolific repositories of videos available is YouTube [7]. In order to access an array of videos all one needs is internet access and a computer or mobile device on which to view these videos. While YouTube does not have a specific instructional focus, YouTube's one billion users need only search for "how to…" almost anything and a variety of videos will likely appear that will literally walk one through a process. It could be argued that YouTube is the world's largest repository of learning content, video or otherwise. Some videos are geared towards specifically completing a task while others might be informational about the concept itself. A person in need of baking tips, car repair instructions, makeup application advice, or help solving complex algorithms has access to a huge range of information.

Provider's major contribution to the ecosystem is content. Of course, this content is meaningless without also providing the ability to search that content and find relevant results. YouTube and other providers give video creators a place to store videos, the ability to control how videos are watched, and the ability to grow a community of viewers. In many cases, content creators are gaining significant income through others watching their video, thus providing an incentive to improve the quality of the created content.

3.2 Channels

Channels are individual pages that contain collections of videos. Content creators create a channel and post relevant videos there. Of particular interest is the Let's Play community and its channels centered around videos of people playing through video games. These videos are generally created for one of a few reasons: showing others how to play through a game, and exploring if a game is worth playing at all, and doing something interesting with the game.

Most video game players understand how frustrating it can be to get stuck within a game. Video games offer problem solving and puzzle like encounters that sometimes exceed the ability of their players. A player might feel that they have tried everything and exhausted all of their resources within the game, but still not be able to proceed. This led to the genesis of some Let's Plays where players explore a game from start to finish showing others how to play the entire game. It was not uncommon for players to video tape themselves successfully navigating portions of a video game that could be problematic for other players in order to share their knowledge and skills on how to be successful. Later, this evolved into a dedicated space for video game walkthroughs named Let's Play [8].

Some Let's Plays focus on playing the game in ways the designers did not intend them to be played. One of the largest of these communities is the speed run community. These are players who attempt to finish a game in as fast a way as possible. These players find exploits and paths that could cut huge games down in fractions of the normal time.

Today Let's Play often includes videos of the game being played, but also of the players while they play it (think picture in picture). This allows players to gain notoriety and to attract followers of their specific videos. Some players have millions of followers, giving them a certain level of celebrity and in some cases monetary gain through sponsorship. While many of these videos might center on humorous or critical narrative of the game being played, they still demonstrate tips and tricks for successfully navigating games.

3.3 Streams

While outlets for videos such as YouTube provide an archive of previously recorded educational material, many players are moving to live streams of their gameplay. These live events can draw more viewers than televised sporting events and are studied by the viewers who are attempting to learn new techniques and strategies. The finals of League of Legends, a tournament played by the best players of the year, were watched by 32 million people overall and by 8.5 million concurrent viewers. With 8.5 million concurrent viewers it had more viewers than the Super Bowl with 3 million unique viewers, according to Nielsen's figures [9].

One of the most interesting facets of these videos is that they are often created by players themselves. These players, combined with their viewers, are creating personal learning networks that can harness the same power that esteemed academies geared towards providing educational content are harnessing. They are similarly authentic, and learners are utilizing them with similar outcomes.

Video streams allow their viewers to watch online in real time, live. This has become very popular both on YouTube via Let's Play, but also for real time learning experiences such as briefings on space missions and live war time reporting on TV. These sorts of experiences allow for synchronous viewing and are often archived for asynchronous viewers who can't be online during the stream.

4   Digital Literacy

Digital Literacy is the ability for people to knowledgeably participate in networked communities [10]. While computer literacy might relate to an individual's ability to understand the working parts of a computer and how it functions, digital literacy relates to an understanding of how to navigate and access the internet from the perspective of utilitarianism. Today's learners must understand where to find the information they need and how to determine if that information is valid when using the internet. Unfortunately, digital literacy is also a factor of availability of the internet and a device from which to access it. This puts students without those resources at a significant disadvantage.

The ability to search for multi-media assets such as "How to" videos requires the ability to use an appropriate term in the search, as well as an ability to refine any videos produced in that search into those that might be most useful. Once determined useful, a user might share that information with other users, often via social media tools such as Facebook or Twitter, or might find a need for more or better content if their search is deemed as not valuable.

Digital literacy in the Let's Play community can be broken down into the three segments, curation, creation, and participation. These three concepts also reflect Schugurensky's three part model of informal learning, self-directed, incidental, and socialization [11].

4.1   Curation

Self-directed informal learners are intentionally learning about a particular concept primarily on their own, or with a group without the assistance of a formal educator [11]. These learners are consuming content, often for selfish goals, like being a better player in an online game. These consumers of content, however, often become curators of the content.

In the process of providing their own self-directed learning they find content that is also useful to others. Content curation happens when a user finds something of perceived value from either a search engine or from a trusted source that they follow and compile it in a useful way. The user may then share that finding with their followers. Curators of content often become valuable resources for those interested in a concept and may be viewed as experts or trusted sources for others. In order for a curator to be considered trusted and valuable, they must review the information they have found and share it with others.

The quality of that sharing over time becomes the basis for their perceived trustworthiness or level of expertise in an area. A curator often also develops a following of persons who are seeking the information they are sharing. This concept of curation allows users to increase their personal knowledge and more importantly their perceived knowledge in a particular area. A follower may share their information with their own followers, further increasing their demonstrated level of expertise through their own curation.

Although curators may have broad shallow knowledge bases on a topic. Curators are often considered experts by others who have already moved past curation into creation. These creators find themselves without the time to stay abreast of all the newest developments and thus rely on curators to keep them informed.

4.2 Creation

In order to demonstrate true digital literacy, a user must be able to find the information they need and curate it meaningfully. Curators of content might perform this in order to find the information they need, or to share information with their followers. Sometimes, however, in the process of locating high quality information, a user may find the available assets lacking. This provides a tertiary opportunity for a user or curator to become a creator of content. For example, a user seeking a recipe online might find a recipe that indicates amounts, but not the steps required to make a cake. Similarly, a viewer of a video game walkthrough might find that the player/creator of a video doesn't sufficiently cover the details needed to successfully defeat a boss. In these cases, a user/curator has found a need for better video to be made and posted. Some users/curators take this opportunity to become creators of their own videos, with the goal of making a more cohesive of better video.

Content creators often have specific deep knowledge to share. They may not have the same breadth of knowledge as a curator, but they have the need or ability to fill in games in the knowledge base of the community. Neilson describes this level of participation in a community with the 90-9-1 rule of participation inequality [12]. This rule stipulates that 90 % of a community is made up of lurkers. These are people who read everything but don't participate in any meaningful way. Then 9 % are creators of content, and 1 % are heavy contributors of content.

Creators often learn through the process of creation. They develop deep knowledge through the process. The learning they achieve is considered incidental learning [11] as they are learning as a side effect of the creation process as opposed to setting out to learn.

4.3 Participation

In determining what videos might be most helpful or the highest quality representations of a desired process, a user will often consider three things:

1. The rating of the video
2. The number of views the video has had
3. The comments left on the video by other users.

Video rating is often done in a typical 5 star format. The more the viewers like the video, the more stars they assign it. This often is considered in conjunction with the number of views however. A video that receives 5 stars, but has only been viewed 10 times might not carry the same value as a video that receives 4 stars but has had 150,000 views. Often these two values are considered together. A user might also choose to read or perhaps contribute to the comments for a particular video. Comments often discuss the strengths or shortcomings of a video and are often fairly honest due to the anonymity of online commenting.

These groups, while fitting into to the 9 % on Nielsen's scale [12], are learning through socialization. They are gaining tacit knowledge through interacting with others in a social environment. They may or may not be setting out to learn, but through discourse and participation they are learning [11].

5   Game Design Education Through Videos and Let's Plays

To visualize the process of curation, creation, and participation students in DIG 4720 Casual Games Production at the University of Central Florida are introduced to major concepts in casual game design primarily through lecture, but also through a series of curated videos describing various aspects of casual game design. These include, paper prototyping, design mechanics for casual games, play testing to inform design, and many other topics. These videos act as supplement to the course presented by often times famous game design professionals with multiple game credits to their name. In some cases the videos are previous students in the course, often held in the same regard as the video from clear professionals. All of the videos are relevant to their major task of developing a casual game. In this case the curator is their professor.

Students also get in on the curation process and are asked to participate in the curation of development tutorials that they find useful in the creation of their projects. Early on this sharing is difficult to spark, but once students realize they will be recognized for their contribution by the rest of the class, more sharing occurs.

Students are encouraged to explore casual games in general. This course is one of the earlier classes in the program's game design curriculum, so students are often less experienced with a varied array of games often including casual games, and are commonly primarily players of core game titles. As they explore casual game design it is also clear that their tastes in games are also changing to include more genres.

Their primary objective in the course is to work in a team to develop a casual game, but they are also assigned to make a Let's Play video of a casual game of their choosing. These Let's Play videos are short, roughly 5 min in length, and concentrate on the design of the core game mechanics of the game. This is a popular assignment, where is it clear that the students are enjoying the process of playing but are also articulating their new game design knowledge as well. The act of filming the video is simultaneously allowing them to entertain themselves, entertain others, and practice articulating their newly formed design analysis skills.

After the videos are created they are shared with the rest of the class and also kept for future classes. This allows students to explore each other's work and participate in the social aspect of learning. This peer to peer exploration of the topic has allowed some students, who often do not have a voice, to begin to articulate their ideas to the group, and improved the overall educational outcomes of the course.

6   Conclusion

The resurgence in videos for learning as a topic of interest for educators and researchers has necessitated consideration of new tools available for learners. Following models that include both formal education, the upside down classroom, and informal education the aggregate of these resources have begun to allow a new educational paradigm for user created content to exist in the same ecosystem as formal learning constructs. Consumers of these videos are more interested in authenticity and trust than the credentials of the presenter and bring instructors and students into similar roles.

By design viewers can easily become curators of content and then eventually become creators. Creators of content are able to demonstrate their expertise but are also subjected to the scrutiny of the community. The community becomes more valuable as raters. Further, the ability for content creators to identify gaps and attempt to close them has valuable underpinnings in this educational model. The ability for those gaps to be closed and juried by peers is the tip of the spear for a new era of digital literacy where consumerism is not as valuable as creation.

References

1. Mojang. Minecraft Statistics (2015). https://minecraft.net/stats
2. Wikipedia top selling games. http://en.wikipedia.org/wiki/List_of_best-selling_PC_games
3. Mojang. Yes we're being bought by Microsoft. Mojang blog (2014). https://mojang.com/2014/09/yes-were-being-bought-by-microsoft/
4. pc gamer. http://www.pcgamer.com/27-million-people-play-league-of-legends-every-day/
5. Loffreto, D.: Kids Learning Code Minecon (2013). http://kidoyo.com/minecon2013.php
6. Khan Academy (2015). www.khanacademy.org
7. You Tube (2015). http://www.youtube.com
8. YouTube. Let's Play Cannel (2015). https://www.youtube.com/user/LetsPlay
9. McCormick, R.: League of Legends eSports finals watch by 32 million people (2013). http://www.theverge.com/2013/11/19/5123724/league-of-legends-world-championship-32-million-viewers
10. Wikipedia. Digital Literacy (2015). http://en.wikipedia.org/wiki/Digital_literacy
11. Schugurensky, D.: The forms of informal learning: towards a conceptualization of the field (2000)
12. Nielsen, J.: The 90-9-1 rule for participation inequality in social media and online communities (2006)

Human-Human Interaction Modeling of Trainer

Hongjun Xue[✉], Wenxin Zhang, and Xiaoyan Zhang

School of Aeronautics, Northwestern Polytechnical University, Shaanxi Xi'an 710072, China
xuehj@nwpu.edu.cn, {qaz741qaz1,zxyliuyan}@sina.com

Abstract. As the important way to achieve the trainer's teaching function, the design of human-human interaction, especially the interaction between instruct pilot and student pilot should be addressed. For trainers human-human interaction is rather the task itself now than designed for the task. The paper adopts the basic theory of Task Technology Fit (TTF) model to establish human-human interaction model. This model discusses the advantage and disadvantage of three traditional interaction ways and features of three tasks and match the interaction ways with tasks and then get the design requirements and methods to strengthen human-human interaction in trainers. Text message is proposed as a new interaction style for the trainer. The new style is an important complementary for the traditional methods. The new interaction style can give more information to ensure more comprehensive communication between instruct pilot and student pilot and then ensure the teaching function of trainer more effective.

Keywords: Trainer cockpit · Human-human interaction · Ergonomic · Task technology fit model

1 Introduction

Design of Human-human interaction is the key for the design of the trainer. To complete the task of the combat or safe navigation, interaction among the pilots is essential interaction. The basic function of trainer airplane is to help student pilots to learn how to fly the plane. The learning process itself is a form of human-human interaction. The very important task of the instructor pilot in the trainer is to show the student pilots how to fly planes in the context of flying safely. So for trainers human-human interaction is rather the task itself now than designed as the task. The design of the human-human interaction of trainers can't copy the method of fighters or commercial airplanes. We should put forward new design standards and methods for trainers.

2 Features of the Trainer Cockpit

There are always two basic layouts of trainer cockpit, which is tandem two-seat layout and parallel two-seat layout. Tandem two-seat layout trainers have advantages of decreasing the burden of the engine [1], addressing the concerns about observing the student's facial expressions, hand movements and body language [1]

© Springer International Publishing Switzerland 2015
P. Zaphiris and A. Ioannou (Eds.): LCT 2015, LNCS 9192, pp. 528–534, 2015.
DOI: 10.1007/978-3-319-20609-7_50

and the symmetrical field of vision [2] while side-by-side layout trainers are good at the arrangement of instruments, the weight and balance problems [2] and the field of vision [1]. Two pilots are always a student pilot and an instructor pilot (IP). Depending on the different functions, trainers can be also allocated a pilot or weapon operator. The interaction model is built to describe the human-human interaction of tandem two-seat layout trainer cockpit.

Trainers are always equipped with two different control systems for safe flight and effective learn. The relationship between two control systems is related or rejected, which is decided by the requirement of training. In general, control systems of primary trainers and intermediate trainers are related while two control systems of advanced trainers can only have one available in the meantime. The related control systems can help student pilots learn operations from the IP while the rejected control system can help the IP get the control right when dangers occur.

Due to the control system above, the pilot workload is not consistent with time. When student pilot (or IP) control trainers, although IP (or student pilots) has tasks of study or monitoring, the visual or auditory load is still less than driving. This feature leads to the human-human interaction is different from that of two-seat fighters or airlines, which makes it possible to delay interaction and more visual or auditory the interaction.

3   The Model to Describe the Human-Human Interaction of Trainer Cockpit

This chapter develops a matching model of task types-interaction styles to describe the human-human interaction. Basic structure is shown in Fig. 1.

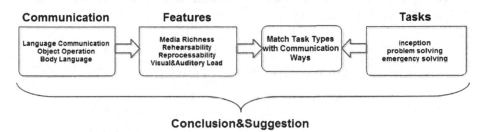

Fig. 1. Matching model of task types-interaction styles

This model firstly discusses three interaction styles of trainers. And then consider different task types from the mission profile and the most suitable interaction ways then can be gotten.

4   Interaction Ways and Media

1. Language Communication
   The media of language communications is radio. Trainer cockpits have two sets. One is for internal communications between the IP and the student pilot while the

other one is for external communications between pilots and ground services [3, 4]. The language communication here refers to internal communications.

2. Object Operation

The media of object operation is control systems. If a trainer is equipped with related control systems, the IP behind can observe the operation from the student pilot in front and vice versa. If a trainer has a rejected control system, there is no such interaction.

3. Body Language

Because of the feature of the tandem trainer, the IP behind can observe the operation of the student pilot in front while the student pilot in front can't see IP's operation behind. As above, tandem trainers have advantages of addressing the concerns about observing the student's facial expressions, hand movements and body language. Body language is single-track, which can only transfer from the student pilot to IP in tandem trainers.

5   Features of Interaction Styles

1. Media richness

Media richness refers to media's ability to enable users to communicate [5]. Better media has immediate feedback, more multiplicity cues, various communication languages, and attracting attention. MRT proposes that if a media is capable of sending "rich" messages which decided by the technology to ensure immediate feedback it is richness [6].

According to the four indexes above, the evaluation of the three interaction media richness is as follows [7] (Table 1):

Table 1. The media richness of three communication ways of trainers

Interaction style	Richness	Features
Language interaction	High	• Synch • Low Symbol Variety • Acoustics Information • Immediacy Feedback
Object operation	Low	• Synch • Single Symbol Variety • Operation Information • No/Delayed Feedback
Body language	Medium	• Synch • Single Symbol Variety • Body Information • No Feedback

2. Information processing ability

   Information processing ability includes information edit ability and information storage ability. Information edit ability is the ability that the media enables the sender to rehearse or fine-tune a message before sending [8]. The media with edit ability can urge senders to consider seriously before sending messages to make sure that the message is accurate, and improve the information effectiveness and reduce the error probability. Three interaction styles available in the present trainers all lack the edit ability.

   Information storage capability is the ability that a message can be reexamined or processed again within the context of the interaction event [8]. The media with storage capability can make it possible for receivers to have sufficient time to consider and quote past messages. Also three interaction styles available in the trainers all lack the storage capability.

3. The visual and auditory interaction features

   The sensory channel of the pilot can be divided into visual channel, auditory channel, and tactile channel. Visual channel and auditory channel is used widely by pilot. For three interaction styles, language interaction have more auditory load while object operation and body language have more visual load. Compared with the auditory load, visual load is heavier when pilot is flying. So while flying the visual interaction should be avoided. However, auditory interaction may have a problem of noises.

6   Features of the Tasks and Matching with Interaction Styles

1. Inception Tasks

   In the trainer mission profile, many tasks, such as taking off, is familiar both to student pilots and IPs, and has been implemented many times. For these tasks, which called inception tasks, receivers will know senders' meanings with short messages and also know subsequent operations.

   For inception tasks, interaction with low richness is efficient. Object operation and body language should be avoided, because the sender should express and transfer messages clearly. If there is only one inception task, there is no demand of edit capability and storage capability, while if there are several inceptions, edit capability and storage capability is essential for the interaction.

   For three interaction styles available now, language interaction is the most suitable style for inception. But three interactions all lack edit capability and storage capability. So trainers need an interaction style that can edit and save like 'short message' and 'email'.

2. Problem Solving

   The aim of problem solving is to take a most suitable method to complete tasks or behave the student. Problem solving emphasizes the selection of methods.

   For problem solving tasks, interaction ways with immediacy feedback will be most suitable. The complex problem solving tasks should match an interaction way that have high media richness while the simple task only need low media richness.

Almost all tasks only have one correct solution because piloting trainers have strict standards. After solving problems there will be no need to reexamine the interaction, so there is no demand of editing for problem solving tasks.

Depending on different tasks, problem solving should match language interaction or object operation. Tasks that can be communicated clearly without the related control system should match the language interaction to release the visual load while tasks that should be communicated using the related control system should match the object operation or both.

3. Emergency Solving

    When an emergency occurs during flying, IP and student pilot should cooperate to solve problem. In the emergency situation all interaction styles should be used to ensure the communication between IP and student pilot. Interaction styles with high media richness and less edit time should be adopted. Finally, with high visual load interaction should be avoided because when an emergency occurs, IP and student pilot need visual interaction to solve problem. Language interaction is the most important way during emergency.

7   Improvement of Interaction Styles

1. Text message interaction

    Three interaction ways available now all lack edit capability and storage capability. For messages that should be considered seriously, reexamined or processed, trainers now can't provide an appropriate interaction way to match. The new interaction style like 'short message' and 'email' should be developed. Such interaction way is called 'text messages interaction' in this paper.

    When the student is piloting, IP can edit a message to conclude the behavior of the student and arrange the command of inception tasks. Because the student is piloting, the visual and auditory load of IP is less than that the situation that IP is driving. IP is possible to divert attention from tasks to edit text messages interaction. In the meantime, When the IP is piloting, the student is possible to read the message of conclusion and reply because of less visual and auditory workload. These situations

Table 2. Features of text messages interaction

Media richness	Low
Features	• Asynch • Single symbol variety • Text information • Delayed feedback
Edit capability	• High
Storage capability	• High
Visual&auditory load	• High visual load

fit with the feature that the pilot workload is not equality with time.

Features of text messages interaction are as follows (Table 2):

Text messages interaction is good at edit and storage. But the media richness is low and visual load is high. So text messages interaction and language interaction is complementary.

The set of text messages interaction include a control and a display. The function of the control is to edit messages while the function of the display is to read messages. The control needs an equipment to input text. The display doesn't need independent equipment. It can be integrated in a multi-function display. Considering that we use text messages interaction to send complex inception, the arrangement of the multi-function display should avoid flight and navigation information.

2. Matching task types with interaction ways

For inception tasks, if messages are easy, we should take language interaction while if messages are complex, we should take text messages interaction.

For problem solving tasks, we should take language interaction or object operation. Tasks that can be communicated clearly without the related control system should match the language interaction to release the visual load while tasks that should be communicated using the related control system should match the object operation or both.

For emergency solving, all ways should be made to ensure the interaction between IP and student pilot while language interaction is the most important ways during emergency.

The matching of task types and interaction ways are as follows (Table 3):

Table 3. Matching of task types and communication ways

Interaction ways	Language interaction	Text-messages interaction	Object operation	Body language
Media richness	High	Low	Low	Medium
Edit capability	Low	High	Low	Low
Storage capability	Low	High	Low	Low
Visual & auditory load	High auditory load	High visual load	High visual load	High visual load
Main matching tasks	1. Easy inception 2. Easy problem solving 3. Emergency solving	Complex inception	Complex problem solving	Single track feedback from student pilot to IP

8   Conclusions

In the design of the trainer, human-human interaction should be addressed. For trainers human-human interaction is rather the task itself now than designed for the task. The design of the human-human interaction of trainers can't copy the method of fighters or commercial airplanes. We should put forward new design standards and methods for trainers. Only adjusting the position of human-human interaction in the design of trainers can we design a better trainer.

Before the design of human-human interaction of trainers, we should be clear about the feature of trainers. The specific operating system makes it possible for delay interaction and the interaction that have much visual or auditory load, which are not available for fighters. We should find out the specific of trainers to find the most suitable human-human interaction ways for trainers.

The paper adopts the basic theory of Task Technology Fit (TTF) model to establish human-human interaction model. This model discusses the advantage and disadvantage of three traditional interaction ways and features of three tasks and match the interaction ways with tasks and then get the design requirements and methods to strengthen human-human interaction in trainers. Text message is proposed as a new interaction style for the trainer. The new style is an important complementary for the traditional methods. The new interaction style can give more information to ensure more comprehensive communication between instruct pilot and student pilot and then ensure the teaching function of trainer more effective.

References

1. Whitford, R.: Preliminary design of a primary training aircraft. In: Aircraft Design and Operations Meeting (1991)
2. Why Tandem Seating in the SGT-300?
3. http://archive.today/FQB9
4. T-38 Talon Twin-Jet Trainer Aircraft, United States of America
5. http://www.airforce-technology.com/projects/t-38/
6. SF-260 Light Trainer/Attack Aircraft
7. http://www.airforce-technology.com/projects/aermacchisf260traine/
8. Sutanto, J., Phang, C.W., Kankanhalli, A., et al.: Towards a process model of media usage in global virtual teams. In: ECIS 2004 Proceedings, p. 167 (2004)
9. Daft, R.L., Lengel, R.H., Trevino, L.K.: Message equivocality, media selection, and manager performance: implications for information systems. MIS Q. **11**, 355–366 (1987)
10. Min, Q., Li, Y., Guo, S.: Global virtual team communication model from the viewpoint TTF: a case study of the chinese software outsourcing industry. J. Manag. Case Stud. **5**(5), 356–367 (2012)
11. Rice, R.E.: Computer-mediated communication and organizational innovation. J. commun. **37**(4), 65–94 (1987)

Serious Games

A Platform for Supporting the Development of Mixed Reality Environments for Educational Games

Luis Arenas, Telmo Zarraonandia$^{(\boxtimes)}$, Paloma Díaz, and Ignacio Aedo

Computer Science Department, Universidad Carlos III, Madrid, Spain
{larenas, tzarraon, pdp}@inf.uc3m.es, aedo@ia.uc3m.es

Abstract. In this work we present MR-GREP, a platform that supports educators in the design and implementation of mixed reality educational games. More specifically the system allows the instructional designers to create game experiences that can be played simultaneously in an augmented reality environment as well as in a virtual space that replicates the physical space. This seeks to support the implementation of collaborative learning experiences that combine the flexibility provided by the virtual worlds with the realism and physical component that training in real scenarios allows. The development of this type of environments usually demand advanced technical knowledge that educators normally lack. The platform aims to overcome this problem by providing a set of authoring tools and applications, which does not require programming skills from the user.

Keywords: Digital Educational Games · Mixed reality · Augmented reality · Virtual reality

1 Introduction

In recent years the development of Digital Educational Games (DEG) has been an active research line. DEGs aim at helping to acquire knowledge and developing skills while maintaining user engagement and motivation. This type of educational resources has proven to be specially useful for the development of skills such as problem-solving and critical thinking [1]. Despite their benefits, the introduction of DEGs in the learning system is not as widespread as one would expect. The development of a digital game requires a variety of skills and specialized knowledge that make necessary the assistance from technical experts. This represents a prohibitive cost for many educators willing to embrace new technology. Although some platforms such as < e-Adventure > [2] and StoryTec [3] provide authoring tools for designing and implementing DEGs without requiring programming skills, the type of DEGs they can produce is restricted to the adventure genre. Action games that train the physical or mental agility of the learner are beyond the scope of these tools, for example.

Current DEGs provide a mock scenario in a virtual environment in which the player performs certain tasks and where she is allowed to explore different courses of action. While this can suit well the training of certain skills such as decision taking, it does not support so well exercising other abilities in which the physical component is key.

© Springer International Publishing Switzerland 2015
P. Zaphiris and A. Ioannou (Eds.): LCT 2015, LNCS 9192, pp. 537–548, 2015.
DOI: 10.1007/978-3-319-20609-7_51

This is the case of those games in which the stamina or speed of the player is a decisive factor in the success of the experience. This scenario could be improved if the game is played in an Augmented Reality (AR) environment, which would allow the enhancement of a physical space with virtual information, supporting the implementation of a situated learning approach. In AR games such as ARQuake [4] or Human Pacman [5] the action of the game takes place in a real setting, and the players are equipped with AR devices that allow them to visualize the game entities as superimposed on their own vision of the environment. In an educational context, this type of games would present unique advantages as they combine the benefits of trainings in a physical space, while retaining the inexpensive management of virtual objects and user safety provided by virtual reality simulations. Unfortunately, the design and implementation of this type of experiences are specially challenging. On top of the difficulties associated to the production of traditional DEGs, they add the complexity of designing a consistent AR environment in which games can be played. The designer could use high level authoring tools like DART [6] and CATOMIR [7], which bring the definition of AR experiences closer to non-experts. However these platforms may still require some programming and are not particularly focused on game development or education.

The objective of this work is to provide educational designers the tools and platforms that facilitate the design and development of DEGs that can be played in a Mixed Reality environment, minimizing dependence from technical assistance in the process. In this case we use the term Mixed Reality (MR) to make reference to an environment which merges physical and virtual worlds, where the elements from both realities coexist and interact with each other. MR extends the interaction possibilities that AR offers by allowing to act not only from the augmented real world but also from a replicated virtual setting.

The type of games whose production we aim to support would allow interacting with the educational experience both from an augmented physical space as well as from a replica of it in a virtual reality environment. The final aim is to allow different players to participate in a gameplay that is simultaneously played in the two types of environments, interacting in real time with each other and with the other game entities included in the game. This type of setting will open exciting possibilities for training and education, as they will offer a more complete training scenario where trainees can interact with the game from the type of environment that better supports the acquisition of the specific skill to develop. Furthermore, it will also deliver unique possibilities for collective trainings and educational experiences where the actions of the players in the virtual world will modify the experience of the players in the real environment and vice versa.

As a first step towards this goal we present MR-GREP (Mixed Reality – Game Rules scEnario Platform). The system provides a set of tools and applications for supporting the design, development and execution of mixed reality DEGs. The current implementation of the platform allows the creation of mixed games where players in the augmented real world act as on-site observers of the game action that takes place in the virtual space. Presently the use of this type of systems in real-world learning environments is restricted due the weight and cumbersomeness of current models of fully immersive AR headmounted displays. However, this work serves as exploratory research to enable the study of the potential usefulness, difficulties and limitations of mixed reality educational games. The insights obtained through the use of this platform will help to develop better games to be used when the technology matures and reaches the general public.

The rest of the document is structured as follows: Sect. 2 presents related work in educational game development, Sect. 3 details MR-GREP platform and its components, Sect. 4 presents a use case created for illustrating the proposal, and Sect. 5 describes the conclusions and future lines of work.

2 Related Work

Even though there already exist several AR and MR games both for entertainment and education, these applications tend to be produced as standalone projects tailored for specific domain [8]. To the best of our knowledge, there is little support for the development of these kinds of games by the hands of end users (EUD).

Efforts have been made in order to alleviate the complexities of AR and MR application programming through the implementation of libraries and frameworks like ARToolkit [9] and OSGART [11]. However, these tools are not suited for end users since programming skills are required. Higher level authoring tools such as DART and CATOMIR allow the definition of interactive AR and MR experiences. These authoring tools bring the development closer to end users by allowing the use of visual programming techniques instead of coding. However, they do not specifically support the creation of games but isolated experiences, and they are not specially oriented to educational environments.

With regards to DEGs, game development has typically been delegated to experts in C or C ++ programming and low level graphical libraries like DirectX and OpenGL. This scenario has been improved with the advent of game engines such as Unity or Unreal Engine [10]. These platforms provide specific support for game aspects like sound, animation, physics, behaviours and game deployment. Although they contribute to lower the level of difficulty of programming digital games, they are only appropriate for programmers. StoryTec and < eAdventure > are two of the few existing authoring tools that do focus on end user game development. StoryTec allows the creation and execution of interactive stories through an authoring platform and a runtime engine. Its authoring platform is composed of five visual components that let users define story logic, stage, action set, assets and properties. On the other hand, < eAdventure > specifically concentrates on providing instructors with the required tools for creating story-driven games as well as to integrate these games and the associated results into e-learning environments. Unfortunately, these tools are restricted to the development of adventure games.

3 MR-GREP

The MR-GREP system integrates different tools and applications for supporting both the design and development of mixed DEGs as well as their execution. Figure 1 depicts the relations between these tools and presents them organized by type of environment and activity supported. This way, the tools depicted in the top half of the diagram (GREP Editor, GREP Player) provide support for the definition and execution of the game action that takes place in the virtual world, whereas the ones included in the lower half (Augmented Scene Editor, Augmented Scene Player) allow the translation of these actions into an augmented real environment. In the same way, the modules on the left hand side of the picture (GREP Editor, AS Editor, AS Player), assist the designers in the process of creation of the EGs, while those on the right (GREP Player, AS Player) allow the players the retrieval and execution of the EG produced. EG definitions are stored in the platform's game server (middle of the diagram), which also ensures that the state of the virtual game elements and their corresponding augmented representations are synchronized.

The process of defining a mixed reality game involves the following steps:

1. Virtual scene and game definition: As a first step, the user designs a virtual reality game replicating a real world space. This process includes the definition of the game scene as well as the game rules.
2. Augmented scene definition: The replicated area in the real world space is augmented with digital graphical representations.
3. Matching between virtual and augmented scene elements: Finally, the elements of the virtual and augmented scenes are matched so that changes in the positions and states of the entities of the virtual games are translated into changes of the graphical representations added to the augmented scene.

The following sections describe the different parts of the system that support the definition of the virtual world and the game rules, the augmentation of the counterpart scenes in the real world, and the matching between the virtual and augmented scenarios.

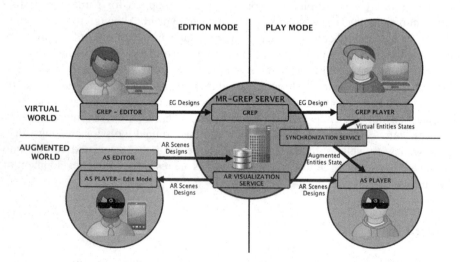

Fig. 1. System diagram

3.1 Virtual World and EG Definition: GREP

The definition of the EG is carried out using GREP (Game Rules scEnario Platform): a system able to interpret descriptions of EGs expressed in XML files and to generate 3D games based on them. The platform has been implemented using the Unity 3D engine. The descriptions of the games the platform interprets should follow the schema of the GREM model (Game Rules scEnario Model) [11], which provides a set of components and design entities for defining EGs. GREP provides different types of implementations for these game components, activating for each game the ones that suit better their descriptions in the XML files. For example, and with regards to the game interface, GREP provides different types of inventory windows, score sections, status bars and a mini-map view. For supporting different types of game mechanics, the platform provides listeners based on entities' current positions, thresholds of attribute values, collisions and the triggering of actions, among others. In the same way, it includes device components implementations for supporting the definition of games compatible with a keyboard, a mouse and a Microsoft Kinect device. In addition, the platform also counts with different repositories that the designers can populate with resources for their games.

The designer defines an EG and generates its corresponding XML description file using a graphical authoring tool named GREP Editor (Fig. 2). The process of defining an EG using the editor involves four steps:

1. *Definition of static scenes*: The process starts by setting up the main elements and parameters of the game scenes. This includes the specification of the size of the scenes, the lighting, and the definition of the floors and walls and the other non-interactive background elements included in them.
2. *Definition of game entities*: The designer continues defining all the interactive elements of the game or *game entities*. These definitions should include the entity name, the lists of attributes, states and actions that the entity can carry out, and the graphical models and animations of the platform repository that will be used to represent those actions and states.
3. *Definition of the game scenes:* The designer completes the definition of the game scenes by placing in the static scenes instances of the game entities previously specified. To aid the designer in this process the editor provides a *scene view*, which allows to navigate through the scene, to add and remove entities to it, and to modify their position, size and orientation.
4. *Definition of the game rules:* The designer specifies the rules of the game. These are described as a collection of game events that capture conditions of success and failure, as well as the triggering of the entities actions, the modification of their attributes, or their appearance or removal from the scene, for example.

The XML description files are stored in the GREP repository and made available to the learners through the GREP Player (Fig. 2). Using a web browser the learners launch the GREP Player and select an EG to play. The platform starts processing the corresponding XML file of the game, and adjusts the components of the platform to the requirements specified in it.

Fig. 2. GREP Editor (left) and GREP Player (right)

3.2 Augmentation of the Real World

To transform an EG played in a virtual environment into a mixed-reality experience it is necessary to specify the augmented representations that will be used to represent the game entities and to place them in a real world environment that replicates the virtual world scene. To support the designers in this process and to allow players in the real world to visualize the game action, the platform provides two different tools: the Augmented Scene Editor (AS Editor) and the Augmented Scenes Player (AS Player).

3.2.1 Augmented Scenes Editor (AS Editor)

The AS Editor is an authoring tool for supporting the design of the *augmented scenes* in which the EG will be played. An *augmented scene* is a real-world environment augmented with 3D virtual elements, which are placed at fixed positions with fixed orientations and scales. To aid in the process of definition of the *augmented scenes* the AS editor provides three different modules: the scene manager, the model manager, and the scene editor:

The *model manager* module provides the designers a repository of graphical models to be used in their augmented scenes.

The *scene manager* allows the designers to describe the physical space to be augmented. This description should include the real dimensions of the place to augment, and a scaled top view plan of it.

Finally, the *scene editor* allows to define the augmented view of the scene. The editor uses the top view plan previously introduced to obtain references of the positions at which the physical space should be augmented. The designer defines virtual elements to display in those positions, and assigns them identifiers, names and the graphical models from the repository that better represent them. Figure 3 depicts a screenshot of the scene editor, where the framed icons represent the virtual elements placed by the user in the scene. Once a virtual element has been specified, the user can complete its definition by modifying their default distance from the floor, orientation and size.

In order to tackle the problem of providing visual feedback about the elevation on a two dimensional space, a color gradient is implemented. The background color of framed icons are set with an elevation-color mapping from ground level to the highest elevation in the scene. This value is set through a slider. Even though users may find it hard to infer the absolute elevation only from the color, the color gradient eases the identification of elements at the same elevation and the identification of which element is set higher than another. Nevertheless, the exact value in centimeters may be seen by selecting a virtual object and observing the value displayed on the elevation slider.

The orientation of the virtual elements defines the direction they are facing. The user controls the orientation by using a slider, which adjusts the rotation with respect to the vertical axis. This allows the user to regulate the yaw of the virtual element, making the element pivot on itself, effectively turning it left or right. The orientation is displayed with an arrow head pointing outwards.

Finally, the size of the virtual elements is set by defining a scaling factor with respect to the original size specified by the model. Once again, a slider is used to specify the scale, which will be represented in the scene by the size of the icon that represents the virtual element.

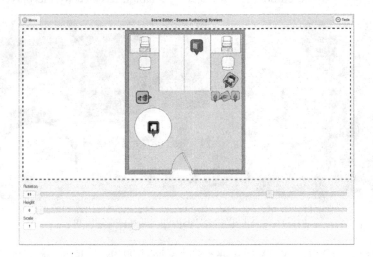

Fig. 3. Screenshot of the scene authoring tool

To ease the edition of multiple virtual elements at once the *scene editor* features multiple selection.

The scene authoring tool is implemented as a HTML5 website for multi-platform compatibility. It is mainly designed for touch interaction on medium-sized screens such as those in tablets, although interaction with a mouse and keyboard on bigger displays is also supported. Specifically, JQuery Mobile was used to design the web interface. The server is implemented in PHP5 with asynchronous AJAX calls and a MySQL database.

3.2.2   Augmented Scenes Player (AS Player)

The AS Player is the subsystem of the platform in charge of augmenting the user view of the physical environment by rendering graphical representations of virtual objects on top of the user view. The system requires the user to be equipped with an optical see-through AR headmounted display, which should permit the augmentation of the whole visual field. In addition he/she should place in the space to augment fiducial markers to be used as references. With regards of these markers it is necessary to note that they are not directly linked to virtual elements, but they encode reference locations, whose coordinates and orientation are stored in a database. To track the user position and orientation in the area it is necessary that at least one fiducial marker is captured by the camera at any given time. Therefore, the user should distribute the markers in the environment to augment in a way that allows him/her to move around freely, being able to observe the augmented elements from any position. To assist the user in this process, the player can be used in combination with the AS Editor. Thanks to tablet portability, the user of the AS editor may wander around the environment, testing different configurations of the markers positions, and visualizing through the AS Player the different views that the system generates based on them. Figure 4 shows a user placing markers and performing on-site edition of a scene with a tablet, assisted by the player.

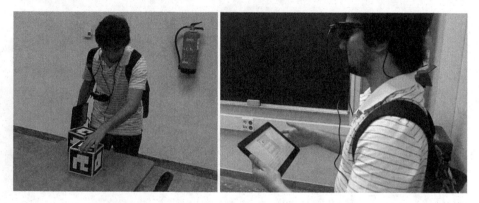

Fig. 4. AS Player-assisted on-site scene edition

The user can improve the accuracy of the location tracking using cubic markers whose six faces provide references of the same position from the six orthogonal perspectives. Figure 4 depicts these cubic markers used as references.

3.2.3   Virtual and Augmented Scenes Matching

Once we have defined an augmented scene and a virtual scene it is possible to define matchings between them in order to have *mixed scenes*. Thus, a mixed scene establishes a correspondence between elements of a virtual scene and elements of an augmented scene (Fig. 5). This way the actions and changes that occur in one scene are replicated in the corresponding elements of the other scene.

The matchings between the virtual reality entities (GREP game entities) and their corresponding elements in augmented scenes are managed through relations in a database. The database schema permits maintaining different matchings between virtual scenes and augmented scenes. This means that one virtual scene can be linked to different augmented reality scenes, each including different representations to suit the requirements of different learner profiles. The connections between *scenes* are static, meaning that they define the initial position of all the elements that are present both in the virtual world (in GREP) and in the real world (through the augmented reality gear).

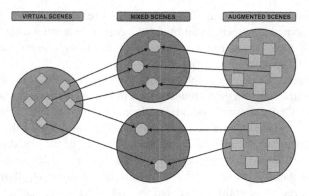

Fig. 5. Mixed scene creation by virtual and augmented scenes matching

Once a matching is done it is possible to define plays in mixed mode, where players could either execute their actions and interactions with the game in the virtual or the real scenes. Consequently, two kinds of users would exist, those who act in the virtual world and those who act in the real world.

A fully mixed game could allow the following:

- A player that plays in the virtual world is able to modify the augmented scene with her actions.
- A player that plays in the augmented scene is able to modify the elements in the virtual world with her actions.

The platform currently supports the first type of interactions. The actions performed by a virtual player affect the virtual objects which, in turn, affect the augmented representations in the augmented scene.

The synchronization of changes in the virtual world affecting the augmented world has been implemented through an event system in GREP. Changes detected on the state of GREP elements are applied to the corresponding augmented scene elements observable by augmented scene players. This implementation consists of a javascript module extending GREP that executes calls to a PHP-based state update service.

4 Use Case: Firefighter Simulation

To evaluate the system a use case has been developed consisting in the implementation of a firefighter and rescue training game in mixed reality modality. The game simulates emergency scenarios that firefighters may stumble upon. In these contexts physical factors are fundamental and time is critical. Firefighters need to wear special protections and gear, whose weight critically reduce their movement freedom and put their stamina to the limit. Additionally, heat and smoke pose obstacles to the realization of their tasks. The implementation of a virtual reality game for firefighter training may be useful for consolidating the studied courses of action to be taken during emergencies, but they lack the real-world characteristics that are so important in these emergency scenarios. On the contrary, a mixed reality game brings these situations closer to the real emergency situation by having the user play in a real physical environment rather than through a computer screen. In addition, the cost of executing these simulations is rather low since victims and fire may be simulated through augmented reality, and firefighter and victim safety is not risked.

Having defined the rationale behind this use case context selection, the design process of the game with the implemented system is now detailed. As a first step, the real world where the simulation would take place is virtualized and designed in GREP. For this use case, we designed a virtual scene that replicates one of the classrooms of our university, including the disposition of the tables, size of the blackboard, windows, etc. Once the virtual environment is defined, the game entities were defined. The objective of the game is to save a kid from the flames by controlling a firefighter. Consequently, three game entities were defined and added to this game: a firefighter, a kid and flames. Instances of these entities were placed in the classroom scenes replicating a situation that required the firefighter to extinguish the flames to reach the kid. After this, the rules that govern the entities and game execution are created. In our case, one of the rules stated that when a firefighter approaches the flames, his/her health level decreases by some amount per second. Finally, when all game rules are defined a playable GREP virtual game is ready.

Once the virtual game had been defined we proceeded to define the augmented scene following the process detailed in the Sect. 3.2. This way, a simple top view plan of the real classroom was uploaded to the tool to create an empty augmented scene, together with the graphical models to represent the entities of the game. Next, the on-site edition of the scene was performed using an augmented reality headset, specifically Vuzixs Star 1200 model was used for this project. In this case two cubic markers were enough to obtain references of the whole space to augment. With regards to the placement of the augmented entities, the kid was positioned on top of a table, trapped behind some flames, and with the firefighter located on the opposite side of the room.

Finally, the matching between the virtual scene created in GREP and the augmented scene defined with the scene authoring tool was performed, linking the entities that represent the kid, the firefighter and the flames in the two types of environments.

Gameplay.
The current implementation of the mixed game considers two roles: player and observer. The player is in charge of controlling the firefighter and plays the game in the virtual world using a laptop. Meanwhile an observer in the classroom can observe the equivalent game action in the real classroom using AR gear. Figure 6 depicts the firefighter and fire as perceived by the viewer (right) while the virtual reality player plays (left). While the virtual reality player moves along the corridor, so does the augmented reality representation in the viewer perspective. Accordingly, when the firefighter extinguishes the flames, the fire disappears from viewer sight. Finally, the test ends when the firefighter approaches the freed victim and leads him out of the building.

Fig. 6. Virtual view (left), observer direct view (upper-right) and augmented view (lower-right)

5 Conclusions and Future Work

Mixed reality technology offers the possibility to take advantage of the physical characteristics of a real environment that virtual reality systems fail to capture or simulate. These advantages can be exploited in the form of mixed reality DEGs, which allow to combine the flexibility provided by virtual DEGs and the benefits of delivering instructions in a real context. Unfortunately, the technical knowledge required to create this type of experiences often poses an unsurmountable barrier for educators. This work has presented MR-GREP, a platform that supports the design and development of mixed reality DEGs with minimal programming involved. The platform is able to reproduce the action of the game in a real context by means of AR technology.

Current work is carried out with the aim of extending the possibilities of interaction supported by the mixed reality environments created by the platform. On the one hand, a wearable gesture recognition system for the players in the real world is currently under development. The system will allow to translate the gestures and movements of the players into changes of their representations in the virtual world. On the other hand, work is being carried out to integrate the platform with an interaction toolkit for developing cross-reality experiences. This will allow to interconnect the physical and virtual actions in the game with changes and readings in real objects placed in the scenario of the game.

References

1. Johnson, L., Adams, S., Cummins, M.: The NMC horizon report: 2013 higher education edition. New Media Consortium (2013)

2. Torrente, J., Del Blanco, Á., Marchiori, E.J., Moreno-Ger, P., Fernández-Manjón, B.: < e-Adventure > : introducing educational games in the learning process. In: 2010 IEEE Education Engineering (EDUCON), pp. 1121–1126. IEEE (2010)

3. Göbel, S., Salvatore, L., Konrad, R.A., Mehm, F.: StoryTec: a digital storytelling platform for the authoring and experiencing of interactive and non-linear stories. In: Spierling, U., Szilas, N. (eds.) ICIDS 2008. LNCS, vol. 5334, pp. 325–328. Springer, Heidelberg (2008)

4. Thomas, B., Close, B., Donoghue, J., Squires, J., De Bondi, P., Morris, M., Piekarski, W.: ARQuake: an outdoor/indoor augmented reality first person application. In: The Fourth International Symposium on. Wearable Computers, pp. 139–146. IEEE (2000)

5. Cheok, A.D., Goh, K.H., Liu, W., Farbiz, F., Fong, S.W., Teo, S.L., Li, Y., Yang, X.: Human Pacman: a mobile, wide-area entertainment system based on physical, social, and ubiquitous computing. Pers. Ubiquitous Comput. **8**, 71–81 (2004)

6. MacIntyre, B., Gandy, M., Dow, S., Bolter, J.D.: DART: a toolkit for rapid design exploration of augmented reality experiences. In: Proceedings of the 17th Annual ACM symposium on User Interface Software and Technology, pp. 197–206. ACM (2004)

7. Zauner, J., Haller, M.: Authoring of mixed reality applications including multi-marker calibration for mobile devices. In: 10th Eurographics Symposium on Virtual Environments, EGVE, pp. 87–90 (2004)

8. Brederode, B., Markopoulos, P., Gielen, M., Vermeeren, A., de Ridder, H.: Powerball: the design of a novel mixed-reality game for children with mixed abilities. In: Proceedings of the 2005 Conference on Interaction Design and Children, pp. 32–39. ACM (2005)

9. ARToolKit Home Page. http://www.hitl.washington.edu/artoolkit/

10. Game Engine Technology by Unreal. https://www.unrealengine.com/

11. Zarraonandia, T., Diaz, P., Aedo, I., Ruiz, M.R.: Designing educational games through a conceptual model based on rules and scenarios. Multimedia Tools and Appl. 1–25 (2014)

Can Games Motivate Urban Youth
for Civic Engagement?

Alma L. Culén[1(✉)], Sumit Pandey[1], Swati Srivastava[1],
and Katie Coughlin[2]

[1] Department of Informatics, University of Oslo, Oslo, Norway
{almira,sumitp,swatisr}@ifi.uio.no
[2] Oslo Children's Museum, Oslo, Norway
katie@oslobarnemuseum.org

Abstract. In this paper, we explore the possibility of using games as a way of engaging youth in environmentally-oriented participatory art or other cooperative urban projects. Our approach was design-led, and youth participated in evaluating games that we proposed from the perspective of motivation and engagement, both in the environmental issues in the games themselves and in the likelihood of subsequent real life involvement stimulated by the games. The findings show that ultimately, personal passion for the cause that the game represents, and not the game itself, would be the central factor in a youth's decision to engage in real life. Social embeddedness was also valued high, as well as the possibility to make a real difference.

Keywords: Urban youth · Participatory art · Collaborative culture · Co-creativity

1 Introduction

Participatory art and collaborative urban cultural processes are no longer only engaging artists and other participants in cultural productions, but are increasingly also representing ways of taking action towards improving the quality of urban life. Worldwide, people are engaging as co-creatives alongside artists and researchers, exploring ways to improve their urban environments. Ingram describes in [1, 2], how New York artists and youth joined forces to reclaim some of the Bronx riverbank, and further how a bioremediation project in Chicago and other environmentally-oriented art projects sought solutions to real life urban ecological challenges. Such projects frequently become multidisciplinary efforts, involving designers, artists, engineers, researchers and most importantly, people who get engaged as collaborators, co-designers or citizen scientists [3, 4].

Technology, and in particular the Internet, has come to play a central role in these participatory, collaborative processes. One can say that the Internet was already central to civic engagement when it comes to youth [5, 6], the Internet natives. The initial research presented in [6] finds that *"… online communities aimed at promoting civic engagement, activism, or community involvement among youth are generally facilitators*

© Springer International Publishing Switzerland 2015
P. Zaphiris and A. Ioannou (Eds.): LCT 2015, LNCS 9192, pp. 549–560, 2015.
DOI: 10.1007/978-3-319-20609-7_52

of the civic engagement that occurs in the offline world, but not necessarily the places where that engagement occurs". Online communities and the tools they offer, e.g., TakingItGlobal [7], may give a valuable starting point for youth engagement, especially for those who are already civic-minded.

However, technology that youth use, or could use, in co-creative urban participatory culture processes, has evolved far beyond the Internet. Understanding the role of technology and how it can support youth when it comes to civic and politically-oriented art and culture is both timely and interesting. Timely, because the dominant discourse when addressing the role of technology has been focused on motivating an individual to be more aware of resources and to act more consciously (for example, diverse feedback and awareness devices designed to give feedback on the use of electricity [8]). Design for increased awareness has also led to re-focusing research in the direction of daily practices and how they can be understood as design material and as such, be redesigned [9]. Interesting, because many cultural institutions such as museums, libraries and theaters have increased their efforts to interact with audiences, and to support visitors' social interactions in meaningful ways [10–12], often using digital platforms. These efforts, however, are not easy to sustain over time and sometimes put the quality of an institution's offerings at risk. Cultural institutions are seeking to understand emerging practices, such as discussed in [13], where the meaning of curatorship is questioned in light of current "outsourcing" of the work to "amateurs" (and the Internet).

Understanding and producing knowledge on technology-supported participatory culture is not simple and has not been researched adequately. In particular, human-computer interaction design research, a field concerned with design of new technologies and interaction modes, had little to say until relatively recently about technologies that support sustained engagement in urban co-development, or about methods and practices for broader engagement and participation in culture or in public interactive spaces [14–16].

This paper presents our initial design-led research, conducted in preparation for a long-term European project exploring the development of participatory culture and related practices across Europe. The project links technology and culture, participation and design in urban living. It draws on a diversity of approaches as possibilities to discover successful practices and meaningful patterns. In the Norwegian subproject, we focus on youth and ways of motivating them towards increased engagement in envisioning a better and more sustainable urban life through interaction design, participatory art and other culture forms.

This paper reports from the first study in which gaming is explored as a motivating factor towards increased engagement among youth in reflection and possible action, concerning sustainability and quality of urban life. Since our approach is design-led, several tools (games) were made for use in workshops and as interview aids that simultaneously allowed us to assess levels of understanding youth had related to the complexity of balancing environmentally friendly urban solutions, economic health, and quality of life. Participants ranged in age from 7 (4) to between 10–15 (23). Although the total number of youth engaged in this study through focus groups, workshops and interviews was small (27), we uncovered clear insights into how well our methods and tools worked to understand issues of motivation and engagement, and in which way these tools could be employed further to raise awareness around the environment, sustainability and most importantly, participation.

The paper is structured as follows: the next chapter presents the results from the use of an interactive game surface – CityCrafter, followed by a description of three exploratory workshops and short interviews where we report results of working with three open-ended games. Thereafter, we present a discussion of our findings from the workshops and interviews in the context of existing literature, ending with a few ideas on future directions and finally, our conclusions from this work.

2   Game Prototypes and Engagement

A recent study [17] shows that for youth aged 16–19, volunteerism has more than doubled in the past 30 + years, while empathy has decreased. The study shows that youth participate in voluntary work primarily in response to outside pressures and requirements. For example, they are often motivated to do voluntary work in order to improve their CVs. The type of motivation that we are interested to stimulate is related, conversely, to passion [18] and creative, innovative expressions [19, 20]. Study [21] considers high school students' motivation for learning in relation to their socio-digital participation. The study indicates that for some students, levels of social activities and gaming outside of school can correlate positively with indifference towards school. Considering results of studies into gaming and its positive effects on behavior in real life [22], the passion youth exhibit for gaming [18], and that we are interested in investigating participatory culture co-creation with youth, we chose to explore the possibilities that gaming offers towards appropriate motivation for civic engagement, possibly also in the school arena. The scope or the "playing field" of the games was kept at a citywide level to promote learning and understanding of resource allocation and consumption at a wider social or at a supra-individual level (see [9]). Our hypothesis was built on research presented in [9, 23], which shows that understanding resource consumption and allocation is best done within a broader socio-cultural context as opposed to specific actions or behaviors.

2.1   The CityCrafter

The initial step for two of the authors of this paper was to make a design brief and propose and supervise a student project in an interaction design course, related to topics presented above. We did not want an online solution, but rather a hybrid or a tangible one. A group of three undergraduate students took up the challenge [24].

The students started their work by organizing two focus groups at the local elementary school. Their first focus group involved children from the first and the second grades. The children were asked to draw buildings and tell about the workings of a city. It was found this age group was too young to have a desired level of understanding. There is an organization in Norway, Miljøagentene [25], working to increase children's awareness around environmental issues, specifically in this age group. The organization works towards a cleaner environment and a better future, by engaging children. It provides activities in nature, collection of batteries, learning about climate changes and most importantly, it motivates children to act and realize that they can make a difference.

The second focus group consisted of third and fourth grade children, age 10–11, and this group was more engaged, understood issues and was interested in more advanced games. The students also inquired about games that the children liked to play.

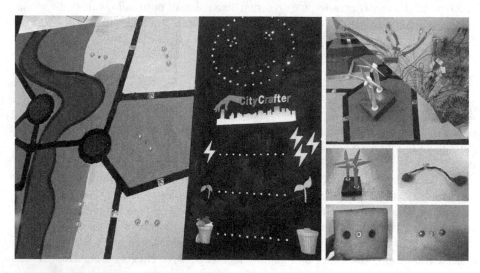

Fig. 1. The portion of the table representing an area of the city, with feedback on environmental issues. Elements to place on the table, and their design, are shown in small images on the right.

The main finding from this focus group was that a game with elements of SimCity, Minecraft and Monopoly could be understood, and could be engaging for this age group. Thus, the students made an interactive prototype based on an open city game that focused on the effects of buildings on the environment and on energy use in the city. Interaction with the designed prototype took place around a large table with tangible elements such as factories, skyscrapers, family homes, windmills, sports arenas, etc. that could be pinned to the table and given a certain amount of energy, see Fig. 1. The feedback, a large smiley face, was built into the tabletop and gave clear and simple feedback on the use of energy and the environmental impact as elements are placed on the table.

The prototype was tested at the Norwegian Technical Museum with 15 participants in the age group between 10–12. From a usability point of view, the results of the test were very positive. There was no confusion as to what to do with the tangible components, how the game was to be played, or how to understand the feedback. The prototype was sufficiently sturdy, and there were no technology problems during the testing, which would have lowered the user experience of the game.

On the other hand, we found that the prototype had serious limitations as a tool to study motivation. As can be seen from Fig. 1, the prototype consisted of numerous components and making the interactions more meaningful by adding additional components would have been difficult. At the same time, the feedback and gameplay was so simple that it could not support the idea of sustained engagement and motivation that we describe in the Introduction and want to evaluate.

2.2 Open Explorations

Shifting the focus from technology towards deeper exploration of our primary objective related to understanding motivation and how it could be stimulated, we made a set of three paper-based prototypes suitable for open exploration and more in the style of traditional games. The games still explored urban living and what it entails, including reflections on balance between investments and economic health, ecological friendliness and life quality. The three prototypes were based on three types of games: co-operative, competitive and explorative, see Figs. 2 and 3. The first one was made very large, so that many participants could sit around the board. The second one was smaller and utilized point system advancement from a start position towards a goal. Both games used an actual map of an area in Oslo as the board background. Icons representing transportation (buses, trams, bikes), roads (city streets, highways), hotels, restaurants, shopping malls, food stores, houses, factories, schools, pesticide use, green areas, power from water, windmills, sewage systems, waste (with or without recycling) and so on were made (around 100 pieces, with some duplicates). Neither game was defined completely. Rather, participants could help make game rules and decide if adding apps or technology might make a positive difference on the experience of the game. The third game explored synergies between different factors, which would lead to either positive or negative results on the environment, such as how an oil spill would harm marine life in nearby waters. The icons for this game were similar to the other two games but the participants were allowed to combine them freely and in creative ways, giving them a chance to explore open possibilities.

Fig. 2. Making a sustainable city: goal of the game is to balance economic health, people's satisfaction and good sustainable solutions. Images are from all three sessions held.

Fig. 3. A competitive game to the left, awarding positive and negative points when choosing a token. The image on the right explores how different (non)sustainable elements mix.

Three workshop sessions were organized with short follow-up interviews. Two of the sessions ran between 1–2 h with 2 participants age 14 and 15 in the first, and 3 participants age 11, 11 and 14 in the second session. The third session was shorter and run with only one participant age 7, to verify the conclusions that students made during their first focus group with children age 7, before prototyping the CityCrafter.

Whereas CityCrafter was tested with participants in a well-balanced mix of gender, the workshop sessions, although planned as mixed-gender, involved only girls. The invited boys were unable to attend for various reasons. Instead of re-scheduling, we held the workshops, aware that our feedback may be gender-biased. However, the findings from these sessions were interesting, and certainly give pointers for further research.

We now give a short summary of the main findings, followed by some interesting points we learned from the interviews.

Workshop Session 1. The participants (girls, age 14 and 15) were told at the start of the session that this was a game in the making. The participants were encouraged to take a look at icons and ask if they did not understand what the icons represent. They could also use wooden blocks in any way their imagination would lead them, but we asked them to talk along, so that we could grasp their reasoning behind actions they took. The girls started playing as competitors, using the blocks to divide the map into districts. Very soon, they gave up this strategy, removed the barriers and started to build open city areas, cooperating on the use of resources (saying, for example, *"For this number of inhabitants, one school should do."* and *"If it is placed mid-way and if there is a public transport from both of their areas, it is the best use of money and it is not so damaging for the environment."*). Soon, the girls were very engaged in trying to determine which decisions would make the most sense for the city they were creating, and their arguments were growing in depth and complexity. Initially, they tried to build a city with all the amenities. The icons concerned with types of electrical power used for houses, hotels and factories made them think about costs of producing clean energy, but also how unpleasant it can be to live, for example, near a windmill, which can be rather noisy. The discussions then considered seriously the environmental consequences of components being added to different areas. After this activity was over, one of the participants shared that she, during the game, realized that the most important factor in the city that she wanted to build was quality of life. She was interested in solutions that enabled people to have, in the long run, sustainable solutions and a good environment. Running a part of the city that is poor, for example, brings challenges, so money is important, and has to flow well. But money was not important in itself; the quality of life was more important. Additionally, both girls would have liked to have access to electronic feedback with immediate, well-reasoned evaluations of their decisions. That would add more drama, as well as learning, to the game. The participants agreed that an opportunity to cooperate and negotiate with one another made this game interesting.

The second, competitive game was experienced as simpler to play after the first one. Here, they wished for electronic point feedback each time they chose an icon. During the session, the Wizard of Oz technique was used to assign points. Participants were very good in using the previous game to evaluate their own choices based on their experiences and thoughts from the previous game, and they evaluated the sustainability impact of their decisions right from the beginning. The Wizard was almost not needed.

The third game was found to be interesting, and the participants indicated that they wanted to know reasons behind the results of mixing the components in more detail. They thought that these synergetic factors were not taught adequately at school and said that they had learned some new things during this game (the relation between de-forestation and flooding, for example). They would have liked to see combinations that gave also positive results, making a positive impact on the environment.

Workshop Session 2. The two 11-year-old girls were friends. From the start of the game, they wanted to co-operate. The 14-year-old girl wanted to compete against them. The dynamics in this session showed some of the same traits as the previous session. All participants were capable of understanding the task to build a city and had discussions around implications of their choices. For example, *"We need to have sewers because people need to go to the toilet."* Further, placement of a sewage treatment plant was made outside of the populated area so that a clean water supply would be assured. Discussing what they liked about the game and what they would change with it, the girls said that it was fun to be your own boss, build, plan, imagine, and consider how things matter. This group liked the tactile and personal engagement with the game and thought that a computerized version would be less appealing. One girl, 11, said that parents do not like children to use the PC all the time. They liked the face-to-face interactions and said that it is fun for people together and that two persons think better than one. They did, however, ask for a set of digital feedback "warnings" that could be either heeded or ignored. They also wanted feedback on how to build a well-functioning economy. This indicates a preference for seamless use of technology in an otherwise traditional board game. The 14-year-old suggested that the game could have many more elements and should be bigger, too. The younger girls agreed, wishing for additional kinds of elements and more colorful game pieces.

The second game received more enthusiasm from this group and was a favorite for one of the 11-year-olds: *"Competition made it a little better, you really understood the point"*. Here, they engaged deeper in discussions such as *"We need to place the solar panels away from the buildings to avoid shadows"*, *"Windmills need lots of room"* and they linked some of their reasoning to memories of lessons learned from their school-work. They also made a point that *"It is good to see how what others do affects you"*.

The engagement with the third game was also good, and the girls expressed that it was different and interesting, but the game was nobody's favorite.

Workshop Session 3. This session engaged only one participant age 7. The goal was to see to what extent earlier observations that students made were correct. The first game was played cooperatively with an adult, but it became clear that while the game was fun, the girl did indeed not yet have the ability to understand the concepts behind the game. The competitive game was thus skipped. In the third game, the adult tried to explain that mixing the bacteria and the food can make people sick, or the city sewage, if dumped too close to the shore may be dangerous for swimmers, and made the first two rows shown in the upper right corner of the Fig. 3. The girl made the remaining two: cutting one tree out of three, leaves only two trees and, a fish plus the plate, makes a good meal. So, again, the concepts required for effective participation in these games were too advanced for this age group.

Follow Up Interviews. After the workshop sessions, we asked some simple questions, that could help us understand engagement, its relation to sustainability, and how could it lead to some real life engagement in co-design and artistic and cultural projects which address some of these issues.

We started by asking our participants what "sustainable" means to them. *"Something that lasts a long time and is stable"*, was the answer.

When asked about any practices at home that contribute to the idea of sustainability and are positive for environment, one of the girls said: *"We all recycle. I also got my parent to buy a car that pollutes less"*. Another girl chimed in: *"We use good power in our homes. Most of it comes from water, and gives good, cheap and clean energy to the whole country"*.

What is the role of the school in teaching you about these issues? *"Occasionally, here and there, we learn about them. But we do not learn about global warming and how to make things that are more environmentally friendly."* *"Maybe, we could have more activities like this at school. They make us remember things that we should do and not do. It is actually also really good to know about small stuff that one can do, like the length of the shower one takes every day, and to take shorter ones."*

What do you think is the most damaging to the urban environment? Here, the girls agreed that factories influence the environment most, and should be made more environmentally friendly. Next in line was transportation, and they saw it as desirable to make people take public transportation in order to reduce the amount of cars, as well as to increase pedestrian areas and bicycle paths.

Do you ever think about freshness of water or air? One girl said: *"Not water. I believe that Norway has great water and the water is still of good quality. But this is not the case with the air. I sometimes really feel the pollution. I also notice trash on the streets which I experience as pollution"*.

What if you heard about an art project, trying to engage people in participation, and the project stands for promoting a cleaner city? Would you participate? The answers here were *"Yes, if I had the time"*, and *"Yes, if I knew what to do"*.

If there were such a project, what would make you most willing to participate: financial reward, social pressure, saving the environment or something else? The participants answered this question sincerely. All of them mentioned that incentives matter. If they had to spend a lot of time, it would be good to make some money. If other friends were engaged, however, making money becomes less relevant. Ultimately, most participants indicated that passion for the cause would be most important, and even voluntary, unpaid participation would be possible if they could make a difference.

3   Making Sense of Motivation to Participate

Participatory art culture with youth is spreading on a global scale [1, 2] with technology and the Internet in particular [6, 7] facilitating action and activism for the civic-minded. The prototypes and workshops discussed in this paper evaluate gaming as a motivator for engagement, good decision-making and better social and environmental awareness. Through experience with the CityCrafter platform we discovered that overly simplistic gameplay is not successful in stimulating sustained engagement even though there may be significant initial interest due to interactive elements. Subsequent workshops benefited from this finding by introducing more complex and varied forms of gameplay and incorporating personal values and emotions as motivating factors. This was done by using the map of Oslo (where all the participants reside) in all the prototypes to test the effects of giving the participants a familiar situation and heartfelt problems. Initially, the emotional and social elements did not seem to create a noticeable impact on the participants' decision-making processes. But as the gameplay proceeded, we noticed that discussions and cognizance of the issues and implications of actions became much greater, particularly in the first game, which had a more complex and exploratory gameplay model. These findings were consistent with the claims of positive emotional impact and social binding in physical settings [22]. It is interesting that during session 1, one of the girls brought in the design of new practices explicitly, using even the example of showering as in [9]. The girl's expression *"the small things that we can do"* implies a willingness to engage personally in new, more sustainable practices in the hope that if everyone does it, it will make a difference. Another participant made an explicit connection between design (*"how to make things that are more environment friendly"*) and a way in which they could potentially participate in making their world a better place. Further, an explicit connection was made with a desire to learn more: *"Maybe we could have more activities like this at school that would help us remember things that we should do and not do"*. Thus, we could notice the connection between design and behavior, and how daily living practices and learning practices could be re-designed to better fit the goal of striving for sustainability. As mentioned in [3], innovations generally come from collaborative and discussion-driven settings. We feel that complex decision-based games placed in social settings like museums and schools could serve very well as a "foot in the door" [26] for engaging youth. Simple activities, which encourage debate and discussions, could lead youth to explore possibilities for getting involved in more difficult and complex tasks. These small engagements could serve as starting points for a "positive spillover" [26]. Practice-oriented design research into sustainable practices [9] provides a concrete example of the above. Our research leads us to conclude that open-ended, decision-based gaming with tangible artifacts is most effective in social, physical settings [22]. Further, it provides an ideal scenario for all three guidelines for practice-oriented design: bodily performance (active integration of learning in practice), crises of routine (the change in routine practices brought about by debate and questioning) and variety of performances (reconfiguration of thoughts and ideas as the game progresses) [9].

In order to get feedback and possibly some further insights into what is motivational, we inquired with a young female activist (23). We engaged her in a conversation about the relation between games and how (or if) games could stimulate broader engagement in participatory art and culture with political and social implications. She is herself a gamer as well. Her perspective was the following: *"Attempts to gamify either serious or educational content often do not work at the personal level. It can somehow end up being not really new and often condescending. However, it works better in the group context of, for example, school, as it is often more fun than the usual ways of learning."* This was in line with what we observed during workshop sessions and is also in line with the suggestions made in [22]. The games would not work, or be interesting for a single person, but the interaction, negotiation and actual learning were fun when involved with others. However, taking the desired step forward from games and engagement in games to actual, physical acts of participation in a real setting are difficult. Further, the activist shared her opinion on why it is hard to start: *"There has to be a space for meeting people. Physical, face-to-face interaction is motivating and inspiring. Online is hard. Then, there needs to be a bridge, bridging the gap of not knowing how to engage in participatory art, as a non-artist, for example. And if engaged, equally important is how to see that your contribution is actually meaningful"*. Hence, possible next steps could be to arrange for follow-up "meet-ups" and collaborative game playing sessions that also include activists and artists (or appropriate persons, depending on the project/game subject matter) and using games as experience-sharing platforms in conjunction with people who already have passion for the cause.

4   Conclusion

Our open exploration of games as motivators for youth engagement in urban settings had environmental sustainability as an overarching theme and additional engagement factor. Through our experiments, we learned that tangible media mixed with interactive gameplay elements serve as a strong motivator for urban youth. Trying out different models of gameplay, such as exploratory, competitive and open-ended, we sought to evaluate the learning processes and the evolution of decision-making processes among the participants, as well as how and what makes their experiences during the game personal and engaging at deeper levels. We discovered that an open-ended model coupled with appropriate feedback led to the highest discussion and debate among the participants. The participants showed a tendency to cooperate rather than compete while making decisions, and they also debated the implications of their decisions for overall satisfaction, environmental impact and economic effects of various amenities created in the city. Moreover, their decision-making was increasingly moving towards trying to create the best possible city by balancing the aforementioned factors. A low-fidelity prototype of the game, CityCrafter, tested at the Norwegian Technical Museum in Oslo, furthers this argument that open-ended, decision-driven play can serve as a strong motivator towards increasing participatory culture among the urban youth. A strong caveat to this argument, however, is our finding from the workshops that engagement is driven primarily through collaborative social settings and peer-to-peer discussions and may not be as effective if used in a solo or closed setting. A second take-away was related to the use of exploratory and discovery-driven gameplay elements, which stimulated questions and increased inquiries about the consequences of different factors such as pollution and deforestation in sustainable practices. Overall, we believe that while these elements might be very effective in aiding a structured inquiry into sustainable practices in a controlled setting such as a game or a school, they do not yet serve as actual strong motivators for a city-specific context in a real life setting. Thus, while our research shows that certain gameplay elements in social settings serve as strong motivators for urban youth to engage, the door is as yet wide open to investigate ways to transpose this engagement into practical, real life urban involvement and contributions.

Acknowledgment. The work is, in part, supported by the EU Creative Europe grant, EC-EACEA 2014-2330.

References

1. Ingram, M.: Sculpting solutions: art-science collaborations in sustainability. Environ.: Sci. Policy Sustain. Dev. **54**, 24–34 (2012)
2. Ingram, M.: Washing urban water: diplomacy in environmental art in the Bronx, New York City. Gend. Place Cult. **21**, 105–122 (2014)
3. Fischer, G., Giaccardi, E., Eden, H., Sugimoto, M., Ye, Y.: Beyond binary choices: integrating individual and social creativity. Int. J. Hum -Comput Stud. **63**, 482–512 (2005)
4. Wiggins, A., Crowston, K.: From conservation to crowdsourcing: a typology of citizen science. In: 2011 44th Hawaii International Conference on System Sciences (HICSS), pp. 1–10. IEEE (2011)
5. Hart, R.A.: Children's Participation: The Theory and Practice of Involving Young Citizens in Community Development and Environmental Care. Routledge, New York (2013)
6. Raynes-Goldie, K., Walker, L.: Our space: online civic engagement tools for youth. In: Bennett, W.L. (ed.) Civic Life Online Learning: How Digital Media Can Engage Youth, pp. 161–188. MIT Press, Boston (2008)
7. Welcome to TakingITGlobal!. https://www.tigweb.org/

8. Froehlich, J., Findlater, L., Landay, J.: The design of eco-feedback technology. In: Proceedings of the SIGCHI Conference on Human Factors in Computing Systems, pp. 1999–2008. ACM, New York (2010)
9. Kuijer, L., de Jong, A., van Eijk, D.: Practices as a unit of design: an exploration of theoretical guidelines in a study on bathing. ACM Trans. Comput.-Hum. Interact. **20**, 21:1–21:22 (2008)
10. Bannon, L., Benford, S., Bowers, J., Heath, C.: Hybrid design creates innovative museum experiences. Commun. ACM **48**, 62–65 (2005)
11. Culén, A.L.: Transforming children´s museums by designing exhibits with children. In: Proceedings of the Transformative Museum, Roskilde Univeristy, Danmark (2012)
12. Garzotto, F., Rizzo, F.: Interaction paradigms in technology-enhanced social spaces: a case study in museums. In: Proceedings of the 2007 Conference on Designing Pleasurable Products and Interfaces, pp. 343–356. ACM, New York (2007)
13. Rodley, E.: "Outsourcing" the curatorial impulse, Part One (2014). https://exhibitdev.wordpress.com/2014/10/29/outsourcing-the-curatorial-impulse-part-one/
14. Culén, A.L., Rosseland, R.: Ecologies of spaces for enjoyable interactions. Int. J. Adv. Netw. Serv. **6**(3 and 4), 361–373 (2014)
15. Kaptelinin, V., Bannon, L.J.: Interaction design beyond the product: creating technology-enhanced activity spaces. Hum.-Comput. Interact. **27**, 277–309 (2012)
16. Fischer, P.T., Hornecker, E.: Urban HCI: spatial aspects in the design of shared encounters for media facades. In: Proceedings of the 2012 ACM Annual Conference on Human Factors in Computing Systems, pp. 307–316 (2012)
17. Brunell, A.B., Tumblin, L., Buelow, M.T.: Narcissism and the motivation to engage in volunteerism. Curr. Psychol. **33**, 365–376 (2014)
18. Fuster, H., Chamarro, A., Carbonell, X., Vallerand, R.J.: Relationship between passion and motivation for gaming in players of massively multiplayer online role-playing games. Cyberpsychol. Behav. Soc. Netw. **17**, 292–297 (2014)
19. Roberts, D., Hughes, M., Kertbo, K.: Exploring consumers' motivations to engage in innovation through co-creation activities. Eur. J. Mark. **48**, 147–169 (2014)
20. Mulder, I.: Living labbing the rotterdam way: co-creation as an enabler for urban innovation. Technol. Innovation Manage. Rev. **2**(9), 39–43 (2012)
21. Hietajärvi, L., Tuominen-Soini, H., Hakkarainen, K., Salmela-Aro, K., Lonka, K.: Is student motivation related to socio-digital participation? a person-oriented approach. Procedia – Soc. Behav. Sci. **171**, 1156–1167 (2015)
22. McGonigal, J.: Reality Is Broken: Why Games Make Us Better and How They Can Change the World. Penguin, New York (2011)
23. Brynjarsdottir, H., Håkansson, M., Pierce, J., Baumer, E., DiSalvo, C., Sengers, P.: Sustainably unpersuaded: how persuasion narrows our vision of sustainability. In: Proceedings of the SIGCHI Conference on Human Factors in Computing Systems, pp. 947–956. ACM, New York (2012)
24. Larsen, E., Svendsen, Ø., Åmodt, J.: CityCrafter. http://www.uio.no/studier/emner/matnat/ifi/INF2260/h14/presentations/City%20Crafter/index.html
25. Miljøagentene - barnas miljøvernorganisasjon!. http://miljoagentene.no/
26. Thøgersen, J., Crompton, T.: Simple and painless? the limitations of spillover in environmental campaigning. J. Consum. Policy **32**, 141–163 (2009)

H-Treasure Hunt: A Location and Object-Based Serious Game for Cultural Heritage Learning at a Historic Site

Hayun Kim[✉], Sungeun An, Sangeun Keum, and Wontack Woo

Graduate School of Culture Technology, KAIST, Daejeon, 305-701, South Korea
{hayunkim,imsung110,keums,wwoo}@kaist.ac.kr

Abstract. Serious game is commonly used to support cultural heritage such as historical teaching and learning, and enhancing historic site visits. Nowadays most of in situ serious games have been supported by GPS but it is not suitable for a small-scale historic site. In this paper, we propose a location and object-based serious game application H-Treasure Hunt. H-Treasure hunt integrates location-based service with object-based sensors to find more exact location of artifacts at a historic site. In the game, the players wear Head Mounted Display (HMD) and explore a historic site interacting with artifacts to complete missions. In this way, H-Treasure Hunt will act as a tour guide helping users learn about the historic site and artifacts. The use of this application is to support cultural heritage teaching and learning as well as enhancing historical site visits.

Keywords: Collaboration technology and informal learning · Mobile and/or ubiquitous learning · Serious games and 3D virtual worlds for learning · User-generated content

1 Introduction

Serious game is commonly used to support cultural heritage such as historical teaching and learning, and enhancing historic site visits. Its playful characteristic not only increases motivation to learn but also raises interest of children and young adults in cultural heritage. Serious games for particular sites help players to find historical or geographical significance of the site and to learn more information than when they just observe. While playing the game, visitors are able to have immersive experience and construct personal meaning as well.

Nowadays most of serious games at outdoor sites have been supported by GPS based location technologies for in situ experience. However, using GPS at a historic site may result in GPS confusion areas, since artfiacts are located close to each other. Therefore, we improved location-based technologies with object-based sensors to pinpoint the location of artifacts at a historic site.

This paper suggests a location and object-based serious game, Historical Treasure Hunt. H-Treasure Hunt is a treasure hunt like location-based game that allows users to create their own content. Furthermore, H-Treasure hunt integrates location-based

© Springer International Publishing Switzerland 2015
P. Zaphiris and A. Ioannou (Eds.): LCT 2015, LNCS 9192, pp. 561–572, 2015.
DOI: 10.1007/978-3-319-20609-7_53

service with object-based sensors to interact with artifacts at a historic site. The game is composed of two major parts: authoring tool (H-Treasure Hide) and playing tool (H-Treasure Hunt). The overall system will be further described in Sect. 3.

Since the object-based sensor provides pinpoint locational accuracy of the user and the artifact, the user can be provided with information about the artifact at a suitable time and place. In this way, he or she will be able to have a feeling of being connected to the artifact with the sense of interaction. We expect that H-Treasure Hunt can provide a new way to explore a historic site and enhance the visitor's experience.

2 Motivation and Related Work

2.1 Motivation

Unlike the majority of location-based games, we desired to make H-Treasure Hunt not tied to specific gaming contents but playable at any historic site by utilizing authoring tool to satisfy different user groups. How can such a game support exploring a historic site by e.g. students and teachers on a field trip. While students are new to a historic site and naturally interested in sightseeing and learning about the history of a city, teachers might be able to re-evaluate their pre-existing view of the site by exploring it with prior knowledge and research.

According to these traits, H-Treasure Hunt has two roles: hider and hunter (Fig. 1). Teacher's role is the hider who hides sensors around artifacts and creates missions. Students can be the hunter who hunts points through completing the missions to reach their ultimate goal of getting a real treasure as a prize for the winner.

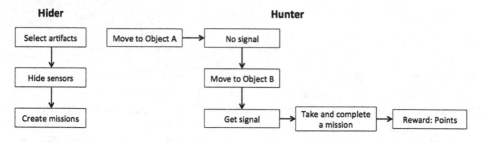

Fig. 1. Overview of the game actions separated by 'Hider' and 'Hunter'

Exploring the site with H-Treasure Hunt, students will be able to discover and learn many interesting facts about history. The game will help them to have an immersive and realistic reconstruction of a real location. As a result, they will be able to appreciate and learn the historical values of the site. It also engages mechanisms to motivate students into a real experience.

2.2 Related Work

Serious games for a historic site are often inflexible because game place is targeted to a certain place and POIs (Point of Interest) are selected in advance. As a result, users have to play the game in one fixed place with the same game content every time they visit the site. One example is mobile tour game that provides location-based service [1]. There are, on the other hand, other location-dependent studies that adopt more flexible approaches towards game place and content [2, 3]. Such studies provide authoring tools allowing user-created content. Instead of relying on already existing content, user creates game content that is relevant to the user's current situation.

H-Treasure Hunt is a close relative to Tidy City [2] and GeoCaching [3]. Tidy City is a scavenger hunt that players need to interpret riddles to find the correct target destination. Geocaching is a hide and seek game where treasures are hidden in the real world focusing more on the real world than in the virtual game world. They are similar to H-Treasure Hunt in that there are two type of user groups including one type of user group who design the gaming content. However, Tidy City and Geocaching focus more on entertaining than learning. On the other hand, H-Treasure Hunt not only has typical entertaining traits of games but also has educational effect.

Typically, these location-based serious games are designed for a wide range of area such as city [2, 3]. Location-based techniques are not oriented to historic site since these techniques are mainly based on GPS, which are robust for outdoor environment. Historic sites are usually smaller than the city scale and artifacts are too close to each other. For example, Bulguksa temple located in South Korea has stone pagodas and stone lanterns as well as buildings. GPS can be used to mark locations of relatively broad area like big objects but is too inexact for small scale positioning. It is not correct for indicating specific artifacts like stone pagodas and lanterns that are only few meters away. Therefore we need to improve location-based technologies to find more exact location of historic site and to interact with artifacts.

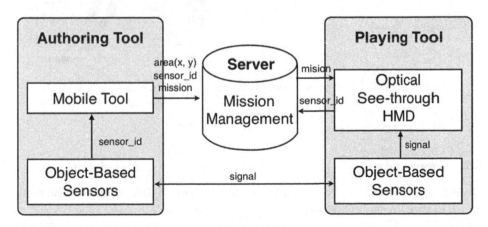

Fig. 2. Overall system diagram

3   System Design

3.1   Basic Architecture

Figure 2 shows a general outline of our system. The game is composed of two major parts: authoring tool (H-Treasure Hide) and playing tool (H-Treasure Hunt).

With authoring tool, designers walk around a historic site carrying object-based sensors. Selecting the artifact, they place the sensor around the artifact and mark a GPS location on mobile authoring tool to give players a rough area. Then designers specify the sensor number and create missions for the artifact. The data is then uploaded to the server and it becomes available for the game.

With playing tool, players hang the user sensor around the neck and wear optical see-through HMD that guide them to the designated area. Then they can freely explore the site to find the object sensors that are scattered around the site as shown on the map on their HMD. As the player gets closer to the hidden object sensor around the artifact, the signal between the object sensor and the user sensor gets stronger. Then, H-Treasure Hunt recognizes the artifact by receiving the unique sensor number from the object sensor and fetch corresponding mission from the server. Finally, HMD displays the mission for the player. After having completed the mission, the player is rewarded with points (Fig. 3).

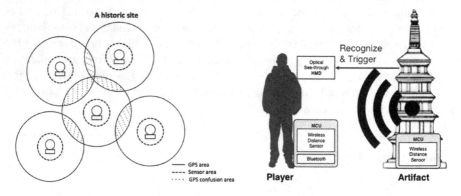

Fig. 3. LBS with object-based sensors (left), and object-based sensor module (right)

3.2   Sensor Design

Object sensor is composed of Arduino and ZigBee (Tx). ZigBee is used to send radio signal to user sensor. User sensor is composed of Arduino, ZigBee (Rx) and Bluetooth. Unfortunately, Google glass can only receive Bluetooth signal. In order to overcome the weakness, the sensor is equipped with Bluetooth and ZigBee. ZigBee calculates the power of radio signal (RISS) then transmits it to user. If the RISS value is high enough, then the Bluetooth sends a signal to Google glass. After that, Google glass creates events.

Beacon is also used to find locations. Bluetooth can connect up to 8 nodes at the same time. ZigBee, however, is suitable when connecting multiple same cell nodes simultaneously (Fig. 4).

Fig. 4. Hardware design (front and back side)

We can read ZigBee RSSI pin using Arduino pulseIn. Pin 6 is PWM0 /RSSI Output PWM Output 0 /RX Signal Strength Indicator on ZigBee and ZigBee-PRO modules. When AT Commands, P0 on the ZigBee module is set to 1 (default), pin 6 outputs the RSSI value as timed electrical pulses (PWM, pulse width modulation.) We can read those pulses using Arduino's pulseIn function. Those pulses will equate to a number in hex. That hex number can then be translated to decibels (dB) which is the unit of measure for our RSSI value.

We fixed the threshold value which allows user sensor to detect object sensor. To get the exact value, we had to perform several tests because wireless signal is easy to be interrupted. Above all, we covered three sides of the sensor box to have only connection from front side. Table 1 shows the results of distance and angle test of the proposed sensor.

Table 1. Relsults of sensor's distance and angle test

	Test1		Test2		Test3		Test4		Average
Sensor	1	2	1	2	1	2	1	2	
Distance(m)	1.1	1.3	0.9	1.7	1.0	1.2	0.7	1.5	1.175
Angle(°)	-30	0	+20	+45	+30	-10	-20	+10	5.625

We designed this device for users to be around 1 m from the object sensor. Programed RSSI setting value is 30(dBm) that is lower than Benkic's result [4] since we covered the sensor box with aluminum foil except front side. We recorded distance and angle between the user and the object sensor every time the user receives the signal from the sensor and gets the mission from the Google glass. The average distance is 1.175 m that is similar to designed value. When testing the device, it was able to detect the sensor within up to about 50 ~ 60 degree. While the test, all the users were able to find the sensor within 0 ~ 45 degree.

3.3   Application

The game accompanies mobile authoring tool that enables users play the game anywhere and with any artifact as well as playing tool application for HMD. Therefore, H-Treasure Hunt is composed of two major software parts: authoring tool (H-Treasure Hide) and playing tool (H-Treasure Hunt).

We incorporated Naver Maps into an Android app, installing the Naver APIs [5]. For exchanging data between android applications and the server, we created PHP classes to connect to MySQL database [6]. The architecture will activate simply by calling a PHP script from android application in order to perform a data operation. The PHP script then connects to MySQL database to perform the operation [7]. The data flows from the Android app to PHP script then finally is stored in our server, MySQL database.

Authoring tool. The game provides mobile authoring tool to let users create their own content anywhere and with any artifact. Designers create missions for each artifact by recording necessary information. There are mainly two activities in mobile authoring tool, Mainactivity.java and CreateQuiz.java. Mainactivity.java shows a list view of registered sensors and missions available, whereas CreateQuiz.java deals with creating missions. Figure 5 shows a screen of CreateQuiz.java. Designers can specify a title, a sensor number, a picture as a clue, answer, and examples. The data is then uploaded to the server and it becomes available for the game. Created missions can also be played by other players.

Fig. 5.   Authoring tool (H-Treasure Hide) and playing tool (H-Treasure Hunt)

HMD. At the historic site, players wear optical see-through Google glass freely explore the site to find treasures that are scattered around the site shown on the map on their Google glass. As the player gets closer to the object sensor attached to the artifact, the object sensor's signal gets stronger [4]. When the player is close enough to the sensor, the sensor attached to the artifacts sends its unique number to the player's Bluetooth that is paired with the Bluetooth mounted on the HMD. These two Bluetooth devices carry out text chat over Bluetooth [8]. Through transferring data over Bluetooth, the Google glass application recognizes the unique sensor number and displays the corresponding mission.

Google glass application is implemented with the Glass Development Kit (GDK) which is an add-on to the Android SDK [9]. For Google glass application, activities are divided into 6 parts: AboutActivity, AnswerActivity, BluetoothChat, Bluetooth-ChatService, DeviceListActivity and SettingsActivity. DeviceListActivity and Setting-sActivity should be preceded prior to game play. SettingsActivity fetches all the necessary information from the server in advance of outdoor activity by extending the range of the game which includes non Wi-Fi zone. The player's Bluetooth can be paired with the Bluetooth mounted on the Google glass through DeviceListActivity. Blue-toothChat and BluetoothChatService are activities for carrying out text chat over Blue-tooth. When BluetoothChat activity receives the number via Bluetooth chat, this activity passes the received number to AboutActivity that displays corresponding mission with the number [10]. AnswerActivity deals with events when the player inputs answer such as A, B, C or D. The following code shows handler that gets information back from the BluetoothChatService and data exchange between activities.

Google glass offers a voice interface as well as gesture interfaces such as tapping, swiping, and scrolling. We implemented Google glass application to support both voice and gesture interfaces. Users can choose to launch the application and manipulate the menu through either voice or gesture interface. In addition, the players checks if he or she is in the right spot by just saying: "Mission!", if so, the corresponding mission is displayed on their screen.

```
private final Handler mHandler = new Handler() {
        public void handleMessage(Message msg) {
        switch (msg.what) {
    begin
        case MESSAGE_READ:
        byte[] readBuf = (byte[]) msg.obj;
        String readMsg = new String(readBuf, 0,
    msg.arg1);

    ((Mission)this.getApplication()).setBt(readMsg);
        Intent intent = new Intent(BluetoothChat.this,
    AboutActivity.class);
        startActivity(intent);
end.
```

Google glass offers a voice interface as well as gesture interfaces such as tapping, swiping, and scrolling. We implemented Google glass application to support both voice and gesture interfaces. Users can choose to launch the application and manipulate the menu through either voice or gesture interface. In addition, the players checks if he or she is in the right spot by just saying: "Mission!", if so, the corresponding mission is displayed on their screen.

4   Experimental Results

4.1   Game Design

We conducted a test to evaluate H-Treasure Hunt application with four test participants and four artifacts at stone sculpture park on KAIST campus. There were more than ten artifacts at the park, and we selected four artifacts in advance to hide sensors: a stone bridge, a stone pagoda, a stone lion and a stone elephant. The test participants had two main tasks of finding the right four artifacts and completing the missions. Before this experiment, with the selection of artifacts, we also played the role of hider by creating missions with authoring tool to focus on evaluating the playing tool (H-Treasure Hunt). Missions were created after reading and understanding the contents of each artifact on panel. After setting the environment for game, hunters were guided to the site as shown on the map on their HMD and they were encouraged to play the H-Treasure Hunt at stone sculpture park (Fig. 6).

 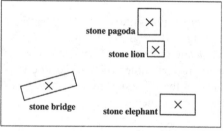

Fig. 6. The Stone sculpture park in KAIST (left), and location of four selected artifacts (right)

4.2   Evaluation Method

We selected four representatives of our target audience to participate in a small-scale, in depth user study for playing tool (H-Treasure Hunt). The group included two male and two female students of KAIST who have never visited the park. All of the participants had no experience using HMD or any AR related devices but they were all familiar with using smartphone.

The evaluation of each participant was approximately a half an hour long and consisted of the following four different stages. First we helped the participants familiarize with gesture and voice interfaces of Google glass by giving them instruction and some time for practice (5 min). We showed them a brief demo of H-Treasure Hunt (3 min) and gave them some time for getting familiar with its environment (5 min). When they are ready, we asked them to freely explore the site playing H-Treasure Hunt (15-20 min). After completing all the missions, we asked them to complete a comprehensive questionnaire that consists of three different parts. The first part evaluates practical benefits of playing the H-Treasure Hunt game at a historic site. The second part evaluates convenience of the H-Treasure Hunt application interface. The third part evaluates participants' emotional experiences. We used Likert-type scale to measure attitude using the following options: Strongly agree, agree, neither agree nor disagree, disagree, strongly disagree.

The goal of this experience is to improve out study by having evaluations from people to find the pros and cons have better insight. Through the experiments and feedback, we can extend our system by developing better game design and system. Especially we focused on the experiential aspects (emotions, feelings, values, meanings, etc.) related to the system.

The reults from Table 2 show that H-Treasure Hunt application was easy to use and understandable on the whole for most of the participants. They also felt that H-Treasure software was supportive for observing artifacts. They believed that the H-Treasure application offered adequate missions to understand the artifacts.

The participants felt that our application was helpful for understanding the historic site and its artifacts. In convenience of the interfaces, participants thought gestural interface was easy to use. However, they felt that voice interface was not much easy to operate. They answered that the interface of the software helped them engage more in the game.

The H-Treasure Hunt offers a new experience, encouraging participants to explore and investigate the site. The result indicates that a combination of fun and challenging assignments creates an effect that leads to deeper engagement and enjoyment. They said this engaging experience provides a link with the artifacts and gives them a chance to appreciate cultural values of the historic site after using the H-Treasure Hunt application. Additionally, they said the H-Treasure Hunt application offers a new and stimulating way to experience the historic site.

Location-based games have been used for educational goals. As an example, Geocaching [3] used GPS for teaching and learning activities. This indicates that the H-Treasure Hunt application can also be applied to the field of education, motivating students to learn about the site while playing the game. The participants expect that the H-Treasure Hunt application would boost motivation and offer educational contents in game design.

4.3 Observations and Interviews

In observations of test participants using our application, they quickly became adept at navigating the interface and completing missions with gestures and voice command. They also had a lot of fun playing H-Treasure Hunt at the historic site showing different playing patterns. In one case, if there is no mission for the artifact, two people passed by the artifact without even observing it. Their playing times were about 12 min, which is relatively shorter than others. On the other hand, the other two participants had a deep

Table 2. H-Treasure Hunt user test statement

	Strongly disagree	Disagree	Neither disagree nor agree	Agree	Strongly agree
Practical Benefits:					
H-Treasure Hunt application is easy to use			25%	75%	
Software supports my actions for observing artifacts		25%	25%	50%	
Software offers adequate missions to understand artifacts				25%	75%
Convenience:					
Gestural interface is easy to use		25%		50%	25%
Voice interface is easy to use		25%	50%	25%	
Software interface supports game immersion		25%	25%	50%	
Emotional Experience:					
Software offers me new experience				50%	50%
H-Treasure hunt was challenging and at the same time interesting			25%	75%	
Software offers stimulation to explore the site			25%	50%	25%
Using the software gave me a sense of connection between me and artifacts		25%		75%	
Software makes me learn more about the site			25%	50%	25%
Software could easily be used in education			25%	75%	
Using the software makes me think about cultural value of the site		25%	25%	50%	

observation of artifacts even though these were not selected artifacts. Therefore, their playing times were around 20 min, which is much longer than previous group's playing time.

The interview process helped us to gain a deeper understanding of each user's personal experience with our system. During the interview, participants most frequently used the words "fun" and "new way to learn" in describing the most positive aspects of H-Treasure Hunt. In negative aspects, participants most frequently mentioned discomfort of HMD with the expression "dizzy" and "unfamiliar".

5   Conclusions and Future Work

In this paper, we proposed a serious game application for cultural heritage learning using location and object-based technologies and accompanying authoring tool for creating flexible game content with smartphones. Preliminary evaluation results confirm that H-Treasure Hunt is new, playful and a stimulating tool that encourages exploration and learning, especially suitable for cultural heritage learning. The element of play proved to be a significant factor that appealed to users, and most of them agreed that the gesture and voice interaction made the experience of exploring more immersive. Remaining frustrating aspects derived from unreliable gesture and voice recognition and the uncomfortable head-mounted hardware. Also some users focused on completing missions rather than exploring the site and observing artifacts. Nevertheless, all participants agreed its playful approach would dramatically increase the motive for learning.

We were encouraged by the detailed feedback we received from our participants, and are eager to forge ahead with intuitive interaction design for exploring the historic site and observing artifacts via IIMD. We will develop the system that help users exploring and observing more in detail with free-hand. And design more game rules which make users could not just pass by the artifacts. In current version of H-Treasure Hunt, in addition, no social element can be found even though it is actually aimed at group activities. The most important component in game design is social experience and co-experience. The group game can be one of the goals in social competition. Users could be more motivated by competing or co-playing with their friend. Therefore we needs to extend and create new tools in H-Treasure Hunt for social experience.

Acknowledgement.   This research was supported by Ministry of Culture, Sports and Tourism (MCST) and Korea Creative Content Agency (KOCCA) in the Culture Technology (CT) Research & Development Program 2014. This paper was supported by the BK21 Plus Postgraduate Organization for Content Science (or BK21 Plus Program) in Korea.

References

1. Kim, Y., Kim, H.: A study of tour game using lbs based on smart phone. J. Digital Policy Manage. **10**(5), 239–244 (2012)
2. Wetzel, R., Blum, L., Oppermann, L.: Tidy city–a location-based game supported by in-situ and web-based authoring tools to enable user-created content .In: Proceedings of the International Conference on the Foundations of Digital Games, pp. 238–241 (2012)
3. O'Hara, K.: Understanding Geocaching Practices and Motivations. In: Proceedings of the SIGCHI Conference on Human Factors in Computing Systems, pp. 1177–1186 (2008)

4. Benkic, K., Malajner, M., Planinsic, P., Cucej, Z.: Using RSSI value for distance estimation in wireless sensor networks based on ZigBee. In: 15th International Conference on Systems Signals and Image Processing (IWSSIP 2008), pp. 303–306 (2008)
5. NHN Corp. NAVER Open API. http://openapi.naver.com
6. Luke, W., Thomson, L.: PHP and MySQL Web Development. Sams Publishing, Carmel (2003)
7. In-gookChun, Android Programming, Saeng Reung Publishing (2012)
8. Android Developers. Bluetooth Chat sample code. http://develop-er.android.com/resources/samples/BluetoothChat/index.html
9. Google. Glass Development Kit. https://developers.google.com/glass/gdk
10. Lauri, A., et al.: Bluetooth and WAP push based location-aware mobile advertising system. In: Proceedings of the 2nd international conference on Mobile systems, applications, and services. ACM (2004)

Developing an Educational Game for Art Education - Gesture Recognition-Based Performance Guidance for Mozart's Opera Magic Flute

Hyung Sook Kim[1,2(✉)], Su Hak Oh[1], and Yong Hyun Park[1]

[1] Human Art & Technology, Graduate Program in Robot Engineering,
Inha University, Incheon, South Korea
khsook12@inha.ac.kr, yhpark81@gmail.com
[2] Dance, Department of Kinesiology, Inha University, Incheon, South Korea
[3] Department of Physical Education, Inha University, Incheon, South Korea

Abstract. The purpose of this study is to develop an educational game, which is used for opera or musical classes. In recent years, art education has been widely emphasized because it helped to develop students' creativity and imagination. Also, many educators and researchers argue that STEM education, which aims to boosting students' interest and competitiveness in science, technology, engineering and mathematics, should be amended to STEAM where the letter "A" refers to the field of Art. The opera consists of many dimensions which makes it unique as a whole such as the human voice, the orchestral music, the visual arts, the drama, and the dance. Hence all, the components of opera theater are included all STEAM fields. The use of a serious game for art education, especially, opera the Mozart's Magic Flute has a number of advantages with respect to increasing student interest. Students play this game to learn and practice the characters of opera by following gesture recognition-based performance guidance for Mozart's Magic Flute. The game is directed by student's movements and gestures which are recognized the RGB-D camera. The context of the game consisted of acting, role playing, singing songs, dancing, doing art, and speaking. The player will be able to learn different activities and enjoy by following Mozart's Magic Flute's guidance in the game. The art education game was exhibited for four days at the 2014 Education Donation Fair. During playing the game, students were passionate to approach the game-based learning and students were thrilled by following most of the components of an art game. Additionally, the students are actively participating in the game-based leaning and the outcome was remarkable. This game doesn't have the automatic evaluation system for students' performance. So, we needed teaching artists for introduce this game-based learning class for opera to students. Their brief guidance and teaching is a component of game-based learning.

Keywords: Game-based learning · Gesture-recognition-based learning · Art education · Mozart's magic flute · KINECT

© Springer International Publishing Switzerland 2015
P. Zaphiris and A. Ioannou (Eds.): LCT 2015, LNCS 9192, pp. 573–582, 2015.
DOI: 10.1007/978-3-319-20609-7_54

1   Introduction

In recent years, art education has been widely accepted by school educators as well as administrators, indicating its importance in providing useful guidelines for all aspects of the modern school curricula on developing students' creativity, imagination, and aesthetics. Nevertheless, many educators also agree that art education allows students to develop the ability to express themselves by covering wide range of subjects and languages that hardly could be offered by other educational means [1].

Creativity is defined as the production of original, unexpected and useful work [2]. Many studies has reported that creative individuals were not only more productive and satisfied with their occupations, they were more flexible and enterprising within their groups [3, 4]. Following these studies of creativity, it seems that creativity and creative skills have now been regarded as highly important in almost every field of work and education in our competitive modern society [5]. In addition, The Organization for Economic Co-operation and Development (OECD) termed modern societies as problem-solving society and to cope with the advancement of technology along with the change in society, the necessity of creative problem-solving ability can be a key to become successful in this unpredictable world [6]. STEM education, which aims to boosting students' interest and competitiveness in science, technology, engineering and mathematics, is a vital part of education policy of many countries. Many educators and researchers, however, argue that STEM is overlooking creativity-related components. They argue that STEM should be amended to STEAM where the letter "A" refers to the field of Art which will contribute in developing students' creativity and imagination.

The learning through digital games is a wave of the future [7]. The curiosity, joy, and pride brought by game have been considered to be the key point of a successful education system and many studies have agreed on that and have reported the positive effect of game-based learning on promoting long-term user engagement and motivation. Actually, the idea of embedding education into entertainment was started in 1954 by Walt Disney. From then onwards, serious games have become more popular in a wide range of educational and training applications and their effectiveness have also been acknowledged in different fields, such as education, health, business, welfare and safety. Previous studies have also reported students who had gameplay in the classroom scored significantly higher citing its ability to engage and motivate learners in the educational process [8]. Therefore, it would certainly have positive benefits and also could impact the player in a real life context.

Microsoft Kinect is motion sensing vision-based sensor. It allows players to interact with their application using a natural interface that employs gestures thus eliminating the game controller. The invention of highly reliable and inexpensive sensors such as Kinect and Wii had boost up the development of serious games including dynamics activities, various sports, and dancing that required gesture movement. Hue reported the potential of Kinect as interactive technology and have discussed how it can facilitate and enhance teaching and learning [7].]. For an instance, players will be able to perform required dance tasks in intuitive manner which is better representative of the real world [8]. Hence, learning to create and appreciate kinetic aesthetics may be more important than ever for the development of the students, especially to those who focus more on studying in STEAM education fields.

This paper reports on the developing a serious game for art education, especially, opera the Mozart's Magic Flute. The primary purpose of this game is educational and complementary for art class rather than just entertainment. Students play this game to learn and practice the characters of opera by following gesture recognition-based performance guidance for Mozart's Magic Flute. The game is directed by student's movements and gestures which are recognized the RGB-D (Kinect) camera. The context of the game consisted of acting, role playing, singing songs, dancing, doing art, and speaking. The player will be able to learn different activities and enjoy by following Mozart's Magic Flute's guidance in the game.

2 STEAM Education

STEAM is an acronym referring to the academic fields of science, technology, engineering, art, and mathematics. Up until now, STEM disciplines have widely been recognized as very important fields with regard to technology and workforce development. However, nowadays STEAM fields, is becoming more essential as arts-based education offers opportunities for students to develop their creativity and imagination.

Today we require professionals and creative thinkers who go beyond disciplines for solving multifaceted issue and complex problems [9]. However in order to do so, teaching and learning through the connecting the arts and sciences is essential. In addition, many historical cases shows that these connections are already innate for the most effective and innovative STEM fielders [10, 11]. In this view point, STEAM education has become an essential paradigm for creative and aesthetic converged teaching and learning in STEM and Arts disciplines [12]. Since 2011, Education Ministry of The Republic of Korea has accepted STEAM education for national policy. In addition, Korea Foundation for the Advancement of Science and Creativity (KOFAC) have been promoting the STEAM campaign and are operating the teacher training for STEAM education nationally. Also, different national organizations and professional communities of science and technology have agreed on the integrative approach of STEAM disciplines as a critical element for restructuring school education which will initially be able to stimulate a domain of the conscience to the students in the field of science and will draw induction for the field of science [13]. Hence, to catch up with increasing the importance of creativity, educators and researchers are accenting the role of Arts disciplines in STEAM education.

3 Mozart's Opera Magic Flute and STEAM Education

The Magic Flute is an opera in two acts by Wolfgang Amadeus Mozart. The opera consists of many dimensions which makes it unique as a whole such as the human voice, the orchestral music, the visual arts (scenery, costumes, and special effects), the drama, and the dance. Hence all, the components of opera theater are included all STEAM fields.

Designing and setting-up stage of scenery is necessary to understanding technology, engineering, and mathematics. Characters, properties, and background (e.g. animals, flute, darkness and lightning,) are good topics of science classes. In addition, learning song and dancing are included not only fine art class but also good themes of science and mathematics class. (e.g. harmonics and newton's laws of motion).

Magic Flute's story is Sarastro who the wise priest of Isis and Osiris, has taken Pamina to the temple for the purpose of releasing her from the influence of her mother, the Queen of the Night. The queen induces the young Prince Tamino to go with Papageno in search of her daughter and free her from the power of Sarastro; Tamino accomplishes his end, but becomes the disciple of Sarastro, whose mild-ness and wisdom he has learned to admire. The prince and the princess are united [15].

4   Development of Game

4.1   System Architecture

Our system consists of a Kinect sensor, a PC, a TV Kiosk, a backlit projection screen, and a projector. In order to develop the game and implement the logics, we have utilized Zigfu, a programming development toolkit and Unity, a cross-platform game creation system [16]. Figure 1 shows the system architecture and user interface of this system (Fig. 2).

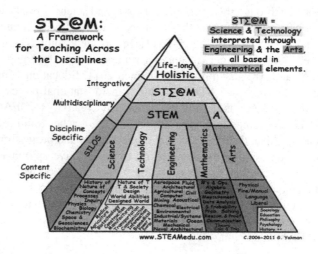

Fig. 1.   STEAM: A framework for teaching across the disciplines [14]

4.2   Game System Setting

The purpose of this research was to develop the educational and essential game by following gesture recognition-based performance guidance for Mozart's Magic Flute for art education. The game was directed by student's movements and gestures by recognizing the RGB-D (Kinect) camera. The context of the game consisted of acting, role playing, singing songs, dancing, doing art, and speaking. The player would learn

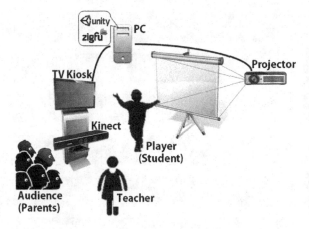

Fig. 2. System architecture and User Interface

everything by enjoying and by following Mozart's Magic Flute's guidance in the game. By participating in the game, it would enable young students in the range of 10 ~ 18 years old to learn and practice performing skills such as dance, acting, speaking progressively and repeatedly. In addition, it is possible that not only playing the game for students but also showing performance for audience at one time. The audience and their parents can watch the students' performance on the simple stage when students, who looking at TV kiosk, are playing at sixth stage of rehearsal mode. At that time, projection screen is a stage background. Teaching artist guides and teaches the students playing the game (Fig. 3).

4.3   Activity-Based Scenarios in Serious Game

The game was designed to be suitable for after school musical theatre classes in public schools, in which students learned Mozart's Magic Flute. Generally, these education programs were designed for preparing the musical style performing art theatre. Students

Fig. 3. Game system set-up, teaching artists, and students participating in the gesture-recognition-based game in exhibition (at 2014 Education Donation Fair, Il-san, Korea).

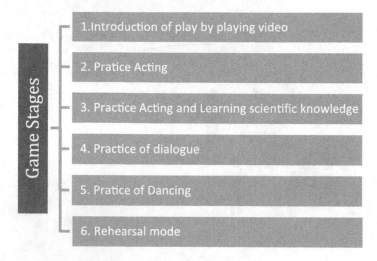

Fig. 4. The scheme of the art educational game, gesture recognition-based performance guidance

learn naturally by completing every level of the game through acting and dancing as characters of the Magic Flute. The prototype game has six levels. Each level was developed and designed to be suitable for many different classes (Fig. 4).

The first stage. The first is introductory and includes a video and briefing about Mozart's Magic Flute. In this mode, players can understand how to play this game and the full story of Magic Flute while watching the video lectures.

The second stage. The second is an acting tutorial which involves gestures by recognition-based game with the Kinect. The player assumes the role of Tamino who is a prince in the story. The story line of the game is that Tamino is running away from a huge serpent. The player acts as Tamino in the game.

The third stage. The third is designed for acting and learning science through the adopted STEAM Educational concepts. The scene of this level is a flock of birds flying in the sky. These birds are dancing and controlled by the sounds of Tamino's magic flute in the story. The player also plays a bird in the game. The player's bird-like gesture is recognized by the Kinect. Plus, the game teaches students how birds fly by showing the four forces of flight – weight, lift, drag, and thrust – affecting the flight of birds. This game concept is designed for STEAM education. Students learn the scientific knowledge while they are playing and acting like the bird in this game (Fig. 5).

The fourth stage. The forth of this game is created for reading and speaking the character's lines in the script. The character in the game and the player are interacting, and speaking following the instructions using arm and hand gestures. The fifth level is a dancing practice game using the Kinect. The player will learn dance moves through watching dancing videos. The arrangement of dance was used in the musical theatre (Fig. 6).

Fig. 5. (Left) The scene in the second level, acting guidance. (Right) The scene in the third level, acting and science knowledge guidance.

Fig. 6. (Left) The scene in the fourth level, script guidance. (Right) The scene in the fifth level, dance guidance.

The final stage. The final mode is designed for preparation for a performance, Mozart's Magic Flute. This final level is cumulative, and require knowledge and practice in the other four levels, which proceeded to successively. By playing the game, students will prepare for the performance of Mozart's Magic Flute (Fig. 7).

4.4 User Experience

We tested the gesture-recognition-based art education game with numerous participants at exhibition. In this part, we report the feedback from a wide range of participants who experienced the game.

The art education game was exhibited for four days at the 2014 Education Donation Fair hosted by the Ministry of Education and the Korea Foundation for the Advancement of Science & Creativity (KOFAC), held at Korea International Exhibition Center (KINTEX, Il-san, Korea) from September 18-21, 2014.

Many students visited our booth and experienced and played the art education game. The participants were mainly students, teachers, and university professors. The students' age was from 7 to 18. During playing the game, students were passionate to approach the game-based learning and students were thrilled by following most of the components of an art game. Additionally, the students are actively participating in the game-based leaning and the outcome was remarkable. A few students initially looked abashed when they were performed acting and dancing but absorbed in it once they tried it.

Fig. 7. (Left up) A player participating in an acting tutorial. (Right up) A player participating in gesture-based script selection. (Left down) A player participating in acting practice and STEAM education mode. (Right down) A player participating in gesture-recognition-based dance practice game (at 2014 Education Donation Fair, Il-san, Korea).

5   Discussions

In our game, scenario of this game is based on Mozart's Magic Flute in order to use it for opera performance class. In exhibition, we succeed in operation of the booth including this game with teaching artist's teaching. This game doesn't have the automatic evaluation system for students' performance. So, we needed teaching artists for introduce this game-based learning class for opera to students. Their brief guidance and teaching is a component of game. Teaching artist's teaching and helping are necessary to progress learning session. It is not enough for student by oneself to start and learn this educational game for Magic Flute. This is because we couldn't make it using all story yet. Now, the game has six stages for learning and practicing the opera, Magic Flute. In the future, we will include the additional stage which has same format, and different story.

6   Conclusion

In this paper, we proposed the educational game by following gesture recognition-based performance guidance for Mozart's Magic Flute for art education. The game was directed by student's movements and gestures by recognizing the RGB-D (Kinect) camera. The game taught students acting, dancing, and STEAM education contents. This game is designed for learning and preparing the musical style performing art theatre. Students learn naturally by completing every stage of the game through acting and dancing as characters of the Magic Flute. The player would learn everything by enjoying and by following Mozart's Magic Flute's guidance in the game. This game could use not only standing alone a game for student but also performing a one-act play for opera theater class. We designed and implemented example system based on the concept of Opera theater class game, and tested with a number of participants at 2014 Education Donation Fair, Il-san, Korea. The feedbacks from the participants confirmed that this game motivated and increased students' activities and learning. We believe that this game is suitable for after school musical theatre classes in public schools, in which students learned Mozart's Magic Flute. Gesture recognition-based performance guidance for Mozart's Magic Flute game by Kinect would be a great answer for the next generation's performing art education. This effort and approach of this project would greatly help the students to understand the importance of art education.

Acknowledgements. This project was financially supported by Inha University. The authors would like to thank the company, JSC games Co. Ltd. who technically supported to make this game and many art teachers who participated in 2014 Education Donation Fair for our booth operation.

References

1. Bajardi, A., Rodríguez, D.Á.: Art education to develop creativity and critical skills in digital society: integrating the tradition in an e-learning environment. In: Communications of the International Conference The Future of Education Conference Proceedings. (2012)
2. Sternberg, R.J., Lubart, T.I.: The concept of creativity: prospects and paradigms. Handb. creativity 1, 3–15 (1999)
3. Amabile, T.M.: The social psychology of creativity: A componential conceptualization. J. Pers. Soc. Psychol. 45, 357 (1983)
4. Littleton, K., Taylor, S., Eteläpelto, A.: Special issue introduction: Creativity and creative work in contemporary working contexts. Vocations Learn. 5, 1–4 (2012)
5. Jo, Doori, Lee, Jae-gil, Lee, Kun Chang: Empirical analysis of changes in human creativity in people who work with humanoid robots and their avatars. In: Zaphiris, Panayiotis, Ioannou, Andri (eds.) LCT 2014, Part I. LNCS, vol. 8523, pp. 273–281. Springer, Heidelberg (2014)
6. OECD: PISA 2012 Results: Creative Problem Solving: Students' Skills in Tackling Real-Life Problems (vol. v). (2014)
7. Hsu, H.-m.J: The potential of kinect in education. Int. J. Inf. Educ. Technol. 1, 365–370 (2011)
8. Kapralos, Bill, Shewaga, Robert, Ng, Gary: Serious Games: customizing the audio-visual interface. In: Shumaker, Randall, Lackey, Stephanie (eds.) VAMR 2014, Part II. LNCS, vol. 8526, pp. 190–199. Springer, Heidelberg (2014)
9. Mishra, P., Terry, C., Henriksen, D., Group, D.-P.R.: Square peg, round hole, good engineering. Tech Trends 57, 22–25 (2013)
10. Root-Bernstein, R.S., Root-Bernstein, M.M.: Sparks of Genius: The Thirteen Thinking Tools of the World's Most Creative People. Houghton Mifflin Harcourt, Boston (2013)
11. Mishra, P., Henriksen, D.: Rethinking technology & creativity in the 21st century: on being in-disciplined. TechTrends 56, 18–21 (2012)

12. Henriksen, D.: Full STEAM ahead: creativity in excellent STEM teaching practices. STEAM J. **1**, 15 (2014)
13. Baek, Y., Kim, Y., Noh, S., Park, H., Lee, J., Jeong, J., Choi, Y., Hand, H., Choi, J.: Basic research for establishing the direction of STEAM education in Korea. Korea Foundation for the Advancement of Science and Creativity (2012)
14. Yakman, G.: STΣ@ M Education: an overview of creating a model of integrative education. In: Pupils Attitudes Towards Technology 2006 Annual Proceedings pp. 341–342 (2008)
15. San Francisco. http://sfopera.com/Learn/Teacher-Resources/Classroom-Materials/The-Magic-Flute.aspx
16. http://en.wikipedia.org/wiki/Unity_%28game_engine%29

Transferring an Educational Board Game to a Multi-user Mobile Learning Game to Increase Shared Situational Awareness

Roland Klemke[1(✉)], Shalini Kurapati[2], Heide Lukosch[2], and Marcus Specht[1]

[1] Welten Institute – Research Center for Learning, Teaching and Technology, Open University of the Netherlands, P.O. Box 2960, 6401 DL Heerlen, The Netherlands
{Roland.Klemke,Marcus.Specht}@ou.nl
[2] Faculty of Technology, Policy and Management, Delft University of Technology, P.O. Box 5015, 2600 GA Delft, The Netherlands
{S.Kurapati,H.K.Lukosch}@tudelft.nl

Abstract. This paper analyses how multi-user mobile games can be beneficial to educational scenarios. It does so in several steps: Firstly, we introduce the field of logistics as a problem domain for an educational challenge. Secondly, we describe the design of an educational board game for the field of disruption handling in logistics processes, which aims to foster shared situational awareness (SSA). Thirdly, we introduce an open-source mobile serious games platform (ARLearn) and fourthly describe how the board game can be realized in this platform. The reader gets to know the problem situation of multi-stakeholder decision situations, learns about the design of a board game, and gets to know the open-source mobile serious game platform ARLearn.

Keywords: Mobile learning · Game-based learning · Multi-user games · Logistics · Multi-role game-design

1 Introduction

Decision-making in sociotechnical systems is complex and error-prone due to inter-dependencies of tasks, conflicting goals in distributed responsibilities and a lack of information among the various stakeholders involved in decision-making [1]. The proactive sharing of relevant situational information might help to improve shared situational awareness (SSA) among the stakeholders involved [2], which can lead to improved decision making processes within sociotechnical systems. Therefore, it is crucial to understand the role of communication among stakeholders [3].

The SALOMO[1] project aims to provide a training solution to create shared situational awareness (SSA) [2] to cope with this situation and to highlight the importance of communication. As multi-stakeholder decision situations confronted with time restrictions and incomplete information such as emergencies have been recognised as a

---

[1] SALOMO: Situational Awareness for LOgistic Multimodal Operations.

© Springer International Publishing Switzerland 2015
P. Zaphiris and A. Ioannou (Eds.): LCT 2015, LNCS 9192, pp. 583–594, 2015.
DOI: 10.1007/978-3-319-20609-7_55

relevant field for training [4–6], a multi-user board game has been designed, which emulates the decision process in the port environment in order to sensitize stakeholders in a value chain about communication and inter-dependencies.

To improve the scalability of the board game, we aim to provide a computerized version of the board game, simplifying the game distribution and execution by providing an automated execution environment for locally distributed players.

While most game-based learning approaches focus on skill development and motivational aspects, little work is reported that focus on multi-user learning situations and decision training. With this work, we also aim to provide new insights to this field of research, illustrated by an example in the logistics domain. The main contribution of this paper is to compare the board game and its mobile derivant from a design, deployment and execution point of view. While we do not report on a comparative study performed to assess the performance of each version, we rather give insights into design and application experiences as well as limitations of each approach.

The remainder of this paper is organised as follows: we start giving background information about the problem situation in logistics followed by an introduction of SSA as theoretical concept in multi-stakeholder decision situations. Based on this, we introduce and discuss our board game design as training game to increase SSA in a logistics decision situation. We continue with an introduction of the mobile serious game platform used and describe the transfer process of the board game to this platform. Finally, we draw conclusions.

2   Problem Situation in Logistics

In a huge international port, like the Port of Rotterdam, thousands of containers are moved every day in and out through several different channels in container terminals. A container terminal is the point of interaction between the different parties involved in container transportation. Containers need to be moved as fast as possible to meet the delivery time expectations of customers. Safety of the port and its operating personnel needs to be guaranteed at all times. To ensure the smooth operation of the port, different stakeholders, equipped with different responsibilities have to interoperate:

- *Control tower* ensures the overall smooth operation,
- *Resource planner* assigns the port personnel,
- *Yard planner* is responsible for the internal storage of containers in the port,
- *Vessel planner* is responsible to deliver containers to and from vessels,
- *Sales manager* is interested in customer satisfaction.

Unplanned and unanticipated events that affect the normal flow of goods and operations in supply and transport networks are termed as disruptions [7]. Unfortunately, disruptions have become common phenomena in port operations. The main categories are port accidents, port equipment failures, dangerous goods mishandling, port congestion, inadequacy of labour skills, hinterland inaccessibility, breach of security, and labour strikes [8]. Disruptions may cause severe ripple effects resulting in high costs, and have dire consequences on the social and economical wellbeing of the surrounding environment [9]. For e.g., a machinery breakdown in the port may lead to a security risk, which may cause an area to be closed. This may cause delays in the unloading of ships, which delays also their loading and planned departure, which affects the trucks, creating traffic jams etc. The operating individuals, mentioned above, need to take decisions to mitigate the disruptions together with external stakeholders. However, they are not always aware of these interdependencies and effects. Given the undesirable ripple effects of the disruptions in seaport operations, it can be deduced that the resilience of seaports, and their terminals, is essential for the resilience and robustness of transport networks as a whole.

As a first step to address this problem, this paper introduces a tabletop simulation game as an approach towards increasing SSA of planners and decision makers in seaport operations during disruption management to improve the resilience of seaport container terminals. In the following, we introduce how we conceptualize shared situational understanding and why it is so crucial in container transportation, before we illustrate how we translated this concept into a simulation board game.

3 Shared Situational Awareness

Situational awareness (SA) is the broadly accepted definition describing the level of awareness that an individual has of a situation, an operator's dynamic understanding of 'what is going on', including the perception and comprehension of a situation and the prediction of its future state [10]. Much has been written about the construct, yet it remains profoundly contentious. Of the definitions and approaches available, Endsley's three level, information-processing-based model has received the most attention [10]. Due to the significant presence of teams in contemporary organizational systems, the construct of team SA is currently receiving increased attention from the human factors community [11]. Distributed teams comprise members interacting over time and space via technology-mediated communication [11]. Team performance itself comprises two components of behaviour, teamwork (team members working together) and task work (team members working individually). SSA is multi-dimensional, comprising individual team member SA, shared SA between team members and also the combined SA of the whole team, the so-called 'common picture'. Add to this the various team processes involved (e.g. communication, coordination, collaboration, etc.) and the complexity of the construct quickly becomes apparent. Most attempts to understand team SA have centred on a 'shared understanding' of the same situation. Nofi, for example, defines team SA as: 'a shared awareness of a particular situation' [12] and Perla et al. suggest that 'when used in the sense of "shared awareness of a situation", shared SA implies that we all understand a given situation in the same way' [13]. In the following, we introduce a study in which we research in how far a simulation game session can support a group of players in developing SSA by providing different levels of communication and cooperation. The increased level of SSA should lead to improved resilience in container terminal operations.

4 Board Game Design and Experience

Simulation games can be defined as 'conscious endeavour to reproduce the central characteristics of a system in order to understand, experiment with and/or predict the behaviour of that system' [14]. It is a method in which human participants enact a specific role in a simulated environment [15]. In our case, we focus on the use of simulation games as a training tool, which is meant to improve communication between stakeholders, and to improve their SSA in seaport container terminals as an example of a complex system. For the conceptualization of our game, we follow a framework by Meijer [16], which is based on the work of Klabbers [17]. According to this, a simulation game is always designed with an objective (for learning purposes) or based on a research question (research purposes). The game consists of objectives, rules, roles, constraints, load and situation, which are controlled by the game designer as shown in Fig. 1 [16]. The framework presented in this figure forms the basis of the simulation game session presented in this research work.

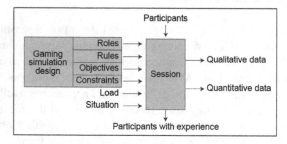

Fig. 1. Input and output elements of a simulation game session [16]

The disruption management game for intermodal transport operations in ports is a 5-player tabletop board game. Resilience is the ability for a system or organization to bounce back to normality even when affected by a disruption [18]. For seaport container terminals, bouncing back to normal can be quantified in terms of the Key Performance Indicators (KPIs). The KPIs can be categorized as efficiency of operations and costs, safety, customer relationship, sustainability, strategic/competitive position in the market, profits and losses [19]. As the game only focuses on operations, the KPIs considered for the game are safety, efficiency of operations, and customer satisfaction. Based on literature and brainstorming sessions with professionals in the container terminal business, the challenges in disruption management in container terminal operations have been translated into contextualized game play, based on the framework described in Fig. 1. The development of the game took over 8 months, as it was an iterative process following design, evaluation and validation cycles.

The game is presented to the participants in the form of a game session (see Fig. 2). One game master facilitates the game play. Every game session begins with a briefing lecture, introducing the concept and motivation, rules, set-up and scoring of the game (see Table 1).

Fig. 2. The board game in action

Table 1. Input and Output elements in the disruption management game

Input/output	Description in the game
Roles	Vessel planner, Yard planner, resource planner, control tower manager, sales
Rules	• There are individual game boards for each participant as well as an overall game board for the container terminal system with KPIs, contain varying information and rules based on the level of the game play • The KPIs are all maximum at the start of the game, they deteriorate after every round, and can be increased by mitigation actions of participants • Participants have information cards as well as action cards, the former used for communication, the latter for performing mitigation actions • Communication can be (virtually) done via e-mail, phone and conference, with differing effectiveness and costs. Limited tokens have to be used to communicate, showing communication costs (time and resources) • The information cards contain disruption details. After a round of information sharing, participants have to perform mitigation actions. • Mitigation cards vary for each round. They contain 3 choices from which participants need to choose one mitigation action card • Based on the actions of the participants the game master changes the scores of the KPIs after every round
Objectives	*Overall:* To maintain resilient transport operations *Individual:* To maintain individual performance indicators as well as the overall KPI of the terminal
Constraints	Information availability, time, resources to communicate
Load	Different disruption situations, different levels of escalation of disruptions, varying channels and cost of communication and information sharing
Situation	University classrooms; Logistics, supply chain and transportation companies; Professional and knowledge institutes
Participants	Academic researchers, students and professionals in the transportation, logistics and supply chain industry
Qualitative data	Observations from the game session by the game master, report of decisions after every round
Quantitative data	Post-game survey

The game play begins after the briefing session. Each level of the game play has five rounds. After every round, the individual and group scores are explained, when the game facilitator reads out the effects of the decisions made by the players on the KPIs. At the end of each level, an overview of the situation based on the participants' decisions is presented. For evaluation purposes, the game play is observed thoroughly by the game facilitator, while the decisions and scores are recorded.

The game session concludes with a de-briefing session, where the game facilitator explains the principles of disruption management, the challenges faced by practitioners, the relationship of the game elements to the challenges, a review of the scores and the reasons for obtaining such scores, alternative strategies, comparison between scores of different play groups and the reasons for it etc. This session is mainly to provide a learning experience for the participants.

After the de-briefing session the game master encourages the participants to provide feedback about the game and their experience, which is recorded. After the game session, the participants fill in an online survey on usefulness on the game.

The data gathered from the game and the survey is then analysed qualitatively to gather insights into disruption management for resilient intermodal port operations. Several game sessions were conducted based on the above design, played with 10 researchers, 15 experts, and 80 graduate students in in supply chain, logistics and transportation. The most important result that emerged from the analyses was the clear difference in the behavioural patterns of players at different game levels. Based on their awareness of the disruption scenario, roles and objectives of others, there was a difference regarding relevant information sharing for mitigating the disruption.

In level 1 of the game play, all the players had limited awareness of the disruption scenario, the effects of their decisions and their objective in the game. In level 2, players made good use of the available communication channels, as they understood where to send and receive information. Several discussions and negotiations were made among the players during level 3. Players teamed up to jointly mitigate the situation. Sometimes, players sacrificed their individual KPIs to boost the overall KPIs. Well-informed decisions were made in level 3.

The results from the mentioned sessions create a helpful learning experience in the field of disruption management and resilience of container terminal operations. While these positive results motivate us to continue, we also observed and collected a number of reasons motivating the transfer of the board game to a mobile version:

- As the board game requires a human game master to be present in order to control the complex game processes, the mobile version should be automated so players can play independent of a game master.
- This automatisation should also simplify the distribution and scalability of the game.
- Game results should be traceable for the necessary debriefing phase. While in the board game only the human memory is available for debriefing, the mobile version should track all user interactions and decisions.
- The board game requires all players to be present in a single room. While this fosters a common game experience, it imposes an unrealistic situation, as in reality the different persons would be distributed across the port.

In the following, we illustrate how the board-game concept has been translated into a mobile multi-player version, taking into account above-mentioned reasoning.

5   ARLearn Platform for Mobile Serious Games

Based on the board game described above, we aimed to design a computerized version using ARLearn. ARLearn is a platform for the design of mobile process-based learning games [20] comprising an authoring interface which allows to bind a number of content items and task structures to locations, events, and roles and to use game-logic and dependencies to initiate further tasks and activities. The platform has been recently used for several similar pilot studies in the cultural heritage domain [21].

One key reason to use ARLearn for the multi-stakeholder decision training scenario described above is its flexibility in designing games for multiple users organised in different teams and using different roles. In a role-based game design, media artefacts can be bound to roles, meaning that they will be only be visible to players that have the same role assigned. The role-based game-design can be used to model situations with incomplete, personalised information and individualised game processes. Consequently, a multi-role game can be designed in a manner that only a collaborative effort of the players in various roles leads to game success. Thus, the event-based game model of ARLearn allows simulating mission critical real-life situations and conditions, placed in an augmented real life situation. ARLearn also records user activities and allows reviewing game runs for the debriefing stage. Commonly used smartphones (Android, iOS) can be used to play ARLearn games. The authoring interface allows copying and modifying games, allowing creating variations.

Based on its flexible, pattern-based game-design approach [22], ARLearn has already been applied to other learning scenarios, where a number of players need to interact and cooperate in order to reach a satisfying goal in a disruption or emergency situation. For the United Nations High Commissioner for Refugees (UNHCR), we created a role-playing game, which simulates kidnapping situations in order to train employees how to react in such situations [23]. In the EmUrgency project, we designed a game educating bystanders of cardiac arrest how to behave in such a situation [24].

Looking at other approaches for mobile serious games, we find a few related approaches. The ARIS platform [25] offers the possibility to author location-based mobile games. While ARIS has been successfully used in several application examples [26], it does not support multi-player/multi-role games. QuestInSitu is a mobile learning platform including authoring which mainly focuses on assessment [27] in location-based contexts. Robles et al. [28] describe an implementation of a team-enabled mobile gaming platform. The location-based task model allows for linear games, where a new task description follows the previous one.

6   Transfer of the Board Game into a Mobile Serious Game

In the mobile version of the board game, the game master is replaced with the automated ARLearn game logic. The game design follows the board game as described in the section 'Board game design and experience'. Figure 3 depicts one round in the game process. Each level consists of five rounds, which are synchronized after each decision. Each round gives access to a new situation description.

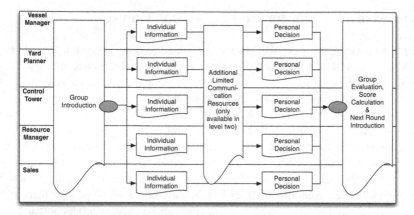

Fig. 3. One round of level one/level two with communication

While level one of the game isolates the different players completely, subsequent levels give access to limited communicative resources. This shall foster the players to exchange information creating awareness for other player's situation and the overall consequences of own decisions (Fig. 3). The ARLearn-based game differs slightly from the board game:

- The five players can potentially play the game in separate locations as their mobile devices are synchronised automatically via ARLearn. The ARLearn game engine automatically synchronizes the game state between the different players.
- No human game master is required, as the game engine automatically updates the game state, evaluates player decisions and distributes information. The game rules, processes, the decisions and all other game resources are encoded as game design script in ARLearn.

Fig. 4. Screenshots of the SALOMO game: message overview and decision point

Table 2. Comparison of board game and mobile game

Dimension	Board game	Mobile game
Execution of game processes	Human game master necessary; scores and game progress are calculated manually.	Game process automatized. No human game master required; scores and game progress are calculated automatically.
Scalability	Game scalability depends on the number of trained game masters available.	Game can be distributed via appstores. Scalability limited to the technical scalability of the game engine.
Location independence	All players need to be at a single location grouped around a table.	Players can be locally distributed. Each player plays with a mobile device. The game engine syncs the game state across devices.
Introduction support	Game master needs to explain the game background, game mechanics and processes as well as the available actions in each situation.	Introduction to the game background is part of the game. Actions are context-dependent: players can only choose from meaningful actions. Game handling needs to be explained (installation, mechanics), e.g. with a tutorial.
Debriefing support	Game master collects decisions and actions for debriefing. The game master is also present during the game phase and can monitor personal or non-verbal feedback.	Logging data for debriefing is automatically collected and can be reviewed. However, despite the data being available, the debriefing session should be guided by a trainer in order to interpret the data and to gather additional personal feedback.
Group experience	As participants play in one location, informal interaction between players takes place, increasing group experience.	Due to the possible local distribution, players can play the game isolated. Communication outside the in-game mechanisms more difficult than in the board game variant.
Realism	In the board game, players are explicitly set in a game setting that differs from their regular work setting. They play around a table – a setting that would normally only be used for meetings.	The mobile game simulates isolated players communicating via different messages (text, image, video, audio). While the game scenario restricts the communication between players, the isolation and the message style communication creates a more realisitc game play situation.
Reusability and variability	The board game supports a fixed number of disruption scenarios. Varying these scenarios requires new versions of the board game to be produced.	The authoring tool used to create the mobile game allows to create variations of the same game. The game design and game processes can be updated and developed continuously to extend the available scenarios or to reflect experiences from previous game trials.

- The mobile devices provide a realistic situation scenario, as the players use communication means similar to their daily activities as the game interaction is based on mobile devices: users receive messages and interact with question items. Multimedia dialogue sequences complement the message driven approach to provide more immersive situations.

Figure 4 displays screenshots of the SALOMO game showing communication messages and decision points.

The ARLearn platform used supports the automatic logging of all player interactions. Through a web-based front-end this data can be retrieved and used for a debriefing session. While the logging data is available, the debriefing itself is not (yet) automatized and has to be performed together with a trained expert.

7 Conclusion

From disruption management processes observed at a large international port, we have designed a board game simulating these processes with a varying degree of communication means available to players. This board game has been successfully trialled with various user groups. Some difficulties of this board game design are that it requires a skilled game master to be available during game play, which leads to decreased scalability of the game, and that it requires all players to be within a single room to play the game, which is unrealistic for the stakeholders in a big port.

Consequently, we have chosen a multi-user, multi-role enabled mobile game environment (ARLearn), to create a computerized version of the game, which can be played by players in the different roles simultaneously. The players play with different mobile devices and do not need to be at the same location.

While we did not perform a comparative study to evaluate the mobile game against the board game directly, the main contribution of this paper is to compare the applicability of the two different game scenarios in various training settings and to assess their value from a design point of view. Table 2 consequently compares the board game and the mobile game along the dimensions execution, scalability, location independence, introduction & debriefing support, group experience, realism, reusability and variability.

Rather than ranking one over the other, the presented table shall guide designers of multi-user decision training games in order to chose their way of implementation according to the training setting at hand. With these dimensions in mind it is possible to create immersive multi-user games simulating complex decision processes gaining SSA among stakeholders and raising awareness for the importance of pro-active communication as a key element of shared decision taking. Where group experience and debriefing support are top priorities, a board game can be seen as preferred option. In scenarios, where realism, location independence, scalability, or reusability are in focus, the mobile game appears to be the preferred solution.

8 Future Work

The work described here represents a starting point for the sound design and implementation of multi-user decision training games for various training scenarios. While we have first results indicating that this kind of games is helpful and can provide effects [29] in other case studies, we are looking for ways to further formalise the design and implementation of multi-user decision training games [30]. Our research therefore follows two directions: firstly, the further development of our game scenarios and technical implementation focuses on enhancing the immersiveness of our games. Secondly, the further evaluation of training scenarios in various settings should deliver stronger evidence about their usefulness and about measurable effects.

Acknowledgements. The Dutch Institute of Advanced Logistics (DINALOG) sponsors the SALOMO project.

References

1. De Bruijn, J.A., Heuvelhof, E.F.: Management in Networks: On Multi-Actor Decision Making. Routledge, New York (2008)
2. Kurapati, S., Kolfschoten, G., Verbraeck, A., Drachsler, H., Specht, M., Brazier, F.: A theoretical framework for shared situational awareness in sociotechnical systems. In: Proceedings of the 2nd Workshop on Awareness and Reflection in TEL, pp. 47–53 (2012)
3. Salmon, P.M., Stanton, N.A., Walker, G.H., Jenkins, D.P., Mcmaster, R., Young, M.S.: What really is going on? Review of situation awareness models for individuals and teams. Theor. Issues Ergon. Sci. **9**(4), 297–323 (2008)
4. Crichton, M.T., Flin, R., Rattray, W.A.: Training decision makers–tactical decision games. J. Contingencies Crisis Manag. **8**(4), 208–217 (2000)
5. Dowell, J., Hoc, J.M.: Coordination in emergency operations and the tabletop training exercise. Le Travail Humain **58**(1), 85–102 (1995)
6. Klemke, R., Ternier, S., Kalz, M., Schmitz, B., Specht, M.: Multi-stakeholder decision training games with ARLearn. In: Proceedings of the Fourth International Conference on eLearning (eLearning 2013), Belgrade, Serbia, 26–27 September 2013
7. Svensson, G.: A conceptual framework for the analysis of vulnerability in supply chains. Int. J. Phys. Distrib. Logist. Manage. **30**(9), 731–750 (2000)
8. Loh, H.S., Thai, V.V.: The role of ports in supply chain disruption management. In: Proceedings of the Int'l Forum on Shipping, Ports and Airports, 325–337. Hong Kong (2012)
9. Yliskyla-Peuralahti, J., Spies, M., Tapaninen, U.: Transport vulnerabilities and critical industries: experiences from a finnish stevedore strike. Int. J. Risk Assess. Manag. **15**(2/3), 222–240 (2011)
10. Endsley, M.R.: Towards a theory of situation awareness in dynamic systems. Hum. Factors **37**(1), 32–64 (1995)
11. Fiore, S.M., Salas, E., Cuevas, H.M., Bowers, C.A.: Distributed coordination space: toward a theory of distributed team process and performance. Theor. Issues Ergon. Sci. **4**(3–4), 340–364 (2003)
12. Nofi, A.: Defining and Measuring Shared Situational Awareness. DARPA. Center for Naval Analyses, Alexandria (2000)
13. Perla, P.P., Markowitz, M., Nofi, A.A., Weuve, C., Loughran, J.: Gaming and shared situation awareness. Center for Naval Analyses, Alexandria (2000)
14. Duke, R.D.: A Paradigm for game design. Simul. Games **11**(3), 364–377 (1980)
15. Duke, R.D., Geurts, J.: Policy Games for Strategic Management. Rozenberg Publishers, Amsterdam (2004)
16. Meijer, S.: The Organisation of Transactions: Studying Supply Networks using Gaming Simulation. Ph.D. thesis, Wageningen University, Netherlands (2009)

17. Klabbers, J.H.: The Magic Circle: Principles of Gaming & Simulation, vol. 12. Sense Publishers, Rotterdam (2006)
18. Chen, L., Miller-Hooks, E.: Resilience: an indicator of recovery capability in intermodal freight transport. Transp. Sci. **46**(1), 109–123 (2012)
19. Port of Rotterdam Authority: Change Your Perspective. Port of Rotterdam, Rotterdam (2012)
20. Ternier, S., Klemke, R., Kalz, M., Van Ulzen, P., Specht, M.: ARLearn: augmented reality meets augmented virtuality. J. Univ. Comput. Sci. **18**(15), 2143–2164 (2012). Special Issue on Technology for learning across physical and virtual spaces
21. Ternier, S., De Vries, F., Börner, D., Specht, M.: Mobile augmented reality with audio. In: SuEdu 2012 workshop, 10th International Conference on Software Engineering and Formal Methods, Thessaloniki, Greece (2012)
22. Kelle, S., Klemke, R., Specht, M.: Design patterns for learning games. Int. J. Technol. Enhanced Learn. **3**(6), 555–569 (2011)
23. Gonsalves, A., Ternier, S., De Vries, F., Specht, M.: Serious games at the UNHCR with ARLearn, a toolkit for mobile and virtual reality applications. In: M. Specht, M. Sharples, & J. Multisilta (Eds.), Proceedings of the 11th World Conference on Mobile and Contextual Learning (mLearn 2012), Helsinki, Finland, pp. 244–247, 16–18 October 2012
24. Schmitz, B., Ternier, S., Kalz, M., Klemke, R., Specht, M.: Designing a mobile learning game to investigate the impact of role-playing on helping behaviour. In: 8th European Conference on Technology Enhanced Learning. Paphos, Cyprus (2013)
25. Gagnon, D.J.: ARIS: An open source platform for developing mobile learning experiences. University of Wisconsin at Madison, Madison (2010). http://goo.gl/ycI7fi
26. Holden, C.L., Sykes, J.M.: Leveraging mobile games for place-based language learning. Int. J. Game-Based Learn. (IJGBL) **1**(2), 1–18 (2011)
27. Santos, P., Pérez-Sanagustín, M., Hernández-Leo, D., Blat, J.: QuesTInSitu: From tests to routes for assessment in situ activities. Comput. Educ. **57**(4), 2517–2534 (2011)
28. Robles, G., Gonzales-Barahona, J. M., Fernandez-Gonzales, J.: Implementing gymkhanas with android smartphones: a multimedia m-learning game. In: 2011 IEEE Global Engineering Education Conference (EDUCON), pp. 960–968. IEEE (2011)
29. Schmitz, B., Schuffelen, P., Kreijns, K., Klemke, R., Specht, M.: Putting Yourself in Someone Else's Shoes: the impact of a location-based, collaborative roleplaying game on behaviour. Manuscript submitted for publication (2014)
30. Klemke, R., Ternier, S., Kalz, M., Schmitz, B., Specht, M.: Immersive Multi-user decision training games with AR-learn. In: Rensing, C., de Freitas, S., Ley, T., Muñoz-Merino, P.J. (eds.) Open Learning and Teaching in Educational Communities. LNCS, vol. 8719, pp. 207–220. Springer, Heidelberg (2014). http://dx.doi.org/10.1007/978-3-319-11200-8_16

Gamification in e-Learning Systems: A Conceptual Model to Engage Students and Its Application in an Adaptive e-Learning System

Ana Carolina Tomé Klock, Lucas Felipe da Cunha, Mayco Farias de Carvalho, Brayan Eduardo Rosa, Andressa Jaqueline Anton, and Isabela Gasparini[✉]

PPGCA, Computer Science Department, Santa Catarina State University (UDESC), Joinville, Santa Catarina, Brazil
{actklock,lucasfelipedacunha,maycofarias.joi, andressaanton51}@gmail.com, brayan_sx@hotmail.com, isabela.gasparini@udesc.br

Abstract. This paper presents a conceptual model to the gamification process of e-learning environments. This model aims to help identify which elements are involved in the gamification process. To understand which game elements is commonly used by e-learning systems, we analyzed ten different gamified e-learning systems. As a proof of concept, our conceptual model was used in a existing adaptive e-learning system. As future work, we propose to extend the conceptual model, focusing on making it adapted to the students profile and preferences.

Keywords: Gamification · e-Learning · Conceptual model · Game elements · Adaptweb®

1 Introduction

Technology enhance learning is an growing area in recent years. For the last decade, a range of technologies was created to improve the learning process. Yet, an old problem still persists. As pointed by Atkin [1], the traditional educational system has many motivational problems: not understanding the curriculum, not understanding the benefits of staying at school, fear, tiredness, among others. According to Visser et al. [2], even with the use of technology, the education still faces the same motivation problems. One of the strategies used that tries to solve this motivational problem is gamification. Gamification is the use of game elements for purposes unrelated to games in order to get people stimulated and engaged to achieve a specific goal [3]. This paper proposes a conceptual model to help the implementation of gamification in different e-learning environments.

This paper is structured as follows: the Sect. 2 shows a definition of what gamification is and some examples of game elements that can be implemented. Section 3 presents the results of an analysis of ten different e-learning environments, explaining how gamification is applied. Section 4 introduces the conceptual model proposed to apply

© Springer International Publishing Switzerland 2015
P. Zaphiris and A. Ioannou (Eds.): LCT 2015, LNCS 9192, pp. 595–607, 2015.
DOI: 10.1007/978-3-319-20609-7_56

gamification in e-learning systems. Section 5 shows how we used this model in the AdapWeb® environment. Finally, Sect. 6 presents the conclusions.

2 Gamification

Gamification defines the use of game elements for purposes unrelated to games in order to get people stimulated and engaged to achieve a specific goal [3]. According to Burke [4], the word "Gamification" was coined by Nick Pelling in 2002, but it only became popular in 2010. In recent years, gamification has been applied in many different areas and it has motivated people to change behaviors, to develop skills and to drive innovation [5].

The key concept in game play is motivation [6]. Motivation is typically divided in two types: intrinsic and extrinsic. Intrinsic motivation refers to the personal internal motivation, which means that someone does something because he/she wants to (e.g. for its own sake, for the enjoyment it provides, for the learning it permits or even for the feeling of accomplishment it evokes) [6]. Extrinsic motivation refers to the external motivation, which means that someone does an activity because he/she seeks to be rewarded with something (e.g., money, high grade, praise from a boss, certification, badge and admiration from others) [6].

If the system promotes a good experience, the players will remain motivated and, consequently, they will keep using it. Some aspects of user experience are desirable like being satisfying, engaging, fun, surprising, provocative, entertaining, challenging, rewarding and emotionally fulfilling [7]. Nevertheless, some others aspects are undesirable like being boring, frustrating, annoying, childish and gimmicky [7]. These experiences are influenced by the users and the system, once users bring their previous experiences, emotions, feelings, values and cognitive elements and the system represents artifacts that influence the experience [8].

Engagement is a goal of user experience that motivates the use of the system and it can be measured by analyzing which are the parts of the system where the users invest more time, attention and emotions. One way to measure engagement is by tracking users while they use the system (e.g. via web analytics tools) [9]. In the web context, click rate, number of pages viewed, time spent on the site, number of times users return to a particular website and number of users are some of the most commonly used metrics for web analytics tools. These metrics do not determine exactly why users are engaged with the system, but they can serve as an indicator: the higher and more frequent use, more engaged the users are [9].

Nowadays, gamification is applied in several different parts of our lives: shopping (e.g. eBay implements points to show users status, reputation as a reward for buyers and sellers and also badges for the best sellers), hanging out (e.g. Swarm enables users to "check in" somewhere and to share their experience about that place, developing their expertise similar to levels), working out (e.g. Nike + rewards users for their training with points that unlock awards, achievements and surprises), recycling (e.g. Recycle-Bank gives points to users when they use less water or energy, when they recycle or even when they go walking to work) and learning (e.g. Duolingo helps students learn a new language using points, levels, rankings, rewards, etc.) [10]. When gamification is applied in educational area, the main difference between gamified and non-gamified systems is that the gamified one promotes another layer of interest and introduces a new way to join game elements in an engaging experience that motivates while educates students [6]. In the next section, we explain different game elements used in the gamification process.

2.1 Game Elements

One of the most known and used framework for game design is the MDA [11]. MDA formalizes the consumption of games by breaking them down into Mechanics, Dynamics and Aesthetics. According to Hunicke et al. [11], the MDA framework provides clear definitions of these terms, explaining how each component is related and their influence in the users experience.

Other framework called MDC (Mechanics, Dynamics and Components) is specific for gamification [12]. Mechanics are the elements that guide and stimulate users interaction and engagement, and they are a way to achieve one or more dynamics. Dynamics are elements that introduces the user to the environment or system, generally this introduction occurs slowly. Components can be defined as a more specific form of mechanics or dynamics [12]. Some examples of game elements available are described below.

Narrative. Werbach [12] defines narrative as a consistent ongoing storyline. The use of stories allows the transmission of information and the guidance of the users, creating interactive experiences to engage users [6].

Rules. A gamified system with rules determines what can and can not be done by the user, what he/she may or may not access and other issues that limit user actions, turning the system manageable [6]. The rules can be divided into operational (defining how the system works), foundational/constituative (defining the formal structure of environmental functionality), implicit/behavior (determining the contract/agreement between two or more users) and instructional (determining the form of learning) [6].

Challenges. They are elements to guide users on the activities that must be performed in the system [13, 14]. It is important to have challenges that users must complete, and the environment should provide many challenges as possible, so users will remain motivated [13].

Integration. It's the act of making a new or inexperienced person enter and get involved into the system [13]. This item is important to engage and encourage the user to stay in a system hitherto unknown and its main benefit is the user engagement for a long term [14].

Reinforcement and Feedback. Resources are used to provide important data to the users, as their location in the environment and the results of their actions within the system. This feedback is important to support the users in their decision making of the situations presented by the system [14].

Loops of Engagement. This element involves creating and maintaining motivating emotions that contribute to the user to keep motivated and engaged in using the system [14], both in the present and in the future interaction [13].

Achievements. Achievements are a virtual or physical representation of having accomplished something. They can be easy, difficult, funny, surprising, accomplished alone or in a group.

Points. They are often used in non-game applications as a way to demonstrate the achievements of users. The points also measure the user's achievements in relation to others and they work to keep the user motivated to the next level or reward. They can be divided into: (a) points of experience, that is the most important type and do not serve as a bargaining chip; (b) points of redeemable, which are used to get locked items; (c) points of skills, that are received for carrying out specific tasks that are not the main system; (d) points of karma, which are points that you need to share to receive some benefit and reputation [13].

Levels. Levels indicate the user's progress within the system [13]. There are three different levels: (a) game level, that must meet the main goals of the history of progress in the system or the advancement of learning (in the case of educational environments), the development of user skills and the motivation of users to continue working toward system to new levels; (b) difficulty level, which could be easy and suitable for beginners with simple challenges and with system help, medium to the most users who need challenges and difficulties in a more balanced way, and difficult for more expert users because the challenges are more complex and there is no help from the system; (c) player levels, that show the user's progress and they can be used to achieve special skills, to acquire new items or as a bargaining chip [6].

Rankings. The main purpose of rankings is to compare the users in the system and they also serve as a way to visualize the progression of the users within the environment. Rankings can be divided into two types: (a) not discourages, which puts the user in the middle of the rankings, except when he/she is in the top rank; (b) infinite, where the goal is to make the user does not get stuck in one position and/or he/she not be exceeded by many users in a short time, so the ranking can be divided into different categories that will cause the user to merge his/her position [13].

Badges. It's a more robust version of points and a visual representation of some accomplishment/achievement of the user in the system [12]. For designers, badges are a way to make social promotion of products and services [13].

Customization. It's the way users transform or personalize items according to their preferences. Customization can promote motivation, engagement, sense of ownership and control over the system [13, 14]. It is important to balance the amount of items available to custom.

Virtual Goods. They are elements present in the system to enable self-expression, where the user can use the points earned to customize the game in general [15]. For example, the user can buy different clothes for his/her "avatar" into the system or change its hair or face, among others characteristics.

3   Gamified e-Learning Systems

In order to verify the use of game elements described in Sect. 2.1, some educational environments were analyzed in the end of 2014. For this, the analysis method adopted was the use and observation of the learning platform, from the registration, through inspection of all areas of the environment, to the perspective of students and teachers, when available in the environment. The e-learning systems evaluated were Khan Academy, PeerWise, QizBox, BrainScape, Peer2Peer University, URI Online Judge, CodeSchool, Duolingo, Passei Direto and MeuTutor, and the game elements found in each educational environment are described below.

Khan Academy is an e-learning focused on teaching math, science, history, art, computer programming, etc., without subscriptions, and free for anyone [16]. The Khan Academy has videos hosted on Youtube to teach content, many exercises to practice the learned content and also allows parents and teachers monitor the student learning process. In the Khan Academy, were found six different gamification elements: the use of points, levels, challenges and the implementation of badges, customization and virtual goods. Experience points are earned when the student completes an activity. These points serve to enable the challenge to evolve the learning level and also to release the characters to customize the avatar of the student, characterizing virtual goods. In addition, there are badges that are won by points or specific challenges.

PeerWise allows students to create multiple choice questions and also answer questions created by others students [17]. It is a free platform where initially the teacher creates the page for the course that will teach and inform students to sign up for the course. PeerWise can be used in a wide range of disciplines, like Anthropology, Biology, Chemistry, Computer Science, Medicine and Physics [18]. It has four gamification elements: points, rankings, badges and challenges. Similar to the Khan Academy, the student achievement badges through completed levels, but in PeerWise there is also a ranking indicating how many students have won that badge previously. Furthermore, PeerWise has reputation scores, the score regarding created questions and answers.

QizBox is a free application to enhance learning in the classroom, allowing the teachers: to present slides, ask and answer questions to the students who are watching the presentation; to discuss the lecture in a chat room; and to provide a real-time feedback [19]. In QizBox, were found two elements: points and levels, where the experience points earned during tasks are used to improve the level of the student.

Brainscape is an online study platform focus on a fast learn by simplifying and accelerating the learning process. The platform, which has free and paid courses, performs questions to students and allows viewing of the answers. This way, learn is based on repetition, active recall and metacognition [20]. In Brainscape we had found two game elements: points and rankings, where points are won during learning through the progress and, based on this progress, there is a ranking of the most advanced students of each content.

Peer2PeerUniversity (P2PU) is an educational project that takes advantage of the internet and educational materials available for free to create a learning model that helps the traditional formal higher education [21]. P2PU is a social platform that allows any member to design and create a course or study group, which can then be accessed by any other member of the online community. Students can participate, complete, and let challenges at any time in P2PU. In P2PU there are two game elements: personalization, where the user can put an avatar photo, and badges won during the execution of the courses offered.

URI Online Judge is a platform to provide programming practice and knowledge sharing, containing more than 700 problems [22]. The platform allows teachers to create courses and exercise lists, which can be solved in C++ or Java. There are four game elements: rankings, badges, challenges and customization. As the P2PU, the URI Online Judge also allows students to customize their avatar. The challenges allow the student to make several badges. There ranking classifies students according to the number of problems solved.

CodeSchool is a site that teaches web technologies and web languages through videos and interactive exercises [23]. Only a few courses offered by the platform are free. In CodeSchool we found the same elements applied to the Khan Academy, offering challenges that once completed, give points to students. These points can be used to "buy" answers when the student has difficulty in completing a challenge. Similar to the Khan Academy, the student level up by completing challenges. In CodeSchool, students earn badges by completing levels, unlike Khan Academy which gives badge to challenges and points. CodeSchool also allows customization of the avatar, such as P2PU and Online Judge URI.

Duolingo is a platform to learn languages for free while helping to translate the web [24]. In Duolingo, there are seven game elements available: points, levels, rankings, challenges, badges, customization and virtual goods. The points earned can be redeemed (lingots) or of experience. These lingots enable the player to buy additional units, "super powers" and practical tests (virtual goods). Experience points are used to reach the daily goal (challenge) stipulated by the student while lingots can be used to purchase virtual goods. Each completed level is entitled to a badge, as in CodeSchool. In addition, there is a ranking by period based on experience points gained by the student, and this ranking only considers other students who are "followed" by the student. Duolingo also allows customization of the avatar.

Passei Direto is a free collaborative social network to connect students and to share knowledge, which allows students to organize their schedule, meet other students, take questions, find study materials and receive invitations to jobs in Brazilian companies [25]. In Passei Direto it was possible to find six game elements: points, levels, rankings, challenges, badges and customization. The student must complete challenges to earn experience points and increase their level in the system. Unlike other environments, Passei Direto increases students level, when they gain a different badge that is displayed next to the avatar and the avatar can be customized by the student. There is a ranking of the students/university which is based on acquired points.

MeuTutor is a partly free educational platform, personalized, focused on the quality of teaching and student performance [26]. The platform social goal is to reduce the discrepancy between the public and private education in Brazil through its use as an aid in preparation tool for the National High School Exam (ENEM). In MeuTutor we had found six game elements: points, levels, rankings, challenges, badges and customization. There are challenges to gain experience points, these points are used to increase the level and to assemble the ranking. There are challenges to win badges and allows the student to customize their avatar.

4   Conceptual Model for Gamification of e-Learning Environments

To help the implementation of gamification in new or existing e-learning systems, our conceptual model aims to assist in identifying which elements are involved in the gamification process. This model provides information of what game elements, actors, data and behavior are involved in the gamification process.

The conceptual model proposed is separated in four main dimensions which defines: who, why, how and what. "Who?" aims to identify the actors of the system that will be involved in the gamification process; "Why?" identifies some of the possible behaviors that gamification can improve during the student's interaction with the system; "How?" defines which game elements will be implemented and; "What?" represents the data that are involved in the gamification process. These main dimensions are described bellow with more details.

Who?. An e-learning environment can have different types of actors like students, teachers and monitors. This model focuses on the two most important type of actors of an e-learning system: the students and the teacher. The student is the main actor because gamified systems were primarily designed to satisfy students' learning needs [27]. The teachers also have a key role: they have the responsibility to provide the content of the course, to understand the needs of the students and to evaluate the development of the learning. In addition, some e-learning environments often let the teacher evaluate certain aspects of students, and these ratings may have a direct consequence on the gamification process (such as the points system and achievements).

Why?. The use of gamification allows desired behaviors within the system to be promoted [28]. Thus, based on the basic functions that an e-learning system must allow, seven possible behaviors were mapped: (1) Accessing of the concepts, examples, materials and classes; (2) Resolution of exercises and delivery of tasks; (3) Increasing exercise performance; (4) Creating and answering forum threads; (5) Using the chat; (6) Using the message board and; (7) Accessing the system more frequently.

These behaviors were classified in four different categories: *Theoretical*: The theoretical part of the system, such as access to the classes and materials related to the course; *Practical*: It is related with the practical part of the system, such as the resolutions of the exercises; *Social*: It is related to the social aspects of the system, such as using the chat and forum and; *System*: It is related to the system itself, as the amount of hits and the usage time of the environment by the students.

How?. The introduction of gamification in an e-learning environment is done through the use of game elements and these elements encourages certain behaviors that can benefit students. Different elements are discussed in Sect. 2.1.

What?. To implement gamification in an existing e-learning environment, some data modifications are necessary to enable the support to the game elements.

To implement the points system, the student model must be updated to allow control and storage of the points received. The update is done through the database, creating tables to keep the information related to the system, and through callback functions that are triggered after an action is performed in the system. For levels, it is also used a database table that defines how the levels are structured. The ranking is just a visual element that has relation with other elements already implemented, such as points and achievements. For challenges, a model must be created to define the characteristics of the challenges according to the system requirements, it is also necessary to implement a way to find out if the challenges were completed or not. For that, analytics tool and system log can be used. Badges and achievements, as well as rankings, are graphical elements, and their implementation is necessary to maintain the database updated about what challenges have been carried out by the students. The narrative can be introduced to adapt the educational content based with the plot created for the environment. Finally, rules are a part of all gamified systems, so teachers and designers have to define during the planning process what rules the system will follow. Figure 1 presents our proposed conceptual model.

Fig. 1. The four dimensions of our conceptual model for gamification of e-learning environments.

An important part of the model is the relationship between each of the four dimensions. There is a relation between the "Why?" (desired behaviors in the system) and the dimensions "How?" (game elements that are used in gamification) and "Who?" (actors).

In addition, according to the identified techniques, it is possible to make a relationship with the dimension "What?" (data involved). This relationship will be based on the possible behaviors mapped before, as follows:

Accessing concepts, examples, materials and classes: All of the elements "How" can be used to encourage this student's behavior. The work of Barata et al. [29] rewards the students with points, levels and rankings for watching classes. The authors also use achievements and challenges to encourage users to read the materials and report any error encountered on them. The work of O'Donovan [30], uses a steampunk bases story that is revealed in the process of accessing the materials and classes in the system. The student is the only actor involved in this process, he/she decides when and if he/she is going to watch or access any of the material/classes.

Resolution of exercises and delivery of tasks: A common practice in gamified e-learning systems is to reward student's with points, levels and rankings for solving exercises or delivering homework [31, 32]. Using achievements and challenges can improve this behavior on students [33]. In the work of O'Donovan [30], each solved exercised would give the student a clue to solve the mystery behind the narrative introduced in the system. Both the student and the teacher are involved in this behavior, the student solving exercises and delivering homework and the teacher evaluating the student answers.

Increasing exercise performance: Besides encouraging the students to solve exercises, it's important to encourage them to make less mistakes and improve their performance. One way of doing this is introducing challenges and achievements. The work of Denny [33] encourages users to answers a long list of questions without making any mistake. The only actor involved in this behavior is the student, only he/she can try to follow the incentives of challenges and achievements and increase his/her performance when solving exercises.

Creating and answering forum threads: Points, levels, rankings, achievements and challenges is a great way to encourage students to create and answer threads in a forum. StackOverflow is a very successful tool that rewards people for creating and answering question with those elements. Both the student and the teacher is involved in this behavior. The student creating and answering question, while the teacher acts as a moderator of the tool.

Using of the chat and the message board: Using achievements and challenges, for example, trying the chat for a first time with a colleague, posting something interesting in the message board, like an important date is a good way to incentive students to use those tools. We believe that rewarding points and levels for using those tools might make the student use those tools arbitrary, and those kind of behavior it's not desired in an e-learning environment. Both student and teacher are involved in this behavior, the student chatting with other students or the teacher and posting important stuff in the class message board, and teachers being the moderator of this tool.

Accessing the system more frequently: One of the challenges of e-learning systems is to improve students attendance. Using gamification throughout the system can improve indirectly this behavior. Using challenges and achievements can improve students access to the system, like rewarding the student for accessing the system during a certain period.

5   Gamification of AdaptWeb® Environment

Based on the foregoing model, it was implemented the gamification model in an adaptive and open source learning environment called AdaptWeb® (Adaptive Web-based learning environment). The AdaptWeb® aims to adapt disciplines presentations of courses on the web, giving many students the content presentation in different ways, tailored to their individual preferences [34]. AdaptWeb® was originally developed through a partnership between the Federal University of Rio Grande do Sul and the State University of Londrina in collaboration with the Brazilian Council CNPq (National Council for Scientific and Technological Development) and nowadays it has been continuously developed, improved and used by the Santa Catarina State University [35].

AdaptWeb® has an architecture based on four distinct modules: the authoring module, the storage module, the content adaptation module and adaptive interface module [36]. The authoring module helps authors to organize their class materials inside the system, defining categories and prerequisites for their materials and choosing which courses will have access to their content (avoiding material duplication) [36]. The storage module creates and organizes files in XML (eXtensible Markup Language) with the data entered in the authoring module [36]. The content adaptation module, as the name suggests, is responsible for adapting the material inserted in the authoring module to the students by filtering the existing XML files in the storage module, generating different presentations for the same content [36]. The adaptive interface module is responsible for adapting the environment interface and navigation, according to the students course/background, their navigation preferences and their knowledge [36].

In the system itself, the students access the course and they can (1) view the content inserted by the author: they can access the content freely or in the tutorial mode that follows the prerequisites set by the author, (2) check the message boards: a fast communication mode between the students and the author and (3) access the discussion forum: asynchronous communication tool that allows the class to share ideas, questions, among other uses.

Following the dimensions described in the previous session, we defined who, why, what and how before start the gamification implementation on AdaptWeb®.

Who. It was defined "who" through a questionnaire answered by thirty-eight students from the Department of Computer Science of the State University of Santa Catarina. Through this questionnaire, we found that most of them (54 %) have a profile directed to solve puzzles and to enjoy the victory achieved with great effort, which can be classified as Achievers according to the Marczewski's user types [37]. Based on that, the main game elements that can be used to attract Achievers are: points, levels, rankings and badges.

Why. To stimulate student behavior, it was possible to identify four of the seven behaviors mapped before that can be encouraged through gamification. The behaviors that can be encouraged are: (1) accessing the concepts/examples/materials/classes, (2) creating and answer forum threads, (3) using of the message board and (4) accessing the system more frequently. However, some behaviors can not be gamified in

AdaptWeb®: (1) resolution of exercises and delivery of work, (2) increasing of the exercise performance and (3) using the chat, because AdaptWeb® does not support the problem solving system and synchronous chat yet.

What and How. The gamification has been implemented in the system through elements that generate a sense of progress, competition and achievement in order to increase engagement and motivation. Points, that are displayed by a progress bar, can be achieved when students access the system (the first access of the day) and materials (the first time), when they use the message board, when they create and reply topics in the forum, when they receive a good ranking from the teacher in the forum and when they complete challenges. Levels are based on the amount of points the student earned (level 1: 50 points, level 2: 150 points, level 3: 300 points, and so on). Rankings are also determined by the amount of points, showing the top five students on AdaptWeb® homepage. Challenges (access the system every day for a certain period, access all available content, win a position in the ranking, the use of the message board, according to the number of responses in the forum and the evaluation of the teacher on them), Badges (visual representations for each completed challenge) and Rules (leading the entire system) were also implemented.

Beyond the game elements, it was implemented some metrics to see what the students are doing in the system and measure their engagement: the number of system visits per student, the frequency of access to the system, the access to concepts, examples, exercises and supplementary materials and the access, creation and response to forum threads. Figure 2 presents AdaptWeb's students profile page.

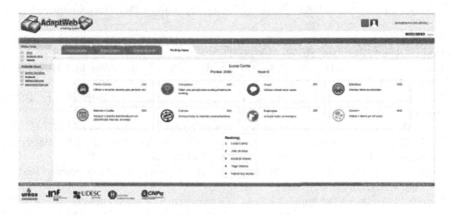

Fig. 2. AdaptWeb's students profile page, which gamification elements available

6 Conclusions

This paper presented a conceptual model to the gamification process of e-learning environments. This model aims to help identify which elements are involved in the gamification process related to four dimensions (Who, Why, What and How). The model provides information of what game elements, actors, data and behavior are involved in the gamification process. It is generic enough to be used by diverse e-learning systems, since it does not focus on the implementation process or induces to one specific game element, thus, this model can be applied to existing e-learning environments and also helps to create others.

To understand which game elements is commonly used by e-learning systems, we analyzed ten different gamified e-learning systems. This analysis was based on our interaction into each system, and the exploration of some course freely available. From the thirteen mostly common game elements described in the literature, the e-learning who had most game elements support seven of them. It can be seen of two ways. On the one hand, we understand the area is new, and besides some e-learning systems have already some gamification process, they are in initial stage and they can be broadly explored. On the other hand, although the theme is new, different environments have incorporated gamification elements to improve engagement and motivation of students. The motivation and engagement in education is an old problem of the teaching-learning process, and different strategies are being used to increase student motivation.

As a proof of concept, our conceptual model was used in a existing adaptive e-learning system named AdaptWeb®. As future work, we propose to extend the conceptual model, aiming to turn it adapted to the students profile and preferences. We plan to evaluate AdaptWeb® and analyze the gamification process with students.

References

1. Atkins, C.: Education and Minorities. Continuum International Publishing Group, New York (2012)
2. Visser, L., et al.: Motivating students at a distance: the case of an international audience. J. Educ. Technol. Res. Dev. **50**, 94–110 (2002)
3. Deterding, S., Dixon, D., Khaled, R.: Gamification: toward a definition. In: CHI 2011, pp. 12–15. ACM, Vancouver (2011)
4. Burke, B.: Gamify: How Gamification Motivates People to do Extraordinary Things. Bibliomotion Inc., Brookline (2014)
5. Burke, B.: Gamification Primer: Life Becomes a Game. Gartner Inc., Stamford (2011)
6. Kapp, K.M.: The Gamification of Learning and Instruction: Game-based Methods and Strategies for Training and Education. Pfeiffer, San Francisco (2012)
7. Rogers, Y., Preece, J., Sharp, H.: Interaction Design: Beyond Human-computer Interaction, 3rd edn. Wiley, Chichester (2011)
8. Forlizzi, J., Ford, S.: The building blocks of experience: an early framework for interaction designers. In: 3rd Conference on Designing Interactive Systems, pp. 419–423. ACM (2000)
9. Lehmann, J., Lalmas, M., Yom-Tov, E., Dupret, G.: Models of user engagement. In: Masthoff, J., Mobasher, B., Desmarais, M.C., Nkambou, R. (eds.) UMAP 2012. LNCS, vol. 7379, pp. 164–175. Springer, Heidelberg (2012)
10. Duggan, K., Shoup, K.: Business Gamification for Dummies. Wiley, Hoboken (2013)
11. Hunicke, R., LeBlanc, M., Zubek, R.: MDA: a formal approach to game design and game research. In: AAAI Workshop on Challenges in Game AI, pp. 1–5. AAAI Press (2004)
12. Werbach, K., Hunter, D.: For the Win: How Game Thinking Can Revolutionize Your Business. Wharton Digital Press, Philadelphia (2012)

13. Zichermann, G., Cunninghan, C.: Gamification by Design: Implementing Game Mechanics in Web and Mobile Apps. O'Reilly Media Inc., Sebastopol (2011)
14. Fazel, L.M., Ulbricht, V.R., Batista, C.R., Vanzin, T.: Gamificação na educação. Pimenta Cultural, São Paulo (2014)
15. Fu, Y.C.: The Game of Life: Designing a Gamification System to Increase Current Volunteer Participation and Retention in Volunteer-based Nonprofit Organizations (2011)
16. Khan Academy. http://www.khanacademy.org
17. Denny, P., Hamer, J., Luxton-Reilly, A., Purchase, H.: PeerWise: students sharing their multiple choice questions. In: ICER 2008, pp. 51–58. ACM, Sydney (2008)
18. Peerwise. https://peerwise.cs.auckland.ac.nz
19. QizBox. http://qizbox.bgsu.edu/public/login
20. Brainscape. https://www.brainscape.com
21. Peer2Peer University. https://p2pu.org/en
22. URI Online Judge. https://www.urionlinejudge.com.br
23. CodeSchool. https://www.codeschool.com
24. Ahn, L.: Duolingo: learn a language for free while helping to translate the web. In: IUI 2013, pp. 1–2. ACM, Santa Monica (2013)
25. Passei Direto. https://www.passeidireto.com
26. MeuTutor. http://www.meututor.com.br
27. Kemczinski, A.: Método de Avaliação de Ambientes E-Learning. Doctoral thesis, UFSC, Florianópolis (2005)
28. Simões, J., Redondo, R.D., Vilas, A.F.: A social gamification framework for a k-6 learning platform. Comput. Hum. Behav. **29**, 345–353 (2013)
29. Barata, G. et al.: Engaging engeneering students with gamification. In: 5th VS-GAMES, pp. 1–8. IEEE Computer Society, Bournemounth (2013)
30. O'Donovan, S., Gain, J., Marais, P.: A case study in the gamification of a university-level games development course. In: South African Institute for Computer Scientists and Information Technologists Conference. ACM, New York (2013)
31. Iosup, A.; Epema, D.: An experience report on using gamification in technical higher education (2013)
32. Li, C., et al.: Engaging computer science students through gamification in an online social network based collaborative learning environment. Int. J. Inf. Educ. Technol. **3**, 72–77 (2013)
33. Denny, P.: The effect of virtual achievements on student engagement. In: CHI 2013, pp. 763–772. ACM, New York (2013)
34. Gasparini, I. et al.: Navegação e apresentação adaptativos em um ambiente de EAD na Web. In: Proceedings of 10th Brazilian Symposium on Multimedia and the Web (2004)
35. Gasparini, I., et al.: AdaptWeb® - Evolução e Desafios. Cadernos de Informática **4**, 47–56 (2009)
36. de Oliveira, P.M., et al.: AdaptWeb®: um ambiente para ensino-aprendizagem adaptativo na web. Educar em Revista **21**, 175–197 (2003)
37. Marczewski's user types hexad. http://www.gamified.co.uk/user-types

Good Newbie or Poor Newbie? Determinants of Video Game Skill Acquisition at an Early Stage

Kevin Koban[✉], Benny Liebold, and Peter Ohler

Institute for Media Research, Chemnitz University of Technology, Chemnitz, Germany
{kevin.koban,benny.liebold,peter.ohler}@phil.tu-chemnitz.de

Abstract. For several years now, game-based learning is deemed as one of the most innovative approaches in educational practice. Nevertheless, little research has been undertaken examining individual determinants of skill acquisition in video games. The presented paper offers empirical data from a nine-week training curriculum for novices in a racing simulation game. Regression analyses revealed that general video game experience and real-world driving experience significantly predicted both initial and later performance. Additionally, perceptual speed also became strongly influential after consistent training. Conversely, while achievement was affected at least occasionally by divided attention, focused attention and dispositions towards aggressive driving showed no effects. Although preliminary, these results provide evidence that those learners without certain beneficial skills may struggle with cutting-edge virtual learning scenarios. Thus, both individual assistance as well as early promotion of video game literacy might be needed to make full use of the potential of game-based learning.

Keywords: Skill acquisition · Individual differences · Game-based learning · Racing simulation games

1 Introduction

Video games have been found to be a promising asset for various learning domains. Recent meta-analyses provide evidence to support this claim by showing, for instance, that learning with serious games evokes substantial effects on declarative knowledge [1] just as simulation games contribute to a better understanding of complex issues [2] and various other video game genres stimulate certain cognitive skills [3, 4]. Most of all, these accomplishments in conjunction with short periods of training foster hopes to resolve important educational problems like the gender gap in science programs [5] or the low popularity of STEM disciplines [6]. Notwithstanding these promising findings, video games do not cause miraculous cognitive achievements. Just as with other technologies that are employed for learning purposes, both intentional and incidental learning with video games require long-term engagement of the learner in order to be effective. A fundamental determinant for such vital dedication lies in player's early performance. According to this, not only the fact that repeated failure is intensely frustrating [7], but also typical features providing rewards for superior initial performances determine whether prospective learners will make

© Springer International Publishing Switzerland 2015
P. Zaphiris and A. Ioannou (Eds.): LCT 2015, LNCS 9192, pp. 608–619, 2015.
DOI: 10.1007/978-3-319-20609-7_57

use of the learning potential [8]. It is therefore crucial to understand which individual attributes influence early performance in novel video game tasks [9]. The presented study investigates those influences in novices' skill acquisition within a virtual training with a racing simulation game. Our main research question was to test which individual characteristics predict early success in an unfamiliar video game task. Thereby, our research is tied to the game-based learning paradigm, in which it provides evidence from a motivational perspective.

2   Determinants of Skill Acquisition

Based upon the seminal work of Fitts and Posner [10] and Anderson [11] skill acquisition processes can be subdivided into three consecutive stages: a declarative stage, an associative stage, and a procedural stage. As stated by Shiffrin and Schneider [12], this delineated skill acquisition process can also be described as a continuous shift from controlled processing in the first stage towards automatic processing in the third stage. Thus, gaining declarative knowledge of a task, especially while performing, usually requires all cognitive resources available. After a considerable amount of training the exact same task can be executed automatically without any effort. Following these well-established frameworks, some authors had reasoned that certain learner characteristics as well as properties of the task have an impact on the progression of this skill acquisition process.

2.1   Personal Features Influencing Skill Acquisition

It is well known that learners with divergent initial capabilities approximate to a joint asymptote over the course of training [13, 14]. Additionally, a substantial body of research deals with the influence of individual cognitive abilities on skill acquisition [15–23]. Extending existing findings, the research group around Ackerman provides a framework for both sensorimotor and intellectual tasks. Based upon the three-staged models, Ackerman and his colleagues [13, 17–19] found evidence for distinct determinants in each acquisition stage. According to their model, general abilities without reference to the actual task affect performance within cognitive stage [20, 21]. Additionally, transferable schemes can have an impact on early achievement as well, if they do not interfere with task-specific requirements. This assumption follows the rationale that even though prior existing schemes might not be optimized for the specific demands of the task, its availability supports accomplishment.

As controlled processing becomes more and more unnecessary, the influence of general abilities and transferable schemes diminishes in the associative stage [22]. Instead, perceptual speed determining the capability to decide efficiently between existing procedures is growing in relevance. Thus, a fast and proper decision, which procedure among several mentally presented procedures needs to be activated determines performance in this skill acquisition stage [23]. Consequently, since these operations no longer occur in fully automatic processing, this effect declines towards third acquisition stage. As a result of automization, differences in diverse mental abilities become negligible in the final stage. Instead, psychomotor skills remain influential.

2.2   Task Properties Influencing Skill Acquisition

Besides learner characteristics, task properties influence the course of skill acquisition. For instance, as a result of the limitations of working memory [24], a high complexity extends the mental effort needed for encoding task requirements or organizing procedures that typically leads to slower improvements [25, 26]. Equally, oversimplified tasks sometimes enable to skip acquisition stages. Even more fundamentally, learning progress is affected by task consistency: Previous research demonstrated that the prototypical three-staged acquisition fully occurs only under the condition of high consistency with demands remaining the same throughout the training [12]. If, however, one or more essential features vary, learning progress will stagnate at some level of controlled processing without ever reaching full automization [21, 27, 28]. Since the distinct influence of certain learner characteristics depends on the current acquisition stage, task consistency strongly affects its effectiveness.

Sophisticated challenges combine both modes by keeping some elements constant while varying others. With regard to the current study, video games often contain repetitive tasks (e.g. operation of the input device) as well as variable tasks (e.g. the challenge itself). After sufficient practice stable elements therefore will be performed automatically, whereas ever-changing elements still have to be processed in a controlled manner.

3   Current Study

The presented study investigates skill acquisition within an unfamiliar video game task. To this end, the framework provided by Ackerman [17] serves as basis, which is utilized for a racing simulation game scenario. Based upon its emphasis in prior research [20], we expected that attention capacity positively predict individual performance in the first training session (H1a). Subsequently, this effect should diminish with consistent practice. Since steady exercise leads to automatic processing, we assumed that perceptual speed becomes a relevant positive predictor after sufficient training (H2). Otherwise, if an unfamiliar challenge is presented, it is expected that attention capacity will be a significant positive predictor at the second time of measurement as well (H3).

Due to apparent correspondences to other video game genres and real-world activities, several prior existing schemes might be relevant in racing simulation games. While genre-specific experience was controlled via selection of both real and virtual racing novices, some evidence supports the assumption that general video game experience also might affect performance in novel video game tasks. For instance, it is assumed that experienced video game players feel more motivated in game-like challenges than non-gamers. This motivational advantage then leads to superior performance [29, but see 30]. Additionally, video game experience might be linked to skills that improve the approach towards unknown problems [31, 32]. In the long term, those advantages of experienced gamers should decrease as feelings of self-efficacy [33] as well as more specialized strategies develop. Thus, we predicted that video game literacy positively only predicts initial performance (H1b).

To our knowledge, no studies investigating the relation between real world driving experiences and racing simulation performance have been presented so far. However, previous findings suggest that experienced drivers possess greater relevant procedural knowledge (e.g. towards the physics of driving or the racing line) and more reliable coping skills than novice drivers [34, 35]. As before, these schemes might be beneficial until more specialized procedures have been established. We therefore assumed that driving experience positively predicts performance solely at the first time of measurement (H1c).

Existing research on racing games focused primarily on its connection with risky driving behavior. Thereby, both longitudinal and cross-sectional studies found alarming effects [36–38] referring to action racing games. Yet, regarding racing simulations no correlation could be found [39–41]. In line with basic assumptions of the General Learning Model [42], these opposing effects can be interpreted as a consequence of differential in-game content. While action racers typically endorse dangerous driving manoeuvres, racing simulation games contribute to behaviors that are in compliance with realistic racing rules. Therefore, to be successful in a racing simulation, it is necessary to follow a more decent way of driving. For that reason, we expected that an individual disposition towards aggressive driving does not positively predict initial or later performance (H4).

Regardless of its popularity, several studies indicated that the use of authentic input devices is accompanied with a loss in performance [43–45]. McMahan and colleagues [45] speculated about possible reasons for these findings (e.g. the use of inadequate muscle groups or an inferior connection quality), but forgot to consider differences in experience with those devices. Even though other findings [43] mentioned this explanation, no evidence can be provided for lack of longitudinal data. Following this, we supposed that controller authenticity negatively predicts initial performance (H1d), but this impact diminishes over the course of training.

4   Method

We conducted an experiment following a $2 \times 2 \times 2 \times 2$ mixed design with controller authenticity (driving wheel vs. gamepad) and in-game vehicle (gokart vs. car) as between-subjects factors and time of measurement (first week vs. ninth week) and familiarity of the track (trained three times vs. trained eight times) as within-subjects factors. Participants with no noteworthy racing simulation game experience played *Gran Turismo 6* [46] on a Playstation 3 console for nine consecutive weeks. As part of a comprehensive study on novices' knowledge transfer, outcomes within vehicle groups were z-standardized to ensure comparability as both conditions used different tracks.

4.1   Participants

Because of rigid requirements towards subjects in the mentioned study on transfer learning, 71 out of 155 participants who completed the recruitment questionnaire were pre-selected according to several criteria (Table 1). Additionally, due to limited resources only 37 candidates could participate in the first cohort. For the study presented here, a total of 27 subjects were selected for the analyses due to a more rigorous exclusion of genre-experienced players. During training four of them aborted, so that the final sample of the first cohort consisted of 23 participants ($f = 15$, age: $M = 24.35$; $SD = 2.39$).

Table 1. Selection criteria for participants taking part in the training

Variable	Criterion
Driving licenses	must have car license must not have motor bike license
Physical fitness	$x \geq .2$ *
Gokart & racing car experience	$x \leq 2$ **
Racing interest	$x \leq 4$ **
Racing simulation game experience	$x \leq 1$ **
Risky driving attitude	$.1 \leq x \leq .6$ *
Reckless driving behavior	$.1 \leq x \leq .6$ *
Sensation seeking	$.1 \leq x \leq .8$ *
State anxiety	$x \leq .6$ *

Note: * scale from 0 to 1; ** Likert rating from 0 to 6.

4.2 Measures

Being part of a more extensive research project, this paper reports only those measures relevant for the purpose of this study. Attention capacity and perceptual speed were assessed using six different cognitive tests. To avoid multicollinearity only three of them were included after checking for significant intercorrelations. Thus, focused attention was measured by the d2 Test of Attention [47]. It consists of 14 lines filled with the letters d and p as well as zero to four dashed above and beneath every letter. Subjects have to highlight only the ds with two dashes while ignoring all the other combinations of letters and dashes ($M_{pre} = 14.00$; $SD_{pre} = 2.45$; $M_{post} = 15.98$; $SD_{post} = 2.69$). In addition, following numerous studies on action video games [e.g. 48] distributed attention was assessed via the Useful Field of View Test [49]. Therein, participants had to solve a decision task presented in the foveal area of the eye and an orientation task in the peripheral vision field simultaneously. The duration of both stimuli decreases until the subject could not give the right answer any longer ($M_{pre} = .76$ ms; $SD_{pre} = .06$; $M_{post} = .76$; $SD_{post} = .04$). In line with Ackerman and Beier [23], a straightforward letter decision task was conducted measuring perceptual speed. Two letters were presented at the same time. Each letter was either a vowel or a consonant in half of the cases. The task was to press the direction key on the keyboard that pointed towards the vowel as fast as possible, but only when both a vowel and a consonant appeared ($M_{pre} = 828.44$ ms; $SD_{pre} = 226.09$; $M_{post} = 741.48$ ms; $SD_{post} = 185.49$).

Participants' video game literacy and driving experience were assessed via single item self-report. We asked the participants for their general experience with video games on a 7-point Likert scale ($M = 3.13$; $SD = 1.89$) and for an estimate of their total amount of driven kilometers ($M = 23482.61$; $SD = 33472.89$). Furthermore, disposition towards aggressive driving was measured using an index with the risk-taking attitude and reckless driving behavior scales provided by Iversen [50]. Because one item of the reckless driving scale was eliminated due to a misleading description and low intercorrelations, the final index consisted of 27 items on a 5-point Likert scale ($\alpha = .838$; $M = 3.02$; $SD = .62$). To measure performance we averaged the subject's best three lap times on each circuit. This mean value was calculated to get a more precise measure of the actual racing capability since novices usually lose time through multiple driving errors. The employed measure reflects a compromise between including the single best lap or each lap and was intended to be less vulnerable to outliers.

4.3 Procedure

Participants were recruited via university mailing lists for a longitudinal study about entertainment media use. After their selection, participants trained at one of two lab rooms equipped identically except for the input device. Training took nine consecutive weeks including 1-hour training per week. Pre- and post-measurements were conducted prior to the first and ninth training session. Cognitive tests were implemented in random order. After a short introduction, participants completed three races for 10 min each, yet of these only the second and third got evaluated. Racetracks were selected to provide a similar difficulty level. The manipulation of consistency was realized through different frequencies with which racetracks were practiced. While one of the evaluated tracks was trained only three times to remain rather unfamiliar (inconsistent condition), the other track was scheduled every week to become well known (consistent condition). Subsequently, participants were debriefed and paid off.

5 Results

The gathered data were analyzed using separate multiple linear regressions for both racetracks at both times of measure (Table 2). All of them used z-standardized performance as criterion and the above-mentioned influence variables as predictors.

Above all, data revealed that video game experience predicted initial performance significantly at the inconsistently trained track ($\beta = -.69$; $t(15) = -3.30$; $p < .01$) as well as marginally significant at the consistently trained track ($\beta = -31$; $t(15) = -1.86$; $p < .10$). Additionally, real-world driving experience ($\beta = -.40$; $t(15) = -2.54$; $p < .05$) and divided attention capacity ($\beta = -.47$; $t(15) = -2.85$; $p < .05$) turned out to be significant predictors of early performance in the consistent condition. Despite low test power, analyses provided support for hypothesis 1b and partial support for hypotheses 1a and 1c. Albeit not at a sufficient level of significance, it has to be noted that the effect of the input device pointed towards the predicted direction with authentic controllers affecting performance negatively ($\beta = -.34$; $t(15) = -1.61$; $p = .13$ at the inconsistently trained track and at the consistently trained track, $\beta = -.22$; $t(15) = -1.30$; $p = .21$). For the second time of measure we predicted that following inconsistent training attention capacity would be a relevant predictor of performance, whereas perceptual speed became influential after consistent practice. Unfortunately, our data yielded no effects of attention capacity. Thus, neither focused attention ($\beta = -.19$; $t(15) = -1.01$; $p = .33$) nor divided attention ($\beta = .14$; $t(15) = .75$; $p = .47$) was significant. As expected, perceptual speed ability, however, turned out to be a significant predictor of performance at a consistently trained racetrack ($\beta = .45$; $t(15) = 2.33$; $p = .03$). Therefore, gathered data provided support for hypothesis 2, but not for hypothesis 3. Interestingly, video game literacy ($\beta = -.58$; $t(15) = -2,92$; $p < .05$ at the inconsistently trained track and $\beta = -.39$; $t(15) = -1.88$; $p = .08$ at the consistently trained track) and real-world driving experience ($\beta = -.33$; $t(15) = -1.82$; $p = .09$ at the inconsistently trained track and $\beta = -.40$; $t(15) = -2.10$; $p = .05$ at the consistently trained track) continued to be significant or marginally significant predictors, regardless of task consistency. Furthermore, the impact of controller authenticity turned out to be irrelevant after training with subjects now being negligible better with the driving wheel ($\beta = .13$; $t(15) = .72$; $p = .48$ at the inconsistently trained track and $\beta = .11$; $t(15) = .56$; $p = .59$ at the consistently trained track).

Table 2. Standardized regression coefficients for both times of measurement

Criterion	Predictor	β_{pre}	t_{pre}	p_{pre}	β_{post}	t_{post}	p_{post}
Lap time (inconsistent condition)	Video game literacy	−.685	−3.299	.005	−.583	−2.922	.011
	Driving experience	−.046	−0.233	.819	−.334	−1.820	.089
	Aggressive driving	−.033	−0.159	.876	.323	1.606	.129
	Input device	−.338	−1.607	.129	.131	0.718	.484
	Focused attention	.203	1.136	.274	−.047	−0.264	.795
	Distributed attention	.188	0.917	.373	−.192	−1.011	.328
	Perceptual speed	.123	0.541	.596	.140	0.746	.467
R^2 /adj. R^2		.579 /.382			.583 /.389		
Lap time (consistent condition)	Video game literacy	−.308	−1.856	.083	−.389	−1.881	.079
	Driving experience	−.398	−2.539	.023	−.400	−2.103	.053
	Aggressive driving	.258	1.568	.138	.104	0.502	.623
	Input device	−.219	−1.303	.212	.105	0.555	.587
	Focused attention	−.153	−1.066	.303	.018	0.099	.923
	Distributed attention	−.467	−2.848	.012	−.185	−0.942	.361
	Perceptual speed	.058	0.318	.755	.453	2.332	.034
R^2 /adj. R^2		.731 /.605			.553 /.345		

Note: Input Device (0 = Gamepad, 1 = Steering Wheel).

Additionally, we performed four equivalence tests to examine null hypothesis (H4) [51]. As expected, due to the low test power, equivalence tests were not significant at all performance measures (Table 3). Nevertheless, although not statistically relevant both regression analyses slightly indicated that an individual disposition towards aggressive driving correlated positively with achieved lap times. Thus, less aggressive race drivers tended to have faster lap times than drivers with a higher disposition for risky driving (e.g. $\beta = .32$; $t(15) = 1.61$; $p = .13$ on the inconsistently trained racetrack).

Table 3. Results of equivalence tests for aggressive driving for both times of measurement

Criterion	r_{pre}	p_{pre}	r_{post}	p_{post}
Lap time (inconsistent condition)	$-.10$	.428	.13	.470
Lap time (consistent condition)	$-.02$	.293	$-.13$	.470

6 Discussion

The presented study explored, which determinants had an impact on novices' skill acquisition in a racing simulation game. For this purpose, we conducted a nine-week virtual training curriculum examining whether individual characteristics predict game performance in the first and last training session. Further, we manipulated the frequency, with which certain racetracks were practiced assuming that familiarity with the task leads to changes in the required skill profile.

In sum, results were partially in line with the framework proposed by Ackerman and colleagues [17, 21]. In accordance with the literature, perceptual speed showed a strong effect within a well-known racetrack. Although the same amount of training was received overall, it remained an insignificant predictor in an unfamiliar task. This result supports the finding that mental abilities ensuring an efficient decision between several possible procedures became predictive of performance after consistent practice [23]. Unfortunately, since our training lasted only for nine weeks, we cannot provide evidence whether this impact will persist for a while or, as predicted by the framework, declines due to further automatization. Prospective studies with long-lasting periods of training therefore have to investigate whether the framework fully applies in this context.

Additionally, prior existing schemes from video game use and actual driving experience were significant predictors not only, as expected, for initial performance, but also for later accomplishment. Thus, gamers outperformed non-gamers in a video game task, even though both were equally inexperienced with the specific video game genre. Existing literature provides several possible explanations. Whereas some authors argued for motivational benefits [29], others hold cognitive or strategic advantages accountable for this effect [31, 32]. Indicating a subtle distortion in measure, regular video game players might also have underestimated their experience by comparing it directly to their favorite video game genre. As consequence of this anchoring effect, gamers might actually be more experienced causing performance differences. Consequently, re-analyzing the collected data after the completion of the second cohort might shed some light on this subject. However, the surprisingly stable impact of video game experience can be explained by the moderate duration of training. Apparently, about six hours of training were not enough to override experience differences.

The positive impact of real-world driving experience can be interpreted in conjunction with the findings concerning divided attention. Interindividual differences in divided attention strongly affected performance in a single measure that took place at a dark and fairly confusing racetrack. Considering these requirements within a continuously changing setting, visual orientation becomes critical explaining the effect. In parallel, subjects might have taken advantage of a similar higher-order capacity associated with driving expertise. Several studies have demonstrated that expert drivers dispose more efficient visual scanning schemes than inexperienced drivers—particularly in demanding situations [52, 53]. This indicates that experienced drivers might have benefitted due to a constant need for orientation. Further research is needed to validate this interpretation among other possible explanations.

Focused attention revealed no significant effect. The reason behind this unexpected result might be related to task complexity. Some studies dealing with cognitively and sensomotorically demanding tasks demonstrated that harsh requirements easily overstrain novices at the outset [20, 22]. On this account, cognitive advantages like a superior focused attention capacity might be of little relevance until basic requirements are fully comprehended. The first time of measure might have been too early to detect an effect.

Furthermore, our analyses provided information about often-assumed deficiencies of authentic input devices [44, 45]. We argued that these disadvantages could be attributed to limited experience with those controls [43]. Our findings supported this argument as performance differences vanished after moderate practice. Since our investigation lacked statistical power, future longitudinal studies will have to validate our results. Additionally, in line with recent findings [39, 42], we found no significant effect of reckless driving. However, it should be noted that dispositions towards aggressive driving tended to predict performance negatively. Even though we cannot provide statistical support, this slight trend indicates that racing simulation games reward accurate driving rather than risky maneuvers.

Several limitations have to be mentioned. Firstly, owing to the fact that the results presented here only contain the first of two cohorts, the small sample size goes hand in hand with low test power. Therefore, only moderate to strong effects could accomplish reliable statistical analyses with acceptable type 2 errors. Additionally, as being part of a more comprehensive study on knowledge transfer, an irrelevant variation in condition had to be z-standardized and with this a possible distortion in data might have occurred. Furthermore, a nine week-long training with little more than six hours of practice and only two times of measurement does not claim to cover the whole skill acquisition process in detail. Thus, it remains unclear whether and how the influence of the chosen predictors changes between both measures or to a prolonged training.

7 Conclusion

The presented research examined the impact of individual features on novices' performance during a nine-week training curriculum using a racing simulation. Results suggest that general video game experience and real-world driving experience strongly influenced early task performance. Additionally, after some consistent training perceptual speed was rapidly growing in importance. Conversely, neither focused attention nor a disposition towards reckless driving predicted any virtual racing capability. These findings suggest that learners without those beneficial skills might struggle deeply with game-based learning scenarios. Being highly acclaimed in intentional and incidental learning contexts by now, this provides a challenge for educators ranging from immediate instructional support to early promotion of video game literacy.

Acknowledgements. This study was partially funded by the German Research Foundation (DFG) under grant 1760 ("CrossWorlds: Connecting Virtual and Real Social Worlds").

References

1. Wouters, P., van Nimwegen, C., van Oostendorp, H., van der Spek, E.D.: A meta-analysis of the cognitive and motivational effects of serious games. J. Educ. Psychol. **105**, 249–265 (2013)
2. Sitzmann, T.: A meta-analytic examination of the instructional effectiveness of computer-based simulation games. Pers. Psychol. **64**, 489–528 (2011)
3. Powers, K.L., Brooks, P.J.: Evaluating the specificy of effects of video game training. In: Blumberg, F.C. (ed.) Learning by Playing. Video Gaming in Education, pp. 302–332. Oxford University Press, Oxford (1989)
4. Uttal, D.H., Meadow, N.G., Tipton, E., Hand, L.L., Alden, A.R., Warren, C., et al.: The malleability of spatial skills: a meta-analysis of training studies. Psychol. Bull. **139**, 352–402 (2013)
5. Feng, J., Spence, I., Pratt, J.: Playing an action video game reduces gender differences in spatial cognition. Psychol. Sci. **18**, 850–855 (2007)
6. Sanchez, C.A.: Enhancing visuospatial performance through video game training to increase learning in visuospatial science domains. Psychon. Bull. Rev. **19**, 58–65 (2012)
7. van den Hoogen, W., Poels, K., Ijsselsteijn, W., de Kort, Y.: Between challenge and defeat: repeated player-death and game enjoyment. Media Psychol. **15**, 443–459 (2012)
8. Peng, W., Lin, J.-H., Pfeiffer, K.A., Winn, B.: Need satisfaction supportive game features as motivational determinants: an experimental study of a self-determination theory guided exergame. Media Psychol. **15**, 175–196 (2012)
9. Bisoglio, J., Michaels, T.I., Mervis, J.E., Ashinoff, B.K.: Cognitive enhancement through action video game training: great expectations require greater evidence. Front. Psychol. **5**, 1–6 (2014)
10. Fitts, P.M., Posner, M.I.: Human Performance. Brooks/Cole, Oxford (1967)
11. Anderson, J.R.: Acquisition of cognitive skill. Psychol. Rev. **89**, 369–406 (1982)
12. Shiffrin, R.M., Schneider, W.: Controlled and automatic human information processing: II. perceptual learning, automatic attending, and a general theory. Psychol. Rev. **84**, 127–190 (1977)
13. Ackerman, P.L.: Individual differences in skill learning: an integration of psychometric and information processing perspectives. Psychol. Bull. **102**, 3–27 (1987)
14. Adams, J.A.: Historical review and appraisal of research on the learning, retention, and transfer of human motor skills. Psychol. Bull. **101**, 41–74 (1987)

618 K. Koban et al.

15. Fleishman, E.A., Mumford, M.D.: Abilities as causes of individual differences in skill acquisition. Hum. Perfom. **2**, 201–223 (1989)
16. Kyllonen, P.C., Woltz, D.J.: Role of cognitive factors in the acquisition of cognitive skill. In: Kanfer, R., Ackerman, P.L., Cudeck, R. (eds.) Abilities, Motivation and Methodology: The Minnesota Symposium on Learning and Individual Differences, pp. 239–268. Lawrence Erlbaum Associates, Hillsdale (1989)
17. Ackerman, P.L.: Determinants of individual differences during skill acquisition: cognitive abilities and information processing. J. Exp. Psychol. Gen. **117**, 288–318 (1988)
18. Ackerman, P.L.: New developments in understanding skilled performance. Curr. Dir. Psychol. Sci. **16**, 235–239 (2007)
19. Ackerman, P.L., Cianciolo, A.T.: Cognitive, perceptual-speed, and psychomotor determinants of individual differences during skill acquisition. J. Exp. Psychol. Appl. **6**, 259–290 (2000)
20. Ackerman, P.L.: Predicting individual differences in complex skill acquisition: dynamics of ability determinants. J. Appl. Psychol. **77**, 598–614 (1992)
21. Ackerman, P.L., Cianciolo, A.T.: Ability and task constraint determinants of complex task performance. J. Exp. Psychol. Appl. **8**, 194–208 (2002)
22. Keehner, M., Lippa, Y., Montello, D.R., Tendick, F., Hegarty, M.: Learning a spatial skill for surgery: how the contributions of abilities change with practice. Appl. Cognit. Psychol. **20**, 487–503 (2006)
23. Ackerman, P.L., Beier, M.: Further explorations of perceptual speed abilities in the context of assessment methods, cognitive abilities, and individual differences during skill acquisition. J. Exp. Psychol. Appl. **13**, 249–272 (2007)
24. Cowan, N.: The magical mystery four: how is working memory capacity limited, and why? Curr. Dir. Psychol. Sci. **19**, 51–57 (2010)
25. Newell, A., Rosenbloom, P.S.: Mechanisms of skill acquisition and the law of practice. In: Anderson, J.R. (ed.) Cognitive Skills and Their Acquisition, pp. 1–56. Lawrence Erlbaum Associates, Hillsdale (1981)
26. Sweller, J.: Element interactivity and intrinsic, extraneous, and germane cognitive load. Educ. Psychol. Rev. **22**, 123–138 (2010)
27. Fisk, A.D., Schneider, W.: Category and word search: generalizing search principles to complex processing. J. Exp. Psychol. Learn. Mem. Cogn. **9**, 177–195 (1983)
28. Schneider, W., Fisk, A.D.: Degree of consistent training: improvements in search performance and automatic process development. Perc. Psychophys. **31**, 160–168 (1982)
29. Boot, W.R., Blakely, D.P., Simons, D.J.: Do action video games improve perception and cognition? Front. Psychol. **2**, 1–6 (2011)
30. Poels, K., van den Hoogen, W., Ijsselsteijn, W., de Kort, Y.: Pleasure to play, arousal to stay: the effect of player emotions on digital game preferences and playing time. Cyberpsychol. Behav. Soc. Netw. **15**, 1–6 (2012)
31. Green, C.S., Pouget, A., Bavelier, D.: Improved probabilistic inference as a general learning mechanism with action video games. Curr. Biol. **20**, 1573–1579 (2010)
32. Ohler, P., Nieding, G.: Why play? an evolutionary perspective. In: Vorderer, P., Bryant, J. (eds.) Playing Video Games. Motives, Responses, and Consequences, pp. 101–113. Lawrence Erlbaum Associates, New York (2006)
33. Klimmt, C., Hartmann, T., Frey, A.: Effectance and control as determinants of video game enjoyment. Cyberpsychol. Behav. **10**, 845–847 (2007)
34. Gugerty, L.J.: Situation awareness during driving: explicit and implicit knowledge in dynamic spatial memory. J. Exp. Psychol. Appl. **3**, 42–66 (1997)

35. Underwood, G.: Visual attention and the transition from novice to advanced driver. Ergon. **50**, 1235–1249 (2007)
36. Beullens, K., Roe, K., van den Bulck, J.: Excellent gamer, excellent driver? The impact of adolescents' video game playing on driving behavior: a two-wave panel study. Accid. Anal. Prev. **43**, 58–65 (2011)
37. Fischer, P., Kubitzki, J., Guter, S., Frey, D.: Virtual driving and risk taking: do racing games increase risk-taking cognitions, affect, and behaviors? J. Exp. Psychol. Appl. **13**, 22–31 (2007)
38. Kastenmüller, A., Fischer, P., Fischer, J.: Video racing games increase actual health-related risk-taking behavior. Psychol. Pop. Media Cult. **3**, 190–194 (2014)
39. Beullens, K., van den Bulck, J.: Predicting young drivers' car crashes: the role of music video viewing and the playing of driving games. Results from a prospective cohort study. Media Psychol. **16**, 88–114 (2013)
40. Fischer, P., Greitemeyer, T., Morton, T., Kastenmüller, A., Postmes, T., Frey, D., et al.: The racing-game effect: why do video racing games increase risk-taking inclinations? Pers. Soc. Psychol. Bull. **35**, 1395–1409 (2009)
41. Vingilis, E., Seeley, J., Wiesenthal, D.L., Wickens, C.M., Fischer, P., Mann, R.E.: Street racing video games and risk-taking driving: an Internet survey of automobile enthusiasts. Accid. Anal. Prev. **50**, 1–7 (2013)
42. Buckley, K.E., Anderson, C.A.: A theoretical model of the effects and consequences of playing video games. In: Vorderer, P., Bryant, J. (eds.) Playing Video Games – Motives, Responses, and Consequences, pp. 363–378. Lawrence Erlbaum Associates, Mahwah (2006)
43. Johnson, D., Gardner, J., Wiles, J., Sweetser, P., Hollingsworth, K.: The inherent appeal of physically controlled peripherals. In: Nakatsu, R., Hoshino, J. (eds.) Entertainment Computing. IFIP, vol. 112, pp. 371–378. Springer, Boston (2003)
44. Limperos, A.M., Schmierbach, M.G., Kegerise, A.D., Dardis, F.E.: Gaming across different consoles: exploring the influence of control scheme on game-player enjoyment. Cyberpsychol. Behav. Soc. Netw. **14**, 345–350 (2011)
45. McMahan, R.P., Alon, A.J., Lazem, S., Beaton, R.J., Machaj, D., Schaefer, M., et al.: Evaluating natural interaction techniques in video games. In: 2010 IEEE Symposium on 3D User Interfaces (3DUI), pp. 11–14 (2010)
46. Polyphony Digital: Gran Turismo 6 (2013)
47. Brickenkamp, R.: Test d2. Aufmerksamkeits-Belastungs-Test. Hogrefe, Göttingen (2002)
48. Green, C.S., Bavelier, D.: Action video game modifies visual selective attention. Nature **423**, 534–537 (2003)
49. Ball, K., Owsley, C.: The useful field of view test: a new technique for evaluating age-related declines in visual function. J. Am. Optom. Assoc. **64**, 71–79 (1993)
50. Iversen, H.: Risk-taking attitudes and risky driving behavior. Transp. Res. Part F Traffic Psychol. Behav. **7**, 135–150 (2004)
51. Weber, R., Popova, L.: Testing equivalence in communication research: theory and application. Commun. Methods Meas. **6**, 190–213 (2012)
52. Kass, S.J., Cole, K.S., Stanny, C.J.: Effects of distraction and experience on situation awareness and simulated driving. Transp. Res. Part F Traffic Psychol. Behav. **10**, 321–329 (2007)
53. Underwood, G., Chapman, P., Brocklehurst, N., Underwood, J., Crundall, D.: Visual attention while driving: sequences of eye fixations made by experienced and novice drivers. Ergon. **46**, 629–646 (2003)

Inspecting Quality of Games Designed for Learning Programming

Tihomir Orehovački[1(✉)] and Snježana Babić[2]

[1] Faculty of Organization and Informatics, University of Zagreb,
Pavlinska 2, 42000 Varaždin, Croatia
tihomir.orehovacki@foi.hr
[2] Polytechnic of Rijeka, Trpimirova 2/V, 51000 Rijeka, Croatia
snjezana.babic@veleri.hr

Abstract. Educational games are specific piece of slow technology that enables students to enhance their competences through fun and play. Taking into account their features, games are widely used in diverse educational settings, including programming. This paper discusses findings of the empirical study that was carried out with an objective to examine quality of two educational games meant for learning programming concepts. Participants in the study were students from two Croatian higher education institutions. Subjective data was collected with pre- and post-use online questionnaires whereas objective data was gathered with reports in the form of in-game progress screenshots. The analysis of collected data uncovered: (1) to what extent students with different background knowledge differ in their perception of programming and attitudes towards using games for educational purposes, and (2) which pragmatic and hedonic facets of quality are relevant for the assessment of games designed for learning programming.

Keywords: Educational games · Quality evaluation · Learning programming · Subjective and objective measuring instruments · Empirical findings

1 Introduction

Quality refers to the extent to which a piece of software meets user needs or expectations [13]. In the current international standard on software quality evaluation [14], these needs are represented by two quality models. The first one is product quality model which consist of 31 attributes that constitute eight categories aimed for measuring static software properties. The second one is quality in use model which is decomposed into five categories that deal with the assessment of the outcomes of the interaction with a software in a particular context of use. Evaluation is a systematic process of measuring the value and importance of software features [9]. Apart from being used for the identification of certain usability issues during the interaction with the software, evaluation is also meant for testing the availability of software functionalities as well as for measuring the user experience [7]. Consequently, quality evaluation should not be reserved only for the end of the development process but has to be carried out continuously through all stages of the software life cycle.

© Springer International Publishing Switzerland 2015
P. Zaphiris and A. Ioannou (Eds.): LCT 2015, LNCS 9192, pp. 620–631, 2015.
DOI: 10.1007/978-3-319-20609-7_58

Computer games are specific breed of software. Given that their features reflect hedonic facets of quality, computer games are often referred to as an example of slow technology [24]. The employment of computer games in educational settings enables students to acquire new knowledge and skills through fun and play which increases their motivation throughout the learning process [30]. This is because computer games stimulate interaction which is one of the essential aspects of the learning process [31]. Educational computer games must be designed in a way to serve as a valuable pedagogical tool for enhancing learning outcomes [34]. According to Sharda [32], design of the educational content, the plot, and the game itself represents a foundation for the assessment of user experience. In that respect, when development of educational computer games is considered, special attention should be paid to the efficient interplay of these three design domains. Taking into account that educational games are useful means for learning and teaching programming concepts [31], a number of them have been developed specifically for programming courses. Detailed overview of educational games focused on teaching programming can be found in [19].

This paper has several objectives. First, to discover to what extent students with different educational background differ in their perception of programming as a discipline at university level and in their attitude towards employing games for the purpose of learning programming concepts. Second, to examine if there is a significant difference between programming novices and experienced programmers in terms of their in-game progress within given time interval. Third, to identify which subjective and objective quality attributes are relevant for the assessment of games designed for learning programming.

The remainder of the paper is organized as follows. Next section offers overview of relevant advances in the field. Brief description of all constructs which constitute research framework is provided in the third section. Findings of an empirical study are reported in the fourth section. Practical implications of our work and study limitations are discussed in the last section.

2   Rationale and Background

Recent HCI literature offers a number of studies aimed for evaluating the various aspects of quality in the context of web sites [8], Web 2.0 applications [27], cloud based applications [23], mashups [4], mashup tools [28], mobile applications [21], and educational artefacts [29]. On the other hand, current research related to educational games is mostly focused on exploring predictors of their adoption while studies on quality assessment are rather rare. Drawing on motivation theory [6], Long [18] found that intrinsic motivation factors such as expectation of fun and opportunity to learn new programming skills significantly contribute to users' behavior related to playing the educational game Robocode whereas extrinsic factors ("to win the game", "to win the prize in the con-test" and "to gain peer recognition") proved to be less important in that respect. With an objective to examine hedonic quality of slow technology (such as computer game Braid), Orehovački et al. [24] have proposed a model which reflects an interplay among constructs adopted from expectation-confirmation theory [20], theory of flow [3], and technology acceptance model [5]. Outcomes of the study carried out by Tao et al. [33] revealed that in the context of business simulation game: (1) perceived attractiveness significantly contributes to perceived ease of use and perceived usefulness; (2) perceived usefulness has a significant influence on learning perform- ance; (3) perceived playfulness is significantly affected by perceived attractiveness and perceived ease of use; (4) learning performance impacts confirmation of expectations; and (5) learning performance and playfulness are significant predictors of students' satisfaction. As a follow up, Liao and Wang [17] discovered that learning motivation is a strong predictor of learning expectations which in turn together with perceived playfulness contribute to the perceived learning performance, learning confirmation is affected by perceived learning performance, while learning expectation, learning confirmation, and perceived learning performance have strong influence on learning satisfaction. By employing AttrakDiff2 questionnaire [11] and a scale adapted from ARCS motivational design model [15], Zaharias and Chatzeparaskevaidou [36] found that pragmatic quality, hedonic quality stimulation, hedonic quality identification, and attraction are significant predictors of students' motivation to learn. Finally, Ibrahim et al. [12] discovered that only two (effort expectancy and attitude) of four constructs introduced in the UTAUT [35] model, significantly affect students' preferences related to online educational games.

3   Research Framework

The success of certain technology greatly depends on users' continuance intentions and satisfaction that is influenced by confirmation of their expectations with respect to the technology employment [25]. The research framework introduced in this paper is composed of attributes that reflect students' attitudes towards playing games and programming as well as of attributes meant for measuring quality of educational games designed for learning programming concepts.

Based on the model proposed in [27] and refined in [26], a set of pragmatic and hedonic quality attributes was identified and adopted to the context of educational games. The extent to which students are ready to adopt games for the purpose of learning programming concepts was evaluated with attributes aimed for measuring playfulness, satisfaction, aesthetics, and loyalty. Quality of educational games considered from the perspective of a system was examined with items meant for assessing consistency. Attributes such as helpfulness, reliability, and feedback were employed for exploring quality of interaction between selected games and users. The extent to which the use of educational games enhances students' performances in learning programming concepts was investigated with attributes designed for measuring effectiveness, usefulness and efficiency. The effortlessness in employing educational games for learning programming was assessed with attributes meant for measuring minimal action, minimal memory load, accessibility, ease of use, learnability, memorability, and understandability.

Scales for measuring users' attitudes towards use, self-efficacy, gameplay anxiety, programming anxiety, perceived behavioural control, result demonstrability, and the perception of programming complexity were adopted from UTAUT model [35].

The degree to which educational games involved in an empirical study are distinctive among games with the same purpose was determined with items meant for measuring uniqueness [22]. The level to which students like to inform themselves and play new games was identified with items assigned to the attribute "resistance to changes" [22]. Dimensions of popularity in the context of educational games for learning programming were explored with items meant for measuring reputation [22]. The extent to which students believe that employment of games can provide them with opportunities for learning programming concepts was measured with items proposed in [12]. Preferences for using games in educational ecosystem, which appeared to be strong predictor of learning opportunities, were evaluated with items proposed by Bourgonjon et al. [1]. Finally, the intrinsic motivational factor which reflects the degree of difficulty and challenge a user experiences when playing a game was measured with items that were adopted from Hainey et al. [10].

4   Results

Participants. A total of 175 subjects were involved in the study. The sample was comprised of 61.71 % male and 38.29 % female participants. They ranged in age from 18 to 45 years (M = 19.72, SD = 2.286). Majority of them (70.86 %) were students at Polytechnic of Rijeka (POLYRI) while remaining 29.14 % studied at University of Zagreb, Faculty of Organization and Informatics (FOI). Most of the sample (96.57 %) were full-time students. Majority of study participants (56.01 %) play computer games at least once a week where 54.86 % of them spend between one and three hours a week on a game play. Study participants are also loyal players of mobile games. Most of them (51.43 %) play mobile games between once and twice a week where 36.57 % of students spend less than an hour on interaction with mobile games. Only 20.58 % and 11.43 % of research subjects play computer and mobile games, respectively, on daily basis.

Procedure. Prior to the implementation of the study, FOI students have completed one course related to the programming and at the time when the study took place they were enrolled in additional two programming courses. In that respect, they can be referred to as experienced programmers. On the other hand, general programming concepts were introduced to POLYRI students several weeks before the study was carried out. Therefore, they can be appointed as programming novices.

The study was composed of three main parts. At the beginning, participants were briefly informed about the purpose of the study which was followed by the explanation of the procedure that was employed. The participants were then asked to complete a pre-use questionnaire that consisted of 60 items related to research subjects' demographics, frequency of using computer and mobile games, their interest for advances in the field as well as prior experience in playing games, their perception about programming and preferences related to the use of games in educational ecosystem, and perceived fear of programming and playing games. Thereafter, students were asked to play each of two educational games for 30 minutes. The first one was LightBot 2.0[1] in which study

---

[1] http://armorgames.com/play/6061/light-bot-20.

participants had to use programming logic to solve assignments that were presented in the form of puzzles. The second one was CodeCombat[2] in which research subjects had to write and execute snippets of code in Python programming language in order to solve implemented quests. Examples of assignments from both games are shown in Fig. 1. As soon as the predefined time for playing each game had elapsed, participants had to make a report in the form of screenshot that illustrated which level they managed to reach. Examples of these reports for both games are presented in Fig. 2. At the end of the study, participants were asked to complete a post-use questionnaire that was composed of 150 items related to 28 different dimensions of quality adapted to the context of games designed for learning programming.

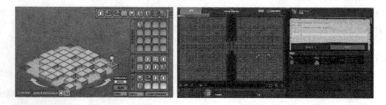

Fig. 1. Examples of assignments which constitute games aimed for learning programming (left: LightBot 2.0, right: CodeCombat).

Fig. 2. Examples of screenshots that indicate which level particular student reached within predefined time interval (left: LightBot 2.0, right: CodeCombat).

Apparatus. Both pre- and post-use questionnaires were administered online using the KwikSurveys[3] questionnaire builder. Responses to the questionnaire items were scored on a four point Likert scale (1– strongly agree, 4 – strongly disagree). The sum of responses to items assigned to particular attribute represent a composite measure which reflects relevant quality dimension. Differences between POLYRI and FOI students in terms of frequency of playing computer games, their prior experience with and preferences for computer games, and perceived anxiety related to programming and gameplay were explored with Mann-Whitney U statistics. The reason why we employed this non-parametric alternative to the independent t-test is because results of Shapiro-Wilk Tests uncovered that variables which constituted pre-use questionnaire together with variables that reflect game level which students reached within predefined time interval

---

[2] https://codecombat.com/.
[3] https://kwiksurveys.com.

significantly deviate from a normal distribution (p < .05). The analysis of data collected with post-use questionnaire adopted a within-subjects design contrasting two games meant for learning programming. Considering that the results of Shapiro-Wilk Tests revealed that at least one of the variables in a pairwise comparison violates the assumption of normality in data (p < .05), differences between evaluated games were examined by means of Wilcoxon Signed-Rank Tests. Taking into account the afore-mentioned, all reported results are expressed as median values. According to Cohen [2], values of .10, .30, or .50 for the size of an effect (r) can be, as a rule of thumb, interpreted as small, medium, or large, respectively.

Findings. The analysis of data collected with the pre-use questionnaire revealed that FOI students (Mdn = 13) are in general significantly less resistant (U = 2456.50, p < .05, r = −.18) to technological advances in terms of novel computer games than POLYRI students (Mdn = 14). More specifically, findings indicate that FOI students (Mdn = 2) like to discuss (U = 2505.50, p < .05, r = −.17) and browse information (U = 2498.00, p < .05, r = −.17) about new computer games significantly more often than POLYRI students do (Mdn = 3). On the other hand, there was no significant difference between these two groups of students (Mdn = 2) in terms of the extent to which they are interested in novel computer games (U = 2801.50, ns, r = −.09), the degree to which they are willing to inform themselves about new computer games (U = 2605.50, ns, r = −.15), the level to which they like to try novel computer games (U = 2785.50, ns, r = −.10), and the extent to which they are inclined to change a game they play in their leisure time (U = 2657.00, ns, r = −.13). According to the study results, FOI students (Mdn = 11) have significantly more experience (U = 2291.00, p < .005, r = −.22) in playing computer games than POLYRI students (Mdn = 14) have. Namely, compared to POLYRI students (Mdn = 2, 3, and 3, respectively), FOI students (Mdn = 2, 3, and 2, respectively) like to play computer games significantly more (U = 2424.00, p < .01, r = −.20), spend significantly more time in interaction with computer games (U = 2436.50, p = .01, r = −.19), and play significantly more diverse genres of computer games (U = 2586.50, p < .05, r = −.22). However, no significant difference was found between these two groups of students (Mdn = 2 and 3, respectively) in terms of the perceived frequency of playing computer games (U = 2726.00, ns, r = −.12) and perception of themselves as game play addicts (U = 2599.00, ns, r = −.15). Significant difference between FOI (Mdn = 4) and POLYRI students (Mdn = 6) was also found in terms of the extent to which people surrounding them play computer games (U = 1774.00, p < .0001, r = −.36). The set forth is particularly true for colleagues (U = 1481.50, p < .0001, r = −.48), friends (U = 2250.00, p = .001, r = −.26), and acquaintances (U = 2578.50, p < .05, r = −.17) of FOI students (Mdn = 1, 1, and 2, respectively).

The study results imply that FOI and POLYRI students (Mdn = 9) do not differ significantly (U = 2637.50, ns, r = -.13) in terms of the degree to which the reputation of a computer game affects their decision to play it. This is specifically true for the number of active game players (U = 3031.00, ns, r = -.04) as well as for position of a particular game on top lists (U = 3046.00, ns, r = -.03). However, it appeared that developer's name has significantly higher impact (U = 2277.50, p = .001, r = -.24) on

POLYRI students' decision (Mdn = 3) to play a particular game than it has on decision making process in that respect of FOI students (Mdn = 4). It was also discovered that FOI students (Mdn = 5) in general have significantly stronger (U = 1898.00, p < . 0001, r = -.32) preference for the implementation of computer games in the educational settings than POLYRI students (Mdn = 6). Namely, significantly more FOI students (Mdn = 2, 2, and 2, respectively) was delighted with the idea of employing computer games for the educational purposes (U = 2400.00, p < .01, r = -.20) and would enroll (U = 1763.50, p < .0001, r = -.37) and actively participate (U = 2085.50, p < .0001, r = -.28) in courses on which games are played as a part of a syllabus. In general, there is no significant difference (U = 3038.50, ns, r = -.03) between FOI and POLYRI students (Mdn = 16) in terms of their reasoning about programming proficiency which is particularly affected by the fact that both groups of students (Mdn = 3) believe that intelligence plays an important role in the process of learning programming concepts (U = 2745.00, ns, r = -.12). However, significantly more POLYRI students (Mdn = 2, 2, and 2, respectively) believe that programming is a complex discipline (U = 2421.50, p < .01, r = -.21), that is difficult to learn programming concepts (U = 2001.00, p < . 0001, r = -.31), and that one have to write large amount of programming code in order to solve relatively simple assignments (U = 1453.00, p < .0001, r = -.46). On the other hand, significantly more FOI students (Mdn = 1, 1, 1, and 1, respectively) think that programming is a comprehensive discipline (U = 2539.00, p < .05, r = -.18), that it requires a special way of thinking (U = 2045.50, p < .0001, r = -.31), that it must be learned with understanding (U = 2302.00, p = .001, r = -.25), and that in cannot be learned by heart (U = 1609.50, p < .0001, r = -.43).

Both POLYRI and FOI students (Mdn = 9) agree that educational background has an important role in learning programming concepts at university level (U = 3039.00, ns, r = -.03). The set forth especially refers to the knowledge of mathematics (Mdn = 2, U = 3137.50, ns, r = -.01). However, significantly more POLYRI students (Mdn = 2) believe that prior knowledge strongly affects the understanding of programming concepts (U = 2251.50, p = .001, r = -.24). On the other hand, significantly more FOI students (Mdn = 2) perceive programming as an interdisciplinary mastery (U = 2457.00, p < .005, r = -.23). The analysis of collected data revealed that POLYRI students (Mdn = 15) generally have significantly higher level of perceived programming anxiety (U = 1841.50, p < .0001, r = -.33) than FOI students (Mdn = 18). This is because significantly more POLYRI students (Mdn = 3, 3, 3, 3, and 3, respectively) feel nervous (U = 2400.00, p < .01, r = -.20), discomfort (U = 1938.00, p < .0001, r = -.33), agitation (U = 2222.00, p = .001, r = -.25), worry (U = 2513.50, p < .05, r = -.17), and aversion (U = 1547.00, p < .0001, r = -.43) when thinking about programming. It was also discovered that POLYRI students (Mdn = 12) in general feel significantly higher level (U = 1891.00, p < .0001, r = -.32) of game play anxiety than FOI students (Mdn = 15). Namely, significantly more POLYRI students (Mdn = 2, 2, 2, and 3, respectively) were worried that they will not be able to successfully complete assignments which constitute games aimed for learning programming (U = 1803.00, p < .0001, r = -.36), that the level of their prior knowledge will reduce their productivity in completing game assignments (U = 1816.00, p < .0001, r = -.35), that they will not be able to complete game assignments from the first attempt (U = 2268.50, p = .001, r = -.24), and that they will not be able to concentrate on solving quests implemented in games (U = 2262.00, p = .001, r = -.24). Finally, FOI and POLYRI students (Mdn = 3) were equally worried that, compared to them, their peers will achieve better results in solving game assignments (U = 2634.50, ns, r = -.14).

The analysis of data collected from screenshots revealed that FOI students (Mdn = 11) were significantly more successful (U = 555.50, p < .0001, r = -.65) in completing assignments which constitute Light Bot 2.0 game than POLYRI students (Mdn = 8) were. It was also discovered that POLYRI students (Mdn = 7) completed significantly lower count of levels (U = 1108.00, p < .0001, r = -.51) of CodeCombat game than FOI students (Mdn = 14) did.

A Wilcoxon Signed-Rank Test showed that study participants have positive attitude towards the employment of both LightBot 2.0 and CodeCombat (Z = -.536, p = .592) for the purpose of learning programming concepts at the university level. It was also found that LightBot 2.0 (Mdn = 18) enhances the perceived self-efficacy of players to the significantly higher extent (Z = -2.573, p = .01, r = -.14) than CodeCombat (Mdn = 14). Moreover, it appeared that is significantly easier (Z = -3.417, p = .001, r = -.18) to figure out how to solve quests which constitute CodeCombat (Mdn = 6) than to learn how to complete assignments that are implemented into LightBot 2.0 (Mdn = 6). On the other hand, a Wilcoxon Signed-Rank Test did not elicit a statistically significant difference (Z = -.454, p = .650) between LightBot 2.0 (Mdn = 7) and CodeCombat (Mdn = 7) in terms of the degree to which is easy to memorize and recall how to solve game assignments. The analysis of data revealed that study participants had significantly less difficulties (Z = -3.039, p = .002, r = -.16) in completing quests integrated into CodeCombat (Mdn = 8) than solving assignments that are included into LightBot 2.0 (Mdn = 9). Study results also imply that players had to make significantly less physical effort related to the frequency of using a keyboard and mouse (Z = -9.191, p = .000, r = -.49) when they were completing tasks which are part of the CodeCombat (Mdn = 13) than when they were addressing assignments that are implemented into LightBot 2.0 (Mdn = 15). On the other hand, the study participants had to invest significantly more (Z = -4.722, p = .000, r = -.25) mental effort in terms of thinking and decision making when they were dealing with quests that constitute CodeCombat (Mdn = 17) than when they were solving assignments that are included into LightBot 2.0 (Mdn = 16). It was also discovered that user interface of CodeCombat (Mdn = 10) has been perceived by players as significantly more visually appealing (Z = -1.996, p = .046, r = -.11) than those of LightBot 2.0 (Mdn = 10). Moreover, the analysis of collected data yielded that CodeCombat (Mdn = 6) and LightBot (Mdn = 6) do not differ significantly (Z = -.652, p = .515) in terms of distinctive features. However, it was discovered that LightBot 2.0 (Mdn = 10) employs significantly more uniform interface structure, design, and terminology (Z = -2.934, p = .003, r = -.16) than CodeCombat (Mdn = 10) does. Furthermore, it appeared that players perceived Code-Combat (Mdn = 9) as significantly less dependable, stable, and bug-free game (Z = -6.753, p = .000, r = -.36) than LightBot 2.0 (Mdn = 7).

According to the results of the analysis of data collected with the post-use questionnaire, LightBot 2.0 (Mdn = 5) is significantly more (Z = -3.339, p = .001, r = -. 18) usable to players with the widest range of characteristics and capabilities than

CodeCombat (Mdn = 5). However, LightBot 2.0 (Mdn = 7) and CodeCombat (Mdn = 6) do not differ significantly (Z = -.895, p = .371) in the extent to which their interface functionalities are clear and unambiguous to players. On the other hand, it was found that CodeCombat (Mdn = 10) offers significantly better and more diverse help materials (Z = -2.741, p = .006, r = -.15) than LightBot 2.0 (Mdn = 11) does. In addition, the quality of messages provided by CodeCombat (Mdn = 13) is significantly higher (Z = -2.679, p = .007, r = -.14) than those shown by LightBot 2.0 (Mdn = 14). Games meant for learning programming (Mdn = 9) do not differ significantly (Z = -. 262, p = .793) in the degree to which they reduce the amount of time needed for learning specific programming concept. There was also no significant difference (Z = -1.854, p = .064) between evaluated games (Mdn = 14) in the extent to which they improve player's effectiveness in learning programming concepts. Moreover, LightBot 2.0 (Mdn = 10) and CodeCombat (Mdn = 10) do not differ significantly (Z = -.441, p = .659) in the degree to which their use contributes to the improvement of programming skills and habits. The level of perceived external control over addressing assignments was not significantly affected (Z = -.654, p = .513) by educational game (Mdn = 8) that was employed for that purpose. Evaluated games (Mdn = 7) do not differ significantly (Z = -1.102, p = .270) in terms of perceived learning outcomes that are result of their employment. No significant difference (Z = -1.567, p = .117) exist between evaluated games (Mdn = 13) regarding learning opportunities (e.g. evolution of logical and critical thinking, personalization of learning process, etc.) they offer to their players. Moreover, it was found that quality of implemented assignments is not significantly influenced (Z = -1.290, p = .197) by the game (Mdn = 12) that was used for learning programming concepts. However, it appeared that LightBot 2.0 (Mdn = 7) was significantly more challenging (Z = -4.593, p = .000, r = -.25) for study participants than CodeCombat (Mdn = 6).

Games aimed for learning programming (Mdn = 8) do not differ significantly (Z = -.941, p = .347) in the extent to which they have met expectations of research subjects. Nevertheless, the study results uncovered that LightBot 2.0 (Mdn = 15) was significantly more successful (Z = -2.260, p = .024, r = -.12) in arousing participants' imagination and stimulating they creativity in completing assignments than Code-Combat (Mdn = 16) was. There was no significant difference (Z = -.729, p = .466) between LightBot 2.0 (Mdn = 11) and CodeCombat (Mdn = 12) in terms of the enjoyment the study participants experienced when they were dealing with implemented assignments. CodeCombat (Mdn = 9) and LightBot 2.0 (Mdn = 8) do not differ significantly (Z = -1.714, p = .086) in the extent to which they made an overall impression on research subjects. Finally, it appeared that LightBot 2.0 (Mdn = 16) and CodeCombat (Mdn = 17) do not differ significantly (Z = -1.478, p = .139) in the degree to which study participants are willing to play them regularly and recommend them to others. Considering all the aforementioned, no significant difference (Z = -.076, p = . 939) was found between CodeCombat (Mdn = 285) and LightBot 2.0 (Mdn = 287) in the overall perceived quality.

5 Discussion and Conclusion

This paper provides several contributions and implications to both scientific and professional communities. To begin with, the concept of quality introduced in current and relevant international standard [14] has been enhanced and adapted to the context of educational games. In addition, the validity of the employed research design and measuring instruments (reports in form of screenshots, pre- and post-use questionnaires) was empirically confirmed. Following the guidelines suggested by Lewis [16], the sensitivity of the pre-use questionnaire was explored through comparison of two groups of students which differed in terms of their prior knowledge related to programming whereas the sensitivity of reports and post-use questionnaire was examined by benchmarking two games meant for learning programming. All constructs that have met the criteria of sensitivity have shown small, medium, or large effect in size thus confirming the validity of measuring instruments.

Drawing on the results of validity testing, relevance of dimensions in testing differences among students with different educational background and examining games meant for learning programming was determined. Measure that reflects the number of levels which can be completed within predefined time interval revealed large in size differences between the groups of study participants. Items meant for measuring the influence of subjective norms on adoption of a game, programming anxiety, preference for the implementation of games in educational settings, and game play anxiety elicited medium in size differences between the groups of research subjects. Constructs that measure how often participants play games and to what extent they are interested in novel games uncovered small in size differences between groups they belong to. Measures that indicate to what degree students perceive programming as complex and inter-disciplinary proficiency as well as to what degree reputation of a game affects their decision to play it have not detected significant differences between groups of study participants.

In the context of the quality assessment, it appeared that: (a) 3.57 % of proposed constructs revealed large (minimal action) and 3.57 % medium (reliability) in size differences between evaluated games; (b) 7.14 % of introduced constructs (minimal memory load and challenge) uncovered between small and medium in size effects between educational games; (c) 32.14 % of employed constructs (learnability, accessibility, ease of use, consistency, helpfulness, feedback, self-efficacy, and playfulness) elicited small in size differences between games; and (d) 53.57 % of remaining constructs (attitude towards behavior, memorability, uniqueness, understandability, efficiency, effectiveness, usefulness, external control, result demonstrability, learning opportunities, quality of assignments, confirmation of expectations, pleasure, satisfaction, and loyalty) did not show significant differences between evaluated games.

As in the case of most empirical studies, work presented in this paper has limitations. The first one is related to the homogeneity of study participants. Although students are representative users of educational games, heterogeneous sample could have importantly different perception about the quality of games that are used for learning programming concepts. The second one concerns the generalizability of reported findings. Considering that each genre of educational games has specific features which might affect one or several quality dimensions, the empirical results should be interpreted with caution. Taking the aforementioned into account, further studies should be carried out in order to draw sound conclusions.

References

1. Bourgonjon, J., Valcke, M., Soetaert, R., De Wever, B., Schellens, T.: Parental acceptance of digital game-based learning. Comput. Educ. **57**(1), 1434–1444 (2011)
2. Cohen, J.: A power primer. Psychol. Bull. **112**(1), 155–159 (1992)
3. Csikszentmihalyi, M.: Beyond Boredom and Anxiety. Jossey-Bass, San Francisco (1975)
4. Daniel, F., Matera, M.: Quality in mashup development. In: Daniel, F., Matera, M. (eds.) Mashups: Concepts, Models, and Architectures, pp. 269–291. Springer, Heidelberg (2014)
5. Davis, F.D.: Perceived usefulness, perceived ease of use, and user acceptance of information technology. MIS Q. **13**(3), 319–340 (1989)
6. Deci, E.L.: Intrinsic Motivation. Plenum Press, New York (1975)
7. Dix, A., Finlay, J., Abowd, G.D., Beale, R.: Human-Computer Interaction, 3rd edn. Prentice-Hall, Haddington (2004)
8. Fogli, D., Guida, G.: A practical approach to the assessment of quality in use of corporate web sites. J. Syst. Softw. **99**, 52–65 (2015)
9. Gena, C., Weibelzahl, S.: Usability Engineering for the Adaptive Web. In: Brusilovsky, P., Kobsa, A., Nejdl, W. (eds.) Adaptive Web 2007. LNCS, vol. 4321, pp. 720–762. Springer, Heidelberg (2007)
10. Hainey, T., Westera, W., Connolly, T.M., Boyle, L., Baxter, G., Beeby, R.B., Soflano, M.: Students' attitudes toward playing games and using games in education: Comparing Scotland and the Netherlands. Comput. Educ. **69**, 474–484 (2013)
11. Hassenzahl, M., Burmester, M., Koller, F.: AttrakDiff: ein fragebogen zur messung wahrgenommener hedonischer und pragmatischer qualität. In: Ziegler, J., Szwillus, G. (eds.) Mensch & Computer 2003: Interaktion in Bewegung, pp. 187–196. B.G. Teubner, Stuttgart (2003)
12. Ibrahim, R., Wahab, S., Khalil, K., Jaafar, A.: Student perceptions of educational games in higher education: An empirical study. Issues Inf. Syst. **12**(1), 120–133 (2011)
13. Institute of Electrical and Electronics Engineers (IEEE) std. 610.12-1990. IEEE standard glossary of software engineering terminology (1990)
14. ISO/IEC 25010: Systems and software engineering - Systems and software Quality Requirements and Evaluation (SQuaRE) - System and software quality models (2011)
15. Keller, J.M.: Development and use of the ARCS model of motivational design. J. Instr. Dev. **10**(3), 2–10 (1987)
16. Lewis, J.R.: IBM computer usability satisfaction questionnaires: psychometric evaluation and instructions for use. Int. J. Human-Comput. Interact. **7**(1), 57–78 (1995)
17. Liao, Y.W., Wang, Y.S.: Investigating the factors affecting students' continuance intention to use business simulation games in the context of digital learning. In: International Conference on Innovation, Management and Service, pp. 119–124. IACSIT Press, Singapore (2011)
18. Long, J.: Just for fun: using programming games in software programming training and education. J. Inf. Technol. Educ.: Res. **6**, 279–290 (2007)
19. Malliarakis, C., Satratzemi, M., Xinogalos, S.: Educational games for teaching computer programming. In: Karagiannidis, C., Politis, P., Karasavvidis, I. (eds.) Research on e-Learning and ICT in Education, pp. 87–98. Springer, Heidelberg (2014)

20. Oliver, R.L.: A cognitive model for the antecedents and consequences of satisfaction. J. Mark. Res. **17**(4), 460–469 (1980)
21. Olsina, L., Santos, L., Lew, P.: Evaluating mobileapp usability: a holistic quality approach. In: Casteleyn, S., Rossi, G., Winckler, M. (eds.) ICWE 2014. LNCS, vol. 8541, pp. 111–129. Springer, Heidelberg (2014)
22. Orehovački, T.: Methodology for evaluating the quality in use of Web 2.0 applications, Ph.D. thesis. University of Zagreb, Faculty of Organization & Informatics, Varaždin (2013)
23. Orehovački, T.: Perceived quality of cloud based applications for collaborative writing. In: Pokorny, J., et al. (eds.) Information Systems Development – Business Systems and Services: Modeling and Development, pp. 575–586. Springer, Heidelberg (2011)
24. Orehovački, T., Al Sokkar, A.A., Derboven, J., Khan, A.: Exploring the hedonic quality of slow technology. In: CHI 2013 workshop on Changing Perspectives of Time in HCI, http://bib.irb.hr/datoteka/617623.workshop_paper_final3.pdf (2013)
25. Orehovački, T., Babić, S.: Predicting students' continuance intention related to the use of collaborative Web 2.0 applications. In: Proceedings of the 23rd International Conference on Information Systems Development, pp. 112–122. Faculty of Organization and Informatics, Varaždin (2014)
26. Orchovački, T., Babić, S., Jadrić, M.: Exploring the validity of an instrument to measure the perceived quality in use of Web 2.0 applications with educational potential. In: Zaphiris, P., Ioannou, A. (eds.) LCT 2014, Part I. LNCS, vol. 8523, pp. 192–203. Springer, Heidelberg (2014)
27. Orehovački, T., Granić, A., Kermek, D.: Evaluating the Perceived and Estimated Quality in Use of Web 2.0 Applications. J. Syst. Softw. **86**(12), 3039–3059 (2013)
28. Orehovački, T., Granollers, T.: Subjective and objective assessment of mashup tools. In: Marcus, A. (ed.) DUXU 2014, Part I. LNCS, vol. 8517, pp. 340–351. Springer, Heidelberg (2014)
29. Orehovački, T., Žajdela Hrustek, N.: Development and validation of an instrument to measure the usability of educational artifacts created with Web 2.0 applications. In: Marcus, A. (ed.) DUXU 2013, Part I. LNCS, vol. 8012, pp. 369–378. Springer, Heidelberg (2013)
30. Prensky, M.: Computer games and learning: digital game-based learning. Handb. comput. Game stud. **18**, 97–122 (2005)
31. Seng, W.Y., Yatim, M.H.M.: Computer game as learning and teaching tool for object oriented programming in higher education institution. Procedia – Soc. Behav. Sci. **123**, 215–224 (2014)
32. Sharda, N.K.: Designing, Using and Evaluating Educational Games: Challenges, Some Solutions and Future Research. http://ceur-ws.org/Vol-386/p08.pdf (2008)
33. Tao, Y.H., Cheng, C.J., Sun, S.Y.: What influences college students to continue using business simulation games? Taiwan Experience. Comput. Educ. **53**(3), 929–939 (2009)
34. Torrente, J., Del Blanco, Á., Marchiori, E.J., Moreno-Ger, P., Fernández-Manjón, B.: < e-Adventure >: Introducing educational games in the learning process. In: 1st Annual Engineering Education Conference (EDUCON), pp. 1121–1126. IEEE, Madrid (2010)
35. Venkatesh, V., Morris, M.G., Davis, G.B., Davis, F.D.: User acceptance of information technology: toward a unified view. MIS Q. **27**(3), 425–478 (2003)
36. Zaharias, P., Chatzeparaskevaidou, I.: Hedonic and pragmatic qualities as predictors for motivation to learn in serious educational games. In: 8th International Conference on the Foundations of Digital Games (FDG) (2013). http://www.fdg2013.org/program/workshops/papers/G4L2013/g4l2013_04.pdf

E-Learning and Serious Games

New Trends in Architectural and Urban Design Education

Francesc Valls[1(✉)], Ernest Redondo[1], and David Fonseca[2]

[1] Barcelona School of Architecture, UPC - BarcelonaTech, Barcelona, Spain
{francesc.valls,ernesto.redondo}@upc.edu
[2] Architecture School, La Salle Universitat Ramon Llull, Barcelona, Spain
fonsi@salle.url.edu

Abstract. The complexity of urban processes needs professionals trained in understanding and managing the design of its spaces and the implementation of urban policies. This paper discusses an educational methodology to complement the standard Project-Based Learning approach with an experience using serious games with gamification elements to stimulate critical thinking in urban planning and urban design students, to promote designing spaces more adaptable and usable for a wide range of users and situations of public life. The proposed methodology uses five "mini games" that place students in different situations: (1) finding an unknown landmark, (2) reaching goal avoiding obstacles, (3) navigating with artificial lighting, (4) simulating the point of view of a person with a disability, and (5) simulating group behaviour. As a secondary objective the experience will track the participants' behaviour to extract data to be incorporated into an agent-based model rule set.

Keywords: Serious games · Gamification · Simulation · E-Learning · Urban space

1 Introduction

As the total number of people living in cities increases, as well as the percentage of urban dwellers relative to people living in rural areas [1, p. 12], the necessity to improve the quality urban life becomes more important.

The formation of the city is unlike a manufacturing process; it is an artifact created by society, through the interactions between its inhabitants, consciously and unconsciously, with different levels of coordination, in a constant state of change, adapting itself over time.

Urban planning and urban design shape the complexity of the city, through building codes, housing policies or urban regulations; planners and designers establish the guidelines of what they think the city should be, but ultimately what the city will become depends on a number of factors: social, economic and historical. Urban planners and designers need to interpret the past of the city, know with precision its present state, and understand the nature of the factors that drive its processes to plan its future.

© Springer International Publishing Switzerland 2015
P. Zaphiris and A. Ioannou (Eds.): LCT 2015, LNCS 9192, pp. 632–643, 2015.
DOI: 10.1007/978-3-319-20609-7_59

Information about the past gives us valuable insight on the underlying mechanisms of the transformation of the city, usually in the form of historic maps that can be georeferenced to generate a timeline of its (physical) evolution. As we get closer to the present, historic data gets more rich and precise, especially since the generalization of digital storage technologies in the decade of 1980. Data about the present situation is vast and it is essential to filter, summarize and visualize them to be understood. Correctly interpreting the current state of the city allows planners to identify areas of improvement and anticipate future necessities, which is crucial considering the slow pace of urban transformation processes compared to the increasingly rapidly changing world.

Planning involves addressing the future challenges of the city. This requires the evaluation of multiple what-if scenarios, generally using informal mental models acquired by practitioners throughout their training, both academic and professional. However, the availability of (synthetic) formal models of urban phenomena, using knowledge of events in its past (to train or calibrate the model) applied to the information gathered about its current state, should be a valuable tool for urban management professionals; in their education, the use of models to explain urban phenomena should allow a deeper comprehension of the subject matter.

This paper explain an educational proposal using a serious games in a gamified educational environment to teach complex concepts regarding urban planning and design to architecture students. It is structured as follows: first the challenges of training professionals in urban planning and design are discussed, followed by an introduction to gamification and serious games, after which the proposed experience outline is discussed and the conclusions are presented.

2   Urban Planning and Urban Design Training

Cities are very complex, and it is precisely this complexity that makes them attractive and fascinates us. The morphology of the city is a multi-scale mosaic in which the architecture of buildings – which are themselves complex – interplay, articulating themselves through public spaces. This physical configuration of the built environment and its empty spaces not only affects the image of the city [2], but has implications on environmental factors such as the available solar radiation, the optimal mix of modes of transportation, the development of specific economic or residential activities in specific areas, the flow of energy, matter and information, as well as its safety.

Moreover, if grasping the complexity of the morphology of the city is a difficult task, understanding the myriad of events that take part simultaneously in the city and their interrelations is extremely difficult, even with today's technology.

In this scenario, education on topics related to urban planning (managing the development of the city) or urban design (shaping the elements of the city: buildings, streets and public spaces) needs to explain the concepts urban planners and designers handle in their professional practice. The educational strategy followed is usually Project-Based Learning (PBL), where students learn as they develop a – fictional but grounded on reality – project. This methodology allows the students to develop critical-thinking skills, which will be useful later in their career to tackle problems effectively.

In the standard PBL approach in urban space design training, where students make proposals which are discussed by the instructor as well as their fellow students, we propose the addition of two introductory activities before the PBL: (1) an analytical approximation to the attributes of the space in which the PBL will be developed, and (2) a gamified experience simulating different aspects of the urban environment.

This paper discusses this educational approach, to promote critical thinking in urban planning and urban design students in their project workflow using serious games in a gamified environment. The strategy is to place students in a virtual reality (VR) environment to simulate different scenarios, to bring up several issues seldom discussed in their training. In addition, the proposal also wants to give students the instruments to manage the complexity of urban data in three – not necessarily geometric – dimensions: (1) physical dimension, (2) data dimension, and (3) human behavior dimension.

3 Gamification and Serious Games as Learning Strategies

For the vast majority of students today, videogames are an integral part of their daily life, especially since the emergence of casual games on smartphones have broadened the audience of people playing games. Thus, it is not unreasonable to argue that incorporating game elements into their education can be beneficial.

A search using Google Trends comparing the trends of the searches "gamification" and "serious games" shows a sharp increase in the amount of queries of the term "gamification" since 2011, overtaking the term "serious games" just one year later and quadrupling the amount of queries as of today (February 2015), and revealing a slight decline in the interest on the term "serious games" over the last four years (Fig. 1).

Gamification is the use of game mechanics in non-game situations [3], taking advantage of some aspects of gaming that make them engaging, generally using a reward system to place the player in a positive reinforcement loop. Gamification can be used to promote a desire to improve using the competitive aspects of playing, and to make an experience more enjoyable and as a consequence reducing abandonment rates.

Serious games usually involve the simulation of real-world phenomena to practice specific skills, and have been traditionally used in areas where it is difficult to train effectively in the real word, such as life-threatening situations (e.g. military tactics, crisis management) or situations which are very rare, such as space exploration. Serious games can also be used in research to test hypotheses.

Both methodologies applied to learning are not mutually exclusive, and serious games can incorporate gamification elements to make the experience more engaging, such as using scoreboards to encourage the competitive spirit among participants, or use game elements to make the experience more entertaining, avoiding procrastination.

The benefits of using simulations cannot be neglected either [4]; as distilled abstractions that model reality, they can enlighten the comprehension of complex phenomena and help us interpret them. In addition, performing experiments though simulations ("in silico") is usually more cost-effective and sometimes allows conducting research that would otherwise be impossible in the real world.

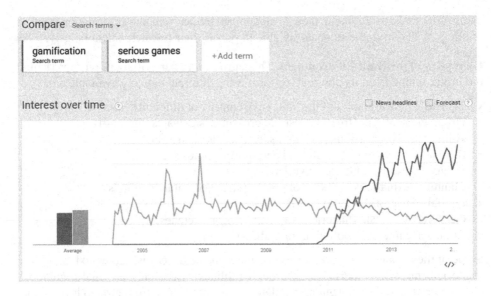

Fig. 1. Terms "gamification" and "serious games" on the Google Trends™ tool (screenshot retrieved on February 10th 2015).

The proposed experience uses elements from serious games mixed with gamification aspects to place learners in a simulated environment, with the objective of helping them reflect on the consequences of different design decisions on the usability of public spaces. As a secondary objective, their (virtual) actions will be tracked by the simulation software to gather data to research on the behavior of pedestrians in urban spaces.

4   Understanding the Multiple Facets of Urban Spaces

Approaching the many aspects of urban spaces may seem an easy task, after all, we are trying to understand the spaces of the human habitat that we experience every day. However, gaining a deep knowledge requires sharp observational skills [5], and many phenomena is not visible, at least not directly or without spending lengthy periods.

Prior to the main chunk of the training consisting on developing the design of an urban space using the standard and time-tested PBL method used in urban planning and design courses, the students will perform two introductory activities: (1) an introductory activity where the students will be asked to analyze the case of study – which will change with every edition of the course – using publicly available data, and (2) a serious game experience with gamified elements where they will be placed in different situations in a setting similar to the one where they will develop their proposal.

The analysis of the case of study is articulated in two sections – the geometry of the built environment and the compilation of the publicly available data on the site – that will use geolocation as their link, using a Geographic Information System (GIS) to integrate and analyze these heterogeneous data. This workflow is very similar to the approach urban planners and designers have traditionally used, but in this case assisted using GIS tools to augment their analysis capabilities. All the information used is publicly available so the students are able to pursue their research autonomously.

Geometry of the Built Environment. This introductory part will focus on approaching the urban setting from its physical [6] form using different publicly available data:

- 2D and 2.5 cartography of the built environment, at different scales
- Urban elements (i.e. trees, pedestrian crossings, sidewalks, lighting)
- Administrative divisions (city limits, census tracts, districts)
- Remote sensed data (land use and aerial orthophotos)
- Utility and transportation networks
- Planning regulations, location of green spaces and public facilities
- Digital Elevation Models (DEM)
- Georeferenced data (historic maps, hand-drawn sketches)
- Environmental data (pollution, rainfall, geology)

Some of these data are not directly observable in the field, because either no longer exist (historical maps), are buried underground (utilities), exist only as legal regulations (administrative limits or planning regulations), are not visible from ground level (aerial or satellite imagery), or require extensive topographic surveying. The integration these cartographic data into the same environment should give the students a robust set of tools to approach the setting where their proposal will be developed. Special emphasis will be placed on analyzing the perceptual qualities of the physical environment from the pedestrians' point of view [7] and analyzing its visibility using space-syntax [8,9], although the usefulness of this technique is somewhat controversial [10,11].

Non-cartographic Data Sources. There is a plethora of publicly available urban data [12] from government open data initiatives, volunteered geographic information (VGI) [13,14] and geolocated social media.

The Spanish Cadastre offers information about the whole built stock in Spain with the same semantics, which allow comparing different regions, and allows obtaining information about their quality, types of uses, and year of construction, as well as identifying vacant lots.

In addition to Cadastral databases, other databases offer valuable information for urban planning as they provide information about population and economic activity such as census, transportation and other publicly available socio-economic data.

Finally, social media (i.e. Twitter, Flickr, Instagram) offers a treasure trove of information waiting to be explored, with some caveats considering that geolocated social media represents a fraction of what constitutes itself a biased sample [15] of all users, even though some studies have shown success in assigning location to data even without geotagging [16].

Human Behavior in the Public Space. Even though people are very diverse in their physical traits or thought processes, their aggregate behavior is known to follow some patterns. To be able to successfully design a space that fulfills the expectations of its users, an urban designer must be capable of understanding the behavior(s) of the people that will use his or her design, during a length of time which, considering the pace of urban change, will most likely be measured in decades. The aspects that influence the behavior and perception of urban spaces are multiple, encompassing from the physical characteristics of the space itself (materials, shapes) to the physical traits of its users, their knowledgeability of the space, environmental factors, the presence of temporary elements, etc.

While the pedestrians' perception of the space depends on subjective aspects such as colors, materials or composition, it also depends on their visual field of view at eye-level, which can be conceptualized using space-syntax. However, this general built envelope is not immutable but is altered by temporary (outdoor markets, public performances, other pedestrians, vehicles, terraces) or permanent (furnishing, vegetation) obstacles.

The physical characteristics of people have implications on their walking speed, their capacity to climb or descend steep slopes or steps, and their capacity to detect and avoid obstacles, narrow passages, traverse uneven or slippery surfaces or walk long stretches without resting. Regarding their attitude, pedestrian behavior varies depending on multiple factors: whether they walk alone or in groups, their activity at any given time (i.e. jogging, working, shopping, cycling), their knowledgeability of the space (i.e. frequent users compared to tourists), etc.

To understand the flows in the public space, information about the uses of buildings at the ground floor facing the public space (e.g. restaurants, shops and kindergartens) is necessary, as well as other factors such as the location of public transport stops or pedestrian crossings, and the population and workplace density. Other environmental factors include nighttime/daytime cycles (related to security), weather conditions (capacity to provide shelter for rain or wind, or avoid slippery surfaces) or seasonal changes (which dictate preference for sun or shade).

Understanding the logic of the combination of these and other factors and the interaction of different people gives designers insight when proposing new public spaces that can fulfill the needs of their users and will endure the test of time.

5   Proposed Experience Outline

The introductory exploration of the site using cartographic and attribute data described in the previous section will be followed by the gamification experience. These two preliminary activities should lay the groundwork to develop the main part of the course – the development of an urban design proposal – successfully, allowing the student to easily integrate information about the site. The main objectives of the gamified experience are threefold: (1) promote critical thinking when designing urban spaces, (2) make the experience more engaging, and (3) gather experimental data about the behavior of students in a virtual environment.

5.1   Serious Game Proposal

The primary objective of the experience is to promote critical thinking [17] in the design process of urban spaces using serious games. The five proposed "mini games" are designed to simulate a limited set of synthetic behaviors in a virtual environment, to stimulate the students to consider specific issues of public life, and compelling them to consider them when developing their designs:

1. Finding an unknown landmark in the least time possible
2. Reaching a known goal quickly, avoiding obstacles
3. Navigating the space with artificial lighting only
4. Simulating the perception of a person with a physical disability
5. Simulating group behavior

These "mini games" incorporate two different attitudes, one change in the environmental conditions and two different profiles of users, and share some common features:

- Each simulation should not be longer than five minutes
- The participants will be asked to participate at least twice in each simulation, to evaluate the effects of experience in repeated tests
- The games will be presented in random order for each participant, but will follow the same order in both runs
- After the compulsory two runs, the students will be allowed to repeat any game more times if they desire so, to find out which experience they find more engaging

Finding an Unknown Landmark in the Least Time Possible. The educational objective of this game is to motivate the students to reflect on the spatial understandability of the spaces for users without complete knowledge, as well as the visibility of landmarks [18,19]. Its research objective is to gather data on search patterns of pedestrians seeking an element they don't know the location of.

The environment of the simulation will be seeded with as set of elements with different physical attributes in different positions, and the participants will be asked to locate a specific – unique – landmark whose description will change every time they run the simulation:

- Relative position to another element (i.e. the element next to the bench)
- Element color, absolute (i.e. the red element) or relative (i.e. the darker element)
- Height of the element, absolute or relative to others
- Element shape

Therefore, the participants may be asked to find "the tall red cylinder next to a tree". This description will be displayed as a reminder on their screens, as well as a time counter that will stop once they have clicked the correct landmark and will increase in a specific amount of time every time they select an incorrect landmark. The final time score will be displayed on a scoreboard with the participant alias.

Reaching a Known Goal Quickly Avoiding Obstacles. In this case the simulation mimics the behavior at the rush hour. The educational objective of this game is to reflect on the physical and visual obstacles in urban spaces, while avoiding of an (artificial) crowd. The research objective is to track the trajectories of the participants and their strategies to achieve their goals.

- The participants will be placed in the flow of a virtual crowd.
- The space will contain static obstacles (i.e. trees, benches, vehicles), some of which will also be visual occlusions
- The avatars will have a finite acceleration and deceleration as well as a steering penalty. Each collision will stop the participant momentarily
- Some paving surfaces allow walking faster than others (pavement opposed to grass)

The participants will be displayed a countdown with the time they have left before the departure of a train, once the countdown reaches zero the simulation ends. The time spent in reaching the goal is displayed in a scoreboard.

Navigating the Space with Artificial Lighting Only. The educational objective of this game is to promote the students' reflection on the importance of adequate lighting [20, pp. 122–125]. The research objective is to compare the change in behavior of users in limited visibility conditions, as the settings will be the same ones described in Sects. 5.1.1 and 5.1.2 above:

- The scene is darker resulting from the light intensity falloff
- The color reproduction is poorer
- The participants will face an unspecified threat to simulate decreased safety

Using the same cases as in the "find a landmark" and "reach the goal quickly" should encourage the students to think about the different space perception depending on the day/night cycle, the seasonal changes or the weather conditions. The data gathered will allow to compare their behavior with and without reduced spatial awareness.

Simulating the Perception of a Person with a Disability. Its educational goal is to place the participants in the role of a person in a wheelchair, to internalize the difficulties that these users face if the urban design does not adapt to their necessities. Using the same environment and objectives described in Sects. 5.1.1 and 5.1.2 above but changing the user profile should raise awareness on the specific needs of people with disabilities. As a research objective, it will gather data on the changes in the participants' behavior when evaluating different itineraries with a time/effort tradeoff. The game will incorporate the following elements to emulate some aspects the experience of a person in a wheelchair:

- The participants have to press two opposite keys alternatively to steer and move their avatar, simulating pushing each wheel of the wheelchair with alternating hands
- Uphill slopes will reduce their speed and therefore increase their effort, forcing the participants to press the keys more quickly and hampering their maneuvers
- Downhill slopes increase their speed and will have to press simultaneously both keys at the same time, otherwise their trajectory gets jerkier and their speed higher
- Some obstacles cannot be avoided
- Their point of view is lower

Simulating Group Behavior. The educational objective is to show the participants that the public space can be understood differently when walking individually or in groups. As a research objective, it should allow to gather data about "flocking" behavior in groups [21]. In this game the participants will be asked to reach a goal without colliding with other people or the environment, and avoid getting separated from the group:

- The environment and goal is the same as in Sect. 5.1.2, but in a group of 3 people (two computer-controlled and the participant avatar)
- The participants hear a conversation, which gets played with a lower volume as the avatar distance to the group increases, so they must be close enough to hear it
- Collision and steering speed reduction results in increased separation from the group
- At the end of the simulation, participants are asked a question about the conversation

5.2   Gamification Elements

The proposed educational experience uses serious games with gamification elements. These gamification elements have the objective of making the experience more engaging and natural –easier to use– for the students. Using a game engine for the simulation translates to indirectly incorporating some game elements familiar to the participants and associated with a play environment:

- User interface (on screen heads-up display, game menus)
- Controls (gamepad, keyboard, mouse)
- Visual language (geometry, shading)
- Use of a – subjective– first person perspective
- Audio cues
- Physical behavior of the elements in the virtual world and of the avatar
- Behavior of the computer-controlled AI (artificial intelligence), using navigation meshes and FSM (finite state machines) for NPC (non-player characters)

These metaphors, ingrained in the player attitude in their experience playing computer games, contribute to a greater acceptance of the limitations of the virtual world – stylized design, simplified behaviors, appearance of artificial actors– to avoid falling into the uncanny valley [22].

In addition some time-tested game mechanics are employed to improve the entertainment value of the experience, facilitating the incorporation of the educational content of the serious game:

- Providing scoreboards for each activity, where participants can compare their results with the results of other participants and compete to get the top score
- Incorporating challenging elements, where participants have to overcome some difficulties
- Introducing novel experiences, where the students are placed in situations outside their daily routine
- Using elements of tension, such as timed countdowns or hit counters

5.3   Participants' Behavior Data Collection

The educational experience will have a data collection counterpart, which will log the participants' behavior in order to gather data about their interactions in the virtual world and investigate whether it can be extrapolated to pedestrians' behavior in the real world. This data collection in a virtual environment does not exclude gathering data in real settings, but can be a valuable complementary source of information due to the difficulties in collecting data in a public environment.

The objective of this data collection is to infer a set of rules to be fed into an agent-based model to simulate pedestrian behavior [23,24] in public spaces and will consist on tracking over time the following data over successive runs:

- Trajectory tracking
- Heatmap of participants' location in all runs
- View direction of the avatar (azimuth and altitude)
- Objects inside the users perspective

Finally, data about user satisfaction will also be collected [25–27] to compare the proposed methodology perceived advantages and disadvantages relative to traditional learning methodologies.

6   Conclusions and Future Work

The proposed educational methodology describes an experience using serious games with gamification elements to stimulate critical thinking in urban planning and urban design students, to promote designing spaces more adaptable and usable [28] for a wide range of users and situations of public life. To improve the proposal, some ideas will remain to be explored in future editions of the course:

- Simulating the perception of a visually impaired person [30], using audio cues and haptic technology using a force-feedback controller
- Generation of the geometry of the simulated urban environment using data acquired using a Terrestrial Laser Scanner (TLS) or procedurally from a set of rules
- Allowing students to visit each other proposals in a virtual environment
- Use an agent-based model to simulate the behavior of pedestrians in each of the students' designs
- Implementing remote participation in the games over the Internet

In addition to the educational experience, data gathered from the behavior of participants in the virtual world, along with tracking data of people's behavior in actual public spaces using infrared cameras or GPS, should be able to help develop a set of rules to be incorporated into an agent-based model to simulate pedestrian behavior, assuming that structure a the macro level arises from interactions at the micro level [29].

Acknowledgments. This research was supported by the Non-Oriented Fundamental Research Project EDU2012-37247/EDUC of the VI National Plan for Scientific Research, Development and Technological Innovation 2008-2011, Government of Spain, titled "E-learning 3.0 in the teaching of architecture. Case studies of educational research for the foreseeable future".

References

1. United Nations Human Settlements Programme (UN-HABITAT), State of the World's Cities 2010/2011 - Cities for All: Bridging the Urban Divide. London: Earthscan (2010)
2. Lynch, K.: The Image of the City. The MIT Press, Cambridge (1960)
3. Deterding, S., Dixon, D., Khaled, R., Nacke, L.: From game design elements to gamefulness: defining 'gamification'. In: Proceedings of the 15th International Academic MindTrek Conference: Envisioning Future Media Environments, New York, NY, USA, pp. 9–15 (2011)
4. Aldrich, C.: Simulations and the Future of Learning: An Innovative (and Perhaps Revolutionary) Approach to e-Learning, 1st edn. Pfeiffer, San Francisco (2003)
5. Gehl, J., Svarre, B.: How to Study Public Life, 2nd edn. Island Press, Washington (2013)
6. Valls Dalmau, F., Garcia-Almirall, P., Redondo Domínguez, E., Fonseca Escudero, D.: From raw data to meaningful information: a representational approach to cadastral databases in relation to urban planning. Future Internet 6(4), 612–639 (2014)
7. Gehl, J., Kaefer, L.J., Reigstad, S.: Close encounters with buildings. Urban Des. Int. 11(1), 29–47 (2006)
8. Hillier, B.: Space is the Machine: A Configurational Theory of Architecture. Space Syntax, London (2007)
9. Sevtsuk, A., Mekonnen, M.: Urban network analysis. a new toolbox for ArcGIS. Rev. Int. Géomat. 22(2), 287–305 (2012)
10. Ratti, C.: Space syntax: some inconsistencies. Environ. Plan. B Plan. Des. 31(4), 487–499 (2004)
11. Hillier, B., Penn, A.: Rejoinder to carlo ratti. Environ. Plan. B Plan. Des. 31(4), 501–511 (2004)
12. Offenhuber, D., Ratti, C.: Decoding the City: Urbanism in the Age of Big Data, 1st edn. Birkhauser Verlag AG, Basel (2014)
13. Goodchild, M.F.: Citizens as sensors: the world of volunteered geography. GeoJournal 69(4), 211–221 (2007)
14. Haklay, M.: How good is volunteered geographical information? a comparative study of openstreetmap and ordnance survey datasets. Environ. Plan. B Plan. Des. 37(4), 682–703 (2010)
15. Ruths, D., Pfeffer, J.: Social media for large studies of behavior. Science 346(6213), 1063–1064 (2014)
16. Mahmud, J., Nichols, J., Drews, C.: Where is this Tweet from? inferring home locations of Twitter users. In: Sixth International AAAI Conference on Weblogs and Social Media (2012)
17. Holbert, N.R., Wilensky, U.: Constructible authentic representations: designing video games that enable players to utilize knowledge developed in-game to reason about science. Technol. Knowl. Learn. 19(1–2), 53–79 (2014)
18. Gibson, D.: The Wayfinding Handbook: Information Design for Public Places, 1st edn. Princeton Architectural Press, New York (2009)
19. Passini, R.: Wayfinding in Architecture. Van Nostrand Reinhold, New York (1984)
20. Great Britain Department for Transport: Manual for Streets. Thomas Telford Pub, London (2007)
21. Moussaid, M., Helbing, D., Garnier, S., Johansson, A., Combe, M., Theraulaz, G.: Experimental study of the behavioural mechanisms underlying self-organization in human crowds. Proc. R. Soc. B Biol. Sci. 276(1668), 2755–2762 (2009)
22. Mori, M., MacDorman, K.F., Kageki, N.: The uncanny valley [from the field]. IEEE Robot. Autom. Mag. 19(2), 98–100 (2012)

23. Bezbradica, M., Ruskin, H.J.: Modelling impact of morphological urban structure and cognitive behaviour on pedestrian flows. In: Murgante, B., Misra, S., Rocha, A.M.A., Torre, C., Rocha, J.G., Falcão, M.I., Taniar, D., Apduhan, B.O., Gervasi, O. (eds.) ICCSA 2014, Part IV. LNCS, vol. 8582, pp. 268–283. Springer, Heidelberg (2014)

24. Duives, D.C., Daamen, W., Hoogendoorn, S.P.: State-of-the-art crowd motion simulation models. Transp. Res. Part C Emerg. Technol. **37**, 193–209 (2013)

25. Garcia-Almirall, P., Redondo Domínguez, E., Valls Dalmau, F., Corso Sarmiento, J.M.: Experiencia docente en la enseñanza de sistemas de información geográfica en arquitectura. In: 9th Iberian Conference on Information Systems and Technologies, Barcelona, pp. 407–412 (2014)

26. Fonseca, D., Villagrasa, S., Valls, F., Redondo, E., Climent, A., Vicent, L.: Motivation assessment in engineering students using hybrid technologies for 3D visualization. In: 2014 International Symposium on Computers in Education (SIIE), pp. 111–116 (2014)

27. Redondo, E., Valls, F., Fonseca, D., Navarro, I., Villagrasa, S., Olivares, A., Peredo, A.: Educational Qualitative Assessment of Augmented Reality Models and Digital Sketching Applied to Urban Planning. In: Proceedings of the Second International Conference on Technological Ecosystems for Enhancing Multiculturality, New York, NY, USA, pp. 447–454 (2014)

28. Myhill, C.: Commercial success by looking for desire lines. In: Masoodian, M., Jones, S., Rogers, B. (eds.) APCHI 2004. LNCS, vol. 3101, pp. 293–304. Springer, Heidelberg (2004)

29. Schelling, T.C.: Micromotives and Macrobehavior. W. W. Norton & Company, New York (1978). Revised

30. Heylighen, A., Herssens, J.: Designerly ways of not knowing: what designers can learn about space from people who are blind. J. Urban Des. **19**(3), 317–332 (2014)

Game Rhetoric: Interaction Design Model of Persuasive Learning for Serious Games

Zarwina Yusoff[⊠] and Amirrudin Kamsin

Department of Computer System and Technology, Faculty of Computer Science
and Information Technology, University of Malaya, 50603 Kuala Lumpur,
Malaysia
zarwina.utm@gmail.com, amir@um.edu.my

Abstract. Serious Games is an emerging technology that can be used in a
learning environment. This technology is an effective interaction design paradigm which can be embedded as a persuasive learning tool to attract learners'
attention. This article will explore the concept of game rhetoric as an element in
game systems for persuading students to engage with the learning context. We
identified three types of rhetorical concept that can be integrated with the current
game rhetoric model to support attention elements: visual, procedural and digital
rhetoric. Three interaction design elements have been used in the model to
support learners' attention: cognition, emotion and social interaction. In this
paper, we propose a new interaction design model based on game rhetoric perspectives to support user interaction in Serious Games for persuasive learning.

Keywords: Game rhetoric · Serious game · Interaction design · Persuasive
learning

1 Introduction

The embedding of persuasion is undoubtedly very important in today's learning
environments. The technology can enhance social interaction among students when the
computer application is used for interaction among them in the classroom (Daud et al.
2013). Human Computer Interaction (HCI) emerged in the late 1970s, and generated
much research into interactive systems intended to persuade user interest (Carroll
2014). Following from this, there has been much more research into persuasion
technology, which has contributed to changing student behaviors, attitudes, and generating learning outcomes. Serious Games (SG) is the one an interactive media technologies that combines animation with narration to improve player performance based
on a games rule system (Sorden 2005). The emergence of SG in the late 1970s changed
the traditional concepts of education when captology was embedded in various computer platforms as a type of educational persuasive technology for achieving learning

---

Please note that the LNCS Editorial assumes that all authors have used the western naming
convention, with given names preceding surnames. This determines the structure of the names in the
running heads and the author index.

© Springer International Publishing Switzerland 2015
P. Zaphiris and A. Ioannou (Eds.): LCT 2015, LNCS 9192, pp. 644–654, 2015.
DOI: 10.1007/978-3-319-20609-7_60

outcomes (Fogg 2003). A number of researchers have noted the effectiveness of persuasion in learning environment (Daud et al. 2013; Bakri et al. 2014; Zulkifli et al. 2013). Based on this, we aim to develop a persuasive learning model for Serious Games which aims to implement the concept of game rhetoric as a learning tool to support the concept of persuasion. In order to instill persuasion in the gaming context, we have identified previous research that has applied the persuasive element in learning environments. Much of the research has discussed the impact of persuasion on users, such as motivation, personalization, emotion, ethical issues, experiences, and the cognitive process of comprehension (Zulkifli et al. 2013). Additional works by Bakri et al. (2013) have proven that a persuasive system design can be used to develop the interactive Al-Furqan Courseware for early childhood learning using Toddlers Learning theory and multimedia principles.

Based on the persuasive elements inspired by Aristotle, the Greek philosopher, we propose to include a 'game rhetoric' concept in order to persuade learners through the interaction design model. He stated that there are three main elements of persuasion, which consist of pathos, ethos and logos. The concept of game rhetoric can be used to persuade players to interact with the games and to maintain players' interest in the game's goal and challenges. In order to construct the proposed model, we used the three elements of interaction design which were proposed by Rogers et al. (2011). Cognitive interaction, emotional interaction and social interaction make up the graphical user interface (GUI) paradigm which will be integrated into the proposed model to support learners' attention.

1.1 Objectives of This Paper

The objectives of this paper are as follows:

1. To review existing models or frameworks of game rhetoric in the persuasion learning context.
2. To propose an interaction design model of persuasive learning for Serious Games based on game rhetoric perspectives.

1.2 Structure of Paper

This article will present the use of the interaction design concept in SG through the representation of game rhetoric. Section 1 introduces previous research on the concept of persuasion and provides a brief introduction to game rhetoric. It is followed by the literature review in Sect. 2 which explains the study of game design. Section 3 explains how the cognitive element contributes to the persuasive environment through the concept of interaction design. Section 4 elaborates the proposed model and Sect. 5 discusses the strengths and limitations of the study. Lastly, Sect. 6 provides a conclusion and recommendations for future work to address the limitations of this study.

2 Study of Game Design

The study of Game Design has indicated that pedagogical issues are an important element to be embedded in game design. Regarding this issue, Hunicke (2000) proposed the MDA framework of games, which consists of mechanics, dynamics and aesthetics, as one of the formal approaches to understanding game design and development. In contrast, Jarvinen (2008), proposed two components of game design, game rhetoric and mechanics, as strong components in designing a game system. Figure 1 shows the concept of game design.

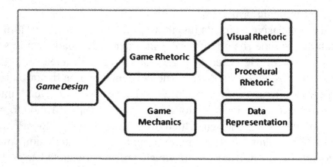

Fig. 1. A study of game design

This study has adopted the two components of game design from Jarvinen (2008), game mechanics and game rhetoric,for its direction. Game Rhetoric has been included to overcome the limitations of persuasive learning. Based on this, the interaction design paradigm has been used to attract learners' attention while playing games.

2.1 Game Mechanics

Game mechanics can be defined as a method invoked by agents for interacting with the game world. According to Hunicke (2000), game mechanics comprises the visual representations and algorithm for the game system. It acts as the main interface for the user to interact with the game's rules in creating experiences. Besides that, it also takes on the role of game system, for example connecting game hardware as part of the user's controllers. Besides that, the interaction between user and game system through run time behavior is a function of the game dynamic, which acts with players' inputs and others' outputs over time.

Game aesthetics is an element that can generate emotional responses among users when they interact with the system. In persuading learners, emotion is an important element in evaluating players' experiences via their attention. Bogost (2007) stated that the four main elements in Serious Games, emotion and sobriety, consequences and demand for consideration, severity and foreboding, and intellectualism and profundity are important aspects for players to engage by in after playing the games. Another work by Hesther (2010) identified three techniques for evaluating users' emotions when playing games. These are self-assessment mannequin, emoticons and affective grid for measuring emotions. Based on this, attention is an important element in creating learners' emotions while playing games. It is useful to connect the role of game mechanics with player behavior when it is an important element in supporting learner's behavior (Hunicke et al. 2004). Behaviorism is one of the pedagogical theories about learner behavior in a learning environment. In this theory, learning occurs through conditioning via the game element, and the player gets rewards based on the stimuli (Schunk 2012).

2.2 Game Rhetoric

Rhetoric is the art of persuasion. Jarvinen (2008) has explained the importance of using communication theories and semiotic element to engage players with the game. Text, animation, sound effect, image, material props are examples of semiotics. The 1, 2, 3 countdown at the beginning of the Mario Kart DS game is one example of the semiotic approach in games.

Besides that, Zookeeper games developed by Success Corporation (2003), has embedded the semiotic approach through communicating player progress and simulating animals' emotional reactions in order to make the game more attractive. Based on the game rhetoric model developed by Sundness (2008), we have proposed the interaction design model of persuasive learning for serious game. The model has been divided into three categories to represent each of the elements in persuasion via game rhetoric: legitimization, authenticity and identification. Figure 2 indicates the game rhetoric model of persuasive games which was proposed by Sundnes (2008).

	Constraints	◄ — — — — — ►	Affordances
Rules	*Legitimization*	◄ — — — — — ►	*Opposition*
Player roles	*Identification*	◄ — — — — — ►	*Identity play*
Gameworld	*Authenticity*	◄ — — — — — ►	*Autonomy*

Fig. 2. Game rhetoric model for persuasive games

We derive three main important elements from the Sundnes model (2008) consisting of rules, player roles and the game world, as the core elements for the game rhetoric in our proposed model. AMERICAN ARMY is a prime example of a persuasive game which embeds rules, player roles and game world concepts (Fig. 3). Game Rhetoric has been proposed as the main element in interaction design in this article because of the effectiveness of the rhetorical element in expressing the concept of persuasion through exemplification in the learning environment (Bogost 2007). We categorized game rhetoric into three types of categories, visual rhetoric (advertisements, photograph, illusion), procedural rhetoric (rules based representation and interaction) and digital rhetoric (text and image), as shown in Fig. 4.

Fig. 3. AMERICA'S ARMY persuasive games (Gamespot 2002)

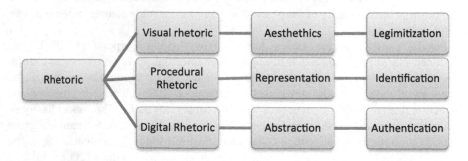

Fig. 4. Rhetoric perspectives

Creating new forms in terms of advertisements or photographs is a useful lesson in visual rhetoric, which can generate users' illusions. In this study, we have mapped visual rhetoric in the context of aesthetics, the function of which is to capture learner emotion through the rules of the game system. As a result, rule based representation and interaction are examples of procedural rhetoric involving the reasoning for a user to perform an action while playing a game. Presenting abstractions of the computer application such as game warnings when the learner does not follow the game rules is an example of digital rhetoric applications which enable to the learner to experience greater authenticity and ownership. In order to enhance the current game rhetoric model, we implemented three mediums of interaction design: cognitive, emotional and social, to create persuasion in the game.

3   Interaction Design: Cognition into Persuasion

3.1   The Persuasive Element in Games

As defined by Bogost (2007), a serious game must contain four elements. Firstly, it must have the *emotion* and *sobriety* element to attract player attention. This is followed by *consequence* and the demand for *consideration* through the steps or actions in the game environment. *Severity* and *foreboding* are the third elements in SG, which invoke the learner's cognition to perform the next action. The last element in SG is how effectively the game will generate knowledge for user. Bogost strongly supports the persuasion element in serious games, and this follows Visch (2003) who defined persuasive games by their effects on users' experiences and behavior.

"Persuasive games design aiming to create a user experienced game
World to change the user behavior in the real world" (Visch 2003)

Persuasion can generate both argumentation and information to change individuals' beliefs, attitudes and behaviors and persuasions. It can also be defined as "human communication designed to influence the autonomous judgments an action of others" (Visch 2013). Based on this, a persuasive game is one example of a serious game through the representation of interaction by using procedural rhetoric effectively (Bogost 2007).

Designing a SG must align with the cognitive issues. This is because a SG must engage with pedagogy in generating learning experiences. Regarding this issue, Van Dijk et al. (2011) proposed a successful SG according to the cognitive aspect; where knowledge acquisition and construction is measured based on three aspects: learning, cognitive load and enjoyment factors. Van Dijk et al. (2011) discovered two types of learning that are embedded in SG design. They are deep learning and surface learning. The function of deep learning is to construct the features of the mental model and to prove the structure of knowledge assessment. Surface learning, combines two types of knowledge: declarative and procedural knowledge in constructing the attributes of the mental model of. Based on Van Dijk et al. (2011) results cognition is an important element that instructs the SG to generate a persuasive learning environment.

3.2   From Interaction into Persuasion

Cognition is the psychological result of perception and learning which is affected by emotions through mental operations. In order to persuade attention as a persuasive element, we identified the relationship between interaction design and persuasion in generating the attention element for the learning environment, as presented in Fig. 5.

Based on Fig. 5, the process of interaction design involves the cognitive process to achieve the persuasion element. In this process, knowledge is provided about the user's actions and expectations in carrying out a hospital priority task. Through the cognitive process, several learner attitudes or behaviors can be generated, as presented in Fig. 5. Many attributes can generate learner attention, such as color, space, and multimedia elements as a representation of visual rhetoric. The attention element introduced by the Keller ARCS Model has been used in this study to support the proposed model. Kakabadse et al. (2003) presented the mental model as a cognitive style in the taxonomies of knowledge management while Yusoff et al. (2013) identified the relationships among mental models in constructing learning engagement through three attributes: cognitive engagement, interactivity, and multimedia learning, to enhance a learner's engagement through knowledge visualization.

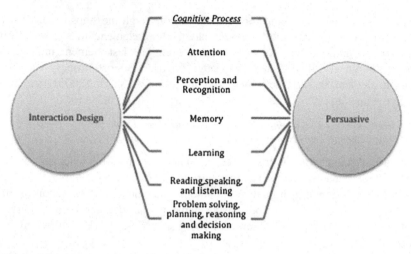

Fig. 5. Cognitive process

4 Proposed Model

This article proposes the interaction design model for persuasive learning which is derived from the current game rhetoric model of Sundnes (2008). We overcame the limitations of the model by adding the learning context integrated with the interaction design paradigm to control learner's attention while playing the game. Figure 6 presents the interaction design model of persuasive learning in SG.

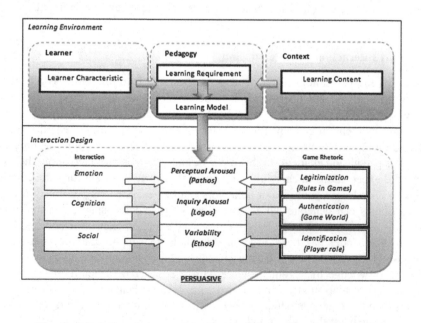

Fig. 6. Interaction design model of persuasive learning in serious game

The proposed model consists of two phases: learning environment and interaction design, to construct the persuasive learning environment.

4.1 Learner Characteristics

For learner characteristics, we have adopted four elements from Drachsler (2000), who defined the characteristics of the learner according to four categories, personal, academic, social/emotional, and cognitive. Demographic issues such as age, gender, level of maturity, and the skills of the learner are the criteria for the personal element. Prior knowledge, educational level and type are the specific criteria for the academic element. Learner's feelings or mood are the social or emotional aspects of a learner's characteristics.

In order to generate learner cognition, Guilford (1967) stated that human intellectual abilities can be divided according to three main dimensions: operations, content and products. In designing the model, we have chosen visual, auditory and kinesthetic as the learning styles required to fulfill learners' requirements through the game environment.

4.2 Pedagogy

We have identified six paradigms of learning theories and models in constructing the pedagogical elements of the learning theory, such as behaviorism, cognitivism, constructivism, design-based, humanism, and 21st Century Skills (Learning Theories and Models (2005). Learning theory must support learner requirements to influence the learning process. Significantly, to support the concept of persuasion, we used humanistic theory to construct the attention element in the model. We followed the Attention criteria from the ARCS Motivation model by Keller (2000) in evaluating learner's attention to construct the persuasive element. These criteria are perceptual arousal (PA), Inquiry Arousal (IA) and Variability (V) to achieve persuasion.

4.3 Context

According to Dias (2005), context is the set of circumstances that are relevant for the learner to generate knowledge when referring to the content. The graphic element is content for attracting players' attention to engage with the game environment. Text, symbols, image, animation, sound, music and touch are a combination of graphic elements which are utilized to provide emotional experiences through challenges in the games. As a result, the interaction between content and context will generate users' knowledge.

4.4 Interaction Design

We have derived three elements of interaction design from Rogers' et al. (2011) consisting of emotion, cognition and social interaction as agents of interaction design.

We adapted the attention element from the Keller ARCS Model (2000) in order to construct the attention in persuasion element. The Game Rhetoric element was also integrated in the proposed model to produce the persuasive learning environment. Three elements of persuasion which were derived from Aristotle consisting of pathos (emotional effects), ethos (moral character) and logos (generate reasoning) were generated through the interaction design paradigm; emotion, cognition and social interaction. Table 1 explains the relationship between attributes in the proposed model.

Table 1. Explanation of proposed model

Persuasion through attention elements	Interaction design	Game rhetoric elements
Perceptual arousal (PA) *What can I do to capture learner interest and affect their emotions?*	*Emotion* Learners feeling confident, secure, comfortable and curious are the features that fall within the emotional category as indicators of learning engagement. (Wang et al. 2006)	*Legitimization* The rules in games have settings to generate user's interest using aesthetic elements such as graphics, sound, text, narration to represent the games.
Inquiry arousal *How I can stimulate attitude through interaction between game and learners?*	*Cognition* Students can generate their own self regulated learning, construct their own knowledge, and take ownership of their learning to be stored in mental models for knowledge storage. (Wang et al. 2006)	*Authentication* The adaptive concept in games which influences the game flow, outcomes and feedback from games can generate learning outcomes after learners interact with the game system.
Variability *How I can use a variety of tactics to maintain attention?*	*Social* External environment; such as sharing resources with others through collaborative learning and acceptance (Wang et al. 2006). Moral character in games will provides learners the opportunity to interact with other' players in achieving learning outcomes.	*Identification* Multiplayer games will develop social interaction among groups which can create intense and passionate involvement in learners' skills.

5   Discussion

This article enhances the design of the interaction design model to strengthen the current model through the use of game rhetoric. In the proposed model, the game rhetoric element is identified as the element generating the persuasive learning environment in Serious Games. We have mapped the concept of game rhetoric onto persuasion to support learner attention. The proposed model provides a strong guideline for developing persuasive games based on the rhetorical element integrated with the attention element in the interaction design concept, *Perceptual Arousal* (emotional), *Inquiry Arousal* (cognitive) and *Variability* (social interaction). As a result in the proposed model, visual rhetoric can generate learners' emotions, procedural rhetoric will affect learners' cognition and digital rhetoric will create social interaction among learners in multiplayer games. Significantly, game rhetoric is a suitable concept to be used in implementing persuasive learning through the Serious Game environment.

6 Conclusion

The proposed interaction design model of persuasive learning which is based on game rhetoric,provides new guidelines for researchers to develop game prototypes. In order to construct learner attention, we proposed the concept of game rhetoric as a means to persuade players through the three core elements of persuasion: pathos, ethos and logos. In further research we want to proceed to building serious game prototypes based on the proposed model by incorporating the concept of learner' attention in history education.

Acknowledgement. We would like to thank University of Malaya Research Grant (UMRG) for sponsoring this project under (RP006A-14HNE), Usability of Serious Game Application for History Education.

References

Bakri, A., Zakaria, N.H., Muhamad Zainuldin, S.N., Abu Safia, A.H.: A conceptual model of Al_Furqan courseware using persuasive system design for early learning Childhood. In: 2014 8th Malaysian Software Engineering Conferences (MySEC), pp. 336–341 (2014). doi:10.1109/MySec.2014.6986040

Bogost, I.: Persuasive Games: The Expressive Power of Videogames. MIT Press, Cambridge (2007)

Carroll, J.M.: Human Computer Interaction - brief intro. In: Soegaard, M., Dam, R.F. (eds.) The Encyclopedia of Human-Computer Interaction, vol. 2. IGI Global, US (2014)

Daud, N.A., Ashaari, N.S., Muda, Z.: An initial model of persuasive design in web based learning environment. Procedia Technol. **11**, 895–902 (2013). doi:10.1016/j.protcy.2013.12.273

Dunwell, I., de Freitas, S., Jarvis, S.: Four-dimensional consideration of feedback in serious games. In: de Freitas, S., Maharg, P. (eds.) Digital Games and Learning, pp. 42–62. Continuum Publishing, New York (2011)

Drachsler, H., Kirschner, P.A.: Learner Characteristics. Centre for Learning Science andTechnology. Open University of Netherlands (n.d.)

Fogg, B.: Persuasive Technology: Using Computers to Change What We Think and do. Morgan Kaufman Publishers, CA (2003)

Guilford, J.P.: The Nature of Human Intelligence. Mc Graw-Hill, New York (1967)

Hunicke, R., LeBlanc, M., Zubek, R.: MDA.: A formal approach to game design and game research. In: Proceedings of the Challenges in Game AI Workshop, Nineteenth National Conference on Artificial Intelligence (AAAI 2004). AAAI Press, San Jose (2004)

Heather, D., Charlotte, W.: User experience design for inexperienced gamers: gap- game approachability principles, evaluating user experience in games. In: Bernhaupt, R. (ed.) Human Computer Interaction Series. Springer-Verlag, London (2010)

Jarvinen, A.: Games without Frontiers: Theories and methods for game studies and design. Tampere University Press, Tampere (2008)

Kakabadse, N.K., Kakabadse, A., Kouzmin, A.: Reviewing the knowledge management literature towards a taxanomy. J. Knowl. Manag. 7(4), 75–91 (2003)

America's Army Operation Reviews (2002). http://www.gamespot.com

Paper, S., Paiva, A.: Learning to interact : connecting perception with action in virtual environments. In: Aamas, pp. 1257–1260 (2008)

Bernhaupt, R.: Evaluating User Experience in Games, Human-Computer Interaction Series. Springer-Verlag, London (2010)

Rogers, Y., Sharp, H., Preece, J.: Interaction Design: Beyond Human Computer Interaction, 3rd edn. Wiley, New York (2011)

Schunk, D.H.: Learning Theories: An Educational perspective, 6th edn. Pearson, Boston (2012)

Løvlie, A.S.: The Rhetoric of Persuasive Games: Freedom and Discipline in America's Army (2007). http://www.duo.uio.no/sok/work.html?WORKID=54268&lang=en

Sorden, Stephen D.: A cognitive approach to instructional design for multimedia learning. Informing Sci. Int. J. Emerg. Transdiscipline 8, 263–279 (2005)

Van Dijk, V., Van der Spek, E.D., Van Oostendorp, H. Erkens, G.: Serious games versus tradition instruction; learning, enjoyment and cognitive load. Experiments in serious game design a cognitive approach. SIKS dissertation Series No. 2011–36

Visch, V., Vegt, N., Anderiesen, H., Van der Kooji, K.: Persuasive game design: A model and its definitions. CHI conference publication, Paris (2013)

Wang, M., Kang, M.: Cybergogy for engaged learning: a framework for creating learner engagement through information and communication technology. In: Hung, D., Khine, M.S. (eds.) Engaged Learning with emerging Technologies, pp. 225–253. Springer, Dordrecht (2006)

Yusoff, Z., Katmon, S.A., Ahmad, M.N., Miswan, S.H.M.: Visual representation: enhancing students learning engagement through knowledge visualization. Int. Conf. Inf. Creative Multimed. 2013, 242–247 (2013). doi:10.1109/ICICM.2013.48

Zulkifli, A.N., Noor, N.M., Bakar, J.A.A., Mat, R.C., Ahmad, M.: A conceptual model of interactive persuasive learning system for elderly to encourage computer-based learning process. Int. Conf. Inf. Creative Multimed. 2013, 7–12 (2013). doi:10.1109/ICICM.2013.10

Success Corporation, Japanese Video Game and Online Game (2003). http://www.success-corp.co.jp/

Summaries of Learning Theories and Models (2005). http://www.learning-theories.com/

Keller, J.M.: How to integrate learner motivation planning into lesson planning: The ARCS model approach. Paper presented at VII Semanario, Santiago, Cuba (2000)

Dias, A., Figueiredo, D.: Learning Contexts: a Blueprint for Research. Interactive Educational Multimedia, Number II, pp. 127–139, October 2005

Lottridge, D., Chignell, M., Jovicic, A.: Affective interaction: understanding, evaluating and designing for human emotion. Rev. Hum. Factors Ergon. 7, 376 pp. (2011)

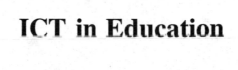

ICT in Education

Just-in-Case or Just-in-Time Training? – Excerpts from a Doctoral Research Study

Devshikha Bose[(✉)]

Instructional Design and Educational Assessment,
Boise State University, Boise, ID, USA
devshikhabose@boisestate.edu

Abstract. This paper is an excerpt on the author's doctoral study titled "Effects of Just-in-Time online training on knowledge and application of the Sheltered Instruction Observation Protocol (SIOP®) Model among in-service teachers." The specific focus of the report is on an aspect of the study, which sought to determine whether there was any statistically significant difference between learners who received Just-in-Time (JiT) versus those who received Just-in-Case (JiC) instruction. Results from the data analysis revealed no significant difference in knowledge or application skills between the JiT and JiC groups. However, there was an increase in learner application of SIOP® Model principles in classroom teaching, for both groups. JiT training did not emerge as a better training strategy than JiC training. The main benefit of the training delivered through this study seemed to be in increasing application and not knowledge.

Keywords: Just-in-Time training · Just-in-Case training · SIOP® · Dick and carey systems approach model · Online teacher professional development

1 Introduction

The timing of training may have an impact on the learners' motivation for using it [1]. Just-in-Time (JiT) training provides learners with the information required to complete a job at the moment it is needed [2], rather than training people just in case they may need the knowledge and skills in future. Just-in-Case (JiC) training may be a wasteful use of resources [3]. JiT training is a form of inductive teaching that occurs in situations in which the instructor starts by challenging the student with a specific problem situation [4]. Students faced with a problem feel the need for gaining access to facts, skills, and concepts, which are then provided by the instructor as the situation demands. This may lead to a deeper level of learning.

The primary outcome of JiT training is a context-specific improvement of knowledge and performance [5]. A meta-analysis of the effectiveness of JiT training as an adult learning method revealed that this training method was most effective when used with actual practitioners who had the opportunity to apply their training to their professions.

The advantages of JiT training appear to be many [1]. JiT reduces the time lapse between learning and the application, ensuring that a minimum amount of forgetting

© Springer International Publishing Switzerland 2015
P. Zaphiris and A. Ioannou (Eds.): LCT 2015, LNCS 9192, pp. 657–667, 2015.
DOI: 10.1007/978-3-319-20609-7_61

takes place [2]. JiT training delivered in small chunks is often more relevant to the needs of the learner, and therefore may be more efficient than lengthier courses. Although the costs of creating electronic JiT training packages may be high initially, it is more cost effective in the long run when factors like the time and money spent in travelling are considered. However, JiT training is not a "panacea" [2] training solution, especially when the training does not meet the needs of the situation. While materials used for on-going training are developed and updated on a regular basis, materials for JiT training are "mandated by an emerging situation" [6].

2 Purpose of Study

The phenomenon under study in this research was the efficacy of the JiT inductive training context versus the JiC training context, through an online medium, on learner knowledge acquisition and application abilities [1]. It is important to compare the JiT training context versus the JiC training context because such research will add to the existing literature in the field of teacher professional development training methods, with specific emphasis on how optimum timing of training can prevent waste of resources.

The purpose of this study was to determine whether there was a difference in knowledge and application of the SIOP® Model among in-service teachers who participated in an online professional development course on the SIOP® Model [1]. Although these teachers all participated in the same course, information on the number of English Language Learners (ELLs) in their classrooms was used to distinguish teachers who received the training in a JiT context, as opposed to those who received the training in a JiC context. This research may help establish the effects of providing JiT instruction on the teachers' knowledge and application skills of the SIOP® Model as compared to the knowledge acquisition and application potential of JiC training. The following research questions guided the focus of the quantitative portion of the study pertaining to the impact of JiT verses JiC training on learning:

1. Is there a significant difference in achievement between Just-in-Time recipients and Just-in-Case recipients of SIOP® Model training, as measured by a knowledge posttest, after controlling for pre-treatment knowledge?
2. Is there a significant difference in application of SIOP® principles between Just-in-Time recipients and Just-in-Case recipients of SIOP® Model training, as measured by the SIOP® protocol and the SIOP® Usage Survey, after controlling for pre-treatment application?

3 Review of Literature

A survey of existing research on JiT and JiC training revealed that there are only a few empirical studies published in this area [1]. Most of the available studies are anecdotal and suggestive in nature. In areas of human resource training such as that of emotional intelligence, it has been reported that there is hardly any literature on short-term JiT training programs [7]. The following review is based on the available empirical, anecdotal and suggestive publications. This literature base suggests that JiT training may be more effective than JiC training.

JiT training provides a learner with the information required to complete a job when it is required [2]. JiT learning systems provide training when and where it is needed rather than providing training to learners through extensive traditional classroom courses well before such knowledge is required [6] It has been suggested that JiT training is more feasible because it minimizes chances of "training waste" [3]. Leaners get the training they need, when they need it for immediate use rather than when training happens to be available. Thus, training people "just in case" they will need the knowledge and skills in future may be a wasteful use of resources [3]. Moreover, JiT learning enables learning in more meaningful or authentic situations, when the learner has a professional context in which the relevant training can be immediately applied [8].

JiT learning can be helpful for adult learners who are trying to take a refresher course on certain skill sets in areas like mathematics instead of taking complete courses which might be time consuming [9] Also, JiT can help learners solve specific problems by making very specific knowledge sets immediately available [10, 11]. With adult learners, JiT learning methods reflect the changing nature of adult learning in the "internet era" where the "old model of learning" or the "warehouse" is being replaced by the "Just-in-Time system of information acquisition" [12].

People usually learn in response to a 'need' [13]. When the need for learning a particular topic is not evident, the learner ignores, rejects, or fails to assimilate it in any meaningful manner. However, when learners feel the need for learning a particular thing they usually make effective use of training resources. Sometimes it is possible for teachers to act as facilitators and providers of JiT scaffolding to students [14]. Students indicated that teacher scaffolding was beneficial when they actually needed it rather than being always available. Thus "delayed scaffolding and feedback" were identified as being more beneficial to learning [14].

Pilot studies of a National Science Foundation (NSF) funded project called The Math you Need when You Need it (TMYN), using the JiT and the necessity principle of teaching, revealed that online, asynchronous learning modules were successful in remediating community college and university student learning in geosciences [15]. Increases in scores from the pre to the posttest, as well as students' reported perceptions of the usefulness of TMYN, demonstrated the success of JiT teaching in this research study.

4 Method

Research Question 1 (see above) sought to determine whether there was a significant difference in knowledge achievement after participation in an online SIOP® training course, between in-service teachers who received JiT training in the SIOP® Model and in-service teachers who received JiC training in the SIOP® Model [1]. The answer was determined through an analysis of differences in scores between Pre and Post-instruction Knowledge Tests taken by the participants. Also, the change in knowledge of SIOP® Model principles after participation in the instruction for the JiT group, was compared with the change in knowledge of SIOP® Model principles for the JiC group. This helped establish whether learners acquire more knowledge through training if they receive training in a JiT context as opposed to training in a JiC context.

Research Question 2 (see above) sought to determine whether there was a significant difference in application of SIOP® Model principles after participation in an online SIOP® training course, between in-service teachers who received training in the JiT context versus teachers who received training in the JiC context [1]. The answer was determined through an analysis of differences in scores between Lesson Plans and SIOP® Usage Surveys submitted by participants before and after instruction. Also, the change in application of SIOP® Model principles after participation in the instruction for the JiT group, was compared with the change in application of SIOP® Model principles for the JiC group though an analysis of a SIOP® Usage Survey. These comparisons helped establish whether learners increase application of SIOP® principles after they receive training in a JiT context versus training in a JiC context.

5   Research Design

A mixed research design was used for this study such that both quantitative as well as qualitative data was collected [1]. In order to gain a better understanding of the research problem, triangulation of numeric data from a quantitative perspective and analytical data from a qualitative view [16] was completed.

This paper focuses on the quantitative and not the qualitative aspects of the study. As such, it does not discuss the data obtained from the Focus Group Meetings. The data from the Demographic Information Survey is referenced as appropriate to the context of discussion. The following paragraph summarizes the Research Design of the entire study:

Participants completed a Demographic Information Survey on the basis of which they were split into two distinct groups – JiT and JiC. Both groups completed the Pre-Instruction Knowledge Test and submitted the Pre-Instruction Lesson Plan [1]. They also took the SIOP® Usage Survey. Then, both groups received the treatment instruction (online SIOP® course). After completing the course, both group participants took the Post-Instruction Knowledge Test and submitted the Post-Instruction Lesson Plan. They also took the SIOP® Usage Survey and participated in the Focus Group Meetings.

6   Participants and Sampling

The participants in this study included K-12 in-service teachers from the state of Idaho, who registered for an online SIOP® professional development course during the summer 2012 semester [1]. The teachers self-selected to participate in this course offered by the research institution (a public Intermountain West university). Invitations to register for the online professional development course were emailed to every K-12 teacher in Idaho. The teachers who enrolled in the course constituted a self-selected sample of convenience. A total of 43 (N = 43) participants were included for data collection purposes in this study. However, different phases of the study had different participant numbers depending on their response rates on data collection instruments.

7 Instruments

While a total of seven assessment instruments were used in the dissertation study only four instruments were used to gather quantitative data data on the JiT and JiC training aspects: A Demographic Information Survey, Pre and Post-instruction SIOP® Knowledge Tests; a lesson plan evaluation rubric (the SIOP® protocol); and a researcher-created self-reported SIOP® Usage Survey instruments, based on the components of the SIOP® Model [1].

8 Procedures

The treatment instruction used in this study consisted of an online training on the SIOP® Model. The course was self-paced and was of four weeks duration. It had four modules. Students earned a single professional development credit upon completing its requirements [1].

Before gaining access to the treatment instruction (online SIOP® curriculum) both JiT and JiC groups completed the Demographic Information Survey, the Pre-instruction Knowledge Test, submitted the Pre-instruction Lesson Plan, and completed the SIOP® Usage Survey [1]. Participants were assessed on their pre-instruction knowledge (determined by the Pre-instruction Knowledge Test) and application (determined by analysis of their Pre-instruction Lesson Plan and SIOP® Usage Survey). After receiving the treatment instruction, both JiT and JiC groups completed a Post-instruction Knowledge Test, submitted a Post-instruction Lesson Plan, completed a SIOP® Usage Survey, and participated in a Focus Group Meeting (data not reported here).

9 Treatment Development and Data Collection

The online curriculum was developed keeping in mind the principles of good Instructional Systems Design [1]. Instructional System refers to the arrangement of resources and procedures used to facilitate learning [17]. This study used the Dick and Carey Systems Approach Model of instructional design. The phases in this design model include: Identification of instructional goals, instructional analysis, analysis of the learners and the context; writing of performance objectives; development of criterion referenced assessment instruments; development of an instructional strategy; development and selection of instructional materials; design and delivery of formative and summative evaluations [18]. In order to answer the research questions focusing on the JiT and JiC training modalities, data were collected in five phases using the five instruments (only four reported in this paper).

10 Data Analysis

A Repeated Measures Analysis of Variance was used to analyze data [19]. This statistical analysis procedure was chosen because the same participants were tested twice, generating three sets of pre and post-treatment instruction scores using three different test instruments [20]. This data were analyzed for within and between subjects effects.

Research Question 1.   In order to answer Research Question 1, a repeated measures ANOVA with one between and one within subjects factor, was used to determine any significant difference in achievement on the posttest between the two groups, while controlling for pre-instruction differences [21].

Research Question 2.   In order to answer Research Question 2, an analysis of the lessons submitted by the JiT and JiC groups before and after the delivery of the treatment instruction was conducted using the SIOP$^{®}$ protocol, in order to determine difference in performance which may be attributed to level of need for the online treatment instruction [1].

The difference in mean scores between the Pre and Post-instruction Lesson Plans was calculated for both JiT and JiC groups to ascertain significant differences in participant SIOP$^{®}$ application [1]. A repeated measures ANOVA, with one between and one within subjects factor, was used to determine any significant difference in application of SIOP$^{®}$ principles between the two groups on the post-instruction lesson plan, while controlling for differences on the pre-instruction lesson plan [21].

Research Question 2 was also answered using the SIOP$^{®}$ Usage Survey [1]. For both JiT and JiC groups, an analysis of the results from the SIOP$^{®}$ Usage Survey administered before and after the delivery of instruction was used to determine changes in implementation levels of SIOP$^{®}$ Model principles in actual classroom practice.

The difference in mean scores between the Pre and Post-instruction SIOP$^{®}$ Usage Survey was calculated for both JiT and JiC groups to ascertain significant differences in participant application of SIOP$^{®}$ principles [1]. A Repeated Measures ANOVA with one between and one within subjects factor, was used to determine any significant difference between the two groups [21].

11 Results

11.1 Data Analysis for Research Question 1

The Pre and Post-instruction Knowledge Test instrument provided data to answer Research Question 1 of this study [1]. Thirty-nine or 90.6 % ($n = 39$) participants completed the Pre and Post-instruction Knowledge Tests. Out of this number, there were 21 participants in the JiT group and 18 in the JiC group who completed both the pre and posttest. Scores from these tests and a value for the JiC versus the JiT variable were obtained. Research Question 1 was addressed by using the total score from all the assessment items in the Pre and Post-instruction Knowledge Tests. There were 28 multiple-choice items in both the Pre and Post-instruction Knowledge Tests. The total score was calculated as a percentage correct.

The Pre-instruction Knowledge Test, the JiT group had a higher average performance ($M = 86.9$, $SD = 9.0$) than the JiC group ($M = 84.5$, $SD = 5.9$) [1]. In the Post-instruction Knowledge Test, the JiT group had a higher average performance

($M = 87.6$, $SD = 10.9$) than the JiC group ($M = 86.5$, $SD = 12.0$). Both groups improved from pre to post test in terms of SIOP® knowledge; however, it was determined (see below) that this improvement was not significant for either group.

Since there were violations to the assumptions of Normality and Homogeneity of Variances, the same comparisons were made using the non-parametric equivalent tests with a Bonferroni Correction for the p-value [1]. Two Mann-Whitney U Tests, which is the non-parametric equivalent of the independent samples t-test, were calculated to compare the JiC and the JiT groups on the pretest scores and the posttest scores. Two Wilcoxon Signed Ranks tests, which is the non-parametric equivalent of paired t-test, were conducted [20] to compare the pre- and post- test scores for the JiT group and for the JiC group. The results were similar to that of the parametric RMANOVA.

The sample size for the Mann-Whitney U test was 39 ($n_{JIT} = 21$, $n_{JIC} = 18$) [1]. No statistically significant difference was found between the two groups for the Pre-instruction Knowledge Test ($Z = -1.054$, $p = .292$, $p_{Bonferroni} = 1$) or for the Post-instruction Knowledge Test ($Z = -0.242$, $p = .809$, $p_{Bonferroni} = 1$).

For the Wilcoxon Signed Rank test, the sample size for the JiT group was 21 ($n = 21$) and the JiC group was 18 ($n = 18$) [1]. There was no significant difference from the pre-test to the posttest scores for either the JiT ($Z = -1.551$, $p = .121$, $p_{Bonferroni} = .484$) or JiC groups (-0.586, $p = .558$, $p_{Bonferroni} = 1$).

RMANOVA Results. A repeated measures analysis of variance was used to assess whether there was a significant difference in performance before and after instruction, whether there was a difference in the groups, and whether there was a significant interaction between groups and pre – versus - posttests, as demonstrated by scores in the Pre and Post-instruction Knowledge Tests [1]. There was no statistically significant interaction with $F (1, 37) = .08$, and $p = .76$, between participant performance and whether participants were in the JiT or JiC groups. There was no statistically significant increase in knowledge after instruction with $F (1, 37) = .36$, and $p = .55$. The JiT and the JiC groups did not perform significantly different from each other on average with $F (1, 37) = .08$, and $p = .76$.

11.2   Data Analysis for Research Question 2

Pre and Post-instruction Lesson Plans were used to answer Research Question 2 of this study [1]. Pre and Post-instruction Lesson Plan data were collected from 36 or 83.7 % participants. Out of this number, there were 19 participants in the JiT group and 17 in the JiC group. Scores from these lesson plans and a value for the JiC versus the JiT variable were obtained.

Research Question 2 was addressed by analyzing performance scores on the Pre and Post-instruction Lesson Plans submitted by the participants as well as by analyzing their scores on the researcher-created SIOP® Usage Survey [1]. The grading rubric used for the Pre and Post-instruction Lesson Plans was the SIOP® protocol which has already been found to be a reliable and valid instrument with an inter-rater correlation of .99 [22].

The Pre-instruction Lesson Plan, the JiT group had a higher average performance ($M = 18.7$, $SD = 14.0$) than the JiC group ($M = 15.6$, $SD = 10.0$) [1]. In the

Post-instruction Lesson Plan, the JiT group had a higher average performance ($M = 58.3, SD = 10.8$) than the JiC group ($M = 58.1, SD = 12.3$). Both groups improved significantly from pre to post test in terms of SIOP® application.

RMANOVA Results. A repeated measures analysis of variance was used to assess whether there was a significant difference in performance before and after instruction, whether there was a difference in the groups, and whether there was a significant interaction between groups and pre-versus-post-tests as demonstrated by scores in the Pre and Post-instruction Lesson Plans [1].

There was no statistically significant interaction with $F (1, 34) = .26$, and $p = .61$ between participant performance and whether participants were in the JiT or JiC groups [1]. There was a statistically significant increase in SIOP® application after instruction for both groups, as demonstrated by increased scores in the Post-instruction Lesson Plan with $F (1, 34) = 210.73$, and $p = \le .001$. However, the JiT and the JiC groups did not perform significantly different from each other with $F (1, 34) = .26$, and $p = .61$.

Pre and Post-instruction SIOP® Usage Surveys were also used to answer Research Question 2 of this study [1]. Pre and Post-instruction SIOP® Usage Survey Data were collected from 33 or 76.7 % ($n = 33$) participants. Out of this number, 17 participants were from the JiT group and 16 from the JiC group. Scores from these surveys and a value for the JiC versus the JiT variable were obtained. Both groups displayed a statistically significant improvement from pre to post test in terms of SIOP® application.

The Pre-instruction SIOP® Usage Survey, the JiT group had a higher average performance ($M = 3.9, SD = .37$) than the JiC group ($M = 3.8, SD = .32$) [1]. In the Post-instruction SIOP® Usage Survey, the JiT group had a higher average performance ($M = 4.1, SD = .38$) than the JiC group ($M = 4.0, SD = .39$). Both groups improved significantly from pre to post test in terms of intended SIOP® application.

RMANOVA Results. A repeated measures analysis of variance was used to assess whether there was a significant difference in performance before and after instruction, whether there was a difference in the groups, and whether there was a significant interaction between groups and pre- versus post-tests as demonstrated by scores in the Pre and Post-instruction SIOP® Usage Survey [1].

There was no statistically significant interaction with $F (1, 31) = .00$, and $p = .94$ between participant performance and whether participants were in the JiT or JiC groups [1]. There was a statistically significant increase in SIOP® application after instruction, as demonstrated by increased scores in the SIOP® Usage Survey, for both the JiT and JiC groups with $F (1, 31) = 8.42$, and $p = < .01$. However, the JiT and the JiC groups did not perform significantly different from each other with $F (1, 31) = .00$, and $p = .94$.

12   Findings and Conclusions

This study did not produce evidence to answer Research Question 1 affirmatively [1]; that is, there appears to be no difference in knowledge acquisition between the JiT and JiC groups. However, the timing of the training, the high pre-instruction SIOP® knowledge within each group, the small number of participants, and other limitations noted for this study may have led to the non-significant results. Alternatively, this study may provide support for the hypothesis that JiC training is as effective for knowledge acquisition as training in a JiT context, and that training, in the absence of an immediate need, does not necessarily waste time or resources. Further research to examine this perspective is needed.

Similarly, this study also did not produce evidence to answer Research Question 2 affirmatively [1]; that is, there appears to be no difference in SIOP® application after receiving training between the JiT and JiC groups. However, the timing of the training, the high pre-instruction SIOP® application within each group, the small number of participants, and other limitations noted for this study, may have led to the non-significant results. Alternatively, this study may provide support for the hypothesis that JiC training is as effective for application as training in a JiT context, and that training, without an immediate need, does not necessarily waste time or resources.

13   Recommendations for Further Research

The findings of this research study lead to various potential opportunities for further research [1]. This study was restricted to participants within the state of Idaho. Therefore the generalizability of this study is limited. A future study could be conducted which could include in-service teachers from states outside Idaho. Since this course was delivered online, including participants at large distances should not be a problem.

The sample size (N = 43) of this study was relatively small [1]. Further research could be conducted with more participants. Discussions during the Focus Group Meetings revealed that the timing of the course was unsuitable for most teachers since it was the end of the school year, when teachers are usually busy with their professional duties. This may be one reason why some potential participants did not register for the course. Therefore it is recommended that future courses should be delivered at a more suitable time.

While some of the instruments in this study (Lesson Plans based on the SIOP® Model, Usage Survey) demonstrate how participants plan to implement the SIOP® training acquired from this course, they do not demonstrate whether the teachers actually implemented SIOP® principles in their classroom [1]. A future study is recommended where teachers can be video-recorded delivering lessons in their actual classrooms, before and after receiving instruction. It is further recommended that a time-delayed posttest or evaluation be made to see the long-term retention and implementation levels of the training.

The duration of this course was only four weeks [1]. Within this short time, learners had to complete many reading assignments, quizzes, activities, lesson plans, surveys, and tests. Some experts suggest that short and isolated professional development workshops should be avoided [23]. Future courses should contain more regular opportunities for participant interaction and collaboration through activities like group discussions and projects.

Some participants mentioned in the Focus Group Meeting sessions (results not reported in this paper) that the online format of the course was a challenge, because they did not have any prior experience in using *Moodle*, which was the delivery Learning Management System (LMS) of this course [1]. It is recommended that future courses should contain an in-built training module on the use of *Moodle* for learners who are not familiar with its use.

This study examined Just-in-Time training within the specific context of the SIOP® Model [1]. Additional research needs to be conducted to determine if the findings from this study could be replicated in other subject areas.

References

1. Bose, D.: Effects of Just-in-Time online training on knowledge and application of the Sheltered Instruction Observation Protocol (SIOP®) model among in-service teachers (Doctoral dissertation). Available from ProQuest Dissertations and Theses database. (UMI No. 3536205) (2012)
2. Woodford, J.: Just In Time Training or Point-of-use Information. Vega Group PLC, Bristol (2004)
3. Rushby, N.: Editorial: avoiding training waste. Br. J. Educ. Technol. **37**(2), 161–162 (2006)
4. Prince, M., Felder, R.: The many facets of inductive teaching and learning. J. Coll. Sci. Teach. **36**(5), 14–18 (2007)
5. Dunst, C.J., Trivette, C.M., Hamby, D.W.: Meta-analysis of the effectiveness of four adult learning methods and strategies. Int. J. Continuing Educ. Lifelong Learn. **3**(1), 91–112 (2010)
6. Iannarelli, B.: JiT Training (JITT) and its implications for teaching and learning. In: Rogers, P.L., Berg, G.A., Boettcher, J.V., Howard, C., Justice, L., Schenk, K.D. (Eds.) Encyclopedia of Distance Learning, Second Edition, pp. 1297–1305 (2009). doi:10.4018/978-1-60566-198-8.ch186
7. Carrick, L.A.: Demystifying the EI quick fix. T+D **64**(11), 60–63 (2010)
8. Ikseon, C., Hyeonjin, K., Jong Won, J., Clinton, G., Jeongwan, K.: A case-based e-Learning model for professional education: Anesthesiology for dental students. Educ. Media Technol. Yearb. **31**, 109–118 (2006)
9. Southwood, S.: Taking the fear out of math. Adults Learn. **22**(6), 14–15 (2011)
10. Samarajiva, R., Gamage, S.: Bridging the divide: Building Asia-Pacific capacity for effective reforms. Inf. Soc. **23**(2), 109–117 (2007). doi:10.1080/01972240701224200
11. Mkhize, P., Huisman, M., Lubbe, S.: An analysis of collaborative learning as a prevalent instructional strategy of south african government eLearning practices. In: Proceedings Of The European Conference On E-Learning, pp. 492–501 (2011)
12. Miller, J.D.: Adult science learning in the internet era. Curator **53**(2), 191–208 (2010). doi:10.1111/j.2151-6952.2010.00019.x
13. Brown, J.S., Duguid, P.: The Social Life of Information. Harvard Business School Press, Boston (2000)
14. Ramaekers, S., van Keulen, H., Kremer, W., Pilot, A., van Beukelen, P.: Effective teaching in case-based education: patterns in teacher behavior and their impact on the students' clinical problem solving and learning. Int. J. Teach. Learn. High. Educ. **23**(3), 303–313 (2011)
15. Wenner, J.M., Burn, H.E., Baer, E.M.: The math you need, when you need it: online modules that remediate mathematical skills in introductory geoscience courses. J. Coll. Sci. Teach. **41**(1), 16–24 (2011)

16. Creswell, J.W.: Research design: Qualitative, Quantitative, and Mixed Methods Approaches. Sage Publications, Thousand Oaks (2003)
17. Gagne, R.M., Wager, W.W., Golas, K.C., Keller, J.M.: Principles of Instructional Design, 5th edn. Wadsworth/Thomson Learning, Belmont (2005)
18. Dick, W., Carey, L., Carey, J.O.: The Systematic Design of Instruction. Allyn and Bacon, Boston (2005)
19. Aron, A., Aron, E.N.: Statistics for Psychology. Prentice Hall, Upper Saddle River (1999)
20. Gravetter, F.J., Wallnau, L.B.: Statistics for the Behavioral Sciences. Thomson Higher Education, Belmont (2007)
21. Field, A.: Discovering Statistics using SPSS. Sage Publications, Thousand Oaks (2009)
22. Guarino, A.J., Echevarria, J., Short, D., Schick, J.E., Forbes, S., Rueda, R.: The sheltered instruction observation protocol. J. Res. Educ. **11**(1), 138–140 (2001)
23. Echevarria, J., Short, D.J., Vogt, M.: Implementing the SIOP® Model through Effective Professional Development and Coaching. Pearson Education Inc, Boston (2008)

Users and Technologies in Education: A Pending Course

Cristóbal Fernández Robin[1(✉)], Scott McCoy[2], and Diego Yáñez Martínez[1]

[1] Departamento de Industrias, Universidad Técnica Federico Santa María, Valparaíso, Chile
{cristobal.fernandez,diego.yanez}@usm.cl
[2] Mason School of Business, Williamsburg, VA, USA
scott.mccoy@mason.wm.edu

Abstract. This research aims to determine which factors influence the Intention to Use Technologies in the education sphere, by using Technology Acceptance Model with university students across two technologies having similar characteristics: SIGA and SGDI. The results shows that the most important factor when determining Intention to Use of an educational technology is Perceived Usefulness. Subsequently, TAM is applied considering the moderating effect of intensity, finding that for intensive SGDI users, the influence of Perceived Usefulness is greater than in normal users, and conversely, the influence of Perceived Ease of Use in intensive users of SIGA is greater than that in normal users, whereas the impact of Perceived Usefulness decreases. Recommendations states that future investigations should focus on the study of the impact generated by the use of software in classrooms, both for students during their training process and for professors in their educational work.

Keywords: Technology in education · Intention to use · Technology acceptance model

1 Introduction

Information technologies have great potential to improve all education spheres, from basic education to university teaching, including continuous education and technical training, both traditional and online. Indeed, while technology is still altering teaching and learning, professors face increased expectations to take advantage of technology [11], promoting their experimentation with simple ways to cope with the need to alternate between pedagogy and technology [9].

Chile has been one of the pioneers in Latin America in the use of computers and networks at the primary and secondary school level. However, the educational process at the primary and secondary level has not changed significantly, and a similar effect is occurring at the university level. For this reason, the factors that influence Intention to Use information and communications technologies in the sphere of education need to be studied.

© Springer International Publishing Switzerland 2015
P. Zaphiris and A. Ioannou (Eds.): LCT 2015, LNCS 9192, pp. 668–675, 2015.
DOI: 10.1007/978-3-319-20609-7_62

2   Literature Review

The Technology Acceptance Model (TAM) [1] is an adaptation of the Rational Action Theory [3] to the specific case of technology adoption, where two factors, Perceived Usefulness and Perceived Ease of Use, are presented as predictors of Intention to Use for the system or technology in question and a parallel causal relationship exists between Perceived Ease of Use and Perceived Usefulness [1].

In recent decades, research has focused on improving the predictive capacity of the model, leading to the emergence of the TAM 2 [13], which introduces external or social influences (subjective norm, voluntariness, image) and the cognitive process (job relevance, output quality, result demonstrability, Perceived Ease of Use) to the model as factors influencing Perceived Usefulness and subsequent Intention to Use. According to Venkatesh & Davis [13], TAM 2 can explain between 40 % and 60 % of the variance, subject to a context of mandatory use. In the same way, various studies have been conducted to validate or refute the TAM in various environments and with different research subjects, obtaining results that converge and validate the model typically by explaining 40 % of the variance presented by Intention to Use [8]. To reconcile the various existing models, the Unified Theory of Acceptance and Use of Technology emerged [14], where Performance Expectations, Effort Expectancy, and Social Influence determine Intention to Use, which together with Facilitating Conditions determine the Use Behavior. With the aim of complementing the study conducted on influencing variables for Perceived Usefulness, Venkatesh and Bala [15] proposed the TAM 3 by adding influencing variables to Perceived Ease of Use (computer self-efficacy, perception of external control, computer anxiety, computer playfulness, perceived satisfaction, objective Usefulness). Turner et al. [12] reviewed previous studies of the TAM, finding a strong correlation between Intention to Use and current use but a weak correlation between Perceived Ease of Use and Perceived Usefulness in terms of current use. On this basis, Turner et al. [12] suggest exercising caution when using the model outside of the context where it has been validated. Venkatesh et al. [16] adapted the Unified Theory of Acceptance and Use of Technology to a context of consumption by adding a series of variables (hedonic motivation, price value, habit) to the original model.

In the sphere of education, Hu et al. [5] studied the level of acceptance of classroom technologies by professors, and the results suggest that Perceived Usefulness directly affects and Perceived Ease of Use indirectly affects Intention to Use, similar to subsequent findings of Teo [11]. Gibson et al. [4] studied the acceptance of online education using the TAM, finding that Perceived Usefulness is a strong indicator of Intention to Use, and although significant, Perceived Ease of Use does not constitute a relevant contribution, which is similar to the results of Teo [10] in terms of the importance of Perceived Usefulness. Similarly, Un Jan and Contreras [6] studied university students and found that Perceived Ease of Use is not an influencing factor in the model, which makes sense because students perceive a certain difficulty in the use of the study technology, although they are willing to use it as part of their training as engineers [6]. Likewise, Escobar-Rodríguez and Monge-Lozano [2] also demonstrate that Perceived Usefulness is more important for Intention to Use than Perceived Ease of Use.

3 Theoretical Model Developed

The model developed corresponds to the TAM applied to higher education students in Chile, where the following relationships are found: Perceived Usefulness with Intention to Use, Perceived Ease of Use with Intention to Use and Perceived Ease of Use with Perceived Usefulness. These relationships lead to the following hypotheses.

H1: Perceived Usefulness positively influences the Intention to Use a given information or technology system.

Perceived Usefulness is defined as the degree to which a person thinks that the use of a technology will improve his or her labor performance [1]. Considering the importance of work performance, a technology perceived as useful will have greater Intention to Use.

H2: Perceived Ease of Use positively influences the Intention to Use a given information or technology system.

Perceived Ease of Use is defined as the degree to which a person thinks that the use of a given technology will be effortless [1]. Considering that effort is a limited resource that must be assigned to multiple tasks, a technology that does not require use effort will have greater Intention to Use.

H3: Perceived Ease of Use positively influences the Perceived Usefulness of a given information or technology system.

If a system or technology requires less effort (taking effort as a limited resource), more effort can be assigned to other tasks, increasing productivity or labor performance [2].

H4: Use Intensiveness has a significant impact on Intention to Use a given information or technology system.

The assessment and behavior of a user with regard to a system evolves as he or she gains experience with the use of technology [7]. Thus, Intention to Use is expected to be greater for intensive users than normal users.

4 Methodology

The first stage of the study pursues exploratory research to delve deeper into the knowledge about the TAM and its application in the education model, specifically for university students. Conclusive research was subsequently performed involving the analysis of structural equations and factorial confirmatory analysis. At this point, the results of the survey of Federico Santa María Technical University students were reviewed to verify the TAM (Fig. 1) in two information systems owned by the University: the Academic Information and Management System (SIGA) and the Industry Department Management System (SGDI). Both systems are used both by students and the Industry Department of Federico Santa María Technical University. Finally, we evaluated the study model by comparing the results obtained for the information systems contained in the study and conducted an analysis of Use Intensiveness for each study technology.

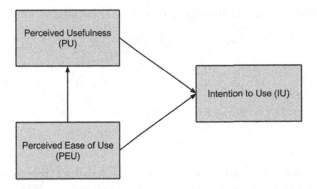

Fig. 1. Proposed model. Source: authors' research with IBM SPSS Amos 20

5   Analysis and Results

The results of the proposed model reveal an adequate fit of the model in terms of reliability and validity tests to which the model was subjected, obtaining statistically significant relationships at the level of the measurement model (the relationship between
observable variables and latent variables) and the structural model (the relationship
between the proposed factors or latent variables) for the case of SGDI, thus proving H1,
H2 and H3.

Table 1 indicates that Perceived Usefulness greatly influences Intention to Use,
whereas Perceived Ease of Use has somewhat less direct influence on Intention to Use.
Likewise, we emphasize the significant impact Perceived Ease of Use has on Perceived
Usefulness, i.e., if SGDI requires less effort (taking effort as a limited resource), more
effort can be assigned to other tasks, increasing productivity or performance due to this
information system.

Table 1. Standardized coefficients of latent variables for SGDI

SGDI	Estimate	P
PU ← PEU	.707	***
IU ← PEU	.290	***
IU ← PU	.526	***

Source: Authors' research with IBM
SPSS Amos 20

In the case of SIGA, Perceived Ease of Use does not have a statistically significant
influence on Intention to Use, disproving H2 in this case, even if the strong impact of
Perceived Usefulness on Intention to Use is noteworthy.

Table 2 depicts how the low impact of Perceived Ease of Use on Perceived Usefulness is also noteworthy. Ultimately, Perceived Ease of Use does not appear to be a
relevant construct when predicting the Intention to Use SIGA.

Table 2. Standardized coefficients of latent variables for SIGA

SIGA	Estimate	P
PU ← PEU	.239	***
IU ← PEU	.004	.937
IU ← PU	.606	***

Source: Authors' research with IBM SPSS Amos 20

These two study technologies have similar characteristics. The apparent difference between these two information systems is Use Intensiveness, as SIGA is a system used intensively at the start of each academic term during the course registration phase for students, whereas students use SGDI on a daily basis to review the news, guidelines and notes in their courses.

Figure 2 indicates the difference in Use Intensiveness between SGDI and SIGA, both in weekly hours and times used per week. Whereas SGDI is used more than SIGA, less time is dedicated to the use of SGDI each time it is used. When determining a ratio between hours and usage times per week, we obtain an average of 0.52 for each student who uses SIGA, and students only need 0.42 h to use SGDI.

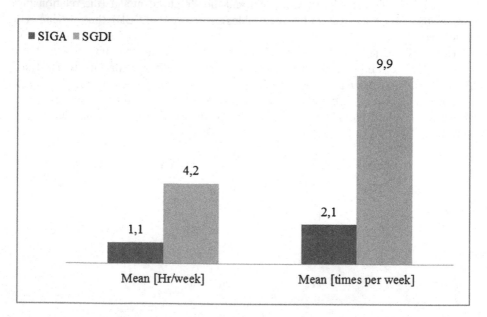

Fig. 2. Use intensiveness. Source: authors' research

Analyzing the predictive capacity of the model reveals that SGDI yields better results than SIGA. The TAM explains 58 % of the total Intention to Use variance for SGDI and 37 % of the total Intention to Use variance for SIGA (Table 3).

Table 3. R^2 Comparison of intention to use for SIGA and SGDI.

	R^2
SIGA	0.369
SGDI	0.576

Source: Authors'
research with IBM
SPSS Amos

These findings suggest that the greater the Use Intensiveness of the study technology is, the better the predictive capacity of the model (H4). To verify this assumption, we performed a comparison of means in the Intention to Use factor according to Use Intensiveness measured in usage times per week in each of the study systems (Table 4).

Table 4. Independent Samples Test of Intention to Use for SIGA and SGDI.

		Levene's Test for Equality of Variances		t-test for Equality of Means		
		F	Sig.	t	df	Sig. (2-tailed)
Intention to Use SGDI	Equal variances assumed	13.486	.000	−5.241	425	.000
	Equal variances not assumed			−5.448	323.311	.000
Intention to Use SIGA	Equal variances assumed	5.229	.023	−7.144	425	.000
	Equal variances not assumed			−7.559	201.758	.000

Source: Authors' research with IBM SPSS Statistics

In this way, we can demonstrate a statistically significant difference for SIGA and SGDI, proving H4, i.e., Intention to Use is different for normal and intensive users.

To reinforce this last hypothesis, we divided the surveyed students into intensive and normal users, subsequently reviewing the results obtained for each of the study technologies in the TAM.

In the case of SGDI, Table 5 reveals how the impact generated by Perceived Usefulness increases in intensive users, i.e., the more the user gains experience using SGDI, the greater benefit he or she derives from the tools offered by it, thus increasing Intention to Use.

Table 5. Standardized coefficients of latent variables according to Use Intensiveness.

	SGDI		SIGA	
	Normal	Intensivo	Normal	Intensivo
PU ← PEU	.705***	.702***	.210**	.230*
IU ← PEU	.322***	.281***	−.116*	.235*
IU ← PU	.472***	.580***	.635***	.514***
R^2	.541	.644	.385	.375

Source: Authors' research with IBM SPSS Amos

Conversely, in the case of SIGA, Perceived Ease of Use has a greater influence on Intention to Use, which is negative in normal users and positive in intensive users. Therefore, in this case, Use Intensiveness appears to encourage the perception of Ease of Use for SIGA but decreases the impact of Perceived Usefulness.

Finally, although Use Intensiveness has a significant impact on the Intention to Use a given information system in the educational sphere, we cannot know whether this impact is direct or whether it works through the PEU and PU constructs.

6   Discussion

The TAM is an excellent tool for predicting and explaining behavior, or Intention to Use, for a given technology. Specifically, in education, where technology use is mandatory, Perceived Usefulness explains Intention to Use to a greater extent, and Perceived Ease of Use is a non-significant factor for Intention to Use in some cases.

Conversely, TAM is not sufficiently effective when explaining differences in Intention to Use for various technologies, which is why we use Intensiveness as a moderating effect. SGDI displays fit, reliability indicators, estimators and determination coefficients that are similar to SIGA. Both technologies are mandatory for university students to use and are designed with similar goals and functions. The greatest difference between SIGA and SGDI is based on Use Intensiveness; SGDI is for everyday use and thus it is not irrational to think that students have a higher level of familiarity with it than SIGA, whose seasonal use presents peaks during course registration periods. In this way, we can see that the results of the TAM vary according to Use Intensiveness, as demonstrated by the results of the mean comparison. The assessment and behavior of a user with regard to a system evolves as he or she gains experience with the use of a technology [7]. Therefore, we should note that the intensive use of SGDI generates a greater impact of Perceived Usefulness on Intention to Use, whereas the intensive use of SIGA decreases this relationship and increases the influence of Perceived Ease of Use on Intention to Use. Future research on the impact of Use Intensiveness should focus on how this relationship is generated, i.e., a direct relationship on the Intention to Use factor or an indirect relationship through Perceived Ease of Use or Perceived Usefulness.

Another point to be considered is that the TAM can only explain the Intention to Use a given education technology, and measuring the impact generated by the use of information and communications technologies (ICTs) in the classroom is insufficient. Consequently, the next step of this research seeks to measure the level of acceptance of ICTs in education and determine the real impact generated by the use of software in the classroom. We plan to conduct an experiment with university students in a marketing class where an online business simulator is used, verifying the extended version of the Unified Technology Acceptance and Use Theory [16] and searching for measures for the impact that technology has on the educational process.

References

1. Davis, F.D.: Perceived usefulness, perceived ease of use, and user acceptance of information technology. MIS Q. **13**(1), 319–340 (1989)
2. Escobar-Rodriguez, T., Monge-Lozano, P.: The acceptance of moodle technology by business administration students. Comput. Educ. **58**(4), 1085–1093 (2012)
3. Fishbein, M., Ajzen, I.: Belief, Attitude, Intention, and Behavior: An Introduction to Theory and Research. Addison-Wesley, Boston (1975)
4. Gibson, S.G., Harris, M.L., Colaric, S.M.: Technology acceptance in an academic context: faculty acceptance of online education. J. Educ. Bus. **83**(6), 355–359 (2008)
5. Hu, P.J.H., Clark, T.H., Ma, W.W.: Examining technology acceptance by school teachers: a longitudinal study. Inf. Manag. **41**(2), 227–241 (2003)
6. Jan, A.U., Contreras, V.: Technology acceptance model for the use of information technology in universities. Comput. Hum. Behav. **27**(2), 845–851 (2011)
7. Kim, S.S., Malhotra, N.K.: A longitudinal model of continued IS use: an integrative view of four mechanisms underlying postadoption phenomena. Manag. Sci. **51**(5), 741–755 (2005)
8. Legris, P., Ingham, J., Collerette, P.: Why do people use information technology? A critical review of the technology acceptance model. Inf. Manag. **40**(3), 191–204 (2003)
9. Pelgrum, W.J.: Obstacles to the integration of ICT in education: results from a worldwide educational assessment. Comput. Educ. **37**(2), 163–178 (2001)
10. Teo, T.: Modelling technology acceptance in education: a study of pre-service teachers. Comput. Educ. **52**(2), 302–312 (2009)
11. Teo, T., Noyes, J.: An assessment of the influence of perceived enjoyment and attitude on the intention to use technology among pre-service teachers: a structural equation modeling approach. Comput. Educ. **57**(2), 1645–1653 (2011)
12. Turner, M., Kitchenham, B., Brereton, P., Charters, S., Budgen, D.: Does the technology acceptance model predict actual use? A systematic literature review. Inf. Softw. Technol. **52**(5), 463–479 (2010)
13. Venkatesh, V., Davis, F.D.: A theoretical extension of the technology acceptance model: four longitudinal field studies. Manag. Sci. **46**(2), 186–204 (2000)
14. Venkatesh, V., Morris, M.G., Davis, G.B., Davis, F.D.: User acceptance of information technology: Toward a unified view. MIS Q. **27**(3), 425–478 (2003)
15. Venkatesh, V., Bala, H.: Technology acceptance model 3 and a research agenda on interventions. Decis. Sci. **39**(2), 273–315 (2008)
16. Venkatesh, V., Thong, J.Y., Xu, X.: Consumer acceptance and use of information technology: extending the unified theory of acceptance and use of technology. MIS Q. **36**(1), 157–178 (2012)

Free Software User Interfaces: Usability and Aesthetics

Edmund Laugasson[✉] and Mati Mõttus

Institute of Informatics, Tallinn University, Narva Road 25, 10120 Tallinn, Estonia
edmund.laugasson@gmail.com, mati@foti.ee

Abstract. Using free software has been one of the discussion topics for time to time. There are several desktop environments available for nowadays modern GNU/Linux (hereinafter: Linux) distributions with different usability levels. However it seems that some of the users are not satisfied with current graphical user interfaces. We present a qualitative analysis of four different Linux distributions using different desktop environments. We find that most usable desktop is XFCE, then comes Mate, KDE and last one is LXDE. The results are a bit surprising as the LXDE is very similar to famous and recently widely used MS Windows XP. Our findings lead us into understanding that Microsoft has designed the past user experience of computer use and its user interface design is affecting also other operating systems based on users perception.

Keywords: User experience · Usability · Aesthetics · Free software · Digital literacy

1 Introduction

Estonia is living in the breaking times. In spring of 2011 the World Bank announced that Estonia is now high income country (World Bank, 2014). This is subject of discussion but based on that decision in turn Microsoft decided to increase prices of software licences for Estonia more than 20 and up to 60 times depending on which licensing scheme to choose and what is the former situation of licences in specific institution. For time to time Microsoft is doing special offers but this is not the sustainable basis on which government can rely. The first deadline of price increase was 30th June 2014, which has been extended now for 30th June 2017. This fact started discussion and activities in Estonian society. First step was free software pilot project organized by Tallinn City Municipality Education Board (EPL, 2014). This project involved five educational institutions: 3 schools and 2 kindergartens from Tallinn city. The project ended successfully in April 2014 and continues currently in next phases were already some more schools are involved.

During the project for time to time people has been claimed that GNU/Linux distribution Lubuntu 12.04 LTS and also 14.04 LTS user interface (LXDE desktop environment) lacks of usability compared with previous successor Microsoft Windows from versions of XP till 8. In that reason we conducted a research of different Linux desktop environments. We formulated two main research questions: "does the Linux

© Springer International Publishing Switzerland 2015
P. Zaphiris and A. Ioannou (Eds.): LCT 2015, LNCS 9192, pp. 676–686, 2015.
DOI: 10.1007/978-3-319-20609-7_63

user interface have poor user experience" and "which desktop environment would be most suitable for educational institutions".

Users dissatisfaction was a little surprise as the LXDE desktop environment was chosen based on its similarity of famous MS Windows XP user interface. Based on our study the LXDE got the worst user rating. This also explains the user dissatisfaction that were experienced during the free software project.

2 Literature Review

There are many articles about free software. One of the most comprehensive look is book "Handbook of Research on Open Source Software: Technological, Economic, and Social Perspectives" in 767 pages (St. Amant et al., 2007). This book has 110 contributors from different point of views over all the world. It introduces the philosophy, challenges, innovation, social, developing and so many other aspects of free software. In chapter 3 there are descriptions of how free software can be much better improved due to its open sourcecode. Main strengths are freedom to use, which gives also reliability even if there are some difficulties as well. These aspects do not prevent the use of software.

Reliability for users usually means that applications works as expected - this means the application does not crash every second or not cause data loss (Garvin, 1984). In our study overall reliability was good only very few times virtual machines crashed during shut down.

In security user need to know the application trustworthy that it does not contain malware or network features are secured (Hoepman et al., 2007). From user perspective the openness is good for security, especially if the developer community is active.

On the efficiency side for user it means that the application has clear, easy to follow user interface (Glott et al., 2010). Also features should be documented so users can search and find them. Functions should meet user needs and the application must be responsive on user actions.

Also open-source software would be much more interoperable thaln closed source one (Money et al., 2012). Interoperability itself has a crucial importance, especially when free office suite should open proprietary file formats. This also helps to avoid vendor lock-in when producing documents in open formats and spreading them with suggestion download also free office suite like LibreOffice and use it.

There are not many studies of free software and aesthetics based on ACM, IEEE, Google Scholar databases. Leach et al. mostly describes morality and aesthetics in free software design (Leach et al., 2009). It is a quite philosophical article and even says, that free and open-source software development and community life (as "social machine") is like we should live in 21th century.

3 Evaluation of UX

The goal of evaluation is to acknowledge competitiveness of free and open source software (FOSS). Evaluation of UX can be used to prove FOSS to be pragmatically usable and satisfying, but also attractive and pleasing.

Pragmatic qualities of UX denote, how users perceive the technology's ability to help them in completing their task and reaching the goal. The way, how pragmatics is experienced, may be expressed with opposing word pairs: e.g. confusing-structured, impractical-practical, unpredictable-predictable, complicated-simple (Hassenzahl, 2010).

Besides pragmatic qualities are also user's feelings that play important role to engage users. These are the hedonic qualities, described by the emotional attributes (e.g., 'exciting', 'impressive', 'presentable'), emphasizing psychological well-being through non-instrumental, self-oriented product qualities (Diefenbach, 2013). First impression, for example has crucial role in user's decision making: affect, caused by first impression happens so quickly that pragmatic usage can not even happen (Lindgaard, 2006). Hedonic qualities of UX can be expressed as word pairs: dull-captivating, tacky-stylish, cheap-premium, unimaginativ-creative, good-bad and beautiful-ugly.

Aesthetics of interaction has significant role while modifying hedonic quality of interactive product. Considering the effect, it has on engaging the users, current study will use aesthetic dimensions for assessing the UX of FOSS besides the traditional, pragmatic usability study.

4   Method

4.1   Evaluating Usability

Usability, in terms of UX, is a parameter of interactive product, that describes user's ability to complete intended task. It integrates both - the features of interface and users ability to use the interface. The value of usability expresses how effective and efficient is the interface in completing the intended task. Usability data is pragmatic, quantitative and it can be objectively assessed/analysed.

Usability evaluation includes three general components: time to complete the task, number of errors during the task completion and ability to complete the task (whether the task was completed or not). Usability data can be collected via observation. The procedures for observation are: taking time, counting errors and keeping notes. Supportive techniques can be video and audio recording, screen recording, key/mouse logging and eye tracking. Some of the data, collected during observation can be used for evaluating hedonic UX.

System Usability Scale (Brooke, 1996) is quick and dirty questionnaire that has been used successfully since 1996. It can be used for evaluating pragmatic satisfaction. It comprises of 10 questions on 5p Likert scale (agree-disagree), addressing the user's perceptions about using the product. Completing the questionnaire takes max 5 min and the questions are easily understood.

4.2   Evaluating Hedonic Qualities

According to suggested definition (Djajadiningrat, 2004), the aesthetic interaction refers to "things that are beautiful in use" and comprises of two components, neither of which should be addressed separately. These components are beauty of appearance and beauty of action. Traditional methods of evaluating perceived aesthetics collect user reported data about beauty of interface. According to definition, interaction aesthetics comprises of two types: beauty of appearance and beauty of use.

Simplest way of collecting data is single question like: do You find the interface appealing? The answer provides quantitative data where the scale varies from "beautiful" to "ugly". Such a question is suitable for assessing user's feeling at any moment throughout the study or retrospectively after the study. The answer does not define the type of stimuli and collected data allows to determine general aesthetic value, perceived and reported by user.

Hedonic qualities were evaluated with questionnaire, comprising of 18 questions, of which 5 questions were open ended and 6 questions were mandatory. One open ended question out of 5 was mandatory. Questionnaire included one question about first impression, one question about credibility, two questions about general aesthetics, two questions about style, five questions about visual aesthetics, five questions about aesthetics of action/dynamics, two questions about sound.

4.3   The Procedure

The procedure describes the way we used four different operating systems based on Ubuntu and running them in one desktop computer. The hardware had 8 GB of operating memory, 500 GB of hard drive and quad-core 2,66 GHz Intel processor.

We have chosen the most used Linux distribution Ubuntu and its flavours: Kubuntu with KDE -, Lubuntu with LXDE -, Ubuntu Mate with Mate - and Xubuntu with XFCE desktop environment (Ryan, 2010). During four months in the beginning of 2014 the Tallinn City Government in Estonia performed a successful pilot project of free software using Lubuntu Linux as operating system and LibreOffice as office suite (Tallinn City Municipality ICT information, 2014). We also tested other flavours of Ubuntu to understand which desktop environment would suits better for everyday usage.

Testing environment were built in top of Oracle's VirtualBox virtualization software using the built-in screencasting feature to record user activities during certain tasks. We created four different virtual machines with latest available versions in testing period of February 2015:

- Kubuntu 14.04.1 LTS 32-bit
- Lubuntu 14.04.1 LTS 32-bit
- Ubuntu Mate 14.04.1 LTS 32-bit
- Xubuntu 14.04.1 LTS 32-bit

We prepared virtual machines as much similar situation as it would be in normal life - made software updates for whole operating system, installed latest versions of used software (newest versions of LibreOffice, Firefox, Thunderbird, VLC Media Player, Adobe Flash plugin, Java plugin, PDF-printer and also some other printers installed). Also VirtualBox Guest Additions were installed for smooth perfomance of virtual machines - all that software were downloaded from Oracle servers using Ubuntu repository and also website for VirtualBox extension pack. Actually virtualization gives pretty much real feeling and the most significant difference users notice is that operating system is working in program window and not in full screen.

Virtual machine had 2 GB of operating memory, 8 GB of hard drive. Most of these desktop environments require less but for more convenient and seamless user experience we used a bit more operating memory.

Testing were started by running each virtual machine separately and filling the questionnaire. Virtual machines were configured so that also screen recording of virtual machine started. The first question was required to answer prior using and rest of after filling certain tasks on the virtual machine. During the virtual machine run all activities were recorded into video file for later analysis.

Tasks were separated into three parts: operating system basic functions, file manager tasks and office suite tasks. In parallel participants filled questionnaire, which was in two parts: SUS (System Usability Scale) and hedonics. Also users compared tested operating system and office suite with former used ones - first impression and how it feels with already used systems.

Participants were each one by own computer and solving tasks in own pace (Fig. 1).

Fig. 1. Participants in tests

5 Results

During testing approximately 24 h video recordings were collected from 46 different computers. There was quite comprehensive challenge to collect all data from different computers and analyze it.

Testing went almost smoothly - only few participants had problems. These problems were related with virtualization software VirtualBox, which very rare cases crashed during virtual machine shut down. Luckily it did not affect ability to run virtual machine again.

Participants had to solve three parts of tasks: operating system -, file manager - and office suite basic tasks. With each virtual machine were same tasks. Last test was office suite with last virtual machine. All results are summarized and collected into Tables 1 and 2.

The tasks were as follows:

- operating system:
  - change wallpaper
  - make shortcuts to Firefox, LibreOffice, Thunderbird, VLC Media Player
  - set default printer as PDF
  - change default program of the given file type: set VLC as default MP4
  - change mouse working scheme as single click
- file manager:
  - find a file by name, open it and then close again
  - navigate to location by path
  - create a directory with given name
  - copy the given file into previously created directory
  - rename the copied file with given name
- office suite:
  - open previously renamed file and save in another file format
  - change whole document to default style
  - change first three paragraph titles as heading 1
  - find a given phrase from text and change font attributes
  - change page layout
  - print to default printer and open created PDF-file for a while and then close it

In video recordings (Table 1, Fig. 2) there were measured completeness of tasks and spent time. Surprisingly the LibreOffice had quite high completeness and relatively small time footprint.

Comparing different desktop environments tasks completeness the XFCE-based Xubuntu 14.04.1 LTS got the best results. Then follows Mate desktop, KDE and last is LXDE.

At the same time accomplishing tasks in Mate desktop were a bit faster than XFCE-based Xubuntu (Table 1, Fig. 3). Also based on completeness the LXDE-based Lubuntu took less time than KDE-based Kubuntu.

So the completeness and spent time are different and here the Mate desktop seems to be fastest and XFCE desktop seems to be easiest to use.

At hedonics side overall results are as follows: the best one is XFCE-based Xubuntu, then not much less comes Mate desktop based Ubuntu (Table 2, Fig. 4). A slightly more difference are with rest of two desktop environments: KDE-based Kubuntu is on third place and LXDE-based Lubuntu is on the last place. Also SUS (System Usability Scale) results are in the same order (Table 2, Fig. 5).

Table 1. Video recording statistics

	Completeness	Average time
Kubuntu 14.04.1 LTS	0,86	00:19:52
Lubuntu 14.04.1 LTS	0,77	00:13:00
Ubuntu Mate 14.04.1 LTS	0,90	00:10:40
Xubuntu 14.04.1 LTS	0,92	00:13:07
LibreOffice 4.3.5	0,97	00:05:57

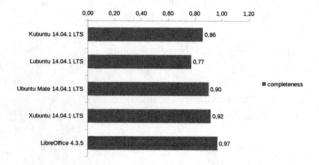

Fig. 2. Virtual machine tasks completeness

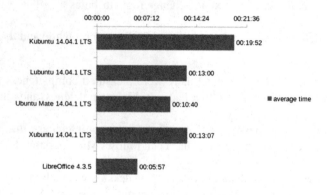

Fig. 3. Virtual machine task average time

5.1 Usability and SUS Analysis

Participants said that XFCE has the most clear user interface but also more untranslated menus. XFCE seemed also more modern than others. Also expected behaviour were in XFCE the best. Even users also appreciated KDE it seemed too many opportunities for most of users. XFCE also reminded a bit Mac OS for some users. As we see from video recording results also XFCE got the best results - the highest completeness rate and but not the fastest time to complete tasks. Several users said that they would prefer in future with XFCE-based Xubuntu instead of MS Windows.

Table 2. Questionnaire statistics

	Kubuntu	Xubuntu	Mate	Lubuntu	LibreOffice
First impression	0,65	0,79	0,74	0,60	0,65
Reliability	0,58	0,68	0,66	0,56	0,64
Aesthetics after use	0,68	0,76	0,71	0,57	0,56
Style aesthetics	0,65	0,79	0,74	0,51	0,56
Visual beauty	0,63	0,78	0,72	0,52	0,53
Placement	0,61	0,76	0,67	0,55	0,61
Shape	0,60	0,79	0,73	0,54	0,58
Color	0,70	0,77	0,73	0,49	0,54
Dynamics/movements	0,69	0,76	0,69	0,55	0,53
Transitions	0,70	0,74	0,71	0,50	0,58
Mouse	0,71	0,77	0,73	0,58	0,63
User activities	0,69	0,78	0,73	0,52	0,63
Sound	0,54	0,66	0,64	0,48	
SUS total	60,35	72,39	67,15	57,45	63,62

Mostly LXDE lacks of usability were common feedback by participants. At the same time LXDE has been found as most simplistic and logical but aged desktop environment. Most complicated were to find different tasks from menus and also some participants did not find the search feature. Also missing graphical sound mixer were one of the claims. This all reflects also in results of worst completeness but almost same time spent for tasks. Several users said that they would never replace MS Windows with LXDE-based Lubuntu.

The Mate desktop were only slightly less usable than XFCE by completeness and fastest by spent time for tasks. Some users found main menu opening at top unfamiliar. At the same time some users appreciated two panels - one for applications and one for taskbar. Overal look and feel were modern and usable by testers. Also most testers found that they could use Mate desktop instead of MS Windows.

The KDE desktop seemed nice and modern but also a little bit overbloated with different bells and whistles eagerly consuming computer resources. Some testers were disturbed of transparency used in most of windows when moved. Also quite big similarity with MS Windows were mentioned. Mac OS X were mentioned by some users as to similar with KDE. Overall feedback was that some people would even replace their existing operating system with KDE-based Kubuntu.

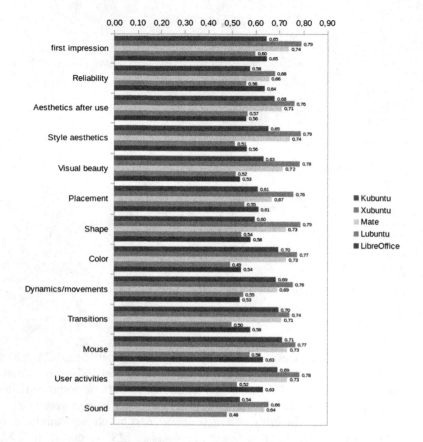

Fig. 4. Hedonics statistics (scale 0…1)

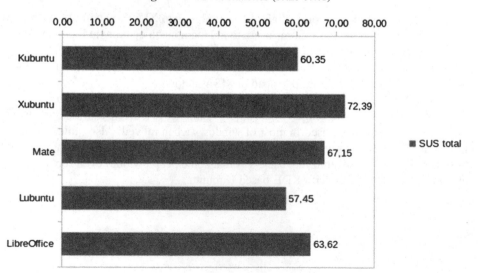

Fig. 5. SUS statistics (scale 0…100)

6 Conclusion

In current study we tested four different graphical Linux desktop environments usability and aesthetics based on appropriate Ubuntu versions. Participants were tested using previously prepared virtual machines and by analysing screen recordings made during tests. Also questionnaire were prepared to collect testers feedback based on System Usability Score (SUS) and usability (hedonic) questions.

Overall results did show, that XFCE-based Xubuntu were performed most well. It had the best usability and SUS results but not the best in time completion of tasks. Most shallow reason of good results was similarity with currently used system.

The second best result was in Mate desktop based Ubuntu Mate, which had the best result in time of task completion and quite close results in usability and SUS.

The third best result were performed by KDE-based Kubuntu. Testers spent most time to complete tasks on Kubuntu but overall rating was even quite good.

The fourth and last result were LXDE-based Lubuntu, which got worst overall feedback from testers.

In Tallinn free software pilot project currently LXDE-based Lubuntu were used. But soon it will be switched to Mate desktop based Ubuntu Mate. Also our study showed best perfomance in completing given tasks and very close usability and SUS test results.

Also we realized, that current systems (mostly Microsoft Windows) has influenced participant's perception of how operating system and office suite should work and look. But still testers found that different Linux desktops were quite usable and several said that they would start using Linux in near future.

Acknowledgement. This research was supported by the Tiger University Program of the Information Technology Foundation for Education - http://www.hitsa.ee/ikt-haridus/tiigriulikooli-programm.

The Digital Safety Lab is supported by the Tiger University Program of the Information Technology Foundation for Education - http://www.tlu.ee/dsl.

References

Brooke, J.: SUS-a quick and dirty usability scale. Usability Eval. Ind. **189**, 194 (1996). doi: 10.1002/hbm.20701

Diefenbach, S., Lenz, E., Hassenzahl, M.: An interaction vocabulary. Describing the how of interaction. In: CHI 2013: Extended Abstracts on Human Factors in Computing Systems (CHI EA 2013), pp. 607–612 (2013). doi:10.1145/2468356.2468463

Djajadiningrat, T., Wensveen, S., Frens, J., Overbeeke, K.: Tangible products: Redressing the balance between appearance and action. Pers. Ubiquit. Comput. **8**, 294–309 (2004). doi: 10.1007/s00779-004-0293-8

EPL. (2014). Tallinn is testing Linux in schools and kindergartens. http://epl.delfi.ee/news/eesti/tallinn-katsetab-koolides-ja-lasteaedades-linuxit?id=67556354. Accessed 2 January 2015

Glott, R., Groven, A-K., Haaland, K., Tannenberg, A.: Quality models for free/libre open source software – towards the silver bullet?. In: (2010) 36th EUROMICRO Conference on Software Engineering and Advanced Applications (SEAA), pp. 439–446 (2010)

Hoepman, J.-H., Jacobs, B.: Increased security through open source. commun. ACM **50**(1), 79–83 (2007)

Garvin, D.A.: What does product quality really mean? Sloan Manag. Rev. **26**(1), 25–45 (1984)

Hassenzahl, M.: Experience design: technology for all the right reasons. Synth. Lect. Hum.-Cent. Inform. **3**(1), 49–58 (2010). doi:10.2200/S00261ED1V01Y201003HCI008

Leach, J., Nafus, D., Krieger, B.: Freedom imagined: morality and aesthetics in open source software design. Ethnos **74**(1), 51–71 (2009). doi:10.1080/00141840902751188. http://www.jamesleach.net/downloads/Freedom%20imagined%20draft.pdf. Accessed 15 February 2015

Lindgaard, G., Fernandes, G., Dudek, C., Brown, J.: Attention web designers: you have 50 ms to make a good first impression! Behav. Inf. Technol. **25**(2), 115–126 (2006)

Money, L.P., Praseetha, S., Mohankumar, D.: Open source software: quality benefits, evaluation criteria and adoption methodologies. J. Comput. Model. **2**(3), 1–16 (2012)

Ryan, J.: Linux distribution chart. Linux J. **2010**(194), 4 (2010)

St. Amant, K., Still, B.: Handbook of Research on Open Source Software: Technological, Economic, and Social Perspectives. IGI Publishing Hershey, New York (2007). http://www.researchgate.net/profile/Alfreda_Dudley/publication/215705660_The_Social_and_Economical_Impact_of_OSS_in_Developing_Countries/links/0f317531ddf1a48821000000.pdf. Accessed 12 January 2015

Tallinn City Municipality ICT information. (2014). http://www.tallinn.ee/est/haridusasutused/IKT-info. Accessed 19 February 2015

World Bank. (2014). High income countries. https://web.archive.org/web/20140702131322/http://data.worldbank.org/about/country-and-lending-groups#High_income. Accessed 6 February 2015

Impacting the Digital Divide on a Global Scale - Six Case Studies from Three Continents

Birgy Lorenz[1](✉), Savilla Irene Banister[2], and Kaido Kikkas[1,3]

[1] Institute of Informatics, Tallinn University,
Narva Road 25, 10120 Tallinn, Estonia
{Birgy.lorenz,kaido.kikkas}@tlu.ee
[2] Center of Excellence for 21st Century,
Bowling Green State University, Ohio, USA
sbanist@bgsu.edu
[3] Estonian Information Technology College,
Raja St. 4C, 12616 Tallinn, Estonia

Abstract. This study represents findings from three continents (Asia, Africa and South America) regarding usage of ICT in six rural schools. Our goal was to analyze the current situation regarding digital technologies in these environments, describe similarities and differences relating to the digital divide, and provide a roadmap that could improve teaching and learning, maximizing the use of existing resources. Our case study was carried out with the help of innovative teachers who are supportive of technology integration in teaching, but have less options to utilize this knowledge in their classrooms because of various barriers. Our results show challenges, but also opportunities to embrace new ways of teaching; ways that might allow digital technologies to be employed in innovative ways to encourage student learning and community growth. Our study is based on participating teachers' understanding of the issues and challenges within these countries and areas, relating to schooling.

Keywords: Digital divide · Technology enhanced learning · Usage of ICT in rural areas · Classroom culture · Curricula challenges · Teacher education

1 Context for the International Integration of Digital Technologies in Education: Inequities in Rural Environments

One of the most important goals in the world is to adequately educate every person. The existence of the digital divide expands the challenge inside the country and also between countries [7] relating to equity in educational experiences. Modern countries are moving in the direction of e-governance and are starting to provide services that are available from a distance, but lack of resources and knowledge in rural areas make it impossible to develop access information and services, even when new resources are developed and installed on a daily basis [9]. Access to learning is rapidly changing because of the presence of digital technologies; these technological innovations are beginning to change the way teachers work. On the one hand, leadership is distributed,

© Springer International Publishing Switzerland 2015
P. Zaphiris and A. Ioannou (Eds.): LCT 2015, LNCS 9192, pp. 687–696, 2015.
DOI: 10.1007/978-3-319-20609-7_64

manual work is decreasing and more people are obtaining basic skills and literacy. On the other hand, rural schools and communities still struggle with lack of resources including access to the Internet and computers, but also limited qualified teachers and sparse knowledge of what is needed to create 21st century learning environments. Wealth flourishes only in city areas and people are leaving their birthplace to find a better job and an easier life somewhere else; this raises migration challenges both city and rural areas. Curricula reforms are desperately needed [10] to address these issues.

Rural area schools, especially in remote places throughout the world, share many common traits. Areas of similarity include the amount of students in classes, lack of technology, and the challenges both in social and economic areas. These areas try to improve curricula, set new rules and regulations and try to maximize the results from a traditional teaching model that pays allegiance to the authority of the teacher and a canon of identified knowledge. This model is dedicated to the perception that the teacher knows all, and basic teaching is supposed to be about reading and listening. Rules and regulations developed in city areas are communicated through this model along with curricular standards, developed in the urban regions but applied to the rural areas without appropriate communication and support from the government espousing these rules and standards [11].

Developing countries face not only lack of technology but also endure environmental and social difficulties; education is only one of the concerns challenging these places. At the same time, when implemented properly, education is the most valuable tool to effect change for these populations at once. These issues can be impacted by attending to the teacher's professional education in 21st century teaching and learning [3, 8]. In ICT-related education or usage in that field, impact is being seen in some homes and in the private sector. (e.g. in villages there are 2–3 Internet providers, a lot of cyber cafes and even the poorest family owns at least some kind of mobile phone.) In addition, parents passionately want their children to learn and want them to experience productive, successful lives with multiple options for employment and viability [2]. However, sometimes rural area teachers see technology as a magical fix for all the existing problems at school, which is unrealistic [4]. These phenomena indicate that rural schools are poised to be impacted by an infusion of ICT teaching and learning strategies.

Educational research focused on innovative ways of teaching highlight student achievement gains when new technologies are tested out in their studies [1]. Studies indicate that students focus more, their activity level increases, and they seem to learn more than ever when ICT innovations are employed. These types of practices could implemented in most schools, including rural ones [5]. Still the needed infrastructure is not always available in these rural settings to even bring these technologies into classes, as there is no electricity or sometimes community support. There is also the need for evaluation of adoption, focusing on what and how much has changed in students' ICT skills if they start using new technologies that are provided from the schools and government [6].

Research focus In our study we emphasized two main goals:

- to understand the situation in these 6 rural area cases related to ICT and 21st century teaching and learning practices;

- to suggest possible directions to target involving resources and teaching practices that could help them move closer to embracing technology-enhanced learning. These suggestions have the intention of making the transition less problematic, encouraging the teachers to see hidden resources in a current situation that is also useful to the schools and countries that faces the same issues.

2 Methods

This study included participants from one of the American teacher training programs in teaching excellence in 2013. Innovative teachers from the rural areas of Nepal, India, South-Africa, Jordan, Costa Rica and Venezuela participated in this program and in the study. The data was collected from the participants in three main segments: participant presentations and participant interviews. The following paragraphs describe the data collection process:

- participant presentations - all participants were asked to draw a diagram and briefly describe their country's educational system and curricula development. The information that was provided also covered classifications such as centralized/non centralized curricula development options and how much latitude the classroom teacher had to make decisions regarding curriculum or methods of teaching in their classrooms. Mandatory and optional courses were also discussed during this time;
- participant interviews - we conducted interviews with open-ended question topics focused on participant educational system and curricula, class culture, teacher's education, usage of ICT at homes and schools and challenges for the future. The interview lasted approximately 2 h and covered all the fields that the teachers wanted to talk about, including how they understood their current situations and changes that are made by their government to improve teaching and learning;
- data from the presentations and interviews were analyzed using qualitative techniques. The information was read and re-read, coding the elements and grouping these into themes. Experts of educational technology were invited to participate in discussing the results and to compare findings with the developing countries to see similarities and differences. Each country represented was considered a separate case, so each case was analyzed for key elements and the researchers synthesized this data into short descriptive narratives of the educational environments. The group also worked to develop strategies that could help rural area schools to make better decisions on how to harness technology, change pedagogy and use resources that already exist to improve their situation.

3 Results

The data indicated that rural schools in developing countries, though unique in some ways, possessed striking similarities. For example, on the issue of class size, South African schools reported the most variance (25−80 students per class), which spanned the smallest to the largest amount of students in one class. Other participants noted class sizes between 35–40 (Jordan, Venezuela, Costa Rica, Nepal) and 40–60 (India). There were also some differences in how many years students were mandated to be in school: 8 classes for Nepal, 9 classes Costa Rica and South Africa, 10 classes in India and Jordan and 11 in Venezuela. This is similar to Europe. The main difference between European schools and the rural schools targeted in the study, in regards to length of stay, seemed to be the dropout rate. Because of lack of family support to stay in school, the rural schools studied had a much higher dropout rate than what is noted in Europe (see Table 1 at http://goo.gl/WS7pKu).

In curriculum flexibility, results were varied, as some countries did not support the change (or adaptation) of the curricula or have had no discussion to modify curricula in upcoming years. Other participants stated that teaching methods and books are changed, but overall the content has stayed the same. The overall impression regarding curricula was that teaching is based on the textbooks and when schools buy books from different company or when the government shares a new edition of the old then the "curricula is being updated." Overall, there was not much teacher input into determining what kind of content should be used. In addition, teachers indicated that the standardized testing imposed on their students thwarted any efforts to modify the curricula.

In identifying challenges that were most crucial to address, all participants indicated that issues of poverty and equality were the most pressing. In South Africa, the teacher shared that the school was a safe place for students, but, in many cases, home was not. Participants noted that schools were underequipped. For example, sometimes there was no chalk to write on the board available. Asian countries faced more issues with migration and having too many students in the classroom. Teaching in these rural schools is teacher-driven and behavioral challenges take much of the teacher's time. At the same time, teachers are well respected and the community supports the schools' goals to become better. In the South American countries, migration was not an issue, but an emphasis on better grades, better scores in testing and getting better salaries and professional careers was paramount. In Jordan, the teacher indicated that there was no need to be more flexible in curriculum delivery, at least in female education, when, after married, the girls usually don't attend school any more. If they do decide to continue their education after marriage, it is difficult (see Table 2 at http://goo.gl/WS7pKu).

Teacher training, school culture, homework and using ICT in academic classes the following paragraphs contain the synthesized summary of each of the rural schools used as a case in this study. Particular areas of focus include teacher training, school culture, homework and the use of ICT in day-to-day classes (see extras country by country and Tables 3, 4 at http://goo.gl/WS7pKu).

Prediction for 2013–2016:

- South Africa – mobile technologies is being used, students leave schools age of 18 rather than 24. Technology usage encourages students to learn more. NGOs are involved, some schools have an internet in librarys or in special classes;
- Jordan – government tackles changes in curricula, Facebook is widely used. Technology usage at schools is not supported, but some schools still has it;

- Venezuela – computer usage is rising, solution is to use FOSS, project one laptop for child projects in primary, lots of piracy regarding Microsoft software. Teachers will be rewarded if they use technology in their work;
- Costa Rica – mobile devices usage is on the rise, students get scholarship for learning ICT, government needs help developing curricula, english language learning is getting more important than ever:
- India – more internet usage, testing in classes. Teachers are provided trainings to use ICT. Richer schools are getting use to an idea of e-school and e-learning;
- Nepal – ICT and internet usage development plans is being discussed. Communities are pressuring schools to harness the use of technologies, helps from NGOs. Need for better search provider example Indian language one.

In general, all countries have cyber cafes. City area schools and private schools are better equipped with computers and Internet access. Most of the teacher participants confirm that their government forbids mobile device (mobile phones and tablets) usage at the schools. Bring Your Own Device (BYOD) is out of the picture for these rural schools. Venezuela and South Africa provide ICT lessons for all. Others don't provide elderly people with any ICT experiences.

Experts in ICT were also invited to discuss the findings and predict options that would benefit rural areas in these situations. One of the first notable situations was lack of connection between the teaching of ICT skills and meaningful ICT integration in the classroom. Even when technology teaching is provided, teachers are not usually able to apply that knowledge in their classrooms. In the end of an ICT professional development experience, teachers feel obligated and eager to test everything when they "get back home", but only few of them after one month still are trying to integrate what they learned, and after six months, maybe only one is still using learned tools and options. This phenomenon seems to occur most when skills are presented the first time. Once these skills are reviewed in subsequent professional development sessions, then there is a higher percentage of use in the classroom. Also, when there is an expectation to provide feedback and demonstrate evidence that they are using these tools later, then teachers are more actively trying to change their way of teaching and using more technology in their classes or in their personal life.

Experts and innovative teachers listed several obstacles that exist in their minds to successful implementation of new technology learning. The biggest obstacle for teachers was realizing the time and effort needed to begin to integrate some ICT experiences in their classrooms. To develop expertise and a comfort level in using digital technologies for teaching and learning does require time and extra work that is hard for teachers to find. This is especially hard when no local support for these changes is offered. Secondly, it is hard to combat the traditional school mindsets. Coupled with a teacher's lack of confidence and fear of the "unknown" in the area of ICT integration, making changes is extremely difficult. Finally, teachers believe that they have to learn so many new tools and strategies to implement ICT successfully in teaching. Some teachers felt that they now must be "technology" teachers, as well as English or science content teachers.

4   Discussion

The case studies reveal that rural schools in the six countries investigated demonstrated a lack of ICT integration in teaching and learning at most schools. Through analyzing the data, and reflecting on possible ways to encourage more ICT integration in the classrooms of these nations, the researchers propose the following ideas to encourage additional growth in this area.

BYOD - the researchers conclude that BYOD policies should be implemented soon in most of the schools, because students have mobile phones that they could use. Using the devices that students do possess would allow for a level of ICT integration that is currently unachievable, because of lack of resources. Most of the school systems in the case studies do not allow students to bring digital devices to school at this time. Venezuela teachers may choose to implement BYOD, overriding the government's suggestion, but this type of decision would require strong support from all the teachers within a school. Since there is limited training in how to effectively integrate digital devices in teaching and learning, BYOD policies might be difficult to implement. While computer teachers are using the technologies in their classrooms, teachers of other content have not transitioned into doing so. Jordanian schools might also be able to adopt a BYOD policy in schools, as they have governmental support for doing so, but most teachers are against this plan. Recent changes (8 years ago) in teaching education where ECDL has been implemented as evaluation tool could encourage teachers to be more receptive to the BYOD idea. Results do show some usage of ICT in the areas of presentation software, e-school, typing and Internet searching, but these activities occur only once every few months. Teachers don't have options to use computers and projectors in their classrooms, and this might be the biggest obstacle for all the countries. When schools can provide projectors, then teachers might bring their own laptops to school or think more about educating themselves in ICT integration.

Use of Internet Cafes and Home Computers - internet Cafes may be used to do homework and project work by students, as well as computers that are at home. However, most teachers are against assigning ICT work because they realize most students do not have access at home. Providing the option of completing class work with digital devices might at least encourage some students to develop additional ICT skills for learning. Gifted students might be more challenged if ICT resources were used in their lessons. The participant from South Africa also mentioned that students were more motivated to work and learn when digital technologies were integrated into their schoolwork. At the same time, South African teachers were usually against asking students to use computers for school activities. Finally, the participant from Jordan noted that families might be against their children using ICT for schoolwork, as it undermines tradition and religion and brings more behavioral issues than families do not like to deal with.

Acquiring Five Computers and a Projector for Each School - schools could begin to provide opportunities for increased ICT integration if at least 5 computers and one movable projector could be acquired for each school. Laptops are the preferred type of computer, allowing mobility and greater access. In Costa Rica, where the danger of theft is prevalent, desktop PCs might be more reasonable; these would be less likely to be stolen, as they are harder to carry. Teachers don't want to bring their own computers to school, so providing school computers seems a reasonable beginning. However, in South Africa and Costa Rica there is a problem with weather that is too hot, and schoolrooms don't have glass windows or curtains. Because of these conditions, computers may not be able to be maintained in satisfactory conditions. Theft is also a possibility.

The South African participant also mentioned a lack of other resources to teach, so prioritizing computers/projectors as a need above other items would be difficult. Teacher get a lot of training about teaching, but this training never involves ICT education, so purchasing computers for the schools would seem unwise. The teachers believe that White people usually use computers and Internet, because they are richer and more educated. Providing computers for all schools, therefore, seems unlikely, but this type of mindset can only serve to increase the social and digital divide.

Quality ICT Professional Development - teacher training is needed to test out new technologies (projector, computer). The best learners (teachers) should get awarded with new technologies at their schools. Assessment and feedback should also be a part of this deployment of ICT professional development, and teachers and administrators should openly share their work and successes in ICT integration with other educators across the country.

Using what is Available - it is, no doubt, extremely difficult to move forward with meaningful ICT integration when peers and school administrators are unsupportive. Nonetheless, teachers that have the option to use their own technology should use it when their schools do not have usable ICT equipment. One can point to areas of experimentation and growth in ICT use that can encourage teachers. For example, there are interesting changes happening in India where 10th grade students are provided with digital tablets, as well as in Venezuela, where primary students are provided with laptops and free software. It is interesting that there was no mention by the Venezuelan participant about teachers needing training when the laptops were added, but maybe their programs are just developed. When Internet is present in schools, then Web 2.0 tools should be learned and integrated into lessons. There are a variety of free online resources that would allow teachers and students to be productive learners. When the Internet connections are absent, or not optimal, then Free Open Source Software (FOSS) options should be acquired and utilized. Again, there are many free software applications that can support teaching and learning. There is a logical concern for the price of Internet connections in schools, but if more schools decide to pay for Internet access, the ISP's will eventually drop their prices.

Advice for Action - if parents and students ask for more computer training, the school will provide it. Computer education is needed to be successful in everyday life and for future productivity. There are many times in work and in social times when ICT knowledge and use is beneficial. For example, the participant from Nepal noted that when there was a threat of migration, then using digital technologies was the only way to keep contact with family members. Also, the South African participant stated that the students who used computers had better motivation and knowledge acquisition in school.

For Teachers, there is a need to be proactive and sometimes just bring one's own device to the school. This can save time and effort, as there are a lot of materials online to use for teaching. It is possible to share information and use less time in lesson planning. At the same time, the participant from India noted that students in these classrooms will get more opportunities in differentiated instruction. The teacher can support more students in their learning, not only those who are gifted, but also those who have more challenges; for schools, there is a need to be active in making an effort to employ a computer teacher and then ask the government to provide money for computer class, as the participant from Venezuela noted. School leaders must provide more support and funds, as it is difficult for teachers to adopt new practices on their own. In that sense, they are like the children that need motivated all the time, as the participant from Jordan stated; for governments, curriculum changes need to be made that support innovative teaching strategies. This will give teachers and schools the incentive to improve and integrate more ICT for learning. Schools should be guided and teacher professional development should be free and valued as described by the participant from Costa Rica.

Finally, the primary strategies to impact the world by using innovative digital technologies for teaching and learning are teacher training, motivation and follow-up. Some participant countries did not sense a directive from their governments to provide new methods and technology training. Some even said that it is very difficult to develop when they must pay for their professional development or the school does not provide tools. It is understandable, but teachers should be encouraged to be vocal and push for more adoption of ICT resources and use in their classrooms. If teachers that don't ask for improvements from school administrators, then the necessary changes may not occur.

Through analyzing the data from these case studies, definite interest in using technology was seen from the countries included. Forerunners in providing more resources for teachers and students were Venezuela (providing all primary teachers and students free software-based computers) and India (10th grade students provided with tablets). In addition, Jordan has already implemented ECDL (for teachers and students) and seems to have the government support to implement new technologies, though resistance does exist from some teachers/schools.

5   Conclusion

In order to encourage more ICT integration in classrooms across the world, teacher training must be supported. This is the most important element to drive the change. At the same time, schools should be provided with Internet connection and at least 5–10 computers to use with students. Tools for teachers to continue professional development using online resources should also be available. While some countries in these case studies provided resources only when there was a trained professional (computer teacher), it is evident that now all teachers and students need skills and development in ICT use. Digital technology integration should be infused in every subject, so it might be useful to implement online modules for every subject so teachers could continue to learn.

While it is difficult to direct money to the area of ICT resources when there are other significant problems in the community including poverty, hunger, and safety challenges. However, in these areas using technology provides enormous benefits in students' motivation and learning-teaching quality. There is a possibility to use devices that are already available in these instances - old cell phones, smartphones or other mobile devices (mp3 players etc.). Some countries don't currently allow these types of resources to be used in classrooms, but they do make up free resources that could be used to benefit student learning. For these rural areas, a simple but useful recording audio-video device would make a big difference in language education.

Many teachers in these rural areas are novices in the area of digital technologies and they possess is a lot of misconceptions and fear. When governments create mandates to encourage ICT integration, without appropriate teacher professional development, teacher anxiety increases. It is possible that the difference could be also cultural. For example, in Jordan the technology-integrating schools do not get much support from the parents as some even forbid the use of technology at homes. The change of thinking in this area might be conducted bottom-up or top-down, but it seems that rural area teachers are expected to deal with many serious issues like overpopulated classrooms, behavioral issues and responsibilities that don't allow them to even choose the content that they are teaching, as it is solely provided from the government. In these countries the testing is the primary focus and when the class test results are low, teachers are blamed and suffer consequences of lower salaries or job loss. In cases such as these, it might be advisable for countries to use international consultants to improve the countries curricula and professional development, as teacher's voices are too weak to make difference from inside out.

For the future research endeavors, it would be interesting to examine the differences within each country based on the rural and urban schools' use of technology. Learning more about the steps that teachers and school administrators took to address issues of ICT integration. It would also be interesting to look further into the challenges that successful American and European countries are still facing when integrating digital technologies. Fear of change is certainly a very real obstruction to progress in using digital resources effectively in schools- this fear exists in both rural and urban schools.

Acknowledgements. This research was supported by the help of the Tiger University Program of the Information Technology Foundation for Education.

References

1. Balasubramanian, K., Thamizoli, P., Umar, A., Kanwar, A.: Using mobile phones to promote lifelong learning among rural women in Southern India. Distance Educ. 31(2), 193–209 (2010). ISSN: 0158-7919

2. Gordon, D.: Remote learning: technology in rural schools: making sure students in rural areas get the same quality of educational experience as their counterparts in urban and suburban neighborhoods can be enhanced by the right kind of technology implementation. (FEATURE: rural schools). J. Technol. Horiz. Educ. 38(9), 18 (2011). ISSN: 0192-592X

3. Hong, K.: Computer anxiety and attitudes toward computers among rural secondary school teachers: a Malaysian perspective. J. Res. Technol. Educ. 35(1), 27 (2002). ISSN: 1539-1523

4. Howley, A.: Rural elementary school teachers' technology integration. J. Res. Rural Educ. 26(9), 1–13 (2011). ISSN: 1551-0670

5. Hlodan, O.: Mobile learning anytime, anywhere. Bioscience, 60(9), 682 (2010). ISSN: 0006-3568

6. Judi, H.M.: Rural students skills and attitudes towards information and communication technology. J. Soc. Sci. (New York, N.Y.) 7(4), 619 (2011). ISSN: 1549-3652

7. Palamakumbura, T.: The computer revolution: struggling for survival in rural Cameroon. Int. J. Educ. Dev. Inf. Commun. Technol. 4(3), 166 (2008). ISSN: 1814-0556

8. Salazar, D.: On-line professional learning communities: increasing teacher learning and productivity in isolated rural communities. J. Syst. Cybern. Inf. 8(4), 1 (2010). ISSN: 1690-4532

9. Tripathi, A.M.: Information and communication technology for rural development. Int. J. Comput. Sci. Eng. 4(5), 824 (2012). ISSN: 0975-3397

10. Zhao, Z.: Basic education curriculum reform in rural China. Chin. Educ. Soc. 44(6), 36 (2011). ISSN: 1061-1932

11. Wang, D.: The new curriculum and the urban-rural literacy gap. Chin. Educ. Soc. 44(6), 87 (2011). ISSN: 1061-1932

Differentiation of Student Perceptions for Online Courses, Over Time

Maria Mama-Timotheou[✉]

Postgraduate Program of Educational Studies, Open University of Cyprus,
Nicosia, Cyprus
mamatimo@cantab.net

Abstract. This paper presents the main findings of a study exploring graduate student perceptions of online education, with a specific focus on their change over time, throughout an asynchronous web-based course. The study was conducted in the UK, and data collection methods included content analysis of online messages and interviews. Data analysis was based on systematically contrasting participant early- (at the beginning of the course) and late- (by the end of the course) course perceptions. Several inconsistencies were identified between early- and late- course perceptions, which were categorized according to three emerging themes: managerial, social and cognitive. The findings indicate negative perception change with respect to the managerial and social aspects, whereas positive change was evident in terms of the cognitive aspect. The implications drawn from the study are expected to inform and support the design and implementation of web-based courses.

Keywords: Case studies · Qualitative methods · Educational technology · Attitudes and beliefs · E-learning/online learning · Computer-assisted learning

1 Introduction

Despite its rapid expansion [1], online education is relatively young; research on the impact of online learning is growing but still inconclusive [2]. We argue that a prominent step towards the effective designing and implementation of web-based courses, is the exploration of online students' perceptions, agreeing with other researchers in the field [3].

Several perception themes are identified in existing studies on online environments but they are largely characterized by inconsistencies and controversies [2, 4, 5]. One of the most standard themes refers to the logistical, technical and time demands of a web-based course. Flexibility of time and place is certainly reported as an appealing feature by students [6], although many students find that e-learning is unduly time-demanding, requiring great dedication and commitment [7, 8]. Other issues students phase include overwhelming feelings due to information overload and lack of computer or Internet knowledge [9, 10].

A key perception theme highlighted in the literature is also online interaction [11]. Many students favor the traditional face-to-face context over the online one, mainly due to prompt peer feedback and non-verbal social cues [12]. Nonetheless, evidence of

© Springer International Publishing Switzerland 2015
P. Zaphiris and A. Ioannou (Eds.): LCT 2015, LNCS 9192, pp. 697–703, 2015.
DOI: 10.1007/978-3-319-20609-7_65

positive perceptions about online interaction is also reported in the literature with some students finding that peer feedback is more constructive and discussions are more insightfully developed, due to the opportunity for reflection, provided by the asynchronous format [13, 14]. Moreover, frustration is common among students when guidance and feedback from the tutor is not immediate, regular, unambiguous and constructive [15]. As with peer interaction, many feel that tutor interaction is rather limited online, when others claim that developing a relationship with him/her is easier since anxiety, often encountered in a face-to-face meeting, is not an issue [16].

In terms of performance, students appear to believe that they could achieve the same grades online as in the traditional classroom, and research evidence corroborate that [17–19]. However, satisfaction with and perceptions of the overall learning experience varies among online students. This diversity is sometimes a result of the learning independency required online, which does not suit all learners. Studies shows that self-motivated and self-directed students tend to share positive experiences. Yet, those who feel more comfortable in a structured and closely guided context, expecting to acquire knowledge directly from the tutor without great engagement on their part, share negative experiences [20].

A broad range of facilitative digital tools and a plethora of information sources are additional features widely appreciated by students who find online learning creative and diversified [21]. For some, diversified learning is also achieved through exchanging ideas and evaluating peer responses and methodologies in the approach of specific topics, which is encouraged in an online 'community of inquiry' [13].

Although the literature indicates that perceptions and experiences of web-based education vary, little effort has been made to differentiate between perceptions before and after enrolling an online course. Yet, since perceptions are strong predictors of practice, pre-course attitude may affect the course outcome. In fact, understanding both student perceptions before or at the beginning of the course and by the end or after the course is essential in pointing out key aspects. In view of the limited research in the area, we explored the differentiation of student perceptions of web-based education over time.

2 Methodology

A case study of a 3-month graduate asynchronous online course offered by a UK higher education institute, was conducted. The course was offered through the 'Blackboard' management system, as part of a Master's program in educational technology. Students were expected to weekly contribute to the online discussion and accomplish activities assigned by the tutor. The sample was composed of all 15 participants. Providing basic demographic information about the sample, it is mentioned that 10 participants were female and 5 male, the majority of them (6) fell within the 30–35 age range, four were between 25–30 years old, 2 between 35–40 and 2 between 40–45 years old. Also, 5 of them were full time students while the other 10 were part-time students. 8 of them were foreign, non-native English speakers, with the other 7 being native English speakers. Finally, 6 of them had previous online learning experiences whereas for the other 9, this was their first online course.

A first stage involved collection of students' messages on the discussion board. Expectations or statements of belief in the early messages were classified as early-course perceptions. Late messages, where participants contrasted their experience with initial expectations, were classified as late-course perceptions. In the second stage, semi-structured interviews with seven participants were undertaken immediately after the completion of the course to collect students' post-course perceptions, which would be grouped with the late-course perceptions identified in the online messages. Data were analysed qualitatively, using content and thematic analyses. Three perception themes emerged: managerial, social and cognitive. Systematic contrast of early- and late-course perceptions was then followed to identify change throughout the course.

3 Results

According to the findings, negative perception change was identified with respect to the managerial and social aspects, whereas positive change was evident in terms of the cognitive aspect. Inconsistencies in attitudes were inevitable; not all students experienced the same affordances and constraints. Nonetheless, negative change in managerial perceptions was significant across the sample. Almost all students shared positive perceptions about the time, effort and skill demands of the course, at the time of enrolling. Characteristically a student posted: "One of the reasons I chose this course is that I like the fact that I can be signing in on a beach in the Caribbean.", while another reported during the post-course interview: "I was hoping that the distant format would fit with my busy schedule and was not disappointed.".

Nevertheless, by the end of the course, the majority of them demonstrated a negative attitude. Factors that appeared to influence this outcome included previous online experience, technology knowledge, discussion layout, platform facility and content load. A student mentioned during the post-course interview: "My initial expectation was that it would be much easier. I naively thought that it would be easier, perhaps in terms of time I spent doing it, and so, you know, I would kick it off nice and quickly; unfortunately that turned out not to be the case". Near the end of the course, another student posted: "I am worried about the speed of discussions. It takes a while to read all the postings, and sometimes it seems that everything has been said. It is a bit difficult remembering every point though. I felt more comfortable during the first weeks when we only had one task to complete and not multiple as in lately."

Implications are there for pre-course training which would familiarize students with the course requirements and study protocol but also address any unrealistic expectations. Moreover, we argue that a moderator assistant, who would attend to students' technical difficulties with the platform, would increase their confidence, but also enable the tutor to focus more on ensuring that content and discussions are presented and archived efficiently so as to prevent information overload. Finally, it is important that he assigns frequent activity deadlines monitoring student progress and helping them stay on schedule.

Inconsistencies among students' experiences with respect to the social aspect, were also identified. Some students favoured the 'anonymity' and informal communication usually established in an online environment. For example one wrote in a late message:

"Developing arguments online gave me a sense of anonymity which in turn gave me confidence and made it easier to participate and interact". Another who mentioned in an early message that they are "shy when among strangers and that's a concern" when they "get to meet new people in a new course", later on posted: "If this course was occurring in a face-to-face context I would probably just hear what other people have to say and even if I wanted to engage or interact I wouldn't. I'm so glad this did not prove to be the case here […] I was much more vocal than what I thought I would be."

Yet, noticeable negative change was evident for most participants. Even though they entered the course holding positive perceptions about the quality and level of interaction with peers and tutor, this changed. For them, lack of immediacy/intimacy proved a major disadvantage. Characteristically, a student posted in a late message: "I was concerned a bit; I think it is more difficult for people to work and interact with each other in this way. I was always wondering if people who read my postings understood my point or something totally different; since I couldn't see others I could never be sure about that and that meant problematic interaction". Another message, from a different student, echoing feelings of isolation was: "I was completely alone, did not know anyone. I eagerly waited for the next course to start to have some social contacts. I even counted the days […] And actually it got even worse". More specifically with regards to the student-tutor relationship, several students were not satisfied, requiring a more 'vocal' tutor presence. Others desired more 'personalized' responses, as the following quote from a post-course interview reveals: "Sometimes his replies were not very 'on to the point' and this was maybe because he tried to address all students' concerns in one message. It was like giving feedback to a group of postings instead of my own and this did not encourage interaction with him".

Many suggested the addition of face-to-face meetings or synchronous sessions to the asynchronous format: "Mixed mode please! Much better than taking only one mode, in terms of collaboration, student-teacher interaction, students interaction. And if face-to-face is not feasible then maybe use synchronous discussion on Blackboard" (Post-course interview quote). We would agree that this is a good practice for overcoming student anxiety and enhancing participants' sense of belongingness in the community. Moreover, in agreement with recent studies, establishing a protocol for communication from the beginning may be essential in regulating expectations encouraging mutual understanding. The tutor's presence is key; not only he needs to encourage social interaction among peers, but he should also be involved in the process. Many students acknowledged that the tutor's role is different online than onsite, yet they still expected him to be an active member. Consistent feedback is important, and, as the results of the study suggest, tutors should aim at replying with personal messages and not generic postings.

Interestingly, negative perceptions of social interaction were not found to largely impact upon students' cognitive perceptions of the course. In fact, the positive attitude change towards the online experience is highly promising about the pedagogical potential of e-learning. Major cognitive benefits according to the participants, included opportunities for sharing information and resources, methodically reflecting on own and peer responses, and gradually developing skills for self-directed learning. Evidently a student reported during the post-course interview: "I did feel I learn from others, yes! When I joined the course I didn't know anything about computer-mediated communication, but since I entered the discussions on related topics, read many colleagues' ideas, followed their reading references, it made me learn a lot. I also saved a lot of time from trying to find and learn all those theories. I wasn't alone in trying to sort out things. That was the first time I worked in a collaborative way, it required effort but it was my first experience and I was very satisfied. I really liked that way of learning." Furthermore, an online message from a student reflected satisfaction due to a sense of learning autonomy: "In this new type of learning, what's important is not only the knowledge you obtain but the method of obtaining it. In this sense the learner is taking over responsibilities for his/her own learning".

These possibilities should be considered by designers and tutors, in an attempt to improve educational experiences. Especially in view of self-directed learning, albeit an arduous process, many students seem to be motivated by the opportunity to control their learning pace and paths. Research should capitalize on new theoretical and practical frameworks for autonomous learning online.

Negative change in cognitive perceptions was also noted, however, with problematic group collaboration distressing some students, as the following post-course interview quote suggests: "People were stating their opinions about things and these were relevant to the topic in general, but did not address the main points. I think things get a bit loose and out of the track also because of the text-based format. There's no one to interrupt your thoughts and get you back on track. That's why I cannot say my online experience was as productive as I'd like." Others discussed the low learning curve they experienced throughout the course: "I haven't attended any other similar courses before, so I had no great expectations or opinions for online learning. I was open-minded and just hoped to make the most of it. I found (online) learning difficult. Yes, you can work at your own pace, but you need to keep finding incentives to keep you going and not stay behind. It's very easy to lose motivation and you cannot see the learning curve, it is developed very slowly. Call me 'old head' but you need to be able to 'see' what you're learning. I'm not sure if I acquired any factual knowledge here. No one explained things to me. It was just me reading stuff." (Late message).

It is essential that students' learning styles and personal characteristics are considered before group assignment. As seen, students complained about unstructured/unfocused discussions and they felt that the discussion was often incoherent, with no specific target, but, to a great extent, this was attributed to the tutor's minimal involvement: "It seems to me that tutor's participation is not as frequent and apparent as in face-to-face. He assigns the activity but leaves participants to respond according to their own conceptualization of the activity, while in a face-to-face situation he often guides the discussion. Perhaps this is why I sometimes felt the discussion was not focused on the topic.". Online tutors are generally expected to facilitate rather than lead, but this should not result in underestimating their role. Finally, negative cognitive perceptions were articulated by a student with dyslexia who struggled throughout: "I did find learning really difficult as well because I am dyslexic and I will always have my own issues regarding learning and writing stuff down. I did find that really difficult also because I'm quite slow in reading so it took me a lot of time to go through everything. I was very nervous about writing stuff down because I knew that everybody was ok with spelling, grammar and stuff." This issue certainly places the emphasis on the design of courses which would address learning disabilities like dyslexia and meet the imperative for inclusion and diversity in online higher education.

4 Conclusion and Discussion

Decades after the introduction of online courses, researchers are still trying to evaluate the impact of online education. Our study attempted to contribute to these efforts through the exploration of change in students' perceptions throughout a web-based course. Some of the perceptions presented above contribute to knowledge by corroborating evidence reported in other studies [22].

The added value of this study, though, is highlighted by the fact that it reviews how these perceptions differentiated over time and what implications are there for the design and implementation of web-based courses. It appears that consideration needs to be given on how online and conventional sessions can be effectively blended to establish an optimized educational environment. Moreover, our findings overall seem to suggest that the focus is placed on the development of metacognitive strategies, for supporting students to overcome obstacles and sustain an effective learning experience throughout their course.

References

1. Allen, I.E., Seaman, J.: Changing Course: Ten Years of Tracking Online Education in the United States, ERIC (2013)
2. Rovai, A.P., Downey, J.R.: Why some distance education programs fail while others succeed in a global environment. Internet High. Educ. **13**(3), 141–147 (2010)
3. Rodriguez, M.C., Ooms, A., Montañez, M.: Students' perceptions of online-learning quality given comfort, motivation, satisfaction, and experience. J. Interact. Online Learn. **7**(2), 105–125 (2008)
4. Bernard, R.M., et al.: How does distance education compare with classroom instruction? A meta-analysis of the empirical literature. Rev. Educ. Res. **74**(3), 379–439 (2004)
5. Zhang, P., Goel, L.: Is e-learning for everyone? an internal-external framework of e-learning initiative. J. Online Learn. Teach. **7**(2), 193–206 (2011)
6. An, Y.J., Frick, T.: Student perceptions of asynchronous computer-mediated communication in face-to-face courses. J. Comput. -Mediated Commun. **11**(2), 485–499 (2006)
7. Smart, K., Cappel, J.: Students' perceptions of online learning: a comparative study. J. Inf. Technol. Educ. Res. **5**(1), 201–219 (2006)
8. Sharpe, R., Benfield, G.: The student experience of e-learning in higher education. Brookes eJ. Learn. Teach. **1**(3), 87 (2005)
9. Chen, C.-Y., Pedersen, S., Murphy, K.L.: Learners' perceived information overload in online learning via computer-mediated communication. Res. Learn. Technol. **19**(2), 101–116 (2011)
10. Keller, C., Cernerud, L.: Students' perceptions of e-learning in university education. J. Educ. Media **27**(1–2), 55–67 (2002)
11. van Tryon, P.J.S., Bishop, M.J.: Theoretical foundations for enhancing social connectedness in online learning environments. Distance Educ. **30**(3), 291–315 (2009)

12. Sher, A.: Assessing the relationship of student-instructor and student-student interaction to student learning and satisfaction in web-based online learning environment. J. Interact. Online Learn. **8**(2), 102–120 (2009)
13. Garrison, D.R.: E-learning in the 21st century: A Framework for Research and Practice. Taylor & Francis, London (2011)
14. Yildiz, S., Chang, C.: Case studies of distance students' perceptions of participation and interaction in three asynchronous web-based conferencing classes in the u.s. Turkish Online J. Distance Educ. **4**(2), 1–10 (2003)
15. Watland, P.A.: Students' Experiences of Tutor Support in an Online MBA Programme. University of Lancaster (2007)
16. Vonderwell, S.: An examination of asynchronous communication experiences and perspectives of students in an online course: a case study. Internet High. Educ. **6**(1), 77–90 (2003)
17. Abdous, M.H., Yoshimura, M.: Learner outcomes and satisfaction a comparison of live video-streamed instruction, satellite broadcast instruction, and face-to-face instruction. Comput. Educ. **55**(2), 733–741 (2010)
18. Johnson, S.D., Aragon, S.R., Shaik, N.: Comparative analysis of learner satisfaction and learning outcomes in online and face-to-face learning environments. J. Interact. Learn. Res. **11**(1), 29–49 (2000)
19. Summers, J.J., Waigandt, A., Whittaker, T.A.: A comparison of student achievement and satisfaction in an online versus a traditional face-to-face statistics class. Innov. High. Educ. **29**, 233–250 (2005)
20. Howland, J.L., Moore, J.L.: Student perceptions as distance learners in Internet-based courses. Distance Educ. **23**(2), 183–195 (2002)
21. Carswell, L., et al.: Distance education via the internet: the student experience. British J. Educ. Technol. **31**(1), 29–46 (2000)
22. Song, L., et al.: Improving online learning: student perceptions of useful and challenging characteristics. Internet. High. Educ. **7**(1), 59–70 (2004)

The Future of Electronic Textbooks
from a User Perspective

Kimberly Anne Sheen and Yan Luximon[✉]

School of Design, The Hong Kong Polytechnic University,
Hung Hom, Kowloon, Hong Kong
Kimberly.Sheen@connect.polyu.hk, yan.luximon@polyu.edu.hk

Abstract. Electronic textbooks have been a popular research topic for decades. Yet, research on student perspectives in this area has been conducted in hindsight and focused on the existing technology. Still, future features are decided by publishers, universities, and academics with limited input from the actual students who would use them. This article identifies the components that university students feel facilitate their studies without linking them to a specific form of hardware and presents a general overview of the perception of textbook components. An online survey was designed to collect students' opinion on each component outside of the constraints of technology. The survey found that university students believe that future electronic textbooks should include text, highlighting tools, bookmarks, supplemental multimedia content, language translation capabilities, dictionaries, and encyclopedias. By including the input of students in the design of the textbooks, a better educational tool could be designed.

Keywords: Education/training · Electronic textbooks · User perspective · Human computer interaction · Interface tools

1 Introduction

For decades, electronic textbooks have remained a popular research area globally. Yet, the research has been grounded in the past and current technology. In addition, design of the future features are influenced heavily by publishers, universities, and academics with inadequate input from the actual users, students. Instead, design focus of electronic textbooks has been on the market potential, current technology, and the business surrounding education [1].

Since the current and past research conducted focuses so heavily on technology and tends to be lab based, the longevity and reliability of the research may be questioned. On the most part, the current incarnation of electronic textbooks is similar to those that were used with the archaic technology. Most electronic textbooks still follow the textbook metaphor, remaining a digital version of the physical textbook with the addition of a few additional components. Yet, in contradiction to this very design, students are shown to prefer reading from short blocks of electronic texts [2–4]. Past research has

© Springer International Publishing Switzerland 2015
P. Zaphiris and A. Ioannou (Eds.): LCT 2015, LNCS 9192, pp. 704–713, 2015.
DOI: 10.1007/978-3-319-20609-7_66

found that interface components such as search functions, text displays, and components that control navigation through pages create a negative student perception of electronic textbooks [5]. A similar study found that students prefer graphics to compliment content and favored following hyperlinks when browsing [3]. Some of the dissatisfaction found by students when using electronic textbooks may be attributed to student engagement remaining with the printed medium [6] and the perception that their learning is better supported by a physical medium [7]. While true that students perceive aspects of their electronic textbooks as dissatisfactory, statistics show that use of these textbooks is only rising. It has been reported that between 2010 and 2012, use has increased from less than a quarter to 70 % with 40 % of students desiring more electronic textbooks [8].

The future of electronic textbooks is in its infancy, but the emergence of two distinct models of textbooks, native digital and enhanced print, have been predicted [9]. Enhanced print will follow the textbook metaphor more closely than the native digital with a few changes to layout, inclusion of collaboration tools, and limited additional materials. Alternatively, native digital textbooks would operate as a collection of related software, creating interactive applications. Both models of textbook negate student complaints regarding text and page layout, yet they will introduce the problem of creating supplemental material [10]. Publishers are already integrating some of these design changes in eLearning platforms [1].

While some research has been conducted into the future of electronic textbooks and student perspectives of these textbooks, there is a distinct lack of research into what components the students feel they need included to properly approach their studies. Much of this research is tied closely to current technology, forgetting that technology is a fast moving field which at times revolutionizes user experiences. Whereas the research outlined in this article aims to advance the current debate by identifying components that could be implemented in electronic textbooks to better support the study habits of students without a link to hardware or software. This article gives a general overview and ranking of components perceived as most useful and not useful during university level readings.

2   Method

The main method employed in this research was a survey hosted on the Internet. It was utilized to ascertain student views on conceivable components. An online survey was chosen as it can gather quantitative data quickly, allows for varied questions, has a low cost, and is convenient for students and the researcher alike [11, 12]. The survey was chosen because it also has the benefits of an inherent ability to reach diverse populations and quickly gain a general understanding a subject. The survey was designed to be short and highly targeted, eliciting responses on components students found desirable, those they found undesirable, and ranking them for inclusion in electronic textbooks through a mixture of nominal and ordinal scales. Several students from different departments piloted the survey for question clarity and terminology before it was released.

Prior to the development of this survey, an extensive assessment of the surrounding research and literature was conducted. It was through this review of the literature that the deficiency in this research was identified. The review also allowed for a better understanding of how the future of electronic textbooks is being approached by the industry and scholars. After this information was gathered, informal small group discussion sessions with university students from various departments was undertaken to identify students' thoughts and perceptions on the future of electronic textbooks and which components they believed would assist them in reaching their academic goals. The components that came to light during these sessions and components identified through the literature were then grouped into the seventeen components that were eventually presented to students in the online survey.

2.1 Survey Design

Student perceptions of the desirability, undesirability, and ranking of the seventeen components were gathered using a ten-question survey. The components presented to respondents are as follows: Text; Multimedia (videos and podcasts); Manipulatable and 3-D Images; Interactive Equations; Highlighting Tool; Annotation Tool; Bookmarks; Integration with eLearning Platforms (Blackboard or Moodle); Synchronization Across Devices; Project or Print Annotations; Translation, Dictionary, and Encyclopedia; Link to Experts for answers to questions; Text to Speech; Speech to Text; Time Management System; Supplementary Materials (PowerPoints, chapter summaries, and quizzes); and Hide Unimportant Aspects of the book.

Inclusion and Exclusion of Components. Two questions were used to measure the students' perception of whether components were desirable or undesirable for inclusion in future electronic textbooks. Students were reminded to consider both questions outside of technology currently in use and any future technology they may have read about. The first question requested that respondents check all check boxes of the components they desired to be included in future electronic textbooks. Later in the survey, students were asked to select any components they felt were undesirable in their future electronic textbooks. The reverse order question offered validation to the previous question. Invalid responses were easily identified, as answering the question with the same components was impossible. While using reverse order wording, the question also recognized that students may not want a component excluded but that did not imply that they wanted said component included in their future electronic textbooks, with the converse being true.

Ranking Components. In addition to providing their perception of the seventeen components, respondents were asked to rank those components from one to seventeen. Each component was required to be assigned a unique rank. This ranking question was also used as an additional validation of the student perceptions regarding desirable and undesirable components. The question anticipated that students would rank the components they deemed desirable in the previous question highly while they would rank components that they regarded as undesirable in the exclusion question lower. The question was designed to uncover the general popularity of the components among university students.

Classification and Prior Usage. Five questions of the online survey were utilized to document the nationality, age, gender, education level, and discipline being studied of the university students who responded. These classification questions were not required to obtain the generalized findings and roughly nine percent of respondents refrained from answering one or more of these question. No respondents opted to skip these questions completely. Age was requested by the following categories: Under 18, 18–24, 25–34, 35–50, and 50+ years old.

Following the classification questions were two questions regarding prior usage of electronic textbooks. The first question asked if respondents had used electronic textbooks for their studies previously. The second question inquired into the percentage of time students employed electronic textbooks during their studies.

2.2 Dissemination and Data Protection

The online survey was developed and hosted using Google Forms. It was circulated to all current students at The Hong Kong Polytechnic University via email. Before distribution, ethical approval for this study was obtained. No identifying information, such as email addresses or names, was solicited from any respondents.

3 Results

3.1 Respondent Description

There were 637 students who completed the survey, representing all of the age categories. Male respondents accounted for 51 % of responses while female respondents accounted for the other 49 %. As expected, the majority of respondents (86 %) identified their nationality as Chinese. Prior experience with electronic textbooks was reported by 83 % of students and only 16 % reported that they had no prior experience using electronic textbooks. The majority of respondents were studying at an undergraduate level (60 %), followed by those studying at a masters level (22 %), doctoral level (11 %), and higher diploma (7 %). Students from over thirty different disciplines responded to the survey with the top three being Engineering (27 %), Business (16 %), and Medicine (11 %). A substantial number of student responses also came from other disciplines such as various hard science disciplines, design, tourism, linguistics, and architecture.

3.2   Reliability of Data

During the verification process outlined in Sect. 2.1, 119 survey responses out of the original 637 were found to contain data that was invalid. Further analysis of data only took place on the remaining 518 surveys. Percentages reported in the previous section changed very little. Reported genders remained the same and the percentage of respondents who reported prior usage of electronic textbooks increased to 84 % while those who claimed unfamiliarity fell one percent to 15 %. The main three disciplines percentage of response fluctuated slightly. Engineering responses rose 2 %, respondents that studied Business fell one percent, and the percentage of those studying Medicine rose one percent. Reported levels of education followed a similar trend with only the percentage of those studying for higher diplomas remaining the same. Undergraduates remained the largest group represented (61 %) while masters responses fell slightly to 20 %, and PhD responses rose slightly to 12 %.

3.3   Components Perceived as Desirable

The frequency of components reported as desirable by the university students that responded is displayed in Fig. 1. As shown in that graph, the four components chosen most often were Text (84 % of the population), Highlighting (82.6 % of the population), Bookmarks (79 % of the population), and Multimedia (75.5 % of the population).

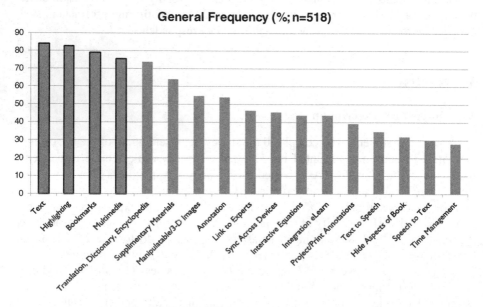

Fig. 1. Graph of desired components (n = 518)

3.4 Components Perceived as Undesirable

The frequency of components perceived by university students as undesirable are found in Fig. 2. As demonstrated in the bar graph, the four components students reported as undesirable are Hide Unimportant Aspects of the Book (22.8 % of the population), Time Management System (22.4 % of the population), Speech to Text (18.5 % of the population), and Text to Speech (16.2 % of the population). The bottom three components found to be undesirable correspond with the three components found to be most desirable in Sect. 3.3 and vice versa.

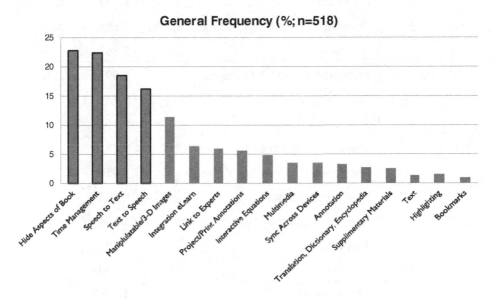

Fig. 2. Graph of undesirable components (n = 518)

3.5 General Rank of Components

In addition to categorizing components as desirable or undesirable, respondents were requested to assign a rank, from one (most desirable) to seventeen (least desirable), to the various components. After identifying the mean rank of each component, an overall ranking of the students' perception of components was established. This ranking is found in Table 1. Text; Highlighting; Multimedia; Bookmarks; and Translation, Dictionary, and Encyclopedia were found to be the five most highly ranked components with a much higher margin than the components following them. Thus, supporting the previous results outlined in Sect. 3.3 on desirable components. The five components that received the lowest ranking were Time Management System, Hiding Unimportant Aspects of the Book, Speech to Text, and Text to Speech. This ranking also supports the earlier findings in Sect. 3.4 regarding the components students selected as undesirable.

Table 1. Rank of the components based on general respondent population (n = 518)

Rank	Components	Means
1	Text	2.676
2	Highlighting tool	5.656
3	Multimedia	6.046
4	Bookmarks	6.923
5	Translation, dictionary, and encyclopedia	7.668
6	Annotation tool	7.861
7	Manipulatable and 3-D images	8.992
8	Interactive equations	9.158
9	Sync across devices	9.164
10	Supplementary materials	9.255
11	Integration in eLearning platforms	9.450
12	Link to experts rank	9.903
13	Project or print annotations	10.349
14	Text to speech	11.971
15	Speech to text	12.394
16	Hide aspects	12.685
17	Time management system	12.828

4 Discussion

4.1 Sampling and Bias

When attempting to evaluate results from surveys, bias related to nonresponse rate must be assessed. Past research related to response rates of university students has found that internet surveys have had a lower response rate among students than paper based surveys [13], but the increased anonymity allowed by online surveys does increase the likelihood for students to report their genuine perceptions [14]. With only 637 responses, the response rate can be considered low but the demographics of the respondents who submitted surveys was similar to the general makeup of the university population. Similar to what was found in the survey respondent demographics, the three main disciplines at the university are Engineering, Business, and Medicine. Percentages of students studying at the various education levels were similar as to those found in the survey results with only a marginally higher percentage of doctoral students and undergraduate students responding and a somewhat lower percentage of masters degree students responding [15]. With a student population of approximately 32,000 students, 400 valid responses are necessary to achieve a five percent error rate necessary to draw appropriate conclusions based on statistics [16]. Since this survey received 518 valid responses, it can be presumed that the amount of responses garnered were acceptable to propose conclusions from the data.

4.2   General Student Perceptions of Components

The desired components recounted by the student respondents varied among the surveys. In the past, researchers have emphasized that students do not engage with their academic materials in the same manner as each other and may use varied support activities to support their studying such as highlighting or taking notes [17]. The results of the survey found that there were many components which could assist in engagement such as highlighting tools, bookmarks, and translation capabilities, dictionaries, and encyclopedias. These findings are supported by similar studies which found that the physical book metaphor, which includes features like bookmarking and highlighting, are understood and embraced by users [18].

While this metaphor is important, employing different components in the design of textbooks may combat the long reported complaint that textbooks are unable to support the two main approaches to studying [19]. These two approaches are the surface approach and the deep approach [20]. The surface approach provides a student with limited understanding of the subject and only allows them to ascertain information which they anticipate being questioned on. While the deep approach allows students to focus and understand the information presented to them. Many of the components students desired in their electronic textbooks support the second approach to reading which allows the student to search for more information on what is presented in the text and relate it to their existing knowledge [19]. The inclusion of dictionaries and encyclopedias, especially, would assist students in expanding their knowledge and finding connections they may not have previously realized.

Overall, the majority of the components listed for inclusion are close to the activities that students utilize to support their readings in physical textbooks while those identified as undesirable are impossible to include in a physical textbook. In addition, some of the components suggested are more related to specific disciplines, such as interactive equations, which accounts for a lower general ranking and preference in those specific components. As electronic textbooks take the place of physical textbooks these support activities may change with the technology; but to currently support students' mental models and assist in their adoption of the new technology, it would be beneficial to continue with the textbook metaphor for the time being.

5   Conclusion

The electronic survey outlined in this study found that students believe that text, highlighting tools, bookmarks, supplemental multimedia content, language translation capabilities, dictionaries, and encyclopedias should be included in future electronic textbooks over the other components available for selection. By including the input of students in the design framework of the textbooks, content and interface designers may create a better educational tool. In addition, examining the components most commonly desired outside of the restrictions of the current physical technology, as this survey did, allows for more flexibility in future applications as technology evolves.

Future research is necessary to identifying the reason students are choosing specific components when using academic texts and the reason they believe one component is more essential in their electronic textbooks than the others. Also, research needs to be undertaken to ascertain how students interact with the components they identified as desirable. Using this research in conjunction with one another, a design framework for use in the creation of electronic textbooks can be developed.

Acknowledgements. Authors would like to thank the Research Grants Council for the Hong Kong Ph.D fellowship Scheme (1-904Z). We would also like to thank the support from the Hong Kong Polytechnic University.

References

1. Tian, X., Martin, B.: Value chain adjustments in educational publishing. Publishing Res. Q. **29**(1), 12–25 (2013)
2. Nicholas, D., Rowlands, I., Clark, D., Huntington, P., Jamali, H.R., Olle, C.: UK scholarly e-book usage: a landmark survey. ASLIB Proc. **60**(4), 311–334 (2008)
3. Chong, P.F., Lim, Y.P., Ling, S.W.: On the design preferences for ebooks. IETE Tech. Rev. **26**(3), 213–222 (2009)
4. Brunet, D.P., Bates, M.L., Gallo, J.R., Strother, E.A.: Incoming dental students' expectations and acceptance of an electronic textbook program. J. Dent. Educ. **75**(5), 646–652 (2011)
5. Kropman, M., Schoch, H.P., Teoh, H.Y.: An experience in e-learning: using an electronic textbook. In: Proceedings of the 21st ASCILITE Conference Beyond the Comfort Zone, pp. 512–515. Perth (2004)
6. Wilson, R., Landoni, M., Gibb, F.: The WEB Book experiments in electronic textbook design. J. Documentation **59**(4), 454–477 (2003)
7. Ganci, A. M.: Redefining the textbook: a user-centered approach to the creation, management and delivery of digital course content in higher education (Doctoral dissertation, The Ohio State University) (2011)
8. EDUCAUSE Center for Applied Research: ECAR National Study of Undergraduate Students and Information Technology, 2012. Educause, Washington, DC (2012)
9. McFadden, C.: Are textbooks dead? making sense of the digital transition. Publishing Res. Q. **28**(2), 93–99 (2012)
10. Defazio, J.: Challenges of electronic textbook authoring: writing in the discipline. Commun. Comput. Inf. Sci. **352**, 8–14 (2012)
11. Wright, K.B.: Researching internet-based populations: advantages and disadvantages of online survey research, online questionnaire authoring software packages, and web survey services. J. Comput. Mediated Commun. **10**(3), 0 (2005). doi:10.1111/j.1083-6101. 2005.tb00259.x
12. Evans, J.R., Mathur, A.: The value of online surveys. Internet Res. **15**(2), 195–219 (2005)
13. Sax, L.J., Gilmartin, S.K., Bryant, A.N.: Assessing response rates and nonresponse bias in web and paper surveys. Res. High. Educ. **44**(4), 409–432 (2003)

14. Lee, R.M.: Unobtrusive Methods in Social Research. Open University Press, Buckingham (2000)
15. PolyU in Figures (2012/13). http://www.polyu.edu.hk/dpoffice/polyu_in_figures/euni_figure_1213.pdf. Accessed 1 December 2013
16. Chandrasekhar, K.: How Many People Do I Need to Take My Survey? (15 September 2011). https://www.surveymonkey.com/blog/en/blog/2011/09/15/how-many-people-do-i-need-to-take-my-survey/. Accessed 1 November 2014
17. Fairbairn, G., Fairbairn, S.: Reading at University. Open University Press, Buckingham (2001)
18. Landoni, M., Wilson, R., Gibb, F.: From the visual book to the WEB book: the importance of design. Electron. Libr. **18**(6), 407–419 (2000)
19. Hartley, J.: Textbook design: current status and future directions. Int. J. Educ. Res. **14**(6), 533–541 (1990)
20. Bowden, J., Marton, F.: The University of Learning. Psychology Press, New York (2003)

Out of Classroom Instruction in the Flipped Classroom: The Tough Task of Engaging the Students

Evangelia Triantafyllou[✉] and Olga Timcenko

Department of Architecture, Design and Media Technology,
Aalborg University Copenhagen, Copenhagen, Denmark
{evt, ot}@create.aau.dk

Abstract. This article presents experiences and student perceptions on the introduction of the flipped classroom model in two consecutive semesters at Media Technology department of Aalborg University, Copenhagen, Denmark. We introduced the flipped instruction model to a statistics course and a mathematics workshop. We collected data by two online survey studies, which show support for student perceptions that out-of-classroom instruction with online resources enhances learning, by providing visual and in depth explanations, and can engage the learner. However, students stated that they miss just-in-time explanations when learning with online resources and they questioned the quality and validity of some of them. Based on these findings and our own experience, we discuss requirements for resources and activities in flipped classrooms in order for the student to engage and learn. Finally, we present a framework for experienced-based learning in flipped classrooms to promote student reflection.

Keywords: Flipped classroom · Mathematics · Screencast technology · Student engagement · Student learning

1 Introduction

One of the recent developments in teaching, which heavily relies on current technology and open resources, is the flipped (or inversed) classroom approach [3]. In a flipped classroom the traditional lecture and homework sessions are inverted. Students are provided with online material in order to gain necessary knowledge before class, while class time is devoted to clarifications and application of this knowledge. The course content, which is provided for self-study, may be delivered in the form of screencasts and/or pre-class reading, exercises or quizzes, while class time is mainly used for group work activities. The hypothesis is that there could be deep and creative discussions when the teacher and students physically meet. This teaching and learning approach endeavors to make students owners of their learning trajectories [8].

Various researchers and instructional designers have sought to investigate the advances in flipped learning environments. Kay and Kletskin introduced problem-based video podcasts covering key areas in mathematics. The video podcasts were created as self-study tools, and used by higher education students to acquire pre-calculus skills [11].

© Springer International Publishing Switzerland 2015
P. Zaphiris and A. Ioannou (Eds.): LCT 2015, LNCS 9192, pp. 714–723, 2015.
DOI: 10.1007/978-3-319-20609-7_67

The results indicated that a majority of students used the video podcasts frequently, viewed them as easy to use, effective learning tools, rated them as useful or very useful, and reported significant knowledge gains in pre-calculus concepts.

Love et al. compared a classroom using the traditional lecture format with a flipped classroom during an applied linear algebra course [17]. Students in the flipped classroom environment had a significant increase between the sequential exams compared to the students in the traditional lecture section, but they performed similarly in the final exam. Moreover, the flipped classroom students were very positive about their experience in the course, and particularly appreciated the student collaboration and instructional video components.

Bates and Galloway conducted a practice-based case study of curriculum redesign in a large-enrolment introductory physics course [2]. The course followed a flipped classroom approach, where lectures were transformed to guided discussion sessions, with focus on peer instruction techniques and discussion facilitated by extensive use of clicker questions. Their results suggest student engagement with pre-class reading and quiz tasks, positive student perceptions of this different instructional format and evidence for high quality learning.

Enfield applied a flipped classroom model of instruction in two classes of a course focusing on web design [7]. Student reports suggested that the approach provided students with an engaging learning experience and was effective in helping students learn the content. They also found that students increased self-efficacy in their ability to learn independently.

While the aforementioned approaches report on benefits of the flipped classroom, there are also critics to this approach [12, 18, 19]. Concerns include among others: criticism about the accessibility to online instructional resources, the growing move towards no homework, increased time requirements without improved pedagogy, teachers concerns that their role will be diminished, lack of accountability for students to complete the out-of-class instruction, poor quality video production, and inability to monitor comprehension and provide just-in-time information when needed.

Our research efforts focus on improving mathematics education in "creative" engineering studies by use of technology [26]. In this context and taking into consideration the reported strengths and weaknesses, we introduced the flipped instructional model during two consecutive semesters for a statistics course and a mathematical workshop at Media Technology department. In both semesters, we collected data on student perceptions on their experience with this new instructional model through survey studies. In this article, we discuss the results and we extract requirements for resources and activities in flipped classrooms that promote student learning and engagement.

This article is organized as follows: the next section discusses the theoretical framework, which we employed for designing the flipped classroom and the related out-of-classroom and classroom activities, the third section reports on the methods we used to design our studies, the fourth presents data from two survey studies on student perception on the flipped classroom and our own experiences, while the fifth section discusses these findings and proposes a framework on experience-based learning that can be used to improve student reflection and engagement in flipped classrooms. We conclude this article with some suggestions for future work.

2   Problem-Based Learning and the Flipped Classroom

In the literature, there have been used various theoretical frameworks to justify the flipped classroom and support the design of in- and out-of-class activities. Such theoretical frameworks typically argue for the benefits of student-centered and collaborative learning (e.g. active learning, problem-based learning, peer-assisted learning) [4].

Throughout our research, we are inspired and guided by the Problem-Based Learning (PBL) pedagogy, which is applied at Aalborg University since its establishment in 1974 [1]. PBL is a student-centered instructional approach, in which learning begins with a problem to be solved. Students need to acquire new knowledge in order to solve the problem and therefore they learn both problem-solving skills and domain knowledge. The goals of PBL are to help the students "...develop flexible knowledge, effective problem solving skills, self-directed learning, effective collaboration skills and intrinsic motivation." [10].

At Aalborg University, PBL is also combined with group work [14]. While working in groups, students try to resolve the problem by defining what they need to know and how they will acquire this knowledge. This procedure fosters the development of communication, collaboration, and self-directed learning skills. Moreover, group work in PBL may enable students to experience a simulated real world working and professional environment, which involves process and communication problems and even conflicts, which all need to be resolved to achieve the desired outcome.

Additionally, PBL represents a paradigm shift from the traditional one way instructional methods. In PBL, the teacher is not an instructor but rather a tutor, who guides, supports, and facilitates the learning process. The tutor has to encourage the students and increasing their understanding during the problem-solving process. Therefore, the PBL teacher facilitates and challenges the learning process rather than strictly transmitting domain knowledge.

Therefore, the flipped classroom that employs computer-based individual instruction outside the classroom and devotes classroom time to group activities with the teacher as facilitator is well justified by the aforementioned principles of PBL. The goal of a flipped classroom is to let the student study individually at her own pace while providing the appropriate support material for out-of-classroom instruction and then come into class, where groups of students engage in group activities facilitated by the teacher. Since our previous research has shown that mathematics courses at Media Technology follow mostly the one way transmission model (lectures as presentation of information) [24], we decided to introduce the flipped classroom approach in mathematics related courses for Media Technology students for aligning them with the PBL pedagogy. In the following sections, we present two studies on the introduction of the flipped classroom at our department with a focus on out-of-classroom instruction.

3   Methodology

We introduced the flipped instructional model during two consecutive semesters at the Media Technology department, Aalborg University Copenhagen. In the first semester, we introduced a flipped classroom approach for a statistics course [25], while in the second semester we used this approach for teaching mathematics related to computer graphics rendering [23]. To facilitate this instructional approach, we provided students with online resources for out of classroom instruction. In the first semester, we created our own screencasts, which were combined with selected sections of the www. mathisfun.com webpage, readings from the www.betterexplained.com webpage, and scanned lecture notes from their past mathematics course covering the relevant subjects. In-class assignments were provided along with each lesson. In the second semester, we substitute our screencasts with selected Khan Academy screencasts and related practice problems, because our experience was that creating quality screencasts is time consuming and hard, since students criticized our won screencasts. Students were required to choose at least one of the proposed resources for studying before lectures. We estimated that going through any of the provided resources would not take more than one hour and a half to complete.

In both semesters, the learning process generally followed the same sequence. Prior to class, students were expected to watch the related video lessons and read the external web resources. In the second semester, students were also provided with some practice problems, which were related to the material they had just studied. In both cases, students were provided with a reading guide in order for students to not get lost in the provided information. During class, a question round took place, in order to clarify aspects that students found challenging. Then, students were provided in-class assignments to reflect on, discuss, and practice what they had learned. The classroom activity was mainly not teacher led; instead, students in groups worked on the assignments while the instructor provided individual guidance as needed. The in-class activities were structured so as to provide students with a variation of the tasks they completed when watching the video, providing opportunity for both practice and transfer of learning to new situations. Additionally, some activities were teacher led demonstrations. Since students were expected to already know some content from previous mathematics courses, the teacher was calling on individuals to explain what to do to complete the task.

During both semesters, we conducted a survey study in order to further investigate student acceptance and experiences in the flipped model, and student perceptions and preferences on screencasts. These online surveys used a Likert scale in order to collect student responses. Items in the survey were measured using 5-point rating scales, with the range of answers from "strongly disagree" to "strongly agree." Moreover, there were items, which gave students the opportunity to provide further information in an open-ended manner.

4 Combining Experiences and Results from Two Survey Studies

In the first semester, we collected answers from 104 fourth-semester students, while in the second semester 46 fifth-semester and master students responded to the survey ($N_1 = 104$, $N_2 = 46$). The results of these two survey studies and their analysis are described in [23, 25]. In the following, we present results from both studies (quantitative and qualitative data). For better presenting the results, we have analyzed the responses and extracted the main topics raised by the questionnaire statements and students' comments.

4.1   Impact on Learning and Understanding

The majority of students who were exposed to out-of-classroom instruction reported that using screencasts and other online resources contributed to improved learning and understanding. In their responses, students mentioned the following characteristics of such resources as improving their learning and understanding. Firstly, online resources can be seen or read multiple times and they give the learner the opportunity to only focus on specific parts of it. This feature allows for recapitulation of challenging parts of the reading curriculum and focusing on what the individual student perceive as important. Regarding adapted instruction, another important feature of online resources is that they provide different means and approaches for explaining the same thing. For that reason, students reported that such resources also contribute to understanding the course material, since they can find alternative explanation in case they are not satisfied with ones provided in the material chosen by the teacher to cover course-related topics. Students also mentioned that screencasts increase understanding because they provide step-by-step explanations and an overview of the process of solving a specific problem. When Khan Academy material was used, students favored also the fact that they are provided with hierarchically organized mathematical knowledge and the connection between topics in mathematics.

Nevertheless, there were students, who criticized the effect of screencasts and online resources in better understanding. Some of them argued that watching a screencast or reading a solved mathematics example does not necessarily lead to improved learning, if learners are not forced to practice themselves. Some others reported that out-of-classroom instruction can be difficult to follow for weak students with gaps in their mathematical knowledge or who don't understand the terminology used. Finally, a student expressed even a more general concern regarding online resources. He feared that getting used to find solutions and explanations on the internet, the learner becomes lazy – as he mentioned: "*...on a philosophic point of view, we could end up as "google-heads" where the things we look up on the net are not really remembered at all, since our brain might fall into a sleep in which it's accustomed to be given the answer instead of remembering it...*".

4.2   Self-reported Engagement

In the survey studies, students were asked if different resources help them to engage during out-of-classroom instruction. Students gave screencasts a better engagement mark compared to text-based online resources. They also favored the fact that they can follow out-of-classroom instruction at their own convenience and they can control the pace instruction. Furthermore, they mentioned that they felt engaged in the classroom, because they could on their own try things out before the lecture and then ask more relevant and specific questions to the teacher. However, few students said that it was boring and tiresome to watch screencasts.

4.3 Information Overload and Filtering

Although we provided the students with a detailed reading guide and we selected only relevant sections from the online resources we proposed to them, there were still students who complained about the time they had to spend on out-of-classroom instruction. Others criticized the screencasts for being too long and others said that they feel overwhelmed by the plethora of information on the internet, when they are searching for alternatives explanations. Finally, many students challenged the validity of the available information on the internet. They argued that not all sources can be trusted and that in some cases information is misleading. A student summarized both problems of information overload and validity as follows: *"It may take a long time to find the right resources for you and you cannot be 100 % sure they are actually correct."*

4.4 Out-of-Classroom and Classroom Instruction

Regarding out-of-classroom instruction, students appreciated the fact that they could be introduced to lecture material and practice with it before going to the class, because according to their comments they were able to ask more in-depth and meaningful questions. They also mentioned that it felt as they had more time for the course compared to traditional lectures. In general, we got positive feedback for the new instruction model and students mentioned that they liked the combination of out-of-classroom and classroom instruction.

What students missed in out-of-classroom instruction was mostly the ability for just-in-time explanations. Students said that it would be nice to be able to get answers to questions raised while studying alone. Moreover, the students mentioned that in-classroom explanations are paramount and they underlined the importance of inter-action with the teacher. Finally, there were students who said that they were not sure how they feel about the flipped classroom, since it was the first time they experienced this instruction model.

5 Discussion

Our results so far indicate that online resources were seen by students as valuable and useful as an aid to learning. We also believe that out-of-classroom instruction can contribute to improved understanding, since it has been found that working with mathematics by themselves is perceived by students the most important learning [22]. Screencasts, visualizations and other online resources are also powerful media and provide different ways to engage with mathematical thinking. Nevertheless, it is imperative that teachers make sure that students practice while going through all this material, otherwise they cannot be sure that authentic learning takes place [21]. Providing practice tests and quizzes can help in making the students study and come to class prepared. Moreover, out-of-classroom and classroom (typically group) activities should be carefully chosen and always being part of a pedagogical framework, which justifies this kind of activities. Otherwise, teachers cannot be sure that such activities will result in meaningful mathematical work and student learning. If these preconditions are met, then the lecture time can be devoted to in-depth discussions and the teacher will be able to offer personalized and meaningful feedback. Otherwise, the lecture time has to be spent for presenting the information the students should have studied before classroom, and this eliminates the added value of a flipped classroom.

A flipped classroom may also contribute to more engaged students. Our results show some evidence for that, since students reported that working with online resources increased their engagement. We also experienced that in-group and in-class discussions during lectures unfolded more smoothly, students participated more actively and asked not only more but also more advanced questions compared to our previous classes. The group classroom activities were another engagement factor, especially for weaker or more introvert students.

However, the decision of which tools should support the out-of-classroom learning is a crucial one not only in terms of learning but also for engaging the student. Based on our experience, we propose that the time devoted to out-of-classroom activities is estimated and kept in mind, when choosing the material given to students or when producing resources (e.g. screencasts). A guided reading curriculum will also help students structure their out-of-classroom studying and not get lost in the provided information. Moreover, providing all the necessary information is important in order to avoid students spending their time looking for it on the web. Finally, as far as online resources in general are concerned, we recommend that students are taught how to determine the validity and affordances of such resources.

In their responses, students reported that they lacked the ability for clarifying challenging parts during out-of-classroom instruction. In order to deal with such problems, researchers have introduced the holistic flipped classroom, where teachers support students both in- and out-of- classroom [5]. Nevertheless, such approaches increase the burden of the teacher, who has already a tight schedule in a flipped classroom (production or selection of online resources, planning of activities and actual lectures). Moreover, we believe that letting the student think about the challenging parts is not per se a disadvantage, because it provides time for students to reflect before coming to the classroom, where the teacher can help. Of course, clear instructions about how and when answers and clarifications will be given are required, in order to avoid student frustration. Practice tests can also help the students check their comprehension, while studying by their own.

All in all, we received positive feedback for the new flipped instruction model. Students were in favor of the blending character of this model, in accordance with results of other studies (e.g. [16]), although there were some students who underlined the importance of the teacher's role and of in-classroom explanations. This may be attributed to the fact that this was their first experience in a flipped classroom, where the teacher's role is different compared to the traditional lectures, where he uses most of the classroom time. In the literature, there have been reported similar comments from students who think that the teacher's role is reduced in flipped classrooms [9], but we believe that they can be attributed to the transition phase from a traditional to a flipped setting. In such transitional phases, students will need time to get used to their teacher's new role.

By applying the flipped classroom, we have also noted that it has another important potential, which has not been emphasized in the literature. The flipped learning model can be used to support a continuous cycle of student reflection over practice and experimentation [15]. We use the term reflection, as used in the Cowan model (Fig. 1) [6]. Cowan combines the analytical reflection from Kolb's experienced-based learning cycle "experience-reflect-generalize-test" [13], with Schön's evaluative reflection for creating this model of reflection loops [20]. Schön's reflection-for-action is the reflection that takes place prior to actions, while his reflection-in-action and the actual action take place at the same time. Kolb's reflection-on-action is more systematic than reflection-in-action and a means to get from experience to conceptualization. We propose that provided that the out-of-classroom and classroom activities are designed properly and the reflection process is facilitated by the teacher, the flipped instruction model with its out-of-classroom, in-classroom and after-classroom phases can be used to involve students in reflection loops and to progress experienced-based learning. However, we still have to apply this framework for data collection in order to prove our assumption.

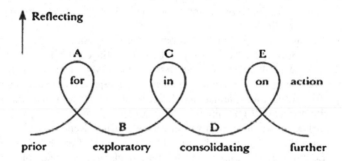

Fig. 1. Cowan's model with reflection loops (taken from [6])

6 Conclusions

In this article, we presented results from two survey studies conducted in two consecutive semesters at the Media Technology department of Aalborg University Copenhagen. Taking inspiration from the PBL pedagogy, we applied the flipped instruction model in a statistics course and then at a mathematics workshop. The studies addressed student perceptions on the flipped classroom approach, they had just experienced. We discussed the results of these studies in four dimensions: self-reported impact on student learning and engagement, information overload and filtering and out-of-classroom and classroom instruction. This discussion revealed some of the advantages and disadvantages of the flipped classroom according to students and according to our own experience. Based on these findings, we proposed design requirements for out-of-classroom instruction. We believe that the flipped classroom can increase student engagement and motivation, encourage deeper though and provide confidence for weaker students, provided the aforementioned design requirements are taken into consideration. Our results suggest also that the resources and activities in such classrooms may determine if the student will engage and learn. Therefore, we presented a framework for student reflection that can be used for designing resources and activities at flipped classroom to promote experienced-based learning. Although the results revealed that students perceive out-of-classroom instruction as contributing to their learning and understanding, it is difficult to draw firm conclusions in terms of improvements to student learning as at this stage it has not been possible to measure this quantitatively. In the future, we aim at applying the presented framework in order to collect data on student reflection in the flipped classroom, and at conducting a quantitative study, in order to compare student attainment in traditional and flipped settings.

References

1. Barge, S.: Principles of problem and project based learning, the aalborg PBL model (2010). http://www.aau.dk/digitalAssets/62/62747_pbl_aalborg_modellen.pdf
2. Bates, S., Galloway, R.: The inverted classroom in a large enrolment introductory physics course: a case study (2012)
3. Bergmann, J., Sams, A.: Flip your Classroom Reach Every Student in Every Class Every day. International Society for Technology in Education, Eugene (2012)
4. Bishop, J.L., Verleger, M.A.: The flipped classroom: a survey of the research (2013)
5. Chen, H.Y., Nian-Shing, C.: Design and evaluation of a flipped course adopting the holistic flipped. In: 2014 IEEE 14th International Conference on Classroom Approach Advanced Learning Technologies (ICALT), pp. 627–631 (2014)
6. Cowan, J.: On Becoming an Innovative University Teacher: Reflection in Action. Society for Research into Higher education & Open University Press, Cambridge (1998)
7. Enfield, J.: Looking at the impact of the flipped classroom model of instruction on undergraduate multimedia students at CSUN. TechTrends 57, 14–27 (2013)
8. Fulton, K.: Upside down and inside out: flip your classroom to improve student learning. Learn. Lead. Technol. 39, 12–17 (2012)
9. Gnaur, D., Hüttel, H.: How a flipped learning environment affects learning in a course on theoretical computer science. In: Popescu, E., Lau, R.W., Pata, K., Leung, H., Laanpere, M. (eds.) ICWL 2014. LNCS, vol. 8613, pp. 219–228. Springer, Heidelberg (2014)
10. Hmelo-Silver, C.E.: Problem-based learning: what and how do students learn? Educ. Psychol. Rev. 16, 235–266 (2004)
11. Kay, R., Kletskin, I.: Evaluating the use of problem-based video podcasts to teach mathematics in higher education. Comput. Educ. 59, 619–627 (2012)
12. Kellinger, J.J.: The flipside: concerns about the "new literacies" paths educators might take. Educ. Forum 76(4), 524–536 (2012)
13. Kolb, D.A.: Experiential Learning: Experience as the Source of Learning and Development. Prentice-Hall, Englewood Cliffs (1984)
14. Kolmos, A.: Reflections on project work and problem-based learning. Eur. J. Eng. Educ. 21, 141–148 (1996)
15. Kolmos, A., Kofoed, L.B.: Development of process competencies by reflection, experimentation and creativity. In: International Conference on Teaching and Learning in Higher Education: New Trends and Innovations (2003)

16. Llorens, M., Nevin, E., Eileen, M.: Online resource platform for mathematics education. IEEE Front. Educ. Conf. **2014**, 1865–1872 (2014)
17. Love, B., Hodge, A., Grandgenett, N., et al.: Student learning and perceptions in a flipped linear algebra course. Int. J. Math. Educ. Sci. Technol. **45**, 317–324 (2014)
18. Milman, N.B.: The flipped classroom strategy: what is it and how can it best be used. Distance Learn. **9**, 85–87 (2012)
19. Nielsen, L.: Five reasons I'M not flipping over the flipped classroom. Technol. Learn. **32**, 10–46 (2012)
20. Schön, D.A.: The Reflective Practitioner: How Professionals Think in Action, vol. 5126. Basic books, New York (1983)
21. Schwartz, M.: Khan Academy: the illusion of understanding. Online Learn. Formerly J. Asynchronous Learn. Netw. **17**(4), 1–14 (2013)
22. Sikko, S.A., Pepin, B.: Students' perceptions of how they learn best in higher education mathematics courses. In: Proceedings of the 8th Congress of the European Society for Research in Mathematics Education, pp. 1980–2446 (2013)
23. Triantafyllou, E., Timcenko, O.: Student perceptions on learning with online resources in a flipped mathematics classroom. In: Proceedings of the 9th Congress of the European Society for Research in Mathematics Education (2015) (to appear)
24. Triantafyllou, E., Timcenko, O.: Developing digital technologies for undergraduate university mathematics: challenges, issues and perspectives. In: Proceedings of the 21st International Conference on Computers in Education, pp. 971–976 (2013)
25. Triantafyllou, E., Timcenko, O.: Introducing a flipped classroom for a statistics course: a case study. In: Proceedings of the 25th EAEEIE Annual Conference, pp. 5–8 (2014)
26. Triantafyllou, E., Timcenko, O.: Opportunities and challenges of using technology in mathematics education of creative engineering studies. In: Stephanidis, C. (ed.) HCI 2014, Part II. CCIS, vol. 435, pp. 171–176. Springer, Heidelberg (2014)

Understanding Nomophobia: A Modern Age Phobia Among College Students

Caglar Yildirim[1]([⊠]) and Ana-Paula Correia[2]

[1] Human Computer Interaction, Iowa State University, Ames, IA, USA
caglar@iastate.edu
[2] School of Education, Iowa State University, Ames, IA, USA
acorreia@iastate.edu

Abstract. Nomophobia, or no mobile phone phobia, is the fear of being out of mobile phone contact and considered a modern age phobia particularly common among young smartphone users. This qualitative study sought to identify the dimensions of nomophobia as described by college students and adopted a phenomenological approach to qualitative exploration. Semi-structured interviews were conducted with nine undergraduate students at a large Midwestern university in the U.S. Based on the findings, four dimensions of nomophobia were identified: not being able to communicate, losing connectedness, not being able to access information and giving up convenience. Given the widespread adoption of smartphones and integration of smartphones into educational settings, findings of this study can help educators better understand learners' inclination to use their smartphones at all times.

Keywords: Nomophobia · Dimensions of nomophobia · Smartphones · Phobia

1 Introduction

As the most recent evolution of mobile information and communication technologies [1], smartphones have been widely and rapidly adopted. 58 % of American adult population are reported to own a smartphone [2]. Of these smartphone users, 83 % are aged between 18 and 29. Thus, smartphones are particularly popular among young adults. As a matter of fact, college students are considered as the early adopters of smartphones [3].

While the proliferation of smartphones can be attributed to numerous benefits and features they provide, there are certain problems associated with mobile phone use in general and smartphone use in particular. One such problem is nomophobia. Nomophobia, or no mobile phone phobia, is "the fear of being out of mobile phone contact" [4]. It is considered a modern age phobia resulting from the interactions between people and new ICTs and is used to refer to the feelings of anxiety and/or discomfort caused by being out of reach of a smartphone [5].

Given the widespread use of smartphones by college students, it should come as no surprise that they are prone to nomophobia. However, nomophobia has received little attention and has not been thoroughly investigated as a theoretical construct.

© Springer International Publishing Switzerland 2015
P. Zaphiris and A. Ioannou (Eds.): LCT 2015, LNCS 9192, pp. 724–735, 2015.
DOI: 10.1007/978-3-319-20609-7_68

Thus, the purpose of this qualitative study was to explore the dimensions nomophobia through the experiences of college students. Specifically, this study sought to address the following research question: What are the dimensions of nomophobia as described by college students?

2 Method

2.1 Design

To address the guiding research question, this study adopted a phenomenological approach to qualitative exploration because the purpose was to explore the dimensions of nomophobia by describing the lived experiences of college students about the phenomenon, nomophobia [6]. Phenomenology, as a qualitative inquiry approach, attempts to explore a phenomenon through participants' narrative descriptions of their own lived experience [7, 8]. Hence, semi-structured interviews were conducted with a sample from college students to better understand the dimensions of nomophobia based on the lived experiences of the interviewees.

2.2 Participants

Participants were recruited for the interviews using purposive sampling strategy, with the purpose of identifying the participants who had experienced the phenomenon and therefore who could provide the most accurate narrative description of the phenomenon. That is why a criterion sampling strategy was used for purposive sampling. For this purpose, a screening questionnaire was distributed through email messages, using snowballing strategies.

The screening questionnaire was composed of questions related to smartphone ownership, duration of ownership, and smartphone use. Also, the questionnaire included eight items from a previously developed and validated questionnaire, Test of Mobile Phone Dependence (TMD) [9]. The reason for the use of this questionnaire was to determine the respondents who heavily depended on their smartphones based on their dependence score obtained from the TMD items.

The selection of the respondents was based upon the following criteria: (1) the respondent owned a smartphone for a year or more, (2) the respondent had a mobile data plan providing access to the Internet via the smartphone, (3) the respondent spent more than an hour using his or her smartphone, and (4) the respondent had a dependence score, calculated using the responses to the TMD items, greater than the mean of the scores of all respondents.

Those respondents meeting these criteria were contacted and invited for an interview. As a result, nine undergraduate students (four males, five females), aged 19–24, were recruited as participants for the interviews.

2.3   Materials

Prior to the onset of the study, an interview guide was prepared to be reviewed by the Institutional Review Board at the university where this study was conducted. The interview guide contained a variety of questions, starting with general questions about college students' smartphone use habits (e.g., *for what purposes do you usually use your smartphone?*), and delving into the feelings associated with the availability and unavailability of the smartphone (e.g., *how would you feel if you left your smartphone at home and had to spend your day without it?*, and *would you feel anxious if you could not use your smartphone for some reason when you wanted to do so?*).

2.4   Procedures

One-on-one, semi-structured interviews were conducted with the nine participants individually in a university office on campus. Upon their arrival at the interview location, the participants were informed about the study. Then, they were given an informed consent form with all the information about the scope of the study and instructed to sign it if they agreed with the procedures outlined in the form. After the interviews' permission was granted, all the interviews were audio-recorded and the interviewees were assured about confidentiality of their information. During the interviews, the interview guide was followed to make sure that all the interviewees were given the same information about the study and were asked the questions. After the interviews, the recordings were transcribed verbatim and pseudonyms were used to protect the identity of the participants.

2.5   Data Analysis

To analyze the qualitative data from the interviews, phenomenological data analysis steps as described by Moustakas [8] were followed. In essence, phenomenological data analysis consists of three main steps: phenomenological reduction, imaginative variation, and construction of the essence of the experience [6, 8]. The initial step in phenomenological reduction is horizonalization, which basically encompasses identifying significant statements about the interviewees' experience while giving equal amount of importance to all the statements in regards to their contribution to understanding the interviewees' experience [6, 8]. This step is followed by the elimination of repetitive and overlapping statements [6] to divulge the interviewees' narrative description of their lived experience, which are commonly referred to as invariant constituents [8]. Later on, these invariant constituents are grouped into themes representing meaning units [6]. Incorporating these themes and interviewees' statements, a textural description of the experience is written.

Imaginative variation is a process in which a structural description of participants' experience with the phenomenon is constructed by using the textural descriptions from the phenomenological reduction [8]. The essence of experience is constructed through the synthesis of the textural descriptions and the structural description [6, 8].

After reading the transcriptions of all the interviews repeatedly and thoroughly, horizons were extracted from each interviewee's transcription. Then, these horizons, or significant statements about the participants' experience, were grouped into meaning units through thematic clustering. Consequently, the textural description of the experience for interviewees was obtained. Later, a structural description of the interviewees' experience was written, which was then used to construct the essence of the phenomenon, nomophobia, through the narrative descriptions of the interviewees [7].

2.6 Trustworthiness

In qualitative research, member-checking is important for the verification of the accuracy and trustworthiness of the findings by requesting input from participants [10]. Member checking was used to make sure that the findings of the phenomenological analysis reflected accurately the interviewees' experience. All interviewees were invited for member-checking through an email message explaining what they were requested to do. They were asked to read the descriptions of their experience and assess whether the descriptions reflected their experience. Also, they were asked to propose changes or corrections if anything was not accurate enough. Three out of nine interviewees were able to check the descriptions of their experience. They did not make any changes on the descriptions. They confirmed that the descriptions were accurate and valid, alluding to the credibility of the interpretations.

3 Findings

As a result of the phenomenological analysis of the interview transcripts, four dimensions of nomophobia were identified: (1) not being able to communicate, (2) losing connectedness, (3) not being able to access information and (4) giving up convenience.

3.1 Not Being Able to Communicate

This dimension refers to the feelings of losing instant communication with people and not being able to use the services that allow for instant communication. It also encompasses the feelings of not being able to contact people and to be contacted.

The interviews showed that the participants heavily relied on their smartphones and respective features for communication purposes. When asked in what ways he thought his smartphone affected his daily routines, Peter, a 21-year-old junior in Computer Engineering, said:

> It lets me keep in touch with… like my parents who live out of the state. We can text or talk all the day without like setting time aside to devote. We can just message each other as needed. For work and stuff, if someone has a question for me I can respond to them wherever I am.

For the same question, Olivia, who is a 21-year-old junior in Agricultural Education, responded as follows: "It lets me communicate with people more easily. So if my schedule needs to change or I need to ask someone a question, I can do that more easily."

Lily, a 20-year-old sophomore in Elementary Education, said: "I think it enhances [my daily routines] actually. Obviously communication is so much easier. You can just text a group to tell them where to meet up…"

Ted, a 24-year-old senior in Mechanical Engineering, explained the importance of his smartphone as a communication tool as follows:

> It is like a good friend to me. It can help me solve many problems. Also, it is a very important way to connect to other people. For example, I am in the US right now, but most of my friends are in China or somewhere. I have to use my phone to communicate with them. It helps me feel better, feel I am not alone. For example, when I first came to the US, I just felt homesick but my phone helped me communicate with my family so I could feel better. Also, every morning when I wake up, my first thing is to get my phone and check what I got during the night. Since there is a time difference with where my friends live, they may send me something during the night. So every time I wake up I check my phone.

These quotations demonstrate the importance of smartphones as a communication tool for young adults. Owing to the place of smartphones in their lives, the participants expressed that they would feel anxious when they could not use their smartphones as illustrated by the following quotations.

> The part that would be unfortunate is like I can't receive any messages or email. I can't contact people I need to contact. That's not like a nice feeling. (Peter)

Peter's statement about not being able to contact people was recurrently pointed out by other participants, as well. When asked how she would feel if she had left her smartphone at home, Lily said she had forgotten her smartphone at home the day before the interview. She described her experience as follows:

> It is funny I did that yesterday [laughing]. I left it at home. Umm it was kind of weird because I couldn't text my roommate and say "when are you riding the bus home?" I couldn't communicate. For that instant communication, I had to wait until I opened my computer on Wi-Fi and typed out a message. [] The communication one was the hardest for me. [] Not being able to get a hold of people…

Lily's experience provides insight into the importance of instant communication for young adults. To her, instant communication meant being able to get a hold of someone through text messaging.

Similarly, another problem was related to being out of contact. Tracy, a 22-year-old senior in Kinesiology, said that she would feel anxious if she could not use her smartphone based on a recent experience: "I just blew through my first 300 min a couple of days ago. I was like "Now how are people gonna call me?" Even that makes me have a feeling of anxiety."

Tracy also explained how she felt when her smartphone was broken. She said she hated the fact that she depended on her smartphone too much and added:

> The losing of contacts, connection and the losing of information too. Pictures are not a big deal. But I don't have the contacts anywhere else so I was like "how am I gonna contact people to let them know my phone is dead."

Thus, Tracy's statements highlight the value and importance young adults put on both contacting and being contactable by their family and/or friends.

While calls and text messages were highlighted in the participants' statements, email messages were another medium of communication for Astrid, a 22-year-old senior in Microbiology:

> I think I am too attached to my email like I get back to emails really quickly, which is great for some things, but sometimes I feel too plugged in to the email. [] I think that not being able to check my email would probably make me a little anxious just because I know at the end of the day I probably would have a full inbox. I wouldn't be able to check it. If someone like needed me for something, I wouldn't be able to respond right away.

To Astrid, email messages were just as important as calls and text messages. Her statement also shows her desire to respond to people immediately when they try to contact her.

3.2   Losing Connectedness

This dimension is related to the feelings of losing the ubiquitous connectivity that smartphones provide, and being disconnected from one's online identity (especially on social media).

The interviews revealed that connectedness was a driving force for young adults to use a smartphone. Astrid stated that one of the benefits of her smartphone was that it helped her stay connected. She said:

> I think it allows me to stay up-to-date with my friends and all of that. I also have this app that allows me... I went abroad this past summer so I have a lot of friends in Africa that I can't text. So it helps me stay connected to them because there is like this free texting app so I can text them for free through that. And then I think it facilitates my ability to stay connected to my classes like I have a Blackboard app that I check for updates and lecture notes and all of that.

Another important point raised by the participants was related to how they ensured that they saw the notifications from their smartphones. For instance, Peter said:

> When I am on my computer or something, I would leave my phone like facing this way [showing his smartphone facing up so he can see the screen when it is on the desk] and then there is a light here [showing the place of the light]. It would change like if it is olivine, it is a text from my girlfriend. If it is like blue, it is like a friend. If it is purple, it is an email. That way if I notice it and I can decide. If it is purple, I don't care about email right now so I can just work on.

Astrid stated:

> I have my smartphone like next to me on my desk like at home. So if it buzzes because someone like Facebooked me or whatever, I will check that and go back to what it is I am doing. I guess I don't like seeking out to check it while doing something but if I see that someone is like contacting me I will check it.

Lily said:

> If it is just sitting here and I know nothing has happened with it, I don't need to check it. Or if I don't hear it ring, or if it is just in a bag somewhere but if I hear it go off then I had that need of

"what is it? what is the notification?" If I could, I would check. I wouldn't if I am having a meeting with a professor. I wouldn't check it; I would just wait. But if I am just doing something on my own, I would check it.

Ted recurred: "If there is a notification, I would check it as soon as possible. If it is nothing important, I would continue what I was doing."

These quotations illustrate the importance young adults attach to making sure that they notice the notifications they receive from their smartphones and their desire to check their smartphones for notifications. They appear to view notifications as a way of ensuring connectedness: if they have notifications, it means they stay connected to their online identity and networks.

Connectedness seems not only related to their online identity but also to the smartphone itself. Tracy's comment provides an exemplar of this point: "[my smartphone] is very important because of that connectedness and I got used to it. So it is hard to go backwards."

It is worth noting that Tracy brought up a recurrent point - being used to having a smartphone. When asked how she would feel if she did not have her smartphone with her, Olivia said:

Because you are used to having it in your pocket or in your hand and it is like you are always touching your pockets, looking for it and like situations like on the bus or if I am sitting outside the classroom, waiting for the class to start, I don't know what to do with myself cause in that situation I'd be probably on my phone.

Furthermore, Peter commented: "Once you are used to having a smartphone, you don't want to go back to having like an old phone."

These statements suggest an interesting point: not only do young adults, via their smartphones, feel connected to their online connections and networks but they do feel connected to their smartphones, as well.

When asked how she would feel if she had left her phone at home, Olivia said: "Umm I have done that before and I just feel kind of like naked."

For the same question, John said he would feel awful. He added:

Pretty much for me it is just like it becomes twined with your everyday routine and everything. I mean it is just like it is not comfortable to have a day without it. If you went all day without, uhh…, get rid of your backpack and pencils and stuff. Imagine going to a class and it would be just weird, I guess. For me, I lost my cell phone in a classroom one day. I couldn't find for like four hours. In that four hours, I was like I just lost power instead of cost, you know. So I guess losing it versus forgetting it is different but yeah I mean going without it is a huge drawback 'cause it is entwined with everything today. It is also kind of an expectation. I guess for the most part society just kind of expects everybody to have a smartphone. So it is like "yeah, I will send an email. Reply once you get it." You know it is not like five hours later when you get home. They want responses quick.

John's portrayal of his smartphone as being entwined with his daily routine shows how important connectedness is in his life. He brings up a very important point that having a smartphone is an expectation in society. To further explain his point, he added:

It pretty much is considered mandatory in society now. People will complain about people who are on their smartphones too much but if you look around at what everybody else is doing if you didn't have a smartphone or you weren't on your smartphone, that's a lot of less productivity. It is just away from the norm.

Thus, he viewed not having a smartphone as an aberration from the norm.

3.3   Not Being Able to Access Information

The dimension of not being able to access information reflects the discomfort of losing pervasive access to information through smartphones, being unable to retrieve information through smartphones and search for things on smartphones.

The interviews showed that accessing information on smartphones was of great importance for young adults. As a benefit of having a smartphone, Peter said:

I like the ability of... if you are walking around, and you are like "oh, what is this song?" you can pull out an app that figures out what song is playing. If you are thinking about "what did I just learn in the lecture today?" you just pull out and google what the lecture note was and like no matter where you are, if you have a question you don't have to set that question aside. You can just figure out the answer like immediately. Things there most of the Internet, I guess.

Robin, a 21-year-old junior in Elementary Education, described the benefits of her smartphone in terms of how it facilitates access to information as follows:

Benefits would be like I check the weather and check like if I have a question like about I didn't know when the [football] game was, so I could check when that was or questions like someone says something and I am like "what does that mean?" so I check it on my phone. Or "what actor was in that movie?" So that's kind of how I use it for that.

Similarly, Lily said her smartphone was very beneficial for accessing information and added:

I use it for my news. I use CNN and BBC apps to like get the world news. I am constantly googling things, looking things up. So instant gratification in a way. Like I can find things right away if I wanna find or know something.

Ted said:

It benefits me a lot. Just like with a smartphone I can get as much information as I want. Because I am an international student, when I have trouble reading something or I don't know what a word means I can look it up on the Internet. It provides me with a lot of information. Also, it has many features. It has a camera. It can work like an iPod or something. I can listen to music. I can take pictures. It also has GPS or navigation. It is very useful.

Barney, a 22-year-old senior in Aerospace Engineering, described the benefits of his smartphone as follows:

Especially with class projects and stuff like that, it is really nice because I like to be able to look things up. That has come in handy a couple times, as I have been talking about. School projects with other friends.

To further explain how he uses his smartphone to access information, Barney also added:

It is especially nice if I have a test coming up. Sometimes I take my study notes on Evernote. From there I can pull out my notes and just look at them quick. Sometimes I make some study notes. If I don't wanna pull out a bunch of sheets, I can like quick search through them to find different things. So many of my classes have like online stuff. For a good example, I had a German test yesterday. When I was on my way to the class, I just pulled out my smartphone, loaded up the PowerPoint and just started reviewing it while I was walking.

These quotations exemplify the importance put on accessing information through smartphones. Since it is a very essential component of their smartphone use, young adults report problems when they cannot access information through their smartphones. The following statements by Olivia provide an insight into this issue:

I like having information at my fingertips like if I don't know the answer of something, I wanna know it right away. So I'm gonna use my smartphone to look it up. [] And if I couldn't answer a question right away, without that access to the Internet I feel like that would make me uncomfortable.

The same concern was pointed out by Peter, too. He said: "I would feel anxious if I can't google information."

3.4   Giving up Convenience

This dimension is pertinent to the feelings of giving up the convenience smartphones provide and reflects the desire to utilize the convenience of having a smartphone.

The interviews revealed that the participants found their smartphones convenient. When describing his use of his smartphone, John said:

[My smartphone use] has probably been excessive. I mean just because it is so convenient, I mean you have literally everything you need in your pocket. If I didn't have to type papers or play Legal Legend, I probably wouldn't need a laptop. I mean there is research, I suppose too. It is just convenient; you always have everything you need right there. [] I mean having like a 4G LT like everywhere here and having the convenience is really nice to have. Especially being able to drive anywhere now. We don't have like dead spots for the most part. I mean besides like a few spots you have pretty much Internet anywhere, which three years ago even you drive out of a city and there is nothing.

Although John believed that he was using his smartphone excessively, he did not seem to be worried about it because of the convenience it provides. When asked how he would feel if he could not use his smartphone, John stated:

I would say it is kind of situational. For the most part, I would definitely feel anxious. I mean if you are in the middle of the day and if it is 2 o'clock and your class is until 4 or something, you know. It is like snowing outside. You know there is always stuff that can happen. Just being out of the loop completely and not having that right here you know… It is almost like a comfort that you carry around with you. It is like a peace of mind, I guess.

John appeared to associate having a smartphone with relaxing or relieving the stress of "being out of the loop." Barney was also pleased with the convenience his smartphone provided. He described it even further:

It is kind of a freedom. It is the same thing as moving from a desktop to a laptop computer. With desktop, obviously you are stuck wherever that is but with laptop you can freely move about the house or move to a friend's location. The same thing with the smartphone is now suddenly you don't even need the Internet. You can kind of move wherever then and you get access to the

Internet and get access to anything. So it is kind of the same way of freedom. If I wanted to, I could access anything at any time.

These quotations demonstrate that having access to the Internet one of the most convenient commodities smartphones allow for. Both John and Barney touched upon the convenience of constant and instant access to the Internet anywhere and anytime. If this convenience of having constant access to the Internet is not provided, then the feelings of discomfort emerge, as demonstrated by the following statements. Robin said:

It would be kind of annoying because it is just I am used to it again. If I don't have service for the Internet, then I would be like always keep trying to see if I do have service or something like that. If I am in a different state, it doesn't always work out and so that's really annoying. I am always like "oh, I wish I was back in Iowa so I could use my smartphone again." One time my smartphone broke, then I got a non-smartphone to use and then it wasn't as big of a deal because I knew it didn't have those capabilities. But I already knew that. If this one [showing her smartphone] wasn't working, again that would be annoying because I am paying for it and I know that I should be able to use it.

As Robin's statements show, when she knows she should be able to use her smartphone and utilize the convenience it offers, she expects to have it available all the time. If not, she feels annoyed. Based on her experience with the "non-smartphone", it might be that as the expectations from the smartphone increase, the feelings of annoyance and/or anxiety tend to be more severe.

Moreover, Ted stated:

Sometimes I feel anxious but mostly if there is not internet connection, I would try to go somewhere else to get access to the Internet. If my battery goes dead, I would try to charge my phone. I would try to make it alive.

Likewise, Ted, who was an international student, said:

Actually, when I am with my family and friends, I would not feel uncomfortable if my battery is low or dead. I think when I am lonely, I feel my phone is a very important thing. But when I am not alone, or I have something to do, I don't feel the same.

Ted's comment is an exemplar of the effect of loneliness and being with family and friends on the feelings attached to the smartphone.

The importance of having battery in the smartphone was pointed out by another participant, as well. John, who was previously reported to believe that his smartphone was a peace of mind for him, expressed his desire for having a charged battery in his smartphone as follows:

[] If it does go dead, that's the sort of thing when it is like "I need to charge my phone right now". Especially, if I'm not at home and it dies, it is just an uncertainty of like what if I forgot my keys? [] If it does die, you lose a peace of mind.

This statement exemplifies how important it is for young adults to have a charged battery so that their smartphone will be "alive". John appeared to attach the same value to having his smartphone with him as the value to having his keys with him.

Another important point was made by Tracy when asked to describe her smartphone use. She said:

Ummm, I would probably say that I am addicted to my phone based on when my phone died a couple of weeks ago and I had to get a new one and I was like "Oh my Gosh what am I gonna do?". And then within 24 h I had a new phone, just real quick. [] I felt like I was gonna get stranded somewhere [laughing]. [] Like "well, I don't have phone now. What do I do?" Like Dark Ages. Just kidding but yeah [laughing]"

Tracy described herself as being addicted to her smartphone. She appeared to count on her smartphone as a means of ensuring safety.

4 Conclusions

This study provided greater insight into nomophobia and enhanced our understanding of the phenomenon by identifying the dimensions of nomophobia as described by college students. In this study, nomophobia is defined as the fear of not being able to use a smartphone or a mobile phone and/or the services it offers. It refers to the fear of not being able to communicate, losing the connectedness that smartphones allow, not being able to access information through smartphones, and giving up the convenience that smartphones provide.

Owing to the advances in mobile ICTs, smartphones have infiltrated into every aspect of our lives, including teaching and learning environments. Given their endless features, mobile ICTs, especially smartphones and tablet PCs, have been closely integrated into teaching and learning. Thus, it is almost inevitable to think of a classroom setting in which smartphones and tablet PCs are not used. That being said, smartphones are sometimes reported to be counterproductive to instructional practices because of their distractive nature: as the students have constant access to the Internet and thus to their online identity on social media, it becomes challenging for instructors to keep their students engaged in instructional activities, in lieu of their smartphones. In that sense, having a better understanding of why students are so attached to their smartphones can help instructors find better solutions to address the problem of engagement and distraction from the learning activities.

This study contributes to the nomophobia research literature by identifying the dimensions of nomophobia through the experiences of college students. Because smartphones have become an integral part of classrooms and have been extensively used as an instructional technology, it is of great importance for educators to consider the unintended consequences and implications of smartphones in regards to teaching and learning. Future research is warranted to investigate the relationship between nomophobia, and academic success and motivation.

References

1. Oulasvirta, A., Rattenbury, T., Ma, L., Raita, E.: Habits make smartphone use more pervasive. Pers. Ubiquit. Comput. **16**, 105–114 (2012)
2. Pew Research Center. http://www.pewinternet.org/fact-sheets/mobile-technology-fact-sheet/
3. Lee, S.Y.: Examining the factors that influence early adopters' smartphone adoption: the case of college students. Telematics Inform. **31**, 308–318 (2014)

4. SecurEnvoy. http://www.securenvoy.com/blog/2012/02/16/66-of-the-population-suffer-from-nomophobia-the-fear-of-being-without-their-phone/
5. King, A.L.S., Valença, A.M., Nardi, A.E.: Nomophobia: the mobile phone in panic disorder with agoraphobia: reducing phobias or worsening of dependence? Cogn. Behav. Neurol. **23**, 52–54 (2010)
6. Creswell, J.W.: Qualitative Inquiry and Research Design: Choosing Among Five Traditions. Sage, Thousand Oaks (2012)
7. Miles, M.B., Huberman, A.M.: Qualitative Data Analysis: An Expanded Sourcebook, 2nd edn. Sage, Thousand Oaks (1994)
8. Moustakas, C.: Phenomenological Research Methods. Sage Publications, Thousand Oaks (1994)
9. Chóliz, M.: Mobile-phone addiction in adolescence: the Test of Mobile Phone Dependence (TMD). Prog. Health Sci. **2**, 33–44 (2012)
10. Rager, K.B.: Self-care and the qualitative researcher: when collecting data can break your heart. Edu. Res. **34**, 23–27 (2005)

Author Index

Printed in the United States
By Bookmasters